First Farmers
on the Island of Bornholm

Nordiske Fortidsminder
Volume 32

PUBLISHED WITH SUPPORT FROM
Aage og Johanne Louis-Hansens Fond
Dronning Margrethe II's Arkæologiske Fond

Both English and Scandinavian archaeologists have maintained the view that it was the local population of hunters, fishermen and collectors who, through an adaptation process, began to engage in agriculture. This was assumed to have happened in contact with already established farming cultures on the European continent, but with no immigration of importance. However, it is difficult to imagine agriculture introduced on Bornholm without the arrival of already-established farmers who brought domestic animals and seeds as well as knowledge of how to engage in farming. Migration may also have played a role for the introduction of farming in other parts of South Scandinavia. Today there is more willingness to see the transition to agriculture in England and in the Nordic countries as part of a wider expansion that issued from the farming cultures on the continent in 4100-4000 BC, as the second major expansion after the establishment of the first agrarian societies in central Europe around 5500 BC. The development in the British Isles and in South Scandinavia must have taken the form of an encounter between two cultures (Sheridan 2010; Sørensen 2014; M. Larsson 2015).

In addition to understanding the actual Neolithisation process, we would also like to reach an understanding of the social organisation that prevailed in early agrarian society, and how this organisation developed through the first half millennium after the introduction of farming. Many before us have stressed the development towards a more hierarchical society, but we go a step further and attempt to describe the stages in this development. We anticipate that our treatment of this issue will be discussed and will perhaps lead to the emergence of other explanations. In that case one of the aims of this work will have been achieved.

While the excavation at Vallensgård forms the basis for the first two chapters of the book, chapter 3 offers a review of the material from 56 Early Neolithic settlement finds. This is supplemented by chapters 4 and 5 with their treatment of the pointed-butted and thin-butted axes, which appear as stray finds and in hoards that are kept in the Bornholm Museum and in the National Museum as well as among private collectors, and chapter 6 reviews finds of Early Neolithic battle axes and halberds from Bornholm. The presentation of the artifact material in the chapters 4-6 is mainly based on a registration that was conducted by one of the authors of this book (FON) in 1986-89 with support from the Carlsberg Foundation, and these records have been updated with information about new finds that have appeared since then. The registration covers finds of all categories from the Neolithic on Bornholm, partly in the National Museum and the Bornholm Museum, partly in private collections. Find lists for chapters 3-6 appear in the catalogue at the end of the book.

The point of working chronologically with the finds is to arrive at an understanding of the sequence of events and thus at a better basis for describing the settlement and societal development. In chapter 7 we attempt to provide an overview of the development on Bornholm seen in the context of current issues related to the transition from hunting to farming and the development of the early agrarian societies in the north.

The task of writing and editing the texts of the book has fallen upon the other author (PON), who in 2015 received support for this work from HM Queen Margrethe II's Archaeological Foundation and from the Aage and Johanne Louis-Hansen Foundation. We are greatly indebted to the foundations, to whom we hereby express our sincerest gratitude. Warm thanks also go to the former Director of the National Museum, Per Kristian Madsen, for his interest in the project and for the inclusion of this book in the series *Nordiske Fortidsminder*. For encouragement in this collaborative project we similarly thank the director of the Bornholm Museum, Jacob Bjerring-Hansen.

It is our hope that this will be the first of several publications on the results of the project 'The Neolithic Settlement of Bornholm'. The excavation at Vallensgård took place in 1986, and it is now time, 34 years later, to bring out the final publication. The explanation of the late presentation is on the one hand the very large body of find material that is the result of the various excavations in the project, and on the other hand the fact that interesting finds continue to appear. The work with the Neolithic on Bornholm is by no means over, either in the field or at the scholars' desks; well into the future it will provide a basis for new projects. About several of the investigations in the project an extended series of provisional publications has been issued (see the bibliography). A few of them also deal with the settlement at Vallensgård (P.O. Nielsen 2009; Nielsen & Nielsen 2014a, 26-31).

Among those who have helped and supported us in the work with this investigation, we would like in the first instance to thank the landowner Ancher Müller for permission to carry out the excavation of the settlement Vallensgård I and for the interest he

Preface

This book concerns the Early Neolithic on Bornholm, c. 3950-3300 BC. Using archaeological finds and excavations, we will study how the first farming society was established and developed. To write an account of how people lived and what their living conditions were like nearly 6000 years ago is no easy task. The authors felt, however, that the remains and finds from Bornholm dating to this important period may have something to say, and that this could even result in new interpretations. It all began early in our collaboration when excavating the settlement site at Vallensgård, close to the famous Echo Valley (Ekkodalen), near the centre of the island.

The excavation of the Early Neolithic settlement Vallensgård I was one of a number of investigations of Neolithic settlements conducted on the island of Bornholm in 1984-93 as a collaboration between the National Museum and the Bornholm Museum within the framework of the project 'The Neolithic Settlement of Bornholm'. This project was begun after the discovery of Neolithic settlement traces in the Bornholm Museum's excavations of settlements and burials from the Bronze Age, Iron Age and Viking Age. At Runegård in Åker in 1979 Middle Neolithic features were uncovered with hitherto unknown archaeological material. This was repeated during the excavation of burials from the Bronze and Iron Age at Limensgård and at Ndr. Grødbygård in the autumn of 1984. In both places, and at the same time, two-aisled house sites from the Middle Neolithic were uncovered in connection with finds of new pottery material from the end of the Funnel Beaker Culture and from the early Battle Axe Culture. Well preserved Late Neolithic house sites, some of the first large longhouses from the period to be excavated in Denmark, were also found at the Limensgård settlement, and besides the house sites from the Middle and Late Neolithic there also emerged traces of house construction from the beginning of the Neolithic. Because of the unusually favourable conditions at Ndr. Grødbygård and Limensgård for the investigation of house constructions from the Neolithic, the joint effort was concentrated at these two settlements up until 1993. At the same time trial excavations were also conducted at other sites to obtain as varied a body of material as possible from the Neolithic. One of the other settlements was Vallensgård I, which is the point of departure for this book, on the basis of which we offer an overview of the Early Neolithic on Bornholm compared with the contemporaneous development of early farming societies in the rest of northern Europe.

The idea of combining the treatment of the find material from this site with an overview of the Early Neolithic on Bornholm arose when we realized during the work with the finds that precisely this site could form the basis for a division of the Early Neolithic in terms of pottery types. This was done on the basis of the grouping of the Early Neolithic pottery that was presented by Eva Koch in the book *Neolithic Bog Pots* (1998). Although this work is about finds of pots from the Zealand island group, Eva Koch's typological division could also be applied to the Bornholm pottery.

With a division into phases that could be applied to both the pottery and the other find material, it was possible to map and describe the developments on Bornholm in the Early Neolithic. With this as a starting point we discuss how the introduction of agriculture and cattle breeding may have taken place in the area around the western Baltic. We believe that the transition from the Mesolithic to the Neolithic in this area was not, as many believed, a slow, gradual adaptation, but a quick, dynamic process. We share this view today with others who also deal with the events in relation to the developments in the neighbouring parts of Europe (Sørensen 2014; Price 2015, 106 ff.).

5.	Thin-butted axes	113
	Thin-butted axes of flint	113
	Thin-butted flint axes of type I	114
	Thin-butted flint axes of type II	117
	Thin-butted flint axes of type IIIA	117
	Thin-butted flint axes of type IIIB	121
	Thin-butted flint axes of type VI	122
	The early production of thin-butted flint axes	123
	Variation in the size and quantity of thin-butted flint axes	125
	Thin-butted axes of other materials than flint	130
	Argonauts of the Baltic Sea	131
6.	Stone battle axes and flint halberds	139
	Battle axes	139
	Flint halberds	142
7.	The development of the early farming society	147
	Theories about the introduction of farming and cattle breeding in South Scandinavia	147
	The European background of the neolithisation of South Scandinavia	154
	The development on Bornholm during the Early Neolithic	174
	The establishment phase. The earliest Funnel Beaker Culture	175
	Population growth and incipient social differentiation	179
	Adaptation, group formation and centralisation	186
	From Early to Middle Neolithic	193
	Summary: Six stages of social development	200
	Sources of inspiration	201
8.	Catalogue. Finds from the Early Neolithic on Bornholm	207
	Finds list I. Settlement finds	207
	Finds list II. Individual finds of pottery vessels	228
	Finds list III. Finds from burials	229
	Finds list IV. Axes of flint and other stone materials	230
	Finds list V. Stone battle axes	238
	Finds list VI. Flint halberds	240
	Finds list VII. Copper axes	242
Bibliography		243

Contents

Preface 7

1. Vallensgård I. Introduction 11
   Topography and soil type 11
   Reconnaissance and surface collection 14
   The 1986 excavation 14
   Finds from the Late Glacial and Early Postglacial period 18
   Finds from the Early Neolithic 19

2. The Early Neolithic settlement at Vallensgård I, c. 3800-3600 BC 21
   Introduction 21
   Finds from cultural layers and depressions 21
   Finds from remains of tree-throws 22
   Finds from postholes 23
   Finds from pits 25
   Pottery 28
   Flint implements 36
   Implements of other stone types 37
   Pottery depositions 37
   Settlement finds from the Iron Age 38
   Finds from the area around the settlement 38
   Finds of flint axes in Vallensgård Mose 39

3. Early Neolithic settlements on Bornholm, c. 3950-3300 BC 43
   Introduction 43
   Settlements from EN A0, c. 3950-3900 BC 44
   Settlements from EN A1, c. 3900-3800 BC 46
   Settlements from EN A2, c. 3800-3650 BC 54
   Settlements from EN B, c. 3650-3500 BC 62
   Settlements from EN C, c. 3500-3300 BC 71
   Multi-phase settlements 77
   The locations of the settlements and the development of farming 86

4. Pointed-butted axes 101
   Pointed-butted axes of flint 101
   Pointed-butted flint axes of type 1 102
   Pointed-butted flint axes of type 2 103
   Pointed-butted flint axes of type 3 106
   Pointed-butted axes of other material than flint 106
   Pointed-butted axes – summary 110

First Farmers on the Island of Bornholm
© The Royal Society of Northern Antiquaries and University Press
of Southern Denmark 2020
Editors of Nordiske Fortidsminder:
Per Kristian Madsen (resp.) and Ingrid Wass
Prepress and printing: Narayana Press
ISBN: 978-87-408-3297-6

Translation: James Manley and Patrick Marsden

All volumes in this series are peer-reviewed.

Front cover:
Flintaxes found in the wetland close to the Early Neolithic settlement
Vallensgård I. Photo Martin Stoltze.

Back cover:
Early Neolithic funnel beaker from Vallensgård I.
Pia Brejnholt *del.* 1:1.

Distribution:
University Press of Southern Denmark
Campusvej 55
DK-5230 Odense M

First Farmers
on the Island of Bornholm

Poul Otto Nielsen
Finn Ole Sonne Nielsen

The Royal Society of Northern Antiquaries · Copenhagen 2020
University Press of Southern Denmark

has shown towards the project, as well as information he has provided about the history of the bog. We are also indebted to the then museum curator Margrethe Watt, Bornholm Museum, whose patience we tried by spending more time on the excavation than had been set aside.

We have drawn inspiration from many sources (see the section on sources of inspiration at the end of chapter 7). For exchanges of information and for constructive discussions, often from opposite points of view, we also wish to thank Lutz Klassen, Niels H. Andersen, Lars Larsson and Anne Birgitte Gebauer. Peter Rowley-Conwy and Christian Jeunesse are to be thanked for updates and literature references. We thank Christophe Laurelut for access to a still unprinted work on the French Michelsberg settlement at Mairy. Much information has been received from Lasse Sørensen, and our thinking has been influenced particularly by his work *From Hunter to Farmer in Northern Europe* (2014), which opens up a European perspective on the neolithisation in South Scandinavia.

The work on the material has extended over a long period, and we have several draughtsmen to thank for the production of the illustrations in the book: Henning Ørsnes (†), Eva Koch (†), Lars Holten, Tim Grønnegaard, Ole Guldager, Pia Brejnholt, Poul Wöhliche and Freerk Oldenburger. For permission to use illustrations from other publications we thank Lasse Sørensen (maps fig. 4.11 and 7.3) and Christophe Laurelut (fig. 7.4).

1. Vallensgård I. Introduction

Topography and soil type

The settlement Vallensgård I lies on a sandy terrace on the eastern edge of Brødreengen, which is in the same hollow as the bog Vallensgård Mose south of the Almindingen forest and south of the island's highest rock massif with Rytterknægten as its peak, 162 m above sea level (fig. 1.1-1.3). The hollow forms a basin that extends from the valley Ekkodalen towards the south-west. Ekkodalen lies in a rift valley, which extends in a straight line towards the north-east through Kløvedal to Saltuna on the north-eastern coast of the island. It was caused by a fault in the Precambrian. The bedrock consists of Almindingen Granite, but in the bottom of the rift valley there is also a basaltic rock, the dark Kelså Diabase, which forced its way up as a melted mass throughout the length of the rift valley when it was formed in the Precambrian or later. In the middle of the island this material is only rarely found at the surface, but it sees the light of day at the mouth of the rivulet Kelse Å on the north-east coast, where the diabase corridor has a width of c. 60 m (Münther 1945).

The area around Vallensgård Mose has acquired

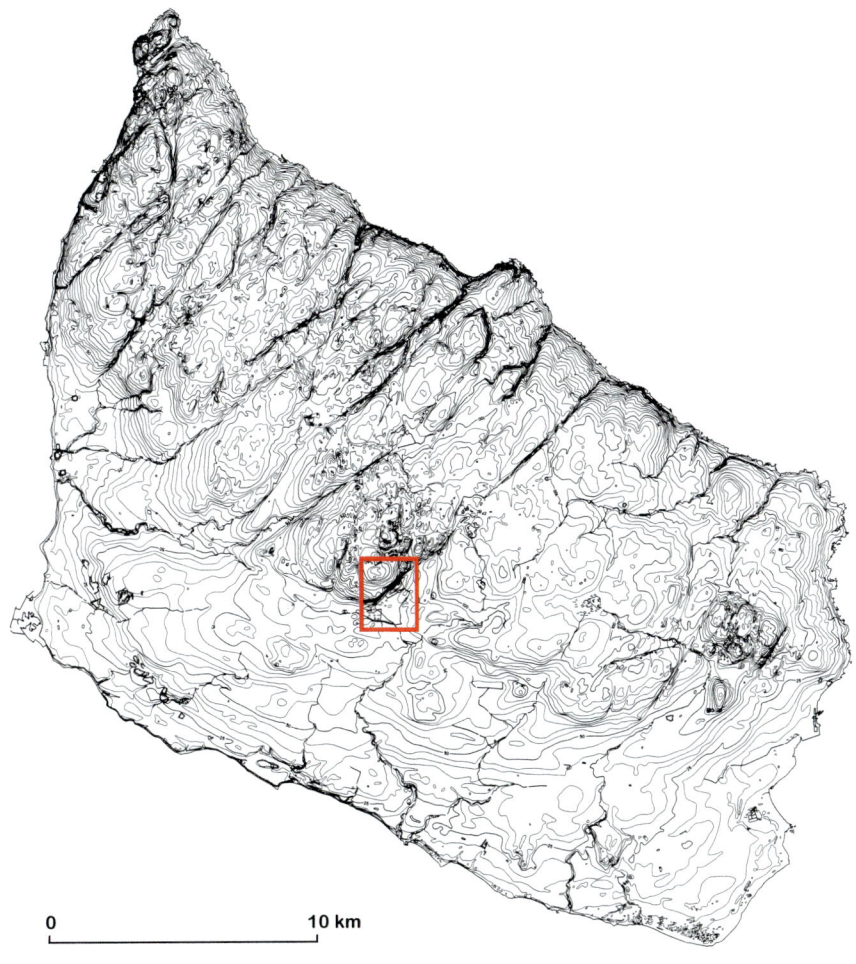

Fig. 1.1. Contour map of Bornholm. The settlement Vallensgård I is located in the centre of the island. The size of the rectangle corresponds with the map sections in figs. 1.2 and 1.3. Map data from the Danish Geodata Agency.

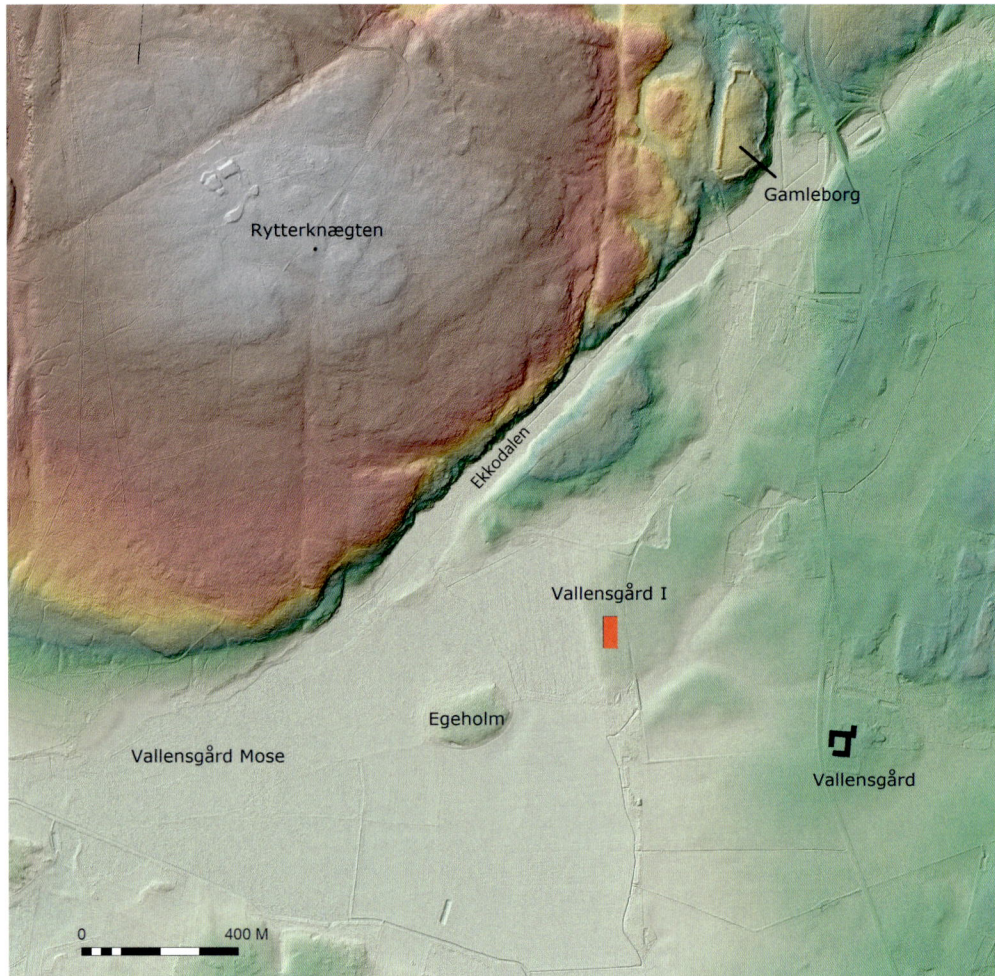

Fig. 1.2. Lidar map showing the location of the settlement Vallensgård I next to a large, low-lying area. From a lake in the early Holocene, this basin gradually became a bog. Most of it is now drained and cultivated. The only remaining bog area, Vallensgård Mose, is today a protected nature reserve. Map data from the Danish Geodata Agency.

its present surface relief both through erosion by glacial ice during the ice ages, and through the flow of material during the melting of the ice. The movement and pressure of the ice has given the rock its rounded surface. Below and between the high rock groups lie large granite cores which were loosened by the pressure of the ice. During the melting of the ice the bottom of the rift valley was eroded by the meltwater, which poured towards the south-west. During the melting, sand and gravel layers were deposited over a large area along the eastern side of Vallensgård Mose.

Once the ice had left the area, there lay a large lake at the place, in which bottom sediments were gradually deposited. Its content of plant remains and pollen bears witness to the advance of vegetation on Bornholm throughout the last stages of the Ice Age and into the present warm age. It speaks of the natural conditions that were encountered by the people who first set foot on Bornholm. The succession of strata extends from the Oldest Dryas until well into the postglacial era, when the older, minerogenic deposits were succeeded by peat. Through sedimentation and the supply of plant remains the lake was gradually transformed into the island's largest peat bog. Both animals and humans frequented the original lake and its surroundings and from time to time left traces. Bones of animals that perished and the implements of the hunters in the form of bone points from the Mesolithic sank to the bottom and were deposited in the bottom sediments. In the Neolithic the farmers lost their flint axes the same way, while other axes were deliberately sacrificed and deposited in the lake. Some of these finds have been gathered without any registration of how deep and in what strata they were found; other finds are better elucidated and can be related to one of the strata deposited at the bottom of the earlier lake, or to the peat layers. At an early stage the older parts of the stratigraphic series became the object of geological and botanical investigations, and the bog is an important site, especially for the study of landscape development in the Late Glacial period (Grönwall & Milthers 1916, 217-22; Iversen 1954, 96; Usinger 1978).

Vallensgård Mose is also the find-site for the oldest artefacts of bone and antler found so far on

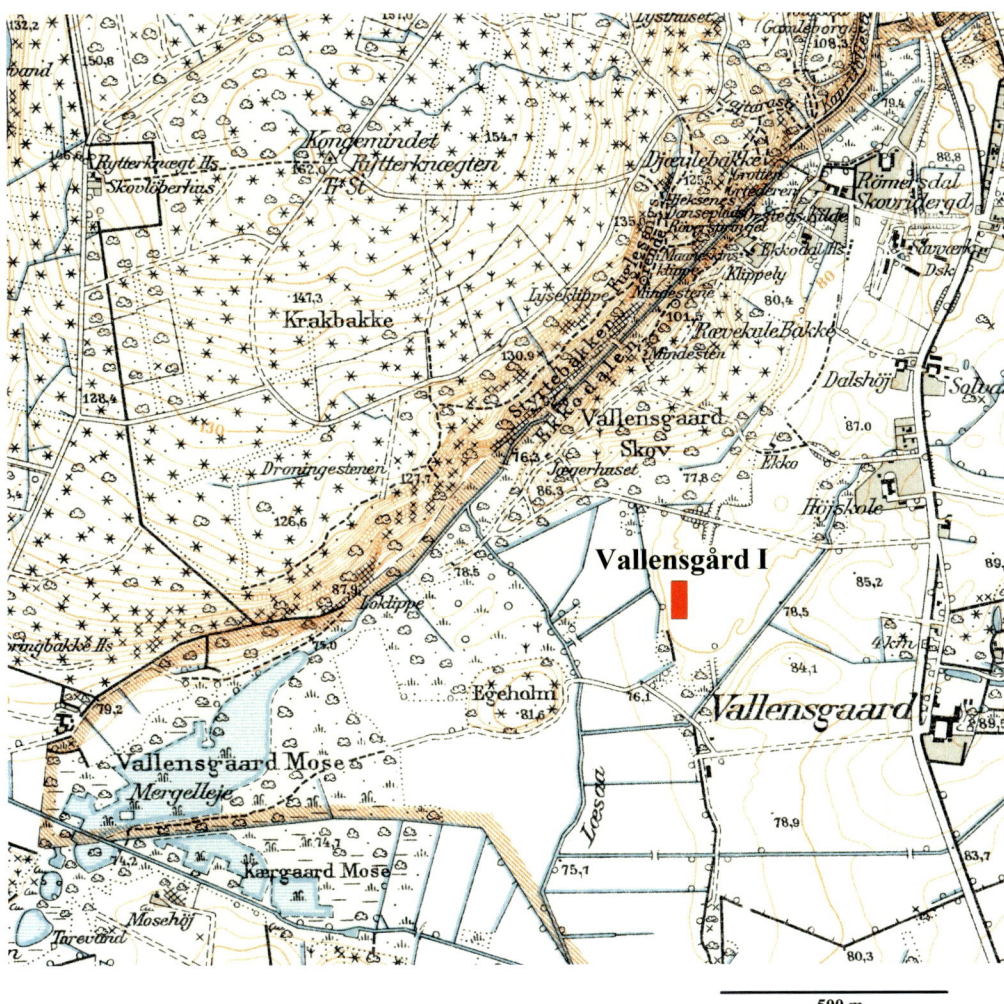

Fig. 1.3. Map from 1946 (issued with minor corrections in 1961) showing the location of the settlement. Map data from the Danish Geodata Agency.

Bornholm. A double harpoon with a spade-shaped base was found in the lime gyttja. It is 16.6 cm long and according to a determination by Herluf Winge is made of elk antler (Becker 1952, 167, fig. 33.3; Casati & Sørensen 2006, 16, fig. 6.9). It has been radiocarbon-dated to the Preboreal period, 9585±55 BP (AAR-9404), calibrated 9150-8800 BC (1σ), 9210-8740 BC (2σ). From the bog too come two fish spears of elk or aurochs bone, each with two short barbs. In addition a single point of elk bone without barbs has been found (Becker 1952, 167-69, fig. 33; Casati & Sørensen 2006, fig. 6.4-8). All these objects are said to have been found in the lime gyttja and are therefore in all likelihood from the Preboreal period.

Only in the southern part of Vallensgård Mose, which has been protected since 1973, can one experience the original character of the bog. The exploitation of the bog peat as fuel came to change the look of the landscape. We have information that in the western part of the bog there was an open water surface until the 1860s, and that the peat was at that time dug from barges. The strata beneath the peat were also exploited, since the postglacial lime gyttja was used to a great extent as marl. The production of marl and peat ended around 1945. But meadow and bog areas were also dried out by draining, so they could be incorporated as agricultural land. On the map from 1887 (fig. 1.4a) Brødreengen, the low-lying meadow area between the settlement and the Læså river, is shown with a meadow/bog symbol. At some point after 1887 cultivation of this water-meadow area must have begun, since it is stated that it was during field work that the first find of thin-butted flint axes was made in 1891 (find no. 1, see page 40, fig. 2.15 no. 175). Between 1904 and 1917 the water level in Læså went down 1 m, and extensive drainage of the adjacent water-meadows was conducted with the aim of gaining some 38 hectares of land for cultivation (Kofod 1917, 162). On the map from 1937 (fig. 1.4b) one can see that the meadow was cultivated in two strips that extend NE-SW between the settlement and Egeholm. It was in 1937 that the Bornholm Museum received an axe deposit found during field work "west of Vallensgård" (find no. 4, see page 41). This presumably comes from one of these fields. In 1952-53 a small area of Brødreengen

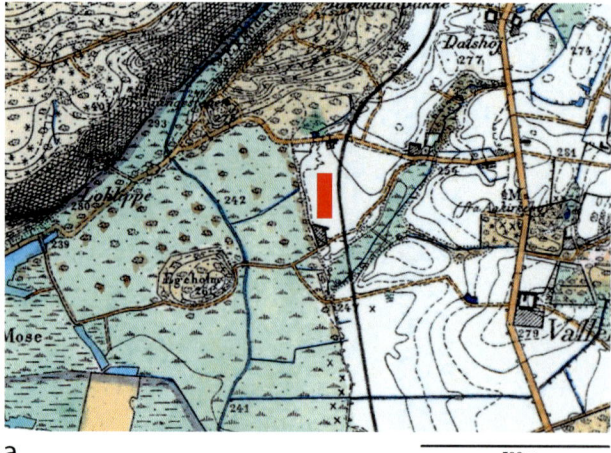

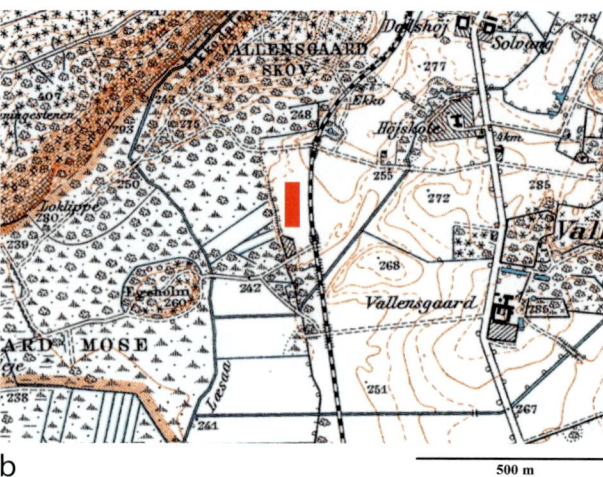

Fig. 1.4a-b. The location of the settlement on maps from 1887 and 1937 respectively, showing the drainage and cultivation of the bog areas. Map data from the Danish Geodata Agency.

was again drained, the rest in 1973. In 1986, when the investigation of the settlement took place, the whole of Brødreengen was under cultivation.

Reconnaissance and surface collection

In 1952 C.J. Becker visited Egeholm, which lies SW of Brødreengen, and at the edge of the high ground he found objects from both the Maglemose Culture and the Middle Neolithic. He prepared an excavation, which was to take place the next year, but for various reasons it was not conducted.[1] In the field east of Brødreengen finds from the Neolithic were registered for the first time in August 1951 by members of Ole Klindt-Jensen's excavation team at Gamleborg. According to a report by Jørgen Meldgaard from December 1951 the settlement area extended to a width of 25-50 m from the edge of the bog and c. 100 metres along it. On that occasion 130 pieces of flint refuse were collected, 5 flakes from polished flint axes, 1 blade knife, 1 broad, irregular blade, 2 cores of Bornholm ball flint nodules and a potsherd of Neolithic character.[2] The place was not investigated again until the beginning of the 1980s, by Finn Ole Nielsen and leisure-time archaeologists from Bornholm – this time too with results, which led to the excavation of which an account is given in the following.

The 1986 excavation

In the years 1984-93 the authors of this monograph conducted several excavations of Neolithic settlements on Bornholm as part of a research project, 'The Neolithic Settlement of Bornholm', which had been launched two years earlier in collaboration between the National Museum and the Bornholm Museum (F.O. Nielsen 1988). The settlement at the edge of Vallensgård Mose became an object of interest in that connection, since an investigation there could provide insight into the Early Neolithic settlement of a place where there seemed to have been no disturbances of significance from later periods of prehistory. In order to evaluate the possibilities for an investigation, the authors conducted an inspection on 19 October 1985 in the company of Margrethe Watt of the Bornholm Museum. The light sandy soil in the field where the settlement lies was being intensively worked by the farm's large tractor plough, and it was obvious that the settlement traces beneath the plough layer were in the danger zone. By agreement with the farm owner, Ancher Müller of Vallensgård, a trial excavation was therefore arranged for the following autumn.

The settlement was named Vallensgård I.[3] It lies 80-81 m above sea level on a slightly sloping plateau at the edge of the north-eastern part of Vallensgård Mose, between the bog and the nature path that has been established on the old railway track between Åkirkeby and Almindingen (fig. 1.4a). The plateau inclines slightly to the west and had a slightly rolling surface (fig. 1.5). The height difference between the present bog surface and the plateau is 5 m. The bog surface west of the plateau is today, after drainage and cultivation, completely flat. Together with the plateau it constituted one large cultivated cornfield at the time of the investigation.

Fig. 1.5. The settlement viewed towards the east, from the edge of the rocks. Photo PON.

The excavation was begun on 25 August 1986 and with interruptions lasted until 25 October. It was supervised on a daily basis by Finn Ole Nielsen, assisted for the first two weeks by the student Ken Hedegaard. The original intention was to carry out a guideline trial excavation. However, this merged into a major investigation because of several interesting finds and observations.

To begin with soil was drawn off by machinery in three parallel sondages just under 2 m in width over a 220 m long stretch extending N-S along the plateau (figs. 1.6-1.7). Just south of the middle of the midmost sondage (B) culture and fill layers emerged with Early Neolithic finds, which prompted an expansion of the sondage in the form of a rectangular field 15-16 m in width and 46 m in length, field D. A smaller widening of the same trench was carried out near its northern termination, where a depression had appeared with remains of a peat layer. Between trench B and C towards the north an extra narrow sondage, F, was dug. Between sondage A and field D a 7m wide connecting passage was dug. In addition, at right angles to sondage A, a 50 m long sondage trench was dug towards the west, sondage E, to ascertain whether there were preserved remains of peat and gyttja on the slope towards the bog surface. In this way a total of c. 1000 m² was exposed level with the subsoil surface.

The subsoil material consists of very coarse yellow sand with much iron precipitation. In the coarse sand there are also pockets of fine, whitish-grey sand as well as greyish, slightly gravelly particles. This subsoil type, which is characterized as meltwater sand and gravel, is found along the eastern edge of the former bog, from which it slopes upwards almost to Vallensgård over a stretch of c. 500 m.

The excavation was primarily conducted in field D and the closest-lying part of sondage A. After the first surface shovelling, it became clear that the settlement was much damaged by ploughing, and that no identifiable structures in the form of house sites belonging to the Early Neolithic settlement were preserved. But various phenomena were registered and investigated:

1. The oldest strata with cultural remains were naturally formed and were the result of processes in the earth's crust during the last ice age. These are *frost wedges* which were formed under permafrost by the contraction of the soil layers such that polygonal soil arose, divided up by deep fissures. When the permafrost thawed, material from the upper soil strata sank down into the frost wedges. This can cause a redistribution of material that lies on the surface, as had happened with flint objects from the Late Glacial which were found in the investigation, and which are discussed below.

2. *Peat formation.* The result of another natural process that took place in stagnant water basins. From the edge of the bog an old gully extends in the north-eastern direction south-east around the plateau, where the settlement lies (figs. 1.1 and 1.4a). At a time when the groundwater level was higher than today, this gully was full of water and was connected to the large lake basin that filled up the later Vallens-

15

Fig. 1.6. Vallensgård I. The start of the excavation seen from the south. The flat area to the left is Brødreengen, the former bog that is now cultivated. In the foreground are Jørgen Skaarup and Finn Ole Sonne Nielsen. Photo PON.

gård Mose. As in the large lake, peat was formed at the bottom of the gully. A similar process, although on a smaller scale, took place in the small depression north of the settlement through which the midmost sondage trench passes, and at the bottom of the depression remains of peat layers were found. Above this there was a cultural layer with finds of flint and pottery from the Early Neolithic. In the Early Neolithic there may have been an open waterhole there. If this was the case, the groundwater surface may have lain around the 80 m contour line, so the water level of the lake may have reached all the way up to the edge of the Early Neolithic settlement. Apart from the one place at the northern end of sondage trench B no preserved peat was found in the investigation. In the 50 m long sondage trench E, which was continued west down the slope to the bottom of the drained bog basin, only pure subsoil sand was identified, which means that the peat that may have been left in this part of the bog has long since been destroyed by drainage and cultivation.

3. *Remains of tree-throws*. There were at least 14 such features in field D (fig. 2.2), and almost all of them contained cultural layer remains and Early Neolithic finds. They testify that forest grew on the plateau after the settlement was abandoned, although we cannot say when. In addition the content of settlement refuse in these features shows that the Early Neolithic cultural layer was originally distributed through the whole of the investigated field D.

4. *Cultural layers* which were dominated by settlement refuse from the Early Neolithic. On the whole they were only preserved up to the 80.5 m contour line. Remains of cultural layers were also preserved in small depressions at a higher level, and the cultural layer must originally have covered a large area. When the ploughing depth was increased by the introduction of the tractor plough, the highest-lying parts of the cultural layer must have been mixed with the cultivation layer with the result that cultural remains became visible on the field surface.

5. *Pits, postholes and unidentifiable features*. 139 fill layers were excavated and documented, and after they were cleared to the level of the subsoil surface, they were assessed as possible postholes or pits and then sectioned and excavated. As a result 68 features could be identified as postholes, 25 as possible postholes, 4 as pits, 2 as fire pits, while 40 had to be designated unidentifiable features. Most of them contained finds from the Early Neolithic settlement, but there were also postholes belonging to much later settlement activity in the Late Iron Age.

6. *Pottery depositions*. A special type of deposition was found in the form of dug holes containing whole pots of the funnel beaker type. These will be discussed in more detail in chapter 2.

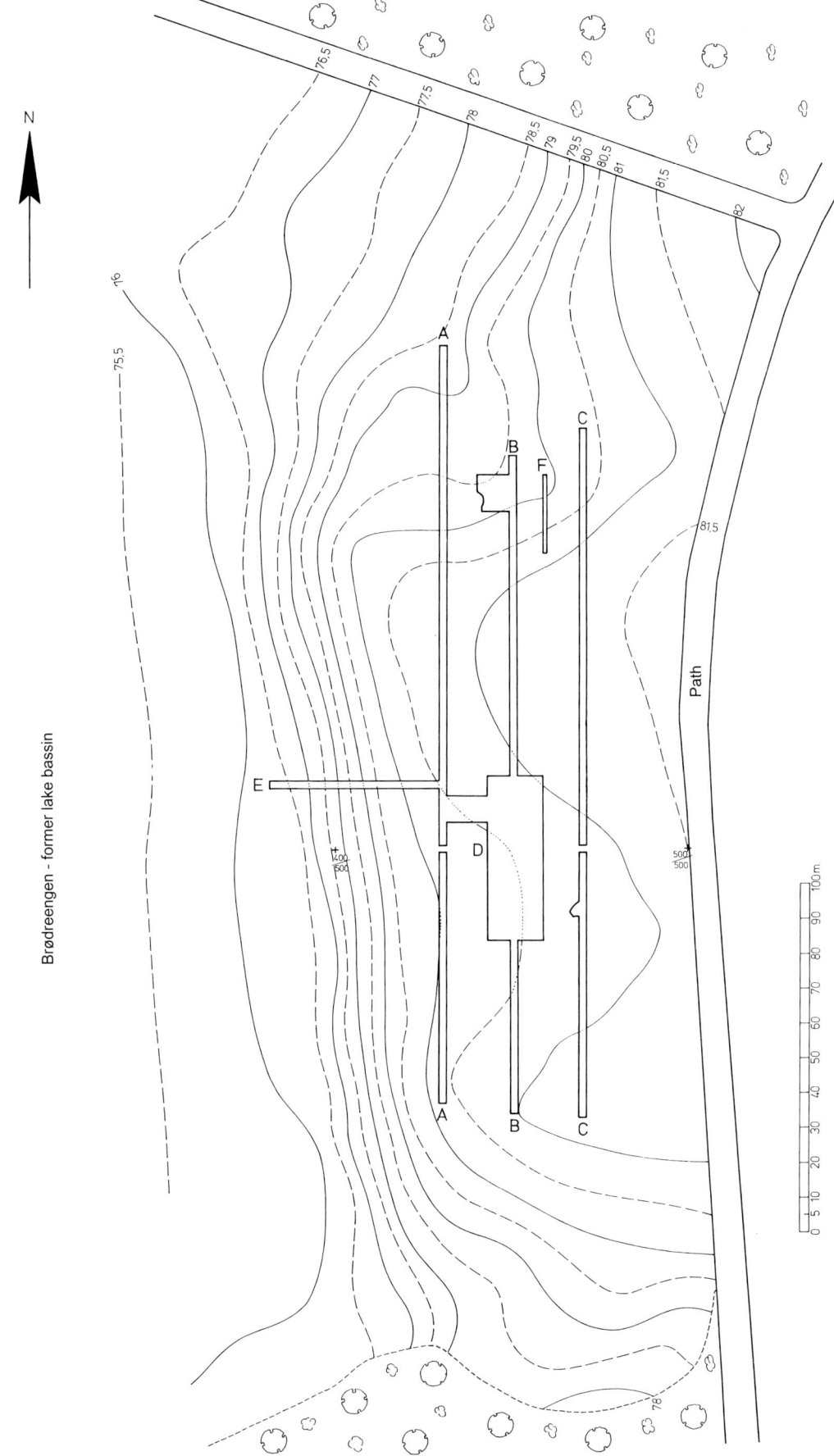

Fig. 1.7. Vallensgård I. Trial trenches and excavation areas. Survey: Poul Erik Skovgård.

Finds from the Late Glacial and Early Postglacial period

As so often happens during excavations on Bornholm, in this investigation more than one interesting archaeological find complex was encountered. The excavation turned up flakes, blades and individual implements of imported Senonian flint with a whitish patina in the uppermost layers of untouched meltwater sand. This means that these flint objects must be very old. Their placing in the untouched sand layers must be due to natural processes such as bioturbation or wind erosion.

In several places in the sondage trenches A, B and C and the middle field D, c. 700 m² in area, patinated and unpatinated worked flint were both found; some of this was embedded in pure subsoil material, while other finds were mixed with Neolithic settlement refuse in cultural layers and hollows. The find conditions in conjunction with the character of the flint and the technique with which it was produced make it possible to distinguish these from the worked flint that belongs to the Early Neolithic settlement. The oldest pieces are of dark, clear Senonian flint, and several of them look fresh and unaffected as if they have come directly from the chalk layers. On several pieces the thin, coarse cortex on the flint surface is preserved and unaffected (fig. 1.8). Other pieces of the originally clear Senonian flint are covered on the cleavage plane by a bluish-white patina. Such pieces must thus have been lying exposed for an extended period before they were embedded in the sand. Finally, some of the older pieces had been struck from flint nodules with an irregular, knocked-off surface, and this may have been flint from the moraine or from beach ridges. On the cleavage planes these pieces have a matt, dark surface.

Among the Neolithic flints there are also some imported, originally clear Senonian flints, but the fracture surface is matt and the colour is light grey. It is characteristic of the Zealand/Scania Senonian flint that in the fracture it changes colour in time from black or dark grey to a light colour, and that the visual impression changes from glossy to matt (Becker 1993a, 125). The older flint must have been in place long before the Neolithic farmers arrived, and this suggests settlement activities in the Late Glacial

Fig. 1.8. Vallensgård I. Blades and flakes from a settlement in the Late Glacial or early Postglacial period found scattered across the excavation areas. Photo John Lee, the National Museum. 2:3.

or Early Postglacial period. This is flint which, as mentioned, may have been imported to the island from areas with open chalk layers, but one also finds pieces that may have come from local moraine deposits and beach ridges. None of the older pieces of flint were made from the local ball flint nodules.

In total, 65 pieces of the older flint were identified, six of which were found in frost wedges, seven in pure subsoil sand and gravel close to the frost wedges; 46 were found during the clearing of the subsoil surface, in cultural layers, pits, postholes or remains of tree-throws, while 6 were found loose on the field surface. Only in the north-eastern part of field D were several pieces found within the same square metre; otherwise the pieces of flint were scattered over an area of at least 100 m² without having accumulated in significant concentrations. They may therefore very well come from more than one settlement presence and may possibly have been due to several visits to the place over a longer period. The blades were split off with a well controlled technique from the core, leaving traces of soft hammering or indirect percussion.

During and after the excavation a few pieces of worked, imported flint were collected from the field surface with patination of the same character as the above-described flint, including a unipolar core (Casati & Sørensen 2006, fig. 5). During later collections at the settlement area a tanged arrowhead was found with a broken-off outer point and a broken-off tang (fig. 1.9). The present length is 4.0 cm and its thickness is 0.3 cm. The tang is retouched on both sides from the back. The point is unretouched. The arrowhead is made from a flake of clear Senonian flint struck from a bipolar core. It falls within the variants of tanged arrowheads of both the Bromme and Ahrensburg type.

With no stratigraphy or opportunity for scientific dating, the dating of the older flint material to the Late Glacial / Early Postglacial period must remain provisional. There are few other finds on Bornholm for comparison. The Maglemose settlement Lundebro in Østerlars belongs to the earliest Maglemosian Culture, and among the stratigraphically oldest material one finds broad, early microliths and regular blades of imported Senonian flint (F.O.S. Nielsen 2001, 92 f.; Casati *et al.* 2004, fig. 6). Over an extended period in the Preboreal, when there was a land connection with the continent to the south, flint may have been imported from the natural occurrences of Senonian flint on Rügen.

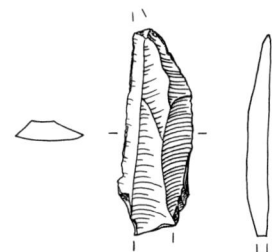

Fig. 1.9. Vallensgård I. Fragmented tanged arrowhead of Bromme or Ahrensburg type found on the surface. Pia Brejnholt del. 2:3.

Finds from the Early Neolithic

During the excavation in 1986 a body of material was found from the Early Neolithic, which is the main subject of this book, and which will be presented in chapter 2. During the registration of the finds and the drawing-up of the report on the investigation it became clear that the pottery finds were distributed over at least two Early Neolithic phases. This observation led to a division of the Early Neolithic pottery from Bornholm settlements that found support in Eva Koch's work from 1998, in which she divided the pottery found in bogs from the Zealand island group into types on the basis of a measurement of the pot profiles. Her division of the Early Neolithic funnel beakers into types 0-III was particularly interesting and was used as a means of dating during the work with the pottery from the Vallensgård settlement. Although this pottery typology was based on material different from that of Bornholm, on the face of it there was a striking convergence which might suggest that the division applied over a larger area of South Scandinavia. It was therefore tempting to test Eva Koch's division on pottery not only from this settlement but from all settlements from the Early Neolithic on Bornholm in an attempt to divide up the find material chronologically.

Notes
1. Åker Parish, sb. 211 and 212. – NM file no. 646/57. – BMR file no. 1396, 1397.
2. Note by Jørgen Meldgaard from December 1951 in the National Museum's Topographic Archive.
3. Åker Parish, sb. 197. – NM A53160.
4. BMR 2076x1.

2. The Early Neolithic settlement at Vallensgård I, c. 3800-3600 BC

Introduction

There were several reasons for the choice of this settlement, after the collection of surface finds, as an object of excavation. In the first place the location at the edge of Brødreengen offered the opportunity to find refuse, possibly in the form of organic material, beneath covered layers in the former lake basin outside the settlement. We also had knowledge of earlier finds – deposits of among other things thin-butted flint axes in the meadow outside the settlement, which underscored the significance of the place in the Early Neolithic. Finally, the surface finds showed that there were features or cultural layers at this place which were being ploughed away.

The excavation only partly fulfilled our expectations. The digging of sondage trench E from the edge of the plateau towards the west out in the meadow revealed that the plough layer ran directly over the subsoil surface, and that any lake deposits that might have been outside the settlement had long since disappeared as a result of drainage and cultivation. For that reason the investigation had to concentrate on the features that emerged after the removal of the plough layer on the plateau which bordered on the edge of the meadow. As described in the introduction, chapter 1, it was a mixture of natural and man-made features that emerged. The finds from there are reviewed in the following.

Finds from cultural layers and depressions

In all the sondage trenches and their extensions, remains of cultural layers appeared with finds from the Neolithic. Apart from a small collection of potsherds belonging to the Late Battle Axe Culture from the northern extension of trench B, all the Neolithic pottery fragments were dated to the Early Neolithic. It is therefore highly likely that the flint material from cultural layers and depressions also mainly comes from the Early Neolithic, with the exception of course of the older flint objects mentioned in chapter 1.

Pottery: In the excavation of cultural layers and depressions a total of 828 fragments of Early Neolithic pottery were found as well as one fragment of a clay disc with finger impressions in the edge (fig. 2.1). The bulk of this material was found during the excavation of the cultural layers in field D.

Most of the potsherds come from small-to-medium-sized funnel beakers. Only exceptionally do sherds of larger, thick-walled pots appear. Parts of two knobs show that a small number of the funnel beakers had been furnished with knobs on the side. Three fragments of lugs were found of a size that occurs on lugged beakers and lugged flasks, so one of these pot types is also represented – if not both.

The small funnel beaker fig. 2.1:1 was found at the top of the cultural layer in trench B south of field D. The pot is unornamented and is 7.0 cm in height. The bottom and most of one side are preserved. It can be identified as a funnel beaker of Eva Koch's type II (Koch 1998, 89-91). In a cultural layer in the southern part of trench C a neck/belly sherd of a similarly unornamented funnel beaker of about the same size was found.

Besides these two pot fragments, 13 unornamented and 53 ornamented rim sherds of funnel beakers were found as well as 758 unornamented side and bottom sherds, as well as 3 lug sherds, in the various cultural layers and depressions. No side sherds are ornamented, which must mean that the material is without elements of funnel beaker pottery from the later part of the Early Neolithic and from the subsequent periods of the Funnel Beaker Culture. Ornaments are exclusively associated with the rim

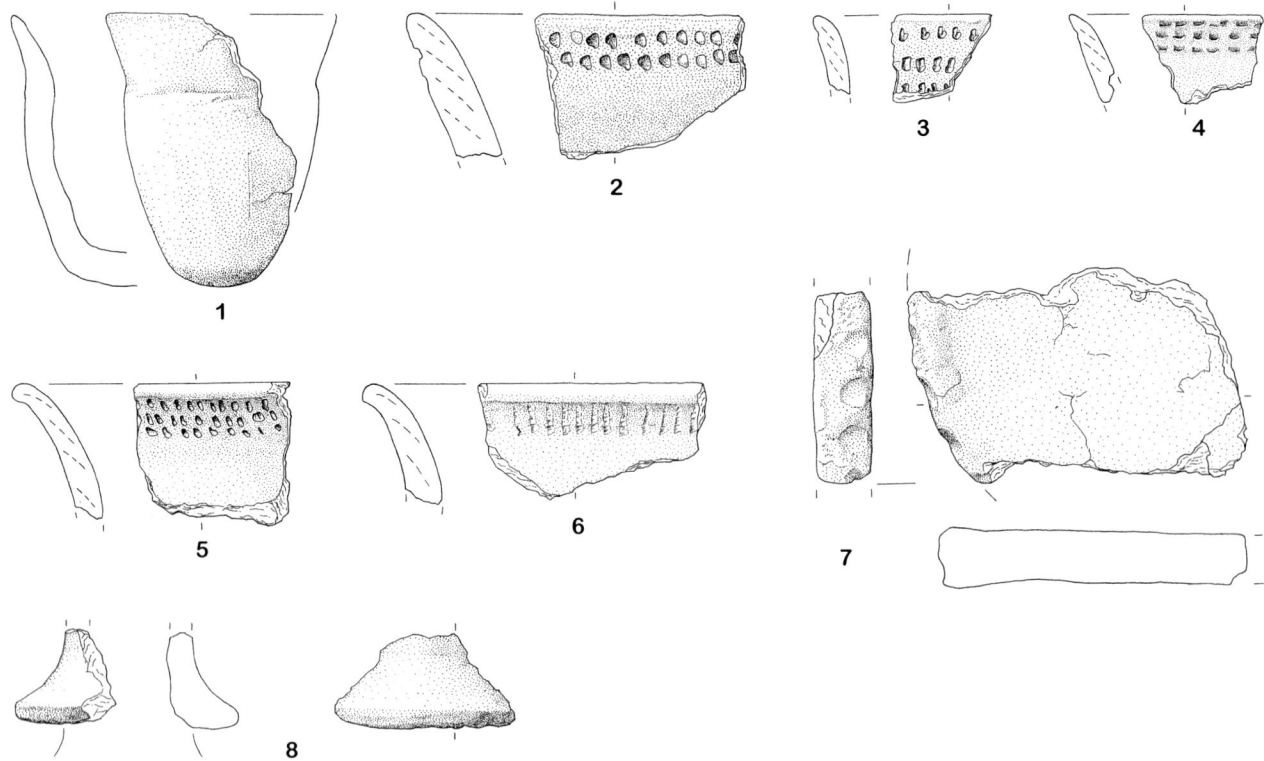

Fig. 2.1. Finds from cultural layers and depressions. Small funnel beaker (1), rim sherds of funnel beakers (2-6), edge fragment of clay disc (7) and collar sherd from a collared flask (8). Pia Brejnholt del. 1:2.

zone of the funnel beakers. Of the 53 ornamented rim sherds, 41 have various kinds of indentations and impressions of fingers or nails, while 12 have impressions of two-ply cord.

The various kinds of indentations and impressions on pot rims from this settlement are shown in fig. 2.8. Of these motifs the following appear on the ornamented rims from cultural layers and depressions: 1a, 2a-b, 3a, 4a-c, 5a-b, 6a, 6c, 8b, 9a-b, 10a, 10c. A selection of the ornamented sherds is shown in fig. 2.1:2-6.

Flint: From cultural layers and depressions, a total of 96 pieces of flint were recovered, which is a strikingly small number, even given that this was not a total excavation of the layers. The flint is distributed over tools and debitage (see table 2.1). The imported flint predominates, and a good quarter of this is fragments and flakes from polished axes. A single flake with a polished facet from the southern part of trench B may come from a pointed-butted flint axe, but the identification is uncertain. Other slightly larger fragments with parts of both the broad side and the narrow side preserved come from axes with quadrilateral cross-sections. The largest fragment of a polished axe was found in a depression in the southern part of trench A (fig. 2.10:1).

Other stone: In the peat-like layer in the northern extension of trench B an almost circular crushing stone of granite was found. This area is also the only place at the site where other Neolithic pottery was found, in the form of sherds of a pot from the Late Battle Axe Culture (F.O. Nielsen 1989 fig. 4f), so it is not certain that the crushing stone belongs to the Early Neolithic settlement. In a soil layer in the northern part of trench A a sandstone grindstone was found, and a fragment of a grindstone emerged from the cultural layer in the southwestern part of field D.

Finds from remains of tree-throws

In field D there were at least 12 disturbances in the form of tree-throws whose fill contained remains of the cultural layer that had covered the area (fig. 2.2). In these pockets of cultural layer there was a total of 107 potsherds of funnel beakers, a sherd possibly of a lugged beaker, a fragment of the collar of a collared flask (fig. 2.1:8) and a rim sherd from a clay disc with finger impressions in the edge (fig. 2.1:7). A neck/belly sherd from a funnel beaker has a knob on the shoulder. Of flint implements a single scraper was found, and otherwise only flint debitage.

Finds from postholes

Of the 139 excavated features 68 were identified as postholes, and 25 assessed as possible postholes. That no more certain identifications were possible was due to the fact that many pits were diffuse, with no clear posthole structure. Even if a hole was clearly contoured in the surface, its downward demarcation could be difficult to ascertain because of the washed-out subsoil sand. Of the 68 postholes it was possible to ascribe 33 to the Iron Age settlement (see below). What remained were 35 postholes and 25 possible postholes, a total of 60 holes, 33 of which contained datable Early Neolithic find material. Of these, 28 were in field D, marked on the plan fig. 2.2. These need not all be features from the Neolithic, even though they contained Neolithic finds since, when later pits were dug, objects may have been transported down into the holes from the cultural layer. In fact only six postholes were identified with certainty as Early Neolithic holes on the basis of a visual assessment of the nature of the fill.

In field D the postholes seemed to be distributed unsystematically over the excavation surface. In only one place, close to the northwestern edge of the field, three clearly Neolithic postholes, features D1, D3 and D4, appeared in a row. This led to an extension of the field between trench A and field D, but no more postholes of this character appeared in the vicinity. Like others of the investigated postholes the three probably formed part of a house structure, although its form and size cannot be determined.

Table 2.2 lists the finds from postholes and possible postholes. Fifteen postholes contained rim sherds or larger fragments of funnel beakers. Of these, five rim sherds were undecorated. As was the case with the pottery finds from the cultural layer, most fragments of funnel beakers had incised ornamentation. Sherds with incised decoration and fingernail impressions appeared in ten postholes; sherds with decoration consisting of impressions of two-ply cord were found in only two of the postholes.

The postholes contained only a small number of

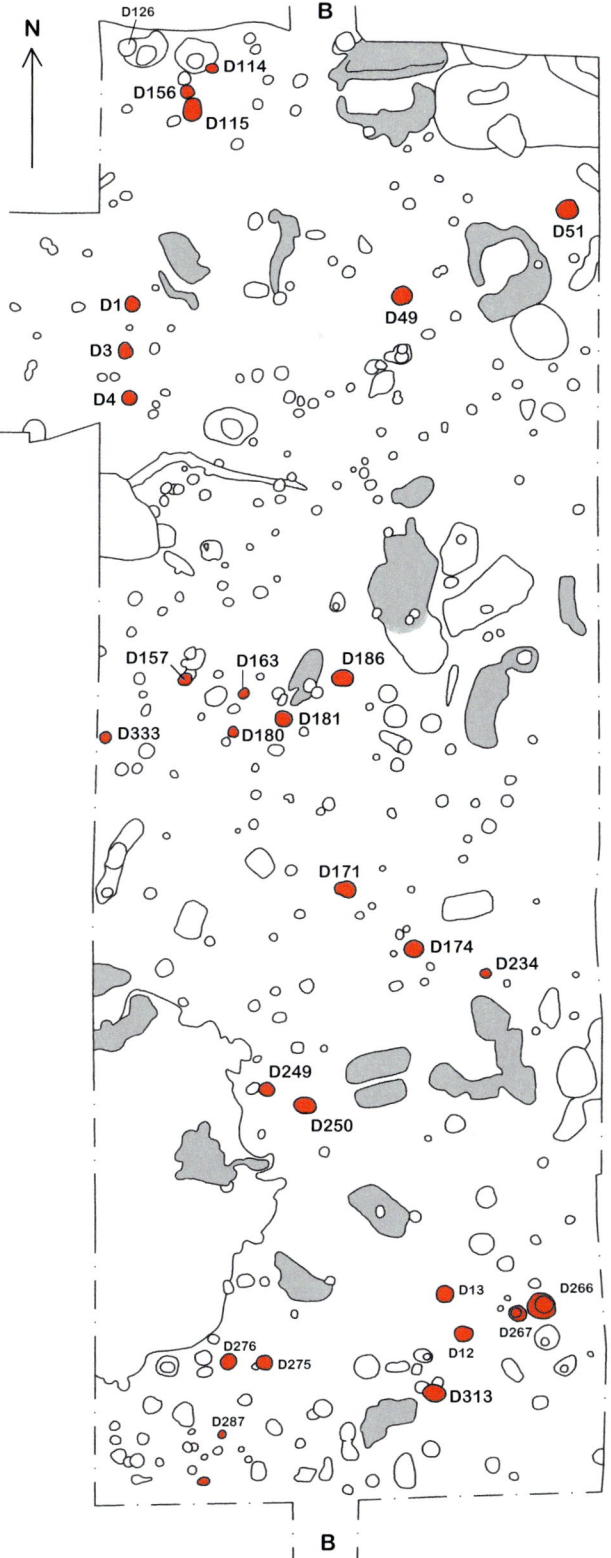

Fig. 2.2. Plan of area D. Postholes and pits associated with the Early Neolithic settlement are marked in red, tree-throws in grey. Graphics: Cecilie Krause/P.O. Nielsen.

flint objects, thus repeating the pattern of the scanty flint material from the cultural layer. Of nine flakes of imported flint, three have polished facets. To these we can add one axe fragment.

Vallensgård I	Cultural layers and depressions	Remains of tree-throws	Post-holes and possible postholes	Pits and indeter-mined features	Other	Sum
Pottery						
Unornamented rim sherds of funnel beakers	13	2	5	5	2	27
Rim sherds with or without indentations	1	-	-	1	-	2
Neck and shoulder of funnel beakers with indentations	-	-	3	-	-	3
Rim sherds with finger/nail impressions	1	-	8	1	3	13
Rim sherds with various indentations	40	3	10	10	10	73
Parts of funnel beakers with two-ply cord impressions	-	-	-	3	-	3
Rim sherds with two-ply cord impressions	12	4	3	8	6	33
Sherds with lugs	3	1	-	2	-	6
Sherds of lugged jars	-	-	-	1	-	1
Sherds of collared flasks	-	1	-	-	-	1
Unornamented sherds	758	96	130	263	211	1455
Clay disc fragments	1	1	-	-	-	2
Pottery vessels and fragments, sum	*829*	*108*	*159*	*293*	*232*	*1619*
Flint						
Flakes of imported flint	47	8	6	28	13	102
Axe fragments	7	-	1	2	-	10
Flakes with polished facets	12	-	3	14	2	31
Blades and blade fragments	5	-	-	1	2	8
Blades and flakes with retouch	2	-	-	1	-	3
Scrapers	3	1	-	-	1	5
Flakes and cores of ball flint	5	2	2	2	3	14
Flakes of other kinds of flint	4	2	1	-	-	7
Fire affected flint	11	-	-	6	1	18
Flint objects, sum	*96*	*13*	*13*	*54*	*22*	*198*
Other materials						
Whole quernstones and fragments	-	-	-	1	-	1
Whole grindstones and fragments	2	-	-	-	-	2
Crushing stones	1	-	-	-	-	1
Pieces of burnt clay	-	12	>12	>130	>11	>165

Table 2.1. Summary of finds from Vallensgård I.

From three of the postholes in which identifiable parts of funnel beakers were found material was AMS ^{14}C dated:

Posthole D1 which had a depth of 0.24 m, contained a neck sherd of a funnel beaker of Eva Koch's type II with three horizontal rows of narrow, oblong indentations below the rim (fig. 2.3:1) and two other sherds. A piece of charcoal from the fill in the posthole was dated and gave the following result:

AAR-8805. Charcoal of alder (*Alnus sp.*), a piece of wood with 6 growth rings, determined by C. Malmros. Dating: 4975±55 BP, cal. 3900-3660 BC (1σ) (with 58.4% probability: 3800-3690 BC), 3950-3640 BC (2σ) (with 75.5% probability: 3820-3640 BC).

Posthole D3 was found just under 1 m south of D1 and was 0.21 m deep. In the top middle part of the fill lay a larger fragment of the neck and shoulder of a funnel beaker of Eva Koch's type II with five rows of small, oval indentations forming a composite pattern, with the indentations alternately vertical and diagonal in each row (fig. 2.3:3). A small rim sherd of a larger, more thick-walled funnel beaker with two horizontal rows of deep fingernail impressions beneath the rim (fig. 2.3:2) was found, as well as three undecorated sherds. A piece of charcoal from the fill in the posthole has been AMS ^{14}C-dated:

AAR-8806. Charcoal of hazel (*Corylus avellana*) branchwood with 5 growth rings without bark edge, determined by C. Malmros. Dating: 4900±49 BP, cal. 3760-3640 BC (1σ) (with 66.4% probability: 3720-3640 BC), 3790-3540 BC (2σ) (with 93.3% probability 3790-3630 BC).

Posthole D181 was found in field D and was 0.30 m deep. In the fill lay a sherd of the neck and the top part of the belly of a largish funnel beaker of Eva

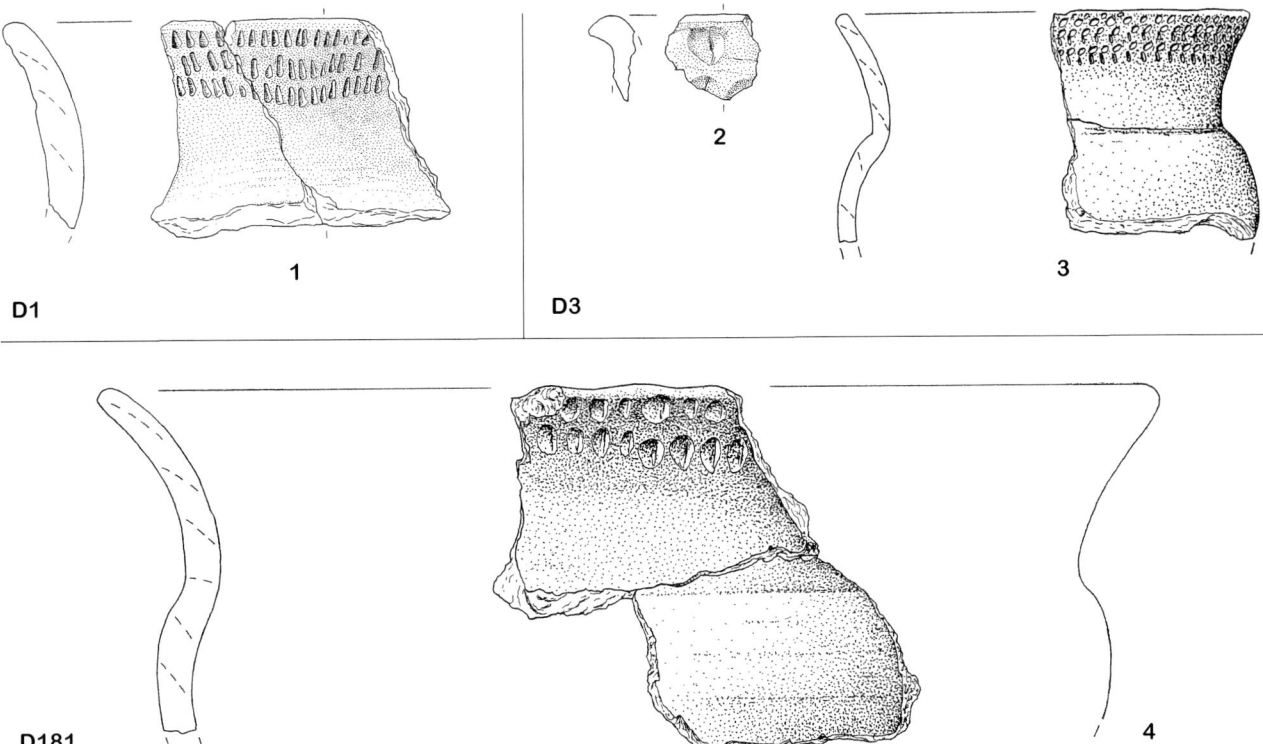

Fig. 2.3. Pottery from postholes D1, D3 and D181. Pia Brejnholt & Ole Guldager del. 1:2.

Koch's type I/II ornamented with two rows of fingernail impressions beneath the rim (fig. 2.3:4). A piece of charcoal from the fill in the posthole has been AMS ^{14}C dated:

AAR-8807. Charcoal of alder (*Alnus sp.*), a piece of wood with 6-7 growth rings, determined by C. Malmros. Dating: 4945 ±55 BP, cal. 3770-3650 BC (1σ, with 68.2% probability), 3940-3630 BC (2σ, with 95.4% probability: 3810-3630 BC).

Finds from pits

Of the 139 investigated holes, four were categorized as pits on the basis of their shape and content, while 40 could only be called unidentifiable dug holes. The latter may include putative bottoms of postholes. The four pits, D115, D171, D249 and D313, lay respectively in the northern, midmost and southern part of field D. Of the other investigated fill layers four were found in sondage trench A, while the rest were spread over field D.

The four pits and 33 of the 40 unidentifiable holes contained finds that are listed in table 2.1. The finds make up a total of 4 unornamented rim sherds of funnel beakers, a whole funnel beaker of type II with two rows of indentations beneath the rim (fig. 2.4:1), one rim sherd with fingernail impressions, and 8 rim sherds with various types of indentation. There are ten sherds or parts of funnel beakers ornamented with two-ply cord, which is proportionally more than were found in the postholes, and there is one sherd of a lugged jar.

Like the cultural layer and the postholes, the pits and the undeterminable fill layers contained a modest amount of flint implements and debitage, although there was more than four times as much flint in the pits as in the postholes. A total of 16 pieces of flint come from polished flint axes, including two axe fragments and 14 flakes with polished facets. Six of the flakes with polished facets come from pit D249, which also contained an axe fragment (fig. 2.6:2). The only quernstone found at the settlement appeared in pit D313 in the form of a fire-brittle fragment.

In the 4 pits, identifiable fragments of funnel beakers were found and there are also AMS ^{14}C datings from three of the pits:

Pit D171 lay slightly south of the middle of field D. In the surface the contour was a little irregular

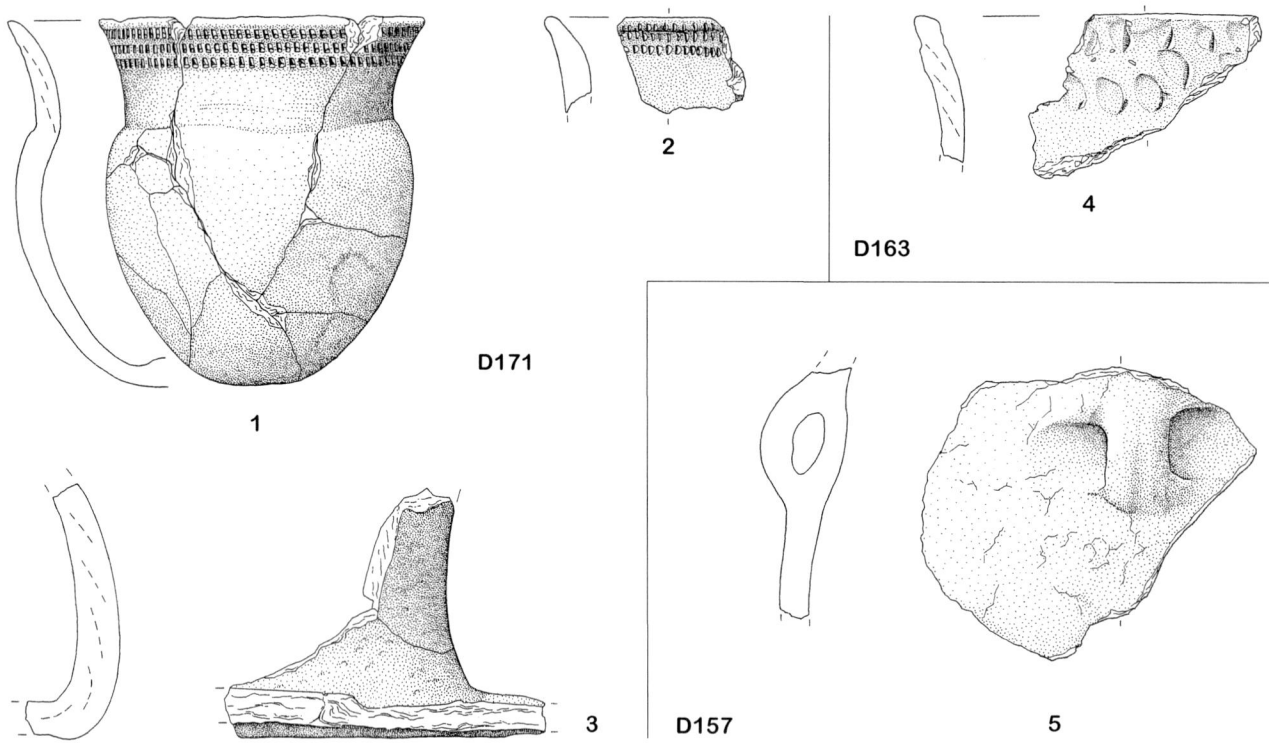

Fig. 2.4. Pottery from pit D171 and postholes/pits D157 and D163. Pia Brejnholt del. 1:2.

and measured 0.65 × 0.55 m. In section the hole has evenly sloping sides and a round bottom. The depth was 0.24 m measured from the surface of the subsoil. The fill in the top half consisted of light-brown to dark-brown sand mixed with clay and soil. In the bottom half the colour was a little lighter. At the top of the fill layer an approximately whole funnel beaker of Eva Koch's type II was found lying almost horizontally. The upward-facing parts of the neck and shoulder area were damaged by ploughing or mechanical excavation. The pot was 10 cm in height and was ornamented with 3 horizontal rows of small, square indentations beneath the rim (fig. 2.4:1). Beside this pot in the pit fill there was a rim sherd of a similar beaker with a slightly thickened rim, in the upper surface of which short indentations had been made, and beneath which there were two horizontal rows of small, oblong indentations (fig. 2.4:2). In addition two neck/belly sherds of funnel beakers, 8 unornamented sherds and a sherd of the neck and shoulder of a large lugged jar were found (fig. 2.4:3). A piece of charcoal from layer 2 has been AMS ^{14}C-dated:

AAR-8802. Charcoal, wood identified by C. Malmros as branchwood with 6 growth rings without bark edge of apple, rowan or hawthorn (*Pomaceae*). Dating: 4990 ± 60 BP, cal. 3940-3690 BC (1σ) (with 52% probability: 3810-3690 BC), 3950-3650 BC (2σ, with 95.4% probability).

Pit D115 was found in the northern part of field D. It was contoured in the surface as an oval fill layer that measured 0.77 × 0.55 m. In section the hole had very steep sides and an irregular bottom. The depth was 0.40 m measured from the surface. The fill is described as grey to light-brown sand mixed with soil with grey-black areas mixed with a few charcoal particles. Some potsherds lay evenly distributed from top to bottom in the fill: several large sherds of the neck of a large funnel beaker of Eva Koch's type III, ornamented beneath the rim with eight horizontal lines in two-ply cord (fig. 2.5:1), two rim sherds of funnel beakers with one horizontal row of oblong indentations beneath the rim (fig. 2.5:2), one rim sherd with several rows of small, oblong diagonal indentations, both on the edge of the actual rim and beneath the rim (fig. 2.5:3) and one rim sherd of a small, thin-walled funnel beaker with horizontal and vertical lines in two-ply cord (fig. 2.5:4). In addition there were several sherds of the bottom part of a large, thick-walled pot. Nine flakes of flint were found, two of these with polished facets. Of organic material there was a charred shell of hazelnut and charcoal.

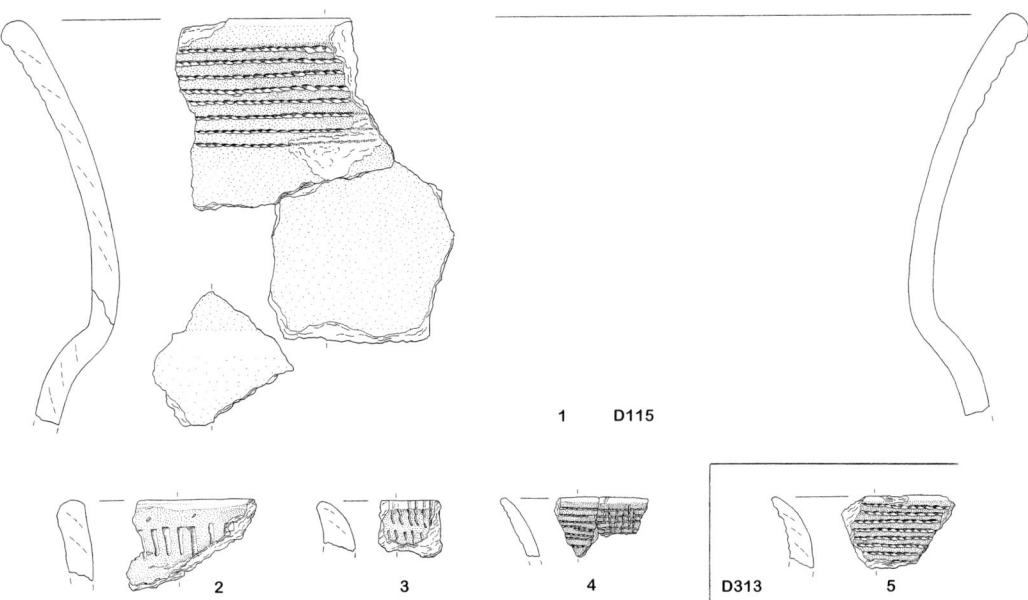

Fig. 2.5. Pottery from pits D115 and D313. Pia Brejnholt del. (1) 2:5, (2-5) 1:2.

Finally, one piece of burnt clay was found. There are two AMS ¹⁴C-datings of material from the pit:

AAR-8803. Charred hazelnut (*Corylus avellana*). Dating: 4865±50 BP, cal. 3710-3540 BC (1σ) (with 62.9% probability: 3710-3630 BC), 3770-3520 BC (2σ) (with 76.2% probability: 3770-3620 BC).

AAR-8804. Charcoal, wood identified by C. Malmros as alder (*Alnus sp.*). Dating: 5048±48 BP, cal. 3950-3780 BC (1σ) (with 52.2% probability: 3950-3840 BC), 3960-3710 BC (2σ, with 95.4% probability).

The datings give us two different ages. The youngest dating of hazel (AAR-8803) must be closest to the time when the material was placed in the pit. The older dating of charcoal (AAR-8804) is not necessarily due to the of the specimen's own age (the wood is alder); it is more likely to be older charcoal which, at the time of the making of the pit, was mixed with its fill.

Pit D313 lay in the southern part of field D. The fill layer had an oval contour in the surface and measured 0.77 × 0.55 m. In section the hole had evenly sloping sides and a flat, irregular bottom. The depth was 0.20 m measured from the surface of the subsoil. The fill consisted of very dark, almost black sand mixed with soil and charcoal and parts of charred apples. In the fill a rim sherd of a funnel beaker was found ornamented beneath the rim with eight horizontal lines in two-ply cord (fig. 2.5:5) as well as seven unornamented sherds. In addition a flint flake and a fire-brittle blade were found, as well as a fire-brittle fragment of a quernstone of reddish granite, three pieces of burnt clay and remains of charred apples. A specimen of the latter has been AMS ¹⁴C-dated:

AAR-9468. Charred apple (*Malus sp.*), identified by C. Malmros. Dating: 4770±46 BP, cal. 3640-3520 BC (1σ, with 68.2% probability), 3650-3370 BC (2σ, with 95.4% probability).

Pit D249 lay in the southern part of field D in the western side near the edge of the cultural layer and had an oval contour at the surface. The pit was cut through at one end by a younger hole but had originally had a length of 0.55 m and a width of 0.45 m. The hole had steeply sloping sides and a flat bottom that reached a depth of 0.28 m measured from the surface of the subsoil. Three layers were distinguishable in the pit. 1) The middle area at the top was filled to a depth of 0.14 m with fragments of clay-and-wattle which together weighed 1.6 kg. 2) Beneath this a layer of light-coloured yellowish-brown sand was found. 3) At the bottom a greyish sand layer was found, coloured dark by charcoal dust containing small pieces of charcoal. Among the clay-and-wattle in the top layer three potsherds were found, one of which had remains of cord ornamentation. In the bottom layer several potsherds were found that could be assembled into most of a 12 cm tall funnel beaker of type II/III with five horizontal lines in two-ply

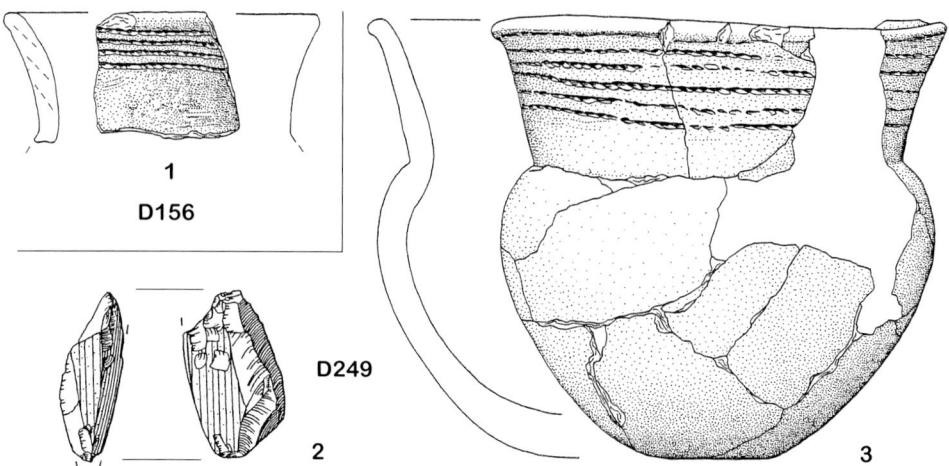

Fig. 2.6. Pottery from post-hole D156 and pit D249. Pia Brejnholt del. 1:2.

cord beneath the rim (fig. 2.6:3). In the same layer a rim sherd and a neck sherd were found with faint indentations and four unornamented sherds, as well as nine pieces of imported flint, including a fragment of one blade corner of a four-sided flint axe with polishing on the broad and narrow surfaces (fig. 2.6:2), and three flakes with traces of polishing. From the pit with no indication of layers come nine flint flakes, three of these with polished facets and two with a milky patina which are possibly Late Palaeolithic, as well as two pieces of fire-brittle flint.

Pottery

Funnel beakers

Funnel beakers and funnel beaker sherds from the settlement fall roughly speaking into two categories. One category has flared necks, indentations at the rim and rounded shoulders, beneath which the lower part narrows towards the bottom. The other category has a tall neck, cord impressions beneath the rim and a rounded lower body. In terms of the original type division into A and B beakers, which was carried out by C.J. Becker (1947), the first category corresponds more or less to an intermediate form between A and B beakers, while the second comes closest to Becker's B beakers.

The most recent typology of funnel beakers based on pot profiles has been drawn up by Eva Koch, who has dealt with bog-found pots from the Zealand Island Group (Koch 1998). She divides funnel beakers from there into ten types (types 0 – IX), the first five of which fall within the Early Neolithic (fig. 2.7). The first of these five types, type 0, has been safely dated by stratigraphy and ^{14}C datings to the beginning of the Early Neolithic, and the last, type IV, has been safely established chronologically in graves and settlements from EN C / EN II. It is not so easy, on the other hand, to place the three intervening types, I, II and III, in a successive order (Koch 1998, 111-113). The ^{14}C datings so far for each of these three types also fall within the same time interval (*idem* fig. 84). Eva Koch's types 0 and I correspond to Becker's type A, her type II rather to an intermediate form, A/B, while type III corresponds to Becker's type B. As will be evident from the preceding review of the features and their find contents, the funnel beakers have been typed according to Eva Koch's classification, and the following will be an account of the principles applied.

Forms and proportions of the funnel beakers

In the settlement discussed here, besides funnel beakers with a full profile which can be identified in terms of Eva Koch's classification into types, there are fragments that cannot be identified in the same way because only part of the profile has been preserved. But a few fragments consist of neck sherds where one can measure the neck height and the diameter of the rim. We have measured Eva Koch's funnel beakers from the Zealand Island Group to gain an idea of how the relationship between these two measurements varies within her types I-III. Calculations have been done for nine of the typed funnel beakers of type I in Eva Koch's catalogue, for 23 funnel beakers of type II and for 25 funnel beakers of type III. No measurements have been taken from lugged beakers, severely fragmented pots or atypical examples. The measurements give the following results:

Fig. 2.7. Eva Koch's funnel beaker types 0-IV (after Koch 1998).

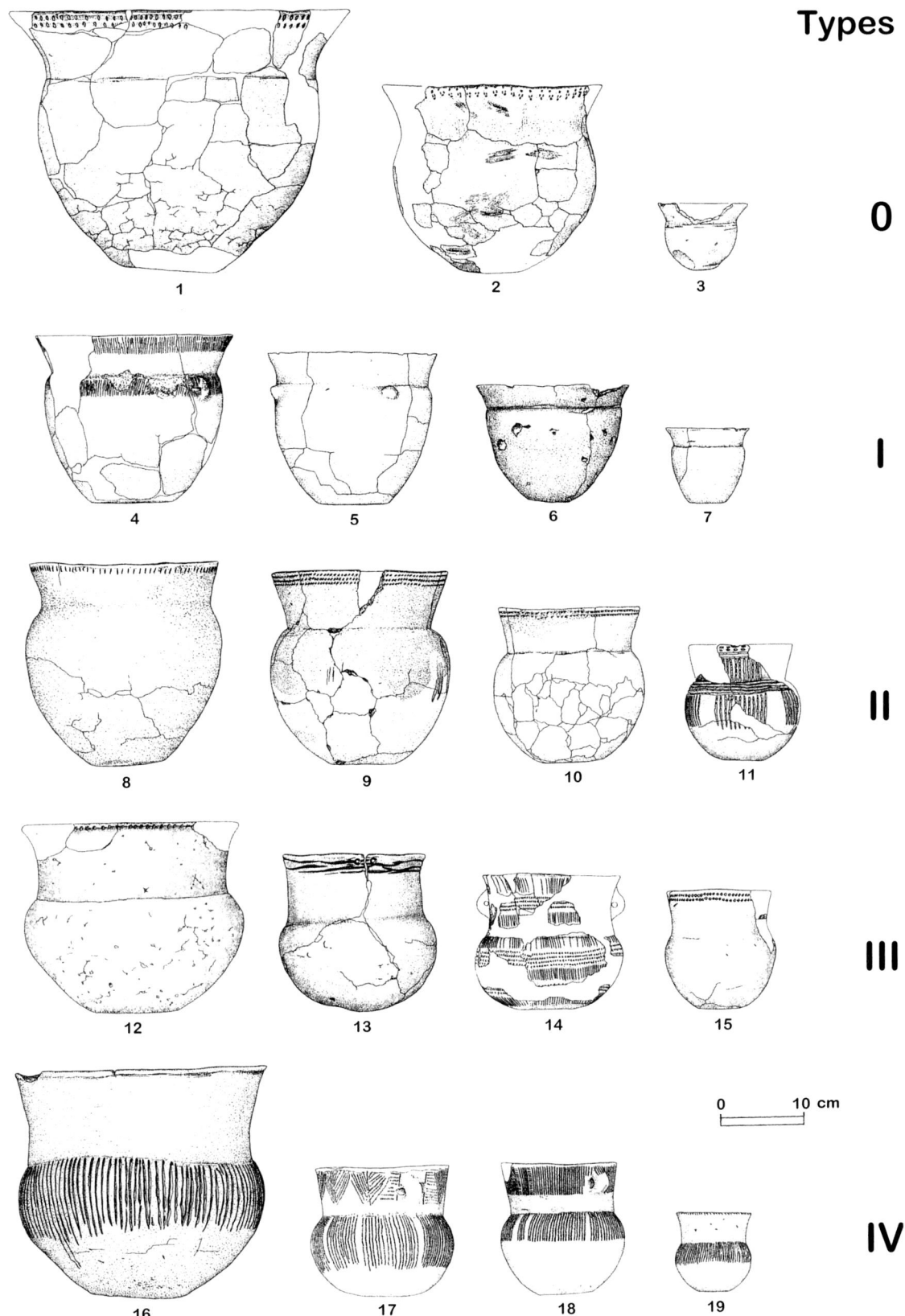

Types

Neck height as % of rim diameter:

Type	Variation	Average
I	12.6 – 20%	16.7%
II	20.4 – 34.5%	28.5%
III	35.4 – 52.6%	43%

There is no overlap among the values for the three types of funnel beaker. In other words they can be distinguished by this one element of proportion, since the borderline values lie at 20% and 35% respectively. No corresponding measurements have been made of funnel beakers of type IV or other

29

types. Although this too would be interesting, the measurements of type IV and the later types overlap with those of type III, so other criteria are necessary to distinguish these types.

The relationship between rim diameter and neck height has been used before, by Bengt Salomonsson, for comparisons among finds of Early Neolithic settlement pottery from various sites on Zealand and in Scania. His measurements showed that the neck height of the funnel beakers from Värby pit V22 in western Scania varies between 10 and 20% of the rim diameter – that is, it corresponds on the whole to that of Eva Koch's type I. Furthermore, it was evident from Salomonsson's measurements that in funnel beakers from St. Valby pit BN and Värby pit V1 it exceeds 20% and thus crosses the boundary between Eva Koch's funnel beakers of type I and II (Salomonsson 1970, 78-80).

If we divide the Bornholm funnel beakers into types with the aid of the borderline values for the Zealand funnel beakers of types I-III, we must assume that the pottery forms in the Early Neolithic on the whole followed the same development on Zealand, in Scania and on Bornholm. Further on in the text, when we include more finds from the Early Neolithic on Bornholm, we shall be better able to evaluate whether this assumption holds. It is necessary, however, to state one reservation when one is using measurements of the pottery. This concerns the largest and the smallest pots, which are difficult to fit into any system. The proportions change, both when the earthenware pots are very small, and when they are very large. The method used here has its limitations, although one cannot say precisely where they lie. It is possible that the measurements of the profiles that Eva Koch uses to distinguish among the funnel beaker types also have their limitations when it comes to the very small and the very large pots. Here and in the following, only funnel beakers will be typed, while funnel bowls and lugged beakers will be excluded.

Neck fragments and whole funnel beakers from the settlement are divided up on the basis of the ratio between neck height and rim diameter, in the following called the neck index, and are in this way classified according to the types of funnel beaker defined by Eva Koch. As will already be evident from the survey of finds, pots and pot fragments from the settlement Vallensgård I are distributed almost exclusively among funnel beaker types II and III.

To *funnel beakers of type II* we can assign five larger and smaller parts of the pots. The pot form can be described on the basis of the whole 10 cm tall beaker from pit D171 (fig. 2.4:1). Its neck index is 34.5, which is close to the borderline between type II and type III. The neck is flared, and its height amounts to a little less than one third of the height of the whole pot. The transition between neck and belly is clearly marked. The lower part is widest 1.5 cm below the point where it begins, and it narrows beneath this towards the relatively small stand. On the inside of the pot the bottom thickens towards the middle. Compared with Eva Koch's Zealand funnel beakers of type II, whose bottom part is described as 'barrel-shaped', this beaker has a wider, more rounded shoulder profile. The beaker fragment from posthole D3, with a neck index of 28.8, has a very similar neck and shoulder profile (fig. 2.3:3). The small fragment no. 83 from posthole D1 (fig. 2.3:1) has a neck index of 21.25 calculated from the reconstructed rim diameter. The small beaker, only 7 cm tall, from the cultural layer, with a neck index of 31.3, has a flatter shoulder profile (fig. 2.1:1). This must be regarded as a miniature beaker which has the main features of this funnel beaker type but which is not a type example. On the neck and shoulder fragment from feature D181 it is hard to measure the rim diameter accurately (fig. 2.3:4). If one assigns to it a rim diameter of 28 cm as it is reconstructed here in the drawing, the neck index becomes only 18-19, and this pot then falls within the variation range of funnel beakers of type I. On the other hand the pot, with its flared, concave neck profile, corresponds to the funnel beakers that have been assigned to type II. Because of the uncertainty about the measurements we must be content to assign this pot fragment to type I/II.

We must regard the small funnel beaker from pit D249 (fig. 2.6:3) as an intermediate form between funnel beakers of type II and funnel beakers of type III. It is slightly uneven in structure, so the neck height varies between 3.9 and 4.3 cm, which makes the neck index vary between 32.5 and 35.8. The pot has a slightly broader shoulder than funnel beakers of type II and is furnished with a slightly thickened, rounded rim, beneath which there are five horizontal lines in two-ply cord.

Funnel beakers of type III included a rim sherd from posthole D156 with four horizontal lines in two-ply cord beneath the rim. This comes from a small funnel beaker with a neck index of 38.7 (fig. 2.6:1). In pit D115 there were neck sherds from a large funnel beaker, ornamented beneath the rim with eight horizontal lines in two-ply cord. The preserved fragment is not large enough for the rim diameter to be measured entirely accurately, but as the neck area of the pot is reconstructed in fig. 2.5:1, the neck index is only 30.0. This is probably because the large pots of type III may have a proportionately shorter neck than the smaller funnel beakers. Despite the low neck index we will regard this neck fragment as belonging to funnel beakers of type III. To indicate that it is a variant of this type which because of its size has a different ratio between rim diameter and neck height from the small and medium-sized funnel beakers, the designation 'large funnel beaker of type III' is used.

Ornamentation on the funnel beakers

The ornamental motifs are also included in Eva Koch's definitions and descriptions of her funnel beaker types (1998, 75-79, 81-108). On funnel beakers and lugged beakers of types I-III there are several examples of ornamentation on both the neck section and the belly section. In the sherd material from the settlement, however, there are hardly any ornamented belly sherds. If we look at the ornamentation of funnel beakers of type I (without lugs) in Eva Koch's catalogue of funnel beakers found in Zealand bogs, fewer than half, six out of 14 examples, are furnished with rim ornaments. Four of the depicted pots have a cordon applied outside on the rim or a little beneath the rim, in which there are finger impressions. Only two pots have other rim ornamentation, in both cases in the form of two horizontal rows of triangular indentations. Pit A at the settlement Sigersted III with funnel beakers of type I contained 111 rim sherds, 41 of which were ornamented (Nielsen 1985a, 99-101), which gives them an ornamentation percentage of only 37%. The rim on large funnel beakers from Sigersted III had a single or double moulded strip beneath the rim with either finger impressions or impressions that form an arcade-like pattern. On rim sherds of medium-sized and smaller funnel beakers, which had no cordon at the rim, there were in 10 cases one horizontal row of indentations and in eight cases two horizontal rows of indentations of different shapes: round, oval, D-shaped and triangular. These rows of indentations were often placed very close to the edge of the rim. In a single case the only ornament was short incisions across the horizontal edge of the rim. The Zealand funnel beakers of type I have sparse, simple rim ornamentation.

Rim ornamentation appears more frequently on Eva Koch's funnel beakers of type II and comprises several kinds of indentation. On the other hand there are no funnel beakers of this type that have cordons at the rim. On 11 of the pots in Eva Koch's catalogue there is one horizontal row of indentations, while in 14 cases there are two rows and in two cases three rows of indentations. These indentations have very varied shapes and composite patterns appear where two parallel rows of indentations have been made with instruments of different shapes. There are also examples of funnel beakers ornamented with two, three or more horizontal lines formed by impressions of two-ply cord. In a single case there are composite patterns consisting of rows of indentations and lines formed with stab-and-drag grooving (Koch 1998 find no. 225).

On funnel beakers of type III from the Zealand bog finds, one also sees horizontal rows of indentations, in nine cases in the form of a single row, in two cases with two rows of indentations. Alongside round and D-shaped indentations oblong, vertical indentations appear. Impressions of two-ply cord occur both as horizontal and vertical lines, and as a new feature there are on some of the pots parallel horizontal lines formed by simple grooves, sometimes interrupted and with blank space in between. In addition there is an ornamentation consisting of both horizontal and vertical lines. On funnel beakers of this type there are also surface-covering ornaments consisting of a combination of indentations and lines which may have been made with grooving. Such patterns on the neck of the pot may be repeated at the top of the belly (Koch 1998, find no. 253). On two cord-ornamented funnel beakers of this type the rim is slightly thickened and turned outward so it forms a 'lip'.

After this brief review of the ornamental motifs on the Zealand funnel beakers of types I-III, we can look at the rim ornaments that appear on the funnel beakers from Vallensgård. The individual motifs are compared in fig. 2.8, where we can note in the first place that there are no examples of pots with cordons at the rim as on large funnel beakers of type I. Nor are there pot fragments with a neck and shoulder profile characteristic of type I. However, one does see a few ornament types that are familiar with that type – on the one hand the short, lateral indentations on the actual horizontal rim (ornament 1a); on the other hand one or two rows of finger impressions with or without clear traces of fingernails (ornament 2a-b). Tellingly enough, this ornament is found on

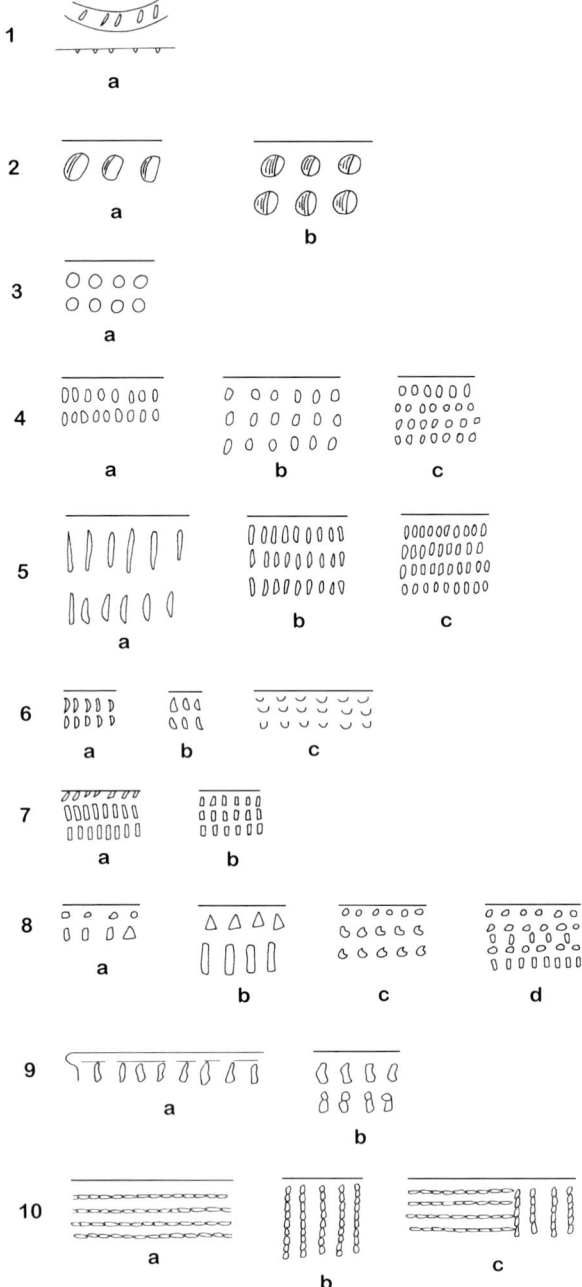

Fig. 2.8. Rim decorations on funnel beakers from Vallensgård I. Freerk Oldenburger del.

among the composite patterns one finds triangular indentations in a few cases along with rectangular ones (ornament 8a-b). Several of the typed funnel beakers and funnel beaker fragments of type II are ornamented with rows of rectangular and oval indentations (figs. 2.3:1 and 3 and 2.4:1-2), including composite patterns where several kinds of indentation have been combined, as in some of the Zealand funnel beakers of this type. Because of the extent of fragmentation it is not possible to distribute the whole total of 86 rim sherds with different indentation ornaments over funnel beakers of type II and type III respectively. But it is likely that the indentation ornaments mainly appear on funnel beakers of type II, while only some of the motifs appear on funnel beakers of type III. One row of oblong, vertical and irregular indentations (ornament 9a) occurs on Zealand beakers of type III (Koch 1998 find no. 32), and here at the settlement this ornament appears on a rim sherd that was found in pit D115 (fig. 2.5:2) together with parts of a large, cord-ornamented funnel beaker (fig. 2.5:1).

Impressions of two-ply cord occur as horizontal lines, as groups of vertical lines and as horizontal and vertical lines combined (ornament 10a-c). In pit D115 sherds were found with two of these patterns, on the one hand the rim sherds of the aforementioned large funnel beaker of type III, which has eight lines in two-ply cord beneath the rim; on the other hand a rim sherd from a small funnel beaker that has both horizontal and vertical lines of cord impressions beneath the rim (ornament 10a and b, figs. 2.5:1 and 4). The funnel beaker of type II/III from pit D249 (fig. 2.6:3) has five horizontal cord impressions beneath the rim. The neck sherd from posthole D156 has four horizontal lines in two-ply cord and is from a funnel beaker of type III (fig. 2.6:1). These examples show that the cord ornamentation is associated with funnel beakers of type III. In addition to these there are 33 rim sherds which are decorated with cord ornamentation, but they are too small for the neck height to be measured. Thus it cannot be easily established whether all these rim sherds belong to funnel beakers of type III.

If one works exclusively with the typed funnel beakers and funnel beaker fragments in this settlement find, one can conclude that the ornamented funnel beakers of type II are decorated with various kinds of indentation beneath the rim (ornaments 1-8), while funnel beakers of type III are ornamented with cord impressions, but also with certain types of

among other items the funnel beaker fragment from posthole D181, whose neck index, insofar as it has been calculated properly, lies close to the borderline between types I and II (fig. 2.3:4). But the nail impression also appears on rim sherds that were found together with neck fragments that clearly belong to funnel beakers of type II, such as the small rim sherds from posthole D3 (fig. 2.3:2).

The various types of indentation include round, oval, pointed-oval, comma-shaped, D-shaped and rectangular indentations (ornament 3-7). Triangular indentations hardly appear at all on their own, but indentation (ornaments 9-10). Looking through the material from the other Bornholm settlement finds from the Early Neolithic, one sees a similar tendency, in some places even more definitively than in the material from the settlement at Vallensgård, where only a small part of the many pot fragments can be typed. From the settlement Lillegård with parts of both unornamented and ornamented funnel beakers of type II (Finds list I, no. 41) there is only a single sherd ornamented with cord, while the remainder of the ornamented sherds have indentations and finger impressions (fig. 3.13). In the Early Neolithic layer in the house site at Pileskoven (Finds list I, no. 10) there is a single rim sherd with finger impressions as well as a few sherds with simple lines, but beyond this only cord impressions in various patterns have been used on the ornamented funnel beakers of type III (fig. 3.20). A similar predominance of cord ornaments on funnel beakers of type III occurs in the settlement find excavated by C.J. Becker at Nr. Sandegård (Finds list I, no. 52), where there are only two rim sherds of funnel beakers ornamented with indentations in the entire material (Becker 1990, 42).

The division noted here into two types of funnel beaker, each with its preferred mode of ornamentation, probably indicates chronological differences. It is important in the Early Neolithic as well as the Middle Neolithic that it is first and foremost the *forms* of the pottery that are used as the basis for the definition of the types, while the ornamentation, which has a tendency to spread over more than one type of pot, must take second place. But the ornamental motifs too must be included in the description of each phase of the pottery's development. If one is to work with settlement material which often includes small fragments of pottery, it is important also to include the ornamental motifs when it comes to a distinction between periods.

It must at the same time be emphasized that the inclusion of the ornamentation as a dating element refers here exclusively to the Bornholm material. While Eva Koch's pottery typology, in terms of the pot shapes, appears to have validity over an area that extends farther than the Zealand Island Group, there appears to be no great uniformity over wider areas when it comes to the use of the various ornamental motifs. Instead there are regional differences. For example, on Zealand one does not find such clear distinctions in the use of ornaments on the funnel beakers as those that can be noted on the Bornholm funnel beakers of types II and III. In the East Zealand settlement finds from Havnelev, where funnel beakers of type III predominate, most pots are ornamented with indentations (P.O. Nielsen 1994, 299-300).

Dating of postholes and pits with funnel beakers

Before we arrive at conclusions about the dating of the settlements and funnel beaker types on the basis of the available ^{14}C datings, it is necessary to look critically at the kind of information the ^{14}C datings offer. In the first place, it is not the pots and potsherds in postholes and pits that are dated, but charred plant material which at some point has come to lie in the same feature. A potsherd and a piece of charcoal may have been embedded in a cultural layer at different times. During the excavation of a posthole or a pit through the cultural layer both objects may come to lie together in a new, mixed soil layer with cultural remains from different times. The datings from pit D115 give an example of how the pit fill may contain charred organic material of different ages.

The most likely result is that in dating such specimens we are dating a human activity at the site which is older than the digging in question. In the case of the postholes one must also consider the opposite possibility, that some of the material has sunk into the hole after the post has been pulled up or has rotted away. This may be material that is later than the time of the digging – for example it may be part of the furnishings or refuse from a house that stood in the place for some time.

The seven ^{14}C datings of samples from postholes and pits can be used to identify the period of time when there has been human activity at the site; in this case the period when there was settlement at the site in the Early Neolithic (fig. 2.9). Wherever possible, for the dating of material from this settlement, samples with little specific age such as charred branchwood, nuts or fruit were deliberately selected. By using several datings we may be fortunate enough to find dated material both from the beginning and from the end of the functional life of the settlement. The datings, which are stated after calibration as intervals of years, do in fact produce varying results, but there is also a high degree of congruity. With the greatest percentage probability within *1 standard deviation* (1σ) we obtain the following dating intervals after calibration:

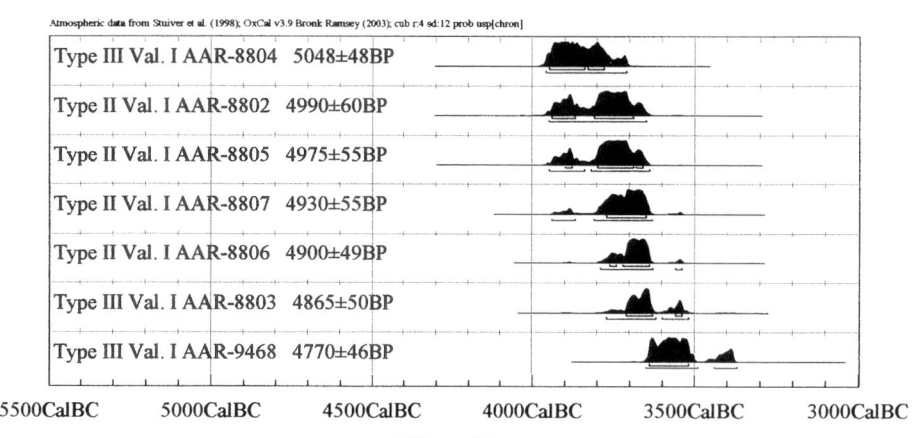

Fig. 2.9. ¹⁴C dates from Vallensgård I.

AAR-8805: 4975±55 BP, cal. 3800-3690 BC (1σ) posthole D1, with funnel beaker type II.
AAR-8806: 4900±49 BP, cal. 3720-3640 BC (1σ) posthole D3, with funnel beaker type II.
AAR-8807: 4945±55 BP, cal. 3770-3650 BC (1σ) posthole D181, with funnel beaker type I/II.
AAR-8803: 4865±50 BP, cal. 3710-3630 BC (1σ) pit D115, with funnel beaker type III.
AAR-8804: 5048±48 BP, cal. 3950-3840 BC (1σ) pit D115, with funnel beaker type III.
AAR-8802: 4990±60 BP, cal. 3810-3690 BC (1σ) pit D171, with funnel beaker type II.
AAR-9468: 4770±46 BP, cal. 3640-3520 BC (1σ) pit D313, with funnel beaker type III.

While the intervals for the individual datings vary somewhat as regards the lower limit, the upper limit of the intervals lies close to the same value. If we except the oldest dating (AAR-8804) and the youngest dating (AAR-9468), five of the dating intervals fall within a period of 60 years, between 3690 and 3630 BC.

With the greatest percentage probability within *2 standard deviations* (2σ) we achieve greater dating reliability but also longer dating intervals:

AAR-8805: 4975±55 BP, cal. 3820-3640 BC (2σ) posthole D1, with funnel beaker type II.
AAR-8806: 4900±49 BP, cal. 3790-3630 BC (2σ) posthole D3, with funnel beaker type II.
AAR-8807: 4945±55 BP, cal. 3810-3630 BC (2σ) posthole D181, with funnel beaker type I/II.
AAR-8803: 4865±50 BP, cal. 3770-3620 BC (2σ) pit D115, with funnel beaker type III.
AAR-8804: 5048±48 BP, cal. 3960-3710 BC (2σ) pit D115, with funnel beaker type III.
AAR-8802: 4990±60 BP, cal. 3950-3650 BC (2σ) pit D171, with funnel beaker type II.
AAR-9468: 4770±46 BP, cal. 3650-3370 BC (2σ) pit D313, with funnel beaker type III.

In this case the beginnings of the intervals for four datings fall within the 50 years between 3820 and 3770 BC, while they end within just 20 years, between 3640 and 3620 BC. Two of the dating intervals start at about the same time all the way back at the beginning of the Neolithic around 3950 BC and end at 3710 and 3650 BC respectively. The placing of the two dating intervals so far back is due to fluctuations, so-called 'wiggles' on the calibration curve for the period c. 3950-3790 BC (c. 5100-5020 BP), which makes it difficult to obtain unambiguous datings from around the beginning of the Neolithic until c. 160 years later. If we eliminate the 'wiggle' effect we must interpret the datings to mean that the settlement activities took place within a period of time that began a little before 3800 BC, and which ended around 3600 BC.

Within this period two of the pottery types, funnel beakers of type II and type III, were in use at the settlement. Since these are types of funnel beaker which are technically structured in different ways, and which are also ornamented in different ways, they were not necessarily in use at the same time; each may represent its own element at the site. However, intermediate forms occur – that is, pots whose neck index lies around the borderline value 35 which distinguishes type II and type III. This could mean that there was a very small time difference between the two elements. The ¹⁴C datings are indeed so close together on the timescale that the dating intervals overlap. If we compare the dating intervals with 1 standard deviation, we get the following:

Features with funnel beakers of type II: The four datings from postholes and pits with funnel beakers of type II (and type I/II) fall within the time interval 3810-3640 BC with an average at 3720 BC.

Funnel-beaker types (Eva Koch)	Periods, South Scandinavia	Periods, Bornholm	Approximate dates in calendar years
Type 0	EN Ia	EN A0	3950-3900 BC
Type I		EN A1	3900-3800 BC
Type II	EN Ib	EN A2	3800-3650 BC
Type III		EN B	3650-3500 BC
Type IV	EN II	EN C	3500-3300 BC

Table 2.2. Chronological scheme.

Features with funnel beakers of type III: The youngest dating of pit D115 with parts of a funnel beaker of type III lies within the time interval 3710-3620 BC with a mean value at 3670 BC. The dating of pit D313 with the neck sherd of a funnel beaker of type III lies in the time interval 3640-3520 BC with a mean value at 3580 BC.

With the ^{14}C datings we are thus able to establish the approximate period for the use of the settlement, while at the same time we obtain a probable dating of the two types of funnel beaker, type II and III, relative to each other. In an earlier work (Nielsen 2009) the Early Neolithic on Bornholm is classified in five periods where it is Eva Koch's division of funnel beakers into the types 0 – IV that forms the basis for the classification. Funnel beakers of type I give us the guide-type for EN A1, type II is the guide-type for EN A2, type III is the guide-type for EN B and type IV is the guide-type for EN C. Determinants for the absolute dating of the various periods are the aforementioned datings of funnel beaker types II and III at the settlement Vallensgård I (see the time scheme, table 2.2). In chapter 3 we will test this time scheme in relation to ^{14}C datings from other Bornholm settlement finds.

Other pottery forms

The sherd material from the excavation comes predominantly from funnel beakers, some of which have been furnished with a knob. No pot profiles have been preserved that can be attributed to funnel bowls, although they may well be represented among the many small rim and neck sherds. Of the six lugged sherds found in the excavation, five consist only of the actual lug, and one cannot tell whether they come from lugged beakers, lugged flasks or lugged jars.

A lug sherd from pit D157 is preserved with a piece of the pot side and may have belonged to a lugged beaker or a lugged flask on which the lugs were placed some way below the transition between neck and belly (fig. 2.4:5). The lug is furnished with a 'soft', vertical groove on the outside. The pot wall is pressed in beneath the lug to increase the diameter of the opening. Lugs with grooving on the outside are known from a lugged beaker of type II from Øgårde 1 (Koch 1998, find no. 86.2) and from several fragmented lugged flasks of the older type with a high lower body, for example from Sigersted III (P.O. Nielsen 1985a fig. 7:1) and Tisvilde Bymose (Koch 1998, find no. 15.3). Grooving on the outside of the lugs is also known from Värby V22 (Salomonsson 1970 Abb. 9C), from Stengade 'house II' (Skaarup 1975 Abb. 64:6-9), from the settlement Siggeneben Süd (Meurers-Balke 1983 Taf. 36:1) and from another East Holstein find with two early lugged flasks (Schwabedissen 1981). It is a small detail but also a widespread diagnostic feature, especially for lugged flasks from the early Funnel Beaker Culture. Impressioning of the pot wall beneath the lugs is an unusual phenomenon, but it can also be seen on the preserved lower body of a lugged flask from Hegnstrup (Koch 1998, find no. 54). We know of a whole lugged flask of the older type with a high lower body and flat bottom from "Bornholm" with no other information about the find-spot (Finds list II no. 1, fig. 8.6).

In pit D171, along with the almost wholly preserved funnel beaker of type II (fig. 2.4:1), a fragment of the neck of a lugged jar (fig. 2.4:3) was found. The neck is slightly flared, and the transition to the belly is marked by a bend that is more pronounced on one side than on the other, as if the neck has inclined a little to one side. The neck diameter at the base is 10.5 cm. The sherd may have belonged to a lugged jar like the complete one found in a bog at Kofoedsgård in Klemensker (Finds list II no. 2, fig. 8.7). This pot has a neck diameter at the base of 9.5 cm and a height of 21.5 cm. It has a flat bottom like the three lugged jars found in the sea around Bornholm (Finds list II no. 6-8, fig. 5.13). As with the two short-necked examples of these, the lugs on the vessel from Kofoedsgård are not located close to the bottom but some way up the side of the pot.

A single fragment of the neck of a collared flask was found in one of the tree-throw remains (fig. 2.1:8). This pot form has not been found in a reliable context with funnel beakers of type I and II but appears for example in pits 1922 and 1933 at Havnelev, in which funnel beakers of type III predominate (P.O. Nielsen 1994 Taf. 7:6-7, Taf. 11:12).

Only two fragments of clay discs were found at the settlement, one fragment from tree-throw remains and one from the cultural layer in field D (fig. 2.1:7), both ornamented with finger impressions at the edge. The latter had a diameter of c. 16 cm.

Burnt clay

In many of the postholes small pieces of burnt clay were found, but there were also larger pieces, as in pit D249, which contained 1.6 kg of burnt clay-and-wattle, and can be dated by a cord-ornamented funnel beaker to EN B (fig. 2.6:3). In postholes associated with the Iron Age settlement, burnt clay-and-wattle was also found.

Flint implements

The limited amount of worked flint comprises a total of 198 items. If we exclude the fire-brittle flint, the rest is distributed over 159 tools and debitage from imported Senonian flint, 14 pieces of ball flint and seven pieces of other flint. As in other Bornholm settlement finds from the Early Neolithic the imported flint predominates over the local ball flint. There are no recognizable tools made of ball flint, but there is a single scraper made of the white-speckled Kristianstad flint (fig. 2.10:2). The other tools and tool blanks are of imported flint: scrapers, blades and retouched flakes (see table 2.1).

The 159 pieces of imported flint include 10 axe fragments and 31 flakes with polished facets. The largest axe fragment comes from a depression in the southern part of trench A (fig. 2.10:1). It is a fragment of a thin-butted, polished axe with slightly convex narrow sides and highly convex broad sides. Given the shape of the cross section this must be a thin-butted axe of type I (P.O. Nielsen 1977, 72 f.). In pit D249, which contained a funnel beaker of type II/III, the edge corner of a four-sided axe was found with polishing on the broad and narrow sides (fig. 2.6:2), together with six flakes with traces of polishing.

No fragments of preliminary work for axes or unpolished examples of flint axes were found, nor were there in the flint material any axe body flakes that could come from the primary production of flint axes. It is therefore unlikely that flint axes were produced at this settlement. On the other hand the many fragments and flakes with polished facets suggest that flint axes were repaired and material from destroyed polished axes was used for smaller implements.

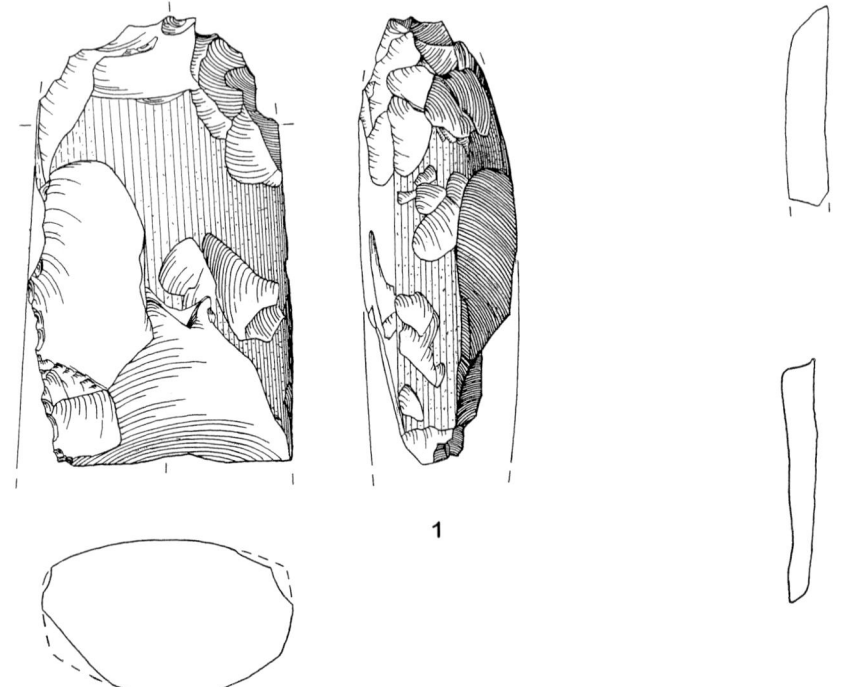
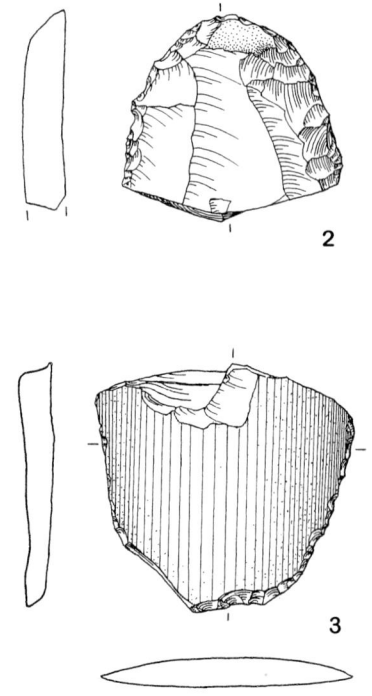

Fig. 2.10. 1) Fragment of thin-butted flint axe from hollow in the southern part of trial trench A. 2) Scraper of Kristianstad flint, unstratified find from area E. 3) Flake of polished flint axe from posthole D126. Pia Brejnholt del. 2:3.

In postholes and pits with pottery, no reliable axe fragments and flakes with traces of polishing were found together with fragments of funnel beakers ornamented with motifs 1-8. By contrast, in a total of five postholes and pits two axe fragments and 12 flakes with traces of polishing were found together with sherds of larger pieces of funnel beakers ornamented with motifs 9-10. Since the ornamental motifs 9-10 are associated with funnel beakers of type III, it is likely that the polished, thin-butted flint axes primarily had been repaired and chopped up for re-use as smaller tools during the later phase of the settlement.

Implements of other stone types

Two grindstones were found, one of which is a fragment found in the cultural layer in the southwestern part of field D. The whole grindstone is a stray find that emerged from surface-shovelling of an old soil layer in the northern part of trench A. Neither of the two pieces is of a size that would make it suitable for overall grinding of axe blanks, but they may have been used for partial polishing of axes that needed resharpening.

An almost circular crushing stone of granite was found in a small investigation of a dark, peat-like soil layer in the northern part of trench B, in which sherds of Early Neolithic pottery were also found, including four rim sherds from a funnel beaker ornamented with horizontal lines in two-ply cord.

In pit D313 a fire-brittle fragment of a quern of reddish granite was found.

Pottery depositions

During the investigation of sondage trench A, pottery was found that had been deposited in two places 45 metres apart in dug holes, A1 and A2. In both cases the hole was just large enough to contain the pot. The pots stood vertically in the holes, but only the lower part which lay below the plough layer was preserved (fig. 2.11-2.12). Both pottery vessels were grown through by plant roots and were full of cracks, which made it difficult to take them up and conserve them afterwards. The scale drawings of the contours of the vessels are shown in fig. 2.13.

Fig. 2.11. Feature A1 with buried pottery vessel in trial trench A. Seen from the south.

A1 contained the lower part of a vessel with no marked base, whose greatest diameter across the belly is c. 35 cm (fig. 2.13:1). The shoulder area is missing. The lower part has straight sides, and this was probably a funnel beaker of type II. Material thickness: 1.2-1.4 cm. In this vessel there was burnt encrustation on the inside.

A2 contained the bottom part of a large funnel beaker with a flat bottom without a marked base (fig. 2.13:2). The greatest diameter across the belly is 33 cm. The vessel is preserved up to the transition between neck and belly, where the diameter is 30.5 cm.

Fig. 2.12. Feature A2 with buried pottery vessel in trial trench A. Seen from the south.

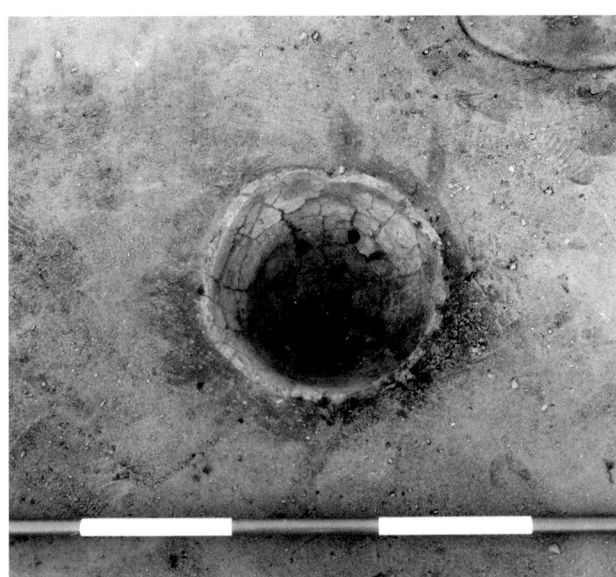

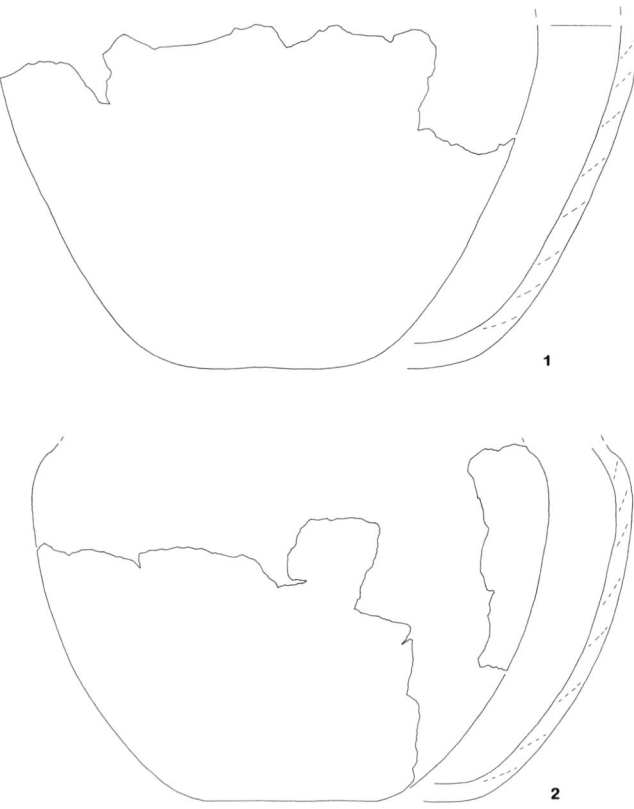

Fig. 2.13. Measurements of the two buried pottery vessels in trial trench A. (1) from A1, (2) from A2. Pia Brejnholt del. 1:5.

The bottom part has a broad, slightly rounded profile, but it is difficult to determine whether this is a funnel beaker of type II or type III. The material thickness is 0.8-1.1 cm. On the inside there is burnt food encrustation.

The fill from both vessels was sieved, but contained nothing that can be identified as original content from the deposition of the pots.

There are several possible explanations for such pottery depositions. One practical explanation might be that old used pots were buried in the soil as containers for food or liquid in order to keep the contents cool. But they could also have been pottery placed on the edge of the bog which, as a parallel to other pots and objects, may have been deposited in or near bog and lake ponds in connection with sacrificial rites (Koch 1998, 132-171). Sondage trench A was closest to the edge of the bog, and the pots were both placed on the part of the flat 'terrace' which projects a little towards the bog. The find of such pottery depositions in two places in the same sondage trench is striking, and one wonders how many of them are in reality to be found in this area beyond the investigated sondages and excavation fields.

Settlement finds from the Iron Age

Both in field D and in the sondage trenches, postholes were found which differed from the Neolithic postholes in that their fill was mixed with clay. They have been interpreted as Iron Age postholes on the basis of observations at other excavations, for example at Limensgård, where the postholes of the Iron Age houses are in fact characterized by containing a clay-mixed fill and sometimes have a compact clay plug in the top part of the hole.

In field D such postholes were found at the northern edge of the field and in the middle part of the field. Two parallel rows of postholes with a distance between them of 3 m ran diagonally through the field in the NE-SW direction (fig. 2.2). In all the postholes in the northwestern row the fill was mixed with clay, while the holes in the southeastern row in most cases contained grey sand mixed with soil. These two rows of posts presumably belong to an Iron Age farm. A total of 33 of the documented postholes were identified as belonging to the Iron Age. Postholes containing clay-mixed fill were also registered, but not more closely investigated, in the southern part of the trenches B and C.

In several layers and postholes, sherds of the Iron Age type were found: sherds of vessels made of micaceous clay, sherds with a smooth, black surface and sherds which were simply Iron Age in character.

Finds from the area around the settlement

Single find of a pottery vessel

From 'Vallensgård' – with no further information – comes a small cord-ornamented funnel beaker of type III (fig. 2.14) (Finds list II no. 5). It measures 12 cm in height, has a tall, flared neck with a slightly thickened rim area, under which one sees eight horizontal lines made with impressions of two-ply cord. The lower part is unornamented apart from the fact that beneath the bottom there are six short, parallel lines in two-ply cord. There are two impressions of cereal grains in the side of the pot, one determined as naked barley (*Hordeum vulgare var. nudum*) and one as einkorn (*Triticum monococcum*) (Brøndsted 1937,

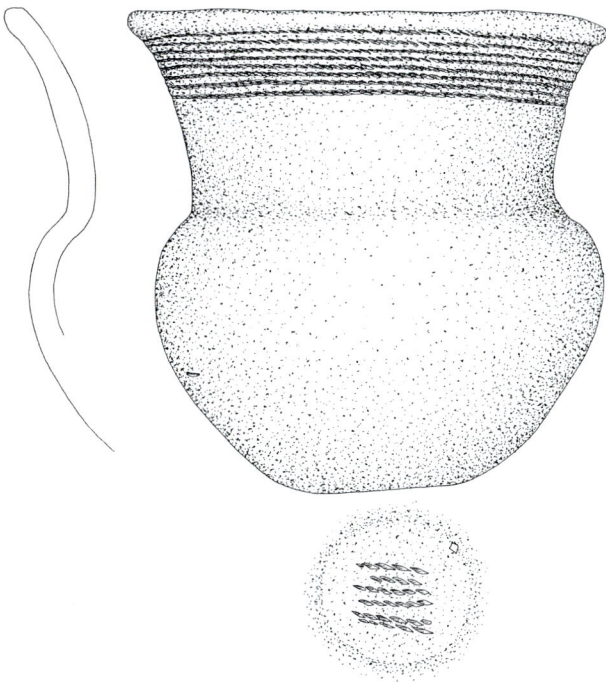

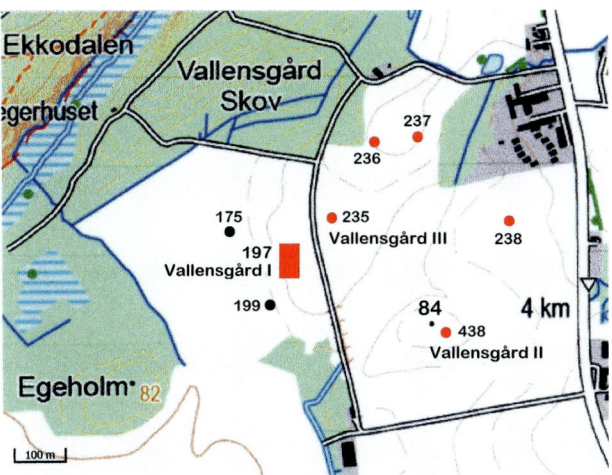

Fig. 2.15. *Settlements identified east of Vallensgård I (red dots) and finds locations of two of the flint hoards (black dots). No. 175 is the location of the axe hoard no. 1 and no. 199 the location of axe hoard no. 2. Map data from the Danish Geodata Agency.*

Fig. 2.14. *Funnel beaker from 'Vallensgård'. Eva Koch del. 1:2.*

Settlements

North-east and east of the settlement, Neolithic flints and potsherds have been found in five places. The finds are all in private ownership. The find-spots have been marked with the site numbers 235-38 and 438 in fig. 2.15. While the excavated settlement Vallensgård I lies at the edge of the plateau near the banks of the earlier lake, the other five sites are more centrally placed on the low hills NW and SE of the watercourse which originally ran in a channel from the NE towards the SW, but which is now in a culvert (*cf.* fig. 1.4a-b). At least two of the registered settlements may have been contemporary with Vallensgård I, since at no. 438 (Vallensgård II) the butt fragment of an Early Neolithic battle axe of an early type was found (Finds list V no. 11, fig. 6.2:1). Another butt fragment of a similar battle axe has been found on the surface during surveys in the area (Finds list V no. 12, fig. 8.11:12). At no. 235 (Vallensgård III) two rim sherds were found ornamented with indentations of the type that appear on funnel beakers of type II.

Finds of flint axes in Vallensgård Mose

339). On preserved areas of the pot's original lustred surface one sees a greyish-black colouring suggesting that the pot has lain in bog soil. The funnel beaker is relevant, although there is no information about its exact find-spot, since in the excavation of the settlement fragments of the same type of pottery were found.

The funnel beaker was probably found in the bog. We know of only a few other examples on Bornholm of Neolithic pottery deposited in lakes and bogs. One is the lugged jar from Kofoedsgård in Klemensker, said to have been found deep in a bog together with bones of humans and animals (Finds list II no. 2, fig. 8.7). On Bornholm, however, whole pots have also been found in dry land – *cf.* the finds of funnel beakers from Kofoedsgård and Simlegård (Finds list II nos. 3 and 4). It is unknown whether these are sacrificial vessels in line with the aforementioned one, since they may also come from graves or façade ditches for long barrows which were not recognized at the time when they were found. Some of the whole pots found at settlements have lain in pits or depressions like the funnel beaker in pit D171 at Vallensgård I (fig. 2.4:1) or like two whole pots found at the multi-phase settlement Smedegade in Klemensker (fig. 3.35-3.37). In other words, on Bornholm more whole Neolithic pots have been found at settlements than in lakes/bogs.

From the bog Vallensgård Mose and its surroundings come several finds of flint axes from the Neolithic, some of which are kept at the National Museum and

Fig. 2.16. Four hoards containing thin-butted flint axes from Vallensgård. From left to right, staggered, finds nos. 1, 2, 3 and 4. Photo Martin Stoltze.

the Bornholm Museum, while others are in private ownership. In the following the focus will be on four finds, each of two thin-butted flint axes, which are of interest in connection with the settlement traces from the Early Neolithic (fig. 2.16).

Find no. 1. The first find to be discussed is described by J.A. Jørgensen in a report of 20 November 1891. It consists of two large, polished, thin-butted flint axes found out in the northeastern part of the bog (fig. 2.15, site no. 175), off the settlement Vallensgård I. The find circumstances are described as follows: "The owner of Vallensgård, Mr. Johannes Müller, found them during digging work just beneath the surface, a little apart from each other, but it is likely that they were torn up from their original place during the working of the soil with farming implements. It may be noted that in the close surrounding area – on Vallensgård's land – antiquities of flint have often been found." The two axes later went to the Bornholm Museum (BMa 378-79) (Vedel 1897, 112). Shown in fig. 2.16. top row, left:

BMa 378. Thin-butted flint axe of type II, polished on all four surfaces but with a sharp-edged, unpolished butt. Length 34.2 cm, blade width 6.7 cm, butt width 5.0 cm. Colour light grey.

BMa 379. Thin-butted flint axe of type II, polished on all four surfaces but with a sharp-edged, unpolished butt. Length 31.2 cm, blade width 6.7 cm, butt width 4.8 cm., with reddish-brown patina.

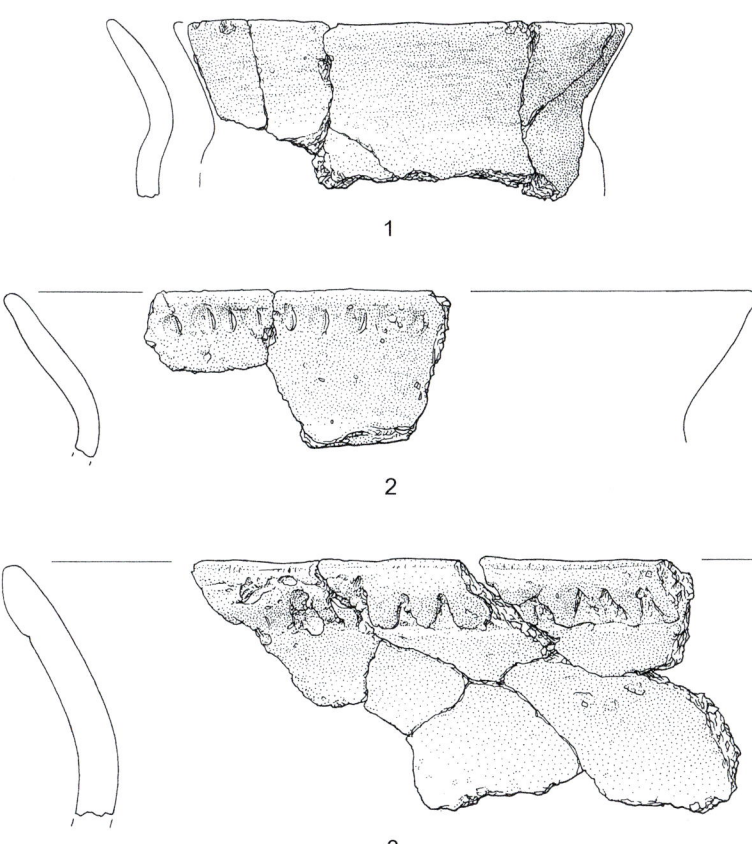

Fig. 3.5. Jættebro, Østermarie (Finds list I no. 56). Remains of funnel beakers from pit A209. Poul Wöhliche del. 1:2.

nection with any particular feature (fig. 3.6). This is one of the rare cases where an axe of another stone type than flint occurs in an Early Neolithic settlement context.

House remains

At several of the settlements from EN A1, postholes were found, but in only one case can they safely be placed in a system that means they can be regarded

Fig. 3.6. Højegård, Nyker (Finds list I no. 40). Axe of diabase. Photo by René Laursen, Bornholms Museum. 2:3.

as traces of two-aisled houses. During excavation of the settlement at Limensgård in Åker (Finds list I no. 34) house remains were found from the Middle and Late Neolithic (Nielsen & Nielsen 1986a; 1986b; P.O. Nielsen 1999; Nielsen & Nielsen 2014c), but in several places in the excavated area traces were also found of settlement in the Early Neolithic periods A1 and B. In the north-eastern part of the excavated area a cultural layer, FK, was found with mixed content from the two periods, and beneath this two house remains were found, FH and FJ, of which FH, which was c. 18 m long, was preserved with holes for both roof-bearing posts and wall posts. House FJ was only preserved as a row of holes for five roof-bearing posts which had stood at regular intervals, and the length of the house can be estimated to have been 12-13 m (fig. 3.7). Both house remains are considered to be from the Early Neolithic, but only FJ has been safely dated. One of the postholes in house FJ contained seven sherds of Early Neolithic pottery, including a rim sherd with a single row of oblique indentations beneath the rim. In another posthole a fragment of an Early Neolithic lugged flask or lugged jar was found. Macrofossils from three postholes in house FJ have been identified by David Robinson and comprise grains of wheat (*Triticum* sp.), bread

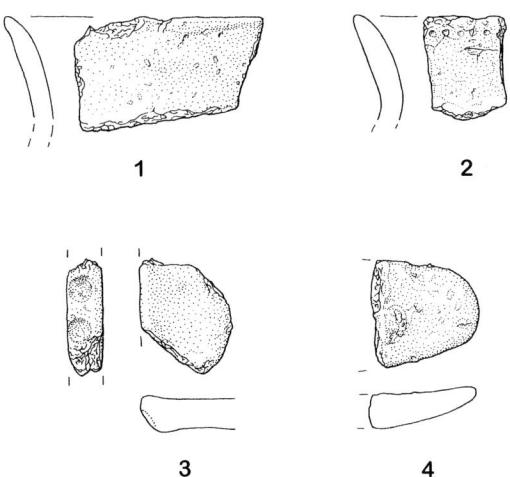

Fig. 3.3. Åløkken, Rø (Finds list I no. 27). Rim sherds (1-2), fragment of clay disc (3) and broken clay spoon handle (4). Poul Wöhliche del. 1:2.

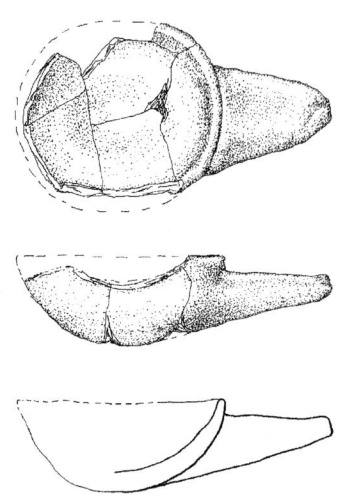

Fig. 3.4. Clay spoon from the Polish settlement from the early Funnel Beaker Culture at Redecz Krukowy, Kuyavia (after Papiernik 2012).

The pit contained a few unornamented rim sherds and a single rim sherd with a number of very small indentations beneath the rim, all from short-necked funnel beakers of type I, a fragment of a clay disc with finger impressions on the edge and a broken-off handle fragment of an earthenware spoon (fig. 3.3). Earthenware spoons are rare, but a few examples are known from Denmark, northern Germany and Poland during this period. Two fragments were found in pit A at Sigersted III in Zealand together with short-necked funnel beakers of type I (P.O. Nielsen 1985, fig. 7:5-6; 1994, Taf. 3:5-6), and a fragment was found in a pit with early funnel beakers with Michelsberg resemblances at Flintbek LA 48 in northeastern Holstein (Zich 1993, 20 ff., Abb. 5:8; Mischka *et al.* 2015a, 469, fig. 3:PU11). Earthenware spoons have also been found in north-eastern Michelsberg contexts such as Wustermark 21 in Brandenburg, a settlement dated to the early Michelsberg Culture with a ^{14}C date of 5305±30 BP, cal. 4225-4002 BC (2σ, with 71,6 % probability: 4174-4040 BC) (Beran & Wetzel 2014, 64). In Poland earthenware spoons are known from settlement layers at Sarnowo (Wiklak 1983, Pl. VII,5) and Redecz Krukowy (Papiernik 2012, Pl. IX), both located in Kujawia and belonging to the earliest Funnel Beaker Culture, the Sarnowo phase (fig. 3.4). With the earthenware spoons we are thus dealing with a utensil common to both the Michelsberg Culture and the early Funnel Beaker Culture.

The largest of the settlement pits was excavated at Jættebro in Østermarie as part of a largish settlement complex with small pits and fill layers containing both Early and Middle Neolithic finds (Finds list I no. 56). Pit A 209 measured 3.50 × 2.15 m at the surface and was 40 cm deep. At the bottom of the pit, sherds of the upper section of a small unornamented funnel beaker were found (fig. 3.5:1), and over 5 kg of sherds were found scattered through the fill, including rim sherds of funnel beakers with a horizontal row of finger impressions beneath the rim (fig. 3.5:2). The largest of them, with an estimated rim diameter of c. 52 cm, has finger impressions on an applied cordon which has been pressed together so that a triangular pattern has arisen (fig. 3.5:3). The pit contained only a few pieces of flint, including seven fragments of polished flint axes, one of which was a fire-brittle fragment of a pointed-butted flint axe of type 1. In addition there were four flakes of Kristianstad flint. Charcoal from the bottom layer of the pit has been AMS ^{14}C dated (see catalogue for details):

(Ua-55180) 5020±33 BP, cal. 3940-3710 BC (1σ), 3950-3700 BC (2σ). Median probability: 3822 BC.[2]

At Højegård in Nyker (Finds list I no. 40) a pit, A16, was excavated which contained parts of pots with the same profiles and rim ornamentation as the above-mentioned, while around the pit a large body of find material had been ploughed up, also containing sherds of a lugged jar and a lugged beaker as well as a fragment of a clay disc. In the ploughed-up material, as in most other contemporary settlement finds, there were flakes from polished flint axes, while in the pit itself there was a blade fragment from a small axe of fine-grained diabase. A whole axe of the same material was also found at the site, but with no con-

Settlements from EN A1, c. 3900-3800 BC

Finds from settlement pits

Twenty settlement elements can be dated to EN A1 on the basis of the occurrence of funnel beakers of type I. At six of the sites the material comes from what we here designate as settlement pits – that is, regularly dug holes which cannot be tree-throw remains, low natural depressions or parts of more extensive cultural layers.

Looking at the pot profiles, we see an almost imperceptible transition from type 0 to type I, where the greatest width of the belly has moved upward, close to the transition between neck and belly (Koch 1998, 86). The large funnel beaker from Hjuleregård pit A9 (Finds list I no. 44), whose upper section could be partly reconstructed, may therefore be assigned to type I (fig. 3.2:1). The parts of this pot were found together with a largish body of sherd material in a small pit where rim sherds of funnel beakers with a cordon applied beneath the rim with finger impressions and rim sherds with horizontal rows of indentations (fig. 3.2:2-3) were also found. Pit A9 is part of a larger complex consisting of different layers and pits with Early Neolithic material within an area of c. 100 × 60 m. Three burnt bones from pit A9 were identified by Pernille Bangsgaard as pig (*Sus* sp.) (domestic pig or wild boar – see catalogue). Charcoal from pit A9 has been identified by Claus Malmros as wood from hazel, the stone fruit family, oak, lime and mistletoe. Of these, two specimens were AMS ^{14}C-dated:

1) Charcoal of hazel (*Corylus avellana*) (AAR-15011) 5064±25 BP, cal. 3943-3801 BC (1σ), 3951-3796 BC (2σ). Median probability: 3870 BC.[2]

2) Charcoal of mistletoe (*Viscum album*) (AAR-15012) 5058±25 BP, cal. 3941-3799 BC (1σ), 3950-3792 BC (2σ). Median probability: 3874 BC.[2]

The two datings match and are at the same time some of the oldest datings of finds from the Neolithic on Bornholm. Not much later is an AMS ^{14}C dating, again from a smallish settlement pit excavated at Åløkken in Rø (Finds list I no. 27):

Charcoal of ash (*Fraxinus excelsior*) (AAR-9466) 5011±46 BP, cal. 3930-3710 BC (1σ), 3950-3700 BC (2σ). Median probability: 3801 BC.[2]

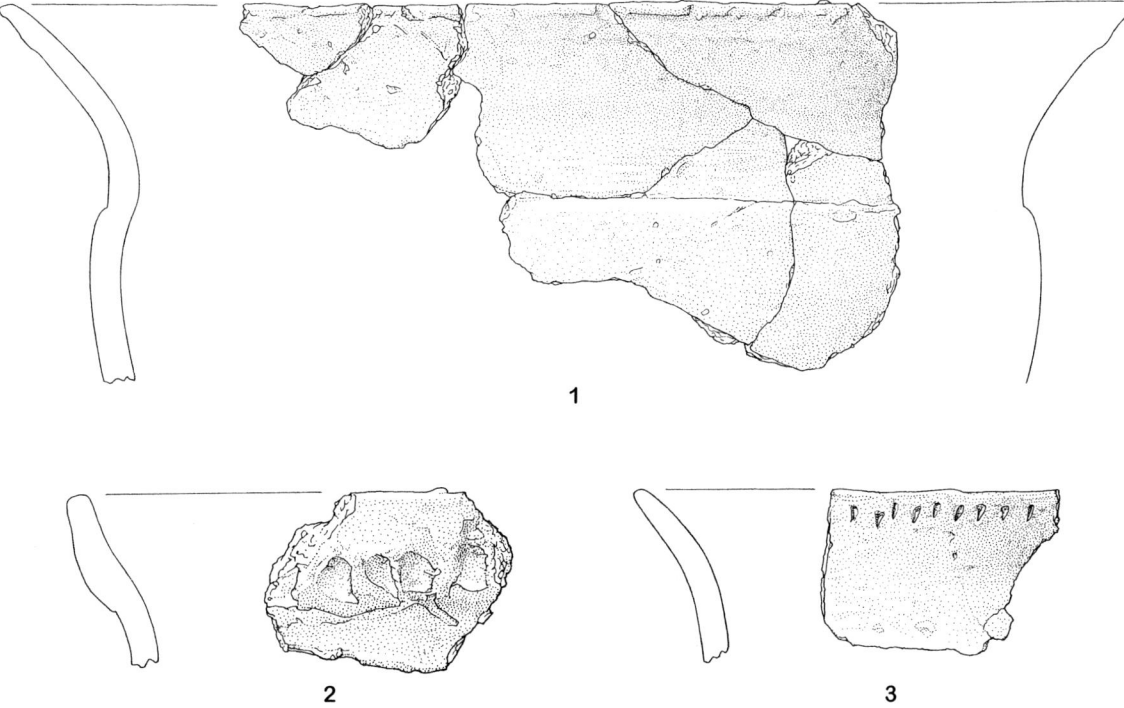

Fig. 3.2. Pottery form Hjuleregård, Nylars (Finds list I no. 44). Poul Wöhliche del. (1) 2:5. (2-3) 1:2.

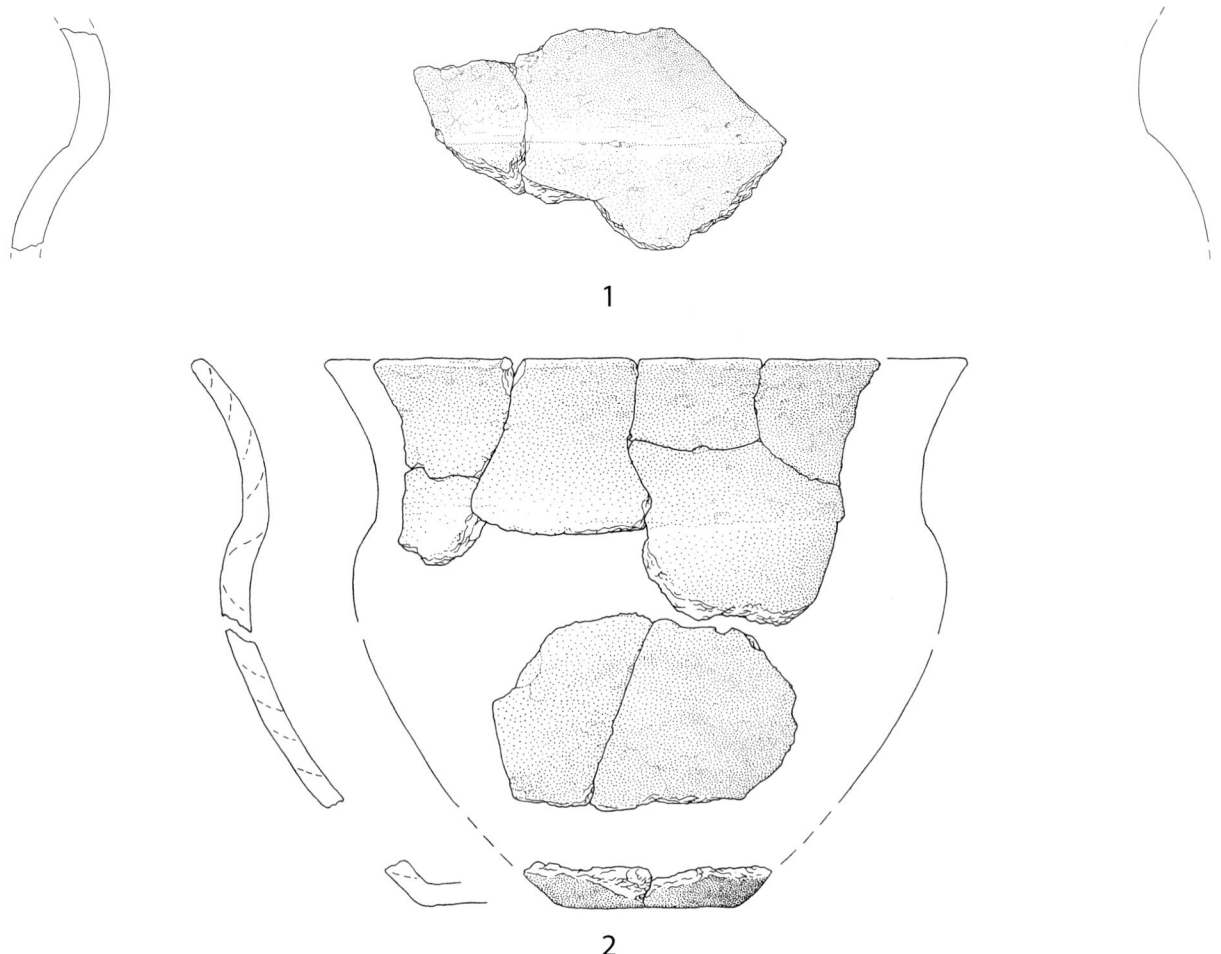

Fig. 3.1. Pottery from St. Myregård (Finds list I no. 42). Poul Wöhliche del. (1) 1:3, (2) 1:2.

ings, funnel beakers of type 0, which must be considered to represent some of the oldest funnel beaker pottery in Denmark, should probably be placed in the interval c. 4000-3900 BC.

The funnel beaker from Sandemandsgård with its faintly marked transition between neck and belly (fig. 3.8:1) may be compared to a c. 20 cm tall funnel beaker with a very similar profile from a post-hole-like feature (A6b) at the edge of one of the find-rich settlement pits at Almhov in western Scania, dated by grain to (Ua-17156) 5000±95 BP, cal. 3940-3690 BC (1σ), 3980-3630 BC (2σ) (Gidlöf et al. 2006, 61 ff., fig. 47b). Together with this funnel beaker, a small funnel beaker was found with a form and profile corresponding to two of the small funnel beakers from Zealand, one from Åkonge, which Eva Koch has also assigned to type 0 (*idem,* fig. 47c; *cf.* Koch 1998, fig. 54, finds no. 154 and 205.1).

A funnel beaker with an S-shaped profile attributed to Eva Koch's type 0 is found together with other vessels with S-shaped profiles, such as Michelsberg *Tulpenbecher*, in an inland settlement context, pit LA 48, at Flintbek in eastern Holstein (Mischka *et al.* 2015a; 2015b). It has been assumed that this indicates the presence of Michelsberg settlers in Holstein at a time corresponding with the Michelsberg II/III transition, c. 4100-4000 BC (Mischka *et al.* 2015b, 249). Even though their bases are flat, Michelsberg influences can easily be detected from the form of type 0 funnel beakers.

In Jutland and on Zealand funnel beakers of type 0 are associated with hunting sites both at the coast and at lake basins inland. Eight of the funnel beakers that Eva Koch identified as belonging to this type were found deposited whole in wetland in Zealand, which must be viewed as the beginning of the deposition practice that continued through the EN. The possible finds of this type of pot at Sandemandsgård and Almhov – if the identification is correct – may mean that it was in this period that farming activities began in inland areas. The number of finds of the dating element, the funnel beaker of type 0, is however still too small for us to posit a settlement pattern characteristic of this period in South Scandinavia.

Period	Settlement phases	Catalogue no.
EN A	4	4, 6, 36, 47
EN A0	2	38, 42
EN A1	20	1, 7, 13, 14, 15, 18, 20, 22, 24, 27, 31, 34, 37, 38, 40, 41, 44, 53, 54, 56
EN A2	12	8, 12, 14, 19, 24, 33, 39, 41, 43, 46, 49, 50
EN B	33	1, 2, 3, 5, 6, 7, 8, 9, 10, 11, 14, 16, 17, 19, 20, 23, 25, 26, 28, 29, 30, 32, 33, 34, 35, 36, 37, 41, 45, 46, 51, 52, 55
EN C	10	1, 6, 17, 21, 22, 35, 36, 41, 48, 52
Sum	81	

Table 3.1 At 19 of the 56 settlements on Bornholm dating to the Early Neolithic, more than one phase is represented. There are a total of 81 separate phases of different dates at the settlements.

In the following chronological review those settlement finds will be mentioned which included characteristic finds, important find combinations and datings, while for the other settlements the reader is referred to finds list I in the Catalogue, chapter 8. In the finds list there are also references to the literature, museum numbers and information on the number of objects.

Settlements from EN A0, c. 3950-3900 BC

To this earliest period of the Nordic Funnel Beaker Culture we can assign only one certain and one presumed find of a settlement character. Both finds were made in the southwestern part of Bornholm.

During trial excavations in 1987 at the Middle Neolithic settlement St. Myregård II in Nylars (Finds list I no. 42) sherds were found within a small area of an unornamented funnel beaker, which could be reconstructed as in fig. 3.1:2. It has a faintly marked transition between the flared neck and the belly, and the shoulder of the pot is only slightly rounded. Eva Koch, who reconstructed the pot, identified it in 2004 as a funnel beaker of her type 0. Together with the sherds of this pot, some sherds were found from the transition between neck and belly of a large, thick-walled funnel beaker which may be of the same type, although it cannot be identified with certainty (fig. 3.1:1).

Several of the pots that Eva Koch identified as funnel beakers of type 0 among the material from the kitchen middens and the Zealand bogs have an evenly flared profile with no marked transition between neck and belly. Most rimsherds from the settlement Sandemandsgård in Knudsker (Finds list I no. 38) can be identified as belonging to funnel beakers of type I, but parts of a funnel beaker with a very faintly marked transition between neck and belly also appear, which should therefore possibly be identified as belonging to type 0 (fig. 3.8:1).

Finds from the same period outside Bornholm

Eva Koch defined type 0 on the basis of measurements of a small number of bog-found pots from Zealand (Koch 1998, 81 ff.), but found the same type represented in the oldest Neolithic layers in the kitchen middens at Norsminde and Bjørnsholm in Jutland (S.H. Andersen 1991, fig. 21:1-2; 1993 fig. 32). Five datings of the oldest Neolithic layer in the kitchen midden at Bjørnsholm fall within the period 3960-3810 BC (S.H. Andersen 1993, 75 and fig. 12; Rasmussen 1993, 94 f.).

At the settlement Åkonge in the western Zealand bog Åmosen, a pot has been found in stratigraphic position that has been assigned to the same type, and which the excavator, Anders Fischer, considers to be the oldest dated funnel beaker from eastern Denmark (Fischer 2002, 357). It has been dated on the basis of charred wood and plant material in the pot wall to (AAR-4395) 5140±70 BP, cal. 4038-3804 BC (1σ), 4224-3715 BC (2σ), median probability: 3936 BC.[1-2]

However, one must not expect any precision in the ^{14}C datings within the interval c. 3950 to 3800 BC because of 'wiggles' in the calibration curve. This means that datings of funnel beakers of both type 0 and type I will lie within the same time interval. However, on the basis of stratigraphy and ^{14}C dat-

3. Early Neolithic settlements on Bornholm, c. 3950-3300 BC

Introduction

In the following Eva Koch's funnel beaker types 0-IV will be used as guide-types in classifying the Early Neolithic on Bornholm into five periods, EN A0, A1, A2, B and C. The period designations used give associations to C.J. Becker's tripartite division into EN A, B and C (1947), which is deliberate, as we regard his original division as fundamental and to a great extent still tenable. At the time it was based on a distinction between types of funnel beaker, and the same is the case today, when Eva Koch's type definitions provide a better basis for the demarcation of the material and have replaced Becker's original definitions. The periodization will contrast with the otherwise-used division of EN into only two periods, EN I-II. However, it is only EN I that is subdivided into more periods in this work, inasmuch as EN C covers EN II.

Eva Koch herself did not think that her types I-III made up a chronological sequence, since neither her ^{14}C datings of food crusts on the pots nor other previous ^{14}C datings (1998) could confirm a chronological separation of the types. Amongst other researchers one finds both the same and the opposite views.

Anders Fischer regards Eva Koch's types as a chronological sequence, and he worked from it in his model for cultural development in EN, as well as with a critically selected series of ^{14}C datings. At the same time he pointed to the uncertainty of earlier ^{14}C datings as a result of inadequate pre-treatment. In addition he found problems with the dating of food crusts which may contain organic material of aquatic origin, and which may therefore have been subject to a reservoir effect (Fischer 2002, 356).

Fredrik Hallgren on the other hand agreed with Eva Koch's view of the contemporaneity of the types. He divided the Early Neolithic funnel beakers in central Sweden (Mälardalen and Bergslagen) partly according to the same method, but with adjustments so one could measure fragments of funnel beakers whose height is unknown. He thus arrived at more or less the same types, which he called Vrå types I-IV (Hallgren 2008, 162). Funnel beakers like those of type 0 were, with some uncertainty, also present. Vrå types III and IV could not be separated using the profiles, only by using the ornamentation. But Hallgren faced the same problems as Eva Koch, as on the basis of the ^{14}C datings one could not separate the types chronologically (Hallgren 2008, fig. 8.23).

When on this occasion we repeat the attempt to divide up the Early Neolithic chronologically by means of the funnel beaker types, we do so partly on the basis of the contexts in which two of the types (II and III) appear at the settlement Vallensgård I, partly from their occurrence in other Bornholm settlement finds, where the types also to some extent appear separately. In this attempt we will not only compare pot types and ^{14}C datings, we will also consider other aspects of development within the EN.

In connection with this investigation, 56 settlement sites with Early Neolithic pottery have been registered on Bornholm (finds list I). Besides excavated settlements, surface-gathered finds have also been included. At 19 of these sites one finds, as at Vallensgård I, examples of more than one type of funnel beaker. Using the periodization that has been set up in the preceding section, this makes a total of 81 dateable settlement features. They are distributed as shown in table 3.1. There are 34 settlement features from EN A with funnel beakers of the types 0, I and II. Of these, two features can be dated to EN A0, 20 to EN A1 and 12 to EN A2. In four cases the fragments of funnel beakers cannot be identified more precisely than as belonging to one of the types 0, I and II. EN B with funnel beakers of type III appears at 33 settlements, while EN C with funnel beakers of type IV has been demonstrated in 10 cases, in one case in a causewayed enclosure.

edge width 6.5 cm, butt width 5.0 cm (allowing for the irregularity of the butt), with a light brown patina.

BMa 2227b. Thin-butted flint axe of type II, polished on all four surfaces but with a sharp-edged, unpolished butt. Length 29.0 cm, edge width 6.8 cm, butt width 5.6 cm, with a light brown patina.

The first of these two axes is of considerable length. Once more they form a pair, and as with finds no. 2 and 3 there is a difference in the lengths of the axes. However, because of the scanty find information we cannot preclude the possibility that several axes of this type were once present among the 'other axes' found in the same place.

The thin-butted flint axes from finds no. 1-4 (fig. 2.16) belong to the narrow, early, thin-butted axes of types I-II (P.O. Nielsen 1977, 72-75). Two of the axes are on the borderline between types I and II, as the angle between the narrow surfaces reaches 5-6° (axe 1 in find no. 2 and axe 1 in find no. 3). The other axes have almost parallel narrow surfaces and are thus situated within type II. There are no other differences between types I and II than the angle between the narrow surfaces, apart from the fact that most of the axes of type II are longer than type I. Characteristic features of these two types of flint axe are the narrow form with an edge width around 7 cm, convex broad sides and a sharply flaked butt. Normally the edge is highly convex, but the Vallensgård axes do not have this feature. Types I and II have a striking eastern distribution and are concentrated on Zealand, in Scania and on Bornholm (P.O. Nielsen 1977, figs. 7-8). Including the aforementioned axes, a total of 50 axes of types I and II have been registered on Bornholm, 32 of which are isolated finds (Find list IV nos. 49-80), and 18 axes come from six find assemblages /hoards whose content of axes was by all indications deposited in the soil at the same time (Finds list IV nos. 174-179). Thin-butted axes of type I-II are dated to the Early Neolithic, EN I / EN A2, c. 3800-3700 BC, which corresponds to the dating of the oldest phase of the settlement. The presence of four finds of axes deposited in pairs in and around Vallensgård Mose represents a striking concentration of hoards not found elsewhere on Bornholm.

None of the four pairs of thin-butted flint axes found at Vallensgård appeared in circumstances that permitted observation of the way the axes were deposited. In other places on Bornholm it has been possible with finds of axes of type I to describe how the axes were placed beneath the soil surface (see p. 115).

Both axes are typical thin-butted axes of type II (Nielsen 1977, 74 f.). The butt width is measured 2 cm from the edge of the butt. As can be seen, the butt and edge widths of the axes are the same, and in other ways too, the two axes match. They may be from the same workshop and may have been laid in the bog at or around the same time. The difference in colour, however, suggests that they did not lie at the same depth.

Find no. 2. In 1966-68, during ploughing in the bog, five flint axes were found. The axes no. 1-4 were ploughed up in the meadow Brødreengen close to the eastern edge of the bog (fig. 2.15, site no. 199) south west of the settlement, which was investigated in 1986. Axe no. 5 was found 2 m south of Egholmen off its southeastern corner. Two of the axes (nos. 1-2) were found on the same day, 13 May 1966, lying close together, and must constitute a single deposition. Shown in fig. 2.16, bottom row, left:

Axe 1. Thin-butted flint axe of type I/II, polished on all four surfaces but with a sharp-edged, unpolished butt. Length 29.4 cm, blade width 6.8 cm, butt width 4.8 cm. Colour light brown to greyish.

Axe 2. Thin-butted flint axe of type II, polished on all four surfaces but with a sharp-edged, unpolished butt and with an unpolished, sharpened edge. Length 25.0 cm, blade width 6.9 cm, butt width 5.0 cm. The colour of the blade area is light brown, on the rest of the axe it is grey.

The thin-butted axes differ a little in proportions. Axe 2 has a wider butt than axe 1, although the standard measure of butt width gives almost the same width. This is because one of the sides of axe 2 curved a little inward in the unpolished area before the end of the butt. The length too is different, which is because of the secondary sharpening done by flaking the edge area of axe 2, probably after a break.

The following axes are not shown here:

Axe 3. Thin-bladed flint axe, unpolished, with rounded butt. The blade is concave on one side. Length 14.1 cm, edge width 4.2 cm, butt width 4.0 cm. This axe is unusual in having the form of a thin-butted, thin-bladed flint axe but with a slightly hollowed edge, something not otherwise found on the early, thin-bladed axes. However, this must be said with reservations for this feature, because of the unfinished, unpolished state of the axe.

Axe 4. Thick-butted flint axe with partially polished broad sides and unpolished narrow surfaces. Length 15 cm.

Axe 5. Large thin-bladed flint axe with polished broad sides and unpolished narrow surfaces. Length 17 cm.

The axes from find no. 2 are in private ownership (axes 1-4 are registered in the National Museum's archive, file no. 525/68).

Find no. 3. Later two flint axes were found during ploughing in Brødreengen at the same place as find no. 2. Shown in fig. 2.16, top row, right:

Axe 1. Thin-butted flint axe of type I/II, polished on all four surfaces but with a sharp-edged, unpolished butt. Length 23.6 cm, edge width 7.0 cm, butt width 5.1 cm. with light brown patina.

Axe 2. Thin-butted flint axe of type II, polished on all four surfaces but with a sharp-edged, unpolished butt. The edge has been knocked off, and the break is fresh. Length 31.0 cm, blade width 6.6 cm, butt width 5.1 cm, with light brown patina and a grey area in the middle of the axe.

The four axes from find no. 2 (axes 1-2) and find no. 3 (axes 1-2) match in both dimensions and formation. The butt is formed in exactly the same way on all four axes with a small concavity making the butt slightly asymmetrical. Both pairs consist of a long axe of around 30 cm and a shorter one of around 25 cm. They may have belonged to one and the same deposition or have been deposited within a short time interval.

The axes from find no. 3 are in private ownership. The same is true of a further two axes, both registered in 1987, also said to have been found in the bog, presumably after 1966. One is a large, thin-butted flint axe, close to the Blandebjerg type (type VII, Finds list IV no. 170), with polished broad sides and unpolished narrow surfaces, 24.2 cm long, with cortex on the butt. One blade corner has been broken off. The second is a thick-butted flint axe with polished broad sides and unpolished narrow surfaces and with a damaged blade.

Find no. 4. In the Bornholm Museum two axes are kept, having entered the museum in 1937, said to have been found during work in the fields together with several other axes. The find-spot is registered as 'west of Vallensgård', that is, the axes may have been found in Vallensgård Mose or somewhere nearby. Shown in fig. 2.16, bottom row, right:

BMa 2227a. Thin-butted flint axe of type II, polished on all four surfaces but with a sharp-edged, somewhat irregular, unpolished butt. Length 37.0 cm,

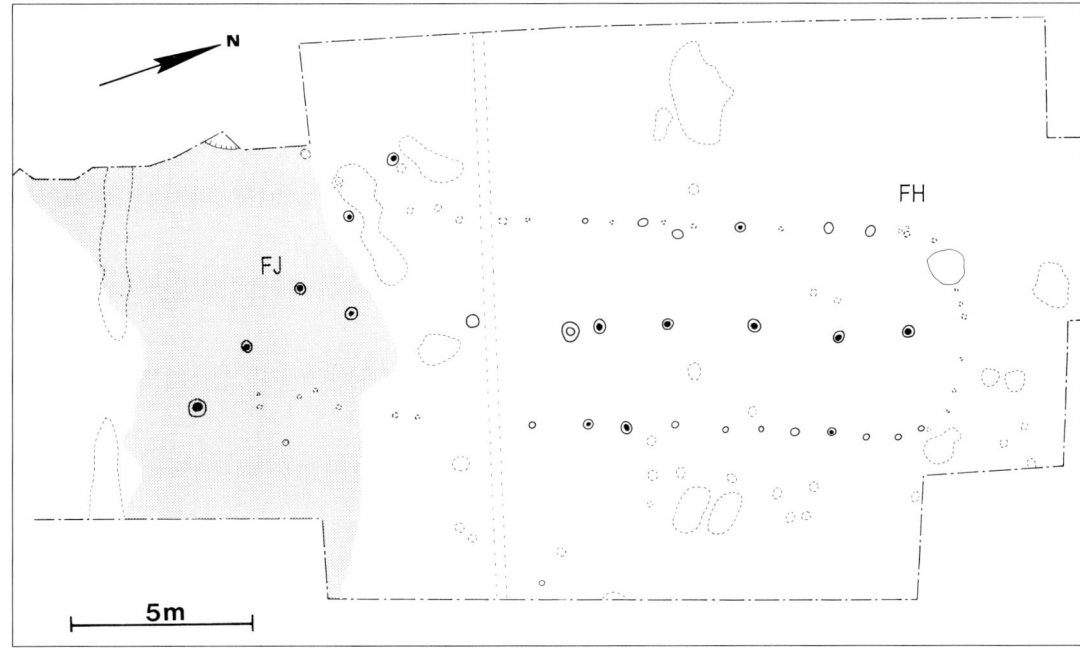

Fig. 3.7. Limensgård, Åker (Finds list I no. 34). Plan of two house sites, respectively with and without preserved wall posts. 1:200.

wheat (*Triticum aestivum*) and naked barley (*Hordeum vulgare var. nudum*). A specimen of barley was AMS ^{14}C-dated:

(OxA-2895) 5000 ±70 BP, cal. 3937-3702 BC (1σ), 3952-3657 BC (2σ) (Hedges *et al.* 1991, 291-92). Median probability: 3794 BC.[2]

Along with datings from Almhof in Scania and Skovgård (see below) this is one of the earliest datings of cereals in Scandinavia. The excavations at Limensgård will be published separately, so beyond these remarks we will go no further into the Early Neolithic material from this settlement.

Finds from cultural layers and depressions

In connection with construction work at Sandemandsgård in Knudsker (Finds list I no. 38) a c. 400 m² area was investigated where one could see fill layers and postholes in the sandy soil that were presumed to be traces of one or more house remains, although their shape and demarcation could not be established. What emerged was a large body of find material from pits and postholes as well as from a cultural layer that was partially investigated. A largish pit, A86, measured c. 1.75 × 2.50 m at the surface and was 30 cm deep. There were traces of later settlement from the Bronze Age and graves from the Iron Age, but the Neolithic find material was highly uniform and can as a whole be dated to EN A. An unornamented pot should possibly be identified as a funnel beaker of type 0 (fig. 3.8:1). Most rimsherds are unornamented, and a small number of them are simply ornamented with 1-4 rows of small round or semicircular indentations (fig. 3.8:2-4). Rows of finger or fingernail impressions also appear, as does an applied cordon with finger impressions. On the other hand, there is not a single sherd from a funnel beaker ornamented with cord. The pottery material is much fragmented, but most rim and neck profiles belong to funnel beakers of type I. The imported flint predominates in quantity over both Kristianstad flint and the local ball flint. The fragments of polished axes are small, but it is most likely that they come from one of the three types of pointed-butted axes. Two cores and 40 flakes of quartzite were found, which is a clear indication that there had been experiments with other stone types than flint for making tools. One of the cores is depicted in fig. 3.9. An overview of the find material is given in table 3.2, which shows finds from the cultural layer, from the large pit A86 and from the other features and scattered finds.

At most Early Neolithic settlements the find material is mixed and reflects repeated human presence, but there are also a few settlements from EN A1 where, as at Sandemandsgård, there are almost only finds from this period, and where there are only insignificant later elements. Such a find was excavated and collected by private individuals in a cultural layer with no further description at Gudhjem Syd in sandy ground close to the coast (Finds list I no. 53). The finds from there comprise parts of funnel beakers with a neck and shoulder profile corresponding

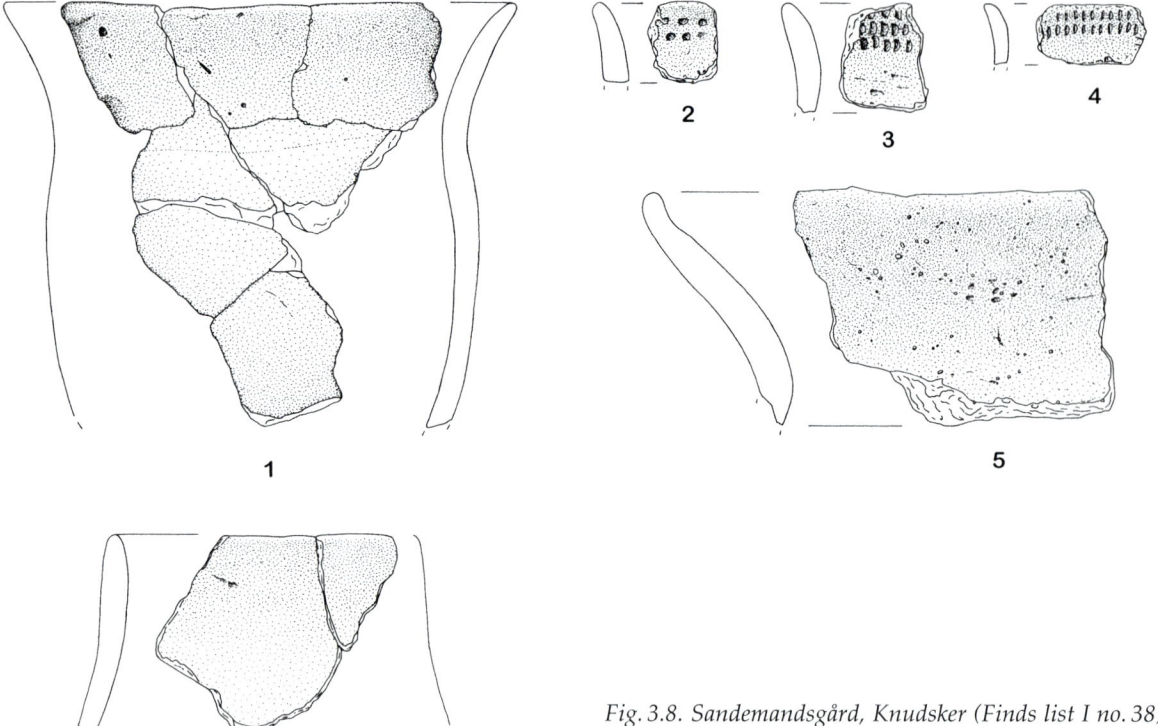

Fig. 3.8. Sandemandsgård, Knudsker (Finds list I no. 38). Sherds from funnel beakers (1-5) and a lugged jar or flask (6). Freerk Oldenburger del. 1:2.

to type I. The sherds of larger pots with a horizontal cordon beneath the rim with finger impressions, and parts of a lugged jar with a short neck also suggest a dating to EN A1 (fig. 8.4). The relationship between neck height and rim diameter do however place a medium-sized funnel beaker (fig. 8.5) at the transition between types I and II. Here too there was not a single sherd with cord ornamentation.

A very similar body of material was also exca-vated and collected by private individuals from an unspecified cultural layer at Borgen in Rø (Finds list I no. 24). Objects were also found from the Middle Neolithic at this site, but the Early Neolithic pottery material that dominated the find comprises parts of funnel beakers with a rim and shoulder profile corresponding to type I (fig. 8.2), which together with applied cordons with finger impressions indicates EN A1. But there are also rim sherds of funnel bea-

Fig. 3.9. Sandemandsgård, Knudsker (Finds list I no. 38). Core of quartzite. Photo John Lee, the National Museum. 1:2.

Table 3.2 Sandemandsgård (Finds list I no. 38). Summary of the finds.

Sandemandsgård	Cultural layers	Pit A 86	Other features and stray finds
Pottery			
Sherds, unornamented	419	557	912
Rim sherds:	38	29	48
unornamented	2	2	7
with 1 row of indentations	4	2	10
with 2 rows of indentations	3	0	1
with 3 rows of indentations	1	0	1
with 4 rows of indentations	0	2	1
with finger/nail impressions	0	0	1
with bead and finger/nail impr.	3	5	17
Lugs	0	0	1
Knops on top of the belly	0	0	1
Clay disc fragments			
Sum	470	597	1000
Flint and other stone			
Imported flint:			
fragments of polished axes	1	2	15
blades	0	0	5
flakes	34	48	92
Kristianstad flint:			
cores	0	1	2
flakes	7	16	28
Ball flint:			
transverse arrow	0	0	1
flakes	1	6	19
Burnt flint, undetermined	6	0	0
Quartzite:			
cores	0	0	2
flakes	0	2	38
Sandstone, fragment of grindstone	1	0	0
Other stone, crushing stones	0	0	2
Sum	50	75	204

kers with a taller, flared neck corresponding to type II (fig. 8.2:4), which along with horizontal rows of fingernail and finger impressions without cordons beneath the rim points to EN A2. A dating of the Early Neolithic finds from this site to pure EN A is supported by the fact that in the very large body of ceramic material there is not a single sherd of pottery ornamented with cord.

In the flint material from the three above-mentioned sites fragments of polished axes occur, but all the pieces are so small that we cannot ascertain with certainty which type of axe they come from. There are however several rounded edge flakings that point towards pointed-butted flint axes. A larger fragment of a pointed-butted flint axe was found at Skovgård in Rutsker (Finds list I no. 23). With the much-rounded broad side this may be a pointed-butted axe of type 1 or 2 (fig. 3.10:7). The material from Skovgård was excavated at the top of a sandhill and comes from cultural layers, tree-throw remains and a few postholes. In most cases it can be dated to EN A1 (fig. 3.10:1-5), but here too there were also a few sherds of funnel beakers of type III and rim sherds ornamented with two-ply cord. In one of the tree-throw remains, besides settlement material, there were 51 charred grains of cereals, 12 of which have been identified by Peter Steen Henriksen as Club Wheat (*Triticum aestivum convar. compactum*). Two grains were ^{14}C dated:

1. (Ua-55726) 5084±32 BP, cal. 3960-3800 BC (1σ), 3970-3790 BC (2σ). Median probability: 3866 BC.[2]

2. (Ua-55727) 5016±30 BP, cal. 3940-3710 BC (1σ), 3950-3700 BC (2σ). Median probability: 3803 BC.[2]

The settlement at Skovgård has thus supplied the oldest datings so far of cereals from Bornholm and at the same time some of the earliest evidence of cereal farming in Scandinavia.

^{14}C datings of the settlements from EN A1 are gathered in fig. 3.11.

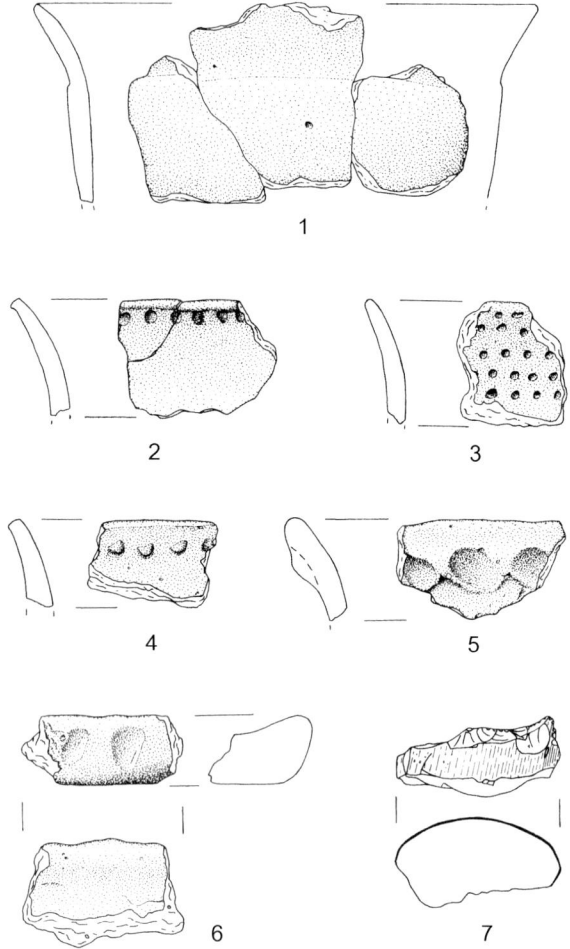

Fig. 3.10. Skovgård, Rutsker (Finds list I no. 23). Fragment of funnel beaker (1), rim sherds (2-5), fragment of clay disc (6) and fragment of pointed-butted flint axe (7). Freerk Oldenburger del. 1:2.

The location of the settlements

The location of the settlements in terms of soil and terrain types is discussed on p. 91 ff. Here it will only be noted that most sites are in the northern and western part of Bornholm, and that only one, Hammeren (Finds list I no. 1) is located directly at the coast (fig. 3.12). This is one of the settlements that have been visited several times, and which is discussed below under 'multi-phase settlements'. At Hammeren finds have been made from the Ertebølle Culture, EN A1 and later periods, as is to be expected because of the location of the settlement opposite the nearest point on the Scanian coast. There are no coastal settlements elsewhere along the Bornholm coast which, like this one, show signs of activities throughout the Neolithic, and this shows that the connections with the surrounding world primarily went from Hammeren in the northwestern direction over to the Scanian coast.

There are only three settlements (nos. 1, 53 and 54) that lie less than 500 m from the coast. The Bornholm coastline has probably not changed much since the beginning of the Neolithic. Coastline changes since the Atlantic period have first and foremost been striking in the southeastern part of the island, where the highest water level of the Littorina Sea has been c. 5 m above the present sea level and thus created something that resembles a fjord or lagoon landscape (F.O.S. Nielsen 2001, fig. 1). A single find of Ertebølle pottery has been registered at Snogebæk (Petersen 2001, fig. 2), where a single pointed-butted axe of rock was also found (Finds list IV no. 43), but otherwise no finds of settlement character from the EN have been found in the same area. Apart from the three settlements located at or near the coast, all other settlements from EN A1 must be considered inland sites. The preferred location is on sandy soil, often high-lying and at a small distance from watercourses or springs. The settlement pattern is thus different on Bornholm from many other parts of South Scandinavia at the beginning of the Neolithic, when settlement seems more or less to have spread from the fjords and coastal areas which were earlier occupied by the

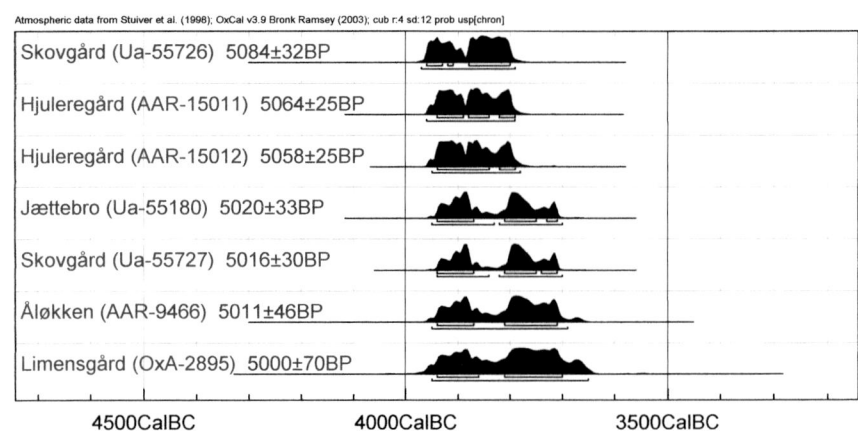

Fig. 3.11. Calibrated ^{14}C dates of settlements dating to EN A1.

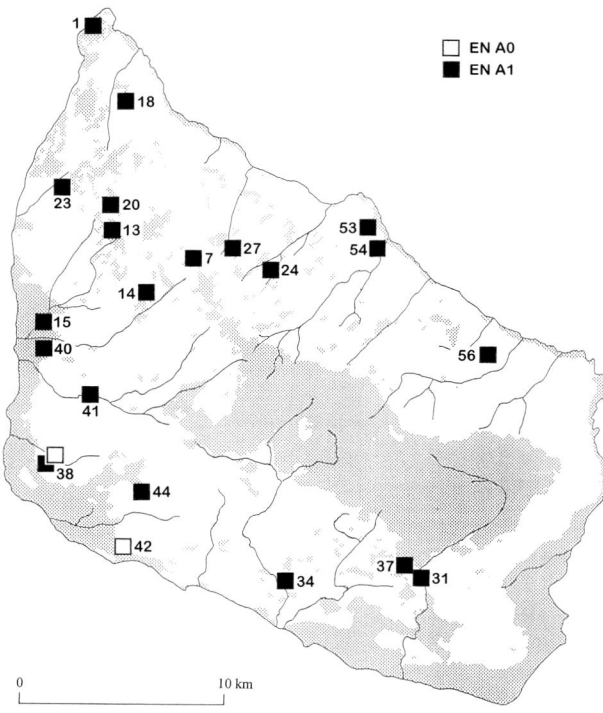

Fig. 3.12. The distribution of settlements where finds from EN A0 and EN A1 have been recovered. In this and the following distribution maps, grey indicates sandy areas (wind-blown, moraine and marine sand).

Ertebølle people, but this may have something to do with the island's different topography.

Finds from the same time outside Bornholm

In her work from 1998, Eva Koch reviewed a number of settlements with funnel beakers of type I: Muldbjerg, Store Valby and Sigersted III on Zealand, Tolstrup II in northern Jutland and Värby pit V 22 in Scania (Koch 1998, 87 with references). In her discussion of the absolute dating of this pottery type, she was greatly influenced by the wide distribution of the ^{14}C datings of both her bog-found pots and the settlements mentioned, insofar as there were ^{14}C datings of them. Her conclusion was therefore that funnel beakers of type I and the find contexts in which they occurred could not be dated more specifically than to EN I, which means a time frame of 450-500 years (*idem*, 89). There is therefore every reason to take up the issue of the dating of funnel beakers of type I again, not least in the light of the datings of Bornholm material presented, here, but also because we have new datings of material from both older and more recent excavations of related find complexes in both Denmark and Sweden.

Sigersted III Pit A (P.O. Nielsen 1985; 1994) contains funnel beakers of type I along with a number of other pottery types which together paint a picture of the ceramic equipment at the beginning of the Neolithic: small and medium-sized funnel beakers with and without rim ornamentation as well as large funnel beakers with cordons beneath the rim in which there are finger impressions; funnel bowls, lugged beakers, lugged flasks, lugged jars, simple bowls, spoons and clay discs. All the pottery types that occur in the course of the Early Neolithic, with the exception of the collared flask, are thus present.

The flint inventory comprises polished, pointed-butted flint axes of type 2, flake axes, scrapers, large and small drills, curved knives and transverse arrowheads (P.O. Nielsen 1985, figs. 8-12). Evidence of cereal cultivation on the sandy soils around the settlement is provided by burnt grains of six-rowed barley (*Hordeum* sp.), while the burnt bone material comes from domestic cattle, pigs and sheep. There are two ^{14}C datings[4] of specimens from the bottom layer of the pit, identified and selected by Claudia Baittinger:

1) Charcoal of ash (*Fraxinus excelsior*), 1 growth ring (Ua-55722) 5219±32 BP, cal. 4045-3980 BC (1σ), 4230-3960 BC (2σ). Median probability: 4017 BC.
2) Charcoal, unidentified, of small twig, 2 mm in diameter and with 1 growth ring (Ua-55723) 5169±33 BP, cal. 4040-3955 BC (1σ), 4050-3820 BC (2σ). Median probability: 3980 BC.

The datings are more precise than the two next dates, which fall in the subsequent period, 5100-5000 BP (3950-3800 BC), where there are wiggles in the calibration curve:

3) Charred seed (unidentified grain) (OxA-39591) 5079±23 BP, cal. 3948-3807 BC (1σ), 3956-3800 BC (2σ). Median probability: 3862 BC.
4) Hazelnut shell (*Corylus avellana*) (OxA-39592) 5065±23 BP, cal. 3942-3802 BC (1σ), 3950-3797 BC (2σ). Median probability: 3870 BC.

Compared with the datings 1) and 2) of short-lived charcoal samples the actual date of the find material from Pit A could fall early in the 'wiggle zone' such as c. 3950-3900 BC. It cannot, however be dated more precisely than 3950-3800 BC.

Important too are finds from the settlement pits at Almhov in southwestern Scania (Gidlöf *et al.* 2006; Rudebeck 2010, 154 ff.; Rudebeck & Macheridis 2015).

The site is interpreted as a gathering and feasting site used by farmers who could also exploit the local flint resources, since the flint mines at Sallerup lie only 11 km from Almhov. Of 190 investigated pits from the Early Neolithic, 34 pits contained Oxie pottery, corresponding to EN AI on Bornholm. In the highly find-rich pit A19049 rimsherds were found with one or more horizontal rows of indentations and neck sherds of a large funnel beaker with a thickened rim with finger impressions, together with fragments of at least two pointed-butted flint axes (Gidlöf *et al.* 2006, 55 ff.). A ^{14}C dating of bread wheat (*Triticum aestivum/compactum*) gave the result (Ua-21383) 5065±60 BP, cal. 3960-3790 BC (1σ), 3970-3710 BC (2σ). Above we have mentioned the dating to around the same time of pit A6b at Almhov with possible funnel beakers of type 0. The datings from Almhov do not contradict a dating of funnel beakers of type I to the time interval c. 3900-3800 BC corresponding to EN A1 on Bornholm.

The same can be said of datings from a complex of settlement pits, A442, excavated at Lisbjerg Skole in eastern Jutland. They contained varied material, including small and large funnel beakers of type I, corresponding to the Oxie phase or the A group, depending which designation one uses. An average of four ^{14}C datings (AAR-8542, 8550, 9227, 9225) taken from shells of hazelnut gave the result 5076±29 BP, cal. 3945-3805 BC (Skousen 2008, 118 ff.).

Finally we can mention AMS ^{14}C datings of the male burial at Dragsholm, in which a funnel beaker of type I was found. The datings correct an earlier conventional dating (K-2291: 4840±100 BP) and are relevant since a special effort was made in this case to obtain the best possible datings (Price *et al.* 2007).

The average of five datings is 5060 BP. With an uncertainty of ±50 years the calibration of the average gives the interval 3964-3760 BC (2σ) with a median probability at 3863 BC.[2]

It seems to be a general tendency that more recent AMS ^{14}C datings produce older datings than the earlier conventional ones. The settlement Muldbjerg I in the western Zealand Åmose has hitherto been the most thoroughly dated of the settlements with funnel beakers of type I. The datings, all of which are conventional and were made before 1986, most of them even as early as 1960, are at least 100 years later than the datings discussed above (see the overview of the Muldbjerg datings in Stafford 1999, Table 5:1). Some of the datings from Muldbjerg I are among the earliest conventional datings ever produced, and the sample material was at that time not pre-treated in the same way as later.[3] With the above-mentioned more recent datings with the AMS method, funnel beakers of type I and the contexts in which they were found have been dated to c. 4000-3800 BC, although with a wide margin of uncertainty because of wiggles in the calibration curve for datings within the period c. 3950-3800 BC.

Settlements from EN A2, c. 3800-3650 BC

Finds from settlement pits

At Lillegård in Nyker (Finds list I no. 41) a pit was excavated that measured 2.55 × 0.90 m, and was c. 0.20 m deep. A soil-mixed cultural layer in the top part of the pit was rich in sherds from Early Neolithic funnel beaker pottery. In the bottom layer of the pit, parts of two funnel beakers of type II were found which may have been deposited whole or as large sherds (fig. 3.13:1, 3). The large funnel beaker with finger impressions beneath the rim was found close to a posthole, and the fill in another posthole contained large pieces of a third pot, an unornamented lugged beaker (fig. 3.13:2). A sample of charcoal from the bottom layer of the pit, identified by Claus Malmros, has been AMS ^{14}C dated:

(AAR-9465) Charcoal of the pome family (*Pomaceae*): 4910±55 BP, cal. 3760-3640 BC (1σ), 3810-3630 BC (2σ). Median probability: 3696 BC.[2]

The function of the pit is difficult to determine. Its oblong shape and the two postholes at its bottom recall the façade ditch of a non-megalithic long barrow. If the pit is nevertheless included here under the category of settlements, this is because of the rich find material, which also contains a few elements from other periods. Besides the three pots mentioned, many of the ornamented rim sherds and neck profiles can be assigned to funnel beakers of type II, but there are also a few sherds of funnel beakers of type I, as well as single sherd ornamented with two-ply cord, which may come from a funnel beaker of type III.

Another oblong pit was excavated at Dalshøj in Ibsker (Finds list I no. 49). This too contained much sherd material, some from funnel beakers of type II.

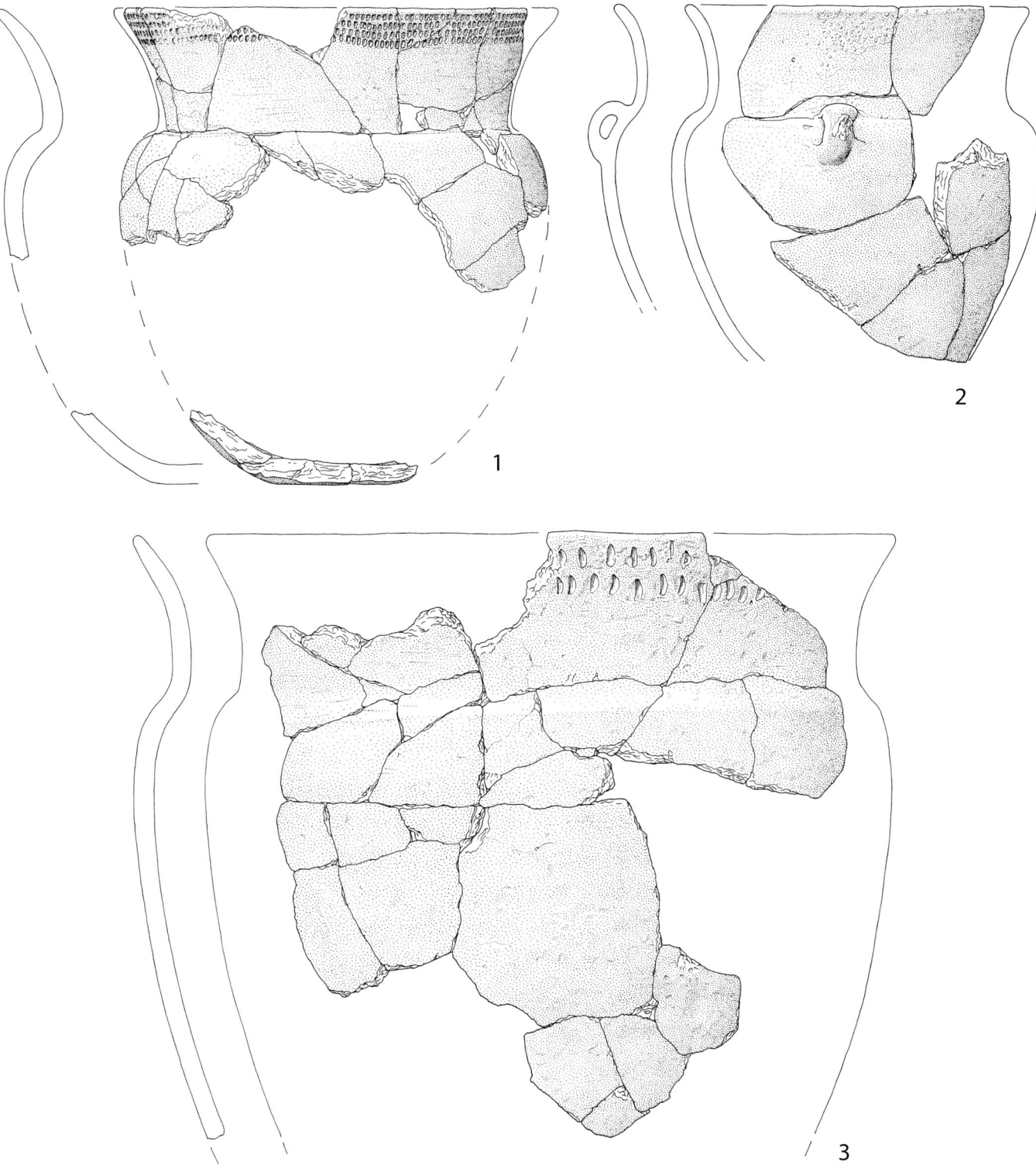

Fig. 3.13. Pottery from Lillegård, Nyker (Finds list I no. 41). Poul Wöhliche del. 2:5.

A settlement pit was excavated at Stubbeløkken in Knudsker (Finds list I no. 39), where pit A98 was 87 cm in diameter and 35 cm deep and was lined with stones at the bottom. It contained among other things several sherds from funnel beakers of type I or II, where the neck index could not be measured, as well as a side sherd of a lugged beaker (fig. 3.14).

A sample from the bottom layer of the pit was AMS ^{14}C dated:

(AAR-25002) Hazelnut (*Corylus avellana*): 4941±28 BP, cal. 3761-3662 BC (1σ), 3775-3655 BC (2σ). Median probability: 3710 BC.[2]

55

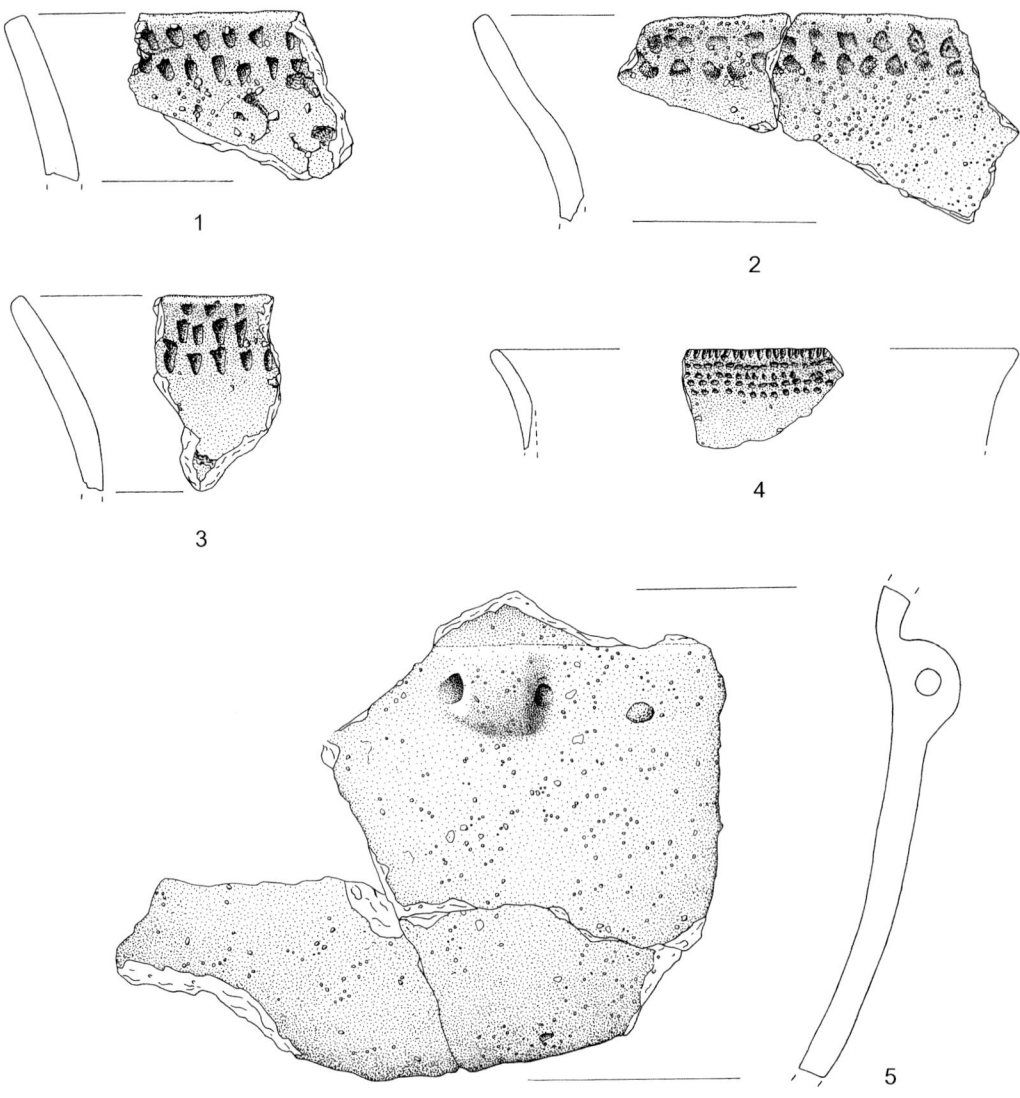

Fig. 3.14. Stubbeløkken, Knudsker (Finds list I no. 39). Sherds of funnel beakers (1-4) and a lugged beaker (5) from pit A98. Freerk Oldenburger del. 1:2.

Charcoal from the upper layer in the same pit was also dated and produced younger datings (see the catalogue). Around the pit scattered sherds and a little flint were found over a large area, including an 8 cm long blade from an unpolished flint axe.

Finds from cultural layers and depressions

Torpebakkerne in Klemensker is an area with sandy soil, where several settlement traces from the Early Neolithic have been found during quarrying for sand and gravel. They have a characteristic location on the hills and one of the settlements is Marevadgård (Finds list I no. 8), where a cultural layer was investigated with finds from the EN, including postholes. In addition, ard tracks were found containing charcoal, which was at first interpreted as traces of slash-and-burn farming in the Early Neolithic, but which after ^{14}C dating turned out to come from farming in the Bronze Age. In a natural depression below the hill old soil layers were also investigated, and ard tracks were registered at several levels. The pottery from the settlement on the hill and from the cultural layers in the depression is much fragmented, so the ratio of rim diameter to neck height on the funnel beakers cannot be measured. Characteristics of funnel beakers of type I, for example rim cordons with finger impressions, seem however to be absent. On the other hand, many of the rim sherds are ornamented with indentations corresponding to the decoration on funnel beakers of type II from the settlement Vallensgård I. The following types of indentation (see fig. 2.8) can be seen on the rimsherds from Marevadgård: 2a and b, 3a, 4a, 5a and b, 6a and b, 7b. In

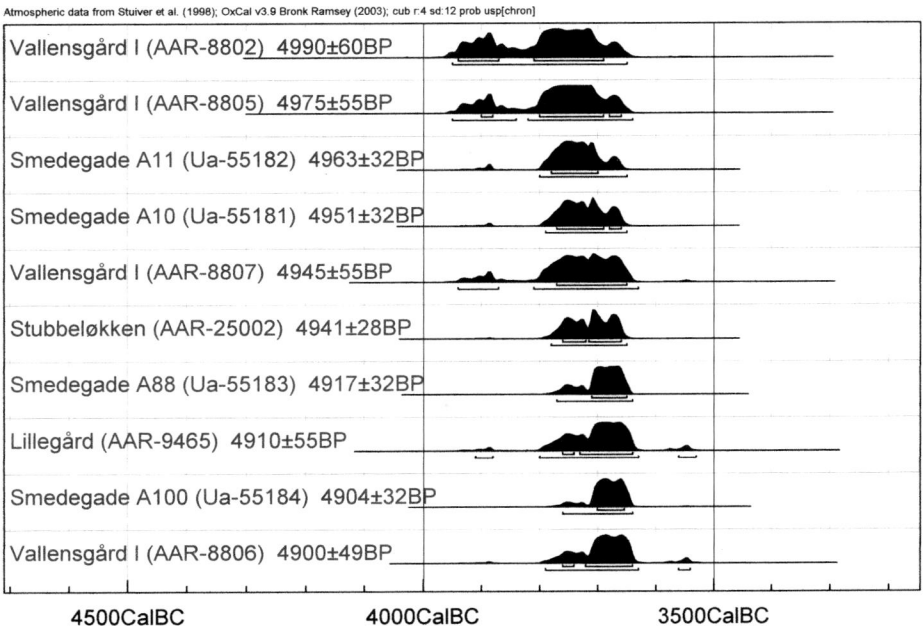

Fig. 3.15. Calibrated 14C dates of settlements dating to EN A2, together with features from the same period at the multi-phase settlement at Smedegade (Finds list I no. 14).

the large body of sherds only a few occur with lines made with impressions of two-ply cord along with fragments of collared flasks. However, the bulk of the finds must be dated to EN A2.

An important body of find material from EN A2 has been excavated at the settlement Smedegade in Klemensker (Finds list I no. 14), and will be discussed below in the section on multi-phase settlements. 14C datings of settlements from EN A2 including dates from features at Smedegade being dated archaeologically to EN A2 are gathered in fig. 3.15.

The location of the settlements

Twelve settlements have been registered with finds from this period, which is fewer than in EN A1. One of the finds consists of a collection of sherds in a beach ridge a short distance from the coast south of Svaneke (Finds list I no. 50), and two other settlements lay in a flat, sandy terrace a few hundred metres from the south coast (nos. 43 and 46). Eight other settlements must be designated inland sites (fig. 3.16). In three cases there are elements at sites where activity in EN A1 was already registered (nos. 14, 24 and 41). The fact that fewer sites are registered from this period than from the preceding one might suggest that the settlement type had become more stationary. But the period was perhaps even shorter than the c. 150 years indicated there. The duration of the individual periods is identified by the 14C datings, which are still limited in number, and only with future datings will it be possible to see whether the time frame is tenable or must be adjusted. EN A2, however, must probably be regarded as a relatively brief transition between the first settlement with the very widespread and uniform find material dominated by short-necked funnel beakers and pointed-butted flint axes in EN A1, and the subsequent period EN B dominated by high-necked funnel beakers and thin-butted flint axes of type IIIA. EN A2 thus comes to represent a period typified by both continuity and change.

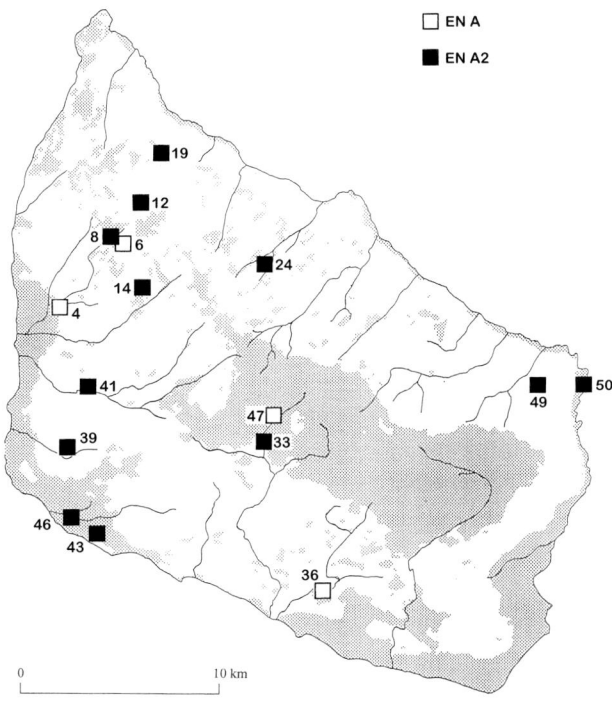

Fig. 3.16. The distribution of settlements where finds dating to EN A2 and to EN A in general were recovered.

Finds from the same period outside Bornholm

When C.J. Becker presented the finds from the settlement pits at Store Valby in western Zealand, he emphasized the difference between the inventory in pit BN, which he identified as belonging to period EN A, and from pit BR, which he considered to be later, and which he thought either lay on the borderline between EN A and B, or was pure EN B (Becker 1955, 151). The reason for this view was Becker's original classification of A-pots as funnel beakers with a soft transition between neck and belly. And in pit BR sherds of funnel beakers were found which had both soft and abrupt transitions between neck and belly (*idem*, fig. 19). In presenting the finds from Värby in Scania, Bengt Salomonsson also emphasized this formal element, and he compared the finds from Värby pits V 1 and V 22 to the finds from Store Valby pit BN because of the soft profiles of the funnel beakers rather than to the finds from Store Valby pit BR (Salomonsson 1970, 77). It is possible that this conceals chronological differences which are not wholly clear today, when differences such as soft and abrupt transitions between neck and belly are not assigned such great importance. In settlement pit A, Sigersted III, sherds of funnel beakers occur with a more or less abrupt transition between neck and belly (Nielsen 1985a, figs. 4-5). Among Eva Koch's funnel beakers of type 1, both elements also appear (Koch 1998, 86 f.). Among the finds from Store Valby pit BR, at least one funnel beaker appears whose neck index is 21 and which thus falls within the range of variation for funnel beakers of type II (Becker 1955, fig. 19a). There is however no doubt that the context otherwise includes funnel beakers which correspond both in form and ornamentation to Eva Koch's funnel beakers of type I (*idem*, figs. 19b-d and 21).

Of interest for the dating of possible early funnel beakers of type II are two close-lying, so-called twin pits at Almhov in SW Scania, pits A3747 and A3748. If the neck index is measured on the two depicted funnel beakers from there (Gidlöf *et al.* 2006, fig. 56 and 58), one gets values that lie close to the transition between types I and II. A ^{14}C dating of grain from one of the pits, A3748, gave the result (Ua-23873) 4930±45 BP, cal. 3760-3650 BC (1σ), 3800-3640 BC (2σ).

In western Scania, parts of pots have also been found with a clearly marked transition between neck and belly and a neck height corresponding to the Bornholm funnel beakers of type II from Lillegård and other sites. At Råga Hörstad one side of a funnel beaker was found with a neck index of 31, indicating type II, ornamented beneath the rim with two horizontal rows of indentations (Petré & Strömberg 1958, 71 f., fig. 4). It lay in a pit in a settlement area that contained several Early Neolithic finds, located on a low sandy ridge.

In Eva Koch's discussion of funnel beakers of type II she mentions the occurrence of the type in a number of Danish settlement finds, including Havnelev (1922), Sølager layer II and Svaleklint (Koch 1998, 90 with references). She further notes that the available ^{14}C datings of settlements along with her datings of food encrustation on funnel beakers of this type fluctuate within the interval 3950-3500 BC – that is, they are spread over the whole of EN I, as was also the case with the datings of funnel beakers of type I. She even hints that the manufacture of funnel beakers of type II may have begun slightly earlier than the manufacture of funnel beakers of type I. She assigns type II to the Svaleklint group, which is defined by Ebbesen & Mahler (1980), partly on the basis of the ornamentation, and partly on the basis of the material from the settlement Svaleklint, which Skaarup (1973, 121) called 'Zealand-West Scanian non-megalithic C', and partly of a comparison of individual pots, including lugged beakers with zoned ornamentation from eastern Denmark (Ebbesen & Mahler 1980, 49).

However, the settlement Svaleklint does not offer a good basis for the definition of either a period or a style. The find material from it comes from a mixed cultural layer which contains finds from most of the EN and the beginning of the MN, including funnel beakers of type I (Skaarup 1973, fig. 43:2) and later funnel beakers such as type V.1 (*idem*, fig. 43:3). Nevertheless, the designation 'Svaleklint group' has entered the terminology and today seems to cover everything within EN I that cannot be identified as belonging to the Oxie group. In one of the most recent chronologies Svaleklint is even placed as the earliest phase of EN I on Zealand and in Scania (Mischka *et al.* 2014, fig. 2).

Zoned ornamentation, which Eva Koch calls complex ornamentation, appears on funnel beakers and lugged beakers of types I, II and III in three different versions: 1.3, 1.1 and 1.2 in that order (Koch 1998, 87, 89, 91 and fig. 49). None of these need to be contemporary, and the pots that have been assigned to the Svaleklint group by Ebbesen & Mahler (1980), are probably not contemporary. Eva Koch is the only person who has presented a closed eastern Danish context which includes sherds of pottery with zoned ornamentation – Pit A at Slotsbjergby Skolehave in western Zealand (Koch 1998, 185 ff., figs. 114-16). The finds from there comprise sherds of pots with complex ornamentation 1.2 corresponding to the kind that appears on funnel beakers of type III. In addition sherds of funnel beakers with vertical belly stripes and vertical moulded ribs on the lower part occur. Eva Koch is undoubtedly right to say that we are here looking at finds from a transitional phase between EN I and EN II, or even more probably from an early phase of EN C (*idem*, 189).

The Svaleklint elements, or rather zoned ornamentation / complex ornamentation, form an integral if not so common part of several successive phases of the EN in eastern Denmark, since these various surface-covering patterns appear on funnel beakers and slender lugged beakers of types I-III. When we begin here by placing these pot types in a chronological order, there is no basis for regarding the 'Svaleklint group' as an independent chronological complex. With that in mind, we could abandon this subject, but it still remains to answer the question why a majority of researchers have acceded to a very early dating of the 'Svaleklint group'. The origin of this view must be sought in an article which because of its early ^{14}C datings turned the chronology of the Early Neolithic on its head and attacked C.J. Becker's division into three periods, A, B and C (Becker 1947). The article was about an Early Neolithic settlement layer beneath a long barrow with dolmen chambers at Mosegården in eastern Jutland (Madsen & Petersen 1984). The long barrow was demarcated by two parallel palisade ditches with remains of large wooden posts, and two samples of charcoal from several of these posts produced very early datings (K-3463) 5080±90 BP, (K-3464) 4890±90 BP). These datings prompted the authors to conclude that the settlement layer beneath the mound must be "among the oldest Early Neolithic settlements immediately after the Ertebølle Culture" (*idem*, 75). However, this did not allow for the fact that the ^{14}C datings were based on charcoal from timber of large dimensions and of unknown own age. The pottery from the settlement was assigned to the Volling group (Ebbesen & Mahler 1980, 40 ff.), and the early datings from Mosegården became important to the determination of the age of this pottery group. Madsen & Petersen also commented on the dating of the eastern Danish 'Svaleklint group', which they considered closely related to the Volling group (1984, 100). In this case they could refer to an early dating of the non-megalithic long barrow at Lindebjerg in western Zealand, which also sealed in an underlying settlement layer. The dating of the long barrow in 1970, (K-1659) 5010±100 BP, was based on charcoal from a piece of oak which measured 30x30 cm and was at the edge of a post-hole in post-ditch C at the eastern end of the long barrow (Liversage 1981, 97, fig. 7). One could say that history repeated itself: here too it was a matter of dating material with an unknown own age. Post-ditch C contained the sherds of one large and four small funnel beakers of type III (*idem*, figs. 24 and 25a). A more likely dating of the long barrow at Lindebjerg will therefore be 3650-3500 BC, and the settlement layer beneath the mound need not be much older (*cf.* Fischer 2002, 366). The same dating may apply to the settlement beneath the long barrow at Mosegården, where the pots with ornaments in Volling style have profiles corresponding to funnel beakers of type III (Madsen & Petersen 1984 figs. 18-20).

Having detached funnel beakers of type II from the concept 'Svaleklint group', we can continue by investigating the variations and dating of the type. In Eva Koch's catalogue of bog-found pottery (1998) 34 funnel beakers of type II have the rim preserved, and only one pot is unornamented beneath it. On the other pots the ornamentation is highly uniform. In 27 cases the pots are decorated with from one to four horizontal rows of indentations beneath the rim. The most frequent kind is vertical, oblong indentations and round or irregular indentations, but one also finds thin, curved indentations which may have been made with a fingernail. In three cases there are 2-3 horizontal rows of impressions with two-ply cord, and in two cases horizontal stab-and-drag ornaments which imitate cord impressions. Finally, there is one pot with zoned / complex ornamentation made with oblong indentations at the rim and vertical and horizontal lines in stab-and-drag technique on the neck and the top half of the belly (Koch 1998, find no. 225). Of a pot which was presumably ornamented in the same way, only the lower part is preserved. In the Zealand Island Group type II is thus mainly ornamented with indentations as on Bornholm, while a small number of the Zealand funnel beakers are ornamented with two-ply cord, which on Bornholm with few exceptions appears exclusively on funnel beakers of type III. A neck fragment of a funnel beaker or lugged beaker of type II with horizontal impressions of two-ply cord beneath the rim was found in the first-excavated pit at the settlement at Havnelev (1922) in eastern Zealand, which contained parts of funnel beakers of both type II and type III (Nielsen 1994, Taf. 7.2). From this pit we have a recent AMS ¹⁴C dating of an ox-bone:

(UBA-300023) 4978±37 BP, cal. 3790-3706 BC (1σ), 3929-3659 BC (2σ) (Gron et al. 2016, 249).

The most thoroughly dated context with funnel beakers of type II, however, is from Præstelyngen in the western Zealand Åmose, where, together with a dugout boat of lime wood (boat II) excavated by Charlie Christensen (1990), parts of two funnel beakers of this type were found – one almost whole (fig. 3.17) and one fragment (Koch 1998, find no. 114). We have chosen to emphasize the datings from Præstelyngen, although these are very early produced, conventional ¹⁴C datings. In the following we use Eva Koch's sample descriptions together with the datings after recalibration. Some of the minor ranges on the calibration curve are omitted; in these cases probability percentages are indicated:[1)]

1) K-1473. Lime (*Tilia* sp.) wood from the prow of the boat: 5010±100 BP, cal. 3942-3705 BC (1σ), 3993-3636 BC (2σ with 99.5% probability). Median probability: 3810 BC.

2) K-1650. Willow (*Salix* sp.) wood from a pointed pole stuck down beside the rail of the boat: 4960±110 BP, cal. 3935-3645 BC (1σ), 3981-3620 BC (2σ with 93.1% probability). Median probability: 3763 BC.

3) K-1651. Moss from the closing of the stern of the boat: 4890±110 BP, cal. 3798-3526 BC (1σ with 98.3% probability), 3951-3499 BC (2σ with 95.1% probability). Median probability: 3687 BC.

4) K-1961. Pole stuck down beside the boat: 4980±110 BP, cal. 3937-3655 BC (1σ), 3992-3626 (2σ with 95.5% probability). Median probability: 3782 BC.

5) K-2057. Charcoal of hazel wood (*Corylus* sp.) from the clay slab in the middle of the boat: 4950±100 BP, cal. 3925-3643 BC (1σ), 3966-3626 BC (2σ with 94.1% probability). Median probability: 3753 BC.

6) K-2058. Charcoal of alder wood (*Alnus* sp.) from the clay slab near the prow of the boat: 4790±100 BP, cal. 3658-3380 BC (1σ), 3776-3361 BC (2σ). Median probability: 3562 BC.

7) K-2056. Sticks from the fish-trap, 10 of them of hazel wood, from the same layer as the boat, partly lying over and resting upon the belly of vessel 1: 4830±100 BP, cal. 3710-3515 BC (1σ with 92% probability), 3800-3368 BC (2σ with 98.9% probability). Median probability: 3603 BC.

8) K-1962. Upright stick, broken off at a higher level than the boat and probably belonging to the culture layer at this higher level: 4750±100 BP, cal. 3639-3378 BC (1σ), 3716-3337 (2σ with 98% probability). Median probability: 3528 BC.

9) K-1963. Worked pole, lying horizontally in the culture layer together with charcoal, cut wood, clay lumps etc., at a higher level than the boat: 4760±100 BP, cal. 3643-3378 BC (1σ), 3770-3344 BC (2σ). Median probability: 3537 BC.

The first seven samples date the boat, the poles that were sunk alongside it, and parts of a fish weir that lay across the boat. The mean of the median probabilities calculated for these seven datings is 3708 BC. The pots cannot be much later than the boat itself. However, dating no. 7, of material from the fish weir that lay in direct contact with pot 1, has a median probability of 3603 BC, which could mean a slightly later dating. So if dating no. 7 is not just a random deviation from the other datings, the dating of the pots should perhaps be placed between 3700 and 3600 BC. This does not appear unlikely, since pot 1 has a neck index of 33, which is close to the borderline of 35 between funnel beakers of types II and III. The last two datings were based on material that is stratigraphically more recent than the boat and the fish weir, and their mean date is 3532 BC.

The dating of the boat and the pots from Præstelyngen was done in 1969-73 with the conventional dating method. One must therefore state the reservation that the datings, here as in other cases, may be around 100 years younger than the datings made today with the AMS method. This issue cannot be elucidated without new datings.

As mentioned, funnel beakers of type II appear at the settlement Havnelev (1922). But other settlements can also be mentioned. At Stengade on Langeland, above a settlement, an oblong/trapezoid stone construction had been built which was at first in-

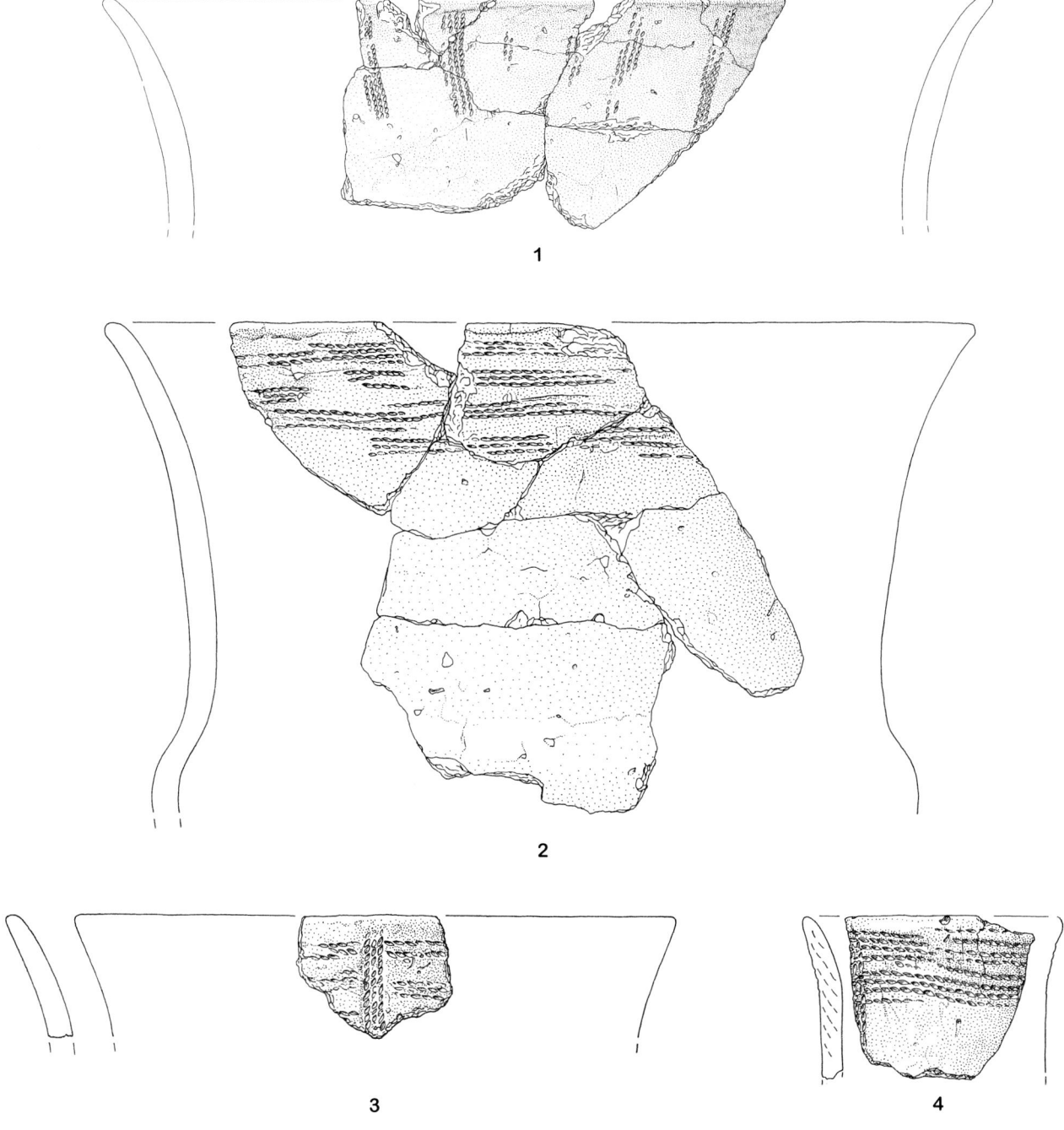

Fig. 3.20. Pottery from Pileskoven, Klemensker (Finds list I no. 10). Poul Wöhliche del. (1) 1:3, (2-4) 1:2.

The feature has been interpreted as the remains of a building with a sunken floor and clay-and-wattle walls. Around the large stone in the western part five crushing stones and hammerstones and four fragments of querns were found. Several of the stones, which were probably used on the spot, were soot-blackened. The building may have housed a workshop space and/or stores, while the actual habitation may have lain on an adjacent hill. In the bottom layer of the depression only sherds of Early Neolithic pottery were found, but in the upper layers of the depression, sherds of pots from MN AII were also found. Several sherds of Middle Neolithic pottery were found in the smaller fill layers E and W of the large depression. It is thus clear that the house site had been established, used and burned down in the EN, and that the place was later used for settlement activities in the MN.

The Early Neolithic finds from the clay daub layer and the ash layer at the bottom of the depression include rim sherds of a large funnel beaker ornamented with vertical lines in two-ply cord separated by blank areas (fig. 3.20:1), several rim and neck sherds with horizontal or both horizontal and vertical lines in

65

two-ply cord (fig. 3.20:3-4), and parts of the neck of a large funnel beaker of type III ornamented with horizontal lines in two-ply cord, gathered in groups of three which were separated by blank areas (fig. 3.20:2). There were many rim sherds of different funnel beakers ornamented with impressions of two-ply cord like the aforementioned examples and a rim sherd of a funnel beaker ornamented with groups of short, thin, vertical lines radiating from the rim. A single rimsherd was ornamented with a horizontal row of finger impressions. In the lower layers of the depression no sherds of beakers with indentations beneath the rim were found together with the cord-ornamented pottery.

There was a conspicuously meagre amount of flint in the bottom of the feature. Of imported flint there were 1 scraper and 1 backed blade flaked off a polished flint axe with rounded narrow sides and convex broad sides, as well as a few flakes. Of Kristianstad flint there were also only a few flakes. In the upper layer of the depression a few flakes of ball flint nodules and Kristianstad flint were found, but hardly any imported flint. On the other hand there were several pieces of quartz.

There are two AMS ^{14}C datings from the bottom layer of the feature:

1) (AAR-10261) Charcoal of apple, rowan or hawthorn (*Pomaceae*): 4960±65 BP, cal. 3800-3650 BC (1σ), 3950-3640 BC (2σ). Median probability: 3750 BC.[2]

2) (AAR-10262) Charcoal of hazel (*Corylus avellana*): 5038±49 BP, cal. 3950-3770 BC (1σ), 3960-3710 BC (2σ). Median probability: 3850 BC.[2]

Both datings are earlier than expected, although the first dating does fall right at the beginning of EN B. But with a median probability of 3750 BC it overlaps the dating of funnel beakers of type II from Vallensgård I and thus EN A2. It is a poor match with this context, where the pottery from the house site is dominated by funnel beakers of type III. Although the charcoal was carefully selected for dating, it may have had a certain intrinsic age. In 2017 two supplementary datings were conducted, both of samples that had been taken from the burnt clay-and-wattle:

3) (Ua-55724) Burnt macrofossil, not further identified: 4513±37 BP, cal. 3350-3110 BC (1σ), 3360-3090 BC (2σ). Median probability: 3213 BC.[2]

4) (Ua-55725) Charcoal, not further identified: 4786±31 BP, cal. 3640-3530 BC (1σ), 3650-3510 BC (2σ). Median probability: 3569 BC.[2]

Dating no. 3 must reflect the activity in the Middle Neolithic, which according to the archaeological dating took place in MN AII. Dating no. 4 on the other hand falls within EN B (3650-3500 BC), whether the uncertainty is calculated with 1 or 2 sigma. We therefore let this dating apply to the settlement at Pileskoven in the EN. It is used in fig. 3.21 together with two datings from Vallensgård I of material from EN B.

The location of the settlements

This period, with 33 settlement finds, is the most frequently represented from the Early Neolithic on Bornholm. There are both more coastal sites and more inland sites than in the preceding periods (fig. 3.22). By and large, the distribution covers the same areas as before, but southern Bornholm is now better represented on the map. Almost half of the sites were also used in EN A. In eight cases they coincide with settlements from EN A1, in six with settlements from EN A2 and twice with settlements that cannot be dated more precisely than EN A.

Finds from the same time outside Bornholm

In eastern Scania, in Blekinge and on Bornholm, the cord-ornamented pottery has been viewed as a connecting factor since C.J. Becker defined his non-megalithic 'Bornholm-South Sweden group', which he considered derived from the pottery in EN B, but which he mainly dated to EN C with support in the finds from Siretorp in western Blekinge (Becker 1947, 161-69; 1990, 43 f.). However, it has not been easy to relate to this late dating of the cord-ornamented pottery. When Berta Stjernquist presented the Early Neolithic finds from the settlement at Simris in southeastern Scania, she found it difficult to date funnel beakers with ornaments in two-ply cord to pure EN C. She dated some of them to EN B together with finds from other settlements, including pots and sherd material from Norra Möinge and Råga Hörstad (Stjernquist 1965, 60).

Becker's dating of the Bornholm-South Sweden group to EN C was however uncritically taken for granted by others (Berglund & Welinder 1972; Skaarup 1973, 130; M. Larsson 1984, 172-73; Jennbert 1984,

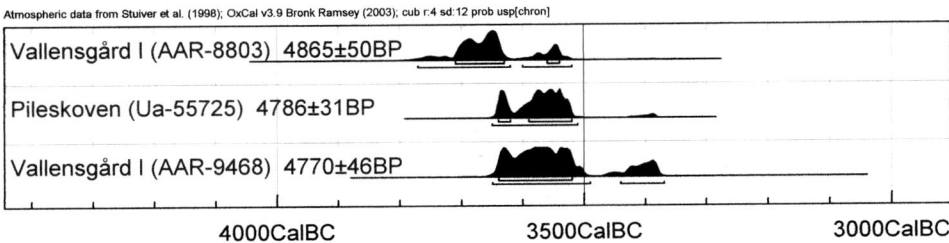

Fig. 3.21. Calibrated ^{14}C dates of settlements dating to EN B. The later dates from Vallensgård I and Pileskoven have been selected.

72; Wyszomirska 1988, 176 f.). In the layers with funnel beaker pottery at Siretorp, though, rim profiles of different types of funnel beakers occur, just as there is variation in ornamental motifs which are best explained by saying that the material from the Early Neolithic does not come from just one settlement, but that the site was visited several times over an extended period. In the area designated 'Furet' (the furrow/groove) rim sherds of funnel beakers were found with lateral indentations in the rim itself. They may belong to funnel beakers of type I, which may also be the case with a sherd with a cordon along the rim in which there are finger-wide impressions (Bagge & Kjellmark 1939, Pl. 68:9, 11-12). Among the rim sherds with various types of indentation, some are dateable to an older part of the Early Neolithic (*idem*, Pl. 61:8-12, 62:1-5, 63, 68:1-10). As at Nr. Sandegård, pot profiles occur which correspond to funnel beakers of type III with simple horizontal lines in two-ply cord (*idem*, Pl. 53, 54, 55:12), and which we date on Bornholm to EN B. Impressions of two-ply cord appear on 33% of the ornamented sherds. But there are also pot profiles with features that recall Early Middle Neolithic funnel beakers of types V-VII, and which are ornamented with various patterns in whipped cord (*idem*, Pl. 56-59). Impression with whipped cord, which does not appear in EN B, but is later, appears on 41% of the ornamented sherds (*idem*, 121) and is thus more frequently present than impression with two-ply cord. Pot parts which are ornamented with whipped cord must be dated to EN C and the beginning of the Middle Neolithic.

That the later elements in the 'S-layers' at Siretorp belong to the beginning of the Middle Neolithic is not a new observation. It has long since been demonstrated by Lili Kaelas (1953, 9-14). The funnel beaker material from Siretorp spans a longer period than Becker and a number of other researchers assumed. The pottery in the 'S-layers' must be distributed over a period that ranges from the older part of the Early Neolithic to some way into the Middle Neolithic (MN AI). Becker was however right in pointing to the similarities between the pottery from Bornholm and from Siretorp.

Before we leave Siretorp there are grounds to remark on the *stratigraphy* and the succession of cultural stages proposed by the excavators, which were to mean so much for the discussion of the transition from the Mesolithic to the Neolithic in South Scandinavia. The excavations were conducted in 1913-15 by Knut Kjellmark and again in 1931-35 by him and Axel Bagge (Bagge & Kjellmark 1939). The stratigraphic observations at Siretorp were acclaimed as one of the most significant breakthroughs in Stone Age research in the 1930s. However, the cultural layers at Siretorp lie in and beneath shifting sand layers and at beach ridges, and some of the layers have been flooded and rebedded, which one has to allow for when the stratigraphy is to be evaluated (*cf.* Berglund & Welinder 1972). Excavation of the sand layers demonstrated

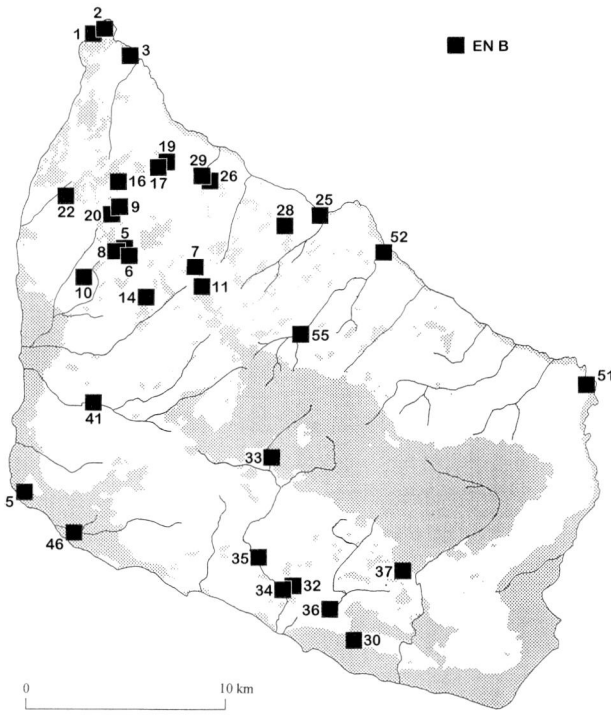

Fig. 3.22. The distribution of settlements where finds dating to EN B have been recovered.

three successive settlement phases with ceramics of the Ertebølle Culture followed by the Early Neolithic Funnel Beaker Culture[5] and the Pitted Ware Culture. This succession can hold no surprises for a present-day observer.

A. Bagge did however add an oldest layer with cord-ornamented funnel beaker pottery which lay beneath the Ertebølle layer. He admitted in the preface to the publication that at the beginning of the investigation he had not taken much notice of the deepest, long undated cultural layer, and it had not occurred to him at all that it could be Neolithic. He added: "Rydbeck's heresies of 1920-28 had not yet won wider acceptance." In this he was referring to a discussion that had been initiated by Otto Rydbeck, and which was about whether the Ertebølle Culture could have continued to exist at the same time as the 'megalithic culture' (see the historical overview of the research by Jennbert 1984, 10-16). The problem with the dating of the allegedly lowest, Neolithic layer in the series led the excavators to pursue it through more trenches. This part of the investigation was not easy, since the layer was extremely poor in dateable material. It is indeed the part of the stratigraphy at Siretorp that is most weakly substantiated and documented. But since Bagge's interpretation of the stratigraphy has long remained undisputed (*cf.* Wyszomirska 1988, 168; Welinder 1997, 95) it is worth looking more closely at the basis of the interpretation, in this case with reference to the profiles in the publication in the order in which they were described by Bagge.

The profiles G and E cut respectively along and across a shifting sand dune in the area 'Furet', a shifting sand area with pine tree vegetation in the eastern part of the Siretorp sandhills (Bagge & Kjellmark 1939, 41 ff., figs. 3 and 25). In the longitudinal profile G there is a distinction between three object-bearing layers, which in the chart between p. 70 and p. 71 are given the letters S, E and S, respectively for 'snörkeramisk' (*i.e.* Early Neolithic cord ornamented ware), Ertebølle Culture and 'snörkeramisk' again. The layers in question are described in more detail on pp. 41-42, where it is stated that the top layer 'a' contained cord-ornamented, Early Neolithic pottery, the middle layer 'c' Ertebølle pottery, while the lowest culture layer 'e', designated with the letter S, in fact only contained flint debitage and no pottery. In profile G the layer is thus undated.

In profile E, which is a longer and more continuous transverse profile through the same dune, Bagge distinguished five cultural layers: at the top a 'cord ornamented ware' layer (EN), beneath this two Ertebølle layers and beneath these again two 'cord ornamented ware' layers (*cf.* the profile drawing between p. 70 and p. 71). In this case there is good reason to distinguish the layers in the dune itself (the m² areas from +T7 to O7) and the layers at the foot of the dune towards the NE (the m² areas from O to ÷K), where there had clearly been a special activity area with fire traces, many stones and more find-rich culture layers than in the dune itself.

The top layer 'a' in profile E was mainly Early Neolithic, but with admixtures from both the Ertebølle Culture and the Pitted Ware Culture. Beneath this lay an upper and a lower layer 'c' with finds from the Ertebølle Culture. The next layer down was the allegedly Early Neolithic layer 'e', which however in its whole southern course, from field T7 to E7, contained no antiquities, only stones. In the northern course of the layer a few flint flakes were found, and in field B7, a sherd of 'cord ornamented ware'. It should be noted that layer 'e' at this point in the profile is not covered by any layer with finds from the Ertebølle Culture, and that field B7 is situated in the transitional zone at the foot of the dune, where one must consider the possibility of disturbances. Layer 'e' is at this point covered directly by a shifting sand layer in which there were many stones. The lowest, coal-black culture layer 'g', which is also designated with S for 'cord ornamented ware', rested directly on marine sand. It has a high phosphate content, but is poor in archaeological finds, containing only a few stones and a little flint debitage as well as, in field C7, an unornamented, *säkert* potsherd of cord ornamented ware. This sherd, so important to the whole sequence, is not described or shown in any more detail in the publication. Nor is it quite clear what is meant by the Swedish word *säkert*, which can mean both 'certainly' and 'probably'. A further sherd of 'cord ornamented ware' was found in field ÷K7 in the deepest culture layer, which is certainly Early Neolithic, but which at this point is not covered by layers with finds from the Ertebølle Culture. Here we are quite outside the stratigraphy of the dune, on the lee side towards the NE, where the sequence of layers cannot be directly compared to the sequence in the dune.

An attempt was made by Bagge and Kjellmark to document a Neolithic horizon older than the Ertebølle phase on the basis of the observations in these two profiles and the find of an unornamented, *säkert* potsherd of cord ornamented ware in a layer otherwise empty of finds older than the sand drift at the place. In all other places in the Siretorp area where there were finds from the Ertebølle Culture and the Early Funnel Beaker Culture in the same excavation fields the Ertebølle layers were at the bottom and the layers with finds from the Early Funnel Beaker Culture were at the top. In other words, a clear, distinct succession like the one we know today from the excavations in the shell mounds (S.H. Andersen 1991; 1993; 1994).

Others have also later questioned Bagge's and Kjellmark's interpretation of the stratigraphy. Persson has pointed to the find-poor layer in profile G (Persson 1998, 156; *cf.* Fischer 2002, 365), and some think that the content of the layers may have been re-bedded (Malmer 2002, 22; M. Larsson *et al.* 2012, 33). It is not possible on the basis of the publication to ascertain all the possible sources of error, which in this landscape of sand dunes at Siretorp may have disturbed the sequence of layers so that the stratigraphy at a single point seems to have been reversed. It can only be said that most stratigraphic observations at Siretorp in fact do not suggest that there is a Neolithic layer older than the Ertebølle layers.

After this digression around Siretorp, where we first looked at the temporal spread of the find material and then at the stratigraphy, we should at least be able to free the Bornholm-South Sweden group with pottery ornamented with two-ply cord from the dating to EN C, and we can return to the issue of the dating of funnel beakers of type III in other contexts. In southeastern Scania the settlement Mossby is relevant as a comparison with Vallensgård I and other Bornholm settlements with cord-ornamented funnel beakers. At Mossby a culture layer was excavated with Early Neolithic finds, including a two-aisled house site (M. Larsson 1992, 66-78). As at Vallensgård, the pots were exclusively ornamented at the rim. Of these, 48% were ornamented with impressions of two-ply cord. In addition there were rim sherds with horizontal rows of thin vertical lines as well as indentations in two or more horizontal rows. The sherds were too small to permit measurement of the neck index. From Mossby we have three very early AMS ^{14}C datings of charred food encrustations from the inside of potsherds (M. Larsson 1992, 74).

As for food-crust datings in general, Persson and Fischer have pointed out the risk that the samples may contain organic material of marine origin, and that they are thus influenced by a reservoir effect (Persson 1999, 101; Fischer 2002, 366; Larsson & Rzepecki 2003, 3). This is also a very likely explanation of the early datings from Mossby, from which we also have two datings of charred grains of barley that come close to the datings from Vallensgård I (M. Larsson 1992, 74)[1] (Ua-755) 4925±115 BP, cal. 3935-3540 BC (1σ), 3967-3383 BC (2σ). Median probability: 3728 BC.[2] – (Ua-753) 4915±100 BP, cal. 3909-3539 BC (1σ), 3958-3387 BC (2σ). Median probability: 3715 BC.[2]

With this great uncertainty, up to ±115 years, the spread of the datings on the calibration curve is very wide. But with a slightly greater uncertainty we may perhaps come closer to a likely dating. With the former dating of barley calibrated with 1σ, 78.3% of the probability distribution lies in the interval 3809-3633 BC, and with the later dating of barley, also calibrated with 1σ, 86.6% of the probability distribution lies in the interval 3802-3633 BC. This best matches the datings of funnel beakers of type II from Vallensgård I, but also overlaps the datings of type III. However, median probabilities for both datings fall within EN A2 on Bornholm. Finally, one must remember that the finds from Mossby do not come from a closed context but from an 'open' culture layer.

In the material from Svenstorp in southwestern Scania there are rim sherds of funnel beakers with many different ornamental motifs, probably reflecting that the finds from the settlement are from different times (Larsson 1984, 103-27). Here 10.3% of the rim sherds are ornamented with impressions of two-ply cord. A cord-ornamented neck fragment had a neck index of only 14, which places the pot within the variation range for funnel beakers of type I (Larsson 1984, 124). M. Larsson compares the pottery from Svenstorp to 'the Svaleklint group' on Zealand and makes the site a type locality for a phase between EN A and C in southwestern Scania (Larsson 1984, 127). There is one ^{14}C dating from feature Ö 51 at Svenstorp (Lu-12): 4780±100 BP, cal. 3653-3379 BC (1σ), 3771-3358 (2σ).[1] With slightly more uncertainty the dating can be narrowed down, as 78.2% of the probability distribution, with a calibration of 1σ, lies between 3653 and 3499 BC, corresponding to EN B on Bornholm. Datings of pits with pottery of the Svenstorp type at Almhov suggest that this phase begins around 3700 BC (Rudebeck & Macheridis 2015, 180).

The problem with Svenstorp is that what were viewed as dug pits during the excavation of the high gravel ridge must in many cases have been tree-throw remains, judging both from plan drawings and profiles (compare the plan drawing Salomonsson 1963, fig. 5 and the profile in fig. 23; see also the survey plan in Larsson 1984, fig. 64). One cannot regard the content of objects in these natural features as closed finds, since half of the tree root presses parts of the culture layers down into the soil with the fall of the tree, and these cultural layers may have contained mixed find material from an extended period at the site.

In the other southwestern Scanian settlement finds from Månasken, V. Kärrstorp, the percentage of rim sherds ornamented with two-ply cord reaches 26.5% (Larsson 1984, 138). A neck sherd of a funnel beaker with this type of ornamentation has a neck index of 33.7 corresponding to that of funnel beakers of type II.

Some of the aforementioned examples give the impression that the use of two-ply cord may have been introduced earlier in Scania than on Bornholm. This also seems to have been the case at other sites in Sweden. Sherds of pottery ornamented with two-ply cord from Skogsmossen in Västmannland have been dated to c. 3800 BC (Hallgren 2008, 139 ff., fig. 8.4).

In the western Scanian settlement material from Råga Hörstad, besides the aforementioned funnel beaker of type II, the top part of a tall-necked funnel beaker with horizontal lines in two-ply cord, interrupted by short, vertical lines was also found. This should most likely be assigned to type III, even though the transition between neck and belly is unmarked (Petré & Strömberg 1958, 70 f., fig. 3).

Among the bog-found pottery from the Zealand Island Group Eva Koch has distinguished 41 funnel beakers of type III (Koch 1998, 91 ff.). Among the pots that have the rim preserved, 10 are without ornaments, while 11 pots have horizontal rows of indentations beneath the rim; of these, six funnel beakers have one row of oblong, vertical indentations as on funnel beakers of type III from Vallensgård I (rim ornament 9a). Three funnel beakers have horizontal lines in the form of narrow, incised grooves beneath the rim; in one case three parallel lines are interrupted by blank spaces. In another case the horizontal lines are combined with short, vertical groups of lines repeated at the top of the belly. Two pots have a horizontal row of indentations just below the transition between neck and belly, in one case interrupted by blank spaces. Four funnel beakers with zoned / complex ornamentation also occur, where the ornaments on the neck are repeated on the belly. A single funnel beaker has moulded ornamentation in the form of short, vertical cordons beneath the rim.

Only five of Eva Koch's funnel beakers of type III have 2-3 horizontal lines of two-ply cord impressions beneath the rim. There are thus great differences in the use of two-ply cord on funnel beakers of type III from the Zealand Island Group and Bornholm respectively. On Bornholm there are settlement finds such as Nr. Sandegård and Pileskoven, where the funnel beakers are almost exclusively ornamented with two-ply cord. It was the frequent use of ornamentation on the Bornholm funnel beakers that prompted C.J. Becker to establish the special Bornholm – South Sweden local group (Becker 1947, 161-69; 1990, 41 ff.).

Funnel beakers of type III very like the Zealand ones also appear at several eastern Jutland settlements. A large amount of pottery was found in the upper Neolithic layer in the kitchen midden at Norsminde, where sherds of c. 150 different funnel beakers were found, only about a third of which were ornamented (S.H. Andersen 1991, 31 ff.; 1994, 30 ff.). The oldest Neolithic pottery in the form of funnel beakers of type 0 and perhaps type I emerged just above layers with finds from the Ertebølle Culture. Later than this pottery are funnel beakers of type III, whose ornamentation, in those cases where it occurs, consists of horizontal lines made with impressions of two-ply cord. Only a few pots are ornamented with indentations. In addition there are funnel beakers with zoned / complex ornamentation which fully match the Zealand funnel beakers with the same ornamentation (*cf.* S.H. Andersen 1991, fig. 20.1-2 with Koch 1998, finds no. 25.2, 187.1 and 253). The material for ^{14}C datings of the layers with this pottery were taken from shells of oysters (*Ostrea edulis*) and cockles (*Cerastoderma edulis*). With recalibration they fall within the time interval c. 3700-3500 BC (S.H. Andersen 1994, Tab. 1).

In the settlement layer beneath the long barrow at Mosegården in eastern Jutland, 2/3 of the funnel beakers were without ornamentation as at Norsminde, and on the rest of the funnel beakers, impressioning with two-ply cord was the most frequent type. In addition there were beakers with surface-covering ornamentation done with stab-and-drag grooving or different types of indentation (Madsen & Petersen 1984, 84 ff.). Such as the pot profiles are shown, there is a strong match between the funnel beakers from Mosegården and the Zealand funnel beakers of type III (for example *idem*, fig. 18b). More recent excavations in eastern Jutland have turned up other examples of funnel beakers which can be directly assigned to Eva Koch's type III. A small, round-bottomed funnel beaker ornamented beneath the rim with two horizontal stab-and-drag lines was excavated at Lindegård Bog (Skousen 2008, 151 and fig. 120), and at Kildevang I and II parts of funnel beakers appeared with the same profile and partly the same ornamentation (*idem*, figs. 132 and 139). Datings of Volling pottery come from Kildevang I, where in the feature A181 a funnel beaker with surface-covering ornamentation was found (Ravn 2011, 139, fig. 7), and from which a sample of charcoal has been dated to (AAR-8511) 4935±55 BP, cal. 3765-3655 BC (1σ), 3929-3637 BC (2σ). Median probability: 3720 BC.[2] In the feature A283 at the same site a funnel beaker was found with two horizontal rows of indentations beneath the rim (Ravn 2011, 142, fig. 10), and from this a sample of charcoal was identified and dated to (AAR-10005) 4913±48 BP, cal. 3758-3645 BC (1σ), 3793-3636 (2σ). Median probability: 3695 BC.[2]

Common to funnel beakers and lugged beakers within the Volling group, both large and small pots, and the eastern Danish funnel beakers and slender lugged beakers of Eva Koch's type III, are the tall neck, the abrupt transition in most cases between neck and belly and the round, often almost spherical lower body, the bottom of which may be round or flat. The way of ornamenting the pots also recurs in both places. Many funnel beakers are unornamented, while some have sparing rim ornamentation in the form of horizontal rows of indentations or horizontal lines made with impressions of two-ply cord or stab-and-drag grooving. A minority of the funnel beakers and lugged beakers are decorated with surface-covering patterns like those for which the Volling-phase pots have become particularly well-known. The richly decorated pots appear in settlement contexts (Madsen & Petersen 1984, figs. 18a and 19a-b; Skousen 2008, 132 ff.; Ravn 2011, fig. 7), but also in grave finds and in the post-trenches of the long barrows, suggesting that this pottery had been selected for specific purposes.

Besides similarities in the form of the funnel beakers, within the time interval c. 3700-3500 BC one can point to strong matches in the composition of the pottery inventory as a whole. This applies to the use of lugged beakers, lugged pots and lugged flasks as well as clay discs with finger impressions in the rim. These are all forms that were introduced in the Oxie phase. New, on the other hand, is the collared flask.

Hitherto, the emphasis has been on pointing out differences and demarcating local groups within the South Scandinavian area in the EN with a particular focus on ornamentation (Ebbesen & Mahler 1980; Madsen & Petersen 1984; Becker 1990, Madsen 1994; Klassen 2004, 232 ff.), while there has been less focus on similarities and parallels in the development. Eva Koch's division into funnel beaker types is a tool for cutting across these factors and showing that the basic design of the pots was determined by the period and was common to a wide area.

Settlements from EN C, c. 3500-3300 BC

Settlements with culture layers and pits

The excavation of the culture layer with Early Neolithic material at Nørre Sandegård in Østerlars (Finds list I no. 52) turned up the sherds of a funnel beaker within a limited area (Becker 1990, pl. 18:362). Becker thought that this pot belonged to the Virum group in EN II (Ebbesen & Mahler 1980) and considered it the only element at the site that could be assigned to this group (*idem*, 44 f.). A funnel beaker of a similar form is known from Tygapil in SE Scania, where it has been dated to the transition EN C / MN AI (Strömberg 1978, 80, fig. 3b). However, judging from the profile of the pot as it is reconstructed in the drawing, the funnel beaker from Nr. Sandegård falls best within Eva Koch's type V.2, which on the basis of find combinations at among other sites Sarup, has been dated to MN AIb (Koch 1998, 101). The same dating applies to two fragmented funnel beakers of type VII which were also found at the site (Becker 1990, pl. 18:1948 E). In this light the basis for including this site among the settlements from EN C is much reduced, although it is possible that we are here close to the transition EN C / MN AI. On the ornamented sherds from Nr. Sandegård, besides impressions with two-ply cord, there are also impressions of whipped cord on at least two pot parts (Becker 1990, 42, pl. 16:92,147, 366 and pl. 17:309). The whipped cord appears on pottery belonging to the Virum group on Zealand and the Bellevuegård group in Scania, which means EN II / EN C, but it also appears frequently at the beginning of MN AI in various pattern combinations (M. Larsson 1992, *passim*).

A large element from EN C was found during the excavation of the culture layer at Ndr. Grødbygård in Åker (Finds list I no. 36). Among the 1200 ornamented potsherds, 68 are ornamented with whipped cord, and 82 sherds come from pots with vertical belly striping. On a small funnel beaker of type IV the belly is vertically striped with deep grooves which almost make the ornamentation look like fluting (fig. 3.29:1). Whipped cord and vertical striping also appear among the pottery from the settlement pit at Vester Rosendalegård in Rutsker (Finds list I no. 22), where there are also elements that can be dated to MN AIa. As no larger parts of pots are preserved, it is therefore not possible to determine how many of the sherds are ornamented with whipped cord, which must be dated to EN C and MN AIa respectively.

A rim sherd from a funnel or lugged beaker from Hammeren (Finds list I no. 1) is ornamented with hanging semicircles in two-ply cord combined with impressions of whipped cord (fig. 3.27:5), which also appear on a slender lugged beaker from Virum (Ebbesen & Mahler 1980, fig. 11:1) and on a fragment of a wide lugged beaker of Eva Koch's type III from Lindbjerggård, western Zealand (*idem*, fig. 19:2; Koch 1998, find no. 36). Among the sherds from Hammeren there is also another neck ornament known from Virum, consisting of 1-1½ cm wide vertical bands demarcated by lines in whipped cord and filled out with dense diagonal lines in whipped cord (fig. 3.27:7, 8; *cf*. Ebbesen & Mahler 1980, fig. 12:6,14). At Hammeren many belly sherds of funnel beakers with vertical striping have also been found, which indicates activity at the site in EN C – MN A1. But otherwise pottery from EN C is not represented very frequently in the find material from the Bornholm settlements.

Causewayed enclosure

On Bornholm one causewayed enclosure has been localized and investigated at Vasagård in Åker on both sides of the stream Læsåen (Finds list I no. 35). One could discuss whether this is one or two enclosures, since there are two parallel rows of segmented ditches with semicircular courses on each side of the watercourse at a distance from each other of 240 m (fig. 3.23). Vasagård East was investigated in 1988, 1993, 2012 and 2015-18, and it turned out that at this site there was not only a causewayed enclosure, but also a later, larger palisade enclosure from the Late Funnel Beaker Culture, MN AV. Also at Vasagård West, which was investigated in 2007 and 2013-19, the ditches belonging to the causewayed enclosure had been superseded by a larger palisade enclosure in MN AV. The extensive activity at both sites in the Late Funnel Beaker Culture left a large quantity of find material, not only in connection with the palisades, but also in the top layer of the ditches of the causewayed enclosure. At Vasagård East, on the other hand, there was not very much material that could date the establishment of the ditches, whose bottom layer contained very few datable cultural remains. In ditch AB a single ornamented sherd at the bottom of the fill could with great probability be dated to MN AII. Ditch AJ farthest to the NW at Vasagård East lay on a slope where ploughing and soil transport had removed most of the fill, so that there were only a few cm left of it. In the thin bottom layer lay a fragment of an unornamented funnel beaker whose profile corresponds to funnel beakers of type IV (fig. 3.24). This is the oldest find from the segmented ditches at Vasagård East and gives us a probable dating of the establishment of the causewayed enclosure to EN II / EN C.

The first segmented ditch investigated at Vasagård West contained a body of find material that was much larger and which provided support for a similar dating. Since the material tells us something about the development in the time after the establishment of the causewayed enclosure, it will be described in more detail here.

Ditch I.1 lay in the outer row of segmented ditches towards the south at Vasagård West. Only the southernmost end of the ditch was exposed, and a 3 m longitudinal section was cut through it, so that a west-oriented section appeared (fig. 3.25). The fill in the ditch west of the profile was excavated layer by layer down to a depth of 130 cm from the surface of the subsoil, where the bottom of the ditch had been dug 15-20 cm down into the firm layer of slate. The top layer above the upper layer of stones contained mixed material from several periods of the Middle Neolithic Funnel Beaker Culture with pottery from MN AV as the latest element. Beneath this, between the stones and all the way down to the bottom, there were finds of the character of settlement material where the pottery was much fragmented. There were no great differences in the quantities of finds in the individual layers. The finds were as follows:

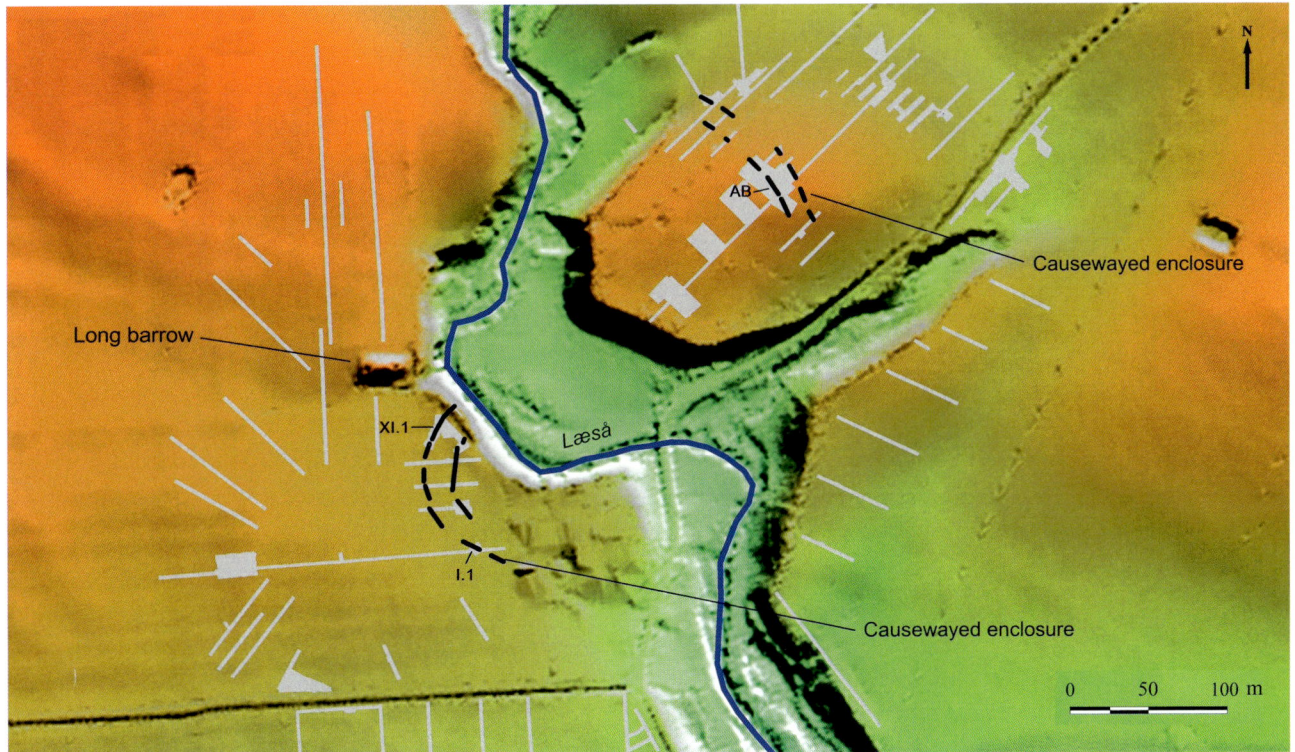

Fig. 3.23. The causewayed enclosures at Vasagård. Graphics: Michael S. Thorsen.

Unornamented side sherds	1420
Unornamented rim sherds	10
Rim sherds with small and medium-sized indentations	13
Rim sherds with large, round indentations	26
Rim and side sherds with cross-hatching	5
Rim and side sherds with angled ornamentation	10
Side sherds with impressions of two-ply cord	2
Side sherds with impressions of whipped cord	3
Side sherd with hanging triangles	1
Belly sherds with vertical striping	97
Sherds with various other ornaments	14
Sherds of collared flasks	1
Lugged sherds	2
Fragments of clay spoons	1
Rim sherds from shallow bowls	2
Sherds of clay discs without visible ornamentation	1
Imported flint	
Flakes	135
Fragments of polished axes	3

Blades	1
Kristianstad flint	
Flakes and cores	25
Scrapers	1
Ball flint	
Flakes and cores	717
Scrapers	2
Flint, unidentified	54
Burnt flint	20
Quartz	137
Crushing stones and fragments of these	5
Querns and fragments of these	3

None of the potsherds are large enough to permit the drawing of pot profiles, so the dating is based on the ornamented sherds. The large number of belly sherds with vertical striping shows that most of the material is from EN C / MN AI. To the early elements belong sherds ornamented with two-ply cord, a very small fragment of a collared flask and a few belly sherds with whipped cord in vertical lines, in one case interrupted by spaces filled out with short, lateral lines (*cf.* belly sherds from Virum, Ebbesen &

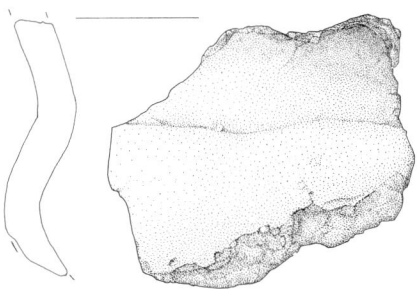

Fig. 3.24. Sherd of funnel or lugged beaker from the bottom of ditch AJ, Vasagård East. Pia Brejnholt del. 1:2.

Mahler 1980, fig. 11:2). To the late elements belong diagonal cross-hatching, which appears for example on funnel bowls from the Scanian megalithic tombs, which have been dated to 'MN I-II', and which in the Danish periodization can be assigned to MN AIb (Bagge & Kaelas 1950, Taf. XI:2, XII, XVII:1 and LXXIII:2). The motif also appears on footed bowls and clay spoons (*idem*, Taf. XIX:3 and LXXVIII:2) as well as on open bowls (Strömberg 1968, Abb. 47) and on shouldered pots that have been dated to MN AII (*idem*, Abb. 42). The most frequent rim ornament consisting of a number of large, round and deep indentations appears on funnel beakers from Bornholm settlements such as Runegård Øst and St. Myregård II and have been dated there to MN AI (Kempfner-Jørgensen & Watt 1985, fig. 15a, b, h; Nielsen & Nielsen 1990, fig. 5a, g; Hansen 2014, fig. 36a, g). Viewing this as a whole, one can only trace a limited element from EN C. It may represent activities that took place when the dolmen chamber was constructed in the long barrow situated only 25 m from the ditches of the causewayed enclosure to the NW (fig. 3.23). The bulk of the material from ditch I.1, however, must be dated to MN AI. This could be interpreted to mean that after the establishment of the segmented ditches in EN C there was a major activity in MN AI. It has been observed at several of the Danish causewayed enclosures that some time after their establishment they were used as settlements, sometimes for a long time and intensively. If their cultural layers have been preserved, such sites are among the most find-rich known Neolithic settlements (P.O. Nielsen 2004). However, massive cultural layers from MN AI have not been found outside the segmented ditches at Vasagård. It is therefore more likely that there was settlement activity during a limited period of time, probably when the passage grave in the long barrow was constructed (Hansen 2014, 48 ff.).

If the ditches were opened on special occasions, during which they were filled with mixed material, this could have happened again after the transition MN AI-II. However, only one very small sherd can with certainty be dated to MN AII. It comes from a small shouldered pottery vessel whose narrow shoulder is ornamented with a double row of angles (as in Glob 1952, no. 167). It was found in the ditch fill at a depth of 80-100 cm beneath the surface of the subsoil. This suggests that the ditch was filled with material at some point in MN AII or later. A sherd of a pottery vessel from MN AII was also found in the lower fill in ditch AB at Vasagård East.

Fig. 3.25. Vasagård West. Section at the south end of ditch I.1. Photo Terrance Slocum.

At the other end of the row of ditches at Vasagård West the outermost ditch XI.1 was dredged in its full length and filled in again in MN AIII; as part of this filling process a compact layer of stones was left on the top at one end to act as a seal (Nielsen *et al.* 2015, 55, fig. 5). The stratigraphy in the segmented ditches is not the same in all the sections, but it would appear that the final closing-off of the ditches with layers of stones took place in all cases in MN AIII, after which cultural layers were formed across the ditches in MN AV (Nielsen *et al.* 2014a; Nielsen *et al.* 2015). This happened concurrently with the building of the palisade features at Vasagård East and West (see chapter 7).

The dating of the establishment of the causewayed enclosure to EN C justifies mentioning it in connection with the settlement finds, since the features at Vasagård must have formed an important element in the settlement structure. But there are also other reasons to include the material reviewed here from ditch I.1 in connection with a review of the settlement finds from the Early Neolithic. Looking at the flint material, there is a significant difference between the quantities of imported and local flint. At the Early Neolithic settlements discussed in the preceding sections the imported flint predominates over the ball flint, but in this case the opposite is true: there are more than five times as many flakes and cores of the local ball flint as there are of imported flint. One finds a similar predominance of the local flint at the Middle Neolithic settlements on Bornholm. At Vasagård this is the case with settlement material, most of which is from the beginning of the Middle Neolithic, MN AI. Another local material group that is more prominent here than at the settlements from the EN, is flakes of quartz, which may come either from the quartz crystals in the granite, from stones in the moraine material or from beach pebbles. This material has not been systematically studied, so at present nothing can be said about the way flakes of quartz were used, except in a single case where one of the round pieces found in the same layer as the 'sunstones' in the top layer of the segmented ditches is made of quartz (Nielsen *et al.* 2015, fig. 8, left). But this layer is from the Late Funnel Beaker Culture, MN AV.

Location of the settlements

In terms of the number of times settlement material can be dated to EN C, this period is the most poorly represented on Bornholm. Only 10 settlements are marked on the map in fig. 3.26, and this even includes

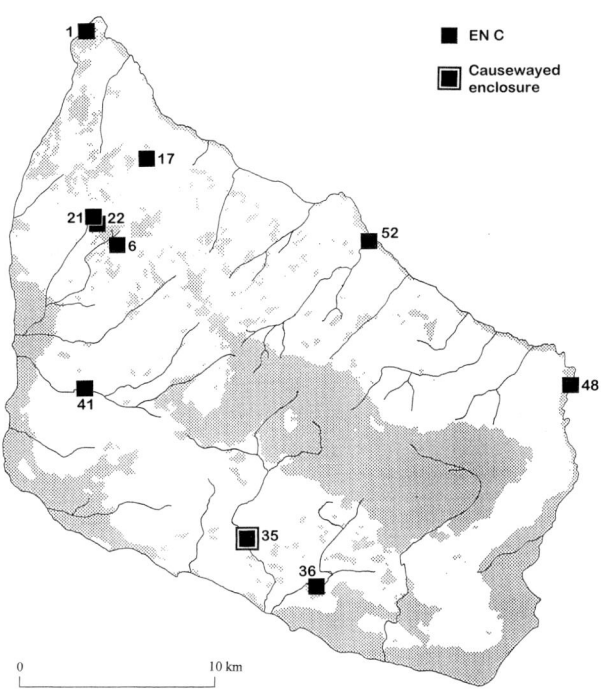

Fig. 3.26. The distribution of settlements where finds dating to EN C have been recovered.

the causewayed enclosure at Vasagård. At eight of these settlements other periods of the EN are also represented, and in all eight cases the sites had been used in the immediately preceding period, EN B. There was thus continuity from the older sites, but at the same time a decline in the number of settlements. It should be noted that three of the settlements are situated at the coast.

Finds from the same time outside Bornholm

With fragments of pottery it can be difficult to distinguish funnel beakers of type IV from funnel beakers of type III. In shape they resemble each other greatly – for example the ratio of neck height to rim diameter is the same for the two types, which precludes the use of this formal criterion. As regards the neck height in relation to the overall height of the pot, there is also a match. The most important difference between type III and type IV is that the greatest width of the lower part moves down to the middle of the belly on funnel beakers of type IV. But the most striking difference of all is in the ornamentation. All Eva Koch's funnel beakers of type IV are ornamented with 'simple ornamentation' on the belly in the form of vertical stripes or vertical ribs. Besides funnel beakers with such 'simple ornamentation', type IV does however also include slender lugged beakers with 'complex ornamentation' of types 1.4 and 2.1 executed as incised lines, impressions of two-ply cord or impressions of whipped cord (Koch 1998, 94 ff.). This continues the tradition from the preceding stages of giving slender lugged beakers 'complex ornamentation'. The rich ornamentation on slender lugged beakers of type IV also appears on wide lugged beakers of type III, which like funnel beakers and slender lugged beakers of type IV have been dated to EN II / EN C (*idem*, 111). There can however be problems with demarcation from MN AI, where vertical belly striping with some of the motifs from 'complex ornamentation' 2.1 is also used, and where the use of whipped cord continues.

The type site for EN II / EN C on Zealand is the settlement find from Virum which has given its name to the Virum style (Ebbesen & Mahler 1980). In the southern part of Scania there are several sites with pot forms and ornamentation that are very close to this style. Towards the west one can point to settlement sites which were assigned by M. Larsson to the Bellevuegård group (M. Larsson 1984, 160 f.) and finds in connection with burial features such as the long barrow Jättegraven (L. Larsson 2002, 28 f., figs. 2.27, 2.28) and Örnakulladösen (Sjöström & Pihl 2002, figs. 4.21-22). In southeastern Scania at the settlements Kabusa I and III sherds were found with ornaments in whipped cord, which also appear at Virum (M. Larsson 1992, figs. 2 and 14a, b; *cf.* Ebbesen & Mahler, 1980 figs. 11:3 and 12:6,14). A characteristic motif from Virum consisting of wide angles made with densely placed lines in whipped cord (Ebbesen & Mahler 1980, fig. 11:3) was found on a high-necked lugged beaker from the long dolmen at Skogsdala in southeastern Scania (Jacobsson 1986, fig. 10:1). In the scanty find material from this period on Bornholm the same ornaments occur, for example on sherds from Hammeren (Finds list I no. 1). There is therefore little doubt that with the Virum style in this period we have a highly homogeneous stylistic group in pottery ranging from Zealand over Scania to Bornholm.

Related to the Virum group is the Fuchsberg pottery west of the Great Belt (Andersen & Madsen 1978), represented for example in the rich find material from the causewayed enclosures Toftum and Sarup I (Madsen 1978; Andersen 1997). The funnel beakers have forms corresponding to Eva Koch's type IV with the 'simple ornamentation', frequently in the form of indentations at the rim and vertical belly stripes. It is characteristic of Fuchsberg pottery that lugged beakers and bowls have 'complex ornamentation' consisting of wide-angled bands often filled out with horizontal lines in whipped cord (Andersen & Madsen 1978, figs. 7-10). Like east of the Great Belt some of the ornamental motifs continue in MN AIa. Bowls with wide-angle bands also appear in combination with finds from MN AIa (Andersen & Madsen 1978, 142 ff.; Ebbesen 1979, 78 ff.), and this is probably why Sarup I has been dated to the transition between EN and MN (Andersen 1997, 27; 1999, 270). But in the case of Sarup I all the ^{14}C datings indicate a date before 3300 BC, which gives a dating of the Fuchsberg pottery at this site to the second half of EN II / EN C (Andersen 1999, fig. 15).

Apart from the fact that in EN II / EN C 'complex ornamentation' also appears on lugged jars from Zealand and from Djursland (Glob 1952, nos. 64 and 65), the rich ornamentation both in the Virum group and on the Fuchsberg pottery was applied to either slender or wide lugged beakers and to open bowls, in other words to a limited part of the pottery inventory, as in the earlier periods.

A survey of the Early Neolithic settlement in southern Scania shows that material from this period is frequently represented, and this may have been due to settlement expansion. In SW Scania the settlement spread from the sandhills inland in EN I to locations closer to the coast in EN II, but without taking on the character of coastal settlement (M. Larsson 1988, 24 ff.). In southern Scania the number of settlements increased from the transition EN II / MN AI, and several of them are now located some way from the coast on light soils, or where the soil alternated between sand and clay. The settlements border on the lagoon areas like in the Late Mesolithic, and on some of the larger watercourses, which suggests the exploitation of a more varied landscape with access to more resources. The placing in the landscape coincides with the spread of megalithic tombs, the erection of which began in EN II. This settlement pattern was maintained until the end of the Funnel Beaker Culture (L. Larsson 1992a).

In Scania, in other words, there was an important reorganization of settlement from the end of the Early Neolithic at the same time as the number of settlements grew. On Bornholm the number of settlements apparently did not increase, but some of the same tendencies can be traced there, where most of the known settlements, as in Scania, are found in the south-facing plain landscape some way from the coast in MN AI-V, where most of the megalithic tombs were also built.

Multi-phase settlements

Hammeren

The settlement at Hammeren (Finds list I no. 1) has been mentioned several times in the preceding sections, since finds were made there from several periods of the EN and from later periods of the Neolithic. The finds come from culture layers covered by shifting sand layers on a gently sloping terrace close to the NW-facing rocky coast. Among the rocks of the coast there are today narrow inlets with a sandy bottom which make it possible to beach small vessels. This may also have been the case in the Stone Age and was so at least in historical times. At the same place as the Stone Age settlement there was a fishing hamlet in the Middle Ages, from which herring were fished in the 13th-15th century. Salomons Kapel, which is known to have existed from the 14th century, is now the only visible trace of it. The holy well of the Middle Ages, Salomons Kilde, may also have existed in the Stone Age. The coastline in the Early Neolithic must have lain higher than the present-day one, as since then there must have been land uplift. The headland Hammerknuden, which is separated from the rest of Bornholm by a rift valley, would have been an island in the early postglacial period, but in the Early Neolithic may well have been connected, although we do not know with certainty.

In his discussion of the hunting stations of the Funnel Beaker Culture, Jørgen Skaarup emphasizes fishing and sealing as the primary reason for the placing of the settlement on the coast of Hammeren (Skaarup 1973, 132 f.). These were probably important activities, and the claim is strengthened by finds of seal bones. But besides these possibilities it must also be stressed that this is the place with the shortest distance from Bornholm to the SE coast of Scania. The importance of the site for sailing to and from the island is therefore obvious.

The settlement at Hammeren is one of the earliest-investigated Stone Age settlements on Bornholm. The first excavations were conducted by E. Vedel and J.A. Jørgensen in 1888. Vedel first describes the excavation of several sandhills, known as *kuller*, from which there emerged layers of black sand with a content of potsherds, flint and burnt bones (Vedel 1897, 105). The excavators probably expected that the low sandhills covered burials, but it appears from the description that what they had was rather several remains of a cultural layer 25-30 cm thick which because of wear and wind erosion had remained as plates covered by shifting sand. In 1892, however, in one of the *kuller* a stone chamber was investigated with an inside area of 2.8 × 1.25 m. The dimensions fit a dolmen chamber or a small stone cist, but it did not contain anything dateable. Excavation of the black sand turned up two rim sherds and two side sherds of Ertebølle pottery, three rim sherds with horizontal rows of indentations, one rim sherd of a small funnel beaker or lugged beaker with 'complex ornamentation', seven side sherds of funnel beakers or lugged beakers with vertical belly striping, one of these with lines in whipped cord, and 19 unornamented side sherds. Among 33 pieces of flint there were imported flint, Kristianstad flint and local ball flint, including flakes of polished axes, but also a pressure-flaked arrowhead. The content of objects in the supposed cultural layer thus reflects human presence at the site over an extended period that ranges from the Late Ertebølle to the end of the EN or the beginning of the MN, and with later elements from the Late Neolithic or the Early Bronze Age.

Continued excavations in 1891-92 also resulted in a broad spectrum of Neolithic finds in cultural layers up to 40 cm thick NE of Salomons Kapel. Vedel carefully listed the finds from there (1897, 106 f.), so here only the parts of pots that belong to the Early Neolithic will be mentioned. These are a few sherds of short-necked funnel beakers of type I, both without ornaments and with one row of small round impressions below the rim (fig. 3.27:1-2). A rim sherd with two horizontal rows of oblong impressions below the rim may come from a funnel beaker of type I or II (fig. 3.27:3). Two assembled sherds form a piece of the neck of a small funnel beaker of type III ornamented with 10 horizontal lines made with fine two-ply cord, interrupted by short vertical lines (fig. 3.27:4). Thus the periods EN A1-2 and EN B are sparingly but clearly represented in the find material. To these we can add a rather larger element of pottery from the subsequent periods, some of which comes from human presence in EN C. This applies to several rim sherds of a large pot, probably a lugged beaker, which has short impressions with whipped cord across the rim, below which are placed concentric hanging semicircles made with impressions of two-ply cord and small horseshoe-shaped impressions (fig. 3.27:5). There are also several sherds of other pots ornamented with various patterns in whipped cord, which like the hanging semicircles

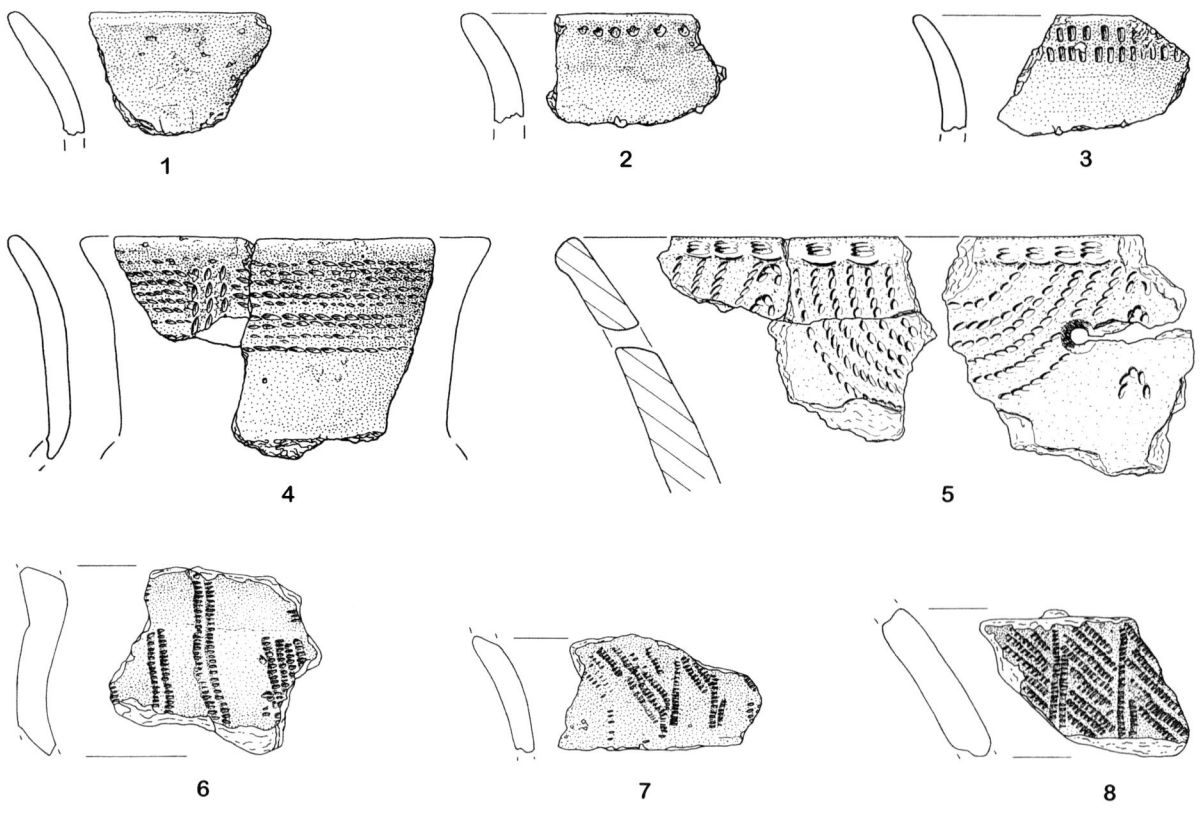

Fig. 3.27. Pottery from Hammeren (Finds list I no. 1). (1-4) Poul Wöhliche del., (5) Eva Koch del., (6-8) Freerk Oldenburger del. 1:2.

are among Eva Koch's 'complex ornamentation' type 2.1, and which recur among the Virum-style motifs, such as vertical bands filled out with diagonal lines in whipped cord (fig. 3.27:7-8). But there are also five sherds from pots with simple parallel lines in whipped cord on the belly or on both neck and belly (fig. 3.27:6). On 27 belly sherds of funnel beakers, 'simple ornamentation' appears in the form of vertical belly striping. Presumably funnel beakers of both type IV and type V are represented. This completes the count of the Early Neolithic pottery material from these excavations, with the reservation that some of the sherds with ornaments in whipped cord and some of those with vertical belly stripes may come from the beginning of the MN.

Ndr. Grødbygård

At Ndr. Grødbygård in Åker (Finds list I no. 36) c. 225 m² of a highly homogeneous cultural layer containing fragments of pottery from EN A1-2, EN B and EN C were investigated. Of the 1200 ornamented sherds of funnel beakers from the cultural layer, 10 rim sherds have a horizontal row of finger impressions below the rim. Of these only one sherd also has a cordon applied beneath the rim. 258 rim sherds have one or more horizontal rows of indentations beneath the rim, and of these 169 sherds have short, while 89 sherds have oblong indentations. Some of the rim sherds with indentations must belong to funnel beakers of types I and II, while some of the rim sherds with oblong indentations may belong to EN B. 769 rim sherds which have impressions of two-ply cord in horizontal lines beneath the rim but also vertical lines and alternating horizontal and vertical lines belong to EN B. The material from EN B thus predominates. An almost completely preserved funnel beaker ornamented with horizontal lines in two-ply cord must however, judging from the neck index, be placed at the transition between types II and III (fig. 3.28).

Among 1200 ornamented potsherds, 68 are ornamented with whipped cord, and 82 sherds come from pots with vertical belly striping. There are also 12 sherds of collared flasks, which may come from both EN B and EN C. In the culture layer an intact 9.5 cm tall funnel beaker of type IV was found, ornamented with a horizontal row of diagonal indentations beneath the rim. On the belly one sees striping with broad grooves that looks like fluting (fig. 3.29:1).

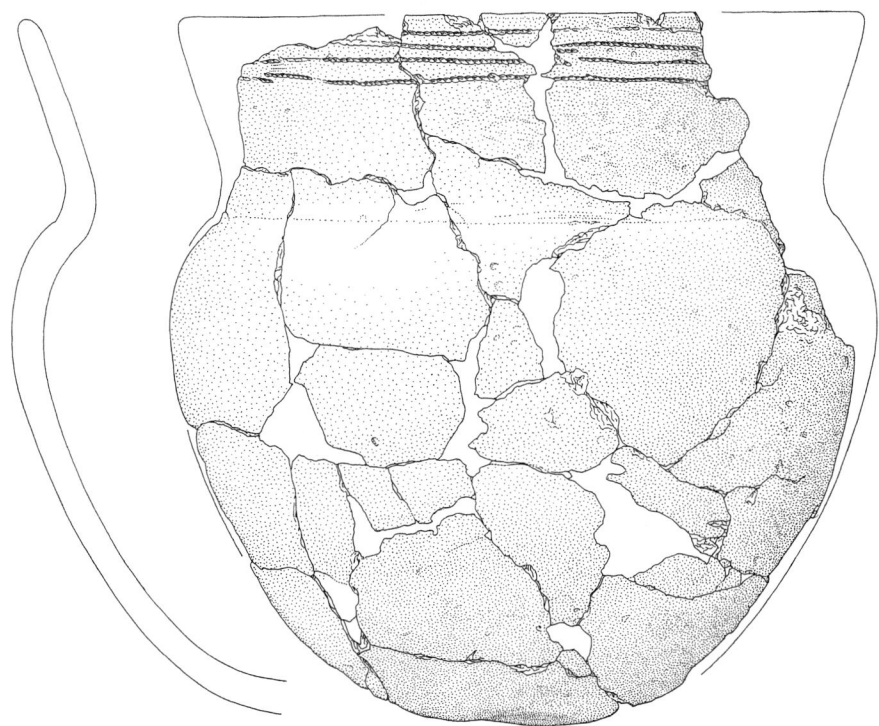

Fig. 3.28. Funnel beaker from Ndr. Grødbygård (Finds list I no. 36). Poul Wöhliche del. 2:5.

The pot was found lying in the culture layer with no visible connection with any feature. The potsherds from the culture layer are otherwise mostly small, so the pottery from this phase cannot be described in any great detail for this period. Impressions of whipped cord appear on rim and neck sherds and on the belly in dense, vertical lines, sometime interrupted by narrow vertical spaces with short transverse impressions. One also sees impressions of whipped cord as vertical lines, the spaces between which are filled out with diagonal lines in alternating directions in the same way as on sherds from Hammeren (fig. 3.27:7-8). The flint material from Ndr. Grødbygård is large, and besides small fragments of polished flint axes the finds from the cultural layer also include a 13.5 cm long butt fragment from a thin-butted flint axe of type IIIA (fig. 3.29:2) and a 9.3 cm long butt fragment from a thin-butted axe of a fine-grained stone type (fig. 3.29:3).

Smedegade

The settlement Smedegade in Klemensker (Finds list I no. 14) is situated high on a sandy hill area now built up with residential properties. The place has not been farmed in recent times, which must be the reason why a thick cultural layer was preserved with finds from the EN, of which c. 500 m² was excavated (fig. 3.30). An overview of the finds from the cultural layer is given in the finds list (a).

A small part of the material from the cultural layer comes from EN A1, since a few sherds can be assigned to funnel beakers of type I. Among other things, there are rim sherds with applied cordons and finger impressions, and one rim sherd has oval indentations of various sizes both on the rim cordon and on the neck of the pot, rather carelessly applied (fig. 3.31.2). Similar indentations can be seen on a fragment of a cordon which is not a rim cordon but which sat vertically on the neck of the pot from the rim down to the top part of the belly (fig. 3.31.1). Viewed from the side, the back of the cordon reproduces the neck of the pot profile. The neck height was at least 7.6 cm, so the vertical cordon must have been on a large funnel beaker, probably of type I. Within the area of the Early Funnel Beaker Culture the vertical cordon from Smedegade is the only find showing such decoration of a funnel beaker.

Almost 2/3 (65.9%) of the ornamented rim sherds from the cultural layer are furnished with horizontal rows of indentations, while the unornamented rims make up 22.8%. Among the pot parts where the ratio of neck height to rim diameter can be measured, there are funnel beakers with a neck index of just under 20, close to the transition between types I and II (fig. 3.32.1). Funnel beakers of type II are however most frequently represented at the settlement and appear both in the cultural layer (fig. 3.32.2) and in the various features and disturbances in the form of tree-throw remains and animal burrows beneath the

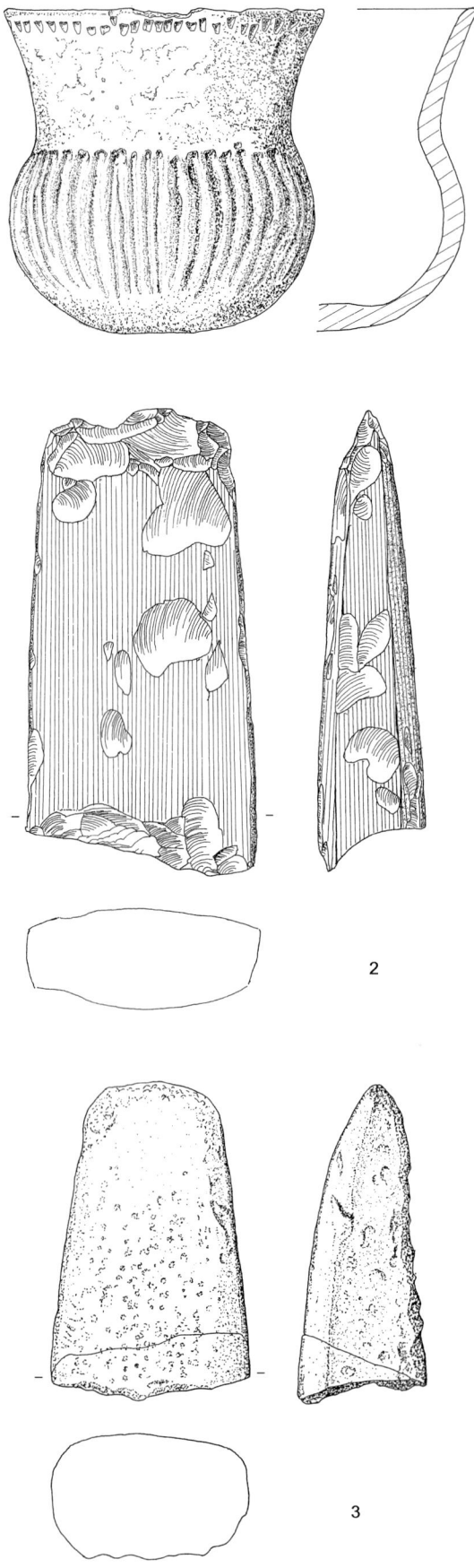

Fig. 3.29. Finds from Ndr. Grødbygård (Finds list I no. 36). From the cultural layer: (1) Funnel beaker, (2) fragment of thin-butted flint axe, and (3) fragment of thin-butted axe of fine-grained rock. Tim Grønnegaard del. 1:2.

cultural layer (figs. 3.32.3; 33.2; 39.1). Sherds ornamented with impressions of two-ply cord make up 6.1% of the ornamented rim sherds from the cultural layer, and they also occur in the features beneath it (fig. 3.32.4). On the whole, in other words, the material from EN A2 predominates, while there are smaller elements from EN A1 and EN B.

In the southwestern part of the excavation c. 8 kg of burnt clay daub was found scattered through the cultural layer, presumed to represent one or more burnt-down buildings at the site. Beneath the cultural layer various fill layers appeared, including postholes, some of which were clearly marked in cross-section, like A40, probably the hole for a roof-bearing post, at the bottom of which there lay a grindstone which may originally have been placed as a wedge to support the post (fig. 3.34). However, the postholes did not form a coherent pattern that could reveal the form and size of the houses. Some fill layers had contours like postholes on the surface, but on sectioning turned out not to have a clear post-hole structure, such as A10 (fig. 3.34), which should perhaps be identified as a refuse pit, given its content of pottery, which comprised neck fragments from funnel beakers of type II and the sherds of most of a clay disc (fig. 3.33). Other fill layers had a more mixed content and should rather be identified as natural disturbances, such as A17, which lay near large tree-throw remains, and contained parts of an unornamented funnel beaker of type II (fig. 3.32:3), but also sherds of both older and more recent pottery. The features A99 and A100 were identified as one animal burrow which contained rather a lot of material that must have sunk down from the cultural layer. The finds from there comprise the upper part of a funnel beaker of type II as well as sherds of various other pots and several pieces of worked flint, including a fragment of a thin-butted flint axe, three transverse arrowheads and six discoid scrapers (fig. 3.39).

Within a small area in the northwestern part of the excavation field two almost intact pots and two contiguous ends of a thin-butted flint axe were found. The largest of the pots (no. 190) lay bottom-up in a low fill layer (fig. 3.35). The 18 cm tall unornamented pot must probably be viewed, on the basis of its wide form and the placing of 'symbolic lugs' on the shoulder, as a wide lugged beaker, which therefore cannot be dated according to the classification of the funnel beakers (fig. 3.36). The profile of the pot corresponds to the profiles one finds among

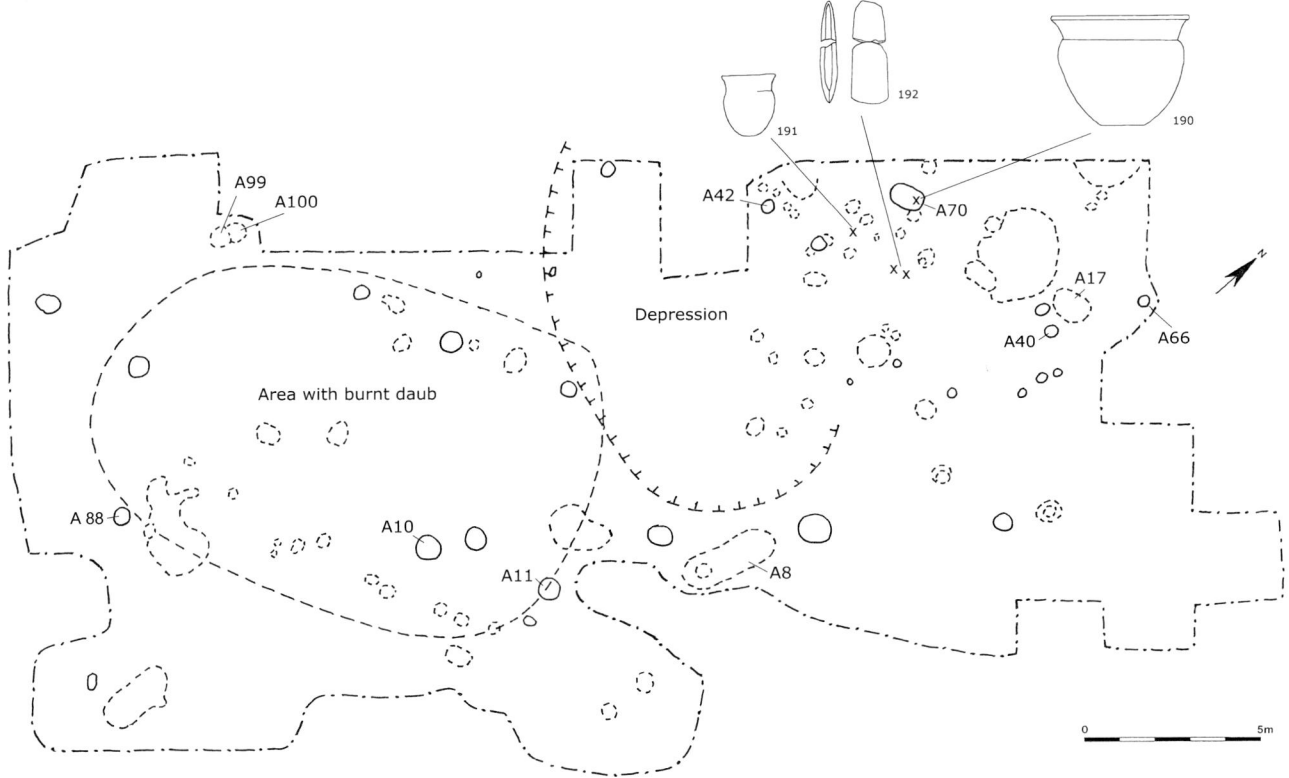

Fig. 3.30. Plan of the excavation at Smedegade, Klemensker (Finds list I no. 14). Neolithic postholes and pits are marked with continuous lines, whilst uncertain fills, tree-throws and other disturbances are marked with stippled lines. Many disturbances have been omitted.

funnel beakers of both type I and type II. The second, almost intact pot lay on its side in the culture layer and only a small part of the rim was missing. It is a small, 10 cm tall funnel beaker of type II with two horizontal rows of oblong, vertical indentations beneath the rim (fig. 3.37). It both resembles and because of its placing recalls the small funnel beaker of type II from Vallensgård I, which was also found intact, lying on its side, but was placed at the top of a pit (fig. 2.4:1).

Both at Vallensgård I and Smedegade the excavations turned up whole pots that may or may not have been deposited in a ritual context. To these we can add another two finds of whole pots, one of which is a small funnel beaker of type II from Simlegårds Bakker (Finds list II no. 4), which possibly comes from a settlement area, while the second is a funnel beaker of type III that comes from a gravel hill at Kofoedsgård (Finds list II no. 3, fig. 8.8) although we cannot say whether it comes from a settlement or a grave. We may also mention the small funnel beaker of type IV that was found in the cultural layer at Ndr. Grødbygård, where it could not be associated with any specific feature (fig. 3.29:1).

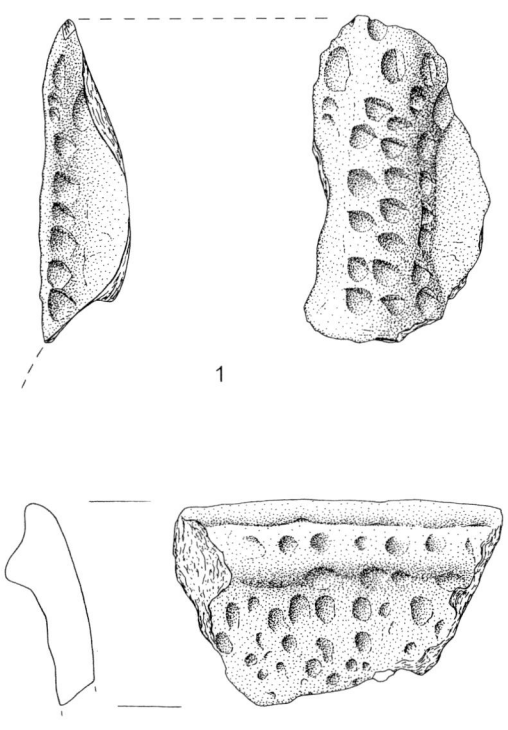

Fig. 3.31. Smedegade. Sherd of vessel with respectively vertical and horizontal cordon on the neck and under the rim. Freerk Oldenburger del. 1:2.

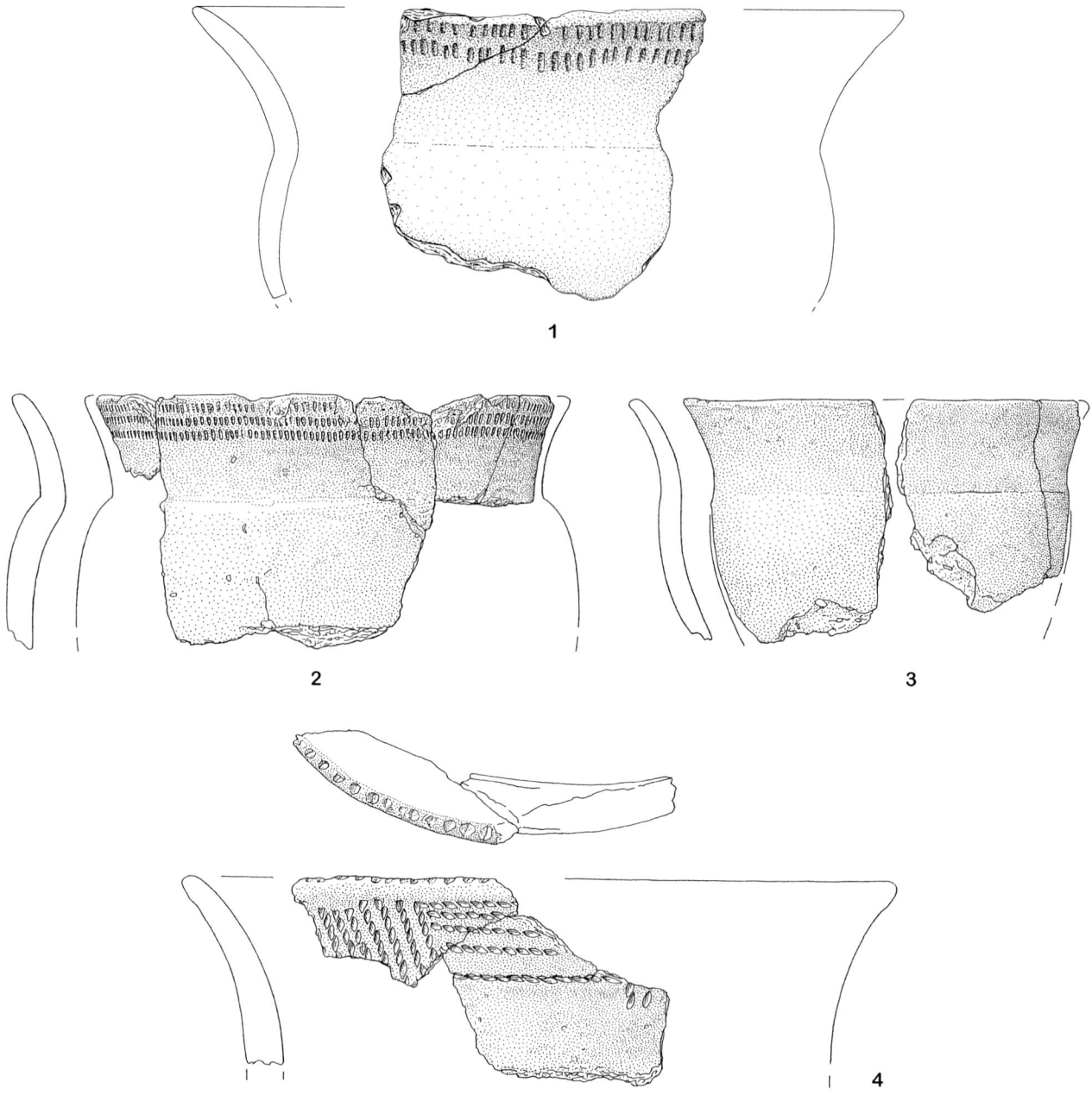

Fig. 3.32. Smedegade. Neck fragments of funnel beakers. (1) from the cultural layer, (2) from feature A11, (3) from A17 and (4) from A42. (1) Freerk Oldenburger, (2-4) Poul Wöhliche del. 1:2.

Only 1.5-2 m from the pots no. 190 and 191, within a distance from each other of 25 cm, two halves of a polished, thin-butted flint axe lay in the cultural layer (fig. 3.38). The axe is 21 cm long but resharpened. With its convex broad faces and not quite parallel narrow surfaces it borrows features from both types I and IIIA of the thin-butted flint axes. It is possible that the axe should be regarded as a deposition, perhaps after deliberate destruction.

The two intact pots and the flint axe were placed in the same area within a short distance of each other, which may indicate that this place had a special meaning and was intended for depositions of a ritual character. The finds emerged from a slightly sloping surface near the edge of a depression which separates this part of the settlement from the area with burnt clay daub where the houses must have stood (see plan, fig. 3.30).

Amongst the flint implements and flakes that were found in the cultural layer, imported flint is dominant over local ball flint and Kristianstad flint. Imported flint also dominates the flint ma-

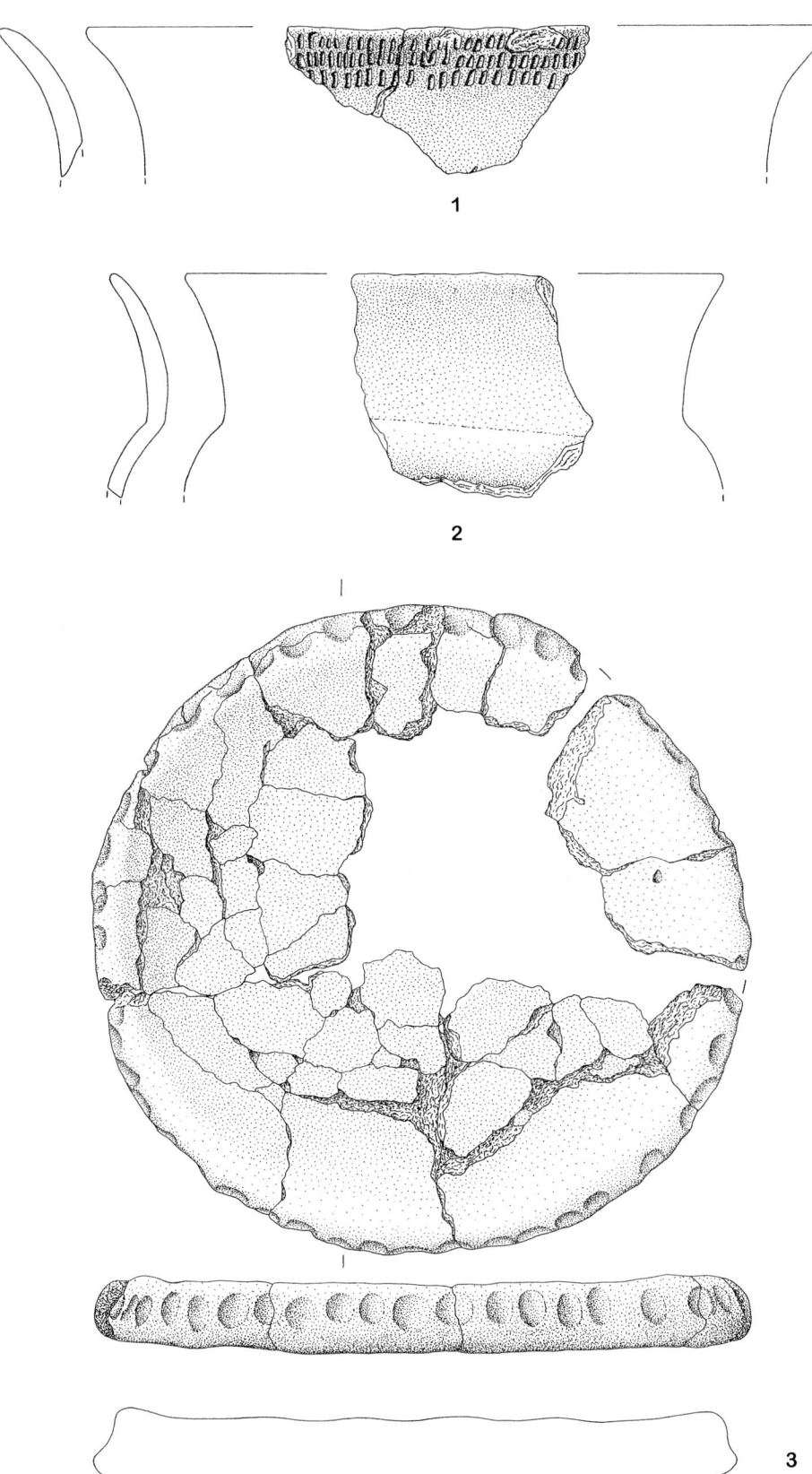

Fig. 3.33. Smedegade. Neck fragments of funnel beakers and joining fragments of a clay disc from feature A10. Freerk Oldenburger del. 1:2.

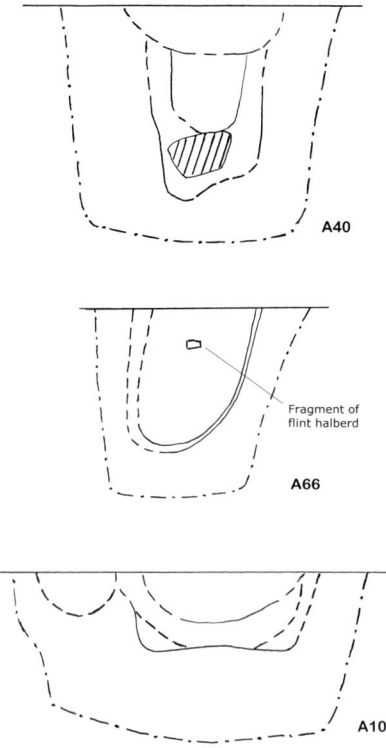

Fig. 3.35. Smedegade. Pottery vessel 190 in situ in fill A70. Photo Bornholms Museum.

Fig. 3.34. Smedegade. Sections of features: Posthole A40 with grindstone at the bottom; posthole A66 with fire-affected fragment of halberd of flint (fig. 3.40.2); and bottom of posthole (or pit) A10 with fragments of a pottery vessels and clay disc (fig. 3.33). 1:20.

terial from some of the features. In feature A99/A100, for instance, the upper part of a type II funnel beaker (fig. 3.39:1) was found together with five polished flint axe fragments (fig. 3.39:2), three transverse arrowheads (fig. 3.39:3-5), six flake scrapers (fig. 3.39:6-8), one atypical backed flake knife and 47 flakes, all mostly of imported flint, whilst there were only five flakes of ball flint and three flakes of Kristianstad flint.

At the site 12 querns and fragments of querns were found, which is evidence of work with cereal products. In eight of the features, including A10, A11, A88 and A100, burnt cereal grains were also

Fig. 3.36. Smedegade. Pottery vessel 190. Poul Wöhliche del. 1:2.

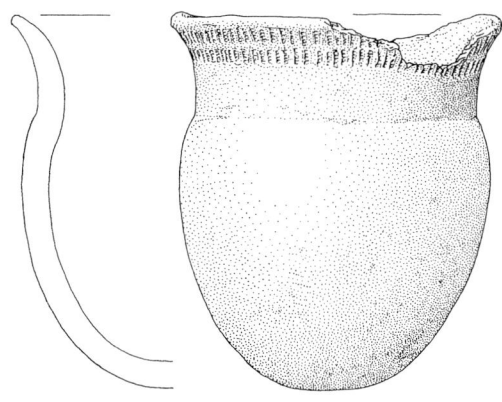

Fig. 3.37. Smedegade. Pottery vessel 191. Poul Wöhliche del. 1:2.

▷ *Fig. 3.38. Smedegade. Thin-butted flint axe 192. Freerk Oldenburger del. 1:2.*

found, most in A88 (14 g). The predominant grain type is naked six-rowed barley (*Hordeum vulgare var. nudum*), but emmer (*Triticum dicoccum*) and common wheat (*Triticum aestivum*) are also represented (identifications by Peter Steen Henriksen – see details in

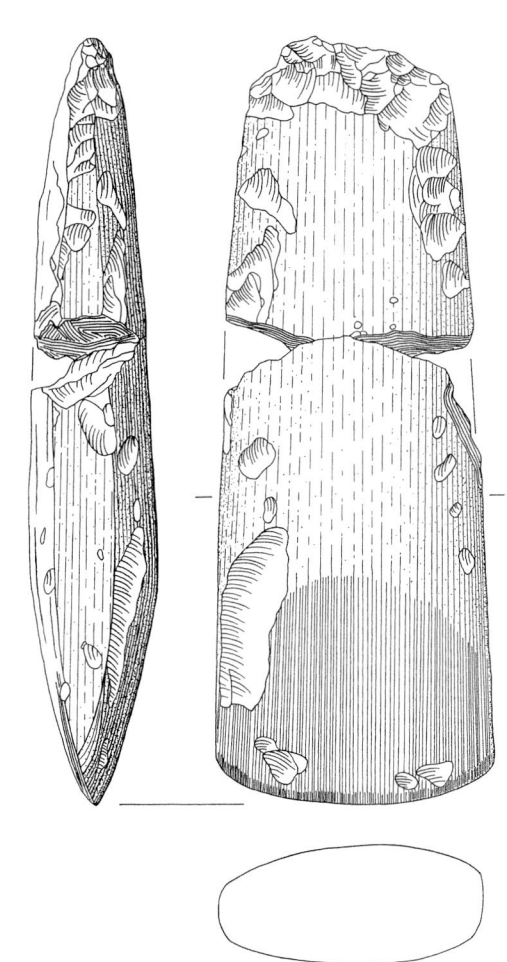

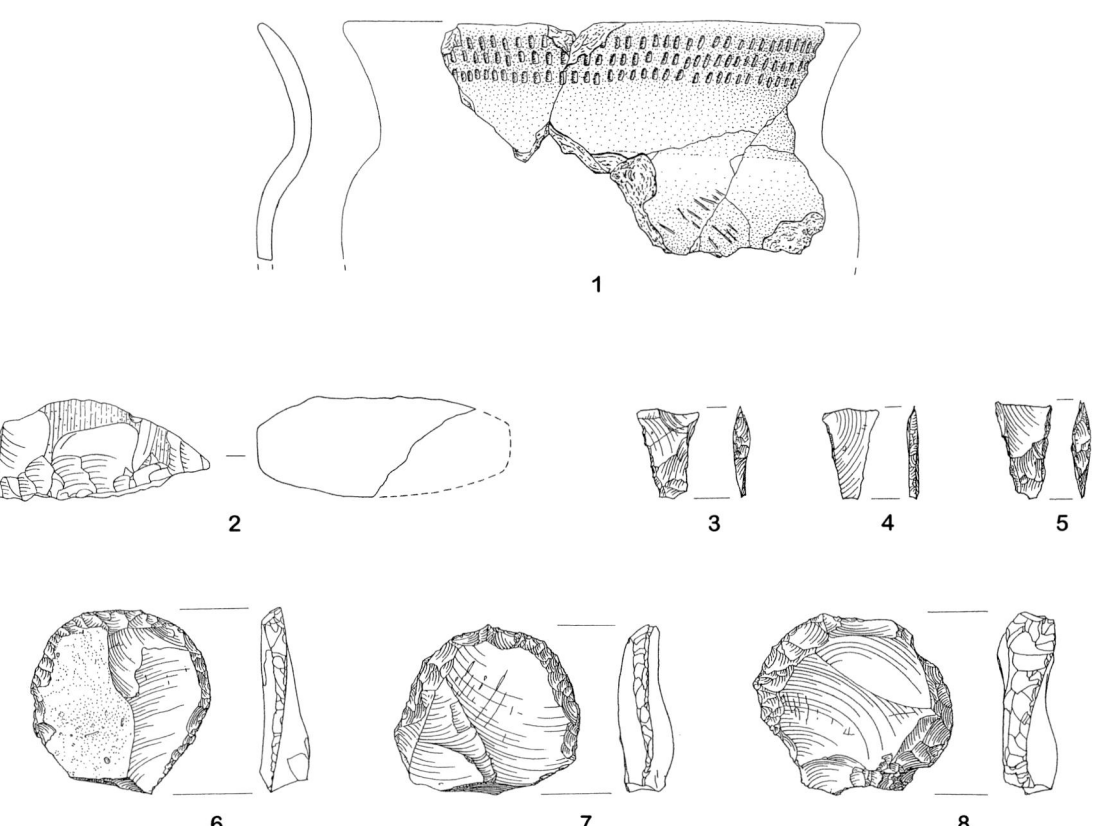

Fig. 3.39. Smedegade. Finds from feature A99/100. (1) Remains of funnel beaker, (2) fragment of four-sided flint axe, (3-5) transverse arrowheads and (6-8) flake scrapers. (1-2) Freerk Oldenburger, (3-8) Poul Wöhliche del. 1:2.

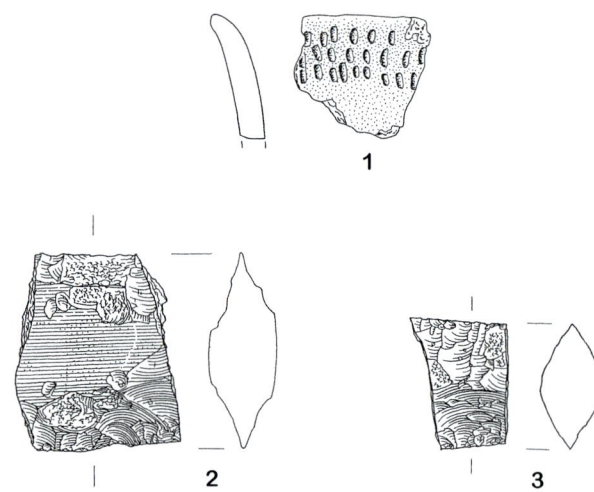

Fig. 3.40. Smedegade. (1) Rim sherd of funnel beaker and (2) fire-affected fragment of flint halberd from posthole A66. (3) Fire-affected fragment of flint halberd from cultural layer. (1) Freerk Oldenburger, (2-3) Poul Wöhliche del. 1:2.

the catalogue). Cereal grains from four features have been AMS ¹⁴C-dated (table 3.4). In 13 features charred shells of hazelnuts were also found. 17 grindstones and fragments of grindstones were found; these may have been used to re-sharpen repaired axes and perhaps also to grind imported, unpolished flint axes. If the last of these is the case, it helps to underscore the significance of the settlement.

At this site seven fire-brittle fragments of halberds were found, one of which lay in posthole A66 along with flint and potsherds, including a rim sherd ornamented with three horizontal rows of indentations, probably from a funnel beaker of type II (fig. 3.40:1-2). The post-hole was the only feature in which such a fragment of a halberd was found; the other six fragments were found in the cultural layer (fig. 3.40:3), where they were concentrated in the area towards the SW with burnt clay daub. The posthole A66 too contained pieces of burnt clay daub. The other Bornholm finds of halberds of the broad, asymmetrical type (Ebbesen's type A) were not found in dateable contexts (see chapter 6). Such a find was made, on the other hand, in Jutland, where it occurs in a grave in combination with finds belonging to the Volling phase (Ebbesen 1994, 110 ff., fig. 14), which corresponds to EN A2 and B on Bornholm. The connection with the burnt clay daub might perhaps mean that this represents an episode when a building was burnt down in connection with an armed struggle.

The ¹⁴C dates of cereals from four features at Smedegade contribute to the dating of EN A2 on Bornholm (table 3.4). Features A10, A11 and A88 contained sherds of funnel beakers that can be identified as type II, while feature A100 contained rimsherds with horizontal rows of indentations as on funnel beakers of type II. The datings of grain from these features fall within a time interval where there is not as much disturbance in the calibration curve, so the uncertainty factor comes close to a normal distribution. If one uses the median probability[2] for each of the four datings, they come to lie within the interval 3738 to 3681 BC – that is, they fall within EN A2 (3800-3650 BC), as do all the datings as well, when they are given with one standard deviation (1σ).

The locations of the settlements and the development of farming

Settlements from the Late Atlantic period

Unlike the Late Ertebølle Culture's coastal settlements, most settlements from the Early Funnel Beaker Culture are located inland. The contrast between the two settlement patterns is reinforced by the fact that it has only been possible to register 11 settlements from the Ertebølle Culture on Bornholm (fig. 3.41). One must of course consider whether the picture this gives of settlement is in fact representative. Although the coasts are generally more exposed

Table 3.4. ¹⁴C dates of cereal grains from Smedegade, identified by Peter Steen Henriksen.

Feature and cereal species	Lab. code	BP uncal.	BC cal. 1σ	BC cal. 2σ	Median probability
A10 *Triticum sp.*	Ua-55181	4951±32	3770-3670	3790-3650	3727 BC
A11 *Triticum sp.*	Ua-55182	4963±32	3780-3700	3800-3650	3738 BC
A88 *Hordeum vulgare var. nudum*	Ua-55183	4917±32	3710-3650	3770-3640	3688 BC
A100 *Triticum dicoccum*	Ua-55184	4904±32	3700-3650	3770-3630	3681 BC

on Bornholm than in inner Danish waters, it is not certain that settlements from the Late Atlantic period have been eroded away by the sea to any great extent. At Grisby on the east coast the coastline of the Littorina Sea has been between 3.5 and 4.5 m higher than today (P.V. Petersen 2001, 166), and along the southern part of the island the same coastline has been at the 5 m contour line. While older settlements, from the Kongemose and the Early Ertebølle Culture, may well have been eroded or washed away by the Atlantic transgressions, the settlements from the Late Atlantic period should have been preserved. Some coastal settlements, however, may have been covered by sand drift, and others may have been destroyed by present-day development, which is concentrated at several points along the coast.

The small number of settlements could perhaps be due to topographical factors, since on Bornholm one does not find the indented coasts and fjord systems whose biodiversity attracted the hunting and fishing population at other places in South Scandinavia in the Atlantic period. In northeastern Scania and along the indented south coast of Blekinge a rich fauna provided a basis for exploitation from the Atlantic to the Subboreal period (Wyszomirska 1988; Welinder 1997). On Bornholm it has not been possible to document exploitation of the coastal resources to the same degree. However, if one follows the 5 m contour line on the southeastern part of the island between Nexø and Snogebæk (fig. 3.41), it veers inland to form a potential lagoon and fjord landscape that might have exerted an attraction on the hunting-collecting-fishing population of the time. But in this area we have only a single find from the Ertebølle Culture. Another place that may have had a different topography in the Atlantic period is the northernmost part of the island. The Hammerknuden headland is cut off from the rest of the island by a rift valley in which there must at some point have been an open sound before the land connection was created as a result of land uplift and sanding-up. Although we cannot say so with certainty, it is probable that in the Atlantic period there was more water in the rift valley that would have made navigation possible. At Hammerknuden three settlements from the Ertebølle Culture have been located, while several may today lie hidden beneath marine deposits and shifting sand.

Most sites with finds from the Ertebølle Culture are on rocky coasts in places where there has been a sandy bottom or low water between the rocks as

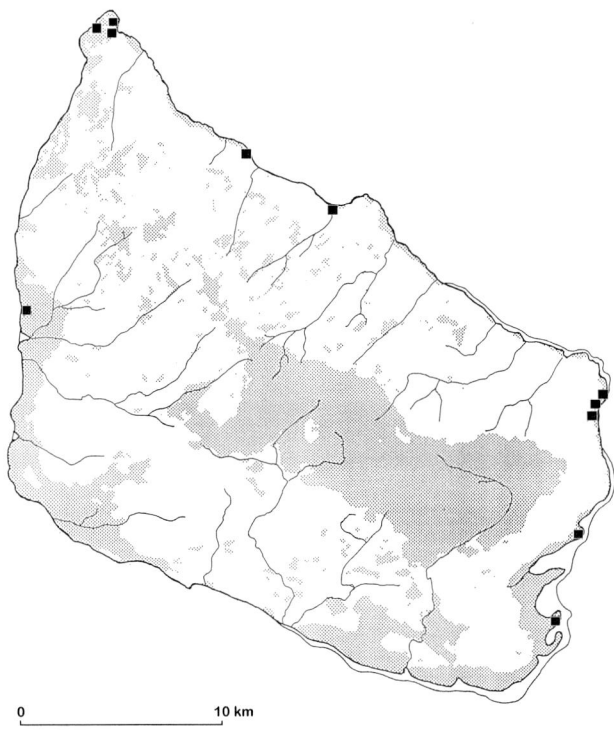

Fig. 3.41. The distribution of settlements dating to the late Ertebølle Culture on Bornholm.

was the case at Hammeren, but also at Frennemark and Grisby south of Svaneke. From there one can very quickly sail out into deep water. The fish bones found at the settlement at Grisby in fact testify that the inhabitants belonged to "the truly great cod fishermen of the Ertebølle period" (P.V. Petersen 2001, 171). But catching sea mammals was also of great importance, since 68% of the mammal bones come from seal and porpoise. The location of the settlement along with the faunal material testify to the use of seaworthy boats and the ability and will to sail over deep water. In the settlement layers at Grisby, flake axes and flakes of imported flint have been found, so in the Late Atlantic period connections must have been maintained with the Swedish mainland.

Settlements from the Early Funnel Beaker Culture

On Bornholm, Early Neolithic elements at the Ertebølle Culture's coastal settlements are few in number. The settlement at Hammeren is one example, but there the traffic over to the Scanian coast may have been the reason why there are elements both from the Late Mesolithic and from most of the Neolithic. At the other three coastal settlements with Ertebølle Culture – Salene, Grisby and Holkemyr/Frennemark

87

– there are Early Neolithic features. None of these elements is particularly common. We therefore lack safely dated Early Neolithic layers at the coastal settlements with faunal remains that can provide answers about the extent to which the Neolithic farmers exploited the potential for fishing and hunting which was exploited in the Ertebølle period. In Scania and western Blekinge, at several coastal settlements from the Late Ertebølle Culture, traces have been found of human presence in the Early Neolithic (see the overview in Jennbert 1984, 64 ff.). But at Skateholm in southern Scania there was no clear continuity from the find-rich settlements of the Ertebølle Culture to settlement in the Early Neolithic, and although one sees a certain geographical congruity from the transition to the Middle Neolithic onward, the faunal finds from the settlements provide no evidence that fishing and sea mammal hunting were very common (L. Larsson 1992a).

When one looks at the locations in the terrain and on soil types (figs. 3.42), there are differences between the coastal settlements and the inland sites from the Early Neolithic on Bornholm. Of the two settlements at Hammeren, one is on a sloping, sandy terrace and the other is in rocky, hilly terrain that does not invite cultivation. Yet it is not certain that the soil conditions at Hammeren had the same character at the beginning of the Neolithic as today, when sand drift has left its mark on the area. Four other coastal localities lie either where the soil consists of mixed glacial layers (Salene), of marine sand and gravel (Svaneke Boldbaner) or of postglacial beach ridge formations (Grisby and Holkemyr/Frennemark). Another two settlements lie close to or not far from the coast respectively on marine sand deposits and shifting sand (Gudhjem Syd and Strandvejen in Rønne). Several northern Bornholm settlements are located on sandy soil formations of other origins (Engvang, Hebro, Gothegård, Åløkken, Borgen). The settlement at Gamleborg in the middle of the island lies on a thin sand layer over the bedrock.

Only a few settlements lie directly on or near moraine clay. These are Skrubbegård and Pileskoven, but both these sites in fact lie where the soil has a changing composition of clay, gravel and sand. The causewayed enclosure at Vasagård lies on moraine

Fig. 3.42. Geological map of Quaternary deposits. Source: GEUS.

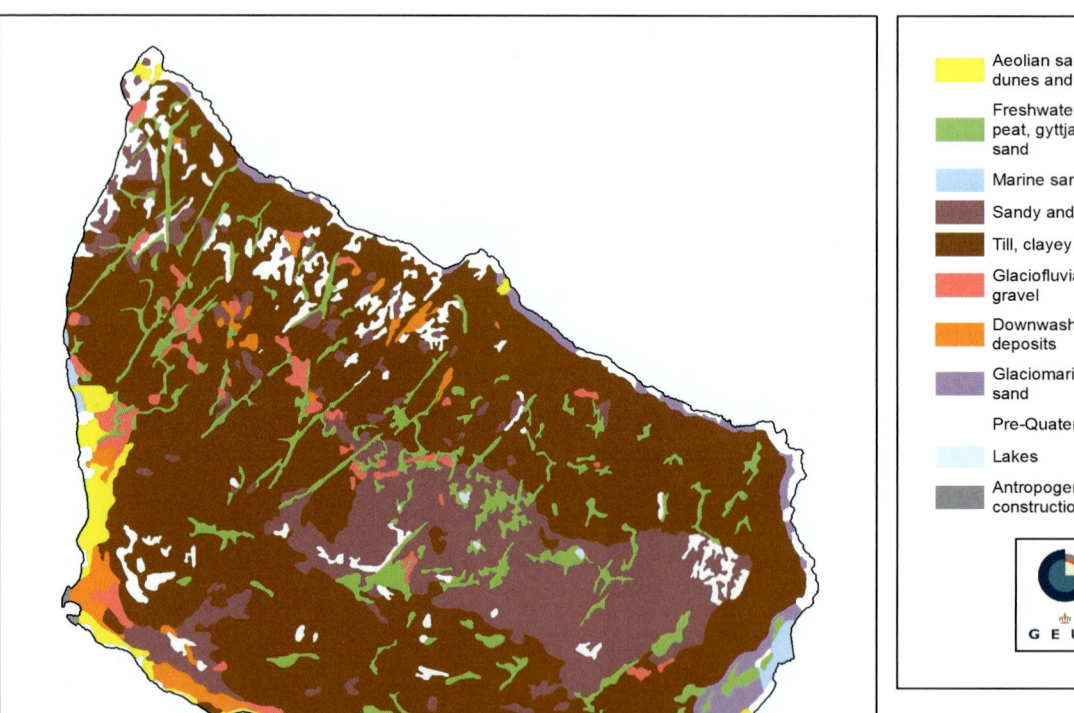

Fig. 3.43. The location of the Early Neolithic settlements in relation to the surface relief. Equidistance 5 m. Map data from the Danish Geodata Agency.

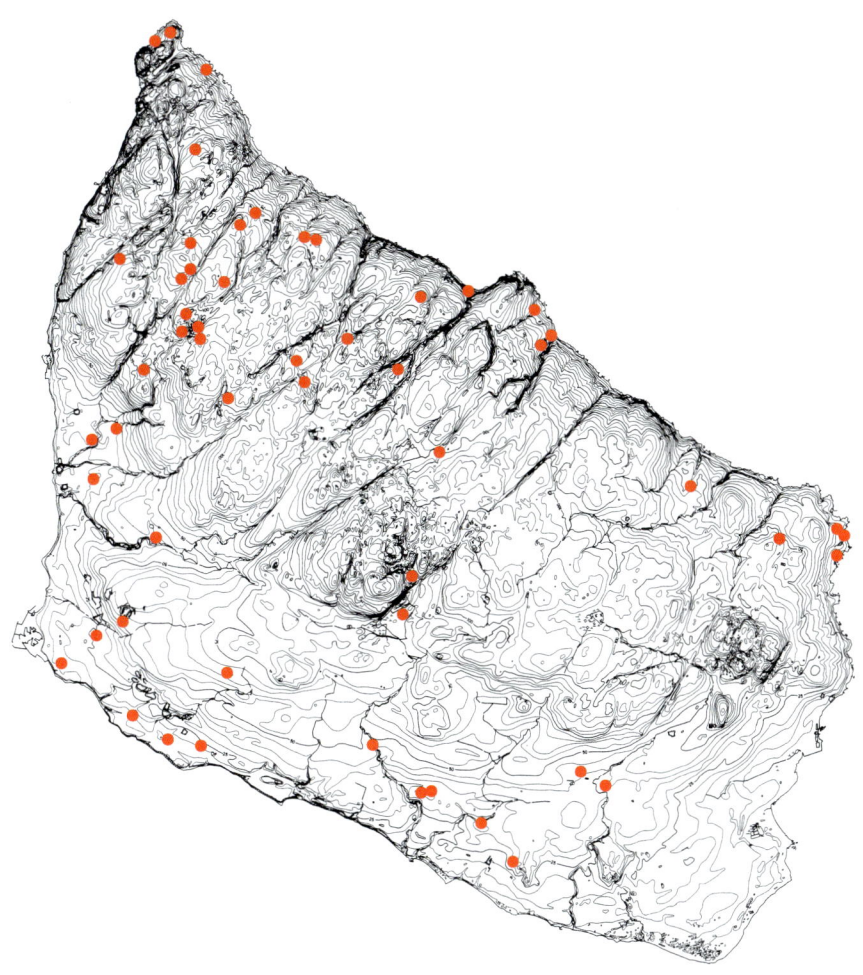

clay mixed with gravel and stones. All other settlements have been found on sandy or gravelly soil.

In southern Bornholm there are several settlements on the low terraces where the soil consists of layered sand and gravel deposited during the Ice Age as bottom sediments in watercourses and lakes (Sandemandsgård, Møllebo, St. Myregård II, Bornholms Lufthavn, Vallensgård I, Limensgård, Solhøj, Bakkegård). These areas have been cultivated up to the present day and have formed a basis for sustainable agriculture since the Stone Age.

Very different from the level country of southern Bornholm is the hilly terrain of northern Bornholm, where several of the settlements from this period are located high up, 11 of them at a height of more than 100 m above sea level (fig. 3.43). Some may be surprised by this placing, but in fact it is not far from the settlements on the sandy hills to one of the nearest watercourses. Close to the settlements, too, there would be a better water supply, since many springs rise on the hillsides. Several of the other finds, which have no demonstrable settlement context, but which must have had connections with the settlements in the vicinity, have in fact been found at some of the highest points of the terrain, more than 100 m above sea level (Simlegård, Bjørnebakkerne, Kofoedgård and Simenehøje).

Both settlements and other Early Neolithic finds are associated in northern Bornholm with the sandhills that were formed at ice front lines (Milthers 1930, 97-103). There are three such ice front lines (fig. 3.44):

1) The Simlegård line stretches from Ruts Kirke over Møllebjerg and Torpebakkerne, where the settlements Torpegård, Marevadgård, St. Knudegård and Kokkedal are located, after which it passes Simlegård and continues towards the SSE (fig. 3.45).

2) The Splitsgård line goes from Møllehøj east – Pilegård, Sorgenfri, Splitsgård and Kofoedgård – and continues over Årsballe and Simenehøje in an arc north of Almindingen (fig. 3.46).

3) The Rø line, which runs parallel with the north coast at a distance of 1-2.5 km, passes the settlements Karlshøj, Grønvang, Båstedbakken and Tyskegård. Pilegård lies near Karlshøj, and thus close to the Rø line, and should perhaps be included in this context.

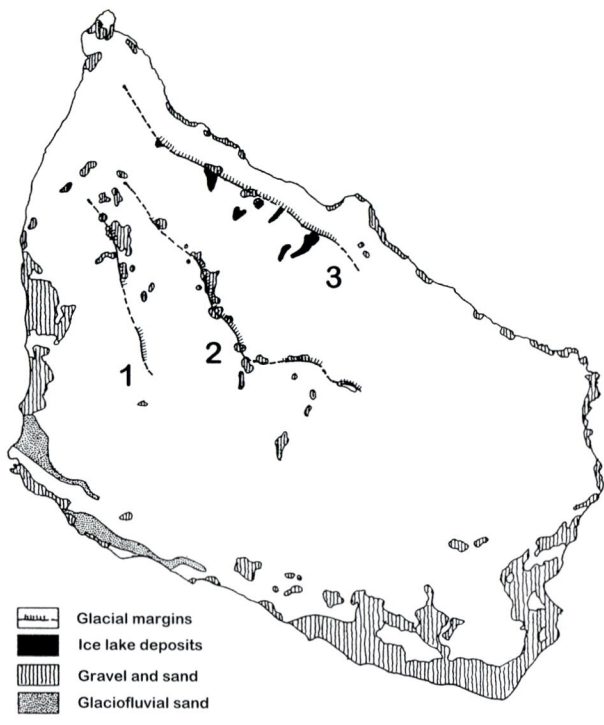

Fig. 3.44. Selected features of the deglaciation on Bornholm. Successive glacial margins on the northern part of the island are numbered 1-3.

How can it be that the great majority of Early Neolithic settlements are found on sandy soil? In the first place it is necessary to look source-critically at this question. Flint and potsherds of such small dimensions as is often the case here are easiest to spot while walking the fields on sandy soil. For that reason the leasure-time archaeologists of the island have often preferred this soil type, not least because the search for Stone Age settlements in fact produced results. But today farming only involves parts of the sandy areas, many of which are planted with forest on Bornholm, from small plantations to the great forested areas: Rø Plantage, Blemme Lyng, Almindingen and Paradisbakkerne. Thus only a small part of the sandy area is easily accessible for reconnaissance. Early Neolithic finds, including several of the settlements, have however also been discovered outside the cultivated areas, in sand and gravel pits (Tingbakke, Bjørnebakkerne, Marevadgård, Kokkedal, Torpegård, Borgen), several of which are in plantations.

The sandhills have been in focus since the beginning of the registration of antiquities. From J.A. Jørgensen's reports from his district inspections in 1882 it is evident that he paid special attention to the archaeological potential of the sandhills. Graves and settlements from other periods of prehistory can also be found on the sandy areas, but not only there. For example, the settlements from the late Iron Age are mainly found in the best clay soil areas in Østerlars, Ibsker, Åker and Klemensker (F.O.S. Nielsen 1996a, fig. 70). While excavations of settlements from the Bronze and Iron Age on sandy soil have also turned up finds of Early Neolithic settlement remains, excavations on clayey soil have only contributed a few finds.

For the time being the picture of sandy soil as the preferred soil type of the Stone Age farmers must stand, at any rate for the first centuries of the Neolithic. It must be assumed that the light soils were

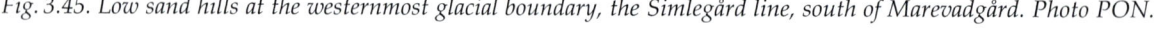

Fig. 3.45. Low sand hills at the westernmost glacial boundary, the Simlegård line, south of Marevadgård. Photo PON.

Fig. 3.46. Sand hills at the middlemost glacial boundary, the Splitsgård line, south-east of Bjergegård. Photo PON.

preferred by the first farmers because they could be cultivated with the technology and the manpower resources that were available. Today the sandy soil areas are considered marginal, but if they were overgrown in the Boreal and Atlantic periods with deciduous forest, around 4000 BC there must have been soil formation that provided sufficient nutrition for cultivation. In other parts of South Scandinavia in the Early Neolithic people in many places also preferred to settle on the light soils. The spread of the Bornholm settlements greatly resembles Early Neolithic settlement in southwestern Scania, where the settlements also lie on sandhills. Mats Larsson believes that it was the composition of the vegetation in this soil type that made it attractive for settlement (M. Larsson 1984, 205; 1985). The early agrarian settlements in Mälardalen in central Sweden are also found on sandy soils adjacent to late glacial gravel ridges (Apel *et al.* 1995, 91, fig. 24; Hallgren 2008, 115). This gives us associations with the placing of the settlements on northern Bornholm, which lie up against the late glacial ice front lines. However, Early Neolithic farming settlements are also known from heavy clay soils, as at Havnelev in eastern Zealand (P.O. Nielsen 1994). With respect to the choice of soil type, though, on Bornholm the light soils were very consistently preferred, perhaps more than in other parts of South Scandinavia.

In the course of EN C, however, there was an expansion of settlement in areas of Bornholm where the soil alternated between sand and clay, and where the clayey soil was predominant. Although the settlements and isolated finds from this period are few, one can see from the locations of the dolmens in eastern, western and southern Bornholm that in these areas there was an expansion of the settlements, and this becomes even clearer at the beginning of the Middle Neolithic.

Soil and vegetation

From Bornholm we lack pollen diagrams from localities near the settlements that could tell us about the composition of the vegetation and the interventions in it that took place with cultivation during the first centuries of the Neolithic, followed by Iversen's *landnam* around 3500 BC. Intensive peat-digging in historical times has meant that most of the peat has been removed from the Bornholm bogs (Jessen 1929, 475), making it difficult to find places where samples can be taken for pollen analyses which reflect the vegetation over extended periods. Valdemar Mikkelsen's diagram from the lake Græssøen in Almindingen shows the development from the Atlantic period until the middle ages. For the Subboreal period it reflects a forest environment where indications of agriculture are few (Mikkelsen 1954). Another pollen diagram has been made on the basis of samples from the sea bed c. 5 km east of Bornholm and must reflect a mean for the development of vegetation

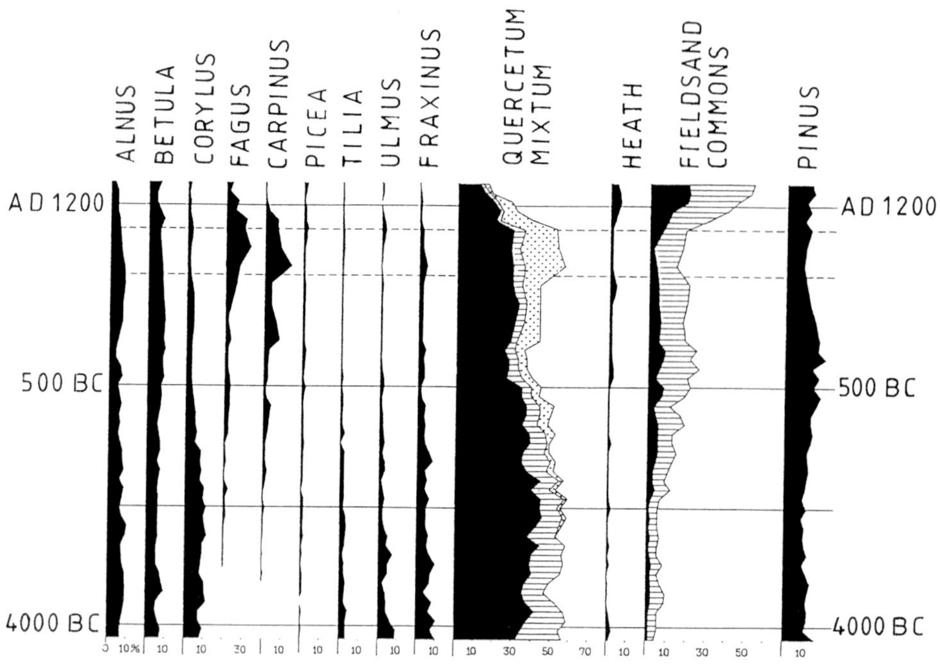

Fig. 3.47. Pollen diagram from the bottom of the Baltic Sea, c. 5 km east of Nexø (after Mikkelsen 1991).

on the whole island between c. 4000 BC and 1200 AD (fig. 3.47) (Mikkelsen 1966; 1991). This gives us a picture of fairly constant forest vegetation dominated by oak, which only yields to open country in the Bronze Age and the Early Iron Age, while the decline in the Neolithic was limited. Cultivation in the Early Neolithic thus did not lead to a deforested landscape. At the beginning of the Neolithic we see a decline in birch, hazel and elm (but not oak) followed by regeneration. The heathland vegetation (*Calluna* heather), which only spread in earnest as a result of intensive grazing in the central parts of the island after AD 1200, is also visible in the diagram around the beginning of the Neolithic and at the beginning of the Iron Age. Heather has probably always been present where the rocks are covered by a thin layer of soil. But the slight increase in *Calluna* around 4000 BC can be seen in connection with forest clearance and intensive grazing on sandy soil.

It can be hard to understand why people in the Early Neolithic preferred the sandy to the clayey soils. The clayey soil, it is true, is heavier to work, but it contains important, plant-available nutrients and retains moisture better. But the latter quality can also be a problem, since without deep soil preparation it will be difficult to drain the water away after heavy showers. Another property of the clayey soil is that it is slower to warm up in the spring but retains the warmth longer towards harvest time. The sandy soil on the other hand has a low content of nutrient-bearing minerals, which in areas with natural vegetation hampers the transformation of detritus, so that sour humus is developed. In addition podsolization occurs – that is, the depositing of humus and iron compounds in deeper layers. The sandy soil warms up quicker in the spring, but also loses warmth quicker. Among the disadvantages of sandy soil is faster leaching-out of nutrients as well as drying-out in rainfall-poor periods with the resultant risk of sand drift.

However, there are some differences between the sandy soils that attracted settlement in the Early Neolithic. In some places the soil may have had a higher content of clay particles and thus more nutrients than it has today. The settlement at Limensgård, which was occupied in the Early, Middle and Late Neolithic as well as the Early Iron Age (Finds list I no. 34), lay on loamy, fine-grained sandy soil whose top layer must have had a higher clay content at the time of settlement in the Early Neolithic. Clay particles sink down in the soil as a result of rainfall, and in several places one could observe a compact layer of washed-down clay at a depth of 60 cm from the surface of the subsoil (fig. 3.48). Some of this washdown may have happened before, during and after the occupation of the settlement in the Early Neolithic. In the bog sections a high clay content has been registered in the peat (pollen zone VII), which according to Mikkelsen reflects heavy rainfall and soil erosion in the Atlantic period (Mikkelsen 1954, 213 f.). From the pollen diagram from Græssøen in Almindingen it is evident, though, that the clay content in the peat endures some way into the Subboreal period (pollen zone VIII) (*idem*, Pl. XX fig. 1).

In most places the sandy soil is more coarse-grained than at Limensgård and now, after millennia of cultivation, is much leached-out and nutrient-poor. These sandy soils are cultivated at present, but only thanks to soil improvement. What kind of soil improvement of the sandy soils can have taken place in the Early Neolithic? In connection with pollen analyses in other places in South Scandinavia the occurrence of charcoal dust in the soil layers alongside the first signs of farming shows that the burning of vegetation took place (S.T. Andersen 1991). The same can be ascertained from the occurrence of deformed tree pollen when one investigates soil layers beneath barrows (S.T. Andersen 1992). The burning of wood and sometimes also of the top parts of the humus layer forms ash that is rich in nutrient salts. If such burning was repeated at intervals, this was one method of improving the soil. Fallowing, where a diversity of plants encroach by themselves, as well as fast-growing trees such as birch and hazel, was another way which, with no great effort, could add new nutrients to the soil.

Fertilizing the fields is another method. To demonstrate this one can measure the nitrogen content of cereal grains found at the settlements, even if they are charred (Kanstrup *et al.* 2012). Analyses of charred grains of emmer, barley and spelt from the Neolithic, Bronze Age and Early Iron Age in Denmark show nitrogen values that point to fertilization, with changing values for the individual cereals and with a rise in the Bronze Age and the Early Iron Age. These analyses included samples that go back to EN II (Kanstrup *et al.* 2014). One of the biggest cereal finds from the Early Neolithic in Scandinavia emerged from excavations of a presumed ritual gathering-place at Stensborg south west of Stockholm (Larsson & Broström 2011). The datings of the charred cereal grains have a spread between 4800±50 BP and 4710±75 BP, cal. c. 3693-3360 BC, corresponding to the time from EN A2 to EN C on Bornholm. 50-80% of the grains are Bread Wheat and Emmer Wheat from Stensborg showing heightened nitrogen values, while for the grains of Naked Barley it was 10-60% (Gron *et al.* 2017). Barley was better able than wheat to grow in fields that were not manured. These analysis results open up the possibility that fertilization may have been practiced right from the beginning of the Neolithic. Today sandy soil is improved with a mixture of compost and animal manure and by the addition of clayey soil. In the Early Neolithic livestock manure was probably mainly used, but it

Fig. 3.48. Profile of posthole AB 26 in Late Neolithic house site at the Limensgård settlement, Åker. The bottom of the posthole was dug down into the top of a layer of washed-down clay particles to a depth of 60 cm. Photo PON.

would also have been possible to fertilize with composted plant material.

The area near Bornholm from which most data have been gathered about the development of vegetation and human interventions in nature in the Neolithic is the Ystad region in Scania. Here, early in the Subboreal period, one can demonstrate a rise in the content of charcoal dust in the bogs, which coincides with a reduction of tree pollen and the appearance of cereals and weed plants. The slow-growing forest trees lime, elm and ash (but not oak) see a striking decline, while birch and hazel thrive on the dry, alder and willow on the wet soils, which reflects the regeneration of the forest (Berglund *et al.* 1991a, 415). The Swedish investigations stress a convergence of natural and human factors. The change to a more open forest environment that took place at the transition from the Atlantic to the Subboreal period is not only attributable to the first farmers' forest clearance and cultivation; it is also viewed as a result of changes to a colder, more unstable climate. The decline in the elms, which is seen as due to elm disease, may have helped to open up the forest (L. Larsson 2014, 205). The culturally determined elements become evident in all the pollen diagrams at the transition from the Atlantic to the Subboreal period in the Ystad area. The cultural influence is strongest in the Early Neolithic and weaker in the Middle Neolithic. This has been interpreted as a sign of shifting cultivation in the Early Neolithic, when small population units engaged in forest clearance and cultivation, which were quickly followed by the regeneration of the forest (*idem*, 421; Berglund *et al.* 1991b, 427 f.).

The development of settlement

It should be possible to apply the conditions in Scania, as they are reflected in the pollen diagrams, to Bornholm, since the developments in the two areas are parallel when one considers the archaeological find material and the pattern the settlements show (M. Larsson 1992). The many small settlements in the first part of the Early Neolithic may not reflect a large population, but may mean that the settlements were moved after some time. A model for settlement in the Early Neolithic based on the excavation of the settlement from the Volling phase at Mosegården in eastern Jutland operates with very short-term occupations (Madsen & Jensen 1982, 82). Such a moveable farming pattern might involve a cyclical return to earlier-cultivated areas. This would explain why, at several of the settlements, one can demonstrate pottery from more than one period of the Early Neolithic. People returned after a period of years.

Another view of settlement and area use in the Early Neolithic prefers to see signs of permanent occupation and fields combined with alternating use of outfields involving clearance and a rotation in the exploitation of the areas (M. Larsson 1988). This view is supported by among other things the now numerous regular house remains known from the beginning of the Neolithic in both Great Britain and South Scandinavia (Rowley-Conwy 2003).

How changeable or permanent were settlements in fact? Of the 56 Bornholm settlements from the Early Neolithic eight must be designated coastal settlements, although some of them border on arable land. The other 48 localities are inland settlements, that is basic settlements where the main occupation must have been agriculture and livestock breeding. Of these, 32 have produced finds from only one period of the Early Neolithic. They are distributed as follows:

EN A	2
EN A0	1
EN A1	11
EN A2	4
EN B	13
EN C	1
Total	32

The number must be taken with reservations, since sites have been included where the area investigated was very limited, for example Åløkken, where the finds come from a single small pit. However, a site like Sandemandsgård, where a major investigation was conducted, has produced an almost pure body of material from a single period.

In the finds from 11 localities there are, as at Vallensgård I, at least two Early Neolithic periods represented, and in the material from four settlements at least three Early Neolithic periods are represented. Finally, the material from two settlements with finds from EN C extend into the beginning of the Middle Neolithic. Three of the settlements with finds from at least three periods are at the same time the most find-rich, that is Kokkedal, Smedegade and Ndr. Grødbygård. One is tempted to say that the larger the area investigated, and the more culture layers preserved, the more periods one finds represented.

At the find-rich settlements where at least three periods are represented, however, the material is not equally distributed over the individual periods. Among the finds from Smedegade the material from EN A2 predominates, while at Kokkedal and Ndr. Grødbygård it is the finds from EN B that are in the majority. At Smedegade and Ndr. Grødbygård the large quantity of find material gives the impression of a continuity that may have extended through several generations. At Smedegade the settlement lasted from the end of EN A1 through EN A2 up to and including EN B. At Ndr. Grødbygård it appears that the activity was limited in EN A, that it was more or less constant in EN B, that it continued in EN C and that it possibly only ended some way into MN AI, after which it continued, however, in the nearby area Runegård East (Kempfner-Jørgensen & Watt 1985).

In other words there are differences among the sites with respect to the duration of the settlement. But most settlements were only used in one of the periods. So which model fits this pattern best? Although at the Bornholm settlements from the Early Neolithic intact house remains are only preserved in exceptional cases, most investigations have found postholes which must come from houses. It is the durability of the earthfast posts that determines how long a house can remain standing – normally no longer than 25-30 years (Zimmermann 1998; Nielsen & Paulsen 2014). At the settlement at Limensgård one certain and one probable Early Neolithic house site have been demonstrated (fig. 3.7), but within the area investigated, c. 150 × 100 m, postholes determined to be from the Early Neolithic, which must come from several house sites, have been dated to EN A1-EN B and may have lasted over a couple of centuries, or settlement may have been resumed during that period. In other places there are problems with the assessment of the actual size of the settlement, since as a rule the excavations cover much smaller areas than those investigated at Limensgård. We must thus make source-critical reservations when we draw conclusions on the basis of the available settlement material.

Returning to the settlement Vallensgård I, within a distance of 100-400 m of it lie five other settlements registered by surface sampling (fig. 2.15). From two of them, Vallensgård II and III, there are finds showing that the sites may have been used concurrently with, or before and after Vallensgård I, at Vallensgård II in the form of a butt fragment of an Early Neolithic battle axe (site no. 438, Finds list V no. 11, fig. 6.2:1). The other three have not been included in the catalogue of settlements, since we have no knowledge of finds from them of dateable pottery. One can imagine changing sitings of the settled area within such a limited area, corresponding to the total area of a single country property. This kind of model would accord best with the picture indicated by most Early Neolithic settlements, which are found on small areas, and which have produced limited find quantities from remains of cultural layers and from a few postholes, tree-throw remains and animal burrows. This might correspond to a duration and activity no longer than the time during which a single house could stand erect. With such a model for settlement – allowing for all uncertainties – it would no longer be a matter of either-or, but of both-and. The settlement may have been permanent within a cultivation area where the residence had a changing location. This accords with the fact that many preserved house-sites from the Early Neolithic in Ireland, England and South Scandinavia have been found individually (Darvill 1996; Rowley-Conwy 2003; Thorpe 2009, 31-41; Smyth 2014; P.O. Nielsen 2019). The designation chosen for the most widespread form of settlement at that time could therefore be the single-farm settlement.

A few settlements have turned out to have been in use for a longer time, perhaps continuously through most of the Early Neolithic, like the multi-phase settlements Ndr. Grødbygård and Smedegade. The settlement at Ndr. Grødbygård lies on a plateau where the soil consists of meltwater sand, in an area of southern Bornholm where clayey soil otherwise predominates. As the preferred soil type the sandy soil here attracted settlement throughout most of the Early Neolithic. Both at Ndr. Grødbygård and at the neighbouring locality Runegård East the settlement also continued into the Middle Neolithic, and at the former of these house-sites and timber-circles from the Late Funnel Beaker Culture have been excavated (Kempfner-Jørgensen & Watt 1985; Nielsen & Nielsen 1991). On southern Bornholm there are settlements with a similar location in areas with sandy soil such as Limensgård and Solhøj.

Besides preferring light sandy soil, the Early Neolithic farmers also made efforts where possible to locate their settlements high in the terrain. A high-lying settlement like Smedegade must have dominated the surroundings, and the settlers may have had their cultivated fields on the sloping terrain on the south side of the ridge where the settlement lay.

Thus we have two settlement models for the Early Neolithic. On the one hand there are the short-term sites where the house moved around within an area and after some generations may have been built at a place used earlier. But there were also more stationary sitings where settlement extended through a long period at the same place. As the examples here show, this may have been due to special soil or topographical conditions, or there may have been historical and social reasons. In the course of the Early Neolithic social differences arose, as reflected in the burial customs, and this may also have been reflected in the settlement, where particular places took on importance as belonging to people in leading positions. In these cases it might play a role that the settlement had a permanent location. One of the activities which here on the island might help to generate status differences, was the procurement and distribution of imported flint and the exchange and ritual deposition of flint axes. These subjects will be taken up in the following chapters.

Find material that sheds light on settlement in the EN C is scanty, which makes it difficult to judge what actually happened in the period. Now dolmens were built, seven of which are known, but only four of which are preserved, and we must expect that they mark where settlement took place. With five of the seven dolmens located in the south of the island, another settlement pattern than in the preceding periods emerges (fig. 7.27). But it is only when one looks at the distribution of the dolmens in relation to the location of passage graves and settlements from the early MN that we can perceive the change that took place (fig. 7.31). The activities were mainly concentrated in four areas where several megalithic tombs were built. Among these, two settlement areas lie in the south – at Nylars to the west and Pedersker, Poulsker and Bodilsker to the south east, where both sandy and clayey soil occur, while the two settlements in western and eastern Bornholm respectively are located on moraine clay. In other words the growth in society moved from the sandhills of the north to areas where crops could be grown on both sandy and clayey soil. This happened concurrently with a concentration of settlement into distinct areas. This change may have had both agricultural and social causes. One possible factor may have been the loss of nutrients in the sandy soil that was cultivated from the start. At the same time the introduction of ploughing may have enhanced the ability to work with the heavier clay soils. The result must have been increased agrarian production and the creation of a production surplus. Some see a connection between the use of extensive ploughing and social differentiation. The cultivation of larger areas requires the work of more hands during the harvesting, which could mean the deployment of non-landowning and thus lower-ranking labour power (Bogaard 2004, 73). The issue of social factors as possible contributory causes of the change in settlement in EN C and the beginning of MN is something we will return to in the concluding chapter.

Arable and cattle farming

Finds of cereals from several sites show that barley and wheat were cultivated in EN A1-A2 on Bornholm. On the other hand no well-preserved bones have been found that can shed light on which domestic animals the Bornholm farmers surrounded themselves with in the Early Neolithic. On Bornholm, unburnt faunal material has only appeared from excavations in recent years at Vasagård and Rispebjerg, but it comes from layers that have been dated to the Middle Neolithic Funnel Beaker Culture. Because of the location of the Early Neolithic settlements on sandy soils which do not encourage the preservation of organic material, at these settlements only small fragments of burnt bones have been preserved, and until now it has only been possible to identify a few of them (Hjuleregård, Finds list I no. 44). Better preserved were the burnt bones from settlement pit A at Sigersted III in central Zealand, where bones of domestic cattle, pigs and sheep could be identified (P.O. Nielsen 1985, 110). Charred macrofossil remains from the pit has been dated to 3950-3800 BC, which shows that the composite livestock pattern that appears in all the subsequent phases of the Funnel Beaker Culture was present from the beginning.

One important find for the elucidation of the livestock farming in this period was made at Almhov in southwestern Scania, which has provided a total of c. 41 kg of animal bones, the largest find of faunal material from the Early Neolithic in South Scandinavia. The material comes from 190 pits, 34 of which can be dated to the Oxie phase, corresponding to EN A1 on Bornholm. In 15 of these, bones of roe-deer were found, and in nine of them fishbones, molluscs or seal bones were found, which shows that hunting, fishing and the catching of sea mammals were practiced. In pit A1854 at Almhov, which is a little later, the pit was wet-sieved, and turned out to contain bones of herring, eel, flatfish and cod, as well as cattle, sheep/goat, otter, dog and harp seal (Rudebeck 2010, 108). The pit contained sherds of funnel beakers ornamented with both rows of indentations and impressions of two-ply cord beneath the rim, and a ^{14}C dating of cereal grains gave the result 4780±50 BP, cal. 3650-3520 BC (1σ) corresponding to EN B on Bornholm (Gidlöf et al. 2006, 79f.). Almhov lies just 3 km from the present coast of the Sound, so there were good possibilities for fishing and sealing nearby. The same possibilities were exploited on Bornholm, where some of the coastal settlements were visited in the Early Neolithic. However, most of the bones in the pits at Almhov come from cattle, almost half as many from pigs and slightly fewer from sheep/goat (Rudebeck & Macheridis 2015). The finds from Almhov demonstrate the importance of cattle farming from the beginning of the Neolithic, and strontium analyses of ox bones from Almhov and Havnelev show that cattle were probably transported both from Zealand to Scania and in the opposite direction (Gron et al. 2016). Transport of cattle and other livestock over the sea cannot have been a problem.

From the beginning of the Early Neolithic livestock farming spread quickly to South Scandinavia and central Sweden (Noe-Nygaard et al. 2005; Price & Noe-Nygaard 2009), and for the first farmers cattle presumably represented the most important resource of all. Studies of isotope data reflecting the diets of cattle lead to the conclusion that the first farmers actively created feeding environments for their animals (Gron & Rowley-Conwy 2017). Cattle not only represented a meat resource: there would also have been dairy cattle, cattle providing hides and cattle that could have been used as draught animals. Since the theory of 'the Secondary Products Revolution' was first proposed, it has been assumed that the consumption of milk and sheep's wool and the use of cloven-footed animals as draught animals began much later than the first domestication, in central and northern Europe corresponding to the fourth and third millennia BC (Sherratt 1981). In Denmark the milking of the animals and the exploitation of their draught power has now been documented from the Early Neolithic on, while sheep's wool was probably first used from the beginning of the Single Grave Culture from c. 2800 BC.

On the European continent milk was probably a nutrient before arable farming was introduced in northern Europe. Traces of butter fat have been demonstrated in potsherds dated to 3700-3300 BC from England (Copley *et al.* 2003, 1527; Copley & Evershed 2007) and in potsherds from the Early Neolithic in Ireland (Smyth & Evershed 2015a and b). Analyses of fat residues in bog pots from Denmark have demonstrated the presence of butter fat in the same period, c. 3700 BC (Robson *et al.* in prep.). In Europe a large part of the adult population is lactose-tolerant, and this tolerance may have been present from the beginning of the Neolithic, as DNA analyses also seem to show (Vigne 2007, 194 f.).

Analyses of the enamel on cow teeth from the Early Neolithic settlement Almhov in SW Scania have been able to demonstrate that cows were manipulated to calve in more than one season, which would have meant an extension of their milk production (Gron *et al.* 2015). We must therefore assume that milk and milk-based products played a major role in the economy. This also means that the farmers in this early period were competent cattle breeders. It is interesting to note from which contexts the samples of cow teeth were selected for the abovementioned analyses. These were four pits at Almhov: A6, A19049, A25594 and A35862. We have already referred to A6, which contained among other things funnel beakers with profiles corresponding to Eva Koch's funnel beakers of type 0 (page 45). The other three pits all contained pottery that belongs to the Oxie group, which is contemporary with EN A1 on Bornholm. The ^{14}C datings of all four pits fall within the first 2-300 years of the Early Neolithic (Gidlöf *et al.* 2006, 61 ff.; Rudebeck 2010, table 17). That methods for controlling the calving of cows and milk had been practiced from the beginning of the Neolithic is a good indication that agriculture was introduced by farmers who came from the outside, and who had know-how based on many generations of experience with livestock farming (Gron *et al.* 2015, 6).

The Neolithic cattle were of large size, judging from bone finds from the late Funnel Beaker Culture (Hatting 1978, 200; Nyegaard 1985, 433), so a slaughtered cow may have provided meat and offal totalling around 300 kg. But beef would not have been everyday fare. In a society with no possibility of long-term storage of meat we must assume that on the whole, livestock was only butchered on special occasions when a large number of people had to be fed, as in the practice of many now-living indigenous peoples. About this the Canadian anthropologist Brian Hayden writes: "That domestic animals are only killed for feasts is one of the strongest relationships that I know of in all of anthropology [….] In fact, there is not one single ethnographic example of a traditional society that I know of where animals are kept primarily to provide meat for daily subsistence" (Hayden 2014, 125; *cf.* also Jeunesse 2016). There is a high probability that this was also the case in the Neolithic, and it is not hard to see a reflection of this in the find material. In the Early and Middle Neolithic concentrations of butchery refuse were left in special places where many people had gathered. Many animal bones resulting from butchery and the consumption of meat, not least from cattle, but also from the other domestic animals and from game have been found for example in the pits at Almhov, in the ditches of the causewayed enclosures and at sacrificial sites by the shores of lakes. They may all be seen as remains of ritual and social gatherings for the sake of which wild and domestic animals were slaughtered.

To maintain life on a daily basis the Neolithic farmers most likely consumed cereal and milk products, meat from wild animals, fish and shellfish as well as gathered fruit and plant parts. δ^{13}C and δ^{15}N analyses of human bones from the Early and Middle Neolithic in Denmark and Sweden indicate a diet with a high proportion of aquatic as well as vegetable food (Craig *et al.* 2011; Sjögren & Price 2013; Sjögren 2017).

Important nutrients were probably cereal products. Today cereal finds are known from many Early Neolithic settlements, including the oldest. Barley was cultivated on sandy soil at Sigersted III on Zea-

Cereal species	Skovgård	Limensgård	Smedegade			
			A10	A11	A88	A100
Club Wheat, *Triticum aestivum convar. compactum*	12					
Emmer, *Triticum dicoccum*			11		148	3
Einkorn, *Triticum monococcum*				1		
Bread/Club wheat, *Triticum aestivum*		22	10		>1	3
Wheat, undetermined, *Triticum sp.*		10	15	1		1
Naked sixrowed barley, *Hordeum vulgare var. nudum*		14	12		1336	11
Hulled sixrowed barley, *Hordeum vulgare var. vulgare*					>1	
^{14}C dates BP uncalibrated	5084±32 5016±30	5000±70	4951±32	4963±32	4917±32	4904±32
Median probability[2]	3866 BC 3803 BC	3795 BC	3727 BC	3738 BC	3688 BC	3681 BC

Table 3.5. Identified and ^{14}C-dated cereal grains from three Early Neolithic settlements on Bornholm (Finds list I nos. 14, 23 and 34). The cereal grains from Limensgård have been identified by David Robinson, and those from Skovgård and Smedegade by Peter Steen Henriksen.

land from 3950-3800 BC (P.O. Nielsen 1985, 110). At Almhov in Scania the datings of cereals, among which emmer and bread wheat could be identified, span the period c. 3980-3630 BC (Rudebeck 2010, 118), and at Lisbjerg Skole in eastern Jutland the datings of wheat and barley fall within the interval c. 3950-3800 BC (Skousen 2008, 123-25). Cereals in the form of charred grains are almost always present when the soil from the Early Neolithic settlements is fine-sieved.

Table 3.5 shows the number of identified and dated cereal grains from three Bornholm settlements – Skovgård, Limensgård and Smedegade. Five different variants of wheat were grown, mostly emmer wheat. The largest number of grains was however of naked barley. There is no reason to believe that cereal farming was less important at the beginning of the Early Neolithic, as many archaeologists write. Cereals are more likely to have been important from the very beginning of the Neolithic as the basic foodstuff that everyone consumed, whether as bread, as gruel or as beer.

Traces of ploughing with the ard have been observed beneath non-megalithic long barrows in Jutland (Beck 2013, 71 f.). The earliest-dated ard tracks were registered, however, under a long barrow on Funen, Højensvej 7, which has been ^{14}C-dated to 3700-3500 BC, and where the ard tracks should probably be dated to 3700-3640 BC (*idem*, 74 ff., 102 f.). It is important that we can establish that ploughing with the ard was among the farming methods from this period on. Ploughing makes it possible to cultivate larger areas and produce more than is necessary to cover the consumption of the individual household. If this possibility was exploited, that might help to explain the expansion of settlement that took place. However, we cannot exclude the possibility that the ard was already in use from the beginning of the Neolithic in South Scandinavia. But since barrows were not built so early, there is little possibility that traces of ploughing are preserved from that time. It is also a question whether ploughing was at all possible in a first cultivation phase using the slash-and-burn method (Schier 2009, 36).

Indications in the bone material of the use of cattle as draught animals have not been found from the beginning of the Neolithic (Johannsen 2006, 40). The oldest ox bone showing traces of any such activity

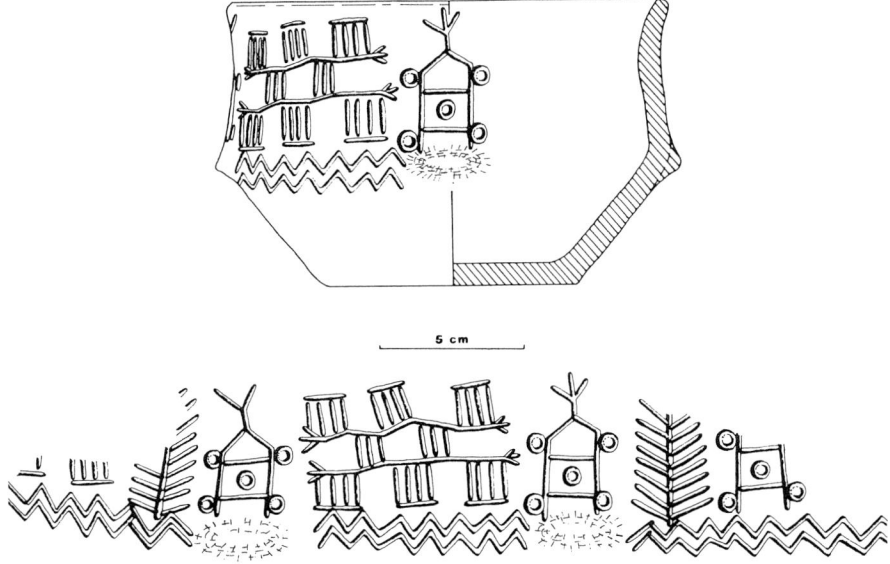

Fig. 3.49. Depiction of a four-wheeled cart on a pottery vessel from Bronocice, Southern Poland, c. 3600-3400 BC (after Milisauskas & Kruk 1982).

was found in northern Jutland and has been dated to 3650-3360 BC (*idem*, 42). From the beginning of the Middle Neolithic we have several symptoms of the use of cattle as draught animals in the form of stress-conditioned deformations of the proximal phalanx, for example in the bone material from some of the large settlements such as Troldebjerg and Bundsø (*idem*, 40). At the same time there is evidence of the castration of young bulls and thus of the probable use of oxen as draught animals. The use of draught animals was however also practiced in EN II/EN C, as is evident from traces of ard furrows beneath long barrows and dolmens. The introduction of this draught power thus coincides with the so-called *landnam*, which was manifested around 3500 BC in the reduction of forest pollen and the advance of grasses and herbs, all of which together gives us a picture of a more open landscape (Iversen 1941; 1949). The use of draught animals for forest clearance may have furthered this process as well as being an important energy factor in connection with the contemporary building of megalithic tombs and causewayed enclosures.

The use of carts has not been reliably documented from South Scandinavia in this interval, but at Flintbek in Holstein possible wheel tracks have been found beneath a long dolmen (Zich 1993). On the side of a pot from Bronocice in southern Poland there are five examples of an image of a four-wheeled cart (fig. 3.49). The find is associated with the southeastern Funnel Beaker Culture in the area around the upper reaches of the Vistula and has been ^{14}C-dated to 4725±50 BP, calibrated 3631-3379 BC (1σ), 3635-3374 BC (2σ) (GrN-19612)[1] (Milisauskas & Kruk 1982; Kruk & Milisauskas 1999, 166 ff.). The dating corresponds to EN Ib/EN II in South Scandinavia. Although there is a great distance from the Baltic to the area from which this find comes, it is probable that technical innovations such as two- and four-wheeled vehicles may at that time have spread over larger areas. There are only scanty signs of connections between Bornholm and the SE group of the Funnel Beaker Culture, but there is one example in the form of a fragment of a battle axe with a butt knob found near the south coast of the island at Myregård in Pedersker. The battle axe can be identified as belonging to Zápotocký's type KVII or type KVIII, the latter of which is dated to the Wiórek phase, corresponding to EN II/EN C, and this type has a distribution that extends to southeastern Poland (p. 141 f., finds list V.14, fig. 8.11:15). Direct or indirect communication with this area may, besides battle axes, have included knowledge of innovations such as carts.

That cattle were significant not only as an important food resource, but now also as draught animals, changed mankind's relations with the animals. This came to expression in the Middle Neolithic in the burials of cattle, which in central and eastern Europe appear at burial sites alongside human burials, but which also appear separately as single or pairwise whole carcasses of male and female cattle as well as oxen, sometimes combined with two-wheeled wagons. They have a spread in time from Salzmünde and the southeastern Funnel Beaker Culture over the Globular Amphora Culture to the Corded Ware and the Schönfelder Culture (Behrens 1973, 243; Pollex 1998; Bogaard 2004, 50; Johannsen & Laursen 2010, 25 ff.; Friederich & Hoffmann 2013). As a parallel phenomenon in Denmark the Jutland stone-packing graves appear, carriage burials with a team of cows or oxen, dated to MN AII-V (Johannsen & Laursen 2010; Johannsen & Kieldsen 2014). To wagon transport belongs the establishment of roads, and kilometre-long rows of stone-packing graves are thought to mark road lines (Johannsen & Laursen 2010, 39 ff.).

Notes

1. The datings have been recalibrated with Calib ver. 7.10 using the intcal13.14c atmospheric curve (Reimer *et al*. 2013).
2. Median probability calculated with Calib ver. 7.10.
3. Three ^{14}C dates of domestic ox are the earliest dates so far obtained from the site of Muldbjerg I (Noe-Nygaard *et al*. 2005, Table 1). The three datings are identical: 5050±50 BP, cal. 3950-3780 BC (1σ).
4. Three samples of material from Sigersted III pit A were AMS ^{14}C-dated in Tucson, Arizona, in 1986, which produced the following uncalibrated datings: 1) grain of barley (*Hordeum* sp.) 4780±70 BP; 2) seed of apple (*Pomaceae*) 4790±70 BP; and 3) charcoal, twig of oak (*Quercus* sp.) 4600±100 BP. The submitter of the specimens (PON) has not published these datings, since they were taken as part of a first series of datings at the newly-started AMS laboratory in Tucson, and because the datings are 2-300 years later than expected. However, they have been mentioned in the literature by others (Koch 1998, 87; Hallgren 2008, 157).
5. In the publication Bagge & Kjellmark 1939 the middle element is called *snörkeramisk*, meaning Early Neolithic cord-ornamented pottery.

4. Pointed-butted axes

In the effort to build up a periodization that applies to Bornholm, and which can be related to other parts of South Scandinavia, there will be a focus in the following sections on objects other than pottery, first and foremost the pointed-butted axes of flint and other materials and the thin-butted flint axes. Both categories of axes are divided into types, and it will be investigated in the following how the individual types relate chronologically to the temporal model drawn up here on the basis of the pottery.

Pointed-butted axes of flint

The pointed-butted flint axe is distributed over a large area in western and northern Europe and can be regarded as a guide type for both the Michelsberg Culture and the Funnel Beaker Culture. Pointed-butted axes in other materials than flint were used in the fifth millennium in the Rössen and Stichbandkeramik cultures, from which axes of various shapes and materials reached South Scandinavia, such as shoe-last axes and pointed-butted axes of amphibolite (Klassen 2004, 63 ff.). Imports of foreign axe types in the Late Mesolithic did not lead, however, to any technological change within the Ertebølle Culture, which continued to make local implement types such as flake and core axes of flint as well as Limhamn axes and related types made of diorite and other stone.

Towards the end of the fifth millennium pointed-butted axes of jade from the western Alps gained wide diffusion and in western and central Europe were imitated in flint (Pétrequin et al. 2010; 2012). Some jade axes may have reached South Scandinavia as exotica as early as the Late Mesolithic, while various types of jade axes must have followed with the expansion that took place around 4100-4000 BC, when arable farming spread to the countries around the western Baltic. In southern and central Scandinavia they were also imitated in flint, as reflected in the design of pointed-butted axes of both flint and other stone materials (Sørensen 2012; 2014, 162 ff.).

The pointed-butted flint axes were the most important working tools of the first farmers in the pioneering phase, when they faced the task of turning forest into arable land. Access to usable raw material for making axes was therefore important, and one can see the opening of a number of flint mines concurrently with the agrarian expansion on the Continent, in South Scandinavia and in England (Sørensen 2014, 169 ff., fig. V.114). Judging from the diffusion of pointed-butted flint axes, the Øresund area with its natural flint deposits played a special role. Most pointed-butted flint axes have been found as intact, fully usable examples which were probably deposited in ritual contexts in the open countryside some way from the settlement, both individually and in hoards with several axes. Most isolated finds and hoards with pointed-butted flint axes have been found in Scania (Jennbert 1984, 108 ff.; Hernek 1989; Karsten 1994, 50-54; Sørensen 2014, fig. V 111). They were produced from the Senonian flint that was extracted from the chalk layers at Södra Sallerup in south-west Scania, where fragments have been found, and from where ^{14}C dates testify to flint mining activities taking place as early as between 4000-3800 BC (Berggren et al. 2016). The distribution of the axes in Scania also reflects the rich resources and surplus in this region from the beginning of the Neolithic.

For more detailed definitions and descriptions of the three types of pointed-butted flint axe, reference is made to P.O. Nielsen 1977, 65-72. In the following description, it is stated whether the flint axes are polished, partially polished or unpolished. In addition, most polished pointed-butted and thin-butted flint axes have been polished intensively in the area of the cutting edge (for description, see B. Madsen 1984, 49 f.). But the presence and extent of this burnishing have not been recorded for this investigation.

Pointed-butted flint axes of type 1

The bifacial pointed-butted flint axe of type 1 with a symmetrical, pointed-oval cross-section (fig. 4.1) is an axe, unlike the Late Ertebølle Culture's core axe with specially treated edge, which is in fact an adze. In the production technique too differences can be demonstrated (Stafford 1999, 48 f.). In the material from Ertebølle Culture settlements in southern Zealand, however, core axes with a specially treated edge and partial polishing have been demonstrated, although one cannot tell whether they belong to the end of the Mesolithic or the beginning of the Early Neolithic (Johansson 1999, 27). They should possibly be regarded as axes and may be a preliminary stage to the bifacial, pointed-butted flint axes. Partial polishing of core axes with a specially treated edge has been demonstrated over a large area in South Scandinavia, which is seen as an indication that the use of polishing on flint axes was one of the influences that reached South Scandinavia from agrarian societies settled on the Continent concurrently with the final phase of the Ertebølle Culture (Sørensen 2014, I, 137, fig. V 75). The fully polished, bifacial, pointed-butted flint axe, which was distributed over a large area of northwestern Europe, was introduced in southern and central Scandinavia at the same time as the introduction of the agrarian economy around 4000 BC (Klassen 2004, 213; Sørensen 2014, I, 164). It superseded the Mesolithic core axes, which after the transition to the Neolithic were no longer made. Core-axe-like pieces found at settlements in the Early Neolithic context, should probably be identified as unpolished preforms for pointed-butted axes (Sørensen 2014, I, 135-37).

On Bornholm five pointed-butted flint axes of type 1 have been found, two of which are unpolished (Finds list IV nos. 1-5). One of the unpolished examples was found close to the east coast, while the remainder were found inland (fig. 4.10). Two axes (nos. 3-4) were found near settlement traces from the Early Neolithic, one in fact close to a spring. A third axe (no. 5) is said to have been found in a meadow. In

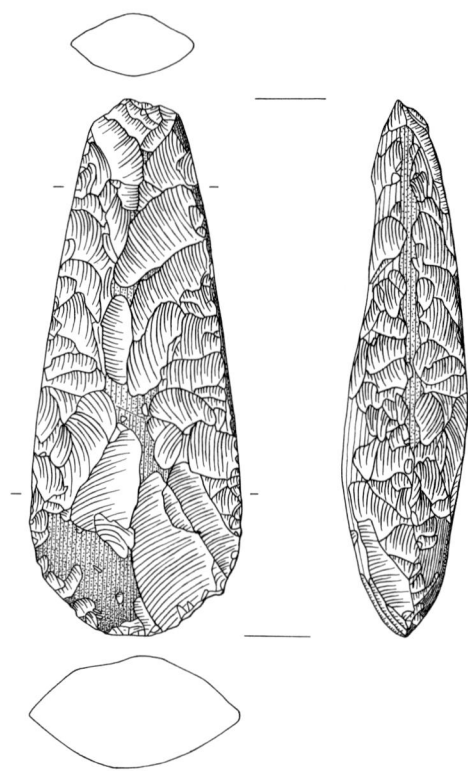

Fig. 4.1. Pointed-butted flint axe of type 1 from Smørmosegård, Vestermarie (Finds list IV no. 1). Freerk Oldenburger del. 1:2.

terms of soil types three axes were found on or near sandy soil, while two were found at places dominated by clayey soil.

At the Bornholm settlements from the Early Neolithic one often finds flakes of polished flint axes, but usually so small that it is not possible to identify from which axe type they have been knocked off. Slightly larger fragments have however made it possible to demonstrate flakes from pointed-butted flint axes. In one of the pits at the settlement Jættebro (Finds list I no. 56) a fire-brittle fragment of a bifacial, ground flint axe of type 1 was found, alongside early funnel beakers of type I (fig. 3.5) which date the piece to EN A1.

The type appears in several other places in settlement contexts. One important site is Oxie no. 7 in western Scania, where the material was not excavated, however, but gathered. It comprises 16 polished and unpolished fragments as well as one intact, fire-brittle example of the type (Forssander 1938, 16 ff.; Althin 1954, 53-58; M. Larsson 1984, 61 f., fig. 32). The settlement material from the site, which includes the often-depicted intact short-necked funnel beaker (Forssander 1938 fig. 5; Althin 1954, 57), was already considered by the first archaeologists who dealt with it to be from the beginning of the Neolithic (Forssander 1938, 24; Althin 1954, 54 f.). The find complex has given its name to the 'Oxie group', which several researchers prefer to use instead of C.J. Becker's period A (M. Larsson 1984, 159; Madsen & Petersen 1984, 96 ff.; Koch 181 f.). In terms of the Bornholm chronology the finds from Oxie no. 7 correspond to EN A1.

At Almhov in southwestern Scania a large complex of pits with find material from the earliest Funnel Beaker Culture was excavated. Of 47 intact and fragmented pointed-butted axes 37 can be identified as belonging to type 1 and 10 as belonging to type 2 (Rudebeck 2010, 174; Sørensen 2014, vol. III Table 59). In pit A 19049 at Almhov two fragments of pointed-butted axes of type 1 were found, as well as sherds of funnel beakers with horizontal rows of indentations beneath the rim and a neck fragment of a funnel beaker with a cordon applied beneath the rim in which there were finger imprints. A grain of bread wheat (*Triticum aestivum/compactum*) from the pit has been ^{14}C-dated to 5065±60 BP, calibrated 3960-3790 (1σ), 3970-3710 (2σ) (Gidlöf *et al.* 2006, 55-59). The find context and the ^{14}C dating thus date the two fragments of pointed-butted axes of type 1 to the Oxie phase, corresponding to EN AI on Bornholm.

Another, but more remotely located find complex was excavated at Tolstrup in northern Jutland, where red-fired clay layers which were covered by the remains of a long barrow contained three fragments of pointed-butted flint axes of type 1 as well as sherds of at least five pots, four of which could be reconstructed as funnel beakers of type I (Madsen 1975, 126-28, 143 f.). The largest find from the early Funnel Beaker Culture yet discovered in Jutland appeared however in 2001-03 during the excavation of cultural layers and pits at Lisbjerg Skole in the Egå valley north of Aarhus. A polished, bifacial pointed-butted axe of type 1 was found there in a flat-bottomed pit (A2247) along with pottery of the Oxie type (Skousen 2008, 131, fig. 97). The axe has been pointed out as an imitation of jade axes of the Durrington type (Sørensen 2014, I, 146).

A stratigraphically registered find comes from the coastal settlement Baabe on Rügen (Hirsch *et al.* 2008). The butt end of a polished, pointed-butted flint axe of type 1 was found there in the upper edge of layer E, which has been ^{14}C-dated on wood to 5203±36 BP, calibrated 4040-3972 BC (1σ). A sample from a fish trap dates the transition from layer E to the more recent layer D to 5134±44 BP, calibrated 3984-3812 BC (1σ).[1] From the same site come parts of early funnel beakers, including a small pot that has been compared to funnel beakers of Eva Koch's type 0, and which also recalls the beakers of the Michelsberg Culture (Hirsch *et al.* 2008, 30 and fig. 9:7,13-14). Lutz Klassen thinks that the bifacial pointed-butted flint axe of type 1 first appeared in South Scandinavia around 3800 BC, which against the background of the datings from Scania and Rügen is questionable (Klassen 2004, 211).

Pointed-butted flint axes of type 1 have thus been found several times with the oldest funnel beaker pottery, which like the available ^{14}C datings strengthens the view that this is the oldest type of pointed-butted axe. Lutz Klassen sees a connection between the emergence of the oldest funnel beaker pottery and that of the pointed-butted flint axe, and he places the origin of both within the Michelsberg Culture, in which pointed-butted flint axes were made with pointed-oval jade axes as a model (Klassen 2004, 211-13). Although there is much to suggest that type 1 is the oldest Nordic type of polished flint axe, at the same time it must be said that type 2 appears in very similar find contexts.

Pointed-butted flint axes of type 2

Of pointed-butted flint axes of type 2 (fig. 4.2) with a triangular to subrectangular or rounded oval cross-section, 23 individual finds and one hoard find of three intact and two reworked pieces have been registered from Bornholm (Finds list IV nos. 6-28, 45). Of the individually found examples, three are stored at the National Museum and 11 at the Bornholm Museum, while nine individually found axes are in private ownership. Only one example (no. 17) has been found less than 1 km from the coast; all the others have been found inland, and about half have been found in the central parts of the island (fig. 4.10). Eleven of the finds have emerged on or near sandy soil, three are from an area with both clay and sand, and eight have been found in a mainly clayey soil. Beyond this, very little is known about the find circumstances. Axes have been found twice on cultivated fields, twice in wetlands and once during construction work. One stray find of an axe (no. 21) is said to have been found in a hollow in the rock,

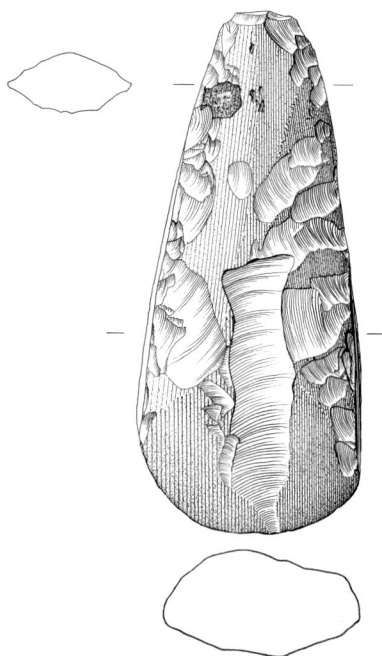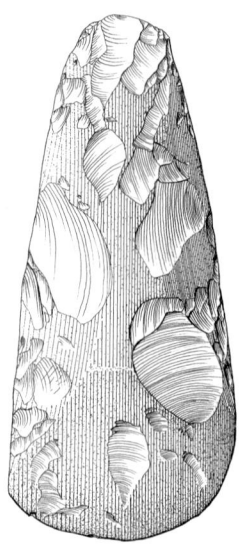

Fig. 4.2. Pointed-butted flint axe of type 2 from Sjælemosen, Olsker (Finds list IV no. 24). Lars Holten del. 1:2.

and as for the hoard from Ravnekær (no. 45) we are told that the axes lay close together in a rock fissure.

With the exception of just one, all the stray finds of axes of this type are polished, and seven are also resharpened. The preforms for axes of type 2 are in principle bifacial, like the unpolished axe from Fredshvile (fig. 4.3) but the faces have been worked without the symmetry characteristic of type 1. The preform has been turned several times during working, and there may be differences in the form of the faces, which tends to give the axe an irregular cross-section (compare the unpolished axe in fig. 4.3 with the polished axe in fig. 4.2). On both the unpolished and the polished axe the edge only has a corner on one side, while on the other side the blade follows the side seam. This makes the blade a little irregular, as can be seen in several examples of type 2. Viewed from the side, most axes of this type are asymmetrical in that one broad side is more convex than the other; see for example the only partially polished axes in the hoard from Ravnekjær, where the edges on two of the axes also curve as on adzes (fig. 4.4:1-2). This

Fig. 4.3. Unpolished preform for pointed-butted flint axe of type 2 from Fredshvile, Klemensker (Finds list IV no. 20). Lars Holten del. 1:2.

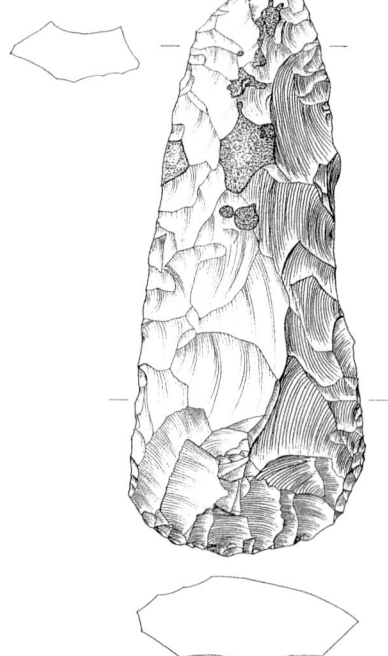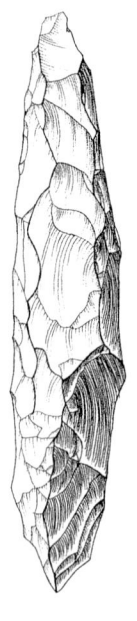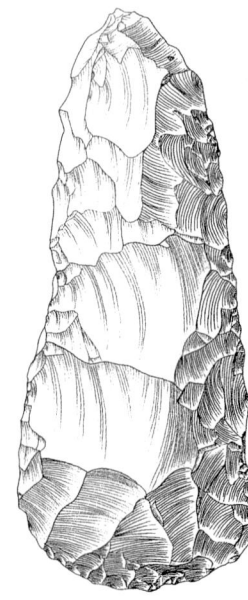

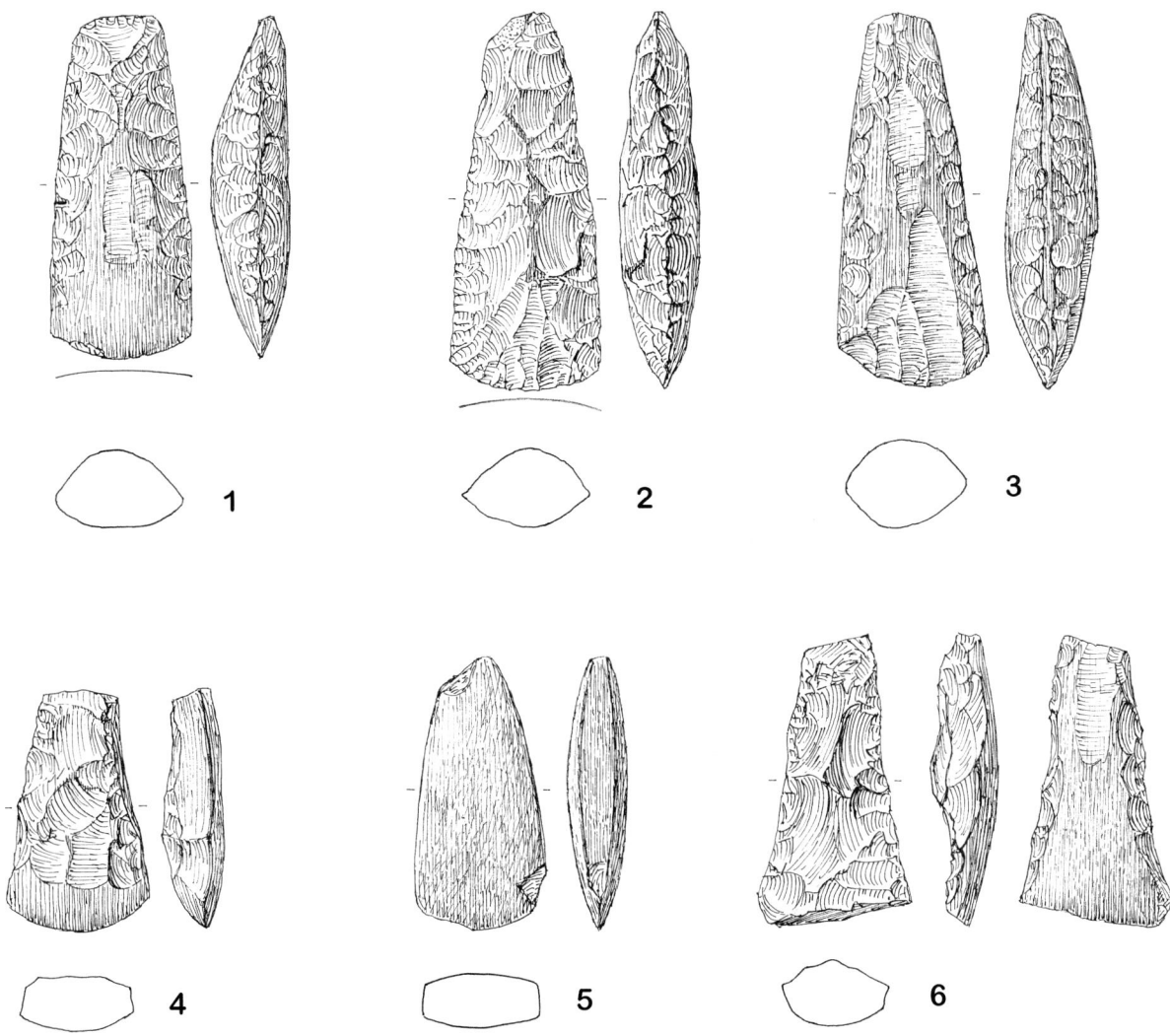

Fig. 4.4. Hoard containing pointed-butted axes from Ravnekær, Vestermarie (Finds list IV no. 45). H. Ørsnes del. 2:5.

opens up the possibility that some axes of type 2 may in fact have been formed and shafted like adzes. Axes of type 2 are formed without the controlled flaking characteristic of the bifacial type 1 and the quadrifacial type 3, and the impression is that preforms for axes of type 2 were made quickly.

Fragments of polished axes which can be identified as axes of type 2 have been found at several Early Neolithic settlements on Bornholm. This applies to the settlement at Skovgård (fig. 3.10:7, Finds list I no. 23), where by far most of the pottery can be dated to EN A1, and the settlements Borgen (no. 24, fig. 8.2:3) and Gudhjem Syd (no. 53, fig. 8.4:9). The latter two settlement sites have not been excavated professionally, no detailed account can be given of the context. But from both sites we have almost consistent inventory from EN A1. At the settlement Sandemandsgård (no. 38) fragments of ground pointed-butted flint axes of either type 2 or 3 also emerged.

Outside Bornholm pointed-butted flint axes of type 2 are known from several settlement contexts, including Muldbjerg (Troels-Smith 1953, 30, fig. 24) and Sigersted III (P.O. Nielsen 1985a, 103-06, fig. 8; 1994, 290, Taf. 4), both on Zealand, and in both places fragments of axes of type 2 have been found together with settlement inventory dominated by funnel beakers of type I. The same is the case at the settlement Värby in Scania, where fragments of type 2 were found in pit V 22 (Salomonsson 1970, Abb. 10A:1-2). Some of the axe fragments that were found during the excavation of the two non-megalithic long barrows at Barkær in eastern Jutland may come from pointed-butted flint axes of type 2 (Liversage 1992, fig. 58:1-2). They appeared as part of the mixed settlement material that was older than the long barrows, and which besides Volling pottery and thin-butted flint axes also included sherds of early funnel beakers (*idem*, fig. 30). Lasse Sørensen (2014) lists several settlement contexts with axes of type 2, including two pits at Almhov in SW Scania. One of these, A32422, contained funnel beakers whose ornaments consist entirely of indentations. The pit has been ^{14}C-dated on grain to 4940±40 BP, calibrated 3800-3650 BC (1σ). The second pit, A1854, contained parts of funnel beakers, some of which were ornamented with indentations, others with two-ply cord. This pit has been ¹⁴C-dated on grain to 4780±50 BP, calibrated 3650-3520 BC (1σ) (Sørensen 2014, fig. V.108; Gidlöf *et al.* 2006, 75-76, 79). The latter dating, in terms of the Bornholm chronology, falls within EN B, which would accord with the occurrence of cord-ornamented pottery in pit A1854, and this is the latest dating of the pointed-butted flint axe of type 2. At a site with intensive settlement in several phases of the EN, however, one must also allow for a certain mixing, for example with the re-use of flint material, which is a possible explanation of the occurrence of the axe in this context.

Similar reservations must apply to the find circumstances at the settlement Svenstorp in southwestern Scania (Salomonsson 1963; Larsson 1984, 103-27). In the material from the excavation in 1962 axe fragments were identified as parts of both pointed- and thin-butted flint axes as well as possible intermediate forms, and some were identified as pointed-butted flint axes of type 2 (Salomonsson 1963, 109, fig. 25). In the treatment of the large body of material from the excavation in 1963 all fragments of polished axes were however determined to be thin-butted and later types (Larsson 1984, 109 f.). As mentioned before, the problem with the settlement Svenstorp is that the find material does not come from regular settlement pits, where the finds can reliably be regarded as contemporary (*cf.* p. 69 f.)

On the basis of the reliable contexts and the number of combinations with pottery types, type 2 must be dated to EN A1.

Pointed-butted flint axes of type 3

Of the quadrifacial pointed-butted flint axes of type 3 (fig. 4.5), 13 have been registered from Bornholm (Finds list IV nos. 29-41). Of these four are stored at the National Museum and three at the Bornholm Museum, while six are in private ownership. About twelve of the axes have find information. Only one axe was found less than 1 km from the coast (no. 33); all the others were found inland at a distance of more than 2 km from the coast (fig. 4.10). Four axes were found on sandy soil, five on clayey soil and three on a soil with both clay and sand. Otherwise there is not much information on the find circumstances beyond the fact that two axes were said to have been found in and beneath burial mounds from later periods. All the axes of this type are polished, and five are also resharpened.

Type 3 can sometimes be difficult to distinguish from type 2, since it is the degree of polishing on the narrow surfaces that determines whether they have a quadrifacial cross-section. So mixed types occur, such as one of the axes from Fredshvile (no. 21). The separation of the two types can also pose problems when one has to identify fragments from the settlements. On Bornholm the type is possibly represented in the material from the settlement Sandemandsgård (Finds list I no. 38), but the fragments are small, and the identification is therefore uncertain.

Type 3 can also be hard to distinguish from the early thin-butted flint axes. The longest of this type of pointed-butted flint axe has a butt width of 3.7 cm and has therefore been classed as pointed-butted, but judging from all the other characteristics it could as easily be classified as a thin-butted flint axe of type I (fig. 4.6) (Finds list IV no. 29).

Outside Bornholm type 3 only appears a few times in settlement contexts. At Kristineberg in southwestern Scania, beneath the remains of a ploughed-over long barrow, a settlement layer was preserved in which there were fragments of a quadrifacial pointed-butted flint axe (Rudebeck 2002, 86). The finds from the layer, which include cord-ornamented pottery, have been dated to the Svenstorp group (*idem*, 89). Type 3 must have been made later than the two preceding types of pointed-butted flint axe – that is, later than or late within the Oxie group, and it may have been wholly or partially contemporary with the Svenstorp group. The find combinations in the hoard finds from Scania suggest the same. There, type 3 appears together with thin-butted flint axes in 11 cases (Karsten 1994, 53).

Pointed-butted axes of other material than flint

In his treatment of the Funnel Beaker Culture's axes of other stone types than flint, Klaus Ebbesen uses a butt width of 4 cm as a dividing-line between pointed-butted and thin-butted axes, in the same way as the flint axes are divided. But at the same time

Fig. 4.5. Pointed-butted flint axe of type 3 from Fredsvile (?), Klemensker (Finds list IV no. 36). Lars Holten del. 1:2.

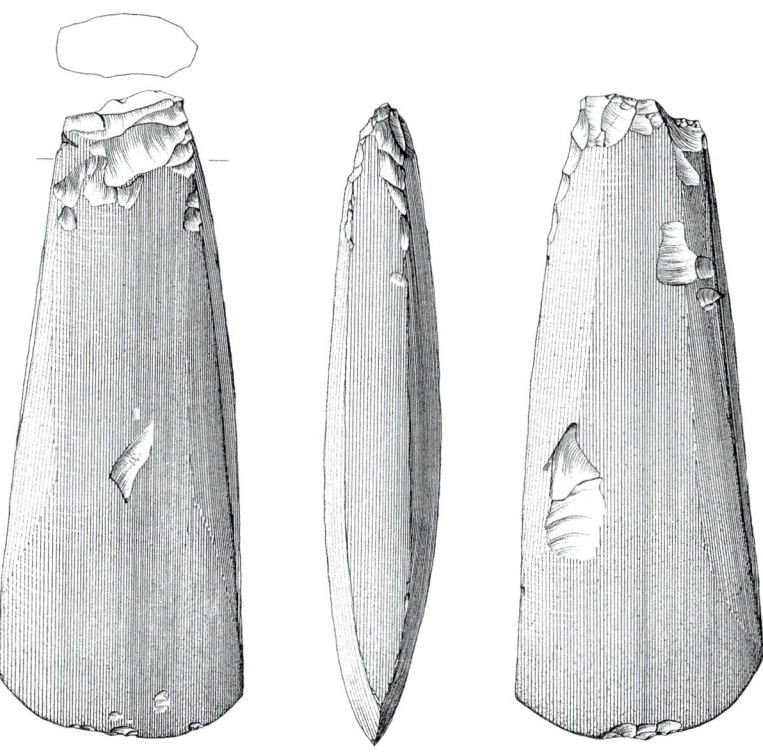

he notes that one cannot use other dimensional and formal criteria from the classification of the flint axes on axes that are made of other materials (Ebbesen 1984, 114 f.). We agree with the view that the two categories of axes did not develop quite in parallel, and that the difference between them must be due both to the properties of the materials and the function of the axes.

On Bornholm ten isolated finds of pointed-butted axes of other stone types than flint have been registered (Finds list IV nos. 42-44.7). In addition there is an axe in the deposition from Ravnekær (fig. 4.4:5, Finds list IV no. 45), where it is combined with pointed-butted flint axes of type 2. At the settlement Højegård (Finds list I no. 40), dated to EN A1, one intact example was found (fig. 3.6) as well as an edge fragment. These twelve axes are all quadrifacial and fall within Ebbesen's type IA (1984, 115 f., fig. 2:2). Although they all have polished facets on the narrow surfaces, the cross-section of the axes is not rectangular, since the broad surfaces are convex. The intact examples measure between 13.5 and 19.9 cm in length. Ten of the axes are made of a fine-grained stone type, diabase or a similar soft stone. One axe

Fig. 4.6. Pointed-butted flint axe of type 3 from Vellensby, Nylars (Finds list IV no. 29). Length: 30.3 cm. Photo John Lee, the National Museum. 2:5.

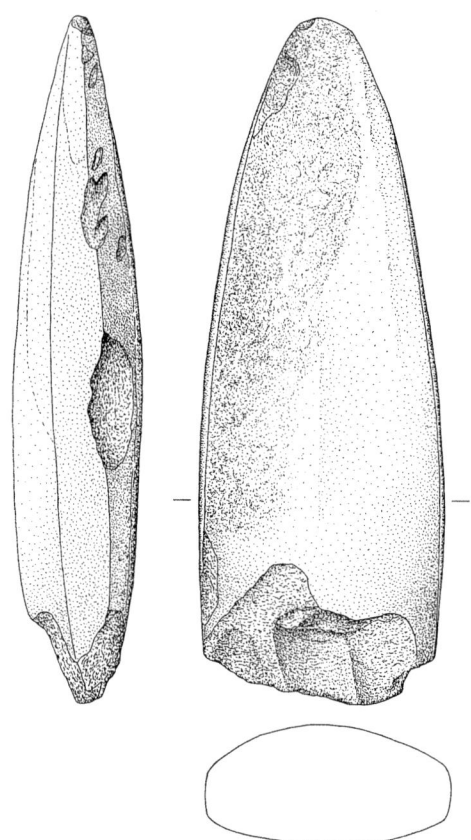

Fig. 4.7. Pointed-butted axe of quartzite from Lillehave (Finds list IV no. 44). Freerk Oldenburger del. 1:2.

from Risbyvang in Klemensker is of sandstone (Finds list IV no. 44.5), and the axe from Lillehave (no. 44) is of quartzite (fig. 4.7).

The find information on the isolated axe finds is scanty. Of two of them we are told that they were found on cultivated soil. However, it has been possible to localize them all to a particular property or a particular landscape area. The distribution is striking (fig. 4.10), as one of the axes was found in Olsker in northern Bornholm, six were found in Nyker and Klemensker, where four of them were found in other places than the pointed-butted flint axes, and another four were found in the southernmost part of the island.

Another axe can be added to the pointed-butted ones: the copper axe with a pointed-oval cross-section from Vester Bedegadegård in Klemensker (fig. 4.8b-c) (Finds list VII no. 1), which has been interpreted as an imitation of a jade axe of the Bégude type (Klassen 2010; Klassen *et al.* 2012, 1286). Alongside the few axes of western Alpine jade that have been found in Denmark (Klassen 1999; 2000, 83 ff.), very many imitations of jade axes of various types have been demonstrated in Denmark and Sweden, but they are of flint and other stone types (Klassen & Nielsen 2010; Sørensen 2014, I, 148). The axe from Vester Bedegadegård is one of the very rare imitations of jade axes in metal. It is made of almost pure copper, which has been identified as Mondsee copper from the eastern Alpine area. It has been stated that most other objects of copper imported to South Scandinavia c. 3800-3300 BC were made of this copper (Klassen 2010, 39). But it has also been suggested that the copper comes from metal deposits in the Balkans (Sørensen 2014, I, 148).

Apart from the axe from Vester Bedegadegård, two other pointed-butted copper axes have been found in southeastern Denmark, one with a quadrifacial cross-section from Vantore on Lolland, and one with an oval cross-section from Pilegård near Varpelev in eastern Zealand (Klassen 2000, nos. 6 and 33). The quadrifacial copper axe from Vantore is of a type and has a metal composition that suggest it was imported from eastern Germany, probably in the period 4100-3900 BC (Klassen *et al.* 2012, 1288). The axe from Pilegård, like the axe from Vester Bedegadegård, is considered to be an imitation of a jade axe (Chelles type). Close to the find-spot for the Pilegård axe in Varpelev Parish, a flint axe has also been found that imitates jade axes of the Saint-Michel type, which come from the Carnac area in Brittany (Klassen & Nielsen 2010, fig. 4).

The copper axe from Vester Bedegadegård has been identified as an imitation of jade axes of the Bégude type, which also belong to the group of axes from Carnac. Axes of the Bégude type are considered some of the oldest jade axes, which were exported in 4700-4300 BC from the western Alps to the area by the Gulf of Morbihan, where they were re-polished, then used in ritual contexts, while others entered circulation and ended up far from their place of origin, for example in Spain, Germany and Italy (fig. 4.9). Some must have reached the western Baltic area to be imitated there in other materials (Pétrequin *et al.* 2012b).

In Brittany other types of jade axes appear in monumental barrows, as in the largest of them, Mont Saint-Michel at Carnac, built between 4700 and 4300 BC, where 48 pointed-butted axes, 12 of jade and 36 of fibrolite, were placed in a stone-built burial chamber standing vertically with the blades upward. Four of the hoard finds from the same area consist wholly or partly of axes of jade, which were also found standing with the blades upward, as at Bernon, where 17 jade axes stood this way in a small

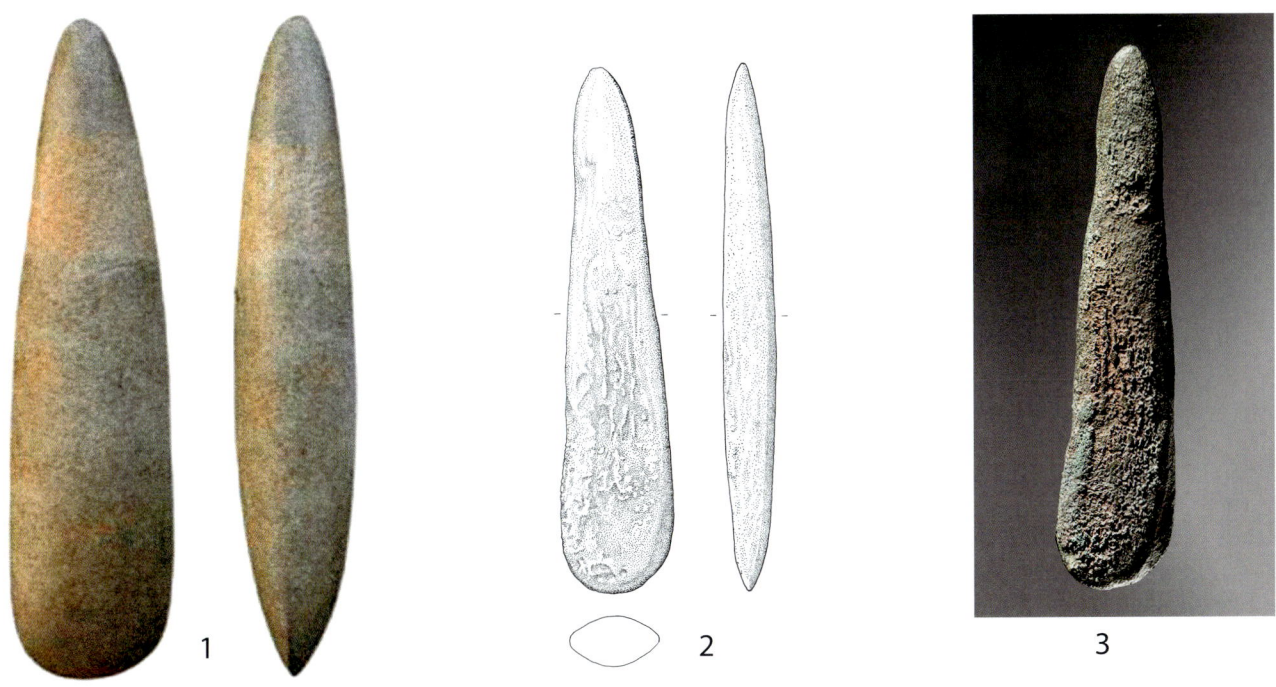

Fig. 4.8. (1) Pointed-butted jade axe from the hoard Bégude-de-Mazenc, Drôme, France. (2-3) Copper axe from Vester Bedegade-gård, Klemensker. (1) after Pétrequin et al. 2012b, (2) after Klassen 2000, (3) photo Arnold Mikkelsen, the National Museum. 2:5.

Fig. 4.9. The distribution of jade axes of Bégude type and imitations of these. Natural deposits of jade are marked with stars. Source: Pétrequin et al. 2012b.

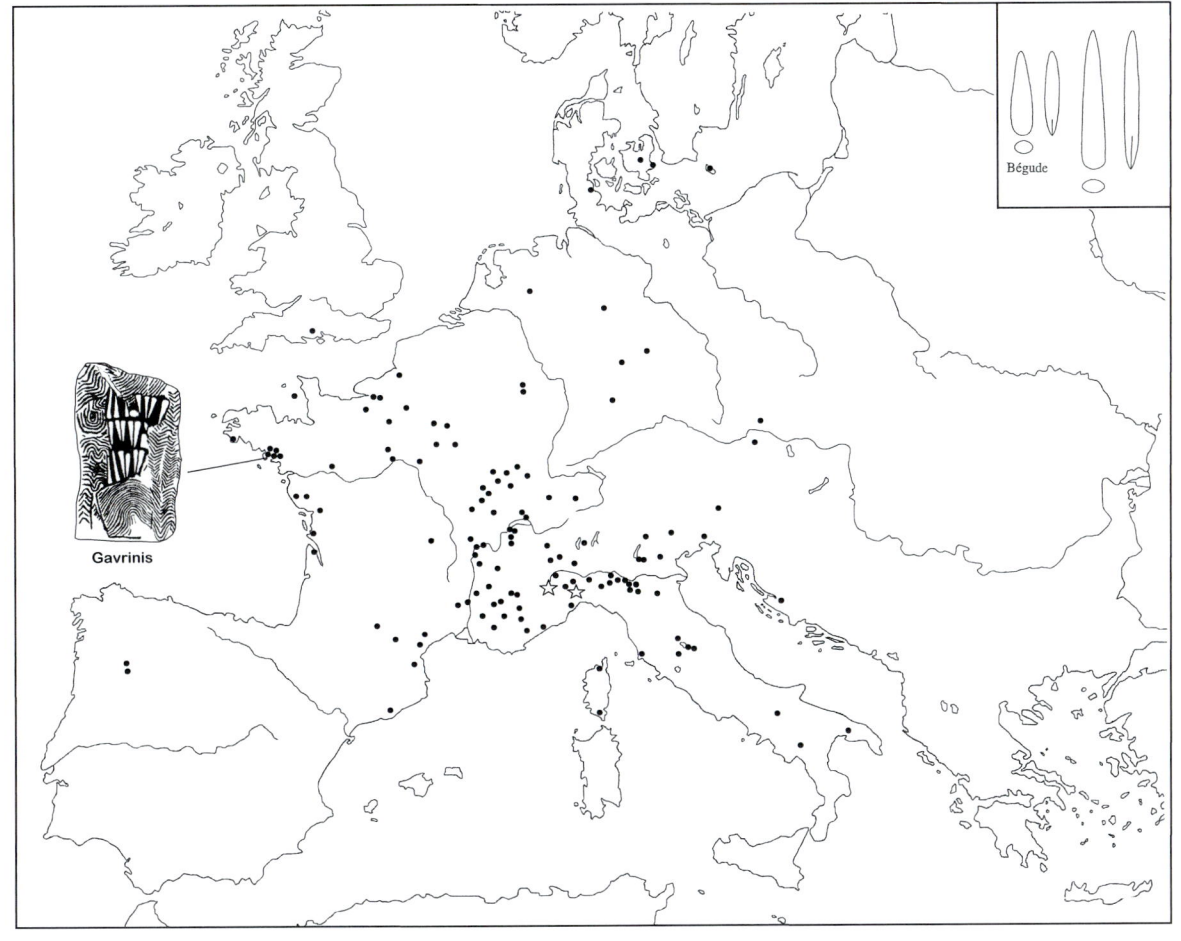

stone cist (Herbaut 2000, 387-95; Cassen *et al.* 2012). A few depictions of axes can be seen on menhirs, some of which were used as construction material in the passage graves in Morbihan from the end of the fifth millennium as in La Table des Marchands. Quite unique is the interior decoration of the passage grave in Gavrinis (Cassen 2012), where depictions of pointed-butted axes are engraved on the uprights together with 'trance imagery' (Bradley 1990, 56).

The jade axe as an object and as a motif has in this case achieved a status as a significant symbol in a society which must have been highly developed and hierarchical. On the long route the jade axes took from western France to South Scandinavia through various societies, a journey that may have taken several hundred years, their meaning and the stories of their origin may have changed many times. But the wide diffusion they attained and the many imitations of them in other materials must mean that they were coveted as prestige objects in the North too. This may be an indication that at the time of the neolithisation of northern Europe a network of connections and power alliances had been formed as a prelude to the hierarchisation of which we have evidence a few centuries later (Sørensen 2012; Nielsen & Sørensen 2018).

The French jade axes can be up to 45 cm long. The longest pointed-butted flint axe found in Denmark is bifacial, measures 37.6 cm and may be an imitation of one of the large jade axes (Klassen 2004, 86, fig. 54C). The longest pointed-butted flint axe found on Bornholm is quadrifacial and measures 30.3 cm (fig. 4.6) (Finds list IV no. 29). Efforts to make record-long axes began in the earliest phases of the Neolithic, and they were encouraged by access to South Scandinavian flint of high quality.

Pointed-butted axes – summary

On Bornholm the three types of pointed-butted flint axes are in some places distributed in terms of the topography of the island like the settlements in EN A1, while in other places they follow a different pattern (fig. 4.10). The greatest convergence between settlements and finds of axes are in northern Bornholm, where both are found on or by the three oblong hills of diluvial sand and gravel that run in the NW-SE direction, and were formed at ice-marginal lines during the melting of the ice (fig. 3.44). The find-spots for seven of the pointed-butted flint axes almost ex-

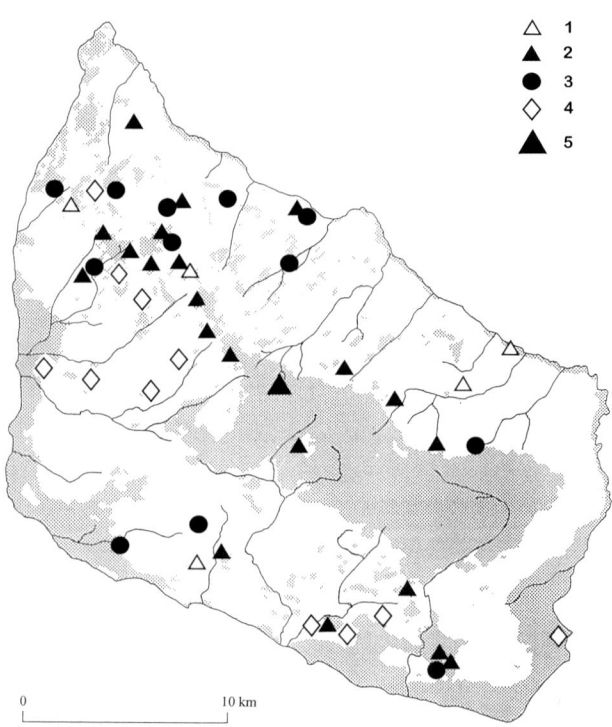

Fig. 4.10. The distribution of pointed-butted axes on Bornholm. (1) Type 1. (2) Type 2. (3) Type 3. (4) Axes of a type of stone other than flint. (5) Hoard.

actly follow the midmost and longest of the sandhills, which is called the Splitsgård Line (Milthers 1930, 97 ff.). Settlements and axes are also concentrated in and around the larger sandy hill area Torpebakkerne, which is a part of the Simblegård Line to the south west.

In the northeastern part of the island there are greater differences in the distribution of settlements and axes. While the settlements lie at the coast or at a short distance from it, four of the pointed-butted flint axes were found inland near the edge of the interior sand and rock area which is today uncultivated and forested. In southern Bornholm, as in northern Bornholm, one sees a tendency for both settlements and pointed-butted axes to be concentrated in areas with sandy soil. Most of eastern Bornholm is without settlements from EN A1 and finds of pointed-butted flint axes. Stray finds of pointed-butted flint axes are also absent from the parishes Knudsker and Nyker in western Bornholm, where settlements with fragments of such axes do occur. The lack of stray finds of pointed-butted flint axes in the western part of the island is however balanced by the stray finds of pointed-butted axes of other materials than flint.

The tendency for settlement in EN A1 to be concentrated in the sandhills corresponds to the settlement pattern one sees in southwestern Scania for

Fig. 4.11. The distribution of pointed-butted flint axes in Scandinavia (after Sørensen 2014).

the settlements belonging to the Oxie and Svenstorp group in the earlier and middle part of the EN (M. Larsson 1984, 207). There are however no sites either on Bornholm or in Scania where there is any great distance from the settlements to a more clayey and thus more nutrient-rich soil.

In Scania a large quantity of pointed-butted flint axes has been registered and mapped. K. Jennbert shows the distribution of 424 axes (1984, 108, fig. 69), while R. Hernek lists 682 axes, which he types as 159 axes of type 1, 263 axes of type 2 and 260 axes of type 3.[2] On Bornholm, where the number of these individual types is respectively 5, 23 and 13, type 1 also shows the lowest find frequency and type 2 the highest. There are, however, striking differences in the numbers of type 3, which in Scania is almost as frequent as type 2. It may be that there is a real difference, but there may also be a difference in the way of typing the axes. On Bornholm a butt width of less than 4 cm is not the only criterion for identifying the pointed-butted axes, since one also considers other formal elements such as the width of the narrow surfaces and the convexity of the broad surfaces. On Bornholm several axes determined to be small and thin-butted have a butt width of less than 4 cm (see below, p. 115.)

Lasse Sørensen has mapped the occurrences of pointed-butted flint axes throughout the Nordic area (fig. 4.11) (Sørensen 2014, I, 162-69). It is evident from this that Scania stands out as the area with the highest find frequency, and that all three types are distributed, if unevenly, over southern and central Scandinavia, also with concentrations on Zealand and in Västergötland. It is noteworthy that the pointed-butted flint axes spread over such a large area when one considers the short time they were in use, from c. 4000 BC to not much later than c. 3800/3750 BC, when the thin-butted flint axes began to appear. This says

111

a lot about how quickly neolithisation took place in the North, and how extensive it was.

At the beginning of neolithisation the North was part of the very large area in northwestern Europe where pointed-butted axes of both flint and other stone, including jade, were in use in the Neolithic societies in the centuries before and after 4000 BC. The North also became part of the area where mines were established to exploit the flint in the underground chalk layers. The flint mines at Sallerup in SW Scania were established at the beginning of the fourth millennium (Rudebeck 1986, 23; Sørensen 2014, fig. V 118). The success that must have been associated with the discovery of these flint deposits may have contributed to the concentration of the early agrarian settlements there, Scania obtaining the status of being a core area for the production and distribution of flint axes for the early farming societies.

There are no natural flint resources on Bornholm besides ball flint nodules, a small amount of Kristianstad flint and of matt Danian flint (Becker 1990, 16-18). These materials are of such limited quantities and dimensions that they could not have been used for making flint axes. The people on the island were therefore completely dependent upon a supply of flint from mainland South Scandinavia or the Continent to the south. Presumably the flint was primarily imported from Scania and the Zealand island group in the form of polished and unpolished axes. Rough axe preforms and blanks are apparently not present, at least not until late in the Middle Neolithic, although even then blanks are only rarely found on Bornholm.

Of hoard finds with pointed-butted axes, one is known from Bornholm (Ravnekær, fig. 4.4), while in Scania 40 have been registered (Karsten 1994, 51). From the Scanian finds, 15 hoards lack reliable find information, while 17 are said to have been found on wetland, and another two were buried by large stones. A whole 96% of the isolated finds of pointed-butted axes from Scania were found on wetland. It plays a major role for the interpretation of the motives behind both the hoards and the isolated finds that they are so closely associated with wet areas. It was at such places that valuable objects were deposited and actions of an indisputably ritual character took place in the Early Neolithic and also in later periods of prehistory. It thus appears that from the start of the Neolithic there were ritual acts where both individual axes and hoards with several axes were buried in wet areas in accordance with a particular pattern. There are no reliable signs that there was a similar deposition practice in the Ertebølle Culture in the Mesolithic.[3] Deposition of axes individually and as groups of several objects is on the other hand known from several Neolithic cultures in the fifth millennium in western Europe, where among other things jade axes, including some of the largest, have been found deposited in a way that indicates a ritual practice (Cassen *et al.* 2012). Depositions consisting of pointed-butted axes of jade, flint and other stone types and sometimes also axes of copper are known from the Michelsberg Culture, c. 4300-3500 BC (Rech 1979, 79 f.), which is the culture whose expansion in 4200-4000 BC laid the foundations of the Funnel Beaker Culture and for the neolithisation of the countries around the western Baltic. It is therefore probable that the ritual practice, which can be observed from the beginning of the Neolithic in South Scandinavia, originated in traditions in the preceding and contemporary Neolithic cultures on the Continent.

Notes

1. Here recalibrated with Calib ver. 7.1. (Reimer *et al.* 2013).
2. For inexplicable reasons R. Hernek (1989) uses Roman numbers in the type designations, and in his figs. 1 and 2 the drawings of the axes of types 1 and 3 have changed places.
3. After completion of the manuscript a paper was published about the coastal site at Syltholm on Lolland, where the finds possibly indicate that ritual depositions took place continuously from the Late Mesolithic to the Early Neolithic (Sørensen 2019).

5. Thin-butted axes

Thin-butted axes of flint

149 thin-butted flint axes have been registered with find-spots on Bornholm. Of these 122 are isolated finds, and 27 come from nine hoard finds with two or more axes (Finds list IV nos. 49-179). The National Museum has 18 and the Bornholm Museum has 60 of the individually found axes, while 44 are registered as being in private ownership. Of the hoards the National Museum owns four and the Bornholm Museum three, while two are in private ownership. There is information about the find-spots for all the axes included here, but the information for the older finds in particular is not very precise. Only nine of the individually found axes and two of the hoards have been localized with a site number in the *Fund og Fortidsminder* database. Many of the axes came to the Bornholm Museum more than a century ago as donations from farmers, and often they cannot be localized more accurately than to the farm in question. About 50 of the 122 individually found axes we have information on the reason for the find (table 5.1), from which we learn that 37 were field finds – that is, they appeared during work in the fields or from gathering on cultivated soil. The second most common reason for finds is the digging of ditches, in most cases drainage ditches on cultivated soil. For 72 of the 122 individually found axes (59%) there is no information on the reason for the find. Against a background of such scanty information one cannot describe a deposition pattern as general. But of 21 individually found axes we learn that they were found on wetland, while four axes were found by a large stone, and two axes were found close to a watercourse. Such information may provide clues to an interpretation of the circumstances of or reasons for the deposition of the axes, although it is unknown how large a proportion of the axes were in fact deposited at such places in the Neolithic.

Because of the imprecise localization of many of

Table 5.1. Finds circumstances of the types of individually found, thin-butted flint axes (Finds list IV nos. 49-170).

Find circumstance	I	I/II	II	II/IIIA	IIIA	IIIA/B	IIIB	IIIB/VI	VI	VI/VII	VII	Sum
Surface of cultivated field	2		6	1	18	3	3		2	1	1	37
Ditch digging, drainage			2	1	3		1	1		1		9
Construction work					3		1					4
Unspecified	11	1	10	4	34	2	2	3	4		1	72
Sum	**13**	**1**	**18**	**6**	**58**	**5**	**7**	**4**	**6**	**2**	**2**	**122**
In meadow, bog or depression	2		5		8		2	1	1		1	21
At large stone	1		1		2							4
At watercourse					1				1			2

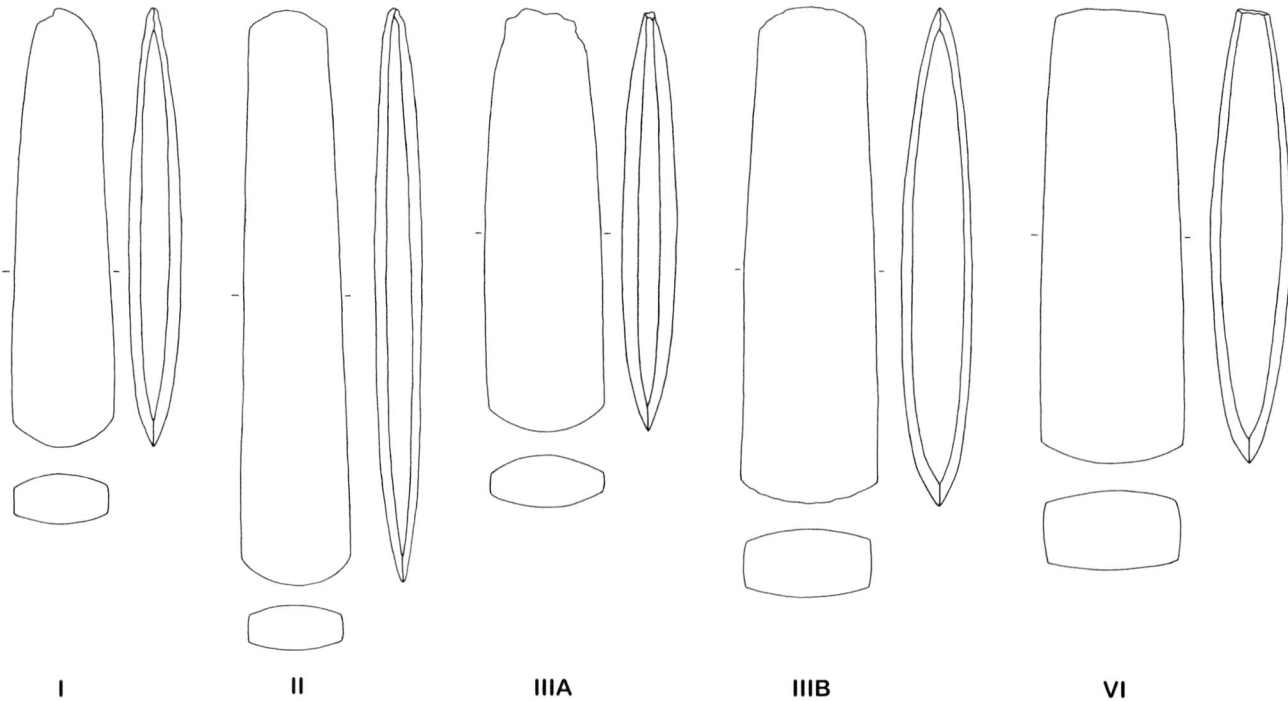

Fig. 5.1. Types of thin-butted flint axes from the Early Neolithic found on Bornholm.

the axes, the finds cannot be used for detailed studies of activities in terms of soil types, distance from settlement sites, etc.; the material must be used for less fine-meshed studies of activities in the various periods. However, these are also significant. As will be evident from the following, stray finds and hoards supplement and strengthen the picture of the occupation of the landscape and its development that is otherwise inferred from the location of the settlement sites.

The axe material discussed in the following is a selection determined by the reliability of the information we have about the find-spot, including approximate find-spots. But the possibility of type determination has of course also played a role, and we have therefore excluded some of the unpolished axes, which have been difficult to type. We have chosen to restrict ourselves to the thick-bladed axes of flint. The thin-bladed axes have not been included.

The thin-butted flint axes are divided into types following P.O. Nielsen 1977. On Bornholm types I, II, IIIA and IIIB, all dated to the EN, and type VI, dated to EN C – MN AI, as well as type VII, dated to MN AII, appear.[1] Here we discuss only the five types that fall wholly or partly within the Early Neolithic (fig. 5.1). It has been possible to type 104 of the 122 individually found axes (85%), while 18 axes could not be identified more closely than as one or the other of two types. They have been included in Finds list IV and on the distribution maps with the designations I/II, II/IIIA, IIIA/B and IIIB/VI. Several unpolished as well as resharpened and otherwise re-formed axes fall within this category.

Thin-butted flint axes of type I

Type I is the earliest of the thin-butted flint axes to appear on Zealand, in Scania and on Bornholm. But it is not the first quadrifacial form. That had already been introduced with type 3 of the pointed-butted flint axes. It is therefore relevant to look at how one distinguishes between pointed-butted flint axes of type 3 and thin-butted flint axes of type I. The butt width, which is measured 2 cm from the butt end, is around 3.5 cm for the pointed-butted axes of type 3. The narrow butt gives the pointed-butted axes a more wedge-shaped contour than the early thin-butted axes. Another difference can be seen in the cross-section of the axes. Because of the width of the narrow surfaces of the pointed-butted axes the cross-section is more rectangular than in the early thin-butted ones, which have more convex broad faces.

However, there are axes that borrow features from both types. The longest of the quadrifacial pointed-butted flint axes of type 3 has a butt width of 3.4 cm, but in design is otherwise very close to thin-butted axes of type I (fig. 4.6).

On the thin-butted axes the butt width is more than 4 cm, but this is not the only criterion for distinguishing the two types, as there are very great differences in the sizes of axes of type I. The large axes have a butt width of 4-5 cm, while on the smaller examples one often measures a butt width of less than 4 cm. In the hoard find from Stavehøl (fig. 5.2) three of the six thin-butted axes have a butt width of less than 4 cm. In the catalogue three axes (Finds list IV no. 46-48) are included whose butt width is 4 cm, and which can be regarded as an intermediate form between the pointed-butted axes of type 3 and the thin-butted axes of type I.

Compared with the other types of thin-butted flint axe, type I is characterized by a wider angle between the narrow surfaces, by its convex broad surfaces, its sharp butt and its often strongly curved edge. On the unpolished as well as some of the polished examples one can sometimes observe the way the concluding flaking of the axe body was done, not always ending with a fully quadrifacial form, because in the end the flint knapper only had two or three edge seams to flake from, alternately towards the broad surface and towards the narrow surface. In the hoard from Stavehøl the unpolished axe (fig. 5.2:1) only has seams along one broad surface, while they are absent from the other one, and on the partially polished axe (fig. 5.2:2) one sees only three seams. In the hoard from Bakkely one of the unpolished axes (fig. 5.3:4) only has seams along one broad surface, and this also applies to the unpolished, short axe (fig. 5.2:5). In the same hoard a bifacially knapped, unpolished axe (fig. 5.3:7) is a preform for a thin-butted axe of type I, whose narrow surfaces will only appear with the grinding and polishing of the axe. Bifacial preforms are not unknown in Scania, where such a piece appears for example in the hoard from Krågeholm together with axes of type I, and where there is also a bifacially flaked preform for a thin-bladed axe (Rydbeck 1918, 16 f. fig. 17a-b; Nielsen 1977, 122 no. 29). These early hoards with thin-butted axes of type I contain polished and unpolished axes with great variations in form. In the deposition from Bakkely for example, axes appear which could formally be classified as thin-butted axes of types I, II and III. This may be an indication that we are looking at an early phase in the production of thin-butted axes, where no fixed formal criteria have yet been established, and where there is still experimentation with the forming of the broad quadrifacial axes.

Thirteen isolated finds (Finds list IV nos. 49-61) and two hoards (nos. 174, 176) have been registered with a total of 23 thin-butted flint axes of type I on Bornholm, and their find-spots are shown in fig. 5.6. Most Bornholm axes of this type are small. The length of axes that have not been re-formed or resharpened varies between 15.4 and 35.8 cm with an average of 22 cm. The longest of the axes measures 35.8 cm and was found at Gammeltoftegård in Østermarie in the soil beside a large stone (Finds list IV no. 50). About the hoard find from Stavehøl (fig. 5.2) the finder states that at a depth of c. 40 cm there was a rectangular frame of small stones covered with two thin slabs like a cist. Inside it the six axes lay so that they formed a star-shaped figure with the blades outward. The find is significant, since it more than suggests a ritual or magical action in connection with the deposition of the axes. There are other hoards in Denmark and Scania where the axes have been observed carefully stacked, crossed over one another or placed in extension of one another (Rech 1979, 15), but the find from Stavehøl is one of those that makes the strongest impression. The same can be said of the deposition with two thin-bladed flint axes from Hallegård in Nyker (fig. 5.4, Finds list IV no. 180), where the axes stood vertically beside one another, also inside a stone cist. There need not be a long time interval between the two finds, as the thin-bladed flint axes, both of type b1 (Nielsen 1977, 113), because of the technical and formal similarities to large, thin-butted flint axes of type I-IIIA, should probably be dated to EN A2 – EN B. The second hoard with thin-butted flint axes of type I from Bakkely (fig. 5.3) was found in a rock fissure like the hoard with pointed-butted axes from Ravnekær (fig. 4.4).

Fragments of thin-butted flint axes do not appear at settlement sites which only have material from EN AI, which means that axes of type I must be later. At the settlement Vallensgård I a large fragment of a polished axe of type I or II with convex broad surfaces (fig. 2.10:1) was found, but it is from the cultural layer that contained finds from both EN A2 and EN B. At the settlement Havnelev, eastern Zealand (excavations 1922 and 1933), several identifiable fragments of type I occur together with funnel beakers of types II and III (Nielsen 1994, 299, Taf. 8:1-2, Taf. 12:1,3). The finds from Havnelev (1922) have been dated to the

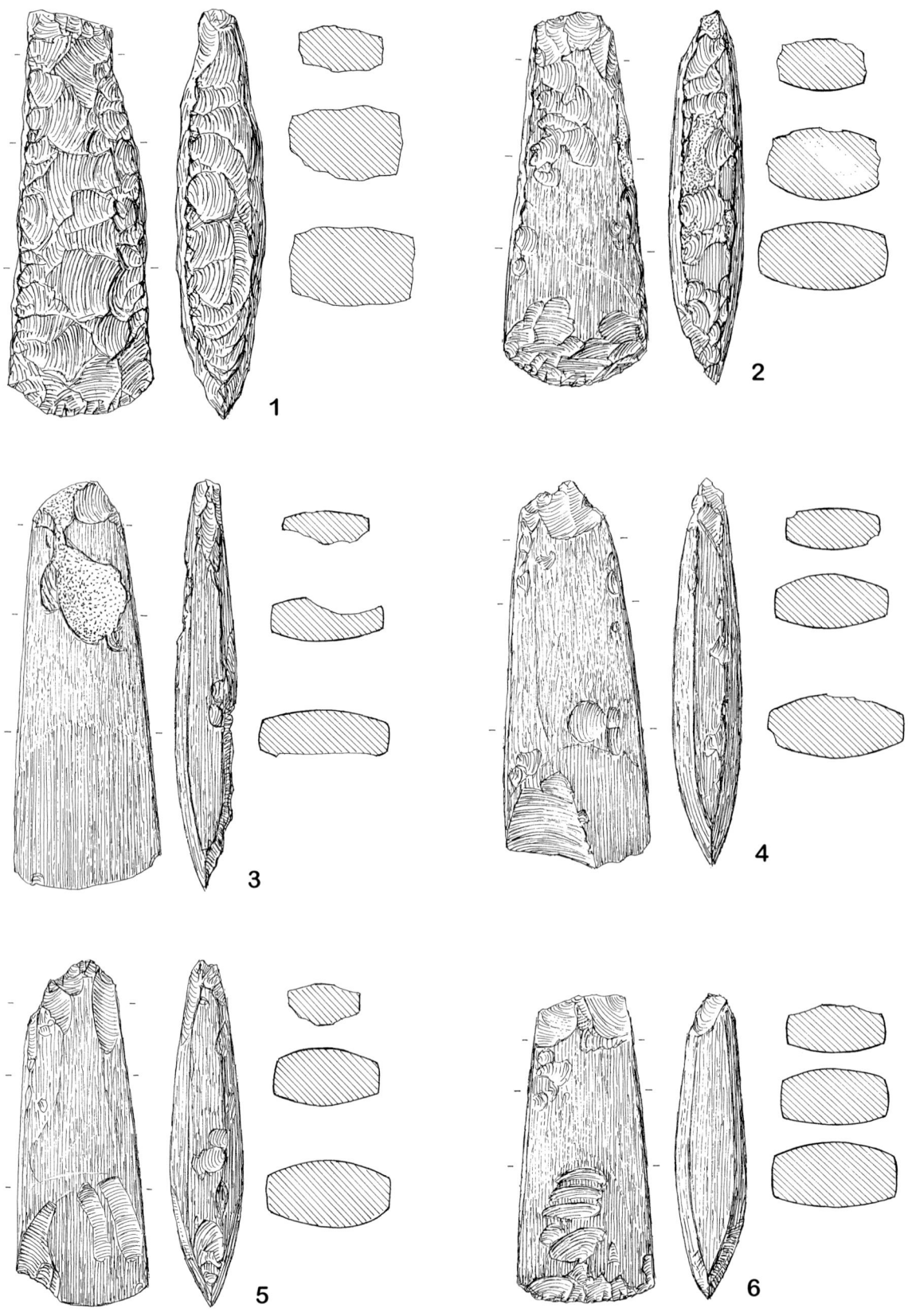

Fig. 5.2. Hoard from Stavehøl, Østerlars (Finds list IV no. 174). H. Ørsnes del. 2:5.

middle of EN I, and this is supported by an AMS ^{14}C dating to 4978±37 BP (Gron *et al.* 2016, 249), a dating that corresponds best to EN A2 on Bornholm.

At Almhov in southwestern Scania remains of Early Neolithic long barrows have been excavated. In connection with long barrow 1 two intact, very similar thin-butted axes have been found with the much-rounded blades characteristic of axes of type I (Gidlöf et al. 2006, 35, fig. 20a; cf. Rudebeck 2010, 174). Long barrow I has been ^{14}C-dated from a fragment of grain to 4990±70 BP, calibrated 3940-3660 BC (1σ), 3950-3650 BC (2σ) (Ua-17158). At 1σ there is a 70.7% probability that the dating lies within the interval 3808-3695 BC. With this interpretation of the dating result, Long barrow 1 becomes one of the earliest features of this type in Scandinavia. However, there is the possibility that the dating of such a small specimen reflects earlier activities in the settlement area. With this cautious reservation the dating in fact accords well with the occurrence of this axe type in other contexts, including possible grave finds (see discussion p. 123).

Thin-butted flint axes of type II

This type shares several characteristics with type I; there is also a single example of an axe that cannot be identified with certainty as belonging to type I or II (Finds list IV no. 62). Common to the two types are the sharp butt, the strongly curved edge and the convex broad surfaces. But the contour is different, since type II has almost parallel, straight sides. One can therefore view this type as a long version of type I or a transitional form between type I and type IIIA. Several of the unpolished axes, however, have been flaked with the same technique often used to make axes of type I, where the flaking of broad and narrow surfaces is concluded by flaking from only two or three edge seams, often leaving only two seams either at the same side or diametrically opposite when the axe is seen in cross-section.

On Bornholm 18 isolated finds of type II have been registered (Finds list IV nos. 63-80), including several long examples (fig. 5.5). Eleven of the axes, which have not been resharpened or re-formed in other ways, are between 26.6 and 36 cm long with an average of 31.8 cm. With such lengths and a maximum width around 7 cm one may well ask whether axes of type II were really intended for working with as ordinary tools. Some of the axes, which are resharpened and 16-20 cm long, must have been used, while the long axes show no signs of use. Along with some of the large axes of type IIIA they are among the most complete and beautifully formed of all the thin-butted flint axes.

There are five hoard finds with thin-butted flint axes of type II (Finds list IV nos. 175-179). In the hoard from Bakkely a polished and resharpened axe of type II appears together with several axes of type I (fig. 5.3:2). As mentioned, the axes were found together in a rock fissure where they were covered with a layer of stones. In each of the four depositions at Vallensgård, all of which were found on wetland, there are two axes of type II, although in two cases one of the two axes has been identified as type I/II. The eight axes have a length between 24 and 37 cm, with an average of 30.4 cm.

The distribution of axes of type II is shown in fig. 5.6 together with the distribution of type I. While type I axes have mainly been found in the northern and eastern part of the island, type II has a more scattered distribution. Axes with a length of 30 cm and more are also evenly distributed, but with a particular concentration in the middle of the island, where two long axes of type II have been found within a short distance of the four depositions near Vallensgård I. We only have information on the find circumstances for a few of the individually found axes of type II. About three of the 11 longest axes it is said that they were found either in a bog or a meadow, and one was found by a large stone. Despite the meagre find information it is reasonable to assume that at least the intact axes of type II are part of the same deposition pattern as the hoard finds. The deposition of these axes individually or several together may have been the ritual ending of their circulation as prestige objects, or they were meant to be used as ceremonial axes from the beginning.

Thin-butted flint axes of type II are like type I widespread on Zealand, in Scania and on Bornholm. But there are no closed finds with other objects that give us a dating of this type. The common features it shares with type I mean that both types must be assigned to an early stage of the production of thin-butted flint axes.

Thin-butted flint axes of type IIIA

Axes of type II and IIIA come close to each other in terms of design. Six axes cannot be identified more precisely than as type II/IIIA: four of these are resharpened (Finds list IV nos. 81-86). One of the differences between the two types is that type IIIA has

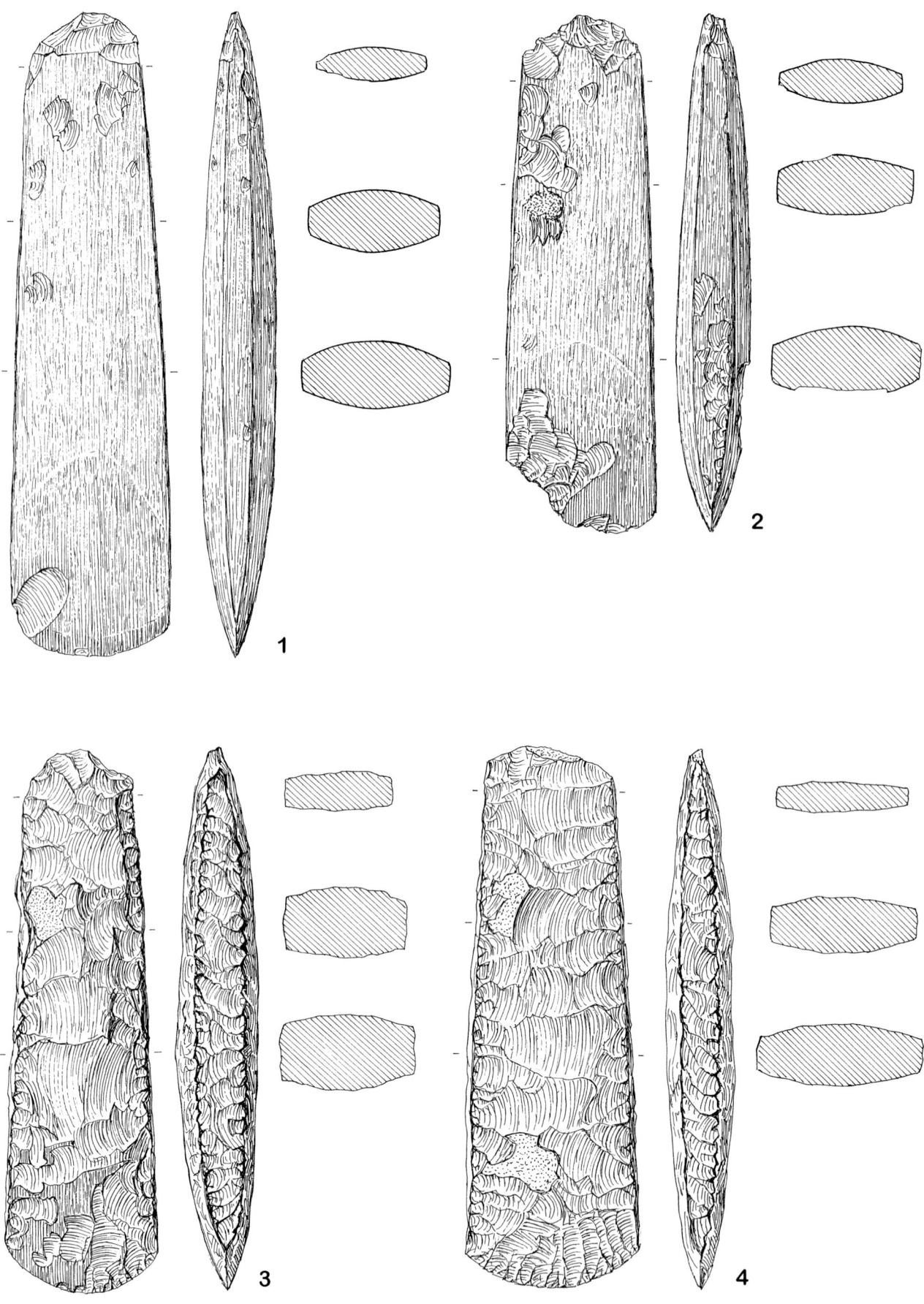

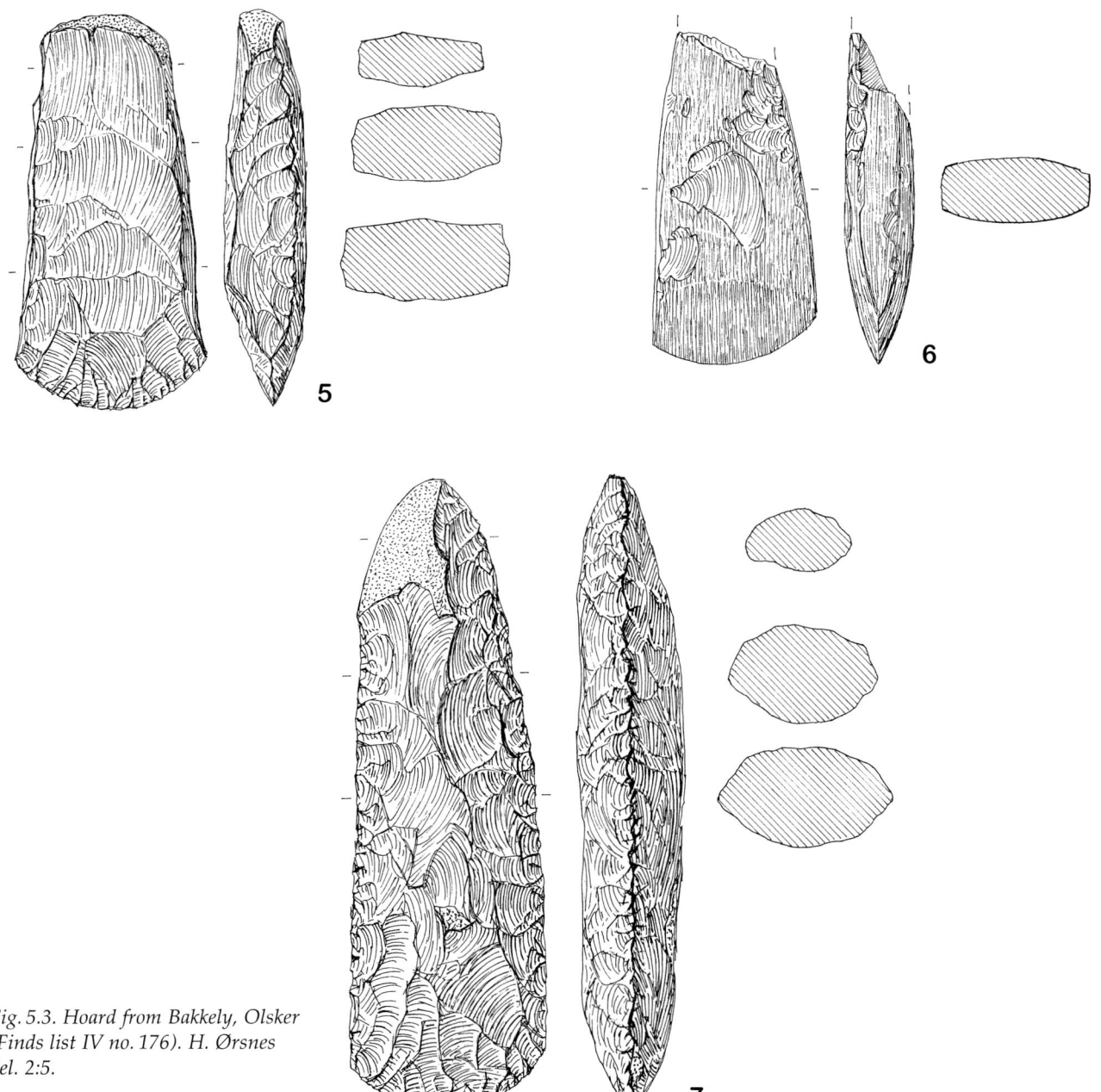

Fig. 5.3. Hoard from Bakkely, Olsker (Finds list IV no. 176). H. Ørsnes del. 2:5.

greater width and often the greatest width is not measured at the blade but in the middle of the axe, so the narrow surfaces become slightly convex (fig. 5.7). The convexity of the broad surfaces is not so marked, and the blade is not as rounded as on axes of type II. One can see on the unpolished axes of type IIIA that they have been formed with the true quadrifacial technique with flaking from all four edge seams.

58 axes of type IIIA have been registered, making it the most frequently occurring type of thin-butted axe on Bornholm (Finds list IV nos. 87-144). In 23 examples which are not resharpened or re-formed in any other way, the length varies between 18.8 and 44 cm, with an average of 28.4 cm. The two longest axes are of 40.5 and 44 cm respectively and are both isolated finds. But otherwise the majority of the axes are of moderate length. Thirteen of the 23 unmodified axes are between 23 and 29 cm long.

Axes of type IIIA appear in two hoard finds (Finds list IV nos. 171-172). The hoard from Almindingen comprises two polished axes, both with a length of 36.6 cm.[1] The deposition from Bredsensgård in Olsker also contains two axes, this time unpolished and being 33.4 and 34.5 cm long, one only identified as type IIIA/B. The latter deposition was found at the edge of a small bog pool.

Fig. 5.4. Two thin-bladed, thin-butted flint axes found in 1869 at Hallegård, Nyker (Finds list IV no.180). The axes were placed upright beside one another in a small stone coffin, which was filled with ash and charcoal. Photo John Lee, the National Museum. 2:5.

For the individually found axes there is very little information on the topography at the find-spot, but eight axes, six of them without resharpening or other re-forming, have been found on wetland, and one was found in the soil by a large stone.

Axes of type IIIA are spread over most of the island (fig. 5.8). Axes with a length of 30 cm and above are not distributed evenly: five are from northern Bornholm, while two are from the southern and two from the eastern part of the island. Fragments of the type have been found at a few of the settlements, and an almost intact example – but broken in two – identified as type I/IIIA, was found at the settlement in Smedegade, Klemensker (fig. 3.38). At this settlement, though, there had been human presence in several periods of the Early Neolithic, and the axe cannot with certainty be assigned to one of these periods.

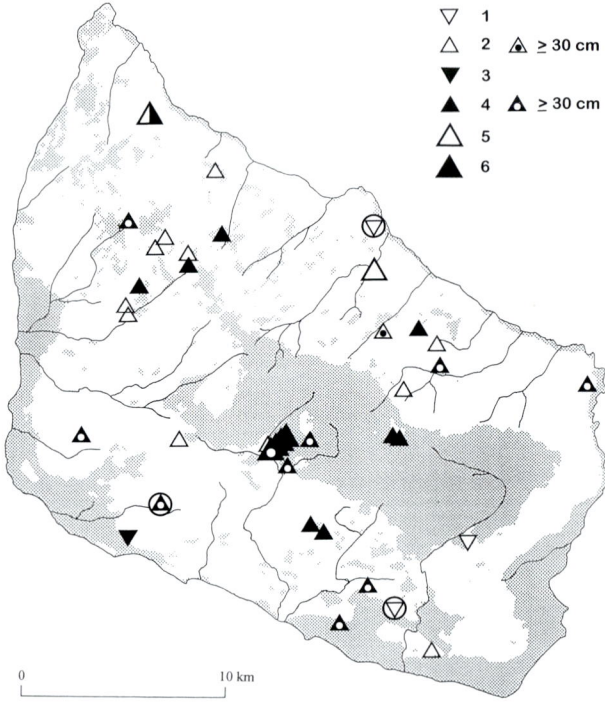

Fig. 5.5. Thin-butted flint axe of type II from St. Knudegård, Klemensker (Finds list IV no. 80). H. Ørsnes del. 2:5.

Fig. 5.6. The distribution of thin-butted flint axes of types I and II. (1) Axes with a butt width of 4 cm. (2) Type I. (3) Type I/II. (4) Type II. (5) Hoards containing axes of type I. (6) Hoards containing axes of type II. Approximate finds location indicated with a circle.

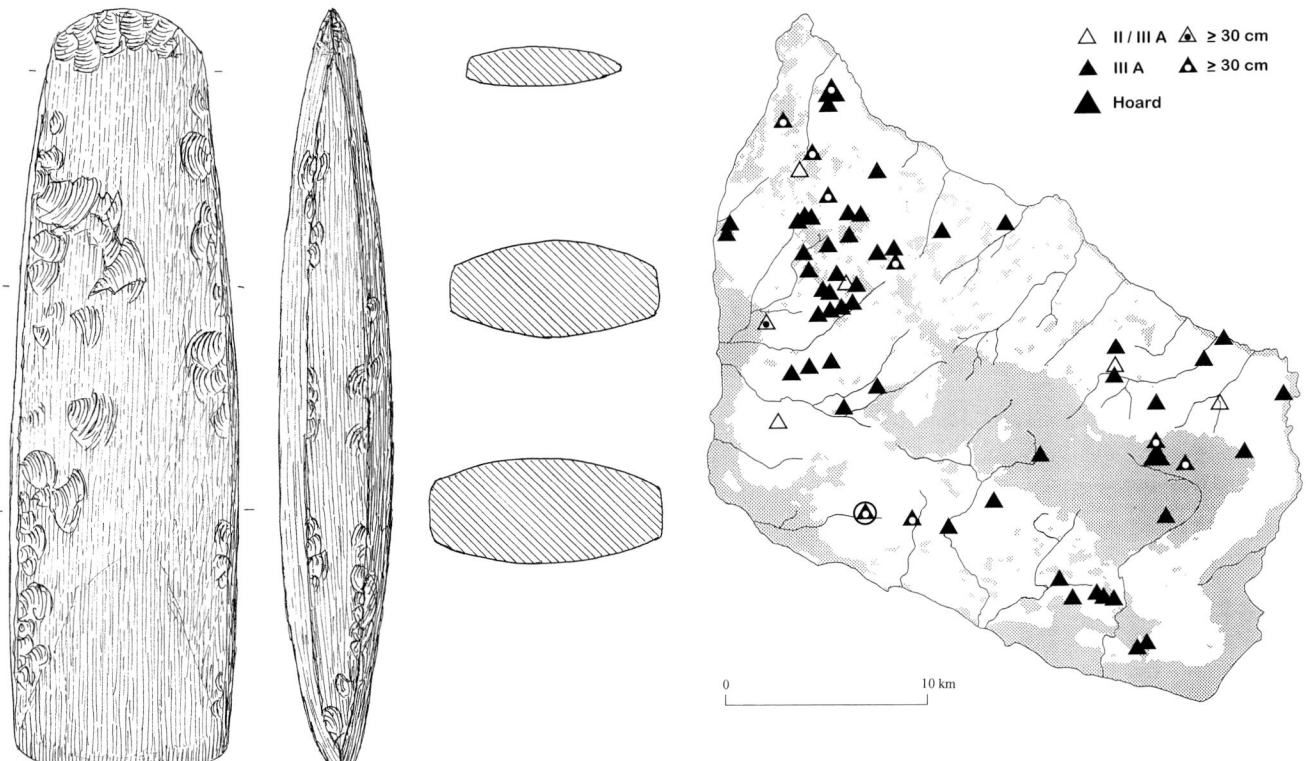

Fig. 5.7 Thin-butted flint axe of type IIIA from Steensgård, Vestermarie (Finds list IV no. 88). H. Ørsnes del. 2:5.

Fig. 5.8. The distribution of thin-butted flint axes of type II/IIIA and IIIA. Approximate finds location is indicated with a circle.

During the excavation of an extensive culture layer at the multi-phase settlement Ndr. Grødbygård a large fragment of the butt of an axe of this type was found (fig. 3.29:2). Nor do axes of type IIIA appear at other Bornholm settlements in any certain context. The type must therefore be dated by looking at its occurrence in other contexts.

Thin-butted flint axes of type IIIA, like the two preceding types, have their main distribution in the east of South Scandinavia (Nielsen 1977, 77, figs. 12 and 37). Unlike the contemporary type IV, which is most widespread in western Denmark, thin-butted flint axes of type IIIA only appear rarely in grave finds. This may be due to a conscious rejection of flint axes as grave goods, as in EN II, since in eastern Denmark flint axes are hardly ever found in the older dolmen chambers (Nielsen 1977, 107). But it may also be because the grave type that was used at the same time as the production and circulation of axes of type IIIA has not so often been found and excavated in the east of South Scandinavia. Type IIIA does appear however in a few grave finds such as the Early Neolithic inhumation grave at Forum in SW Jutland (Johansen 1917, 131-35, fig. 2; Glob 1952, no. 115) and in one of the graves in the Early Neolithic long barrow Højensvej Høj 7 on SE Funen (Beck 2013, fig. 10). Three AMS ^{14}C datings of charcoal from the east façade of this long barrow fall within the interval 3700-3500 BC (*idem*, 52).

Type IIIA, which is the type of thin-butted flint axe most often found on Bornholm, has been dated to EN B, which is also the period of Bornholm's Early Neolithic to which the largest number of settlement sites can be assigned.

Thin-butted flint axes of type IIIB

There was probably a gradual transition from thin-butted flint axes of type IIIA to type IIIB. At all events, five axes cannot be classified more precisely than to type IIIA/B (Finds list IV nos. 145-149). Type IIIB differs otherwise from type IIIA in having broader narrow surfaces, with the result that the broad surfaces are less convex. The butts of axes of type IIIB are rounded as on many axes of type IIIA, but at the same time they have been made sharper, so viewed from the side the axes have a lanceolate appearance.

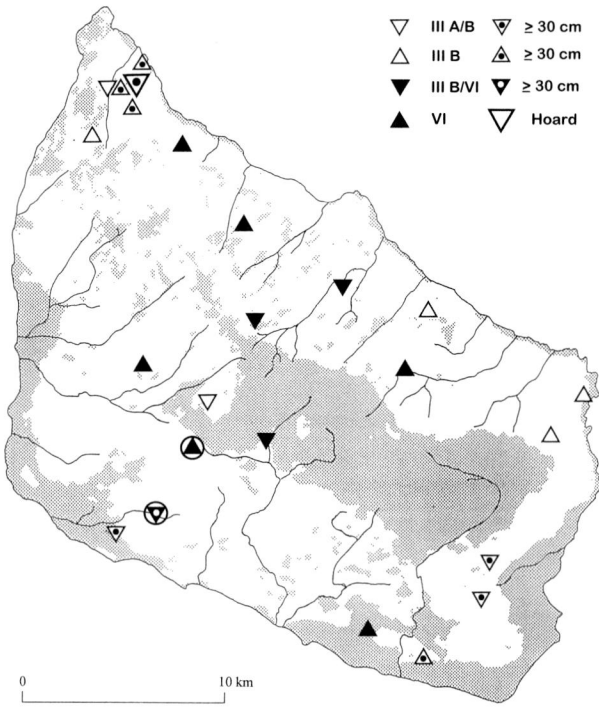

Fig. 5.9. The distribution of thin-butted flint axes of types IIIA/B, IIIB, IIIB/VI and VI. Approximate finds location is indicated with a circle.

Eight axes of this type have been found on Bornholm (Finds list IV nos. 150-156). Four of the axes are unpolished and three only partially polished, and one has a damaged and repaired blade which has not been repolished. The length varies between 23.9 cm and 32 cm, with an average of 29 cm. Two of the axes have been found in a bog and one during the digging of a well c. 1.26 m deep in the ground. Another was found buried close to a rock with a rock carving (Finds list IV no. 151a), and in the same place at a higher level a partially polished thin-butted flint axe of type VII (no. 169) was found. Some points in the landscape must have preserved their special meaning over a long period. In the deposition from Bredsensgård in Olsker (Finds list IV no. 173) a 34.5 cm long axe identified as type IIIA/B was found, while there are no hoards with axes of type IIIB.

The distribution of this type is striking, as the axes have been found either in the north-westernmost or the eastern part of the island (fig. 5.9). Of the five axes identified as type IIIA/B, three were also found within these two separate areas, while two of them are from the area in between, from Nylars and Vestermarie. Striking too is the distribution of axes with a length of 30 cm or more. If we compare the axes identified as type IIIA/B and type IIIB, with a single exception they were found partly in the northwestern part of the island and partly farthest to the south east. This suggests a polarisation reinforced by the fact that most axes of type VI have been found between these two areas (fig. 5.9).

Type IIIB cannot be dated by means of the settlement finds, so as with type IIIA we must turn our attention to other areas to find reference points for a dating. Unpolished examples of type IIIB have been found at the foot of the kerbstones of two long dolmens on two of the islands south of Zealand, Bogø and Møn (Nielsen 1977, 103 f., figs. 45-46). This tells us that we have passed the point in time for the building of the early dolmens with closed chambers and we are thus in EN II (EN C).

Thin-butted flint axes of type VI

Five axes from four finds could not be classified more precisely than to type IIIB/VI (Finds list IV nos. 157-160). Type VI, like type IIIB, has broad narrow surfaces but differs from the latter type in that the butt is not sharp but blunt and it is not rounded but straight or slightly curved. The corners of the blade may be slightly flared. Large examples of type VI are often broad, thick and heavy. Only a few axes of this type are longer than 30 cm. While the preceding types are almost always made of the clear Senonian flint, axes of type VI were also made of the matt, tough Danian flint.

Six axes of type VI have been found on Bornholm (Finds list IV nos. 161-166), two of them unpolished, while three have been re-formed and one is only a fragment. The lengths of the two unpolished examples are 17.8 and 29 cm. Of one of the axes we are told that it is from a wetland area, while another was gathered by a watercourse. There are no hoards with axes of this type, but the hoard from Blæsbjerggård in Nyker (Finds list IV no. 171) contained two axes that cannot be classified more accurately than to type VI/VII. They are said to have been found deep in the soil by a large stone.

The distribution of type VI on Bornholm is just as striking as that of axes of type IIIB (and IIIA/B), since their find-spots fill the gap in the middle of the island between the northwestern and the southeastern distribution of type IIIB. Axes identified as type IIIB/VI have the same distribution (fig. 5.9).

Type VI cannot be dated with reference to the

Bornholm settlements from the EN and must be dated on the basis of its occurrence in burial and settlement sites in the rest of Denmark, where it is the type of thin-butted flint axe that is most widely distributed. It appears there in inhumation graves and closed as well as open dolmens such as Skavange and Gerum in Vendsyssel (Kjærum 1971, fig. 5; Ebbesen 2009, fig. 536:4), while it has not been reliably demonstrated in finds from passage graves (Nielsen 1977, 106 f.; Ebbesen 2011, 318 f.). Among the finds from the causewayed enclosure at Sarup on Funen, type VI has been demonstrated in 43 cases in the Early and Middle Neolithic phases Sarup I-III and it almost occurs as the only type at Sarup I, which is dated to EN II (EN C) (Andersen 1999, 201 f.). On this basis type VI must be dated to EN II (EN C) – MN AIa. It is followed by type VII (Blandebjerg type), which has been dated to MN AII.

The early production of thin-butted flint axes

In the preceding sections a dating of the various types of thin-butted flint axes has been proposed, and it is argued that type I is the oldest. With some individually found axes it can be hard to determine whether they belong to the quadrifacial, pointed-butted type 3 or the thin-butted type I, and in the catalogue three axes are included with a butt width of 4 cm as intermediate forms (Finds list IV nos. 46-48). There are some indications that the thin-butted flint axe arose as a further development of the quadrifacial pointed-butted axe. Nevertheless with the thin-butted axe a new concept was introduced in terms of both form and size. It is therefore relevant to look at the early occurrences of the thin-butted forms in a wider geographical context.

Thin-butted flint axes of type I are widespread in Zealand, in Scania and on Bornholm, where they appear as isolated finds and in hoards. During the first mapping of the distribution of the type only a few examples could be localized on Funen and in Jutland (Nielsen 1977, fig. 7). This might indicate that there were no significant imports of this axe type from the eastern areas to western Denmark, or that there was not the same practice there with depositions. It is hard to imagine, though, that thin-butted flint axes were not made and used in Jutland and on Funen at the same time as the production of type I began on Zealand and in Scania. But they may have been designed in a different way. If one reviews the settlement finds, fragments of axes do occur with a wide angle between the narrow surfaces and convex broad surfaces as on axes of type I, for example in the settlement material from Stengade 'house II' on Langeland (Skaarup 1975, Abb. 46:1, 6-7). The pottery from this settlement includes the same forms and decorative elements as in the first excavated settlement pit at Havnelev (1922, cf. P.O. Nielsen 1994). In eastern Jutland north of Aarhus, where a substantial body of settlement material from the Early Neolithic has emerged, in pit A2242 at Lisbjerg Skole, together with pottery in the Volling style, several axe fragments were found, some of which could be classed as quadrifacial pointed-butted and others as thin-butted of types I and IV (Skousen 2008, 134 f., 105 and note 123). In his review of the finds from the Early Neolithic layers in the kitchenmiddens at Norsminde and Bjørnsholm, S.H. Andersen noted the presence of fragments of thin-butted flint axes of type IV, but in both places "possibly also type I" (Andersen 1991, 31 and fig. 18; 1993, 85). M. Stafford depicts an axe from Norsminde which is designated as pointed-butted, but which is rather a resharpened, thin-butted flint axe of type I (Stafford 1999, fig. 5.29, right). T. Madsen, who has registered Neolithic axes from 43 parishes, an area of 640 km² around and north of Horsens Fjord in eastern Jutland, lists 17 fragments and intact axes of type I, in most cases found in areas around the fjord. At the same time he points out the difficulty of distinguishing safely between fragments of type I and type IV (T. Madsen, pers. comm.).

One of two Early Neolithic grave finds from Sejlflod in northern Jutland (grave PY) contained two thin-butted axes which can be identified on the basis of the narrow surface as belonging to type I, but which lack the curved cutting edge and the convex broad surfaces. Both axes could therefore be a transitional form between type I and type IV. The axes were found together with five transverse arrowheads, two blades and a flake (J.N. Nielsen 2000, I 146, II 123). Two ^{14}C datings of samples taken from a post-hole east of the graves give the following ages: (K-4071) 4850±90 BP, calibrated 3759-3521 BC (1σ), 3909-3374 BC (2σ), and (K-4070) 4800±90 BP, calibrated 3661-3382 BC (1σ), 3762-3369 BC (2σ).[2] The second grave at Sejlflod (AS) contained an axe of a similar form, which was found together with a collared flask with a hollow collar, amber beads and a piece of copper (J.N. Nielsen 2000, I 51, II 37; Klassen 2000, 84, Taf. 29; 2004, 196).

It is therefore probable that there was an early production of thin-butted flint axes in western Denmark too, and that these axes partly had the same characteristics as axes of type I. Type IV of the thin-butted flint axes thus need not be the oldest type in Jutland, as assumed by R. Hernek (1989, 221) and L. Klassen (2004, 210). But it was not until type IV, which was entirely or partly contemporary with type IIIA,[3] that major production began with a centre in northern Jutland, where type IV shows a high find frequency as isolated finds as well as in hoards and grave finds (Nielsen 1977, 77 f., fig. 16A). Type IV has been well dated on the basis of the grave finds to the interval c. 3700-3500 BC (Sørensen 2014, fig. V.135) and cannot, as L. Klassen thinks, have been the model for the first production of thin-butted flint axes in Scania and on Zealand (Klassen 2004, 211). For one thing it is too young, for another there are in terms of both technique and design too great differences between this type and axes of types I-II.

Thin-butted flint axes of type IIIA and IV were always made with the true quadrifacial technique – that is, they were made with an indirect flaking technique alternately against the broad surface and against the narrow surface, so that four characteristic zig-zag seams appeared. The mastery of this technique was the precondition for making the long, perfect 'ceremonial' axes of types IIIA and IV. The axes of type I and to some extent of type II represent a preliminary stage on the way towards the true quadrifacial technique, and they must therefore be regarded as belonging to the incipient production of thin-butted flint axes.

In the hoards with thin-butted flint axes of type I on Zealand, in Scania and on Bornholm one can observe how the flintworker struggled to make large axes with the quadrifacial technique, but did not always succeed, as can be seen in the hoards from Stavehøl and Bakkely on Bornholm (fig. 5.2 and 5.3) and in the deposition from Bjergby Mose on Zealand (Nielsen 1977, fig. 34). These hoards include unpolished examples whose formation was concluded with only two seams, and one even finds bifacially flaked preforms, as we saw in the hoard find from Bakkely (fig. 5.3:7). The quadrifacial form in the case of these preforms had to be accomplished with intensive grinding and polishing of the narrow surfaces.

In the bifacial preforms Lutz Klassen sees an independent type corresponding to Sophus Müller's 'broad-butted' axes (Müller 1888, no. 53), and believes that they represent a version of the western European thin-butted flint axe, which is bifacially flaked (Klassen 2004, 215). It is not improbable that there may have been contacts between the British Isles and South Scandinavia, through which knowledge of the production of flint axes may have been passed on in both directions, since thin-butted axes arose and developed in both places about the same time. But in South Scandinavia no thin-butted flint axes of the English type have yet been demonstrated, just as it is uncertain whether reliable finds have been made in the British Isles of thin-butted flint axes of Scandinavian origin (Pitts 1996, 336). It is therefore more probable that all 'wide-butted' flint axes from Denmark and Scania are unground preforms for quadrifacial, thin-butted flint axes of the Nordic type.

Like other researchers before him, Klassen discussed the issue of how the thin-butted flint axe arose as a form, and he pointed to the possibility that quadrifacial axe blades of copper may have inspired the production of quadrifacial axes of flint (Klassen 2004, 210-15). L. Sørensen shows the diffusion of quadrifacial axes of copper and flint over a large area between South Scandinavia and the Balkans which may support such an assumption (Sørensen 2014, 175, fig. V.136). It may be that knowledge of quadrifacial axes in other materials from other places influenced the formation of the thin-butted flint axes, but it is also a possibility that the inspiration and the urge to work in the quadrifacial form should primarily be sought on both sides of Øresund, on Zealand and in Scania, to which one can localize the most extensive production of early thin-butted flint axes.

The places where the raw materials for the axe production were extracted, whether jade, flint or other stone, must be regarded as centres of innovation and development with regard to the design and size of the axes. So too with the Øresund area, which was the area in South Scandinavia where the flint that was suitable for axe production was most easily accessible in the largest quantities. We have noted earlier that the reason for the early establishment of many agrarian settlements in Scania could have been access to flint and the possibility of working up a production of flint axes that could meet the need for axes as useful tools. But the farmers who immigrated here from the Continent were also aware of the benefits of possessing axes of unusual size and quality. The efforts to produce record-long axes began in South Scandinavia in the early phases of the Neolithic, and they were encouraged by access to usable flint. With the thin-butted flint axes of type II there were already axes with a length up to over 40 cm, which may not have been intended for practical use, but which were applicable for ceremonial use because of their excellent manufacture. With the later production of types IIIA and IV axes were made up to half a metre in length. The longest thin-butted flint axe to be found in Denmark is of type IV and measures 50.5 cm.[4] This corresponds to the dimensions that were achieved with the longest of the jade axes in western Europe. In South Scandinavia the production of oversized axes reached a high point around 3700-3500 BC, a half to a whole millennium later than in western Europe, but in both places the phenomenon was associated with a particular stage in the development of society when the possession of prestigious objects such as axes of exotic foreign stone types and long axes of jade or flint was important for the attainment of status and power. Viewed in that light, the axe production of which the early thin-butted flint axes formed a part must have arisen and developed to meet both practical needs and the need for objects associated with high prestige.

Variation in the size and quantity of thin-butted flint axes

We can get an impression of the size of the thin-butted flint axes and of possible functional differences by looking at the unused polished and unpolished axes. Table 5.2 shows the number and length of 72 intact axes that have not been much resharpened or otherwise re-formed. Both the individually found axes and axes from the hoards are included, and they make up around half (48%) of all registered thin-

Table 5.2. Length variation of complete, polished and unpolished flint axes from Bornholm.

Length in cm	P – polished, U – unpolished									
14-16	P									P
16-18	PPU								U	P
18-20					PU	P				
20-22	U								U	PU
22-24					PU	U				
24-26	P	P			PPPP UU					
26-28			P		PPP		PP			
28-30	P	P	PUU	P	PP		PU		U	
30-32			PPPU		P	PU	UU			
32-34			PPP		PPU	U	P			
34-36	P		PPP			U				
36-38			PP		PPP			P		
38-40										
40-42					P					
42-44					P					
44-46										
Type	I	I/II	II	II/IIIA	IIIA	IIIA/B	IIIB	IIIB/VI	VI	VI/VII

butted flint axes from Bornholm. At the same time it is indicated whether the axes are polished (P), including those with partial polishing, or unpolished (U). It should be possible to see from this how the axes looked when they were introduced to the island.

Most polished and unpolished axes of type I are short, but one also sees long, polished axes up to 36 cm in length. The intact axes of type II, which are contemporary with type I and only differ from it in their smaller narrow-surface angle and greater length, are all between 26 and 38 cm long. The longest examples, 30 cm and longer, are all polished. Of type IIIA there are 25 intact axes, which is the largest number, and half of these are between 22 and 28 cm long. Most of the long axes belong to this type, and the longest that are over 34 cm are all polished. After this the number of intact axes thins out, and there are only a few long axes of types IIIB and VI. Among the safely identified axes of type VI there are no long axes. Most long axes in other words occur among the axes of types II and IIIA.

Can one regard the axe production of the Early Neolithic as a specialised craft? Against the background of modern experiments with the making of flint axes several scholars incline to the view that there was no full-time or part-time specialisation, but that in areas with access to flint this was a widespread occupation in which everyone participated more or less directly. The making of preforms for flint axes before polishing would not have been a long process for experienced flint workers (Hansen & Madsen 1983, 58; B. Madsen 1984; Olausson 1983a-b; 1997; 2000). There is no doubt, however, that the long axes up to 40 cm in length that were made in EN A2 and EN B would have required a particularly expert technique that would not have been mastered by everyone. There may have been particularly able flint workers who were held in high esteem for creating masterpieces in flint. Lars Larsson has suggested on the basis of the great uniformity of the axe production that it was in fact specialists who were responsible for the production of axes, and that they also had a special status in society, among other reasons because they performed some of the rituals that involved axes (L. Larsson 2011a, 212). Jan Apel, who works with the social organisation behind the production of the Nordic flint daggers, goes even further and thinks that there was a specialised craft that was organised in fraternities in a way that corresponded to the guilds of the Middle Ages, which in the same way took care of the training and social welfare of their members (2001, 125 f.). The existence of such social networks might be one of the explanations of the original acceptance of social hierarchization (*idem*). The producers of the Early Neolithic flint axes would have been in a very similar situation to the flint workers who in the Late Neolithic and Early Bronze Age made flint daggers, and they may have been organised in a similar way if we accept Apel's model. Common to the thin-butted flint axes and the pressure-flaked flint daggers is the very high degree of standardization that makes it possible for us to distinguish between the various types and note their wide distribution. There are very few poor imitations. This suggests that the production was organised and kept within certain circles of craftsmen who passed on their knowledge of the material and of the manufacturing technique to a narrow circle of apprentices.

Can we determine when we are dealing with axes for practical use and when they are ceremonial axes whose function and meaning were associated more with the social and religious sphere? Did several categories of axes exist with different functions – as ordinary axes, axes used to pay bride price, and ceremonial axes like those used by the natives of central New Guinea (Strathern 1970; Højlund 1979)? – Deborah Olausson, who has worked most thoroughly with the issue of the function of the thin-butted flint axes, noted that axes over 28 cm in length are at the same time axes of the best flint quality and made with the finest manufacturing technique (Olausson 1983a, 20 f.). But she also investigated traces of use and found them on the blades of even the longest of the axes (*idem*, 30). From experiments with the use of axes she inferred that one could work with axes up to 30 cm in length, although some of them broke, perhaps because of incorrect helving or use (*idem*, 63). She concluded that there was no reason to consider the long axes functionally less useful and thus no reason either to consider that they belonged to a special class of axes for ceremonial or other non-practical use. However, no chopping experiments were performed with axes over 30 cm in length. Olausson's investigation was conducted at a time when there was a strong focus on experimental archaeology and especially imitative experiments with flint knapping, and it has many important observations and reflections about technological aspects. But the aim was not to deal with the axes in terms of their archaeological context and the social context in which they were involved, which is what we will be trying to do here.

So let us first look at the contexts in which the axes were found. During the discussion of the various types of thin-butted flint axes a number of cases have been mentioned where we may assume that they were ritual depositions, given the find-spot and the relative positioning of the axes. The first condition for interpreting the finds as ritual depositions is that they are definitive depositions of objects, which have not been hidden in places from where they were easily retrieved, and which have not been scrapped. Bogs or low-lying places where there may once have been water basins could be places where single axes or hoards were definitively deposited, especially if repeated depositions took place at such places. With axes found on dry land, however, there is also the possibility that the objects were hidden and buried in a place from which they could be retrieved. In the 'life cycle' of a flint axe there may have been many stations where the axe spent some time before it came to play a role as a gift in an exchange relationship or in a sacrificial ceremony.

Of the 122 individually found, thin-butted flint axes registered on Bornholm, there is only detailed information on the find-spots of 27 axes, but 21 of these were found on wetland, while two were found by watercourses (table 5.1). Of the nine hoards with thin-butted flint axes from Bornholm five were found on wetland, including the four depositions in Brødreengen at Vallensgård.

The next thing one might expect of this putative ritual practice is that such depositions have been observed repeatedly, so they reflect a pattern of action. Here again we may refer to the depositions from Brødreengen, which show that four times, at short intervals, at least two thin-butted flint axes at a time were definitively deposited. From the Early Neolithic and on through the periods of prehistory, a large body of find material from South Scandinavia and northern Germany testifying to final depositions has appeared in wetland deposits and this applies to flint axes found individually or several together as well as mixed, cumulative finds. The water was a medium for the exchange of valuables with the higher powers (Nielsen 1977; Rech 1979; Karsten 1994; Koch 1998; L. Larsson 2011b, 70-75).

We can thus answer in the affirmative the question whether there were axes that were used for special purposes, among which we can here point on the one hand to their use in prestige-oriented exchanges, on the other to their use as sacrifices to higher powers. This is particularly true of the long, thin-butted axes. But can they also have been used for other things? The characteristic feature of the thin-butted flint axes is that they are of different sizes, without otherwise differing from the same norm as regards design. On the whole only the length varies. Looking at the axes of type II, they must have been introduced to Bornholm in lengths between 26 and 38 cm (table 5.2). Besides the intact axes without traces of use or resharpening, there have been isolated finds of five sharpened axes of type II and one with a damaged and re-formed blade (Finds list IV nos. 66, 67, 72, 73, 75 and 79). In addition, in one of the depositions from Brødreengen (no. 178) a 25.3 cm long axe of type II with a resharpened but not re-polished blade was found (fig. 2.16, find no. 2, axe 2). These axes are between 16 and 34.2 cm long. None of the resharpened axes of type IIIA, however, is more than 28 cm long. This could in other words indicate that Olausson is right when she says that the long axes were also used. But we cannot know what they were used for. People would hardly have chopped wood with the longest of the axes. It must also be considered that the sharp blade of a polished flint axe is always the place that is most vulnerable and exposed to damage by accidents, irrespective of whether the axe has been in use or not. A knocked-off blade corner may have led to repairs of the axe. That the long axes have been used or have been damaged and then reworked and resharpened, does not deprive them of their original status as especially valuable objects.

It is evident from a review of the Finds list that many of the axes of different types have been used and have been repaired. This also applies to those which from the find circumstances must be supposed to have been ritually deposited. In the deposition from Stavehøl (fig. 5.2, Finds list IV no. 174) three of the axes have a reworked blade area without re-polishing. The same is true of one axe of type II in the deposition from Brødreengen (no. 178), of at least six individually found axes of type IIIA, of one of type IIIB and two of type VI. There have been no investigations of whether these axes too may have been used with an unpolished blade.

Each of the four depositions from Brødreengen (Finds list IV nos. 175, 177, 178 and 179) contains two long, ground axes of types I/II and II. Identical details such as the flaking of the butt suggest that they were made at the same time, as a series. They were therefore probably imported together to Bornholm. Apart from the one re-sharpened without re-polishing the axes were preserved intact until they were deposited pairwise in the bog. All the 72 axes listed in table 5.2, both short and long, appear to have ended their 'life cycle' without being used at any time. The surplus this reflects, however, did not remain constant. Most axes, both short and long, as well as used and unused, are of types I, II and IIIA, which were deposited in the periods EN A2-B (EN I), while the deposition of axes of all sizes declined markedly in EN C (EN II). Either fewer axes were imported to the island in EN C, or the deposition pattern changed. The latter may be connected with changes in the social structure. From EN C on there was a focus on major collective tasks such as the building of megalithic tombs and causewayed enclosures. At the same time one sees signs of a stricter hierarchization and the beginning of group formations, which may have led to a restriction of the axe circulation and limitations on access to imported goods. We will return to this in chapter 7.

The distribution of thin-butted flint axes of types I – IV with a length over 30 cm is a phenomenon which mainly appears in the EN I (on Bornholm in EN A2 and EN B), and which declines in EN II (EN C). The long axes are widespread in South Scandinavia with the greatest concentration in Scania, but they are also found in central Sweden. Three have been found in southern Norway around the Oslo Fjord, and a single one appeared in Öland. On Gotland 32 axes over 30 cm long were found in three depositions (Sørensen 2014, fig. V.144).

If we look at the length of the thin-butted flint axes from both isolated finds and hoards (table 5.3), there is no great difference in variation between Scania and Bornholm. In Scania, where the largest quantity has been registered, the number of long axes gradually declines until the longest reaches 42 cm. On Bornholm there are only two axes longer than 37 cm. On Gotland the 32 axes from the depositions are the longest, but there are also three individually found axes over 30 cm in length. The long axes are in this respect clearly different from the axes of 'normal' length. This tendency is intensified when we move to Södermanland and Närke, where there is a leap from axes of 22 cm to axes of 31 cm, between which there are only three axes of 28-29 cm. The long axes clearly stand out here. In each of the four areas mentioned there are two axes over 40 cm in length. The longest was found on Bornholm and is 44 cm in length (Finds list IV no. 142).

The farther one gets from the production area, Zealand or southwestern Scania, the more the long axes stand out as a special category. Mats Larsson

Fig. 5.10. Map of South and Central Scandinavia.

notes that thin-butted flint axes longer than 40 cm appear in the Ystad area in south-eastern Scania, but not in south-western Scania (M. Larsson 1988b, 52 ff.). Jacqueline Taffinder quotes from a work by Lars Sundström, in which it is also pointed out that in Sweden the number of long, thin-butted flint axes increases proportionally the farther one gets from the raw material deposits (Taffinder 1998, 79; *cf.* Sundström 2003, 147 ff.). An investigation of the distribution of the axes in the landscape north and south of Mälaren shows that the long axes have been found in other places than axes of 'normal' length, and this has been interpreted as an indication that the long axes mark ritual centres (Apel *et al.* 1995, 116). One must suppose that the fewer axes of South Scandinavian flint to be found in an area, the greater the prestige associated with the acquisition and ritual deposition of the long, thin-butted flint axes. The significance of the long axes was the same in South Scandinavia, on Gotland and in central Sweden. In all three areas thin-butted flint axes of the various sizes were used, some having a practical and others a symbolic function.

To the practice of depositing intact axes in particular places one can add the more destructive practice of burning axes and other flint implements, as known from Svartskylle in southern Scania, where thin-butted flint axes and other flint implements were burnt on a hill that is a salient feature of the

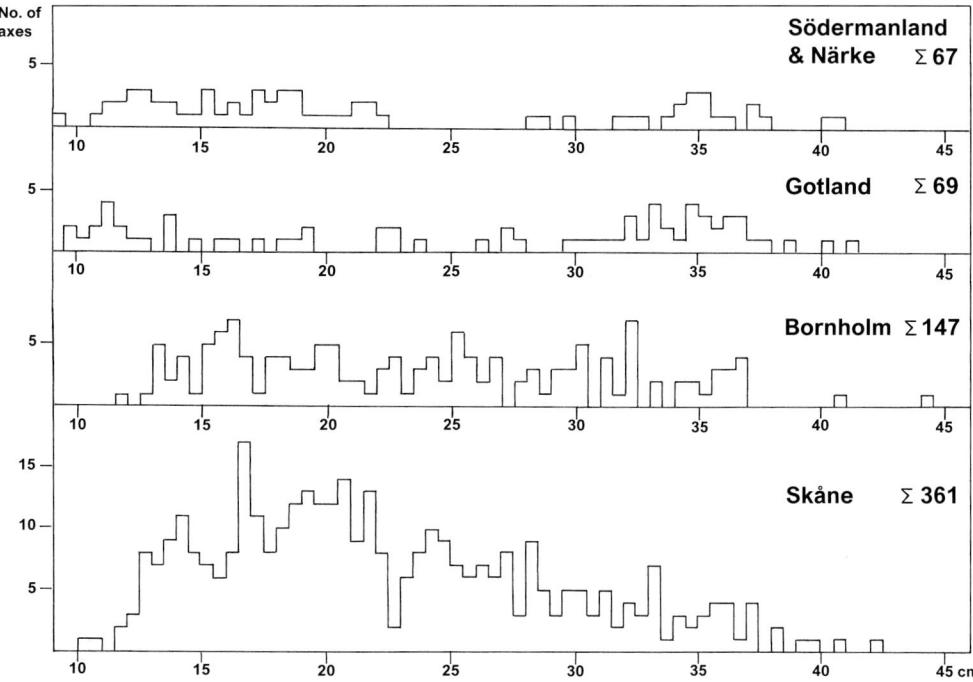

Table 5.3. Length variation of thin-butted flint axes (all types). Fragments not included. Scania after Karsten 1994, Gotland after Lang 1985, Södermanland and Närke after Apel et al. 1995.

landscape (L. Larsson 2002b). But the same kind of destruction by fire of Early Neolithic axes and tools of flint has also been noted at the site Stensborg in Södermanland in central Sweden, and in this case both pointed- and thin-butted flint axes were fire-damaged, presumably as part of sacrificial ceremonies (Larsson & Broström 2011).

The flint axes were coveted objects, were distributed over large areas and were either deposited intact or destroyed by fire as part of ritual acts. That this happened in the same way irrespective of the distance from the primary flint deposits must be an expression of similarities in ideology and ritual practice within the areas where arable and cattle farming were introduced at the beginning of the fourth millennium BC, regardless of what the various occupational conditions were in the individual areas. In Mälardalen people lived by fishing and sealing at the coastal settlements, while inland they bred cattle as well as sheep/goats and pigs. According to ^{14}C datings cattle farming was introduced between 4000 and 3800 BC, which is just as early as in South Scandinavia, while cereal farming perhaps came a little later (Hallgren 2008, 76 ff., figs. 7.1 and 7.3). The parallels with South Scandinavia are conspicuous from the beginning, and come to expression in the occurrence of short-necked funnel beakers and pointed-butted axes of South Scandinavian flint (*idem*, 163 ff., 233 f.). The acquisition, use and ritual treatment of the thin-butted flint axes form another parallel, or in Fredrik Hallgren's formulation, 'Identity in Practice' (the title of his monograph from 2008). This might also indicate that the social structure was the same.

So what can the distribution of the thin-butted flint axes tell us about the social structure? We have seen that to some extent the quantity and sizes of thin-butted flint axes decline the farther one gets from the raw material deposits and the production areas. This might accord well with Colin Renfrew's model of down-the-line distribution among equals in a society without formally organised exchanges, where only some of the axes went on to recipients farther from the production areas (Renfrew 1977). But the occurrence of isolated finds and hoards with long axes of exceptional quality far from the places of production, as on Bornholm, Gotland and in central Sweden, suggests that there were also organised exchanges of prestige objects controlled by people with privileged access to the material. We therefore take the view that the distribution of thin-butted flint axes in the period when it was most intensive, corresponding to EN B on Bornholm, reflects activities controlled by an elite in a society with growing hierarchization.

If we turn our gaze in the opposite direction, deposition finds with thin-butted flint axes also occur south of the Baltic and have been found on Rügen, in Mecklenburg-Vorpommeren, Schleswig-Holstein and Lower Saxony, while their deposition in wet areas such as in South Scandinavia declines the farther one moves away from the Baltic (Rech 1979, Karte 3). The borderlands towards the south west for the deposition on wetland of flint axes which come from Denmark or northern Germany lie within the West Group of the Funnel Beaker Culture in northern Holland (Drenthe), where 60 flint axes have been found deposited individually or several together. Among these are 35 thin-butted flint axes, 20 of which are of the 'old type' – that is, types III-VI (Wentink 2006; Wentink *et al.* 2011). The way they were selected and deposited corresponds to the depositions in South Scandinavia, and this might lead to the assumption that the axes functioned in the same way, as prestige objects with a special symbolic value, perhaps reinforced by the fact that they circulated so far from their place of production. Here, as in South Scandinavia, we do not always have information about where the axes were found, but it is evident that over 50% of the Dutch flint axes with a length over 25 cm have been found on wetland (Wentink 2006, fig. 4.5). The depositions took place in the area where, partly at the same time and partly later, megalithic tombs, the Dutch 'hunebedden' were built (Bakker 1992). This could mean that the people who owned and exchanged such axes, and who carried out the final ritual deposition of them, acted in accordance with the same ideological thinking that prevailed in the Funnel Beaker Culture's North Group. "This knowledge itself was considered an inalienable possession as it constituted TRB world-view, TRB identity" (Wentink 2006, 96).

As in Holland, in South Scandinavia one can note a close correlation between the distribution of thin-butted flint axes and megalithic tombs (Hülthén & Welinder 1981, 163, fig. 18:1-2; Nielsen 1984; Sjögren 2003, 209 ff.). But if we look at the frequency of the various types of thin-butted axe, the deposition and circulation of the longest examples culminated before the building of megalithic tombs began. On Bornholm, on Zealand and in Scania the depositions begin with axes of types I-II, and they culminate with type IIIA, and in Jutland with the contemporary type IV. The most extensive production and distribution took place in EN Ib, at the same time as the building of the non-megalithic long barrows, which are the precursors of the dolmens. On Bornholm there is a conspicuous decline in the number of axe depositions in EN II. It is in this period that the large areas are cleared for cultivation and grazing. In the same period megalithic tombs and causewayed camps are built. This must have required extensive use of axes for practical purposes, and may be one of the explanations for the decline of depositions of costly axes. Other causes than the purely practical one could be constraints on individual exchanges of goods, a centralization of distribution and perhaps a higher degree of social control.

Thin-butted axes of other materials than flint

Nine thin-butted axes of other materials than flint have been found on Bornholm (Finds list IV nos. 181-89). They are all made of fine-grained stone not identified further. Only three of the nine axes are intact and unreworked, and their length varies between 13 and 22.7 cm. One not fully polished preform (no. 185) reaches a length of 28 cm. The thickness of seven of the axes can be measured; it varies between 3 and 4.9 cm, and the average thickness is just about 4 cm. These axes are thicker than the flint axes, and most of them have highly convex broad surfaces. Three of them fall within Ebbesen's type IIA (1984, 121 f., fig. 2.7) because of the thickness and the almost parallel narrow surfaces. This type has been dated to EN C / MN AIa (*idem*, 122). But the butt narrows on four of the axes (nos. 181, 183, 185, 187), which must almost be designated an intermediate form between Ebbesen's types IA and IIA (*idem*, figs. 2.2 and 2.7) – that is, they may be related to the pointed-butted axes. One single axe (no. 187) has a thickness of only 3 cm and rather falls within Ebbesen's type IVA (*idem*, 126, fig. 2.3). The broad, thin-butted axes of the types IIB and IIC, both of which have been dated from the contexts they appear in to EN II-MN AIII (*idem*, 122-24) do not seem to be represented in the material from Bornholm.

On Bornholm a butt fragment was found at the settlement Ndr. Grødbygård (Finds list I no. 36). This axe is one of those that narrow towards the butt (fig. 3.29:3). The thickness cannot be measured accurately, as one broad surface is broken down, but it must have been over 3.7 cm. The axe fragment was found in the culture layer containing finds ranging from EN A1 to EN C, with the main concentration in EN B (p. 78 f.). Axes of this category have otherwise not been found in dateable find contexts on Bornholm. Their distribution (fig. 5.11) is scattered. Five of the nine axes have been found in southern Bornholm, while the northern part of the island, where many

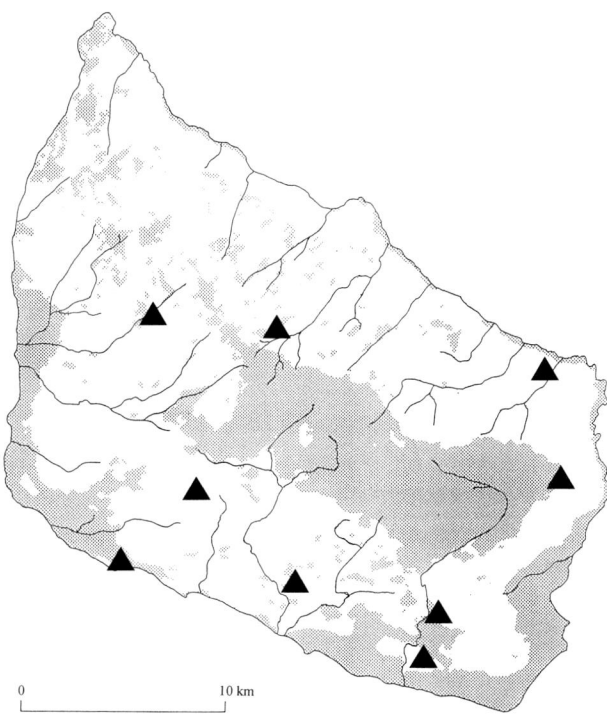

Fig. 5.11. The distribution of thin-butted axes of materials other than flint.

of the thin-butted axes of flint are concentrated, is empty of such finds.

Argonauts of the Baltic Sea

In the subsoil of Bornholm there are no natural flint deposits that can be used to make either pointed-butted or thin-butted flint axes. The local ball flint occurs in large quantities as small, naturally ground pieces, often of the form and size of hens' eggs. Larger pieces of flint can be found in the form of Kristianstad flint, which primarily occurs in northeastern Scania, and which also occurs in the moraine on Bornholm. In very rare cases axes made of this hard flint type have been found (Cederschiöld 1949; Karsten 1994, 340 no. 1111; Knarrström 1997, 9; Högberg & Olausson 2007, 78-87). The Kristianstad flint was probably transported to Bornholm with the glaciers of the Ice Age, but no pieces large enough for making axes have been observed. Nor have finished axes of this flint type been found on the island.

The first farmers who settled on Bornholm must very quickly have become aware of this resource scarcity. It is therefore strange that no major production of axes in other materials was initiated. They could have used the softer diabase, which occurs in fissures in the granite and is easily accessible on the coast at Saltuna and Listed (Münther 1945). This material was used to make axes in the Mesolithic. But among the individually found pointed-butted axes, 41 are of flint and only 10 are of other materials that may be of native origin, eight of these are of diabase and other fine-grained stone, one is of sandstone and one of quartzite (fig. 4.7). The difference is even greater when we look at the individually found thin-butted axes, 122 of which are of flint and only nine of other stone. None of the pointed- or thin-butted axes of other materials than flint that have been found on Bornholm are of a size or quality that ranks them alongside the flint axes we consider to be prestige objects. Some of the axes of other materials than flint may very well have been deposited in ritual contexts in the same way as the flint axes, but this is hard to establish, because for this group of axes we lack information about the find circumstances.

In other places where early farming societies arose at the same time far from the natural flint deposits, axes were made of the local stone, as in central Sweden (Welinder 1985; Hallgren 2008, 199 ff.). We can take another example from the Shetland Islands, where the production of axes in the local felsite comprised both 'everyday' axe heads and 'prestige' axe heads (Ballin 2013). On Bornholm a decision must have been made at an early stage to maintain the connection with the mainland and to be part of a South Scandinavian contact network through which the flint axes circulated.

Most Early Neolithic flint axes were made of flint from the Maastrichtian chalk layers, here called Senonian flint, which were lifted up by the glaciers of the Ice Age on the east-facing coast of Rügen, at Møns Klint and Stevns Klint on Zealand and at Södra Sallerup in southwestern Scania (fig. 5.12). Because of the erosive power of the ice, the flint from these layers was scattered and mixed with the moraine material. There are areas where the moraine is full of many small, crushed pieces of flint, as in central Zealand and eastern Lolland, but the ice also deposited large pieces of usable quality, as along the coasts. This is especially the case on Falster, where flint of a particularly good quality occurs in loose blocks. The great majority of axes found on Bornholm are of Senonian flint, and only a limited number are of the younger, more coarse-grained Danian flint from early tertiary limestone layers as in the upper parts of Stevns Klint. Danian flint also occurs in SW Scania

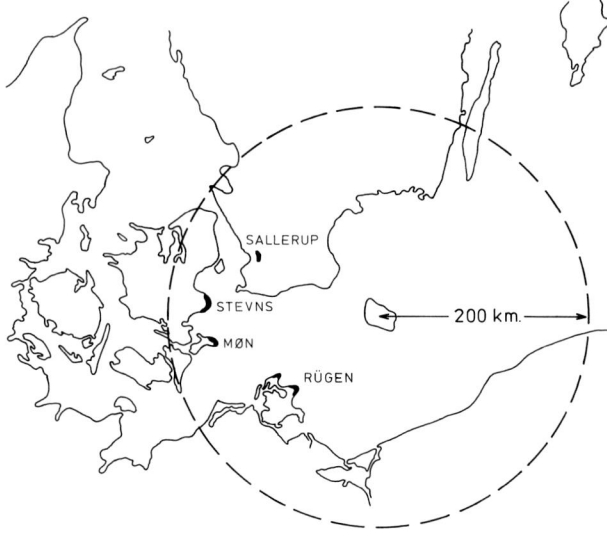

Fig. 5.12. Map of the Baltic Sea, showing the distance between Bornholm and the natural outcrops of Senonian (Maastrichtian) flint.

and can be found as secondary occurrences along the south coast of Scania (Högberg & Olausson 2007, 53).

Theoretically, people could have sailed from Bornholm searching for Senonian flint at the natural deposits on Rügen, on Møn and on the southwestern coast of Scania, made preforms there or stocked up on the raw material and sailed back to the island to finish the axes. But it is doubtful that it happened that way. No flint blanks for making axes have been found from the Early Neolithic on Bornholm,[5] and on the whole there are no indications that there was local fabrication of flint axes at that time on the island. At the Early Neolithic settlements only a few of the flakes that are diagnostic for axe making have been found. On the other hand several flakes from repairs of polished axes have been found, as well as many intact and fragmented grindstones of fine-grained sandstone with which the axes could be re-ground and polished after repairs, but which could also have been used to polish entirely unpolished imported axes. It is therefore most probable that all Early Neolithic flint axes, either polished or unpolished, were imported to Bornholm. All flint axes found on Bornholm are of types that occur on Zealand and in Scania.

Looking at the Early Neolithic alone, Bornholm was for more than half a millennium continuously supplied with such ample quantities of flint axes that a significant number of them could be taken out of circulation to be deposited in ritual contexts. It is on the whole this quantity of axes that we are able to study today. Can we imagine how the transportation of axes over open sea was organised, who did it and what was the motive behind the maintenance of the connection?

As for the distribution of axes, until now we have held to the interpretation that exchanges of prestigious objects took place among people of high status, and that the acquisition of rare objects such as axes of foreign stone types or oversized axes of flint helped to enhance the status and power of the people in question. We have also been able to see that exchanges of axes took place in South Scandinavia at a relatively early stage of the development of Neolithic society, in the same way as it had begun earlier in other places in Europe. There are striking parallels in development between western and northern Europe in terms of grave types and the circulation of status objects, although the individual stages did not come at the same time but at more staggered intervals.

The first farmers on Bornholm were involved in the circulation of flint axes in the same way as in other parts of South Scandinavia. There was simply the difference that in this case they had to cross the sea to transport flint axes. Klaus Ebbesen, who rejects the different models of exchange from ethnographic sources applied when studying prehistoric distribution patterns, finds that sea-borne distribution was fundamentally different from the way things were distributed on land (Ebbesen 2002, 104). We believe that distribution in the Early Neolithic took place in the same way whether it crossed land or sea, because the way distribution was organised was determined by how social contacts and alliances were established.

The closest distance from the mainland was 38 km from Hammeren to the SE coast of Scania. If one stands at a high point in the terrain in clear weather one can see the opposite coast, but this is not possible when one is at sea level. In addition, the current is normally strong in the waters between Hammeren and the Scanian coast. Voyages would therefore have to take place at the most favourable point in time, and even then this could be a challenge that required courage, strength and resolve.

There is little evidence of the size of the vessels that the seafarers used for these transports, or of their cargo capacity. In Denmark 35 Neolithic dugouts have been found, all of which had been used in lake basins inland, and they reach a length of 10 m (Christensen 1990). One dugout from the early Funnel Beaker Culture found in Stralsund by the north-

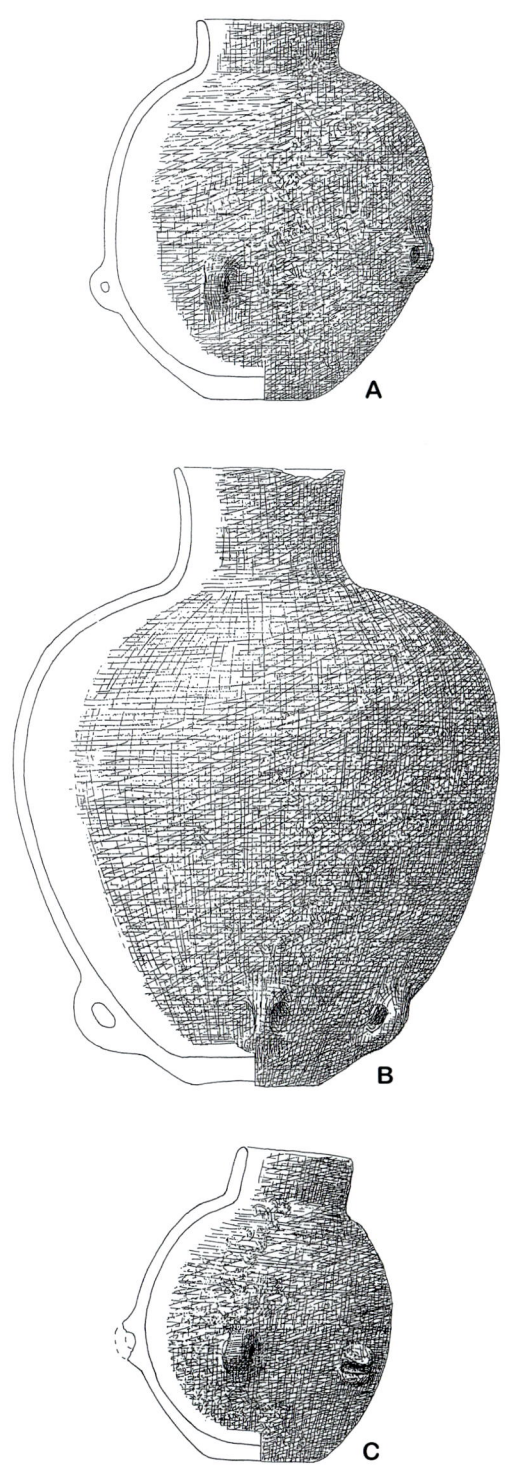

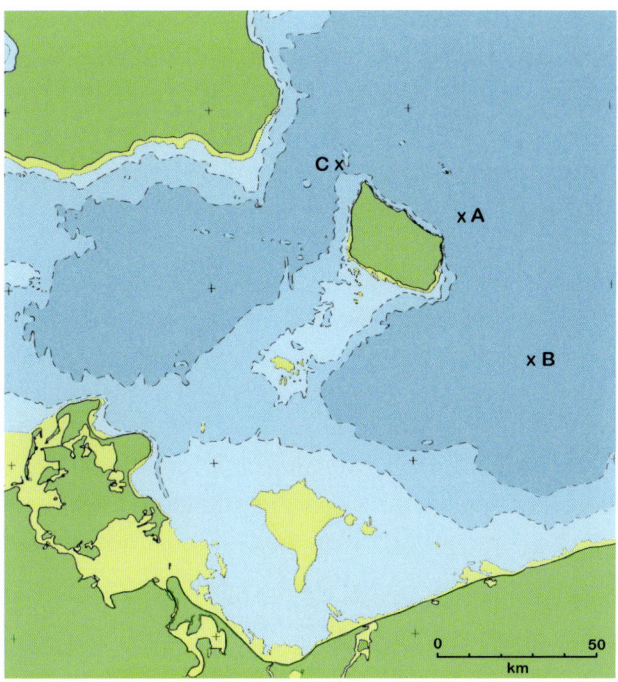

Fig. 5.14. Map of the Baltic Sea showing the sea depths at 10 m intervals. A-C: Finds of the three Early Neolithic lugged jars shown in fig. 5.13. Map illustration: Jesper Jespersen.

Fig. 5.13. Three lugged jars from the bottom of the Baltic Sea. (A) Finds list II no. 6, (B) Finds list II no. 7, (C) Finds list II no. 8. H. Ørsnes del. 1:5.

ern German Baltic coast and ^{14}C-dated to 5040±26 BP (KIA-24234), calibrated 3937-3788 BC (1σ), 3948-3771 BC (2σ)[6] is as long as 12 metres (Kaute *et al.* 2005; Lübke 2005). We imagine that the boats were not primitive given the very fact that the voyages must have been made at regular intervals. But in troubled waters sailing could go wrong. In three places in the Baltic off Bornholm fishermen have found Early Neolithic lugged jars in their nets. They probably contained the boat crew's supply of drinking water (Finds list II nos. 6-8) (fig. 5.13). The two smallest lugged jars correspond approximately in their form to another short-necked lugged jar with the uncertain find-spot 'Bornholm' (Finds list II no. 1, fig. 8.7) and to a fragment of a lugged jar from Gudhjem Syd (fig. 8.4:8), which most probably dates them to EN A1. The largest of the lugged jars found in the sea has a taller neck and a more convex upper part, like a neck fragment found with a funnel beaker of type II at Vallensgård I (fig. 2.4:3), which means that this form could be later, from EN A2 or EN B.

An example of a similar voyage over perilous sea bringing axes from the mainland to an island community can be taken from the Channel Islands, where axes were made in the Neolithic in local stones such as dolerite and fibrolite. Nevertheless there were imports of axes of other materials from the mainland, although it is not evident that these axes were of a better quality than those made on the islands (Patton 1991, 74 ff.; 1993, 27 ff.). But they were different and may have met other needs. Axes only went one way, so this exchange was asymmetrical, unless other objects or services of which we know nothing today went the other way. It is only 24 km from the mainland to the island of Jersey, but the tides there are so strong that a crossing is risky and requires detailed planning and resourceful navigation. This prompts the thought that making the voyage was in itself part of the point of it all. Such an expedition was demanding, and one could undoubtedly win a considerable reputation by accomplishing it successfully. Another objective with sea voyages over long distances might be to forge and maintain social contacts. At least this was originally one of the aims of maintaining the famous Kula Ring, which linked the Trobriand Islands in Melanesia, where the contacts between the voyagers and the permanent residents involved reciprocal obligations such as hospitality, protection and assistance (Malinowski 1922).

There is little doubt that this kind of contact must have taken place when seafarers in the Early Neolithic landed their boats on the coast of Bornholm bringing flint axes and perhaps other important goods. They would have had to visit people with authority and ability to fulfill wishes that could bring balance to the exchanges. This might mean ensuring the voyager a stay on the island until the weather conditions permitted a return journey. It might also mean allowing the voyager to settle permanently on the island, which would have to involve negotiations with other prominent people, including issues of payment. It might involve negotiations about marriage. If we look only at the material values, the importing of flint axes to Bornholm would seem unbalanced without reciprocation with corresponding goods, while there may have been quid pro quos of a social and economic kind that brought balance to the relationship. There is no doubt that the people who were part of this contact network and who regularly received travellers played a central role in relation to the inhabitants of the islands, not least with regard to the further distribution of flint axes. The traffic could have taken place in friendly forms, at least at the beginning. But one can also imagine that a point was reached when it was necessary for the travellers to bring flint axes if they were to have any hope of gaining access to the island at all.

Bornholm is not the only flint-poor island in the Baltic to which travellers brought axes of South Scandinavian flint. The same happened on Öland and Gotland. The distance from the mainland to Öland over the Kalmar Sound is only 4 km, which in the Early Neolithic must have been manageable. Stray finds from the Stone Age in Kalmar Län have been registered by Nils Åberg (1913). They show that in the Mesolithic Öland was more sparsely populated than the mainland opposite, and in the Early Neolithic too the greatest concentration of pointed- and thin-butted flint axes as well as battle axes was found on the mainland at coastal Sörmore south of Kalmar, where the largest Neolithic settlements have also been found in recent investigations. But with 47 thin-butted flint axes the central and southern part of Öland appears richer in finds per unit of area than the mainland, and this might suggest that the island was densely populated. On both sides of the Kalmar Sound, some of the axes were deposited on wetland, while others were burnt, which is an expression of the same ritual practice as we know from the areas towards the south from which the axes came (Gurstad-Nilsson 2001, 149). As for links with the surrounding world, recent investigations have shown that Kristianstad flint predominates at the settlements on the mainland, while the South Scandinavian flint is predominant in the material from the Öland settlements (*idem*, 148). As on Bornholm, in Öland there was no perceptible limitation of the flint supply in the Early Neolithic. Another difference that characterizes the development on Öland in relation to the mainland is the occurrence of four megalithic tombs in the southern part of the island.

The beginning of the Neolithic on Gotland is interesting compared with Bornholm, since on Gotland a much larger body of faunal material is preserved from both the Late Mesolithic and the Early Neolithic than on Bornholm. Bones of domesticated ox, sheep and pigs from the cave Stora Förvar on Stora Karlsö have been ^{14}C-dated to 3900-3550 BC (Lindqvist & Possnert 1997, 46), so Neolithic occupational features were introduced on Gotland at about the same time as on Bornholm. There appears to have been no long-lasting transition period. Christian Lindqvist calls the introduction of domestic animals a sudden occurrence as a result of organised colonisation, and he draws a comparison with the neolithisation process on Cyprus and Crete around 7000 BC (Lindqvist 1997, 373).

On Gotland 27 pointed-butted and around 80 thin-butted axes have been registered, although the figures are given differently, and not all listings distinguish between axes of flint and of other stone (Lang 1985; Österholm 1989; Bägerfeldt 1992). The individually found axes are spread over most of Gotland, although there is a striking concentration of thin-butted axes in the middle of the island (fig. 5.15). The distribution of the two kinds of axes recalls what we find on Bornholm. Of the thin-butted flint axes from Gotland, 33 are distributed over three hoard finds, all of which were found in the central and western parts of the island. They are unusual compared with most contemporary axe depositions in South Scandinavia because of the quantity and sizes of the axes:

(1) Kulstäde in Vall Parish, with 7 axes, 31.2-41.4 cm long.[7]

(2) Djupbrunns (Källgårds) in Hogrän Parish, with 15 axes and a blade fragment. There are 14 intact axes which are 30.9-40.3 cm long (fig. 5.16. See also photographs in Ebbesen 2002, fig. 24).[8]

(3) Kopparsvik outside Visby, with 11 axes, 33.2-37.6 cm long.[9]

The axes are polished and appear to be identical in size and proportions in each of the hoards. They have all been identified as thin-butted axes of type I by Lars Bägerfeldt (1992, 31). It is relevant, however, to look more closely at the typing, since the time when these three impressive collections of axes were imported is interesting both in terms of imports of flint axes to Bornholm and of the distribution and long-distance transport of flint axes in the various periods of the Early Neolithic.

The axes from Kulstäde, Djupbrunns and Kopparsvik on average have a largest width at the cutting edge of 7.3-7.1-7.0 cm respectively (Lang 1985, table 3.2). In comparison only 15% of the South Scandinavian axes of type I have an edge width of 7.0-7.4 cm, while 43% of the axes of type II and 37% of the axes of type III have such a width (P.O. Nielsen 1977, fig. 29). As for the greatest width of the axes, the axes from Kulstäde and Djupbrunns correspond more to types II and III than to type I. If we look at the angle of the narrow surfaces, on the axes from Kulstäde, Djupbrunns and Kopparsvik it is on average 4.1-4.5-4.4° respectively. As a comparison, only 15% of the South Scandinavian axes of type I have a narrow-surface angle in the interval 4-5°, while 47% of the axes of type II and 65% of the axes of type III have values within this interval (idem, fig. 31). Once more we have a better match with axes of types II and III. The longest of the axes in the three Gotland depositions reach 41.4 and 40.3 cm. None of the axes of type I, however, has a length that exceeds 39 cm, whereas some axes of types II and III reach a length between 40 and 43 cm (idem, fig. 24).

In other words the axes in the three depositions are despite great similarities not quite identical. The

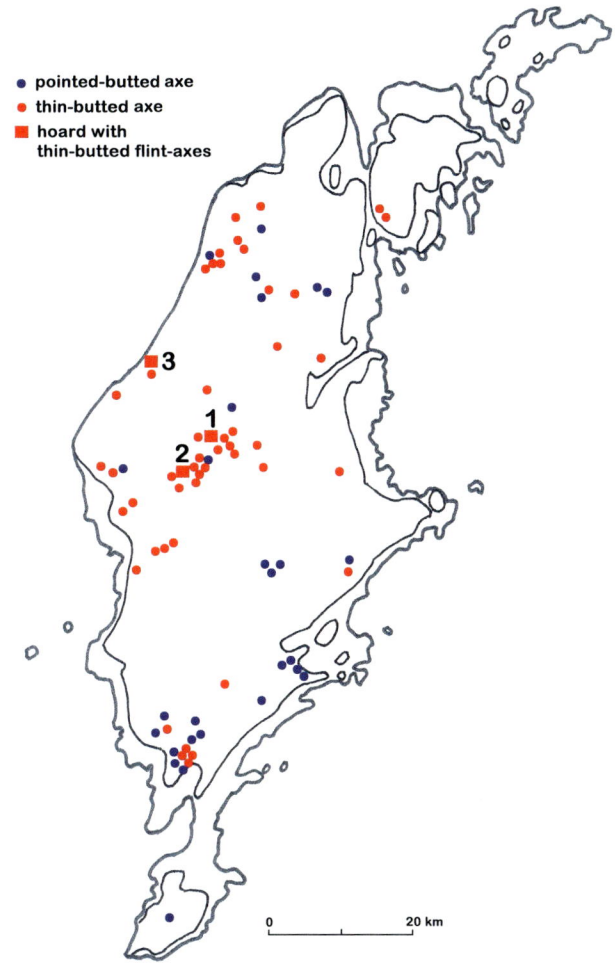

Fig. 5.15. Map of Gotland showing the distribution of pointed-butted and thin-butted flint axes, as well as three hoards containing thin-butted flint axes: (1) Kulstäde, (2) Djupbrunns and (3) Kopparsvik.

axes from Kopparsvik are narrower, have a slightly larger narrow-surface angle than the axes in the other two depositions, and their length does not exceed 37.6 cm. They therefore come closest to type I. The axes from Kulstäde are the broadest, have almost parallel narrow surfaces and are a complete match for type IIIA. The axes from Djupbrunns lie somewhere in between but are most like the axes from Kulstäde.

Because of these differences among the axes in the three Gotland depositions it is not certain that they were made in the same place and come from quite the same area. However, they testify to deliberate, repeated transport of axes of high quality, which must have taken place at relatively short time intervals. The find circumstances for the three depositions are not equally well elucidated, but of the two from Kullstäde and Djupbrunns we learn that they emerged during work in the fields on a low-lying or former

Fig. 5.16. Hoard from Djupbrunns, Gotland. Photo Gabriel Hildebrand, Statens Historiska Museum.

bog area, which is confirmed by the yellowish-brown patina of the axes. This is missing from the axes in the hoard from Kopparsvik, which was found close to the coastal cliff. At Djupbrunns the axes lay on their broad surfaces in three rows with the blades alternately turning in opposite directions. This corresponds to the deposition pattern known from Bornholm and the rest of South Scandinavia, and is an indication not only that Gotland took part in the status-related distribution system that culminated in the middle of the Early Neolithic, but that the treatment of the valuables, including their disposal by ritual deposition, took place in the same way as in South Scandinavia.

The three Gotland depositions must be dated in terms of the Bornholm chronology respectively to EN A2 (Kopparsvik) and EN B (Kullstäde and Djupbrunns). The latter two are from the time when there was major production of flint axes in South Scandinavia with types IIIA and IV of the thin-butted flint axes, and when imports to Bornholm were most extensive. The diffusion of South Scandinavian flint to Gotland was less than to Bornholm, and this may have had to do with the distance from the places of production. The large axes in the three depositions must therefore have represented extraordinarily high value. The depositions at Kullstäde and Djupbrunns took place in an area in the middle of the island, where there is the greatest concentration of the thin-butted axes of flint and stone whose diffusion otherwise covers most of the island (fig. 5.15). If there are no differences due to different gathering frequency, the concentration of axes in one area may be an indication of a concentration of population or a regulation of the circulation of axes, not least when it comes to the exotic long flint axes. The occurrence of long flint axes in the depositions on Gotland reflects a wealth surplus, and their deposition must be viewed as an action whereby the people who performed it achieved considerable prestige. This could be a sign of an incipient hierarchization on Gotland in the period 3700-3500 BC, as was the case in South Scandinavia. However, on Gotland only one megalithic tomb has been registered, the dolmen at Ansarve, Tofta Parish (Bägerfeldt 1992, 7-27; Lindqvist 1997).

The greater distance over the sea would not necessarily have been a hindrance to contacts with the outside. Between the mainland and Gotland the distance is about 85 km, while the distance between Öland and Gotland is about 60 km. Modern sailing in a 7.5 m long dugout with an outrigger has shown that five paddlers can take the trip from Stora Karlsö off the west coast of Gotland to the northern point of Öland on a summer's day in calm weather (Österholm 1997).

But on Gotland ceremonial axes were only imported for a short period, and as on Bornholm the practice declined from the beginning of EN II / EN C. Only one example of each of the late thin-butted flint axes, types VI and VII, appears among the individually found flint axes from Gotland. Imports of flint axes only picked up again at the end of MN A and the beginning of MN B with among other things thick-butted flint axes of groups A and B, and then in a Pitted Ware context (Bägerfeldt 1992, 31).

Until now we have seen imports of flint axes on Bornholm and the other two islands as the result of traffic that came from the outside. But one can also imagine other scenarios. Finds from later periods of prehistory testify that the inhabitants of the islands kept up active contacts with the surrounding world. The very fact that one can hardly demonstrate any chronological difference between the finds from the islands and the finds from other parts of northern Europe in terms of object types, grave types and decorative styles suggests intensive contact with leading societies in other places. One of the few examples of a later transition to something new on Bornholm came with the transition to the Battle Axe Culture around 2600 BC, which is a little later than in Scania. On Bornholm the transition took another course and was perhaps not as abrupt as on the mainland. But if we look forward to the period from the Roman Iron Age through the Viking Era to the Early Middle Ages, the hoard finds testify to a surprising accumulation of wealth through contacts with the surrounding world. The same is true of Öland and Gotland.

In a society where there is competition for power and prestige, knowledge of other worlds plays a significant role. One can imagine that the importance of such knowledge was heightened in island societies with infrequent news of events taking place on the other side of the sea. The first agrarian settlers on Bornholm came with a knowledge of the surrounding world that was kept up through tales and legends, and which the most courageous renewed by journeying away from the island to foreign coasts: knowledge of foreign peoples, languages, landscapes, animals and mysteries can be a powerful means of enhancing one's personal esteem. Esoteric knowledge of the alien and the extraordinary is attributed to heroic figures who journey at the margins of the known world or beyond it such as Jason, Ulysses and Sinbad the Sailor. The mastery of esoteric knowledge can give its possessor political and ideological advantages (Helms 1988, 13). The aim of the journeys of that time would have been the forging of contacts and the acquisition of goods both material and symbolic, but it would also have been to gain the travel experience and knowledge of the foreign that could benefit society and influence the traveller's social status at home.

Notes

1. One of the two thin-butted flint axes in the deposition from Almindingen (Finds list IV no. 172) has thin narrow surfaces and parallel sides like axes of type IV, and both axes were formerly identified as belonging to this type (Nielsen 1977 no. 46), but the identification is uncertain.
2. Here recalibrated with Calib 7.1. (Reimer *et al.* 2013).
3. It is a misunderstanding that type IV has been considered later than type IIIA, as stated by L. Klassen (2004, 110). It has always been considered contemporary, or partly contemporary, with type IIIA (Nielsen 1977, 108 and fig. 48).
4. The 50.5 cm long axe of type IV was found with a mechanical excavator together with a damaged axe of the same type in 2016 at Kardyb, Kobberup Parish, Fjends District, in central Jutland (NM A54528).
5. A Middle Neolithic deposition find from Smedegård in Rø (BMR 986, NM 4688/82) comprises a flint blank for making an axe, and six thick-butted and thin-bladed flint axes (Lind 1936, 243). Another deposition find from Kofoedsminde near Aakirkeby consisted of four unground B-axes and a large piece of partly worked raw flint (in private ownership, F.O.S. Nielsen 1996b, 209 f., fig. 12).
6. Calibrated with Calib ver. 7.1 using the intcal13.14c atmospheric curve (Reimer *et al.* 2013).
7. Statens Historiska Museum, Stockholm, nos. 11117, 11235. Found in 1900.
8. Statens Historiska Museum, Stockholm, no. 20358. Found in 1933.
9. Gotlands Fornsal, Visby, no. C 11177. Found in 1975.

6. Stone battle axes and flint halberds

Battle axes and halberds are both considered weapons of war, although they are very different in character. Each would also have had its cultural associations and each its course of development. They are discussed here together, since they appear at the same time and seem to have been important at about the same point in the Early Neolithic on Bornholm.

Battle axes

The Early Neolithic battle axes of fine-grained stone are often called 'polygonal axes', although only some of the late types are polygonal in cross-section. The axes are furnished with shaft holes and have a blunt butt which on the early types is simple, on the late types supplemented with a circular knob. The German term for the early types is *flache Hammeräxte* (flat hammer axes) or F-axes, for the late types *Knaufhammeräxte* (hammer axes with a knob) or K-axes. These terms come from M. Zápotocký's work on Neolithic battle axes in central and northern Europe (1992). The F-axes, which at first are incredibly identical over a large area, belong to a period that is contemporary with EN I (EN A-B) in South Scandinavia, and on the Continent they occur within cultural groups such as Michelsberg, Pfyn, Altheim, Mondsee, Baalberg and the Northern and Eastern Funnel Beaker Culture. In time local variants of the F-axes develop, and the Nordic axes take on their own character. The K-axes are in general later than the F-axes and have been dated to EN II (EN C) in South Scandinavia, where a few examples have been found in dolmen chambers. Another classification of the Early Neolithic battle axes is used by K. Ebbesen, who divides the Danish material into five types, of which types I-II are axes without a butt knob, and types III-V are axes with a butt knob (Ebbesen 1998).

One K-axe of copper is said to be from Scania, but is otherwise without find information. This prompts the question whether the Early Neolithic battle axes are imitations of axes of copper – a reasonable assumption, especially when one looks at the late K-axes with a curved longitudinal axis and acute lateral angles. But the opposite may also be the case. Lutz Klassen has demonstrated similarities between the Scanian copper axe and battle axes of stone of Zápotocký's type KIB-2 in an area in southern Germany/Austria from which several objects of so-called Mondsee copper reached South Scandinavia in the EN (Klassen 2000, 146 f.).

The battle axe must be regarded as a man's personal weapon, although we know of very few graves with battle axes which confirm this. An important man's grave which contained a battle axe is from the early Funnel Beaker Culture and was found at Dragsholm in western Zealand (see below). The buried person can be identified as a farmer by the funnel beaker in the grave (fig. 7.10a), as a hunter because of his archery equipment and the deer antler point that was placed vertically down by his head, and finally as a warrior by virtue of the battle axe of Ebbesen's type I (fig. 7.10b). The wide dispersal of the early types of battle axe must be a sign of a collective identification with the warrior as a role model in the societies on the Continent and in the North that participated in the agrarian expansion c. 4100-3800 BC. From the start the battle axe was introduced as a mark of status, and continued to be so although in the subsequent centuries it changed its appearance in the various parts of central and northern Europe, where differences arose as within other categories of the material culture (Sørensen 2014, 177).

On Bornholm 15 battle axes that can be dated to the Early Neolithic have been found. Six of these are intact and nine are fragments. Nine examples are kept at the Bornholm Museum, one example at

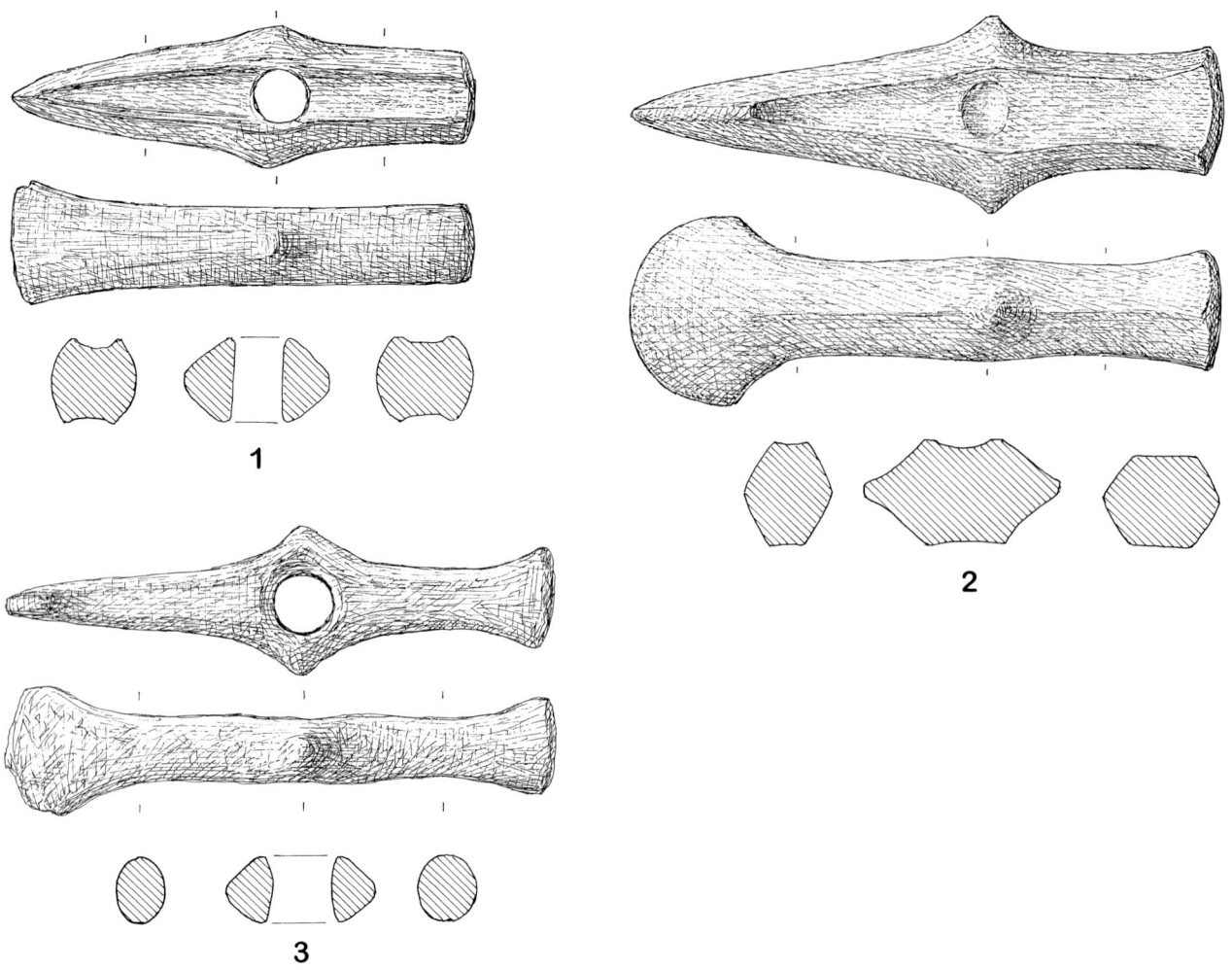

Fig. 6.1. Battle axes of type FIV. (1) Vestermarie (Finds list V no. 5). (2) Smedegård, Åker (no. 7). (3) Ellevang, Vestermarie (no. 6). H. Ørsnes del. 2:5.

the National Museum, while five belong to private collectors (see catalogue, Finds list V). With a few exceptions they are isolated finds without further find information.

The battle axe from Hjorthøj in Østerlars (Finds list V no. 1, fig. 8.11:1) has no parallels in South Scandinavian material and belongs to one of Zápotocký's first groups, among which Group FI is called 'the Continental group' and is spread throughout central Europe (Zápotocký 1992, 23 ff.), while FII is called the 'northeastern German group'. It is not possible to say with certainty to which of these two groups the axe from Hjorthøj belongs. It comes closest to an axe belonging to the subgroup FIIA from Rostock-Peez (Zápotocký, Finds list 1 no. 463, Taf. 19.4). The largest concentration of axes belonging to Zápotocký's group FII is found in north-eastern Germany, and the northernmost example found is from the northern point of Rügen. There are several closed finds with axes of this group, although not all of them are well documented, but in a find from Mützelburg, Uckermünde, an axe of type FIIA-1 is combined with a pointed-butted flint axe with an oval cross-section (Zápotocký 1992, 40, Finds list 1 no. 443 and Taf. 13.3-5). The battle axe from Mützelburg has a form that corresponds to several of the Danish battle axes of Ebbesen's type I, which occurs in South Scandinavia from the beginning of the fourth millennium. There is no doubt that the battle axe from Hjorthøj is one of the oldest Neolithic battle axes found in South Scandinavia, and that it must be dated to EN A1 on Bornholm. It testifies to Continental connections contemporary with the first Neolithic settlement on the island. It is interesting that it was made on Bornholm as a preform.

Three Bornholm battle axes (Finds list V nos. 2-4, fig. 8.11:2-4) correspond to Zápotocký's Group FIII and can also be assigned to Ebbesen's type I. The axes are flat and straight in both planes, have a simple termination of the butt, slightly rounded widening around the shaft hole and no blade corners or only

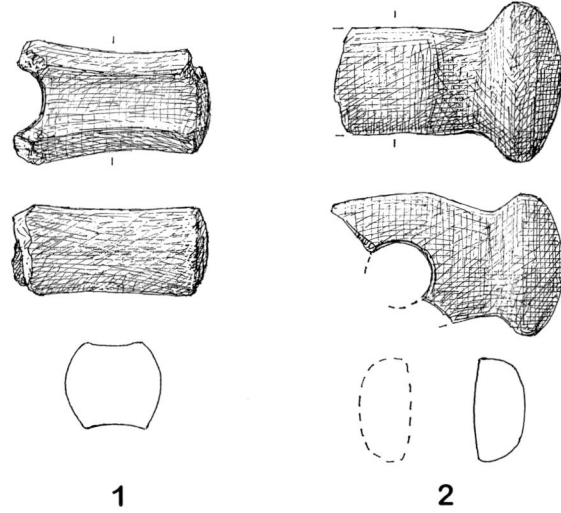

Fig. 6.2. Butt ends of battle axes. (1) Vallensgård II, Åker (Finds list V no. 11). (2) Myregård, Pedersker (no. 15). H. Ørsnes del. 2:5.

slightly widened ones. Ebbesen lists 15 axes of this type from Denmark, one of them found in the man's grave at Dragsholm, which has been dated to early EN I (on the dating see page 54), and where the battle axe appears together with a funnel beaker of Eva Koch's type I. In terms of the Bornholm chronology this type must be dated to EN A1.

Four Bornholm battle axes (Finds list V nos. 5-8, fig. 8.11:5-8) correspond to Zápotocký's Group FIV and belong to Ebbesen's type II (fig. 6.1:1-2). Such axes, like the preceding axes of type I, are straight and symmetrical in both planes and have a simply formed butt which however on some examples is widened and has a circular, blunt termination which anticipates the knobs on Zápotocký's K-axes and Ebbesen's type III (fig. 6.1:3). The extensions on both sides of the shaft hole may be pointed and round, and the blade corners are flared. Ebbesen lists 20 examples of this type from Denmark, one of which was found in a grave in a non-megalithic long barrow at Rustrup in central Jutland. Samples from charred posts in the east façade of the long barrow have been ^{14}C-dated to EN I (Fischer 1976). In terms of the Bornholm chronology battle axes of Ebbesen's type II should by all indications be dated to EN B.

Five fragments of battle axes cannot be classified more accurately than to Zápotocký's Group FIII-

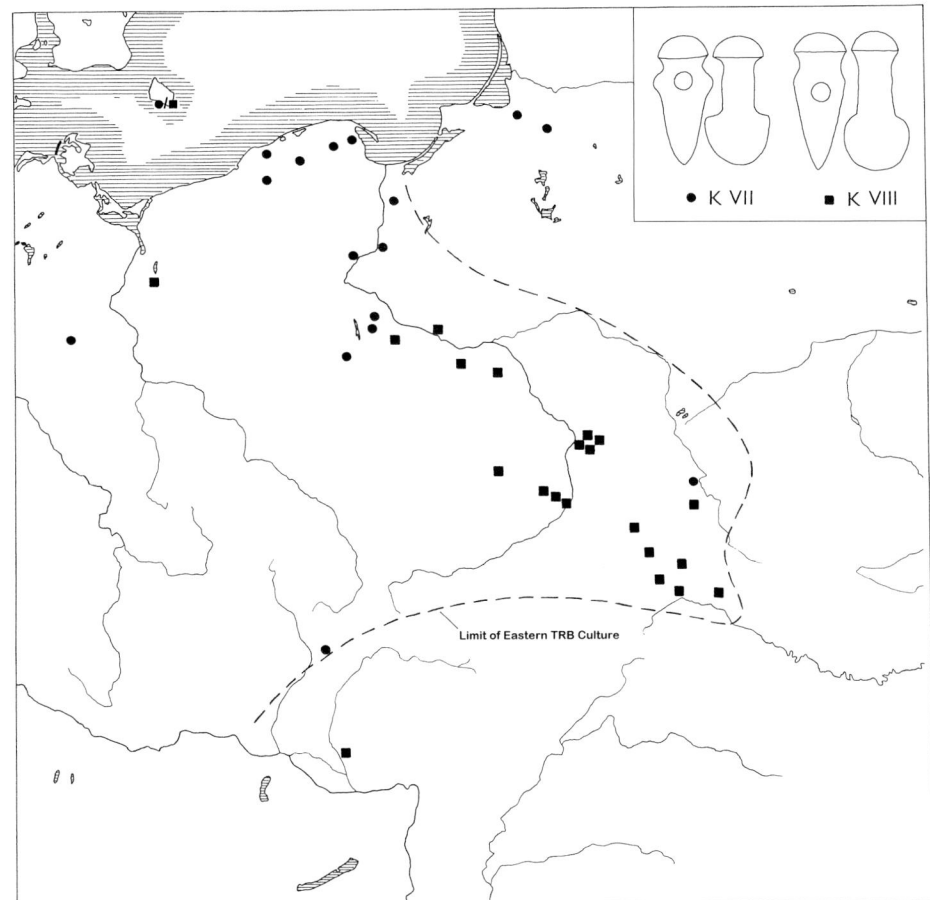

Fig. 6.3. The distribution of battle axes of types KVII and KVIII. After Zápotocký 1992 with additions.

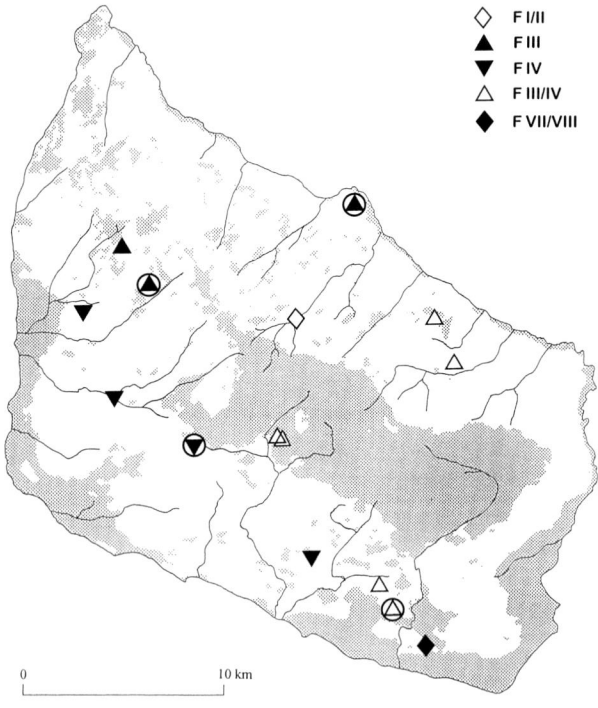

Fig. 6.4. The distribution of Early Neolithic battle axes. Approximate finds location marked with a circle.

IV and Ebbesen's types I-II (Finds list V nos. 9-14, fig. 8.11:9-14). They have thus been dated generally to EN A-B. The fragments are all broken at the shaft hole.

It is striking that none of Ebbesen's types III-V, the battle axes with a butt knob, have been found on Bornholm. One might otherwise have expected that the curved type V (Zápotocký's group KIII), which is the most common type in Sweden, and appears in Scania, Blekinge, Öland, Gotland and in central Sweden, would also be represented on Bornholm. There is however a fragment of a battle axe with a butt knob. It is from Myregård in Pedersker (fig. 6.2:2) (Finds list V no. 15) and has a very conspicuous butt knob and a shaft hole that sits close to the butt. There is no projecting extension of the narrow surfaces at the level of the shaft hole. It is hard to see on the short fragment whether the axe is straight or curved but it looks as if it is straight. With these characteristics, especially the short distance from the shaft hole to the butt, this axe differs from the other Danish axes with a butt knob of Ebbesen's type III-V, and instead matches Zápotocký's eastern groups KVII and KVIII, both of which comprise axes which are short and solid, with a much widened blade. While KVII appears in northern Poland and bordering areas, KVIII is distributed over an area that extends from central Poland along the Vistula and on to southeastern Poland (fig. 6.3). KVIII has been dated by several grave finds to the Wiórek phase of the eastern Funnel Beaker Culture (Zápotocký 1992, 73), corresponding to EN II (EN C). The axe fragment from Myregård was found only c. 1250 m from the coast in the southern part of the island and is thus a possible sign of a direct connection to the south over the Baltic.

The early battle axe from Hjorthøj and the late battle axe from Myregård (Finds list V nos. 1 and 15) both belong to types, which are foreign to the South Scandinavian environment in the Early Neolithic, and whose diffusion extends on the Continent to the south and south-east respectively.

The battle axe finds are evenly distributed on Bornholm (fig. 6.4), although with smaller quantities on the northern part of the island, which was most densely populated in EN A-B. No fewer than nine of the 15 battle axes are fragments, broken at the shaft hole. It is hard to tell whether this destruction happened in prehistory or as a result of contact with field implements. It does however form a striking pattern. The battle axe from Kokkedal (Finds list V no. 2, fig. 8.11:2) has marks from hammering on both sides of the shaft hole. Perhaps there was a tradition for the victor to destroy his opponent's weapon after battle. In that case the axe fragments may have been trophies.

Flint halberds

The halberds were thick, bifacially flaked pointed weapons, almost all of which were made of Senonian flint. This is also the case with the seven Bornholm halberds (Finds list VI, fig. 8.12).

There are three almost intact halberds, nos. 1, 4 and 6, of which nos. 4 and 6 belong to Ebbesen's type A, the asymmetrical type (1994, 112). Only two of the halberds, nos. 1 and 6, are partly polished (fig. 6.5). None of the individually found Bornholm halberds can be dated based on their find circumstances. The oldest dated find of a halberd which given its width may belong to this type is from Almhov in Scania, where a 7.5 cm long fragment lay in a pit which has been dated by charcoal to 5030±50 BP, calibrated 3940-3710 BC (1σ, Ua-23872) (Gidlöf et al. 2006, 60, fig. 45; Rudebeck 2010, 177 f.) corresponding to EN A1 on Bornholm. In grave finds type A first appears in late EN I, corresponding to EN B on Bornholm,

Fig. 6.5. Halberd of flint from Klippely, Klemensker (Finds list VI no. 6). Photo John Lee, the National Museum. Length: 20.6 cm.

as in the grave at Bukkær in Assing, western Jutland, which was covered by a non-megalithic long barrow, and which besides the halberd contained a thin-butted flint axe of type IV, an unusually large hourglass-shaped piece of amber and an amber bead (Rostholm 1982, 22, fig. 11; Ebbesen 1994 fig. 14). This is so far the only grave find from a non-megalithic long barrow to contain a halberd that can be typed. Another long barrow at Rokær in eastern Jutland was built over a grave containing 206 amber beads, two thin-butted flint axes, one of them of type IV, and an atypical halberd made of a c. 16 cm long, large flint blade which was partially polished (A.M. Kristiansen 2000a; 2000b). However, both intact halberds and fragments of halberds have been found in the settlement material under the long barrows at Barkær in Djursland, where they are concentrated in the same area as sherds of pottery in the Volling style, and include an intact halberd of type A (Liversage 1992, 62, fig. 60:1). But at Barkær, besides halberds of type A, symmetrical halberds apparently also appear, so it is not certain that there is a chronological difference between the broad asymmetrical and symmetrical halberds (*idem*, 62). Ebbesen depicts a fragment of an asymmetrical halberd from a dolmen chamber at Grøfte on Zealand (Ebbesen 1990, fig. 25c). Halberds of type A can thus also appear in EN II / EN C.

Of the Bornholm halberds, no. 2 has been identified as type A because of its asymmetry, but it differs from other halberds of that type because of its thickness. It is also coarsely chipped and should possibly be regarded as a preform.

The longest of the halberds, no. 1 from Biskopsenge, is symmetrical and falls outside Ebbesen's definitions, since its thickness is at the same time only 30% of its greatest width. It comes closest to the halberds of type A.

The fragments nos. 3, 5 and 7 are difficult to type, as they lack the widest part, so one cannot measure the ratio of greatest width to thickness that Ebbesen used in his type definitions. Nor can it be determined with full certainty whether they were symmetrical or asymmetrical. They come closest to Ebbesen's type A. None of the Bornholm halberds belongs to the narrow, symmetrical type B.

About the dating of the halberds in general it can be said that the various types overlap chronologically, and that together they cover the period from the early EN to the beginning of MN A. Broad and thin halberds also appear later in a few cases. A broad, symmetrical intact halberd was found at the settlement Blandebjerg on Langeland, where it had been deposited in a pit along with a fragment of a thin-butted flint axe of the Blandebjerg type (Winther 1943, 30, fig. 50-51). With a dating to MN AII this is the latest-dated Danish find so far of a halberd-like object. Similar broad, thin halberds have also been found in Schleswig-Holstein in a Middle Neolithic context (Lübke 1998, types III-IV).

The distribution of the halberds on Bornholm is striking, as five of them have been found in Klemensker (fig. 6.6). Four of them belong with the greatest probability to the Early Neolithic. Two halberds have been found in eastern and southern Bornholm

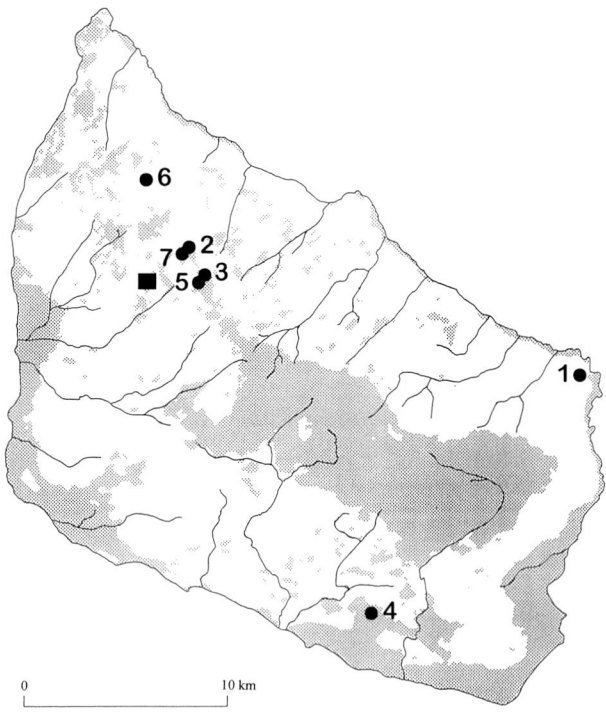

Fig. 6.6. The distribution of flint halberds. The settlement at Smedegade is marked with a square.

respectively. The halberd from Biskopsenge (no. 1) is symmetrical, thin and broad, and is at the same time the longest of them all. We cannot preclude the possibility that it should perhaps be dated to the Middle Neolithic. It is at the same time the only one of the seven individually found halberds whose find circumstances we know, since it was found by a large stone. Judging from its strong dark brown patina no. 2 from Bakkegård may have lain in a wetland deposit. None of the other halberds is very much patinated.

From Scania we know 13 halberds distributed over eight isolated finds and four hoards (Karsten 1994, 58). Of the individually found examples, seven were found in wetland and one was found by a large stone. In the hoards the halberds are combined with thin-butted flint axes.

Four of the Bornholm halberds were found at a short distance from the settlement Smedegade in Klemensker (Finds list I no. 14), which is the only one of the Early Neolithic settlements where halberds appear, in this case in the form of seven fire-brittle fragments (fig. 3.40:2-3). Most of the dateable pottery from this settlement can be dated to EN A2 and EN B. The fragments are small, but they come from very thin, broad halberds, which makes it most probable that they belonged to the broad, asymmetrical type A, which has also been found in an early context in other places such as Barkær. One of the fragments lay in a posthole, while the others were scattered through the cultural layers. They might be connected with one or more burnt constructions of which traces were found in the south-western part of the excavated area (see page 86), and perhaps they were in use during an armed struggle.

P.V. Glob used the term *dolkøkser* ('dagger axes') of the halberds and placed them as a weapon type alongside the Late Neolithic halberds of metal (1952, 23). He does not preclude the possibility that the models should be sought in Mesolithic pointed weapons. Glob and Ebbesen both think that the halberds were shafted at right angles to a wooden shaft, and Ebbesen finds rubbing marks on the base part as evidence of such shafting (1994, 123). Lutz Klassen on the other hand designates the halberds as daggers and finds parallels in the Altheim Culture in southern Germany. He points to the importance of metal daggers as models (Klassen 2000, 260 ff.). However, the halberds are not cutting tools, and given the form alone, there is little doubt of their function as pointed weapons. This kind of weapon is known from both the Mesolithic and the Neolithic. From the Mesolithic we know long, smooth-scraped and in some cases elaborately ornamented rods of deer antler which have been given the designation 'pointed weapons' although they may also have had another function besides possible use as weapons (Mathiassen 1948 nos. 38-40). From the Ertebølle Culture we also know short, unornamented points of deer antler with diagonal cutting and vertical bores through the base for shafting. Four such 'deer antler weapons' have been found at two Jutland and two Holstein coastal settlements (S.H. Andersen 2009, 174, figs. 151-53). Neolithic pointed weapons of deer antler with lateral bores through the base and with a median length of around 30 cm are known from Denmark, Scania, Gotland and Mecklenburg (Stenberger 1943, 87-89; Becker 1956; Bastian 1961, Abb. 71). The Danish pieces have been assigned by Becker to the Pitted Ware Culture, and Malmer has demonstrated that they also appear in graves of the Swedish-Norwegian Battle Axe Culture (1962, 319). About their function there can be little doubt if one trusts old accounts. Becker and Malmer mention two grave finds, one from Taastrup near Keldby on Møn found in 1868 and one from Tygelsjö in Scania from before 1838. A pointed weapon of deer antler is said in both cases to have pierced the skull of the deceased (Becker 1956; Malmer 1962, 318).

Finally we can mention the unusual double-pointed bone tools or pointed weapons from Ostorf-Tannenwerder and Krappmühle in Mecklenburg (Bastian 1961, 40-45, 98-101). Two such appear in the Ostorf-Tannenwerder grave III/35, which has been ^{14}C-dated to c. 3000 BC, corresponding to MN AII/III and to the Walternienburg-Bernburg period in Germany (Lübke et al. 2009). The bodies in the graves at Ostorf belonged to a population of hunters and fishermen at a time when the surrounding country was otherwise populated by farmers. It can therefore come as no surprise that the furnishings of the graves signal a hunter-gatherer identity. The use of pointed weapons of deer antler both here and later in the Pitted Ware Culture can be seen as an indication of the same. Parts of the furnishings of the man's grave at Dragsholm also refer to the hunt. A pointed deer antler was inserted in the ground with the point downward behind the head of the deceased (p. 172, fig. 7.11). The deer antler, of which the tine closest to the point had been cut off, was preserved to a length of 36 cm, while the base end, which turned upward, was broken off. We can therefore determine the function of the item with certainty. That it had a prominent position in the burial must mean that it had a strong inherent meaning. It is very possible that it was a type of pointed weapon.

We believe that the halberds of flint were not inspired by foreign weapon types, but arose at the beginning of the Neolithic as pointed weapons of flint, and that they belong to the same category of weapons as pointed weapons of deer antler. In the Early Neolithic and Early Middle Neolithic, when hunting and fishing were still important, this weapon would thus have been a symbol with archaic connotations. Ebbesen (1994, 123) and Anne Mette Kristiansen (2000b, 9) both use the term 'symbol of dignity' of the halberds. Harald Lübke, who has discussed the halberds from Schleswig-Holstein (1998), considers this a dubious designation, but does think it possible that they may have belonged to men with a special social status.

During the investigation of the remains of a long barrow at Onsved Mark on Zealand, Flemming Kaul found a base fragment of a halberd probably of the symmetrical type B. He remarks that several of the halberds found in and by dolmens are broken halves, which prompts him to assume that the rituals surrounding the deposition of halberds in connection with graves may have required them to be broken (Kaul 1988, 38). Four of the seven Bornholm halberds also appear to have been broken in prehistory (Finds list VI, nos. 2, 3, 5 and 7). The other three halberds, however, are intact. One of the whole ones, given its light brown patina, may have been deposited in wetland (no. 4); another was found by a large stone and also has a brown patina (no. 1). There may have been several ways of depositing the objects, and perhaps this reflects the fact that intact and broken halberds had different meanings. During the treatment of the battle axes a suspicion arose of the systematic destruction of the weapons of opponents. A broken halberd may have been a trophy and may have had a different, but probably just as important meaning as an intact one.

7. The development of the early farming society

Theories about the introduction of farming and cattle breeding in South Scandinavia

There are many publications on the subject of the transition from hunter-gatherer to agricultural societies in Northern Europe. Some of the questions that have been examined in previous works have already been touched upon in the text above, especially in relation to dating. We will now examine some of the theories and opinions that have been of significance to understanding how the cultural change from hunter-gatherer to farmer occurred. This cannot include a presentation of all the details of this discussion, and for those wishing to investigate the question in more depth, other publications can be consulted, that deal with the subject or provide an update regarding the research (Thorpe 1996; Persson 1998; Price 2000; 2015, 104 ff.; Fischer & Kristiansen (eds) 2002; Klassen 2004; Glørstad & Prescott (eds) 2009; Sørensen 2014).

Most Scandinavian scholars believed, at least until recently, that agriculture was introduced to South Scandinavia by the indigenous population of hunters, fishermen and gatherers, who were in contact with agricultural societies south of the Baltic. Others suggest that there was immigration of a large or small population of farmers, and focus upon the question of how the meeting between the indigenous population and immigrants occurred.

One of the proposed scenarios involves a very long-lasting process, during which contacts between the Late Mesolithic Ertebølle Culture's population of hunters and gatherers in South Scandinavia and epi-Linear Pottery Culture groups of farmers in Central Europe led to diffusion of both production technology and prestigious objects, as well as agricultural products. This is described as *the productive gift* (Jennbert 1984). The introduction of pottery within the Ertebølle Culture from c. 4700 BC and the importation of prestige items, such as shaft-hole axes of amphibolite, was regarded as an important expression of the exchange connections with the agricultural societies to the south, leading to the introduction of agriculture (Fischer 1982; 1983; Jennbert 1984; Midgley 2011; M. Larsson 2013). However, today we see the contacts with the epi-Linear Pottery Culture groups and their significance to the introduction of agriculture in the Nordic countries in another light.

It has often been said that the contacts with the farming cultures to the south in the fifth millennium resulted in a transition to the use of pottery in the Ertebølle Culture. But it could not convincingly be explained how this culture's pointed-bottomed pottery vessels and lamps were derived from the Neolithic pottery of the Stichbandkeramik and Rössen cultures. Neither is this so surprising, as the pointed-bottomed pottery does not have any connection with these cultures, but is instead associated with the Mesolithic and partly Neolithic groups in an area from the Dutch Swifterbant Culture west of the Baltic and far into the Russian area to the east (Klassen 2002, 314; 2004, 109-19; Jordan & Zvelebil 2009, 35; Czerniak & Pyzel 2011). Not only in relation to production and form, but also in terms of function, there were major differences between the two ceramic traditions (Müller 2011).

On the other hand, the numerous finds of shoe-last axes from South Scandinavia and North Germany are indisputable evidence of exchange with the epi-Linear Pottery Culture groups, which is thought to have occurred throughout most of the fifth millennium, but ceased before the end of this millennium, so it is uncertain whether the importation of these axes was related to the introduction of agriculture in South Scandinavia (Klassen 2004, 24 ff.; Terberger *et al.* 2009). No imitations of the imported shoe-last axes in other types of stone are found, and they are represented in just one case in a deposit, which can perhaps be interpreted as of ritual type. It is uncertain what function these objects had amongst the hunter-gatherer population, and there are no indications that they circulated as prestige objects, as indicators of the beginnings of social hierarchization (Sørensen 2012).

In 1984, a development model was proposed for the transition to the Neolithic in Northern Europe from the hunter-gatherer perspective. The model involves three phases in the transition to farming: availability, substitution and consolidation (Zvelebil & Rowley-Conwy 1984). The model is still relevant to the description of the transition to agriculture in this part of the world, even though the situation is different today, as the contacts between hunter-gatherers and farmers that occurred during most of the fifth millennium apparently did not open up the possibility of an availability phase. There should, therefore, be a more dynamic sequence of events associated with the expansion of the Michelsberg Culture and the Funnel Beaker Culture's emergence in the geographical areas south of the Baltic, before we can talk about an availability phase.

In later contributions concerning the transition to the Neolithic period in the Baltic area, however, Marek Zvelebil (1996; 1998) places focus upon the actual process of transition. What happens in the cultural meeting between peoples with different kinds of technology, habitation, social structure and life philosophies? A number of ethnographic examples can be cited of the relationship between farming societies and a population that lives off the products of nature. These parallels indicate that the farmers occupy a dominant role and in the long run cause various disruptive effects amongst the hunter-gatherers (Zvelebil 1998, 16 ff.). Peter Rowley-Conwy, however, believes that this is to view the matter from a modern perspective, involving the meeting of cultures at very different levels, and that the transition from the Mesolithic to the Neolithic involved societies that were more equal, and where the hunter-gatherers could equally well have had the upper hand (Rowley-Conwy 2014). The cultural meeting may also have involved conflicts, although Zvelebil proposes that there was more likely to have been collaboration. It may have been crucial to an expanding population of farmers, who settled down in a new area, that the possibility existed of exchanging food materials with the local population before the agricultural production began. Through the contact with the hunter-gatherers, the farmers could quickly obtain knowledge of the natural resources and the places where it was possible to collect raw materials in the new surroundings. Zvelebil's focus was upon the contact zone between the Mesolithic groups in the Baltic area and the epi-Linear Pottery Cultures to the south, in a process that he and others thought led to the initiation of agriculture within the hunter-gatherer population, a transformation that it was responsible for. Even though we have moved away from this interpretation, we will later return to his considerations about the contacts between hunter-gatherers and farmers.

The transition from the Mesolithic to the Early Neolithic in South Scandinavia should mainly be assessed on the basis of to what extent there was continuity or discontinuity in subsistence strategy, settlement, technology and social structure. In addition to this, there is of course the question of population continuity, which can only be answered when the results of sufficient numbers of DNA analyses of human material from either side of the transition become available.

The discussion has long involved a focus upon the Ertebølle Culture and the indications of continuity during the transition from the Mesolithic to the Neolithic, which have been demonstrated by investigations of this culture's predominantly coastal settlements. The settlement remains of the Ertebølle Culture in the form of middens, inland settlements and submarine settlements have been rewarding subjects of study, where the living conditions could be described based upon data relating to the natural conditions of the period and the preserved contemporary faunal remains. The topographical location of the settlements on the coast or near to inland lakes has meant that rich and varied finds are still preserved today. Near the coastal settlements, whose activity area has been eroded away by the transgressions of the Littorina Sea, submarine waste layers have been found, which contain exceptionally well preserved organic material (Andersen 2013).

The Ertebølle Culture's large and long-lasting coastal settlements give an impression of permanent settlement rather than a mobile lifestyle. The adaptation to the natural surroundings appears ideal, given the location of these settlements, especially in relation to the aquatic resources. At some of the coastal settlements, there is evidence of continued hunting and fishing, as well as collection of molluscs long into the Neolithic, which has resulted in the use of the term 'fisherman-farmer' based upon the signs of continued use, as at the settlements at Bjørnsholm and Visborg in North Jutland, where the largest middens are located (Andersen 2000; 2007; 2008). It shows that, in the parts of South Scandinavia where resources were available, a very broad subsistence strategy could be practised at the start of the Early Neolithic. At the Ertebølle settlement Tybrind Vig there is evidence of both active and passive fishing, and finds of traps, leisters, harpoons, fish weirs and fish hooks demonstrate the use of a number of different fishing and catching methods (Pickard & Bonsall 2007; Andersen 2013, 295 f.). This specialised technology continued with the use of fish traps and weirs long into the Neolithic period (Pedersen 1997).

The transition from the Mesolithic to the Neolithic is often described against the background of material from such sites, where in both periods fishing, catching, hunting and the collection of shellfish took place. It is therefore perhaps not so strange that a number of contemporary researchers regard the transition to agricultural activity as a slow process, in which domesticated animals and crops were not of great significance as a nutritional basis in the beginning, as it was clear that the Stone Age population continued to practice hunting, fishing and collection long after the introduction of agriculture (Midgley 1992, 405; Welinder 1997; Persson 1998; Petersson 1999; Price & Gebauer 2005, 148 ff.). Studies of the development of vegetation have helped provide the impression that farming had a limited influence on the environment from the beginning of the Sub-Boreal, contrasting with a later, more extensive clearance phase around 3500 BC, described as 'Iversens landnam' (Iversen 1941; 1949). Only a few flint sickles with definite traces of microwear dating to the Early Neolithic have been identified, which has encouraged the view that cereal cultivation was limited during this period (Jensen 1994, 114 ff.).

But this view of the activity and societal conditions of the early farming culture has primarily been based upon the study of settlements that illuminate the hunting and catching aspect of the early Funnel Beaker Culture. Due to the good preservation at the sites, this aspect has been overrepresented in comparison with the archaeological source material from the agrarian settlements that are located inland. There has therefore been a lack of spatial dimension to the description of the transition from the Mesolithic to the Neolithic (Johansen 2006). Regional archaeological studies of settlements have, however, been undertaken of the overall material, consisting of settlement finds, offerings and stray finds from the Early Neolithic. These indicate that the finds from the first part of the Early Neolithic are not just found at fishing and hunting stations along the coasts, but particularly occur inland on cultivable soils. This has, for instance, been demonstrated on the islands south of Funen, where 'the Neolithisation process occurred quite quickly' (Skaarup 1985, 346-59). Studies from South-West Scania show a marked concentration of settlements dating to the beginning of the Early Neolithic, which are located on the sand hills of the inland area (M. Larsson 1984, 188-215). In Scania, the distribution of pointed-butted flint axes demonstrates that the first agricultural settlement moved away from the coast and followed the water courses far inland (Hernek 1989). Our mapping of the settlements and flint axes on Bornholm gives the same picture, which is in complete contrast to settlement during the Late Mesolithic. Even though finds of many complete, probably deliberately deposited pointed-butted flint axes are unlikely to provide the precise location of the settlements, these locations mark part of the activity areas that the early farmers moved around in. Lasse Sørensen (2014) has mapped the distribution of the three types of pointed-butted flint axes in Scandinavia, which shows the extent of the early farming culture; this partially corresponds with the distribution of the Ertebølle Culture, but also demonstrates extensive expansion into large parts of the inland areas (fig. 4.11). This expansion occurred within 150-200 years and has to be described as a very radical change.

The continuity at the coastal settlements from the Mesolithic to the Neolithic is one of the reasons why it was thought that farming and cattle breeding were initially only introduced as a supplement to hunting, catching, collection and fishing, and were practised more for social and ideological reasons than economic ones (Price 1996; 2000; Welinder 1997; M. Larsson 1997a, 97 ff.; 1997b; Price & Gebauer 2005, 155-57; Stafford 1999, 134; Fischer 2002). Not just in Denmark but also in Great Britain, the transition to the Neolithic period has been described as mainly a social and ideological change, whilst the economic significance of agriculture has been downplayed (Rowley-Conwy 2004 with references). The inspiration for this comes, for example, from Brian Hayden, who believes that it was through the creation and use of food surpluses at prestigious feasts amongst specialised hunter-gatherers that agriculture emerged and spread (Hayden 1990). 'The competitive feasting model' is appropriate for societies where status is achieved by redistribution of foodstuffs and other goods. Gifts create debts, which are the basis for power and control over labour resources. It has been suggested that, against such a background, hierarchization occurred as early as the Late Mesolithic in South Scandinavia, which may have been an important factor in the introduction of farming and cattle breeding (Andersson *et al.* 2016, 25). The model, however, does not fit in very well with the late Ertebølle Culture, in which it is difficult to discern differences in status (Price & Gebauer 2005, 146-48). There is a lack of evidence for the existence of chieftain types, and nor are there any archaeological finds that make the model likely in this cultural context. The accumulation of foodstuffs amongst hunter-gatherer populations is difficult, as large quantities of foods are the result of fortunate hunting or catching, which is unpredictable or dependent upon seasonally-determined large catches. Farmers, on the other hand, always have permanent supplies of food in the form of domesticated animals, which were probably only slaughtered when feasts were held (Hayden 2014, 125). In South Scandinavia, the competitive feasting model is therefore more likely to be relevant in connection with agricultural societies, and we will return to this later.

The continued use of the Ertebølle Culture's hunting and catching places from the Late Mesolithic to the Early Neolithic has made it difficult to imagine that the neolithisation occurred without the participation of the local population of hunters, gatherers and fishermen (*i.a.* Tilley 1996, 86). A continuity within flint technology has also been highlighted, by both Mats Larsson (1984, 162; 1997, 96) and Michael Stafford, who do not find any particularly striking differences between the flint assemblages of the Ertebølle Culture and the earliest Funnel Beaker Culture (Stafford 1999, 124 ff.). Stafford notes that the differences include a change from the use of blades to flakes as the basis for the production of small tools, a transition from soft to hard hammer flaking for the production of blades, a change in the ratios of the small tools, the disappearance of the core axe and the appearance of the polished, pointed-butted flint axe. The similarities include the continued use of the same small tools (scrapers, knives and transverse arrowheads), as well as flake axes and blades, although to a lesser extent than in the Late Mesolithic. To the differences highlighted by Stafford, we can add the larger numbers of flakes at Early Neolithic settlements, which were used for the production of small tools, like scrapers and knives, and often originate from the production and repair of pointed-butted and thin-butted axes. Small 'Havnelev flake axes' are found, which are often made from such flakes, and some flake axes display evidence of polishing, indicating that they were made of flakes from broken polished axes. Typical small tools at the Early Neolithic settlements consist of backed flake knives and small borers (Nielsen 1985). The Early Neolithic range of objects reflects a different approach to flint technology and also includes new tool forms. The most pronounced differences between the two assemblages is the end of very controlled production of blades that characterises the flint technique of the Ertebølle Culture, and the introduction of polished flint axes in the Early Neolithic.

The discussion about the continuity from the Ertebølle to the Funnel Beaker Culture within flint-working has, however, come to be seen in a different light after Lasse Sørensen has demonstrated that the flint assemblage at Early Neolithic settlements like Muldbjerg and Sigersted III (Nielsen 1985) have a composition which corresponds more with the flint assemblages of the Michelsberg Culture than with the Ertebølle Culture. For instance, flake axes are also found in the Michelsberg Culture (Sørensen 2014, 233, fig. V.184). Common to the Michelsberg and Funnel Beaker cultures are also pointed-butted axes of flint and other types of stone, both with and without a perforation through the butt (Sørensen 2012; 2014, 126 ff.), as well as stone battle axes of Zápotockýs Groups FII-III (Ebbesens type I), which appear for the first time at the beginning of the Early Neolithic.

The introduction of the pottery vessels of the Funnel Beaker Culture meant a break with the Ertebølle Culture's ceramic tradition and is perhaps the most clear indication of changes in basic food production. The archaeological finds and dates that are available to illuminate the beginnings of agriculture in Northern Europe suggest that the new ceramic technology was introduced at the same time as the introduction of domesticated animals like sheep/goats, oxen and pigs between c. 4000 and 3800 BC (Price & Noe-Nygaard 2009; Sørensen 2014, 86 ff.). Finds of the earliest cereals date to the same time (Sørensen & Karg 2014). One of the earliest dated context from Denmark containing preserved grains of barley (*Hordeum* sp.) is from the inland settlement of Sigersted III on Zealand, and dates to 5079±23/

5065±23 BP, cal. 3948-3807/3942-3802 BC (1σ) (P.O. Nielsen 1985, 110).

The finds from Bornholm also contribute to the picture of early agriculture during this period. Charred grains of club wheat (*Triticum compactum*) were found at Skovgård, Rutsker, and are dated to 5084±32/5016±30 BP (uncal.). As imprints on pottery club wheat is also known from Store Valby, western Zealand, in contexts dated to EN Ia (Becker's EN A) (Helbæk 1955). Two other types of cereal were found in house site FJ at Limensgård: bread wheat (*Triticum aestivum*) and naked barley (*Hordeum vulgare var. nudum*), dated to 5000±70 BP (see above p. 48 f.). The calibrated dates fall within EN A0-A1 on Bornholm, c. 3950-3800 BC. Equally early finds of bread/club wheat (*Triticum aestivum/compactum*) have been recovered at Almhov, Scania (Gidlöf *et al.* 2006, *passim*; Sørensen 2014, 72 ff.). "The impression gained (…) is that of a pretty complete plant-producing culture, with all the cereals at its disposal which at the time were common in the lands from where we may expect Denmark to have received cultural influences" (Helbæk 1955, 204). The use of different cereal types characterizes both the Funnel Beaker Culture and the Michelsberg Culture (Kreuz *et al.* 2014).

Even though both bones of domesticated animals and cereal grain impressions on the pottery vessels are known from the Ertebølle Culture, there is nothing to suggest consistent agricultural activities in the Late Mesolithic (Jennbert 2011; *cf.* Klassen 2004, 142 f.), and neither do the pollen diagrams from the sites in South Scandinavia show definite signs of changes in the vegetation that can be attributed to human intervention before the transition from the Atlantic to the Sub-Boreal, corresponding chronologically with the introduction of agriculture and cattle breeding (Rasmussen 2005, 1118-19).

Analyses of stable isotopes have helped paint a picture of an abrupt change in food intake after the transition to the Neolithic in South Scandinavia. Firstly, there is the demonstration of δ^{13} levels in human bones as an indicator of the quantities of marine versus terrestrial food. This has shown that the diet was dominated by aquatic food in the Late Mesolithic, whilst in the Neolithic people almost exclusively lived off terrestrial food sources (Tauber 1981). The content of $\delta^{15}N$ compared with $\delta^{13}C$ has pointed towards a similar picture (Schoeninger *et al.* 1983; Tauber 1986; Richards & Koch 2001). These indications of radical changes in diet are hard to dismiss in the discussion of the Mesolithic-Neolithic transition (Schulting 1998). The results have also been confirmed by subsequent investigations, which have indicated that there was limited maritime food intake throughout most of the Neolithic (Fischer *et al.* 2007). How pronounced the transition from marine to terrestrial food was, and precisely when it occurred, however, can only be established when more dates and isotope analyses of human bones around the Mesolithic-Neolithic transition become available.

Up until now, comparison between the $\delta^{13}C$ values of the Mesolithic and Early Neolithic populations has been made more difficult by the considerable chronological differences between the skeletal remains that it has been possible to analyse, which have ranged over a thousand years from the early Ertebølle Culture c. 4700 BC to c. 3700 BC. Only a few skeletons are dated to the period in between. This problem also plays a part in connection with the physical anthropological comparisons between the Mesolithic and Early Neolithic skeletons. Whilst the cranial and bone composition of the Mesolithic population is described as robust, the Early Neolithic population is more gracile. But it cannot solely on the basis of the physical differences be determined whether these were people of different ancestry, or whether, after the transition to the Neolithic, there were changes in the health of the local population, resulting from a different diet and different living conditions (Bennike & Alexandersen 2007).

Alterations in the natural conditions may have helped speed up the change. The transition to the Neolithic corresponds precisely with a significant drop in the numbers of oysters in middens, which may have been associated with changes in the sea level around 4000 BC (Christensen 1995). Changes in tidal amplitude and salinity have previously been suggested as the reasons for the decline in oysters (Petersen 1993). More recent investigations, however, have not identified significant changes in salinity of the waters where the oyster beds were located at the transition from the Mesolithic to the Neolithic. The reason for the decline in oysters has instead been suggested as being lower temperatures and increased sedimentation, which had negative consequences for the oyster populations (Lewis *et al.* 2016). P. Rowley-Conwy (1984) has pointed out that the loss of this food source was a contributing cause to the transition to agriculture. Others, however, have downplayed the significance of this one factor (Price 1996, 354; see also the discussion in Fischer 2002, 369-71). But this was not the only change that took place at the transition from the Atlantic to the Sub-Boreal. Pollen analyses from Sweden show a change to a colder and more unstable climate, accompanied by a lowering of the groundwater level (Berglund *et al.* 1991a, 415). At the same time, a decline in elm trees occurred, which must have been due to the spread of Dutch elm disease in Northern and Western Europe (Rasmussen 2005, 1119). Other changes may have occurred that affected animal behaviour and human access to natural resources. Lars Larsson suggests that the changes in the natural surroundings may have seemed like a sign from the powers above, and that this could have psychologically affected the hunter-gatherers, who faced the choice of either continuing their lifestyle or adopting agriculture (L. Larsson 2007).

In Scandinavia, the transition to the Neolithic has also been examined from an epistemological perspective, which has focused upon conceptualization and theory (Rudebeck 2000), but has also involved questioning the significance and relevance of this approach (Johansson 2003). Meanwhile, in recent years, new explanatory models have been proposed. Two scholars adhere to the same theory of communities of practice, which is intended for modern learning (Wenger 1998), but supports ideas of learning processes within societies of limited size, as formulated by Ralph Linton (1936), an influential American anthropologist from the first half of the 20th century. Fredrik Hallgren (2008) uses the theory to describe how the local population groups in Mälardalen and Bergslagen, Central Sweden, acquire and further develop practices associated with diet technology and crafts at the transition to the Neolithic, and therefore create and become part of a new cultural identity as farmers. No outside actors are involved in the process. The same is proposed based upon the finds and settlement, which point toward continuity of population in Östergötland (Gruber *et al.* 2016). But the knowledge that was acquired must have come from somewhere. We therefore go back to Zvelebil's notion of a possible collaboration across the dividing line between the hunter-gatherers and those that were already practising farming, with the advantages and disadvantages that could be associated with this for both groups. Lasse Sørensen (2014) uses the theory of communities of practice for this scenario. He believes that if a large proportion of the indigenous population of hunter-gatherers wanted to practice agrarian technology, then they could have entered communities of practice, and this could have led to a quick change in material culture and dietary strategy. By being under the influence of people with agrarian competences, the hunter-gatherers would also become part of the farmers' network and the social structure that characterised the Early Neolithic society (Sørensen 2014, 47). This explanatory model would suit the introduction of agriculture in South Scandinavia, which in many ways is characterised by a quick and 'invisible' transition from the Ertebølle to the Funnel Beaker Culture.

Searching explanations for culture change the pendulum can swing back to old, long abandoned theories when new material and dates become available and enable previously concealed sequences of development to be discovered. Diffusion and migration as an explanation of cultural change have long been regarded as a closed chapter in the history of research in Scandinavia. The radiocarbon revolution (Renfrew 1973) helped cement the view that innovation and development of cultural forms could emerge independently of one another and without being influenced by a specific starting point. This has consciously or subconsciously influenced the thinking of archaeologists, including those who have worked on the subject of neolithisation, and has been of great significance to the choice of explanatory models.

If we look outside Europe and examine the consequences that neolithisation has had in various parts of the world, however, there are a number of traits that recur. One of these is that the transition to farming has almost always led to population growth, which has encouraged the hypothesis of Neolithic demographic transition (Bellwood & Oxenham 2008). Inbuilt into this hypothesis is the idea that agriculture has most often been spread by immigration. The most explosive population growth can be observed where migration has occurred in previously uninhabited areas, like Oceania, whilst there has been slower population growth when the area's indigenous population has participated in the neolithisation. In Western and Northern Europe, agriculture was introduced over much larger areas than those inhabited by hunter-gatherers. The spread of farming in these areas was not at all slow, and the growth in population during the Early Neolithic may well be called 'explosive'.

Migration has also been one of the explanatory models, involving the first spreading of agriculture from the Balkan Neolithic by the Linear Pottery Culture over a short period to large parts of Central Europe around 5500 BC. The long standing debate about whether agriculture was adopted in Europe because of cultural contacts or demic diffusion came to a turning point when it was demonstrated that the dominant genes of the people of the Linear Pottery Culture originated from Anatolia and the Levant (Sokal *et al.* 1991). It had an impact on understanding processes of change due to migration of people, but it was also perceived as a support for theories about the spread of Indo-European languages (Renfrew 1987; Bellwood 2005).

The speed with which the establishment of agriculture occurred at this time, has encouraged some to suggest that full-scale migration may not have taken place, but instead that small groups or individual people must have arrived first and communicated knowledge of agriculture to the Mesolithic population, as 'managers of the neolithisation' (Gronenborn 2007; Kind 2010, 457). The DNA analyses that have been undertaken up until now, however, point towards a different picture, as individuals belonging to the Linear Pottery Culture contain only a small amount of haplogroup U, which is dominant amongst the Palaeolithic and Mesolithic hunter-gatherers. The composition of the haplogroups amongst early farmers in the Near East and the Linear Pottery Culture population is very uniform, consisting of haplogroups J, K, T and X, which suggests that the first farmers in Central Europe emigrated from the eastern Mediterranean via the Balkans. It is with the epi-Linear Pottery Culture groups, like Rössen and later on groups like Michelsberg and Baalberge, that the U-haplogroup first appears in the gene material, thus indicating that there was a clear mixing between farmers of south-eastern origin and local hunter-gatherers (Brandt *et al.* 2013; Mathieson *et al.* 2015; Lipson *et al.* 2017; Sørensen 2015).

The admixture of Anatolian/Near Eastern genes with the genes of European hunter-gatherers must have been an outcome of the diverse developments of the epi-Linear Pottery groups during the 5th millennium in western, central and eastern Europe while they were interacting with the surrounding hunter-gatherer societies. Some of these developments took place in Poland, where genes of Mesolithic provenance could be identified in the Brześć Kujawski Group of the late Lengyel Culture in Kuyavia, indicating that both male and female hunter-gatherers became part of the population of farmers. Analyses of succeeding Funnel Beaker Culture individuals from Kuyavia showed that they shared a similar genetic composition as that of the Brześć Kujawski individuals (Fernandes *et al.* 2018). There is still a lot of genetic history to be investigated, but the data available until now lead us to the assumption that an admixture with up till c. 30% of hunter-gatherer genes happened in the farming communities on the European Continent before agriculture spread towards northern and northwestern Europe.

Prior to the introduction of agriculture in Scandinavia, expansion occurred within the Chasséen and Michelsberg cultures in the period c. 4200-4000 BC, which resulted in the formation of new agricultural societies on the European Continent and in the British Isles. This expansion most likely involved migration (Sheridan 2010; Rowley-Conwy 2011; Sørensen 2014). It is supported by recent DNA analyses indicating that agriculture was introduced to Britain by incoming continental farmers, who had small levels of hunter-gatherer ancestry (Brace *et al.* 2019). Sørensen suggests that the starting point for migration to Northern Europe can be found in the Michelsberg Culture, whose expansion into Central Europe in the centuries before 4000 BC may have been the result of population growth and increased tension and competition between population groups, as well as perhaps an agrarian economic crisis, which meant there was a need to take control of and cultivate new areas (Sørensen 2014, 263 ff.). It is a model that can explain why the Funnel Beaker Culture, which was equipped with agrarian technology like the Michelsberg Culture, emerged in Central, Eastern and Northern Europe from c. 4100 BC. Sørensen sees the process as happening in a collaboration between the migrating farmers and the local population groups, which by participating in communities of practice quickly adopted both the agrarian technology and the social behaviour that characterised the immigrant population (Sørensen 2014, 264). The model may explain the indications of continuity, such as seasonal stays at the settlements, which in the Mesolithic period were used for hunting, catching and fishing. On the background of the continuous exploitation of wild resources it has also been suggested that there may have been 'cultural and economic negotiation' between local foragers and immigrating farmers (Gron & Sørensen 2018). We think, however, that any cultural dualism at the beginning of the Neolithic could only have existed for a very short period of time. There is no convincing evidence for a continuation of the Ertebølle *Culture* after 4000/3950 BC. We may therefore ask how much of the Mesolithic *population* did actually survive the Mesolithic-Neolithic transition? (*cf.* Brinch Petersen 2015, 128 ff.) Only new genetic analyses can answer that question.

Sørensen examines the various forms of migration, and its possible causes in the form of push and pull effects (2014, 50 ff.). Push effects could be growing population, increasing competition and conflicts, whilst pull effects include favourable conditions for cultivation, and supplementary food sources or raw materials in the destination areas. One of the factors that perhaps led to migration from the south may have been the possibilities that existed in South Scandinavia to supplement farming and cattle breeding with hunting, fishing and catching sea mammals, which would have provided migrating farmers with the security of being able to survive a transitional phase, before agrarian production properly began. Another factor may have been demand for raw materials like flint for the production of tools, which is suggested by the establishment of flint mines from the beginning of the Neolithic in South Scandinavia.

Movement of entire families, animals and equipment to another location must have been both demanding and risky, so before migration took place, scouting expeditions must have been dispatched to find and explore suitable locations for settlement (Sørensen 2014, 56 f.). Access to high-quality flint in South Scandinavia may have encouraged such scouting expeditions, which were followed by migration to flint-rich areas. We have seen how the production of pointed-butted flint axes developed from the beginning of the Early Neolithic on both sides of Øresund, where there was access to considerable quantities of good-quality flint, and the quantities of finds in exactly these areas must reflect a significant increase in population.

In quite a few cases, open seas must have been crossed to travel from the south coast of the western Baltic to the Danish islands and Southern Sweden. Maritime pioneer colonization was not new to migrating farmers. It took place c. 2000 years earlier from east to west along the coasts of the Mediterranean (Isern *et al.* 2017). And it happened during the neolithisation of the British Isles at approximately the same time as in South Scandinavia (Sheridan 2010). As we have previously mentioned, travelling across the sea did not just take place during the colonisation phase, but was undertaken on many occasions during the first centuries of the Early Neolithic, for example, to Bornholm and Gotland. Journeys over land and water also became part of the way of life of those who were ambitious, and for whom it was important to maintain and establish new status relations.

We believe that Sørensen's migration model is not only suitable for explaining the introduction of agriculture in North Germany and Scandinavia, but that it can also be used as an explanatory model for the whole area in which finds from the early Funnel Beaker Culture occur, and where the finds are composed of elements that either completely or partially can be traced back to the Michelsberg Culture. Migration may have become part of the way of life of the farmer population. People may not have migrated all the time, but migration may have been practised by a new generation. If within societies that had recently begun to live as farmers, the practice emerged of sending young people to other areas to establish farming, then there may have been a domino effect. This would help to explain the quick spread of agriculture, the wide distribution of uniform pottery during the early phase of the Funnel Beaker Culture and objects with symbolic meaning, like the battle axes of Zápotocký's Groups FII-III (Ebbesen's type I).

The European background of the neolithisation of South Scandinavia

Chronological basis

In the following text, the archaeological material from the Early Neolithic on Bornholm will be interpreted and converted into a model for the development of the early agricultural society between c. 4000 and 3300 BC. The basis for this will mainly be provided by the archaeological material, but the development will be compared with the results that elsewhere have helped illuminate the spreading of farming and cattle breeding in Northern, Western and Central Europe, followed by the social and economic development in a number of stages.

Dating is essential for understanding the development. In Denmark, the earliest inland settlements associated with the Funnel Beaker Culture, like Sigersted III, Pit A, in Central Zealand, are dated to 3950-3800 BC (see page 53), with the lake shore settlement Åkonge in Store Åmose, West Zealand, as early as c. 3950 BC (Fischer 2002, 357 ff.). The change from the Ertebølle to the Funnel Beaker Culture can be identified from the stratigraphy of middens in Jutland, most precisely in the midden at Bjørnsholm, North Jutland, where the earliest Neolithic material is dated to 3960-3830 BC (S.H. Andersen 1993, 75).

In Halland, both cereals and Funnel Beaker pottery have been dated to around 4000 BC (Sjögren 2012). In Central Sweden, the transition from the Mesolithic to the Neolithic is dated to 3950-3850 BC (Hallgren 2008, 76-89), whilst in other parts of the Scandinavian peninsula, where the development has followed its own course, there are somewhat later dates. It has been suggested in a number of cases that the appearance of Early Neolithic pottery and polished axes in a given area does not necessarily demonstrate contemporary introduction of farming and cattle breeding. This applies to areas like Bohuslän and Southern Norway (Nordqvist 1997, 106; Persson 1999, 108; Petersson 2009; Glørstad 2009, 150; Schenck 2014).

Also very relevant to the development of early agriculture on Bornholm and in the rest of South Scandinavia are the dates from the south coast of the Baltic Sea for early Funnel Beaker Culture material, including domesticated animals, such as from the settlement at Wangels, where the earliest finds of sheep/goat are dated to c. 4100 BC (Hartz *et al.* 2000; Hartz *et al.* 2002; Hartz & Lübke 2005; 2006).

In order to compare the development on Bornholm and in the rest of South Scandinavia with that in Western, Central and Eastern Europe (fig. 7.1), we will use the following division of the Early Neolithic into three phases, EN Ia, EN Ib and EN II, which are defined in the following way: [1]

EN Ia, 4100-3800/3750 BC. Oxie-/Wangels phase. On Bornholm EN A0-A1. The occurrence of Eva Koch's funnel beakers of type 0 and I. Earliest flint mines. There are no monumental burial monuments and no causewayed enclosures during this phase in South Scandinavia. Outside South Scandinavia, this phase corresponds with the earliest Funnel Beaker finds from Holstein (Flintbek, Wangels and Neustadt) and the Sarnowo phase in Kuyavia, which both begin around 4100 BC. It is contemporary with Michelsberg I-II.

EN Ib, 3800/3750-3500 BC. On Bornholm EN A2 and EN B. The occurrence of Eva Koch's funnel beakers types II and III. Volling style in Jutland. The burial custom includes non-megalithic long barrows in South Scandinavia, Central Germany and Poland. The construction of causewayed enclosures begins in South Scandinavia. Outside Scandinavia, this phase corresponds with Baalberge in Central Germany and the Pikutkowo phase in Poland. It is contemporary with Michelsberg III-V.

EN II, 3500-3300 BC. It corresponds with EN C on Bornholm. The occurrence of Eva Koch's funnel beaker type IV. Fuchsberg and Virum style. The burial custom primarily involves megalithic burials in the form of dolmens and a small number of non-

Fig. 7.1. Chronological scheme.

Calendar years BC	Western France	North-Central France	Western Germany	Sachsen-Anhalt	Great Britain	South Scandinavia and North Germany	Northern Poland	Calender years BC
3200				Salzmünde B	MN	MN A I	Luboń	3200
3300	Kerugou	Seine-Oise-Marne	Wartberg		Peterborough Ware	EN II Fuchsberg / Virum Bellevuegården	Wiórek	3300
3400				Salzmünde A				3400
3500								3500
3600			Michelsberg			EN Ib Volling / Havnelev, Svenstorp / Vallensgård I	Pikutkowo	3600
3700	Chasséen		MK V	Baalberge	EN			3700
3800		Michelsberg / Chasséen	MK IV					3800
3900			MK III	Baalberge amphorae	Carinated Bowl Neolithic	EN Ia Oxie/Wangels	Sarnowo	3900
4000			MK II					4000
4100				Schiepzig (MK)				4100
4200	Castellic		MK I				Late Lengyel / Brzesc Kujawski	4200
4300			Bischheim	Gatersleben	Late Mesolithic	Late Mesolithic		4300
4400	Cerny	Cerny				Ertebølle		4400
4500			Rössen	Rössen				4500
4600	Les Fouaillages / Carn Group						Stichband-Keramik	4600
4700		Villeneuve-Saint-Germain						4700
4800				Stichband-keramik				4800
			Grossgartach					

megalithic long barrows in South Scandinavia and North Germany. The construction of causewayed enclosures reaches its peak in South Scandinavia. Outside Scandinavia, this phase corresponds with Salzmünde A in Central Germany and the Wiórek phase in Poland.

In South Scandinavia, this chronological division is based upon the discussion above regarding dating of the Bornholm settlement contexts and flint axe types. Regarding Central Europe, there are various overviews of the chronology of the individual phases and cultural groups based on ^{14}C dates, with the most detailed study focusing upon the development in the Elb-Saale area (Müller 2001). In relation to Poland, the division of the Funnel Beaker Culture in the extensive Polish lowland area is referred to (Jażdżewski 1984, 161; Midgley 1992, 51-58), as well as the dating of the earliest phase in Kuyavia with recent corrections (see below).

The origin of the Funnel Beaker Culture – east or west?

The origin of the Funnel Beaker Culture has been looked for in eastern Central Europe (Jażdżewski 1932; 1936; Becker 1947, 200 ff.; 1955; Midgley 1992, 47; Price 2000). It ought to have emerged through acculturation of Mesolithic groups on the basis of epi-Linear Pottery Culture groups, like the late Lengyel Brześć Kujawski Group in Central Poland. However, very different interpretations have been proposed in relation to the continuity between these groups, as the composition of the flint assemblage within the earliest Funnel Beaker Culture, the Sarnowo phase, is thought to point back to the Mesolithic (Niesiołowska 1994, 333), but also parallels the flint technology of the late Lengyel (Balcer 1983; Domańska 1995). Regarding the pottery assemblage, Polish researchers place emphasis upon the composition of the pottery fabric and use of grog, which connects the pottery from the Brześć Kujawski Group with the early Funnel Beaker Culture (Rzepecki 2004, 226; Kukawka 2015, 291). The pottery is, however, morphologically different, which must reflect functional differences. Within settlement organisation and house construction, however, the Sarnowo phase represents a clear change. The construction of the Lengyel Culture's trapezoid longhouses ceases and is followed by smaller house constructions that are difficult to recognise (Grygiel 1984; 2008).

The Sarnowo phase has long been regarded as having occurred very early, as the earliest find complex of the Funnel Beaker Culture, a notion based upon a single ^{14}C date of charcoal from a pit under a non-megalithic long barrow at the site of Sarnowo 1A in Kuyavia, which gave a date of c. 4400 BC (GrN-5035, 5570±60 BP) (Bakker *et al.* 1969, 7-9; Gabałówna 1970, 80). Even though the sample was not of sufficient volume for conventional dating, the date has nonetheless been of great importance to the discussion about the beginnings and origins of the Funnel Beaker Culture, and the early dating of the Sarnowo phase has ended up being included in all subsequent chronological schemes.

A sample from a grave, Łącko 6A, in the Bydgoszcz area gave the same date (Gd-6019, 5570±110 BP), which apparently confirmed the date form Sarnowo (Domańska & Kośko 1983; Rzepecki 2004, Table 18). These are, however, the only two dates from the early Funnel Beaker Culture in Poland, which stretches back to around 4400 BC.

It was only after the discovery of new finds and further dates that it became obvious that the above-mentioned dates were too early. The beginning of the Sarnowo phase is now placed 4100-4000 BC (Terberger & Kabaciński 2010; Papiernik 2012; Kukawka 2015; Papiernik & Płaza 2018, 265-72; Czerniak 2018, 121), and an even later date c. 3900/3800 has also been proposed (Grygiel 2018). The Polish finds (fig. 7.2)

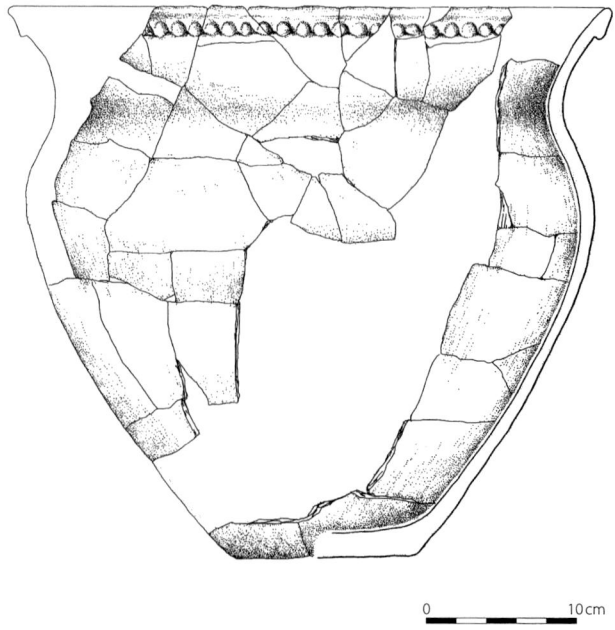

Fig. 7.2. Funnel beaker from the settlement Redecz Krukowy, Kuyavia, Poland. The Sarnowo phase of the early Funnel Beaker Culture c. 4000-3900 BC (after Papiernik 2012). 1:5.

Fig. 7.3. The distribution of the Michelsberg Culture and early Funnel Beaker Culture c. 4100-3800 BC (after Sørensen 2014).

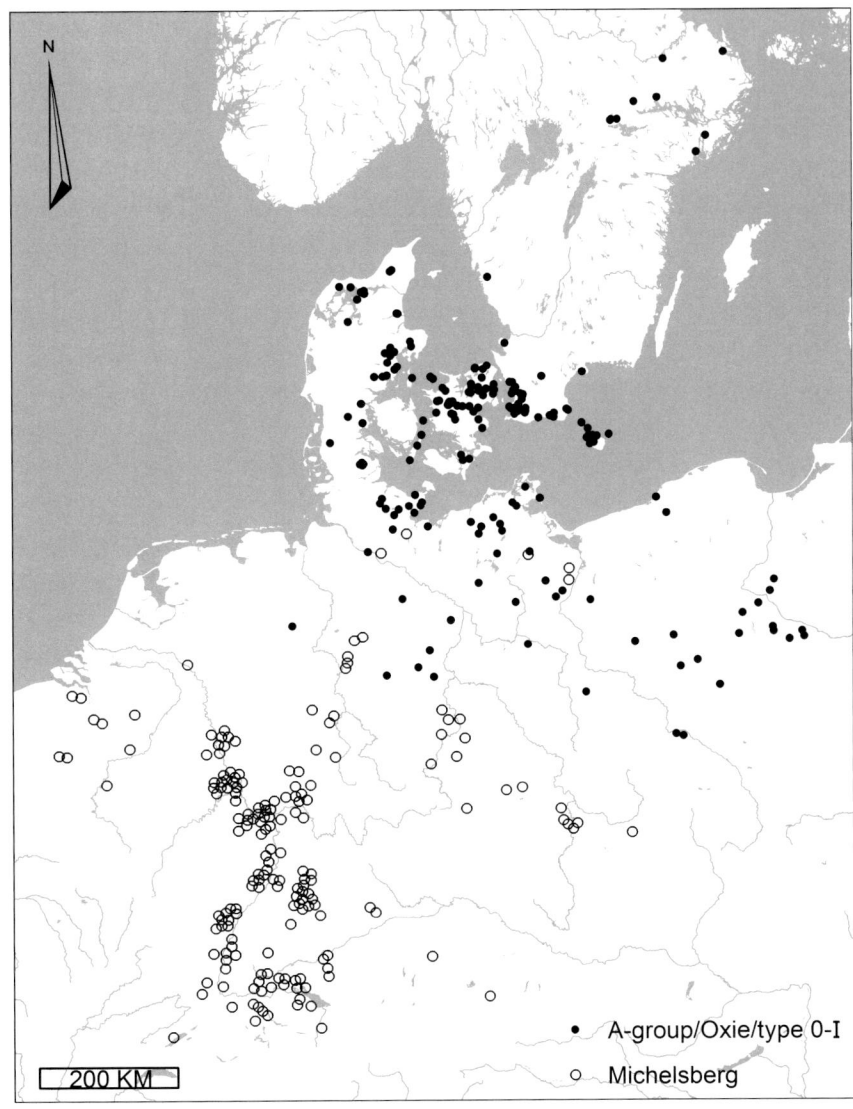

are therefore not earlier than finds from the earliest Funnel Beaker Culture from Flintbek (Zich 1993), Wangels (Hartz *et al.* 2000) and Neustadt in North Germany (Glykou 2016).

The earliest phase of the Funnel Beaker Culture occurred later and covered a much larger geographical area than was previously assumed. The scenario has changed significantly. Similarities between the find assemblages from Kuyavia, North Germany, and Scandinavia as far north as Central Sweden, along with new ^{14}C dates, indicate that the earliest phase of the Funnel Beaker Culture in all of this area dates to c. 4100-3800 BC. None of the material culture from this phase in North Germany and Scandinavia suggests any connection back to the late Linear Pottery Culture groups of the fifth millennium, such as the late Rössen, despite the contacts that existed with these societies in the Late Mesolithic, and which involved the importation of shoe-last axes and other things that may have been considered exotic by the hunter-gatherers (Klassen 2004, 19-108; Terberger & Kabaciński 2010). Neither is it likely that the inspiration to undertake agriculture came from these sources.

The impulses came from elsewhere, and we should turn our attention to Western Europe, where a development occurred in the second half of the fifth millennium that came to accelerate the spread of farming and cattle breeding. It occurred within forms of society that in many areas had become removed from the previous, late Linear Pottery Culture groups. These new societies also became important to the development of social aspects of the Neolithic societies in Western, Central and Northern Europe. The early Funnel Beaker Culture developed parallel with the expansion that took place within the Chasséen and Michelsberg cultures. The Michelsberg Culture, whose earliest phase is dated to 4300-4200 BC, expanded c. 4200-4000 BC in an easterly direction towards Central Europe, and ceramic finds, which are either original types or copies, spread towards Holstein and Mecklenburg-Vorpommern (fig. 7.3). The Michelsberg Culture is therefore of great significance as a potential basis for the emergence of the Funnel Beaker Culture in North Germany, Poland and Scandinavia (Rzepecki 2004; Klassen 2004, 273 ff.; Sørensen 2014; Price 2015, 114).

As in Poland, the construction ended of the large, trapezoid longhouses, which in the fifth millennium were erected within the late Linear Pottery Culture groups, such as Rössen, Großgartach and Villeneuve St Germain, in West and Central Europe (Hampel 1989). At the settlements belonging to both the Michelsberg Culture from 4300-4200 BC and the early Funnel Beaker Culture south of the Baltic dating to c. 4100 BC, only a few and unclear remains of dwellings have been preserved, which point towards another form of settlement and social organisation (Last 2013). The changes also applied to farming, as cultivation not only took place on the loess soils like in the time of Linear Pottery Culture, but also on other soil types.

The bones from the large causewayed enclosures give us an idea of the domesticated animals that were characteristic of the Michelsberg Culture. Cattle, sheep, goats and pigs were kept as domesticated animals within the later Linear Pottery Culture groups, and among the bones from the ditches of the enclosures it is especially cattle that dominate. The slaughtering of the meat-rich animals must have been associated with gatherings at these sites, with the other types of domesticated animals not represented to the same extent. The butchering waste also includes quite large quantities of bones from wild animals, especially red deer and aurochs, which illustrates the continued importance of hunting (Arbogast 1998; Steppan 1998).

There are great similarities between the ceramic assemblages of the Michelsberg and the Funnel Beaker cultures (fig. 7.4). Common forms are the funnel beakers, in Michelsberg 'Tulpenbecher', lugged jars, lugged flasks and clay discs with finger impressions at the edge, as well as more rarely clay spoons. Michelsberg funnel beakers have round bottoms, whilst within the Funnel Beaker Culture these vessels are predominantly flat bottomed. The pottery is generally undecorated or only minimally decorated, but cordons at the rim with finger impressions, 'arcade rims', are found in both cultures. Within the Michelsberg Culture, there are also forms which are not found in the northern, early Funnel Beaker Culture, such as bowls with sharply-angled profiles known from later Michelsberg contexts (fig. 7.4:5).

As mentioned above, there are also similarities in the composition of the flint assemblages of the Michelsberg and Funnel Beaker cultures, but also differences. Leaf-shaped, pressure-flaked arrowheads are widespread within Michelsberg and related groups in Western and Central Europe, but are not found in Scandinavia. The production and use of pointed-butted, polished flint axes is one of the most significant similarities. In the examination of the pointed-butted flint axes above, it is suggested that pointed-butted axes of jade may have been of importance to the form and symbolic significance of flint axes. Ritual deposits of one or more pointed-butted flint axes within the Michelsberg Culture correspond with the widespread deposition of pointed- and thin-butted flint axes in Scandinavia. Exchange of prestigious objects, like axes of jade and flint, characterised societies in Western Europe as far back as the beginning of the fifth millennium, but other phenomena also emerged in the western part of the Continent, which were of significance to the further development of Neolithic society, and came to affect Northern Europe to a considerable degree.

Hierarchisation as a result of neolithisation

Earlier research regarded the occurrence of megalithic tombs in Western and Northern Europe as an indication of cultural connections with the Mediterranean (Montelius 1899; Stjerna 1911, 132 ff.; Childe 1957, 213 ff.; Daniel 1958, 120 ff.), and the spreading of the monumental burial custom has been described as a megalithic mission associated with the worship of a mother goddess (Glob 1967, 75-78). It was with the radiocarbon dating revolution that this theory was invalidated (Renfrew 1973). The diffusionist outlook had to be abandoned and it was accepted that monumental burials were constructed in Western Europe from the fifth millennium, long before any supposed prototypes in Egypt and the Aegean area. The next realisation was that the Western and Northern European megalithic burials were not the first burial monuments, but were a stage in the development of the monumental burial custom within the Early Neolithic societies. The idea of a common religion within the whole of the Western and North European area has gradually been diluted and replaced

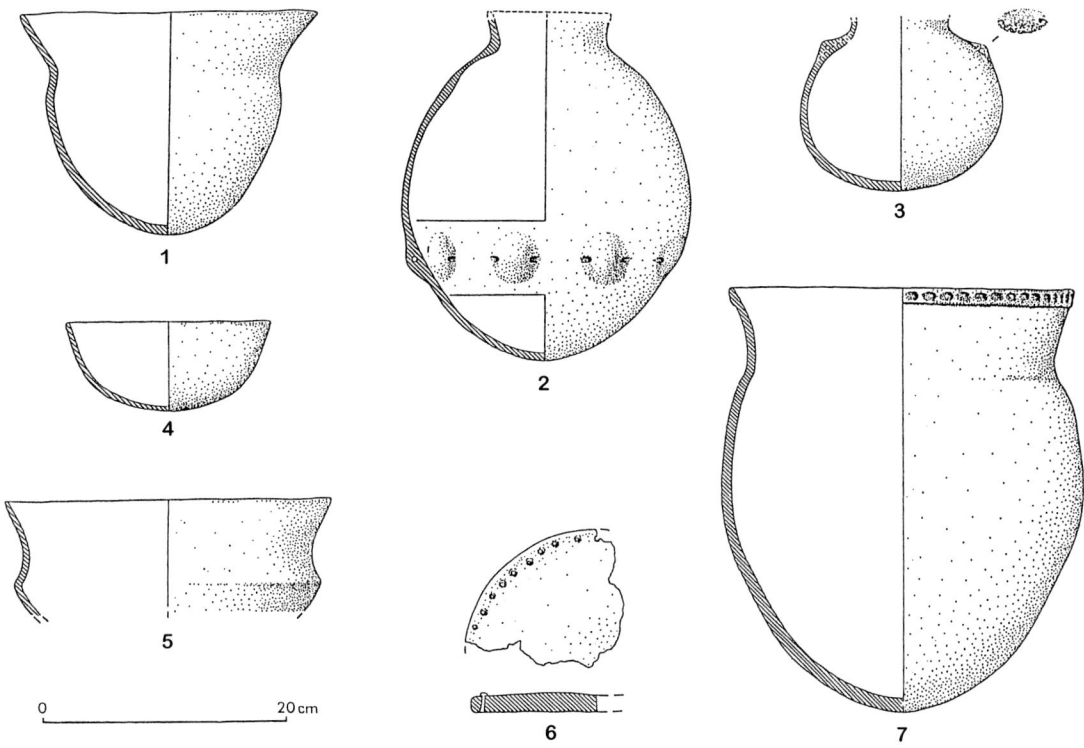

Fig. 7.4. Examples of Michelsberg pottery from Mairy, Western France, belonging to different phases of the settlement, c. 4000-3600 BC (after Laurelut 1989).

by ideas of emerging hierarchies and the worship of ancestors, as common traits amongst the different Neolithic societies.

In Western France and on the Channel Islands, around the middle of the fifth millennium, monumental burials appeared in the form of non-megalithic, trapezoid or rectangular burial mounds, *tertres tumulaires*, with burials in closed burial chambers. In Brittany, there is a concentration of these long barrows on the south coast around the Gulf of Morbihan, where, at the same time, decorated menhirs were also erected, which today can mostly be found as re-used elements in passage graves, such as Gavrinis and La Table des Marchands, where they have been used as capstones. La Table des Marchands was constructed on top of an early ritual structure containing menhirs, the largest of which, le Grand Menhir Brisé, had been 20 m in height. Some of the fragments of menhirs have engraved images of oxen and pointed-butted axes. Standing menhirs are still found today in Brittany, and some, including the long row of menhirs at Carnac, may date back to the time before the construction of megalithic tombs (Scarre 2010).

Impressive long barrows with closed chambers lacking access from outside, *tumulus carnacéens*, are also found in Brittany from the middle of the fifth millennium onwards. The largest, Le Tumulus-Saint-Michel, is 125 m long, 60 m wide and 10 m high. Slightly later come the first passage graves in long barrows or round barrows. The long barrow Barnenez is over 70 m long and contained 11 passage grave chambers, to which there was access via narrow passages. The passage graves in Brittany were constructed from c. 4300 BC and probably up until c. 3200 BC. They are therefore the earliest megalithic tombs in Europe. There can be little doubt that there was a sequence from mounds with single burials to the construction of complex passage grave chambers, which reflects society's development from the beginnings of hierarchisation to a complex social structure (Boujot & Cassen 1993; Cassen *et al.* (eds) 2000). The repeated incorporation of earlier elements into the burial architecture may have been an expression that the connection with the ancestors was maintained and this was transformed into myths about the founders of the society.

As mentioned in the section on the pointed-butted axes previously, it is in Brittany that the richest deposits of pointed-butted axes of jade and other types of stone are found, some of which are associated with menhirs, whilst others have been found in *tumulus*

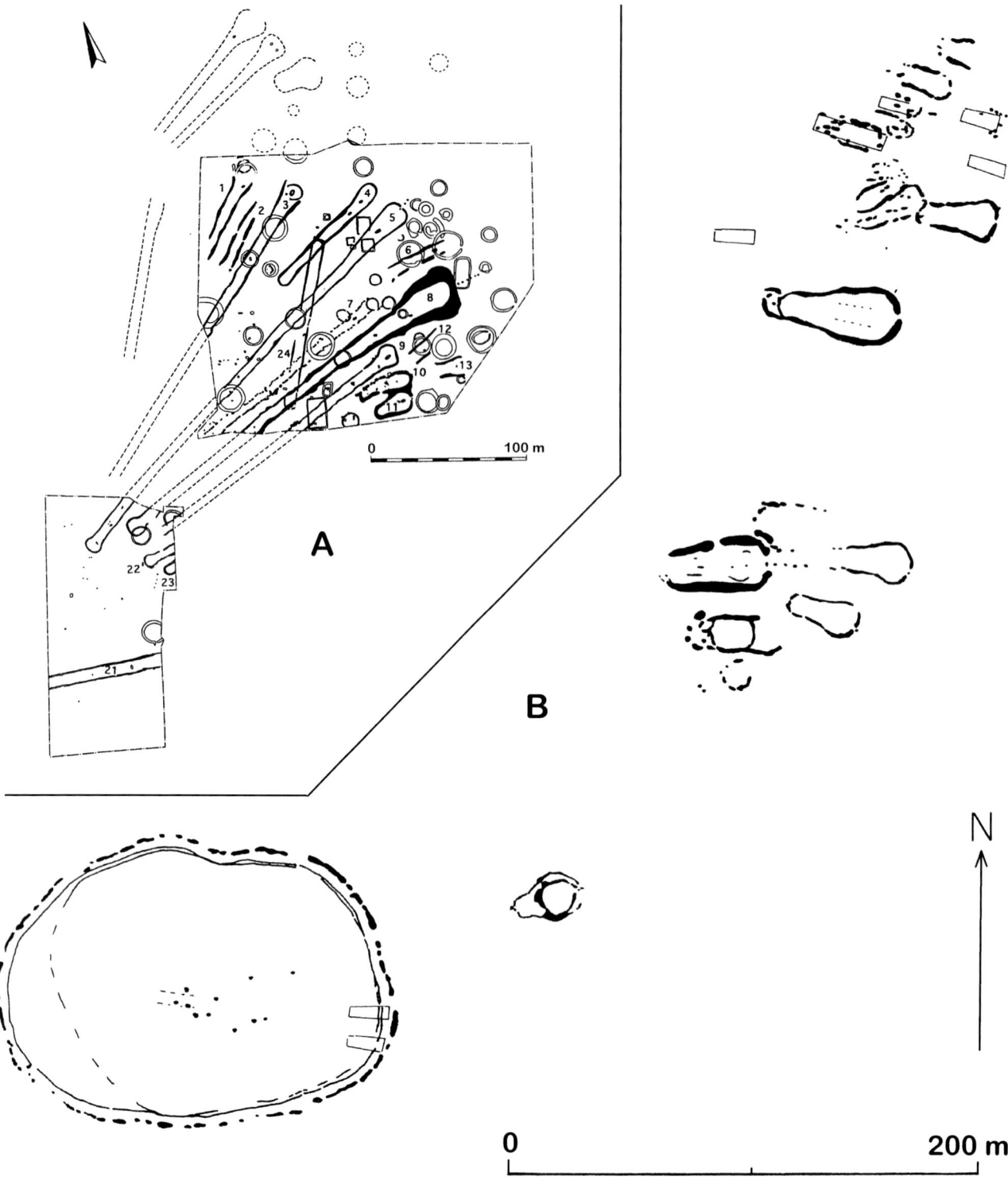

Fig. 7.5. (A) Long barrows of the Cerny Culture at Passy, France (after Duhamel 1997). – (B) Long barrows and causewayed enclosure from the Cerny Culture at Balloy, France (after Mordant 1997).

carnacéens, and there are depictions of these axes in passage graves such as Gavrinis. A significant proportion of the distribution of axes of exotic stone to other parts of Europe is thought to have radiated out from here (Klassen *et al.* 2012). In Brittany we thus observe a number of the traits that also characterised the Early Neolithic societies in other parts of Europe.

As already mentioned, at the same time as the construction of the earliest, non-megalithic long barrows occurred in Brittany, around the middle of the fifth millennium, very similar burial monuments were constructed in North Central France within the Cerny Culture, the so-called long barrows of the Passy type (Duhamel 1997). These appear in groups and can be up to 230 m long (fig. 7.5A). There are 18 long barrows at Balloy in Valle de Seine, which are 13-60 m long and are located at three burial places close to a causewayed enclosure from the same period, c. 4450-4250 BC (fig. 7.5B). Four of the long barrows were constructed on top of the remains of epi-Linear Pottery Culture longhouses belonging to the Villeneuve-Saint-Germain Culture (Mordant 1997; N.H. Andersen 1997, 219 ff.). Of the 45 buried individuals, 36 % were children and there was an approximately equal division between men and women amongst the adults. The burials do not contain many grave goods, but in each of the investigated burial places there is one male grave that stands out from the rest due to its special furnishings, which unexpectedly are associated with hunting (Chambon & Thomas 2010). There are therefore symbolic references both to the previous farming societies, on top of whose dwellings the long barrows were erected, as well as the life as hunter-gatherers, which may indicate that the people of the Cerny Culture had roots in both cultural forms.

The connection between monumental burial mounds and causewayed enclosures suggests that this community was controlled by people from families of special status, whose members, regardless of their age, were buried in the long barrows. In the southern part of the Paris Basin, at least eight sites with long barrows have been recorded, including Chablis, which is also near a causewayed enclosure, and Passy, which has given its name to the burial type, where 24 long barrows were excavated, including some of the longest examples (fig. 7.5A). The sites are spread out and are 30-40 km apart. This gives an impression of the size of the territories whose populations were controlled by an elite (Delor *et al.* 1997, 392).

The long barrows of the Passy type were not followed by the construction of megalithic burials like in Brittany, and long barrows, with a few exceptions, were not subsequently constructed in the Michelsberg and Chasséen cultures. Just a few long barrows are known from the Michelsberg Culture and these are respectively dated to an early and a late phase of this culture (Rzepecki 2011, 171 f.; Colas *et al.* 2007). There is a chronological jump from the construction of the French long barrows to similar structures appearing in other parts of Europe.[2] It is therefore somewhat of a puzzle how non-megalithic long barrows nevertheless came to play a significant role as social markers in communities, which the Michelsberg and Chasséen cultures came into contact with in the British Isles and Central Germany, Poland, North Germany and Scandinavia from c. 3800 BC, long after the Cerny Culture had ended.

During the 2nd half of the 5th millennium metal spread from sources in the Balkans and Eastern Europe, and 'copper age' groups emerged, such as the Brześć Kujawski Group in Central Poland, prior to the emergence of the Funnel Beaker Culture, which seems to have happened in close proximity to Brześć Kujawski settlements. Some of the burials of the Brześć Kujawski Group were richly furnished, and their contents indicate long-distant exchange in exotic objects including ornaments made of copper. It cannot be interpreted otherwise than "emergence of people of an exceptional social status" (Czerniak 2012, 166). Social stratification thus began prior to the advent of the Funnel Beaker Culture in those areas and long before any status markings such as long barrows became visible.

Organised cemeteries are not found within the Michelsberg Culture, where burials often took place in silo-shaped pits. Human and animal skeletons are also found in and near the ditches of the causewayed enclosures but lack the order that can otherwise be expected at cemeteries (Jeunesse 2010a). Common graves containing the remains of men, women and children are interpreted as evidence of attacks and massacres (Wahl 2010). Repeated burials in silo-shaped pits, in which the uppermost body has been randomly placed and lacks grave goods, may represent evidence of a custom of subordinate people or slaves being buried with their masters (Jeunesse 2010a). The human remains thrown into the ditches and in the mass graves point towards conflicts between rival groups.

In the discussion about the neolithisation of the British Isles, at least four different events have been highlighted that all involved migration from the Continent. There may have been limited migration from Brittany to Wales, Western Scotland and Northern Ireland, where simple passage graves of the Breton type were constructed in the period 4300/4200-4000 BC, and in this case these are the earliest megalithic graves in the British Isles (Sheridan 2010, 92 ff.). This may have been associated with the culmination of the passage grave construction in Brittany, which must have been ordered by a powerful elite with connections to distant areas. But it is uncertain whether the proposed migration had consequences for the development of the construction of burials in the British

Isles. There is an early date from County Sligo in Ireland, where, according to the ^{14}C dates, the causewayed enclosure at Magheraboymay should already have been established by c. 4000 BC, in which case it is the earliest example of this type of structure in the British Isles (Danaher 2009; Cooney et al. 2011, 574 ff.).

In Southern England, where the Neolithic begins c. 4000 BC or just before this, the earliest dates for long barrows are shortly after or around 3800 BC, and long barrows apparently appear slightly before the construction of causewayed enclosures, which are first found around 3750 BC (Bayliss et al. 2011, 719 ff.). In the British Isles, the construction of burial monuments continues with both long barrows and different forms of megalithic tombs, culminating in the large passage graves 3400-3200 BC.

The non-megalithic long barrows in Poland have various forms. The long trapezoid, Kuyavian burial mounds very much resemble the Passy type and, like these, are found in large groups (Chmielewski 1952). On the basis of the now revised, early dating of the beginning of the Polish Funnel Beaker Culture, these mounds have also previously been considered to be approximately contemporary with the Passy type (Midgley 1994; 2000). But the ^{14}C dates of the Kuyavian long barrows that are available today, however, are all placed after 4000 BC (Rzepecki 2011, 150 ff.). Despite their chronological difference, however, there is another trait that is shared by the Kuyavian long barrows and long barrows of the Passy type, as in more than one way the barrows are associated with the ancestors' dwellings. The trapezoid Kuyavian long barrows resemble the trapezoid longhouses that were built by the Brześć Kujawski Group in Central Poland (Grygiel 1984; 2008). A number of archaeologists have emphasised the similarity between the earliest long barrows and the trapezoid longhouses of the Rössen, Lengyel and Villeneuve-Saint-Germain cultures in the fifth millennium BC (Kinnes 1982; Midgley 1985, 215; 1997, 684; 2000; Sherratt 1990). Due to the chronological difference with the houses of the Brześć Kujawski Group, for the people who constructed the Kuyavian long barrows it must have been a link to a quite distant, mythological past. In France, on the other hand, the long barrows of the Passy type at Balloy were placed precisely on top of the house remains from the immediately previous Villeneuve-Saint-Germain Culture.

The relationship between house, settlement and burial construction is also a theme that is associated with recent Danish excavations at Frydenlund and Damsbo on Funen, where the house sites were enclosed by oblong structures, with or without mounds, and under dolmens (Eriksen & Andersen 2014, 101 ff.; N.H. Andersen 2015; 2019). Most of the Danish and Swedish non-megalithic long barrows can, on the basis of the available ^{14}C dates and the associated find contexts, be dated to EN Ib, c. 3800/3750-3500 BC (Sørensen 2014, 215 and fig. V.165). There are earlier dates for structures from both Jutland and Scania, but these come from sample material, which is either of an unknown age or from activities that took place before the construction of the long barrow itself (see pages 59 and 184). Later dates indicate that this type of burial monument was also constructed to a limited extent in EN II. There is therefore a considerable degree of accordance between the dates for the earliest non-megalithic long barrows in South Scandinavia and Southern England. Causewayed enclosures begin in Southern England around 3750 BC, whilst the earliest Danish structures are dated to c. 3650 BC (Klassen 2014, 202). Most of the Danish causewayed enclosures, however, were established after 3500 BC in EN II/MN AI, at the same time as megalithic burials were constructed (P.O. Nielsen 2004).

During several periods of the Neolithic and Bronze Age, the development in Central Germany, the *Mittelelbe-Saale Gebiet*, has been of great value as a reference area for the development in South Scandinavia. This also applies to the time we are dealing with, and in which we can now especially focus upon the period 4100-3300 BC, when early agriculture developed in South Scandinavia. Reference can be made to Johannes Müller's socio-chronological division (2001) of the Funnel Beaker Culture in the *Mittelelbe-Saale Gebiet* into five stages, MES I-V. The first three stages, as well as partly the fourth stage, are of significance for comparison with the development in South Scandinavia during the Early Neolithic.

The first phase, 4100-3800 BC, is described as the formation stage of the Funnel Beaker Culture, which occurred at the same time as the latest finds complexes involving the Linear Pottery Culture traditions, Gatersleben and Jordansmühl, disappeared. It can be compared with the development in Central Poland, where the Funnel Beaker Culture's Sarnowo phase replaced the Brześć Kujawski Group of the late Lengyel Culture. The finds from the first phase of the Funnel Beaker Culture are limited, and the graves are only sparsely furnished or contain no finds, and therefore do not suggest a hierarchical division of society. An expansion from the Early Michelsberg Culture (the Schöninger and Schipziger Group) must have influenced the development during this and the subsequent phase (Beran 1998; 2000, 128; Schunke & Viol 2014).

In the second phase, 3800-3500 BC (Baalberge), there are richly-furnished simple inhumation burials, non-megalithic burial structures and large enclosures. Working of imported, Eastern Alpine copper takes place. The construction activities and finds are regarded as early indications of hierarchisation.

In the third phase, 3500-3300 BC (Salzmünde A), there is a tendency towards local group formation, copper quantities decrease, population changes may reflect instability and battle axes are found for the first time in the burials. Decorated pottery becomes more widespread. There is an increase in the numbers of collective burials.

The fourth phase, 3300-3100 BC (Salzmünde B/Walternienburg/early Globular Amphora Culture), is regarded as a period of expansion. Extraction and working of local copper begins. There is a change in the use of enclosures, which are smaller in size, but are apparently inhabited. The cultural diversity is expressed in different forms of burials, including megalithic graves.

The burial monuments and enclosures that are constructed are visible expressions of a gradual hierarchisation within the societies in Western, Central and Northern Europe that succeeded the late Linear Pottery Culture groups. Other factors also played a role, such as the establishment of networks for the exchange of prestige objects. These traits collectively show that there were similarities between a number of areas, in terms of economic, social and religious aspects. Such developments also took place in areas outside those discussed here, such as in Western France, south of the Loire River (Scarre 2007).

The aim of this examination has been to highlight common traits in the social and economic development, and the formation of hierarchies within the different Neolithic societies. The individual stages of the development did not occur at the same time everywhere, but manifested themselves in almost the same sequence of events. In Western France, the British Isles and South Scandinavia, the construction of monumental burial structures can be followed for the longest period and involved the most stages, from non-megalithic burial mounds to passage graves, whilst in other areas such as Poland, where the development of the burial traditions took another direction, there was not a development that led to the construction of elaborate monumental graves such as passage graves. A parallel phenomenon, however, was the construction of causewayed enclosures, which had a similar extensive distribution and also entered a developmental sequence at a point that was determined by the social and economic development within the individual areas.

Indications of the formation of different hierarchies

The individual sequences of development reflect the formation of hierarchies. Social inequality is thought to have characterised Neolithic societies from the very beginning in the Near East (Price & Bar-Yosef 2010) as well as in Northern Europe (Price & Gebauer 2017). We can therefore assume that the possibility of the formation of hierarchies existed at the beginning of the development that we describe here, and which involved the new agrarian societies that emerged within the Funnel Beaker Culture in North Germany and South Scandinavia from c. 4100 BC. How should we describe the hierarchies that emerged and how did they function?

Our starting point is in the development that can be observed with the formation of the Cerny Culture in Northern France around 4500-4400 BC, where burials in non-megalithic long barrows are closely associated with causewayed enclosures. The society that created and used causewayed enclosures was therefore dominated by elite families. This leads us to ask the question: what was the function of the causewayed enclosures? The answer to this is not straightforward. Most scholars consider these structures as primarily ritual centres for the population of a geographical area. But they have also been interpreted as meeting places for the exchange of goods and prestige objects, and locations for the celebration of social events, where the population confirmed their common identity (Andersen 1997, 311 ff.). Recently, the significance of the structures for long-distance communication has been emphasised (Klassen 2014, 239 ff.).

The social structure of these societies has mostly been considered 'flat', like within 'segmented tribes' that lack an elite (Madsen 1991; Andersen 1997, 360; 2000, 42). The modest grave furnishings of the people buried in the long barrows have even led to the assumption that the monuments were purely symbolic and that (material) wealth was no option (Pospieszny 2010). As we have placed focus upon the appearance of hierarchies, however, we should not overlook the connection between monumental burials and causewayed enclosures that can be discerned in the Cerny Culture in France, the Early Neolithic in England, the Baalberge and subsequent groups in Central Germany, and in South Scandinavia in EN II, where megalithic burials are, in many cases, concentrated at causewayed enclosures, like at Sarup and Lønt, for example (Andersen 1997; Gebauer 2014).

François Bertemes states that causewayed enclosures associated with the Michelsberg Culture were, as well as being cultic sites, also political gathering places of regional and multiregional significance, and are indirect evidence for the existence of a complex social structure. Causewayed enclosures would only have been possible if they were planned by a central group, and their construction could fulfil the requirements of the central organisation. The appearance of these sites was probably also a symbol of wealth and power (Bertemes 1991, 456). The causewayed enclosures, like the monumental burial structures, could thus reflect a society led by an elite.

If we follow Bertemes' ideas, then a leader's tasks were to gather the population, acquire sufficient resources and organise the construction of a causewayed enclosure. These structures were erected as common gathering places to be used by a population of farmers, who lived in small settlements spread across the landscape. Even though the causewayed enclosures occupy very different locations, many of them are situated on prominent terrain above the surroundings, such as the site at Sarup on Funen, which, like others, is naturally bounded by water courses, a location which may have been determined by defensive considerations. It is also likely that causewayed enclosures associated with the Michelsberg and Funnel Beaker cultures were located on probable traffic routes, which is confirmed by partial correspondence with modern road networks (Knoche 2013, 210 ff.; Klassen 2014, 146 ff.). The structures are also regarded as centres for long-distance contact, and may thus have been important in the exchange of products and ideas across Europe (Klassen 2014, 239 ff.). None of these things would have been unfamiliar to an elite that wanted to achieve control over its near surroundings, as well as the external influences.

A common trait that is shared by the causewayed enclosures in France, Germany, England and South Scandinavia is that they are surrounded by segmented ditches, and as can be observed at the best-preserved structures, such ditches, as well as the presumably associated earth banks, were located in front of a palisade. The structures could thus be defended, although no obvious defensive logic can be used to explain the segmented ditches. This feature, however, is so widespread that there must have been some logical reason behind it. Niels H. Andersen suggests that society's social structure was reflected by it, as a "microcosm of the settlement surrounding the site" (N.H. Andersen 1997, 307). The term 'sociogram', reflecting the social structure, has been used in this respect, although in connection with more developed societies (Knight 1998). Katherine Spielmann has, in a similar way, interpreted the segmented ditches surrounding the ceremonial gathering places of the Hopewell people in southern Ohio (c. 50 BC-AD 450), and compared these with the English causewayed enclosures (Spielmann 2008, 55). The individual social units, which take the form of families or family-connected communities, each contribute to the construction of the structure by digging one of the segmented ditches. The individual population groups therefore maintain their identity, and perhaps also their demands for influence and ownership.

Does the size of the causewayed enclosures reflect the efforts of the society or elite to build up surpluses? Sarup I, which is one of the largest Danish structures, covers c. 9.5 ha. The largest English causewayed enclosure is Crofton in Wiltshire and covers c. 27 ha (Oswald et al. 2001, 72), whilst the largest structure of the Michelsberg Culture, Urmitz, covers up to 100 ha (fig. 7.6) (Boelicke 1977). The most important resource that could be accumulated at this time must have been livestock, particularly cattle, which could provide meat reserves and dairy supplies, and were subsequently used as draft animals (Bogucki 1993). Tabaczyński links the appearance of causewayed enclosures with the increasing importance of cattle operations. He suggests that the structures cannot have been just defensive, but were suitable for keeping herds of cattle together. This may also explain why some causewayed enclosures are not bounded by ditches where there are natural boundaries, such as water courses, cliffs bordering water courses or wetlands (Tabaczyński 1972, 49 f.). In connection with the theory about the location of the sites along traffic routes, it has also been proposed that cattle were transported along these routes, with the journeys

Fig. 7.6. Examples of German causewayed enclosures from the Michelsberg Culture and the Baalberge/Hutberg Culture (same scale, after Meyer & Raetzel-Fabian 2006).

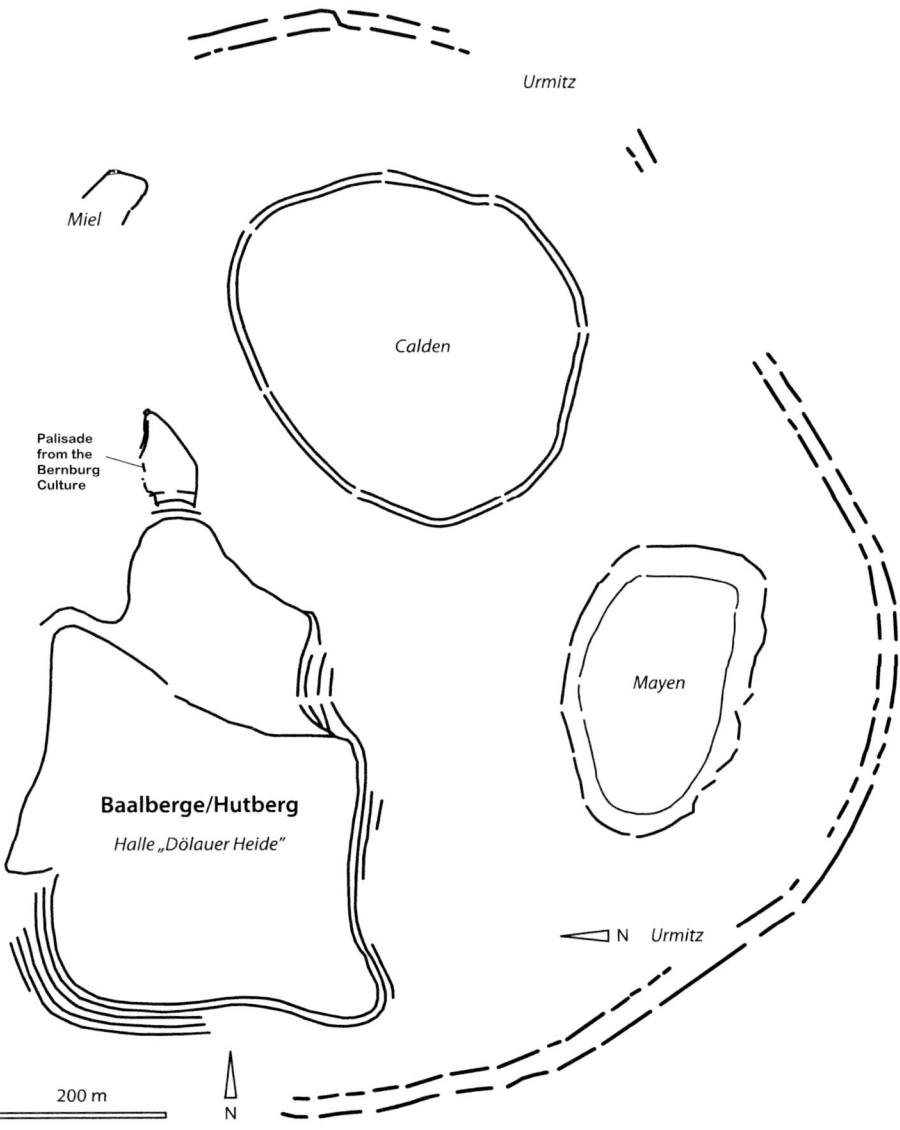

broken up by stays at the causewayed enclosures (Geschwinde & Raetzel-Fabian 2009, 242 ff; Knoche 2013, 212). This so-called 'Braunschweiger model' is inspired by the trading of cattle in historical times. It is, however, likely that cattle, like other domesticated animals, were kept within the causewayed enclosures at times when it was practical or necessary for the society or the elite. The size of the causewayed enclosures could be adjusted to the numbers of grazing domesticated animals and would therefore, both externally and internally, mark the extent of the surplus that the society or its leaders expected to achieve. At the same time, the size of the structures signalled size of the workforce that could be acquired and used for the erection of the causewayed enclosures. The structures may have functioned as a storage place for all the community's livestock when there was the threat of external attack. If this was the case, then their size begins to make sense.

Only in a few cases have recognisable remains of buildings been found at the settlements and causewayed enclosures of the Michelsberg Culture, although there are exceptions. The enclosure Hautes Chanvières at Mairy is located near the Meuse River in the French Ardennes. Here, within several ditches with internal palisades, the remains of 23 rectangular, timber-built houses with wall slots and internal dividing walls were found (fig. 7.7) (Marolle 1989; 1998). The houses were two-aisled, sometimes with a considerable distance between the roof-bearing posts, and with other roof-bearing posts placed in pairs opposite one another inside the walls. The houses were 21-60 m long and 7-13 m wide (fig. 7.8). Outside the houses were 206 circular storage pits, which had been reused as rubbish pits, within a 18 ha area. The settlement can be dated to 4050-3650 BC, based upon the pottery and ^{14}C dates (Laurelut in press). In one of the longhouses (house 7),

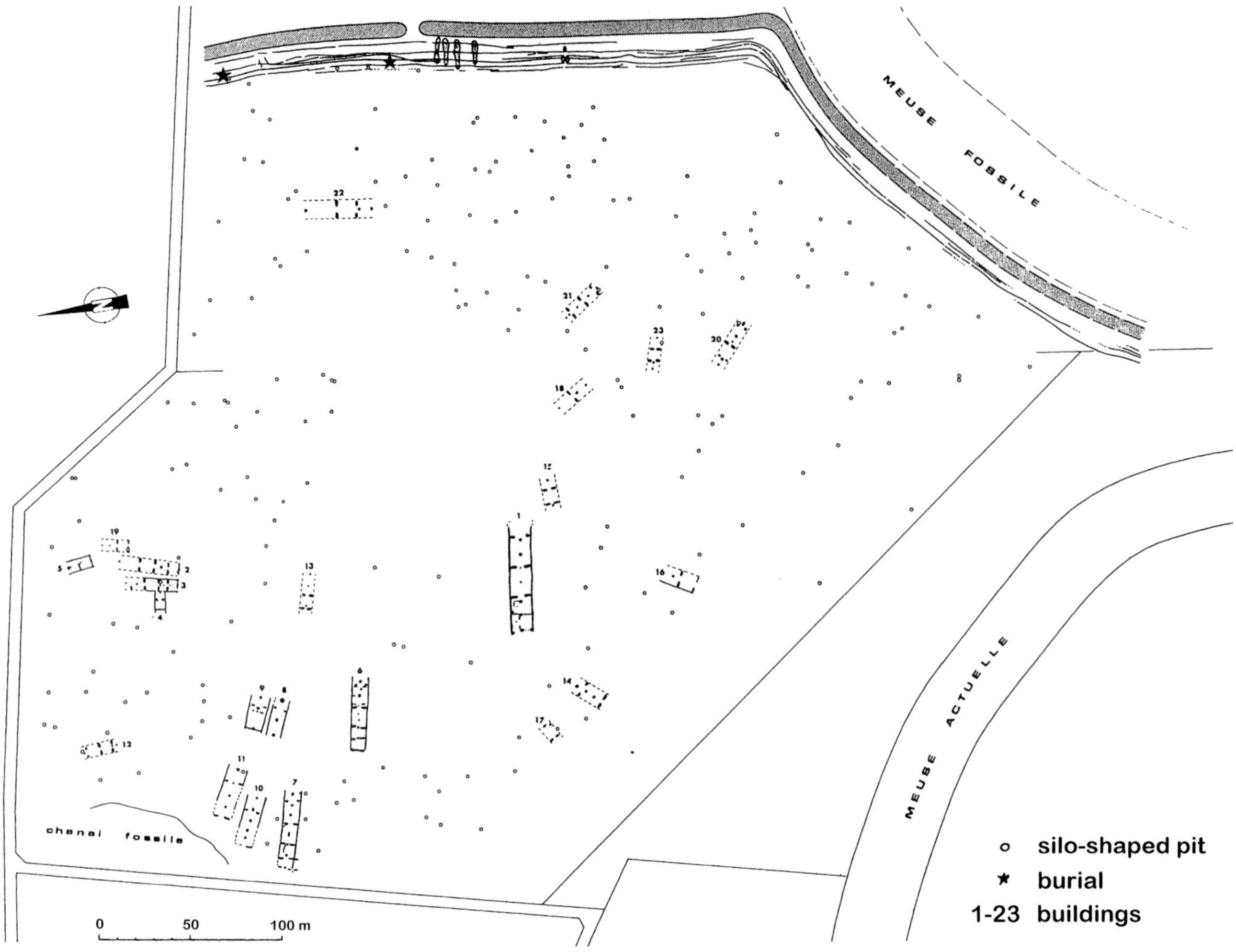

Fig. 7.7. Plan of the excavation at Mairy (after Marolle 1998).

measuring 45 × 8.5-9.5 m, a deposit was found at the bottom of one of the roof-bearing posts; this consisted of three pointed-butted flint axes and two flint chisels (Hamard 1989). The unusual settlement complex at Mairy has been interpreted in different ways. Some researchers propose that the site was a gathering place and that the houses were constructed for cultic purposes (Jeunesse 2010b), whilst others suggest that the large houses were used for the storage and safeguarding of cereal grain resources (Sørensen 2014, 210). The houses at Mairy are probably distributed over most of the 400 years in which the site was used, although several of the buildings may have stood at the same time. It is

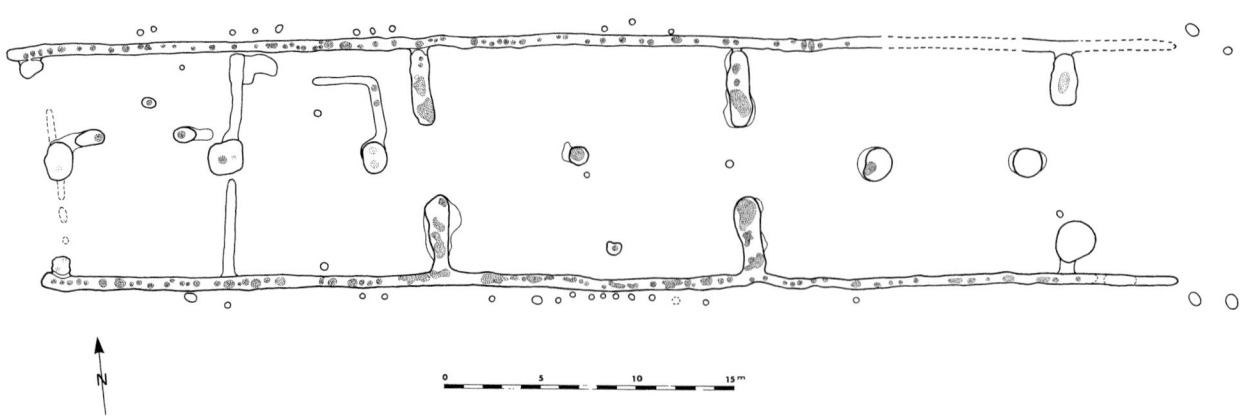

Fig. 7.8. The largest of the longhouses at Mairy (after Marolle 1989).

quite possible that this location was used for the common storage of resources.

Only a few continental parallels have so far been found for the houses at Mairy, although in England and Scotland large longhouses from the same period are also found: 'timber halls', like at Lockerbie Academy, where a longhouse measuring 27 × 8 m and dating to between 3950 and 3630 BC was excavated (Kirby 2011). Other large houses have been excavated at Balbridie and Claish Farm, the dimensions of which are respectively 24 × 12 m and 25 × 9 m (Barclay et al. 2002). Both these buildings are divided into sections internally, like the houses at Mairy, and are dated to 3800-3600 BC. The excavation of the large house at Balbridie uncovered one of largest Neolithic cereal grain deposits found in Great Britain: 20,000 charred grains of emmer, bread wheat and naked barley (Fairweather & Ralston 1993). In England and Ireland, a few cereal grain finds have been dated to between 4000/3950 and 3800 BC, although most early dates of cereal grains are later than 3800 BC (Brown 2007).

It is suggested that the large houses associated with early dates from England and Scotland functioned as common storage places for the first farmers, until they were sufficiently well established and could settle down in small buildings spread across the landscape (Sheridan 2013, 293). But they can also be interpreted as buildings where either the community or the elite safeguarded its surplus, in the form of corn stores in the house at Balbridie. These buildings existed at the same time as the first non-megalithic long barrows were constructed in England. So at this point the elite began to emphasise itself. In England and Scotland, the most far-reaching influence from the Continent was felt at the beginning of the Neolithic, around 4000 BC, prior to the establishment of the Carinated Bowl Neolithic, in Sheridan's migration model described as several different elements of immigrant groups from the Chasséen Culture in France (Sheridan 2010, 95 ff., fig. 9.3). This immigration must have involved planning, organisation of transport and access to resources, in the form of labour, domesticated animals and cereal grain reserves, which may have been based upon a leadership that could build up surpluses and initiate large projects. Neolithisation occurred at the same time in South Scandinavia and may have had a similar social background.

Within both the Chasséen and Michelsberg cultures there was an organisation that enabled the accumulation of sufficient resources for the construction of causewayed enclosures, as well as expansion to distant destinations. But there was apparently not a hierarchical structure of the same type that existed within the Cerny Culture and the societies that developed subsequently in several of the areas which were affected by the expansion of the Chasséen and Michelsberg cultures. The organisation may have been of another character. Within the Michelsberg Culture, there are hardly any burial places that reflect status differences, and neither are there signs that the elite legitimised its position of leadership through its ancestors, as is indicated by the monumental burial structures of the Cerny Culture. The leadership may have been structured in a different way. It may have been a reaction against the form of control that had developed within the Cerny Culture. The ideals may have been different. But organisation took place and causewayed enclosures continued to be constructed within the Michelsberg Culture, even in quite large numbers during the period 4000-3500 BC (Klassen 2014, 209 ff.), which shows that, over a long period, and especially in periods of expansion, there was a need for organisation, which focused upon accumulating and securing resources.

As mentioned above, there are several examples which indicate that violence with a fatal outcome occurred at the causewayed enclosures of the Michelsberg Culture. At the top of and next to the ditches of the causewayed enclosure at Bruchsal-Aue in Baden-Württemberg, over a stretch of c. 70 m, six graves were found that contained one or more bodies, of a total of 16 people, consisting of children of up to 7 years of age and adults over 40 (Nickel 1998). The burials were apparently located in the place where the individuals met their deaths. Meanwhile, at other causewayed enclosures, human skulls and limb bones have been found that are spread out and not associated with one another (Kossian 2005, 155, with references). Evidence of violence has also been identified at many causewayed enclosures in England (Bayliss et al. 2011, 716 ff.). Many of the causewayed enclosures must have been the scene of clashes between rival groups, which suggests that there was competition for resources. An important objective of the construction of causewayed enclosures may have been to defend the values of society.

The emergence of the Funnel Beaker Culture should be seen in connection with the expansion of the Michelsberg Culture c. 4200-3800 BC, and in continuation of this, far beyond the boundaries of agriculture that had existed up until then. From the whole of this period of expansion, which is characterised by the pioneering farmers' creation of the basis of life in new areas, there are no visible signs of the establishment of hierarchies, in the form of richly-furnished or monumental burials. But these appeared shortly after the end of the pioneer phase, in the areas where neolithisation occurred and where it was possible to create surpluses. This possibility is essential for the development and maintenance of social inequality (Price & Gebauer 2017). We must therefore find a model for leadership within the Michelsberg and Funnel Beaker cultures during the expansion phase, in which the leader, unlike in the subsequent consolidation phase, based his power upon surplus and/or lineage. It would have been desirable to choose a leader who behaved as an aggressor like a warrior chieftain.

Associated with the aggressive behaviour of this period was probably a warrior ideal, which was expressed by the use of battle axes of the same type, that, with only minor variations, are found over a very large area, stretching from the Alps in the south to Central Sweden in the north, in the period 4100-3500 BC (battle axes of Group F I-IV, Zápotocký 1992). Around a thousand years later, the same phenomenon occurred with the spreading of early types of battle axes in connection with the Corded Ware groups' expansion and establishment of new agrarian societies.

The formation of simple chiefdoms

"No one has observed the actual origin of a chiefdom" states Elman R. Service in his book Primitive Social Organisation (1971, 135). But we actually have a very good opportunity to reveal the mechanisms that formed the basis for the creation of the earliest chiefdoms. We will suggest a number of conditions to illuminate this, and the starting point is that the outlook and philosophy of life of the Neolithic farmers was more related to our own than to those of the Mesolithic hunter-gatherers (Knutsson 1995).

1. The first condition is that the Neolithic farmers had the same aspirations and set themselves the same goals as modern people: that is to secure the best possible livelihood and if possible to achieve a dominant role in society. Different resources were available during the Neolithic period to achieve these goals and, for example, to reach even further as a leader and achieve a level at which power could be obtained.

2. Another condition is that the Early Neolithic farmer did not live in village-like communities, but in single-family houses at small settlements, that he possessed the right to own his land and its means of production, and this right and the farmer's position in society could be justified by his lineage.

3. Thirdly, it is assumed that the Early Neolithic farmer needed to generate surpluses. It could be the condition for survival that there were sufficient food resources to fall back upon in crisis situations. It was therefore necessary to secure the right to the best land and, if possible, to achieve as large a property, as large an animal herd and access to as many resources as possible.

4. Fourthly, we assume that the people at this stage, like in many existing, indigenous societies, believe that all things and events are determined by supernatural forces. Lars Holten mentions, with reference to Mircea Eliade (1958; 1959), 'the god-fearing person', who lived in a coherent, overall cosmos (Holten 2009). If we accept this, then the use of the terms sacred and profane is inappropriate, as the profane sphere cannot have existed for the people of the time (Bradley 2005, 119 f.). The word profane comes from the Latin (*pro fanum*, outside the temple). It was used in a multicultural and therefore multireligious society like the Roman one, and has subsequently been used in the western world. In archaeology, a distinction is often made between sacred and profane which is based upon a practical and logical view of the archaeological material, but this is based upon our own, modern world of ideas (*cf.* Brück 1999). In indigenous societies, success and failure are regarded as being determined by supernatural powers.

5. The fifth condition that we will propose is the significance of gift giving in expectation of exchange. This is a quite universal principle amongst modern day indigenous peoples, but also looking back from a long historical perspective. The principle of reciprocity as described by Marcel Mauss (1990) was probably dominant in the early agricultural society, as it is amongst indigenous societies in many parts of the world. A person gives to get something back in return, and the person that receives has an obligation to give something back. *Do ut des* (I give so that you can give). It also applies to supernatural forces. In addition, this way of thinking is represented within contemporary religions.

Ethnographic analogies should be used with caution, but can help us understand the relationships that are potentially represented by the archaeological material, but which cannot be deciphered immediately. In the examination of the flint axes and their circulation as prestige objects, we have referred to ethnographic parallels, and we will now also examine some of the mechanisms that help create inequality and various degrees of hierarchisation within modern, indigenous societies.

In social-anthropological theory, social development is most often portrayed as linear, from group to tribe to chiefdom, and as a development towards ever-greater social complexity (Service 1971). The evolutionist outlook is also reflected in archaeological work, where the course from the Neolithic to the Bronze Age in Scandinavia is likened to a development from tribal societies in the Neolithic to chiefdoms in the Bronze Age, with a ranked society emerging that manifests itself in concentration of wealth, establishment of foreign contacts and great social inequality (Randsborg 1974; Kristiansen & Larsson 2005; Kristiansen 2010; Iversen 2015). Others describe the elite formation at the transition to the Bronze Age without using social categories (Vandkilde 1996; 2007). Kristian Kristiansen, who was one of the first scholars to identify signs of a chiefly elite as early as the transition from the Early to Middle Neolithic (1982; 1984), however, warns against the use of fixed categories and instead sees great variation of social organisation unfolding both in chronological and spatial terms (1998, 50).

This is a reasonable starting point. Variation in social structures can be seen reflected in the different parts of the Neolithic in Scandinavia, both from a chronological and a geographical perspective. The latest attempt to describe this measures differences in social complexity within the various cultural groups and phases in the Middle and Late Neolithic in Southern Scandinavia in relation to the status categories 'great man', 'big man' and 'chief', which are borrowed from studies of social structure in Melanesia (Iversen 2015, 158 ff., with reference to Liep 1991).

In our attempt to interpret the development in the Neolithic, we also borrow terms from ethnographic analogies, whilst primarily still using the archaeological material as the starting point. We use the combination of a number of archaeological sources in order to postulate that elite formation at the level of simple chiefdoms emerged within Neolithic cultural groups on the European Continent from around the middle of the fifth millennium BC. We use the term 'archaic chiefdoms' to emphasise that it is a social category defined on the basis of the archaeological association, without reference to any specific theoretically-defined or anthropologically-described hierarchical structure. 'Archaic' (from Greek: original, old) is also used by Helena Knutsson to describe prehistoric societies and prehistoric ways of thinking (1995, 17).

The combination of archaeological sources that we use are from Western, Eastern, Central and Northern Europe, and include the earliest monumental graves, in the form of non-megalithic long barrows and megalithic tombs, the circulation of prestige objects (ceremonial axes) and causewayed enclosures. A chronological sequence is involved, in which non-megalithic long barrows appear as the first indicators of the emergence of an elite in all areas where they are found. The development of a hierarchical society began early and can most clearly be discerned in Western France, where from c. 4500 BC it is reflected in the construction of burial monuments, from simple *tertres tumulaires* to elaborate passage graves. Within the Cerny Culture, non-megalithic long barrows appear, together with the circulation of prestige objects and the first causewayed enclosures. But the development did not take place in the same way in other parts of Western, Central and Northern Europe, where, within the Michelsberg, Chasséen and Funnel Beaker cultures expansion occurred, and instead gave rise to a warrior aristocracy without lasting status markers, as long as the expansion phase lasted. Only in the subsequent consolidation phase from c. 3800 BC do we again see signs of status differences that are marked in the same way as in Western France from the middle of the fifth millennium. Non-megalithic long barrows now appear in Central Europe, like in the Mittelelbe-Saale area, at the same time as the construction of causewayed enclosures, and non-megalithic long barrows are erected in the British Isles and Northern Europe, followed by the construction of causewayed enclosures. In Western France, the British Isles and Northern Europe, non-megalithic long barrows are followed by megalithic burials.

The circulation of prestige objects, and the construction of monumental graves and causewayed enclosures in Western, Eastern, Central and Northern Europe, indicate that ranked societies emerged and leadership developed and manifested itself in the same way. It is noteworthy that over a period of several hundred years, within the Michelsberg and early Funnel Beaker cultures, it was primarily necessary to gain a foothold in new surroundings, whilst maintaining an awareness of how power could be achieved and status emphasised. This suggests that some things were elementary and fundamentally common to these Neolithic societies.

One of the common traits amongst the Neolithic societies was the ability to create and convert surpluses, not only of foodstuffs but also of prestige objects. Both forms of surplus were also apparently used to achieve and maintain prestige. Another common trait was the construction of monumental burials, such as non-megalithic burial mounds and megalithic tombs. The extent that the cult of the dead achieved through the construction of even larger burial monuments demonstrates the importance of ancestry. The construction of such memorials required the common effort of many people and cannot have occurred without providing a large amount of foodstuffs. The person who initiated such a project could achieve prestige.

We have previously touched upon the competitive feasting model, which was originally based upon studies of complex hunter-gathering communities elsewhere in the world (Hayden 1990). There is no doubt that this model is also relevant in a Neolithic context in our part of the world (Hayden 2014, 285 ff.). The person who was able to show the greatest surplus and convert this into extravagant feasts could achieve the greatest prestige and gain the most followers: "…generosity is usefully enlisted as a starting mechanism of leadership *because it creates followership*" (Sahlins 1974, 208).

In South Scandinavia in particular, the favourable conditions for preservation and abundant finds have provided an insight into ritual gatherings and feasts, which took place near lakes and water courses, in 'special places' associated with settlements and burials (Koch 1999; Sparrevohn 2009). Animal bones preserved in waterlogged deposits indicate that meat was consumed from domestic animals, which consisted of oxen, sheep/goats and pigs, as well as game. There is also evidence that complete axes were sacrificed in the Early Neolithic and at the beginning of the Middle Neolithic (Koch 1998, 252 f.).

At the sites that have been mentioned, apart from remains of meals after feasting, the following must have been deposited as offerings to the supernatural powers: pottery vessels, which may have contained foodstuffs, as well as collections of these, complete or partial animal and human skeletons, amber, and tools and weapons of flint or other materials. Some finds may represent common depositions, whilst isolated deposits could be personal offerings. Some of the finds have accumulated during a longer period of time and can consist of different categories of depositions. At locations where feasts were held, sacrifices were also made, so both may have been practised as stages in a sequence of activities. The quantities of waterlogged ritual deposits in South Scandinavia increase from the beginning of the Early Neolithic, culminating in EN Ib – MN AI, at the same time as causewayed enclosures and megalithic burials are constructed (Karsten 1994, 172 ff.; Bennike & Ebbesen 1987, fig. 19; Koch 1989, 132 ff.). Whether the ritual deposits were made in wetlands or other places, the aim was probably the same: to offer something to the supernatural powers in expectation of receiving something back in return.

Other examples of gatherings are the remains of funeral feasts at passage graves, where pottery vessels, usually of high quality, have been left behind, either complete or crushed up, in front of and on either side of the entrance to the chambers (Madsen 2019). Combined finds of pottery, tools and animal bones in the ditches of the causewayed enclosures are probably evidence of feasts that were held for many people at such sites (*idem*, 915-16).

Exchange of prestige objects to form alliances with equal partners from near and far has already been mentioned in the previous text. Production, distribution and ritual deposition of the most sought-after flint axes reached a highpoint in EN Ib in South Scandinavia, and their distribution as prestige objects extended far beyond this region. For the Neolithic farmers, the creation of surpluses and thereby achieving elite status was an objective. Their competition with one another created a society that was characterised by social inequality. The most successful individuals achieved a status that gave them power over people. The driving force behind the competition for power and prestige may have been the possibility of achieving elite status.

Based upon a study of so-called transegalitarian societies in Polynesia, the term 'aggrandizers' has been used for aspiring chiefs, who strive for prestige by practising the same things as a chieftain, like holding lavish feasts, giving gifts in anticipation of receiving, developing myths of lineage and organising costly burial rituals (Hayden & Villeneuve 2010; Hayden 2014, 49 ff.). Aggrandizers act based upon their own interests in order to achieve power and wealth, and personalities of this type are represented in all societies. In Melanesia, the term for a person who strives for personal power is 'big man', but he is also described as a 'man of importance', 'man of renown', 'generous rich-man' and 'center man' (Sahlins 1963, 289). In agrarian societies, the person who is able to create surpluses can hold feasts for a large part of society, and this may have been the motivation for creating surpluses. An aggrandizer or big man, who can appear as the wealthy giver, can also claim that his efforts are favoured by supernatural powers. His feasts are therefore also ritual celebrations. Access to leadership depends upon how near an individual is to the supernatural forces (*cf.* Friedman & Rowlands 1977, 207).

In his examination of the warrior graves of the Funnel Beaker Culture, Erik Brinch Petersen (2008, 37) poses the question: "were such warriors also responsible for pushing the new subsistence and the new way of living further north? Were they perhaps also some kind of entrepreneurs?" We believe that the answer is yes, and that the aggrandizer concept can be used in our part of the world during the period when Neolithisation occurred in Western and Northern Europe, as an allegorical term for the armed, pioneering farmer.

In 1973, Brinch Petersen excavated what at that time until now is the earliest Neolithic burial from Denmark, the male burial at Dragsholm, North-West Zealand (fig. 7.9) (Petersen 1974; Price *et al.* 2007). This burial is especially characteristic of exactly the type of pioneering farmer that we are referring to here. In the discussion about the battle axe from the grave, we used the terms farmer, hunter and warrior for the deceased (p. 139). We can now more closely examine the significant attributes that are associated with him. The decorated, short-necked funnel beaker, which had been placed to the right of the head, is of type I (fig. 7.10a) and shows his association with the early Funnel Beaker Culture, EN Ia, which is also demonstrated by the four most recent ^{14}C dates (median probability: 5053 BP. Price *et al.* 2007, 203 ff.). A number of elements suggest that he was a hunter. Along with a few bone objects and flint blades, three transverse arrowheads were placed to the left of the head and six transverse arrowheads between the legs. None of the arrowheads were situated in a way suggesting that they have been shot into the body of the deceased. Transverse arrowheads are considered to have been hafted on shafts used for hunting. No wood was preserved in the grave, so if a bow was part of the man's equipment it would not have been preserved. The absence of the bow,

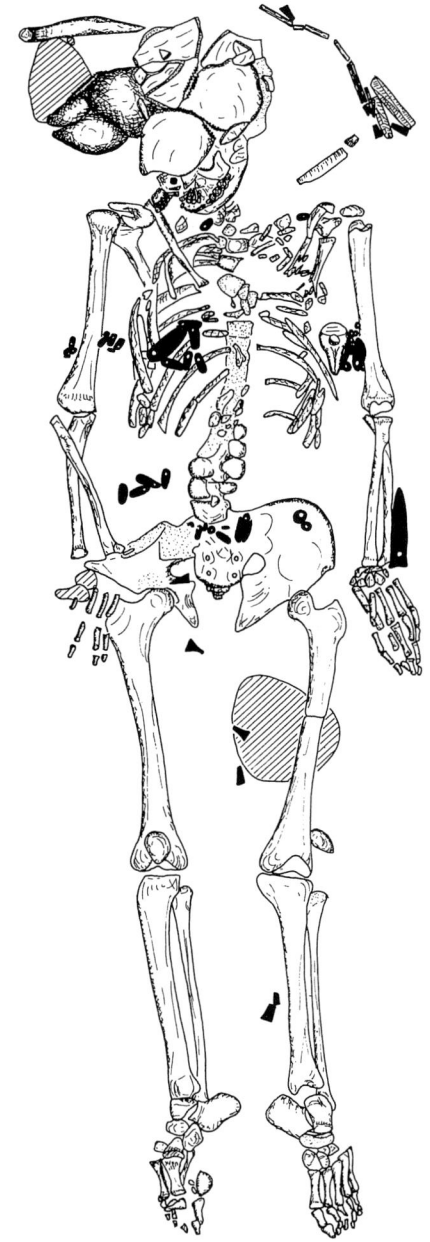

Fig. 7.9. Male burial at Dragsholm (after Petersen 1974).

however, is offset by the presence of a bone wristguard, which was attached to the man's left forearm or wrist. An antler with cut-off side branches was placed with its tip in the ground near the back of the man's head. Its upturned base end was broken, so it could not be determined whether it had been used as a pointed weapon attached to a shaft, although this is a possibility (fig. 7.11). The battle axe, which lay between the chest and left upper arm, indicates the man's warrior status. It was found in a very disintegrated state during the excavation, and was only recognised when the butt of the axe was removed. The preserved part of the axe has, however, enabled

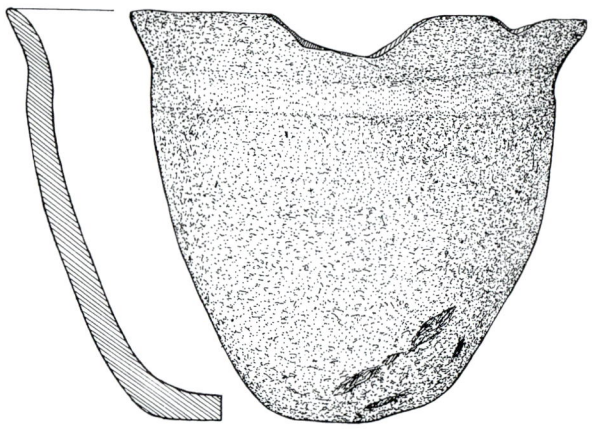

Fig. 7.10a. Funnel beaker from the burial at Dragsholm (after Petersen 1974). 1:2.

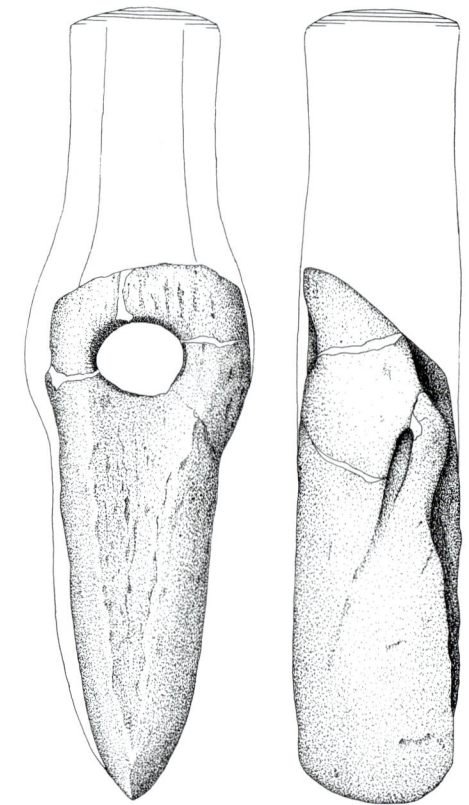

Fig. 7.10b. Battle axe from the grave at Dragsholm, reconstructed. Eva Koch del. 1:2.

it to be reconstructed as an axe of type I (fig. 7.10b). 52 amber beads were also found, most of which were drop shaped, with the largest measuring 7.5 cm in length. These were placed in a way that suggested they may have been attached to the clothing of the deceased. Some of the largest beads were found in the right chest area, whilst others were spread over the abdomen, and two small concentrations were situated near both upper arms, as if they had been sewn onto the sleeves (fig. 7.12). The amber beads from this grave are the only examples that so far have been definitely dated to EN Ia. But they are also significant, as they signal a type of status and wealth that was probably achieved through the exchange of gifts. Amber is found in the greatest quantities as a raw material along the west coast of Jutland, but can also be collected along the Baltic coasts, although here it is more rare. For the early farmers of North-West Zealand, amber beads of this size may have been considered exotic. Brinch Petersen (2015, 133) suggests that the deceased himself may have come from a place near the amber-rich coasts of Jutland such as the eastern Limfjord area.

The neolithisation and subsequent development in South Scandinavia consisted of migration, the establishment of agrarian production in new areas, the

Fig. 7.11. Antler from the grave at Dragsholm. Photo John Lee, the National Museum. Length 36 cm.

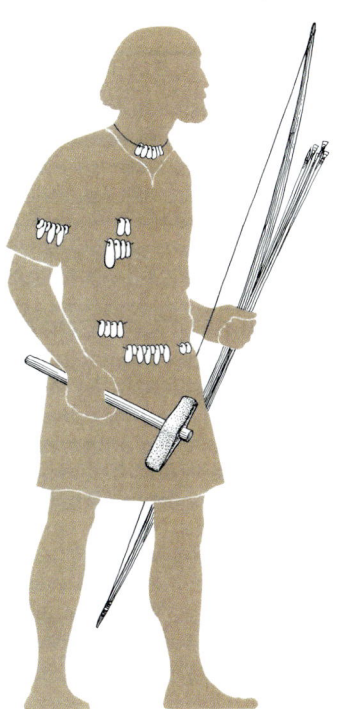

Fig. 7.12. The man from Dragsholm. Illustration by Flemming Bau.

accumulation of surpluses from production, the creation of self-knowledge in the form of myths regarding origins and lineage, the establishment of new social relations and participation in competition for status and power. The people who participated in the introduction of agriculture in new areas, may, as the previously-mentioned aggrandizers, have set themselves ambitious aims of achieving personal success. This may help explain the spreading of agrarian societies across a large area of Northern Europe within a few centuries. Not all aspects of the process can be directly discerned from the archaeological material, but the most important aspects can be, such as the quick spreading of the agrarian societies, exchange of status objects, the holding of ritual feasts and the construction of monumental burials.

The Neolithisation took place in the British Isles and Northern Europe around 4000 BC, when the formation of elites had already occurred on the European Continent, although within different scenarios. This must also have been a condition for the neolithisation to be able to occur. Organisation of travel and transportation to unknown territories, and taking along living animals and cereal grain resources, required planning and coordination on a scale that was far beyond the capabilities of the individual household. Prior to such journeys being made, scouting expeditions were probably dispatched, which were aimed at finding places that were suitable for cultivation, as well as establishing what strategy should be adopted towards native hunter-gatherers (Sørensen 2014, 56 f.). The transportation of people, domesticated animals and cereal grain resources had to involve crossing the sea, in order to reach the British Isles, as well as parts of South Scandinavia, such as the Danish islands, South Sweden and Bornholm. This would have presented those involved with significant logistical challenges (Sørensen in press). We assume that there must have been a dynamic leader who decided on, initiated and undertook such projects, based upon surpluses that were large enough to ensure the projects could be achieved.

In a society corresponding with a 'big man' society, the individual strives after prestige, but not on behalf of society as such. This requires a form of leadership at the level of a chieftain. We will therefore propose that at this point, chieftain-like positions of leadership existed. A good deal of evidence suggests that the term chieftain fits in as a stage in the development of society in the Neolithic, solely because the phenomenon is so widespread and known from most of the world.

We assume that from the middle of the fifth millennium BC and afterwards, elite positions developed in the form of archaic chiefs based upon their lineage, as is also the case in many historical chieftainships. The chieftain's family members would thus also belong to a higher class, and this explains why people of both sexes and all ages were interred in the monumental burials, as can be observed within the Cerny Culture, but also later on in the Funnel Beaker Culture. The chieftain keeps the secret of the family's mythological origins and is familiar with the rituals associated with the ancestral cult. The farmers pay part of the surplus from agrarian production to the chieftain, whereby he accumulates surpluses, which can be redistributed and also used for holding ritual feasts. A surplus can also function as a buffer for society in crisis situations. The chieftain is also responsible for external connections, both in terms of the peaceful exchange of gifts with leaders at the same level, as well in relation to conflicts. The archaic chief's position was not necessarily permanent. His power may have been based upon his ancestral origins, but probably also his extraordinary achievements, such as the organisation and leadership of common projects, which had to satisfy the interests of all of society. During the period that was characterised by expansion and migration, the choice of chief could be justified by the need for a strong leader, who could mobilise both resources and armed forces.

In the previous text, we have pointed out that the development towards a more hierarchical society occurred in a number of places and at different times, but was associated with the same indicators of hierarchy, so the process apparently repeated itself. Detlef Gronenborn has developed a theory that the society in the Neolithic period developed politically and socially in a number of cycles, which began with 'big men', led to elite formation, wealth and power at the chieftain level, and continued to complex chiefdoms, and subsequently there was a break, after which a new cycle began (Gronenborn 2016). Although this model is very generalised, it fits in well with the sequence that we describe here, where the social development occurs in a very similar way in several areas of Western, Central and Northern Europe, even though there are chronological differences. The model is also suitable for the development over a long period in Northern Europe, if we accept that one cycle begins with the introduction of agriculture, a second starts with the emergence of the Single Grave Culture and a third cycle begins in the Early Iron Age.

During the fifth millennium, forms of organisation and hierarchical structures had already been created, and had gone through a number of stages within the Neolithic societies on the European Continent. It is therefore likely that the possibility of achieving higher status and power also characterised the mindset and behaviour of people at the time when agriculture was introduced in Scandinavia. But after the farming culture had gained a foothold in South Scandinavia, the development towards a similar hierarchical structure in this part of Europe began. It was the start of a first cycle towards the development of a more hierarchical society.

The development on Bornholm during the Early Neolithic

Finds and interpretations

In chapter 3, we attempted to shed light upon the connections between Bornholm and the rest of South Scandinavia in the Early Neolithic, which primarily focused upon chronological questions. The starting point for this was a division of the ceramic material on the basis of the funnel beaker types that were proposed by Eva Koch (1998). This has enabled us to divide the material from Bornholm into five phases, as well as to provide a different view of the ceramic development within South Scandinavia. Besides the regional differences that are reflected by the decoration on the pottery vessels, and which have been emphasised by others, comparison of the vessel *forms* in the individual areas has provided a better overview, and an almost contemporary development has been suggested.

The examination of the flint axes has shown that Bornholm was connected with the rest of South Scandinavia by a contact network, through which flint axes were distributed, both in the form of ceremonial axes that circulated in specific circles, as well as axes that were intended for ordinary use. On Bornholm, axes were exchanged and ritually deposited in the same ways as in the rest of South Scandinavia. The study has also identified evidence for the origins of the trade in especially valuable axes within the early cultures of Western Europe. The distribution of axes in Scandinavia can be seen as an extension of a system in which axes of jade and other materials were traded as valuable objects, which characterised a number of the Neolithic cultural groups from early in the fifth millennium BC. The axe was the most important tool of all for Neolithic farmers, and it could also be of special value, as long as it had special qualities, was made of a rare material or had a particularly interesting 'life story'.

We have seen that the competition to acquire prestige objects was one of the factors that led to the hierarchisation of society, and we have also seen how monumental burial forms emerged within Neolithic groups on the Continent, prior to the introduction of farming and cattle breeding in Northern Europe. The development in South Scandinavia progressed in the same way as the development of society towards a more hierarchical and complex society in Western and Northern France, although with a chronological difference of c. 500 years. In South Scandinavia, cultivation of the land began, whilst passage graves were being constructed in France.

In order to compare the development on Bornholm with that in the rest of South Scandinavia and the neighbouring areas of the Continent, in the following summary overview, we will divide the sequence into three stages, which correspond with the period division that is used for South Scandinavia.

The establishment phase. The earliest Funnel Beaker Culture

EN Ia, c. 3950-3800 BC

21 settlements have been recorded from this first phase of the Neolithic, which corresponds with EN A0 and A1 on Bornholm, and these are distributed over most of the island. The location of the settlements, along with finds of pointed-butted axes, is shown on the map fig. 7.13. Only the easternmost part of the island is devoid of finds, with the exception of a single axe from Snogebæk. As was shown by the examination of settlement, most settlements are located on sandy soils.

No burials have been recorded from this period, and with one exception, this also applies to the rest of South Scandinavia. The only securely-dated grave from EN Ia is the male burial at Dragsholm, West Zealand (Price *et al.* 2007), which is a simple, not especially deeply dug inhumation, without a stone lining. Such graves can be difficult to identify if they are located on sandy soils, in which organic remains are hardly ever preserved. The male burial at Dragsholm contained a funnel beaker of type I, a battle axe of Zápotocký's Group FIII and transverse arrowheads, whilst the other objects in the grave were of amber, bone and antler. If such objects are typical of this period, then some of the individual finds of early funnel beakers and battle axes from Bornholm may actually be from burials, which were not recognised, for example, if the objects were uncovered by ploughing.

Seen in relation to the few coastal settlements that are known from the Late Mesolithic (fig. 3.41), it can hardly have been population pressure from within the Ertebølle Culture that formed the background to the Neolithic settlement on the island. Neither is there any evidence amongst the find assemblages from some of the settlements of any contact between the hunter-gatherer-fishermen population and the farmers. The early and quite extensive Neolithic settlement must instead have been due to immigration of groups that possessed fully-developed agrarian technology. The settlement during this early phase must therefore have been associated with the development of early agrarian societies outside Bornholm.

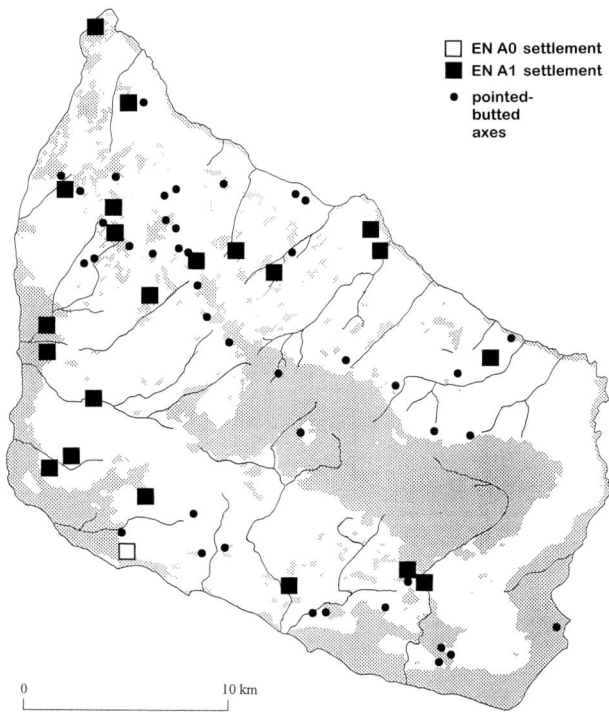

Fig. 7.13. The distribution of settlements from EN A0-A1 and pointed-butted axes.

Ceramic material from EN A1 (fig. 7.14)

There are only a few possible funnel beakers of Eva Koch's type 0 on Bornholm (Finds list I no. 42, fig. 3.1), whereas funnel beakers of type I, combined with other pottery vessel forms, are well represented. Small and medium-sized type I funnel beakers are either undecorated or have indentations on top of the rim itself or in one or more horizontal rows below the rim. Large funnel beakers often have one or two applied strips with finger impressions just below the rim. Lugged beakers are undecorated or decorated in the same way as small and medium-sized funnel beakers, and the lugs are on the upper part of the belly, in the same place as knobs can be present instead of lugs. Lugged flasks have a short neck, in contrast with the lugged flasks of subsequent periods. The lugged jars also have a short neck, rounded or flat bottom, and the lugs may be situated in the middle of the belly or further down the body. Small clay spoons are found occasionally. There are also round clay discs, which always have finger impressions around the edge.

Similar ceramics characterise other settlements associated with the earliest Funnel Beaker Culture, the Oxie/Wangels phase c. 4100-3800 BC, and are found

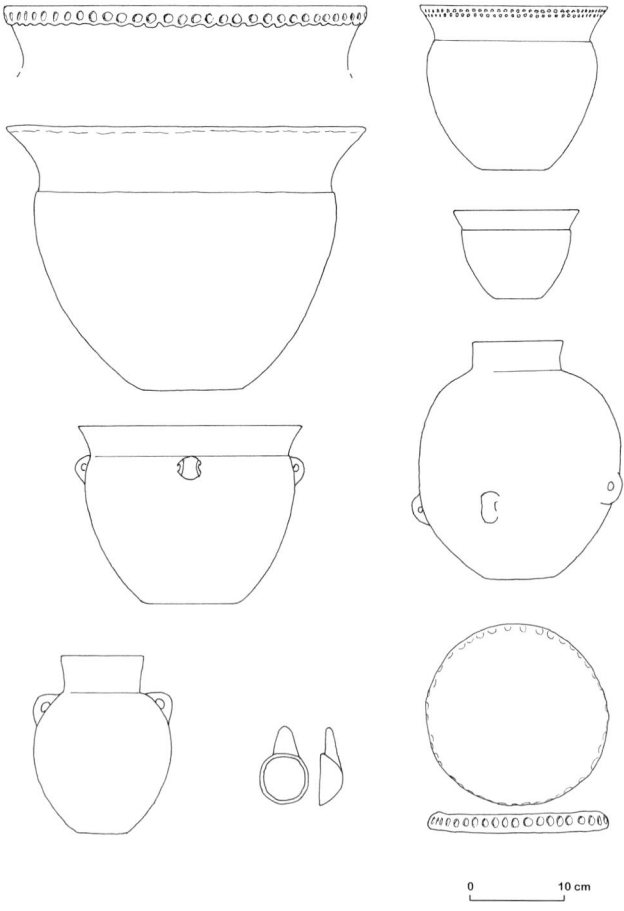

Fig. 7.14. Ceramic forms from EN A1 and Bornholm.

over a large area. As mentioned above, the pottery forms and their composition can be compared with the pottery of the Michelsberg Culture (fig. 7.4), the distribution of which also borders the area where the settlements from the early Funnel Beaker Culture are located (fig. 7.3). The common ceramic forms, such as *Tulpenbecher*, respectively funnel beakers, lugged flasks, lugged jars and clay discs, must reflect the same functionality, and the scanty ornamentation in the form of finger impressions on applied rim strips and at the edge of the clay discs indicates a convergence of taste and aesthetics. There are also similarities in the composition of the flint assemblages at the settlements (Sørensen 2014, 233). Other common traits include smaller settlements containing dwellings of limited size, like those dating to the Early Neolithic in South Scandinavia, but of which there are still a lack of definite traces from within the Michelsberg Culture in general. The animal husbandry within the two cultures was similar, with the domesticated animals consisting of oxen, sheep/goats and pigs, with an emphasis on cattle within the Michelsberg Culture (Jeunesse 2010, 52). The crops are actually better known within the Funnel Beaker Culture, but where plant remains are preserved at the sites of the Michelsberg Culture, these indicate that various wheat species, as well as naked barley, were cultivated (*i.a.* Knoche 2013, 131).

The origins of the Michelsberg Culture should be looked for in northern Central France (the Paris Basin), from where this culture expanded southwards to South-West Germany, to the east to Saxony-Anhalt and northwards to Lower Saxony. But with this, the expansion or its effect did not end. The Neolithisation in South Scandinavia actually began in the area where impulses from the Michelsberg Culture initiated the formation of the early Funnel Beaker settlements in the northern and eastern part of the European Continent. This connection has been confirmed by several elements of Michelsberg-influenced material that have also been identified both north and south of the western Baltic, in the form of rounded- and pointed-bottomed *Tulpenbecher* and other pottery, which was probably influenced by the vessel forms of the Michelsberg Culture (Vogt 2009, Table 26; Sørensen 2014, 124, fig. V.57-59; Mischka *et al.* 2015a; 2015b).

From where did the first farmers come to Bornholm? Throughout the Neolithic, the archaeological finds indicate that there were close connections between Bornholm and Scania, between which the shortest distance is 38 km. It is also finds from Scania that are used for comparison in the previous section on the settlements, and it is in Scania where, from the start of the Early Neolithic, there is the greatest concentration of pointed-butted flint axes. But this does not rule out the possibility that other routes may also have been used. From the Polish coast, which is 94 km away, Bornholm cannot be seen, as there are not any sufficiently high-lying viewing points near the coast. On Rügen, which is 88 km away from Bornholm, the highest point is 161 m above sea level. There are differing views as to whether, from the east-facing cliff at Königstuhl on Rügen, in favourable weather and light conditions, it is possible to see Bornholm, whose highest point is 162 m above sea level. The curvature of the earth means that this is uncertain. But the island's location may have been known, and from the south coast of the Baltic Sea, cloud formations above the island could have been observed. At night, the light from forest fires or the deliberate burning of vegetation may have been reflected in the clouds. On the eastern side of Rügen is the settlement at Baabe, which was active in the Oxie/Wangels phase (Hirsch *et al.* 2008). From here, connections could have been established across the Baltic Sea to Bornholm.

It would, on the other hand, be strange if the people on Bornholm, like elsewhere in South Scandinavia, were not familiar with Rügen, whose east-facing cliffs offered easy access to clear Senonian flint. But as it comes from the same chalk layers as the Senonian flint of East Zealand, imported Rügen flint is difficult to identify. There is, however, one object that points toward early contact between Bornholm and Rügen or Mecklenburg-Vorpommern. A preform for a battle axe from Hjorthøj, Østerlars (Finds list V no. 1, fig. 8.11:1), belongs to Zápotocký's North-East German group FII, which is not otherwise found in South Scandinavia. But there is one example of this type from Rügen (see page 140). No other possible examples of connections between Bornholm and the German coast in this period have been identified. But these can also be difficult to detect, as both the flint and pottery are so uniform over a large area.

There are a few early Funnel Beaker settlements further to the east. One of these, Kosin in the Pyrzyce area (Wiślański & Czarnecki 1970), with its funnel beakers corresponding with Bornholm type II from EN A2, has been previously mentioned (page 62). In recent years, however, much attention has been devoted to the finds from Dąbki, which is located near the coast in central Pomerania (fig. 7.15). The Mesolithic population of this site was in contact with shifting Neolithic groups during the fifth millennium BC, as can be observed from the imported pottery (Terberger *et al.* 2009; Czekaj-Zastawny 2015). Here, local, pointed-bottomed vessels and pointed-oval lamps of the Ertebølle Culture types are also found from as early as around 4800 BC (Czekaj-Zastawny & Kabaciński 2015, 205). In addition, early Funnel Beaker pottery of Sarnowo type is represented, albeit combined with Ertebølle pottery, like in feature 38, where charcoal on one of the funnel beakers gave the date (Poz-49886) 5250±40 BP, cal. 4223-3984 (1σ), with median probability 4061 BC (Czekaj-Zastawny *et al.* 2013a fig. 12). Several of the pointed-oval lamps are decorated with indentations like those on the funnel beakers (*idem*, fig. 8; Czekaj-Zastawny & Kabaciński 2015 fig. 2-3). The examination of the pottery has encouraged the theory that there was a development from pointed-bottomed vessels to funnel beakers, and that this led to the emergence of Funnel Beaker pottery in the Mesolithic environment, prior to the introduction of agriculture (Czekaj-Zastawny *et al.* 2013a, 207; 2013b, 423 ff.).

The same view characterises the analysis of the finds from the submarine site at Neustadt, East Holstein (Glykou 2016). Here, Ertebølle and Funnel Beaker pottery are found in the same submarine layers, which has been interpreted as representing a chronological overlap between the two ceramic traditions from c. 4100 BC (*idem*, 152 ff.). But as these are marine layers, the stratigraphy must be regarded as uncertain. In spite of this, the idea of contempora-

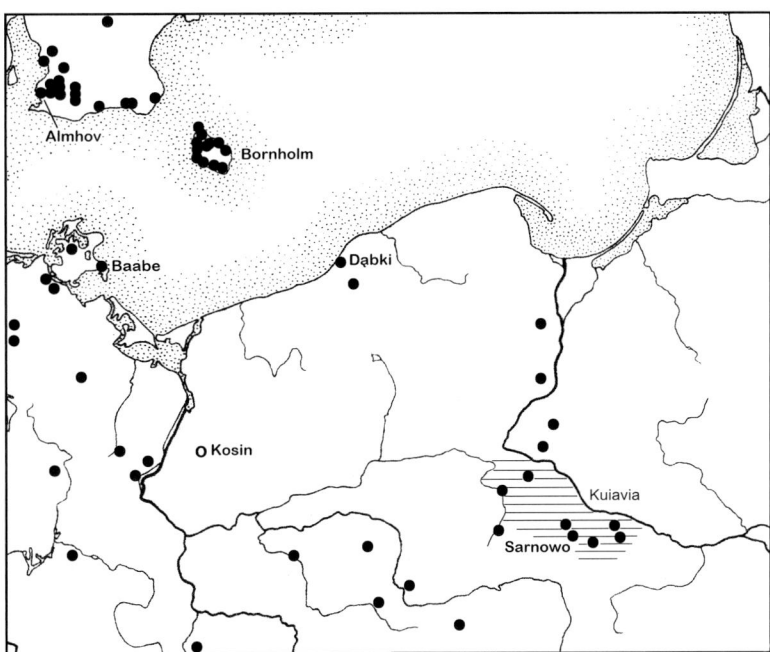

Fig. 7.15. Map of the Baltic showing some of the sites mentioned in the text. Black dots show finds of short-necked funnel beakers from the Oxie/Wangels phase in the Western Baltic and the Sarnowo phase in Poland. Sources: P.O. Nielsen 1985, Sørensen 2014, Czerniak & Rzepecki 2015.

neity between the two ceramic traditions has been maintained, which must have involved a gradual development, technological 'improvement' of the pottery from the pointed-bottomed vessels to the Funnel Beaker pottery, and type 0 funnel beakers representing a transitional phase (*idem*, 357 f.). It reflects the view that the transition to the Neolithic was a gradual development. More importantly, the Ertebølle pottery at Neustadt is dated to before 4000 BC and the Funnel Beaker pottery to after 4000 BC, if the dates of food residues on the vessels, which are affected by the marine reservoir effect, are not included (*idem*, 48 ff.). This corresponds with the dates from the Danish middens for the change between the two ceramic traditions.

In the publications of the find material from Dąbki and Neustadt we find a revival of Troels-Smith's previous view (1953) that C.J. Becker's A-phase of the Funnel Beaker Culture emerged in a settlement context belonging to the Ertebølle Culture. The revival of this view coincides with the rejection of the early dating of the Polish Sarnowo phase of the Funnel Beaker Culture to around 4400 BC, which previously meant that the earliest phase and probably the origin of the Funnel Beaker Culture could be found in the interior of Poland, in Kujawia (Czekaj-Zastawny *et al.* 2013b, 423). The rejection of this chronology now resulted in focus being directed towards the Ertebølle Culture of the western Baltic as the possible starting point for the development of the Funnel Beaker Culture.

This interpretation, however, has been opposed by other Polish scholars, who regard the earliest Funnel Beaker pottery from Dąbki as associated with arable settlements in the inland area belonging to the Sarnowo phase, representing a repetition of what had happened earlier, when pottery elements from distant Neolithic communities were left at the site (Czerniak & Pyzel 2011; Czerniak & Rzepecki 2015, 52). Furthermore, the question is not only about the origin and development of one particular vessel type, the funnel beaker. In the early Funnel Beaker Culture a whole set of ceramic vessels of different shapes and functions was introduced to suit the needs of the farming economy (Czerniak 2018, 106). As we have already argued, the Funnel Beaker Culture emerged at approximately the same time in Poland and along the south coast of the Baltic, in respectively the Sarnowo and Oxie/Wangels phase from c. 4100 BC, after which it spread to the southern part of Scandinavia around 4000 BC. The basis for the emergence of agriculture and new pottery facilities should not be looked for in a Mesolithic context, but in the already established farming societies on the Continent to the south and west, and in association with the expansion of the Michelsberg Culture.

Whatever view of development one adheres to, the observations at Dąbki may indicate that contact existed between the Late Mesolithic communities on the southern coast of the Baltic and the early Funnel Beaker Culture, even if such encounters may not have lasted long. Within the Danish area, Ertebølle pottery disappeared with the introduction of early Funnel Beaker pottery 4000-3950 BC (S.H. Andersen 2011, 210 f.). At Dąbki, it is first after a hiatus of 150-200 years that traces of agriculture appeared in the form of pollen from cereals dating to c. 3700 BC (Czekaj-Zastawny & Kabaciński 2015, 205).

The funnel beakers from Dąbki have been compared with the South Scandinavian forms of Eva Koch's types 0, I and III (*idem*, fig. 6). The site is considered to be the easternmost offshoot of the early Nordic group of the Funnel Beaker Culture, and is located at the intersection between the Nordic and eastern groups of the Funnel Beaker Culture (*idem*, fig. 1). If we examine more closely the vessel forms that were used, such as funnel beakers of type 0, this may, however, be a tulip-shaped beaker of the type found within the Michelsberg Culture, like the tulip-shaped beakers from Brunn 17 in Mecklenburg-Vorpommern (Vogt 2009, Table 26, *cf*. Sørensen 2014, 124). If this is the case, then at Dąbki there could be an overlap of influences, which also includes offshoots of the Michelsberg Culture, with a number of possibilities for the development of the eastern group of the Funnel Beaker Culture.

The Funnel Beaker pottery from Dąbki is very fragmented, although parallels can still be identified with the South Scandinavian funnel beakers of types I and III. There may therefore have been a sequence of development within ceramic production, which paralleled the one we have demonstrated on Bornholm, and contact between the two areas cannot be ruled out. With the dating of the first agriculture at Dąbki to as late as c. 3700 BC, the contacts that might have existed with the Polish coastal communities, however, were probably not associated with the introduction of agriculture on Bornholm. There are many more indications that the first farmers came to the island from Southern Sweden and the Danish islands.

But the development in Northern Poland is nevertheless interesting. The settlement expanded during the Sarnowo phase, apart from in the areas that had been cultivated by the late Linear Pottery Culture societies, and more sandy soils were sought after (Czerniak & Rzepecki 2015, 53). The same occurred in relation to the early Funnel Beaker settlement on Bornholm and in other parts of South Scandinavia. This 'sandy soil agriculture' generally characterised the early Funnel Beaker settlements.

Population growth and incipient social differentiation

EN Ib, c. 3800-3500 BC

On Bornholm, the material from this period is divided into two phases based upon the ceramics, EN A2 and EN B, as two types of funnel beaker, II and III, appear, which each have their own type of decoration. EN A2 corresponds with the distribution of the early, thin-butted type I and II flint axes, and in EN B, the most common thin-butted axes of type IIIA appear. 11 settlements belonging to EN A2 have been identified, including the early material from the Vallensgård I settlement, whilst 33 settlements from EN B have been recorded, including the later material from Vallensgård I. The difference between the quantities of finds from the two phases (figs. 7.16 and 7.18) may reflect a growing population, as the development apparently culminates in EN B, c. 3650-3500 BC. In EN A2 there is still a lack of finds to the east, in the parishes of Ibsker, Bodilsker and Poulsker, while in EN B, the distribution covers almost the entire island.

Ceramic material from EN A2 (fig. 7.17)

The identification of this ceramic phase is based upon the pottery material from the early part of the Vallensgård I settlement, where funnel beakers of type II are found, which are either undecorated or have indentations under the rim, in continuation of the rim decoration from EN A1, although sometimes with several horizontal rows of indentations, which can be of different size and shape (see chapter 3). Medium-sized funnel beakers still have one or two horizontal rows of finger impressions under the rim, but now without added cordons. The lugged beakers can be undecorated or have decoration on the rim like funnel beakers, and the lugs are situated at

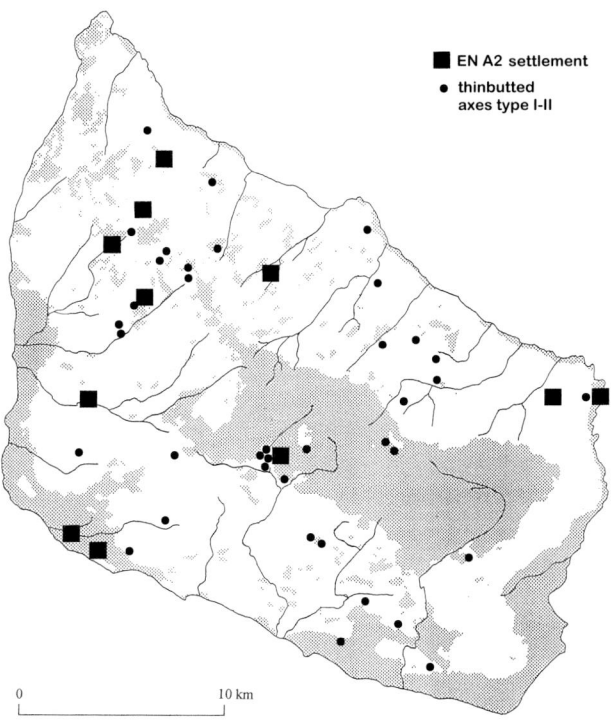

Fig. 7.16. The distribution of settlements from EN A2 and thin-butted flint axes of types I-II.

Fig. 7.17. Ceramic forms from EN A2 on Bornholm.

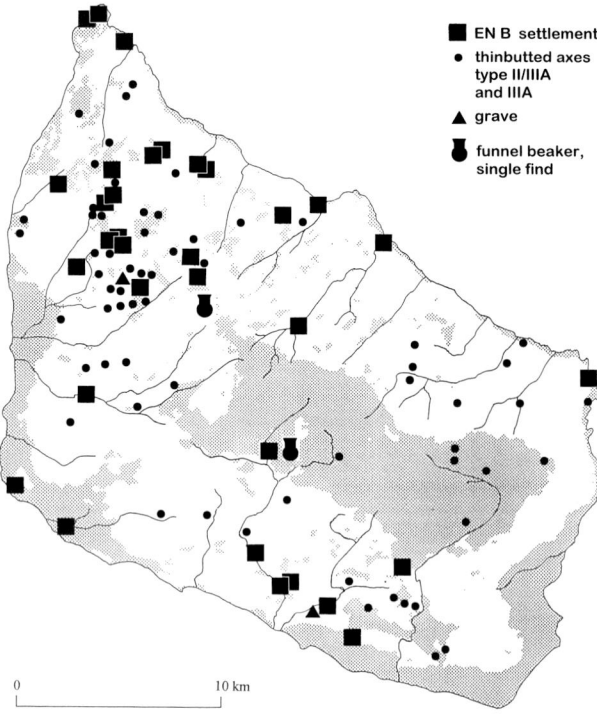

Fig. 7.18. The distribution of settlements, individual finds of pottery vessels and probable grave finds dating to EN B, as well as thin-butted flint axes of type II/IIIA and IIIA.

Fig. 7.19. Ceramic forms dating to EN B on Bornholm.

the top of the belly. Lugged flasks are not securely dated to this period, but were probably present. A fragment of a lugged jar was found together with a complete funnel beaker of type II in one of the pits at Vallensgård I (fig. 2.4:1 and 3), so that we can also add lugged jars with a cylindrical neck to this phase. As in the other phases of the Early Neolithic, clay discs with finger impressions along the edge are found.

Both north and south of the Baltic Sea, the pottery changes in style from c. 3800 BC, and this constitutes the beginning of a regional development of styles. On Bornholm, there is a gentle transition from EN AI, in which the pottery forms and decoration continue with only minor changes in EN A2. The separate forms of vessels and clay discs continue, so the changes do not indicate a functional break in the development of the ceramic assemblage. All over South Scandinavia, there is a tendency towards more high-necked funnel beakers, and the same tendency can be observed in the areas south of the Baltic, like within the Baalberg Group (Preuß 1966) and the Polish Funnel Beaker Culture during the Pikutkowo phase (Niesiołowska 1994). There was apparently a general development, which was not the result of extensive influence from the south. Both in terms of form and ornamentation, the ceramics develop differently within the individual areas.

Ceramic material from EN B (fig. 7.19)

The ceramic material from this phase can be identified in the later phase of the Vallensgård I settlement, which is characterised by funnel beakers of type III that are decorated under the rim with two-ply cord impressions or limited numbers of indentations (see chapter 3). Finger impressions are no longer present on the vessel rims. No lugged beakers or lugged flasks could be reconstructed from the material that was recovered from the settlements, and the decorated sherds did not include any remains of broken lugs. At settlements where material from this phase is dominant, such as Kokkedal (Finds list I no. 6), broken lugs are present, but it is not possible to determine which vessel forms these are associated with.

Lugged jars are, however, likely to be represented in this phase if a comparison is made with other finds, like in EN Ib at Havnelev and Ryomgård, where the lugged jars have a high neck and domed upper body (P.O. Nielsen 1994, Table 11.10 and 14.3). The lugged jar from the seabed south-east of Bornholm probably belongs to this phase (Finds list II no. 7). The collared flask is a new form, if it is not already found in EN A2. Clay discs with finger impressions around the edge are still present.

Two-ply cord decoration has a wide distribution and is found on funnel beakers from Scania, Blekinge, Central Sweden, Zealand and Jutland in EN Ib, although in most areas it is not as dominant as it is on Bornholm, but with great variation, especially in the Swedish areas, combined with various types of indentations (M. Larsson 1997; Nordqvist 1997; Hallgren 2008, 139 ff.). On Zealand, indentations on the rim continue to dominate, and two-ply cord is only used on a small number of vessels (see page 70). In Jutland, the funnel beakers and particularly the lugged beakers of the Volling style are decorated with two-ply cord impressions, stab-and-drag grooving and a variety of indentations (Madsen & Petersen 1984, 84 ff.; Klassen 2004, 189-203).

Burials

Before this investigation, non-megalithic burial mounds from this period were not known of on Bornholm. During the examination of Neolithic finds from excavations of features from other periods, however, two features were identified that can be interpreted as remains of east or north-east-facing façades of non-megalithic long barrows. This, however, is a different interpretation than that which was arrived at during the excavation.

The first feature was uncovered in 1979, in connection with the excavation of cairns dating to the Early Iron Age, on a high-lying gravel ridge, Bjørnebakkerne, Klemensker (Finds list III no. 1). At the edge of the excavation area, an elongated, NW-SE-orientated fill was uncovered, which measured 3.6 × 1.1 m (fig. 7.20). At the SE end were two large stones (not shown in the plan) and beneath these was a concentration of charcoal. Underneath and along the sides of the cut were several small stones. The bottom of the cut was not level. A possible posthole was recorded. The fill of the cut consisted of soil and was fresh in appearance, although it was not interpreted as a modern disturbance. The fill contained

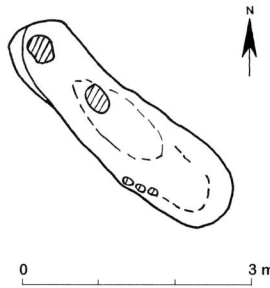

Fig. 7.20. Probable post ditch for the eastern end of a long barrow at Bjørnebakkerne, Klemensker (Finds list III no. 1).

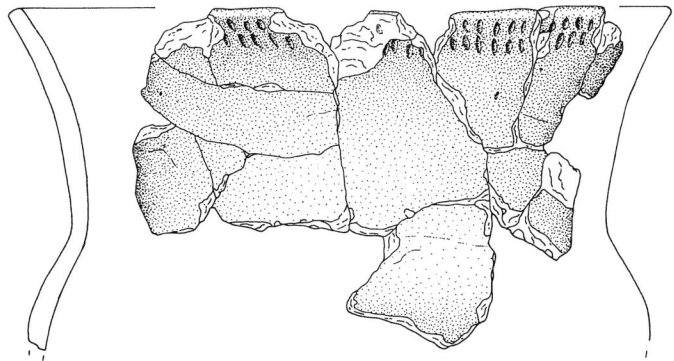

Fig. 7.21. Part of funnel beaker from Bjørnebakkerne (Finds list III no. 1). Freerk Oldenburger del. 1:2.

a transverse arrowhead and sherds from two funnel beakers. Sherds from one of the vessels, which was decorated with two rows of indentations under the rim, could be joined together in parts of the neck area and at transition to the belly (fig. 7.21). With a neck index of 34.8, this vessel is at the boundary between funnel beaker types II and III. The use of two rows of indentations most often characterises funnel beakers of type II, like a few of those from the Vallensgård I settlement (rim decoration 4a). The feature was interpreted as an Early Neolithic burial, but a number of observations suggest that this was a post ditch for an NE-SW-orientated non-megalithic long barrow, from which the posts had been pulled up, and the fill therefore appeared disturbed, see references below in the discussion of the next feature.

The second feature was uncovered in 1982, during an excavation at Runegård East, Åker (Finds list III no. 2). The purpose of the excavation was to investigate settlements containing house sites from the Early Iron Age and Viking period (Watt 1982). The excavation was a combination of full-scale excavation and trial trenches. In one of the trial trenches Neolithic feature 1305 was found, which contained sherds of a small, cord-decorated funnel beaker of type III (fig. 7.23). The feature was interpreted as the remains of a stone-lined grave that had been disturbed by uprooted trees (see the excavator's de-

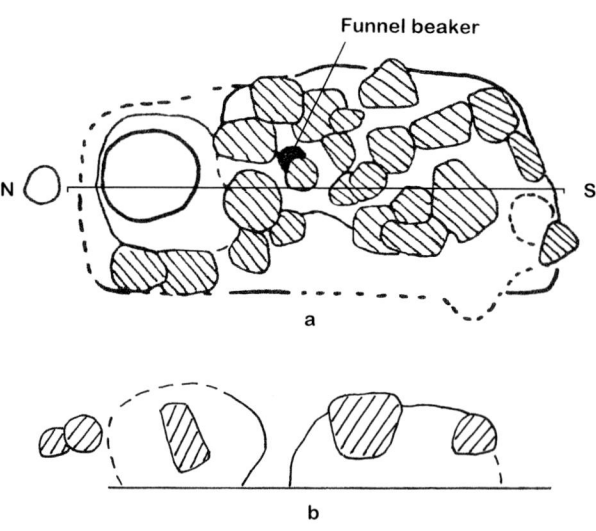

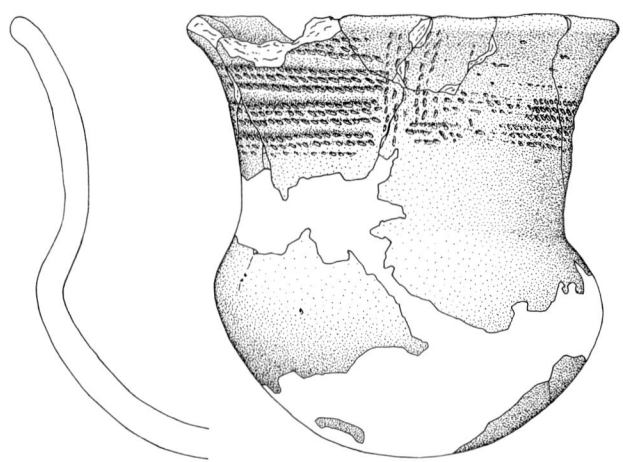

Fig. 7.23. Funnel beaker from Runegård East. Freerk Oldenburger del. 1:2.

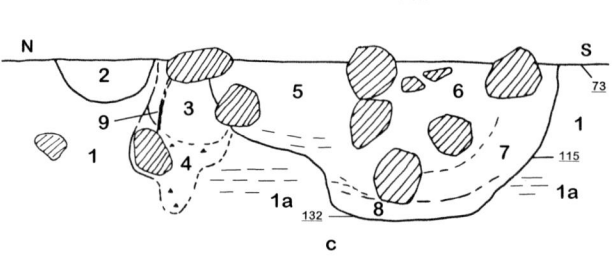

Fig. 7.22. (a) Plan of feature 1305, Runegård East. (b) Plan of the cuts at a depth of 42 cm below the subsoil surface after removal of the western half. (c) Section through the feature. Layer description:

1. Sandy subsoil.
1a. Sandy subsoil with ferruginous stripes.
2. Light brown-grey sand.
3. Grey-yellow to grey-brown charcoal-mixed sand.
4. Greyish charcoal-mixed sand.
5. Grey-brown lightly soil-mixed sand.
6. Light grey-brown sand.
7. Yellow-brown sand.
8. Grey-brown charcoal-mixed sand.
9. Dark brown-red stripe.

scription in the catalogue text). But the feature can perhaps also be interpreted as a short ditch, which contained two substantial posts, each placed in its own posthole (see plan and section of the feature in fig. 7.22). The ditch was subsequently packed with stones and at some point the small funnel beaker was placed on top of the stones in between the posts. The disturbances that were recorded may have occurred when the posts were removed. The feature can therefore be interpreted as a small façade ditch for a non-megalithic long barrow, which was E-W orientated, although no other remains of this were observed during the excavation. This may have been due to disturbances associated with the subsequent, intense settlement at the site during the Neolithic, Early Iron Age and Viking period. Another reason for this may have been the excavation method, which did not involve full excavation, and the area was instead investigated with parallel trial trenches, which were 4.5-5 m apart.

The small, cord-decorated funnel beaker (fig. 7.23) is of type III and can be dated to the period c. 3650-3500 BC, to which most of the excavated non-megalithic long barrows in Denmark can also be dated. Several of these contain evidence of the pulling up of the substantial posts, which stood in the façade ditch at one end of the long barrow. At Højensvej Mound 7, Svendborg, on Funen, a section through the façade ditch indicated that placement and subsequent pulling up of posts occurred three times, which the excavator interpreted as indicating that the posts were erected in connection with the placement of three successive burials in the long barrow (Beck 2013, 57-62). The façade ditch of the non-megalithic long barrow at Onsved Mark, Horns Herred, on Zealand, also contained posts, which apparently had been pulled up (Kaul 1988, 61). At the bottom of the cuts at both Bjørnebakkerne and Runegård Øst, the fill was mixed with charcoal, and this has also been observed elsewhere, such as at the bottom of the façade ditch of the long barrow Storgård IV, North Jutland (Kristensen 1991, 75 and fig. 6).

A characteristic and widespread trait of the Early Neolithic long barrows, which are most often E-W orientated, is that at the eastern end, heavy vertical posts were erected; these were lined with stone and

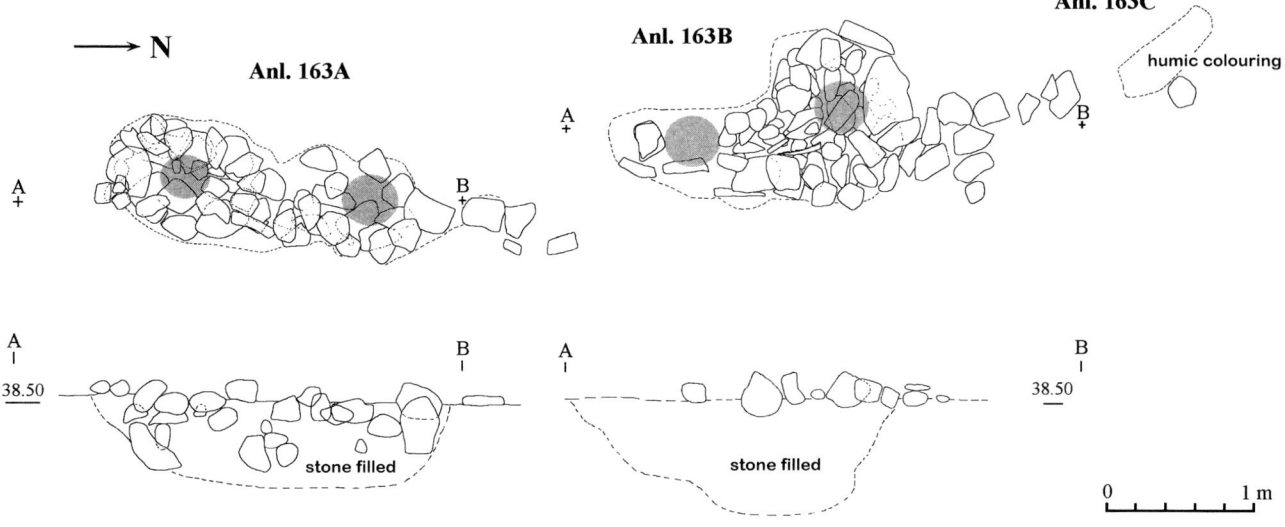

Fig. 7.24. Plan and reconstructed profiles of feature 163A-C at Kristineberg, Scania, interpreted as post pits in the east façade of a long barrow. The grey hatching marks the probable placement of posts (after Rudebeck 2002).

placed in a cut feature, in the form of a ditch which ran across the longitudinal direction of the barrow. Such façade ditches have, for example, been excavated at Barkær in Djursland, where they were up to 7.7 m long (Liversage 1992, 26). But there is great variation in the shape and size of the features that formed the eastern ends of the long barrows. At Kristineberg, South-West Scania, parts of an extensively damaged Early Neolithic long barrow have been excavated, which, just like the structures at Bjørnebakkerne and Runegård Øst, was only recognised after the excavation had been completed. The structure at Kristineberg terminates to the east, not with a ditch, but with two separate, stone-filled cuts, with respective dimensions of 1.8 × 1.5 m and 1.8 × 1.1 m, which probably contained respectively two and three vertical posts (features 160 and 161, Rudebeck 2002, 91 and figs. 5.4 and 5.9) (here fig. 7.25). North of the remains of the long barrow were two similar, stone-filled cut features, which may have constituted the eastern end of yet another long barrow (feature 163, figs. 7.24 and 7.25). The size, shape, depth and disturbed, stony fills of these features are reminiscent of the feature at Runegård East. At Almhov, which is also located in South-West Scania, four-five façade features from Early Neolithic long barrows were also found, where the façades consisted of either two or four such post pits (Rudebeck 2010,

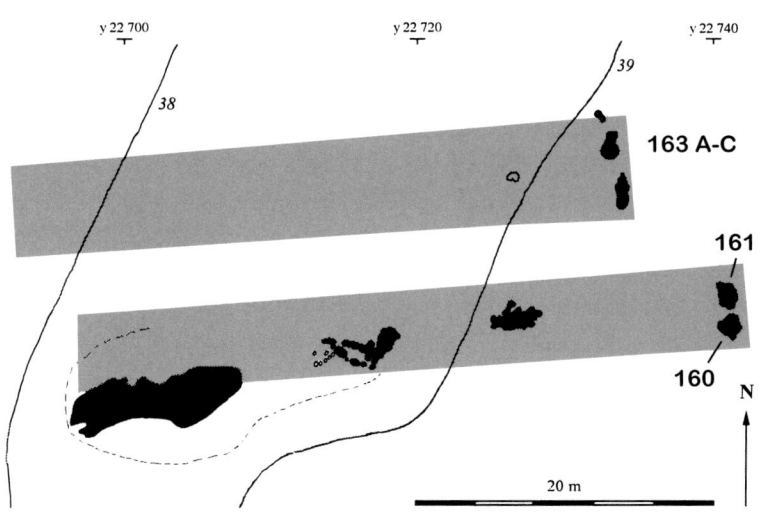

Fig. 7.25. Reconstruction of two long barrows at Kristineberg, Scania (after Rudebeck 2002).

141 ff. and fig. 14). At the eastern end of a long barrow at Bjørnsholm in Northern Jutland, two 80 cm deep, stone-lined postholes, which were connected by a less deep ditch, evidently had supported large, wooden posts marking the eastern façade of the barrow (Andersen & Johansen 1992, 47 ff.). At Vilsund in Thy, three separate pits for substantial posts were found, which were interpreted as the remains of the eastern façade of a long barrow (Klassen 2014, 187). At Runegård East, only one post pit with two postholes was recorded in the narrow trial trench, and it is uncertain whether there originally may have been more such pits.

A further possible burial from this period is from Simenehøje, Nyker Plantage (Finds list III no. 3). The site is located high up on sandy soils, where remains of a large, cord-decorated funnel beaker of type II/III were found on top of a stone pavement, which may have been laid in the façade ditch of a long barrow. But the information about these remains is minimal, and they must therefore be regarded as very uncertain.

The beginnings of elite formation

The burials in non-megalithic long mounds from Scania, the other Danish islands, Jutland, North Germany and Poland are better documented (Rudebeck 2002b; Kossian 2005; Rzepecki 2011). 85 long barrows are known from Denmark and Scania alone. As we have mentioned, some of the ^{14}C dates for the Danish long barrows are very early, but these are also problematic from a source-critical perspective (page 162). In Sweden, it has been assumed that long barrows with façades were constructed from the beginning of the Early Neolithic (Andersson et al. 2016, 79). But this should also be regarded with some scepticism. Long barrow 1 at Almhov is located within a settlement area, where there was activity from the beginning of the Early Neolithic, and one ^{14}C date from the structure: 4990±70 BP, cal. 3940-3660 BC (1σ), is based upon a cereal grain fragment (Gidlöf et al. 2006, 34). Both ^{14}C dates and archaeological contexts now support a dating of the earliest South Scandinavian long barrows to 3800/3750 BC (Sørensen 2014, 215, fig. V.165). This date coincides with the first construction of long barrows in England and Poland, as well as in Central Germany within Baalberge. This accordance is noteworthy and indicates that the social development towards the beginnings of elite formation occurred at the same rate within these areas. After the first phase, in which farming was established, the need arose to legitimise the right to the land, and this was achieved by erecting visible symbols of kinship with ancestors and the founders of the society in question. By creating myths of origin and lineage, social and psychological value formation could also occur. In this stage of the early history of agriculture, it must have been particularly important to be able to trace one's ancestors back to the first settlers.

Despite the paucity of indicators for the construction of long barrows on Bornholm, which may be due to their lack of preservation, this development within the social sphere must also have affected the island. In EN Ib, and especially in the period c. 3650-3500 BC (EN B on Bornholm), the number of settlements indicates that there was an expansion of the settlement compared to the precedent periods, which must reflect an increase in population. Meanwhile, the quantities of flint axes that have been found, both as single finds and hoards of two or more axes, demonstrate that there was a great deal of activity and circulation of valuable items. Both aspects may indicate that there was increased competition. Our settlement model is based upon permanent settlement, although it involves movement of the dwelling within the property at regular intervals (page 95). There are, however, also signs of more permanent settlement in the same place, which may have been intended to signal continuity. An example of more stationary settlement of this kind is found at Smedegade, Klemensker, which is located high up, in a dominating position in the landscape (Finds list I no. 14). Here, remains of one or more burnt-down buildings, as well as burnt fragments of flint halberds, are probably evidence of at least one violent attack.

Metal imports

A very small number of metal objects that have been recovered from Bornholm can be dated to the Early Neolithic. These consist of three copper axes (Finds list VII, 1-3). One is the axe from Vester Bedegadegård, which was discussed in chapter 4 (p. 108). This was possibly cast in Scandinavia from imported Mondsee copper, as a copy of a pointed-butted jade axe of the Begude type (fig. 4.8:1-3). Lutz Klassen gives a broad dating, c. 3800-3300 BC, to the use of Mondsee copper in Scandinavia (2010). As it seems unlikely that this copper axe was made any later than the production and circulation of other

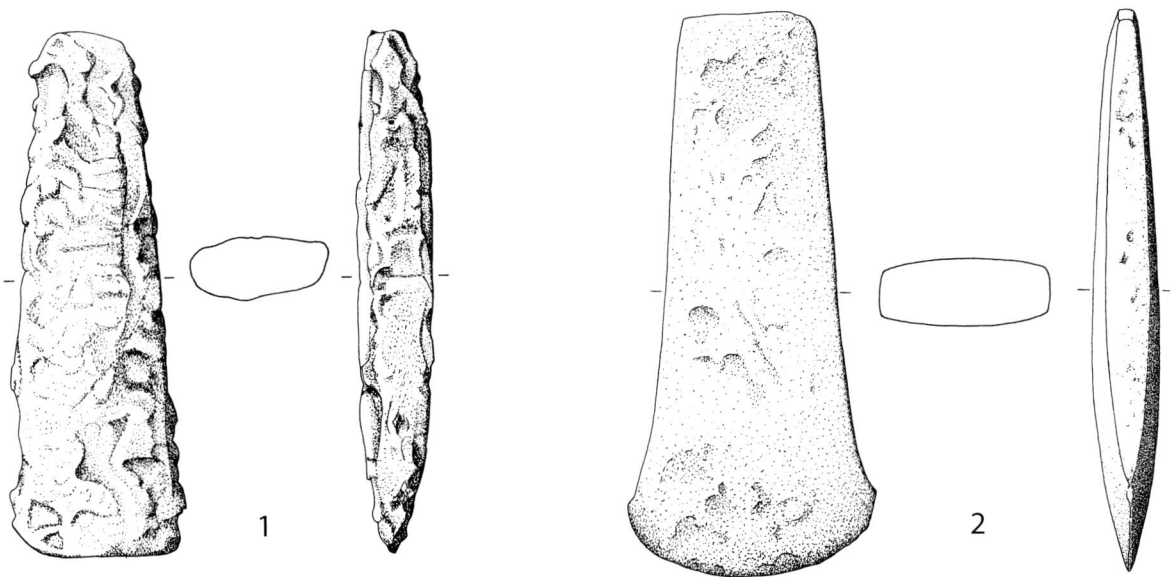

Fig. 7.26. Copper axes from Nexø (1) and Slusegård (2) (after Aner & Kersten 1977). 2:3.

pointed-butted axes occurred, an early date for it is possible, at the latest around 3800 BC. The very corroded copper axe from Nexø (fig. 7.26:1) has not been subjected to metal analysis, but its chisel-like form suggests that it may be amongst the earliest copper axes in Scandinavia (Klassen 2004, 69). This cannot, however, be confirmed without analysis of the metal being undertaken. The copper axe from Slusegård (fig. 7.26:2), on the other hand, on the basis of its form and metal composition, can be dated to c. 3850-3500 BC (Klassen 2004, 71), and thus indicates that there was at least some importation of metals to Bornholm during EN Ib.

The earliest causewayed enclosures

There are no definite remains of causewayed enclosures on Bornholm before some way into EN C/EN II, when the double structure at Vasagård was established (fig. 3.23). Its dating is based upon the earliest pottery that was recovered from the ditches (see page 73 and after). A few metres outside the northernmost ditches at Vasagård East, a small amount of pottery dating to EN Ib was found, including a fragment of a funnel beaker of type III decorated with horizontal two-ply cord impressions, but this is probably evidence of settlement activity prior to the construction of the causewayed enclosure.

Causewayed enclosures, however, appear in Jutland in this period, with two structures providing ^{14}C dates within the period c. 3650-3500 BC: Starup Langelandsvej in South Jutland (Klassen 2014, 202) and Liselund, Thy (Torfing 2016). The ^{14}C dates from the causewayed enclosure Albersdorf LA 68, Dieksknöll, north-western Holstein, are even earlier, with the earliest phase dating to between 3820 and 3630 BC (Klassen 2014, 202; Dibbern 2016, 46). These early dates make it seem likely that causewayed enclosures began to be constructed in North Germany just as early as in England. In South Scandinavia, however, they started to be constructed around 3650 BC and, as in England, 100-150 years after the appearance of monumental grave burial structures in the form of non-megalithic long barrows.

Causewayed enclosures reflect the first formation of territorial groups under common leadership. At this time, in the expanding agrarian communities consisting of autonomous, scattered single farms, the need arose for the establishment of a structure that could create a balance between the territorial demands of the population, deal with conflicts and ensure defence against competing groups. The local leaders may have been chosen from members of the aspirant elite, who could display the most distinguished lineage, create surpluses and who through gift giving had entered into as many alliances as possible. We presume that these were simple chiefdoms, that the power of the chiefs was based upon status, that their position was not hereditary, and that their authority was not so secure that it could not be challenged.

Adaptation, group formation and centralisation

EN II, c. 3500-3300 BC

Only 10 settlements are recorded from EN II / EN C. Three of these are located on the coast or a few hundred metres from the coast. The numbers of settlements and individual flint axe finds are considerably lower than in the previous two periods (fig. 7.27). Although this period lasts two centuries, the quantities of finds are less than from EN A2, which lasts for only 1-1½ century. In continuation of the previous distribution, finds from EN C have also been recovered on East Bornholm.

As is noted in chapter 5 (p. 122), the distribution of the thin-butted axes of types IIIB and VI is noteworthy (fig. 5.9). Most axes of type IIIB (and IIIA/B) are limited to respectively the northern and eastern parts of the island, whilst type VI (and IIIB/VI) is found in the central area. There is probably a chronological difference between types IIIB and VI, even though they may also be partially contemporary. But irrespective of whether they are contemporary or there is a chronological difference between them, both distributions demonstrate a different distribution of the axes than was previously the case. The distribution of type IIIB is mainly in North and East Bornholm, as if control of the distribution of axes was introduced. The fact that the later axes of type VI were only deposited in the middle part of the island may reflect similar control. A number of factors may have been involved, including changes in axe supplies from external sources and variation in deposition practices. It is the first time that the distribution of the flint axes on the island reflects clear local differences.

Ceramic material from EN II (fig. 7.28)

The ceramic material from the few settlements is modest in quantity and is also very fragmented, apart from a single complete vessel, the small funnel beaker with vertical channels on its lower body from Ndr. Grødbygård (fig. 3.29:1). The pottery from Hammeren includes funnel beakers of Eva Koch's type IV with vertical belly stripes, funnel beakers and lugged beakers, and possible lugged jars with complex ornamentation (fig. 3.27), reconstructions of which are shown in fig. 7.28.

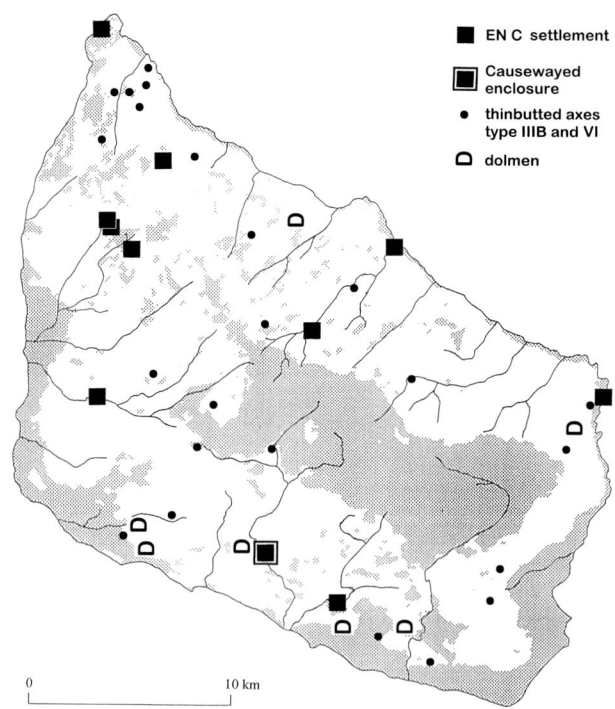

Fig. 7.27. The distribution of settlements dating to EN C, thin-butted flint axes of types IIIB and VI, dolmens and the causewayed enclosure at Vasagård.

The decoration under the rim of one funnel or lugged beaker consists of semicircles formed by two-ply cord, a motif which is also present on a lugged beaker from Virum, a lugged beaker from Lindbjerggård and a lugged jar from Skuerup Mose, all of which are located on Zealand. On the latter vessel

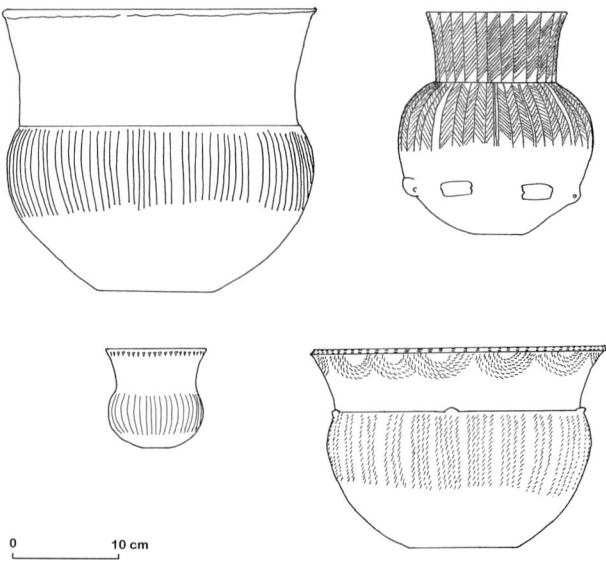

Fig. 7.28. Ceramic forms dating to EN C on Bornholm.

and a lugged beaker from South-West Scania, these consist of whipped cord impressions (Ebbesen & Mahler 1980, figs. 11.1 and 19.1-2; L. Larsson 1992, fig. 6). The lower body of the vessel from Hammeren was probably also decorated with vertical belly stripes of two-ply cord, like a funnel/lugged beaker from Maglelyng 3, Zealand (Koch 1998 Pl. 90:158.3), which was used as the model for the reconstruction drawing for the vessel shown in fig. 7.28.

Another motif represented on the sherds from Hammeren is vertical bands filled with diagonal lines, all formed by whipped cord impressions (fig. 3.27:7-8). The motif occurs on sherds from settlements in the Ystad area (M. Larsson 1992, figs. 37e and 49.11) and on bog finds from Zealand, where it is mostly found on sherd material, although it is sometimes present on almost completely preserved vessels, including three lugged jars (Koch 1998 Pl. 28:58, 32:65 and 144:231), a lugged beaker (*idem*, Pl. 34:68) and possibly also on an open bowl (*idem*, Pl. 27:56). There are thus several forms to choose from, but we have decided to show a lugged jar with this motif as an example of the continued development of this jar type. The lugged jar from Kongsted Lyng, Præstø County, Zealand, has been used as the model (Glob 1952 no. 64; Koch 1998 Pl. 144:231). The lugged beaker with this decorative motif is from Lille Knabstrup Mose, Holbæk County, Zealand, and is used by Eva Koch as one of the examples of type V.2 funnel beakers dating to the beginning of MN A (Koch 1998, 101, fig. 71).

The set of vessels during EN II also includes lugged and collared flasks, but neither of these two vessel forms can be reconstructed based upon the sherd material from the Bornholm settlements. Lastly, clay discs, either with or without decoration, should still be present.

Most of the pottery vessels that can be regarded as being intended for everyday use, such as funnel beakers of various sizes, were still decorated to a lim-

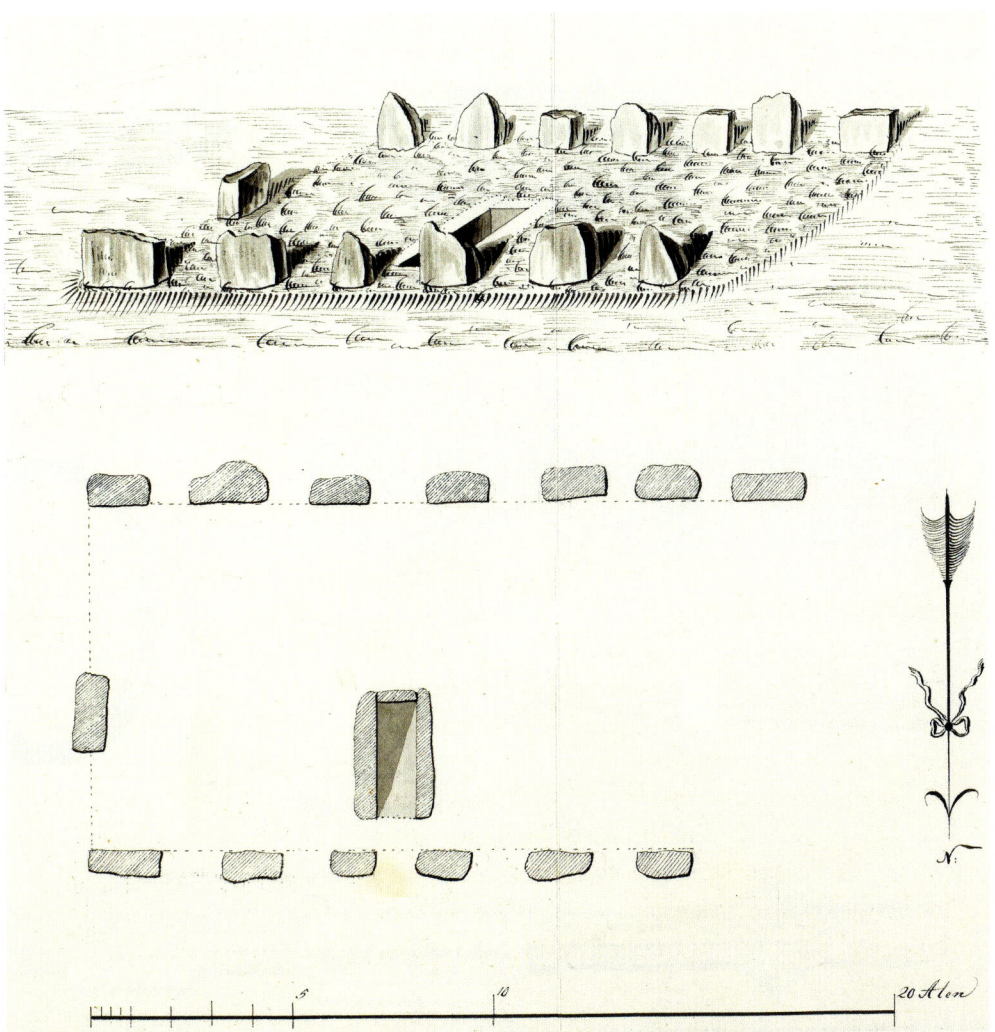

Fig. 7.29. Illustration of the long dolmen 'Stenedansen', Rø, which was subsequently destroyed (after J. Jansen 1820).

187

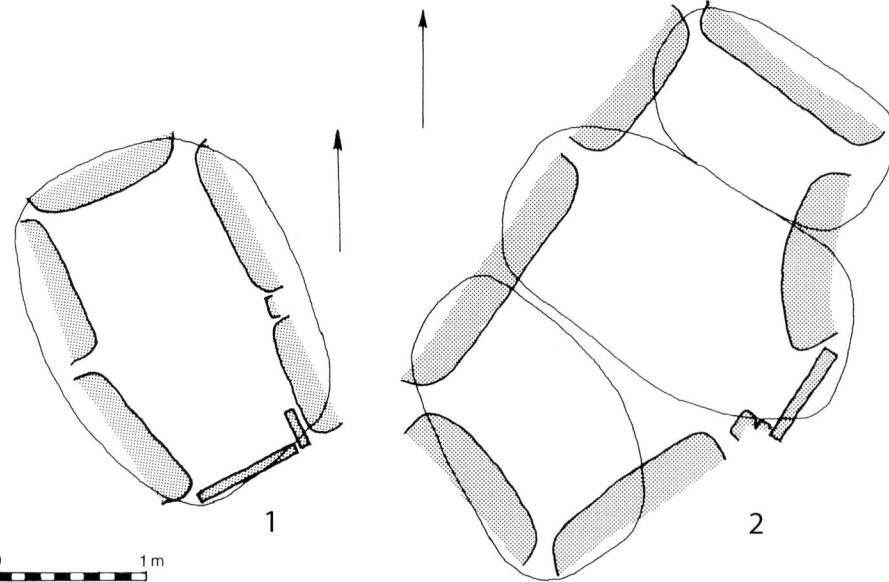

Fig. 7.30. Dolmen chamber (1) and passage grave chamber (2) in the long barrow at Vasagård (after F.O. Nielsen 2006b). 1:50.

ited extent during this period, whilst the decoration increased on certain vessels, such as lugged beakers and lugged jars. These vessels were improved aesthetically, perhaps because of their use in common rituals. At the beginning of MN, the decoration developed significantly, with this leading to a blossoming in pottery production, in terms of the quality, forms and decoration of the clay vessels, during MN AIb. This was contemporary with the construction and first use of passage graves around 3200 BC.

Dolmens

Seven dolmens are marked on map fig. 7.27. Five of these are in the south of the island, and their placement a short distance or a few kilometres from the coast is somewhat similar to that of dolmens in Scania (M. Larsson 1988a, 33 ff.). A now-dismantled dolmen at Saltholmgård, Ibsker, must have been a round dolmen. The dolmen at Vasagård is located in a long barrow, but recent georadar scans have indicated that it was originally a round dolmen (Hansen 2014, 50). The other dolmens were E-W-orientated long dolmens, which were 9-35 m long, 5.5-17 m wide and up to 3.5 m high. The best preserved example is Stenebjerg in Pedersker (F.O.S. Nielsen 1996a, 19). The few ground plans of dolmen chambers that exist show mostly open chambers, like Stenedansen (fig. 7.29) and Vasagård, where the chamber has an entrance stone at its southeastern end (fig. 7.30:1). The dolmens may have been constructed over a long period, during EN II and possibly also at the beginning of MN A. There are no preserved Neolithic burials in the dolmen chambers.

The earliest dolmens were intended for the burial of individual people, and therefore had the same purpose as the non-megalithic long barrows: to create a lasting memorial to people of importance. But the construction of megalithic tombs required more resources and a different form of organisation. The weight of the stones meant that a concentrated input from construction workers was required, as well as the probable use of oxen as draft animals. The construction of megalithic tombs amongst indigenous peoples elsewhere in the world has been identified as being part of the holding of feasts for many people (Harrisson 1958, quoted on page 204). This can provide us with a measure of the surpluses of foodstuffs that were needed to enable such construction activity, which may have required long-term preparation.

3216 dolmens have been recorded in Denmark (Ebbesen 2007, 12), although it is estimated that the original number must have been around 20,000. Assuming that the construction took place c. 3500-3200 BC, that is over 300 years, 67 dolmens would have been constructed every year. Many long barrows, however, contain more than one chamber, and Ebbesen suggests that each mound had an average of three construction phases. In other words, dolmens may have been constructed and dolmen chambers added 200 times a year (*idem*, 19).

Dolmens and passage graves were constructed within the areas of Northern Europe that were covered by moraine deposits from the last ice age. Only a few megalithic tombs were constructed outside these areas. Today, a few protected areas still demonstrate how extensive stone scatters once covered the landscape from which the ice retreated (A.V. Nielsen 1967, 262). Ice-transported stones of all sizes were concentrated at the limits of the ice front, and the largest numbers of megalithic tombs are also located along such terrain, as, for instance, can be observed in North-West Zealand, on and around Røsnæs and Asnæs (Schülke 2009; 2014). Irrespective of whatever religion or social structure was involved, the megalithic tombs are also symbols of large-scale clearance and cultivation.

The development of settlement

The placement of the dolmens in the landscape helps paint a picture of the settlement during EN II. The distance between settlement and burial monument was not great. In several examples from EN Ib, a long barrow was placed on top of settlement remains, as at Barkær, Lindebjerg and Stengade (Liversage 1992; 1981; Skaarup 1975), presumably above the remains of the dwelling in which the deceased had lived. In recent years, attention has been drawn to the fact that long barrows, long barrow-like burial structures and dolmens can be located on top of settlement remains, with some examples involving a gap of a considerable period of time (N.H. Andersen 2009; 2015; 2019).

Four of the seven dolmens on Bornholm are located in the southern part of the island, where the soil alternates between clay and sand. This demonstrates a shift from the previously preferred settlement on the sand hills of North Bornholm. It may suggest that emphasis was now placed upon the cultivation of larger areas, with this including cultivation of the heavier, but more fertile soils in the flat plain landscape of the southern part of the island. We cannot establish the precise details of this development, as only a limited number of pollen analyses have been undertaken on Bornholm, but from pollen studies undertaken elsewhere in South Scandinavia, it can be concluded that there was increasing encroachment into areas of natural vegetation during the Early Neolithic, and that this culminated around 3500 BC in the so-called 'Iversen's Landnam', when larger, open areas for cultivation and grazing were created (Iversen 1949; 1967). This has been associated with the introduc-

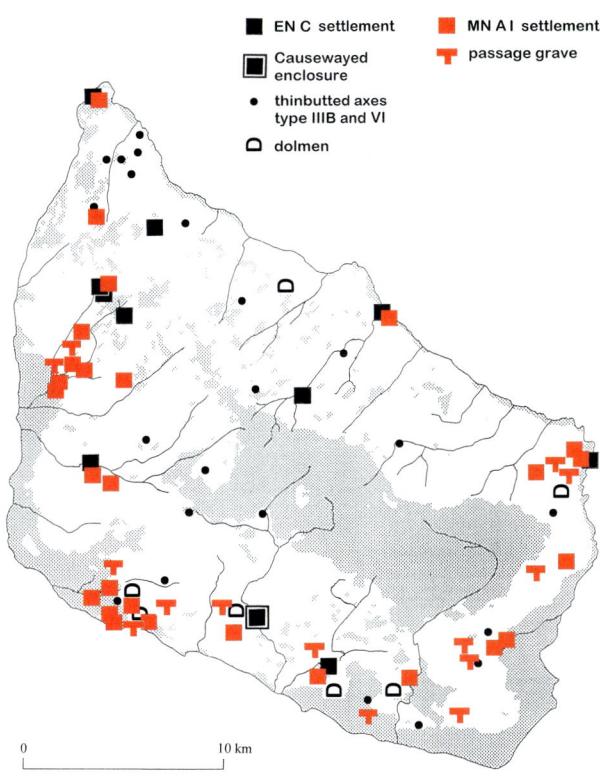

Fig. 7.31. The distribution of passage graves and settlements dating to MN AI (red) on top of map fig. 7.27, which shows settlements, dolmens and thin-butted flint axes from EN C (black).

tion of the plough, with plough marks having been recorded under megalithic tombs, although, as already mentioned, these have also been identified under long barrows during EN Ib. The earliest find of oxen with morphological indications of the use of cattle as draft animals is dated to 3650-3360 BC (Johannsen 2006, 42). It is also likely that carts began to be used during this period, which led to the construction of trackways. The opening up of the cultural landscape, and the increase in areas for cultivation and grazing, can therefore be seen against the background of a technological development.

In order to understand where the development of settlement on Bornholm was heading at the end of the Early Neolithic, we should focus our attention on the situation in the subsequent period. The map fig. 7.31 shows settlements and burials dating to MN AI, c. 3300-3200 BC, combined, for comparative purposes, with the map of finds locations during EN II, c. 3500-3300 BC (fig. 7.27). Collectively, the two distributions show that the settlement in MN AI continued to expand in the areas where the dolmens were located in EN II. This occurred in areas that were not the most densely populated in EN I, as the eastern and southern part of the island were the focus of attention in MN AI, whilst an area of new settlements and megalithic burials appeared in the middle of the western part of the island. The number of settlements increased from 10 in EN II to 27 in MN AI, and the number of megalithic tombs doubled from 7 dolmens to 14 passage graves. Apparent decline and thinning out of the settlement at the end of the Early Neolithic is followed by increased activity at the beginning of the Middle Neolithic. Even though EN II on Bornholm is apparently lacking in finds compared to EN I, it should perhaps not be regarded as a period of decline, but rather a period of reorganization and adaptation.

Causewayed enclosures

Midway between two megalithic settlement areas on South Bornholm is the causewayed enclosure at Vasagård, which is the only structure of this type that has been identified on the island (Finds list I no. 35) (Kaul *et al.* 2012; Nielsen *et al.* 2014a; Nielsen *et al.* 2015). It is perhaps actually two causewayed enclosures, as it consists of two double, semicircular rows of interrupted ditches, Vasagård East and Vasagård West, which are located 240 m apart on either side of the 10 m-deep valley, which the Læså River runs along (fig. 3.23). The two structures are also placed on either side of an 80 m-wide, slightly sloping extension of the river valley and next to a natural river crossing. The assumption that causewayed enclosures are located near trackways is also confirmed here (Klassen 2014). As stated in chapter 3, the digging out of the interrupted ditches is dated to EN II.

Why do causewayed enclosures appear at this time? Lutz Klassen writes: "The primary function of enclosures in Western and Central Europe clearly had to do with the performance of rituals related to culture change" (Klassen 2014, 244). Within the Michelsberg Culture, many causewayed enclosures were constructed in the period c. 4000-3500 BC, which was characterised by expansion. This does not, however, appear to have challenged the cultural foundation to any significant extent. But causewayed enclosures may have been the answer to the challenges that this expansion was faced with. In South Scandinavia, enclosures were established, especially in the period 3500-3300 BC, a time that was also characterised by expansion in the form of the enlargement of cultivated areas. On Bornholm,

a change in the settlement occurred, which, for example, involved taking into use the fertile and cultivable, but also more labour-intensive and heavy clay soils. In EN II, population growth must have continued, even though this is not clearly reflected in the quantities and distribution of the finds on Bornholm. It was marked elsewhere by the erection of thousands of dolmens. Such a development may have led to tensions and conflicts, and resulted in more fixed group formation, which is also reflected in the way the settlement developed in EN II and subsequently. A religious aspect was involved, but more important during this phase must have been the social and political elements that were associated with expansion and reorganisation of the settlement. We therefore instead regard the causewayed enclosures that appear at this point as gathering places, which had a multifunctional purpose in a more fixed and hierarchical organisation of society that was necessary to withstand conflicts and instability. We connected the construction of causewayed enclosures within the Cerny and Michelsberg cultures with the emergence of simple, archaic chiefdoms, whose tasks included organisation and leadership of such common construction projects, which were intended to accommodate the interests of all of society. This type of site originated in France, Germany, the British Isles and South Scandinavia at the same stage of society's development, in connection with the expansion of agriculture and the establishment of a new social order. These causewayed enclosures therefore all became 'sociograms', both for the division of society and settlement into segments, and for the oldest form of institutionalized leadership within the early agrarian societies.

Ritual deposits, including human sacrifices

The deposition of flint axes acquires another character from EN II. The long, slender and polished thin-butted flint axes of types I-IIIA, which were in circulation in EN Ib, are replaced by shorter, wider and heavier, thin-butted axes of types IIIB and VI, with a slight bias towards unpolished examples (table 5.2). This change occurs at the same time as elsewhere in South Scandinavia there is an increase in finds from wetlands, consisting of both flint axes and other groups of objects, such as pottery vessels and meal remains in the form of animal bones. In Scania, 60% of all sacrificial sites are established during the period EN II-MN II. The range of object types also becomes broader and from the beginning of the Middle Neolithic it includes battle axes (Karsten 1994, 173 f.). This can be seen as an indication that competitive feasting increases in extent at the same time as, and probably also in connection with, the construction of the first megalithic burials. On Zealand and in Jutland, a connection can also be demonstrated between the location of the sacrificial sites in the landscape and the placement of contemporary megalithic tombs (Ebbesen 1982, 62; Koch 1998, 139 ff.; Sparrevohn 2009).

This association cannot be identified on Bornholm, however, where virtually no remains of mixed deposits dating to the Early and Middle Neolithic have been found in wetlands. This may be due to the preservation conditions or perhaps that such sites were not located near water. There is, however, one exception to this: the lugged jar from Kofoedsgård, Klemensker, which was acquired by the National Museum in 1827. This was found at a depth of c. 3.75 m in a bog, together with several smaller vessels, "a human head of small dimension" and bones of domestic animals (Finds list II no. 2).

Apart from the lugged jar, which is probably from EN Ib (EN A2), we cannot determine the date of the individual elements of the finds that were recorded in the bog at Kofoedsgård, but other sites from South Scandinavia indicate that human sacrifice took place in the Neolithic, especially within the Funnel Beaker Culture. The best known examples are the bodies of two men from Boelkilde on Als (Bennike et al. 1986) and the two young women from Sigersdal Mose, Zealand (Bennike & Ebbesen 1987). In both cases, the people were forced into the bog/lake, as one individual from each location had a rope tied around their neck. Both examples have until now been dated to the Early Neolithic, but dating based upon the $\delta^{13}C$ and $\delta^{15}N$ content of the bones has placed them slightly later, so that the men from Boelkilde and women from Sigersdal now date to the beginning of MN (Fischer et al. 2007). The corrected and uncorrected dates of human bones found in bogs in Denmark are distributed over a broad period, see table 7.1. In order to provide a summary, the probable mean values of the ^{14}C dates have been used in the table. Of these, the dates of nos. 1-7 are placed in

Table 7.1. Bog finds of human remains from the TRB Culture in Denmark. ^{14}C dates are corrected using reservoir correction model including $\delta^{13}C$ and $\delta^{15}N$ analyses (Fischer et al. 2007). Median probability ages of corrected and uncorrected ^{14}C dates are obtained using Calib vers. 7.10. (6) and (12) from Skaarup 1985, (13) from Koch 1998, (9) and (11) see Bennike 1985 and 2003, the remainder from Fischer et al. 2007.

Name of site	Sex	Lab. no.	^{14}C age BP	Corrected ^{14}C age BP	Calibrated age BC (median probability)
1. Veksø Mose	F	POZ-17006	4985±27	4907±27	3681
2. Bodal K	M	AAR-6826	4970±60	4887±60	3680
3. Ferle Enge	F	K-6299	4940±95	4875±95	3669
4. Tagmosegård	Infant	K-6297	4920±95	4873±95	3667
5. Trudstrupgård	M	AAR-6881	4870±45	4798±45	3571
6. Andemose	F	K-3579	4800±90	-	3571
7. Hesselbjerggårds Mose	F	AAR-7310	4867±32	4778±32	3570
8. Hallebygård	M	POZ-17025	4800±40	4711±40	3497
9. Døjringe II	M	K-3624	4670±90	-	3454
10. Porsmose	M	K-3748	4710±90	4664±90	3449
11. Døjringe I	M	K-3623	4640±90	-	3424
12. Myrebjerg Mose	F	K-3702	4640±320	-	3345
13. Ulvemose	Juv.	K-6306	4580±90	-	3300
14. Sigersdal B	F	K-3745	4680±75	4564±75	3265
15. Sigersdal A	F	K-3744	4650±140	4554±140	3256
16. Øgaarde 13 (at boat III)	M	K-3746	4570±60	4509±60	3208
17. Boelkilde	M	K-4593	4670±65	4487±65	3190
18. Østrup Mose 2	M	K-5741	4530±90	4434±90	3119
19. Østrup Mose 2 'Leda'	F	K-5742	4510±90	4419±90	3097
20. Jordløse Mose XXXVI	M	K-6302	4430±90	4301±90	2937

EN Ib, c. 3700-3500 BC, and the dates of nos. 8-13 fall within EN II, c. 3500-3300 BC, whilst the remainder (nos. 14-20) are placed in MN AI-III, c. 3300-2900 BC. The same explanation does not necessarily apply to all human bones that have been found in the bogs (Bennike 1999, 29). The skeleton of the male from Porsmose (no. 10) is evidence of a killing that involved arrows, and the find from Ulvemose (no. 13) may have resulted from violence, as in addition to the dated femur of a young person, the bones include those of seven other people of all ages (Koch 1998, find no. 216). The table also includes three finds which may be burials (nos. 16 and 18-19) (Koch 1998, 156). If we downplay the importance of these finds of remains due to the uncertainty surrounding their interpretation, we are left with eleven that date to the Early Neolithic and four to MN A, which can be regarded as ritual deposits. Most of the human sacrifices therefore date to the Early Neolithic. The human remains can, however, collectively be regarded as reflecting an increase in violence and the competition for territories from around 3700 BC, which might have resulted in the killing of captured people or human sacrifice in a ritual context. Human sacrifice presupposes the existence of a hierarchy in society (Randsborg 1975, 115). Performing the 'ultimate sacrifice' is a demonstration of power and must be regarded as being associated with the rise of an elite.

The importance of metal

None of the three copper axes that have been found on Bornholm can definitely be dated to EN II. We cannot, however, overlook that it was during this period that the most extensive importation of copper, in the form of flat axe blades and jewellery of hammered-out copper, occurred. Of the 113 individual finds, burial finds and hoards containing copper objects dating to the Early Neolithic from South Scandinavia and the closest parts of Germany, 57 can be dated to EN II (Klassen 2000). A similar concentration of metal finds is not found elsewhere in Central Europe at this time, nor in the Eastern Alps, where most of the metal came from. The nearest concentration of objects of the same type of copper is found in the Elb-Saale area of Central Germany (Klassen 2014, 228, fig. 134). It is also notable that the Nordic copper axes weigh around twice as much as the axes that have been found closest to the source of the raw materials, which suggests that the metal was melted down after it was imported, and therefore metal processing must have taken place in the West Baltic area during the period 3500-3300 BC.

The copper axes can hardly have been used as tools, but are more likely to have functioned as symbols of wealth and status (Randsborg 1979, 318; Klassen 2000, 282). The introduction of metal at this time was an innovation, but should not be regarded as a technological breakthrough. The aim of the importation of metal objects, as well as the probable melting down and working of copper axes, was to satisfy the elite's desire to achieve wealth and prestige. The importation also meant the organisation of foreign contacts and acquisition of valuable items, which could involve exchanges with foreign leaders of the same status. In Scandinavia, copper objects abruptly disappeared at the beginning of the Middle Neolithic. But copper axes continued to be of symbolic importance, as imitations of the flat axe blades with outward-curved blade corners continued to be produced in stone and amber into the Middle Neolithic (Klassen 2000, 258 ff.).

Innovation and adaptation

The transition from the Early to Middle Neolithic in South Scandinavia has been defined on the basis of changes in ceramic forms and decoration, as well as stylistic changes in battle axes. This change is based upon typological and chronological studies of the archaeological material. There is, however, no doubt that the transition which has been defined in this way c. 3300 BC is correctly placed, as around this time there were significant changes in terms of settlement, the burial cult and social structure. From the beginning of the Early Neolithic, there are overall increases within a number of areas in South Scandinavia. On Bornholm, it is clear that the numbers of settlements and individual finds of flint axes, as well as hoards, increase between EN Ia and EN Ib, and that the finds quantities decrease in EN II. This picture differs from the sequence in the rest of South Scandinavia, where the erection of numerous dolmens must indicate continued population growth and increasing expansion of agriculture. It is not clear why there is this difference between Bornholm and the rest of South Scandinavia. We have already suggested that the decline in the deposition of flint axes contributes to a somewhat unimpressive picture of the finds in this period, and there are also only a few recorded examples of settlements dating to EN II. The fact that at least one causewayed enclosure (Vasagård) is constructed, and there is an increase and concentration of settlements, as well as the construction of more megalithic tombs in the form of passage graves at the beginning of Middle Neolithic, however, indicate that on Bornholm the same development occurred as we are familiar with from the rest of Denmark and Scania, even though the finds from EN II do not especially reflect this.

The significance of this period should not be overlooked. The introduction of ploughing, expansion of cultivated areas, increase in ritual feasts, the construction of several thousand monumental burials and the establishment of causewayed enclosures is the culmination of a development that began with the introduction of agriculture half a millennium before. But this also meant the end of expansion, as the settlement pattern changed from scattered to more concentrated settlement. This can be regarded as being associated with a partial regeneration of the forest areas in MN A (S.T. Andersen 1993; Rasmussen *et al.* 1998).

One element that characterises the Early Neolithic in Scandinavia, and particularly EN II, is the accumulation and conversion of surpluses, which were invested in ritual gatherings and construction projects. Johannes Müller identifies similarities between the development in Northern Europe and the Mittelelbe-Saale area in Central Germany during this period, and believes that the increase in ritual activity, the construction of causewayed enclosures and the beginning of metal production testify to changes that affected all areas of society, and that there was an opening up to external influences and innovations (Müller 2004, 257 ff.). One of the possible innovations that made its first appearance within the eastern Funnel Beaker Culture area at this time was the ox-drawn cart. Given the openness and extensive connections that characterise this period, we must assume that it also reached South Scandinavia at the end of the Early Neolithic. Up until now, however, this has only been confirmed by a single possible cart wheel mark under a long barrow in Holstein (Zich 1993). But it has also been suggested that the locations of megalithic tombs in the Netherlands and Northern Germany mark trackways (Bakker 1976).

Much of what unfolded in the Early Neolithic can be explained as resulting from individual attempts to create production surpluses. This led to the construction of individual status markers in the form of earthen long mounds in EN Ib and dolmens in EN II. It can be regarded as expressing that it was the farmer, family and lineage that constituted the focal point throughout this development, and that in EN II a more general structure emerged, in the form of group formation traversing family ties and lineage, which resulted in common construction projects being initiated, in the form of causewayed enclosures. At this stage of the development, we assume that leadership positions emerged, at the level of chieftain, with control over territories. This elite not only dealt with contacts with its nearest neighbours, but probably also legitimised its role of leadership by establishing links with leaders of a similar status in distant areas. This may help explain how prestigious metal was acquired, and why production of metal objects began in Scandinavia, which in terms of their size and magnificence could compete with or even surpass metal products manufactured elsewhere in Europe (Klassen 2000, 225 ff.).

From Early to Middle Neolithic

Passage graves

The development of burial traditions meant that not only on Bornholm, but throughout most of the Funnel Beaker Culture area in South Scandinavia, passage graves were constructed during a short period, c. 3200-3000 BC. The transition from dolmens to passage graves involved a number of phases, from the closed, coffin-shaped burial chambers of the earliest dolmens, to open dolmens, grand dolmens and passage graves. The appearance of burial buildings with an entrance has been regarded as evidence that the burials occurred in stages, and that the burial chambers were ossuaries for skeletal remains which had previously been buried elsewhere. It is, however, most likely that the passage graves continued to be graves intended for primary burial (Strömberg 1971, 285-91; Gräslund 1994, 22 ff.; Ahlström 2009, 81; Sjögren 2014; 2015), and that these graves contained room for successive burials of members of important families. This meant the continued development of the concept that elite status was based upon lineage. The leader's status was consolidated because he was responsible for the burial rituals, was familiar with his ancestors and could describe their achievements, and knew the proper way of conducting the ancestral cult. The megalithic tombs were also very much 'tombs for the living' (Fleming 1973).

In Central and Northern Jutland, the so-called cult houses appear, one of which, at Tustrup, Djursland, has been restored and is located close to two dolmens and a passage grave (Kjærum 1967; Eriksen & Gebauer 2016). 10 of these wooden constructions have been found, having an opening at one end. Six of the structures are located within a small area of Central Jutland. They are all dated to within the periods MN AIa-III. Four of the constructions from Central Jutland are located at sites where there are also long rows of later stone-packing graves (Fabricius & Becker 1996, 277 ff.). Sherds of exquisitely ornamented pottery have been found in the best-preserved cult houses. In four cases, the cult house was burnt down after use, and some house sites have been subsequently covered by a pile of stones (Becker 1993). The close connection with megalithic tombs and other burial structures of the Funnel Beaker Culture makes it likely that the cult houses' function was associated with the burial cult.

In MN AIb, the Klintebakke phase, during which the construction of passage graves began, pottery was produced of a quality and level of decoration that had not been seen before. The background to this may have been that a proportion of the pottery was manufactured for use in connection with burial rituals. The prestigious pottery was used in the cult houses, with footed bowls and spoons indicating particularly luxurious serving of certain foodstuffs. Large quantities of this pottery were also found scattered in front of and on either side of the entrances to passage graves, where the remains of the burial feasts were apparently deposited. The use of cult houses and the mass deposition of high-quality pottery are evidence of burial rituals on a considerable scale, at a level corresponding with that of the burial of a senior leader.

The open burial chamber of the passage graves meant that both physical and spiritual contact could be maintained with the ancestors (Schülke 2014). The largest Irish passage graves, Knowth and Newgrange in the Irish Boyne Valley, like the passage graves in Brittany, feature carved symbols and patterns on the internal upright stones and kerbstones. The significance of these symbols cannot be clearly determined, nor was this likely to have been possible for the ordinary people at the time, but they may have contained the code that was required for the initiated to make contact with the spirits of the dead. The burial cult at this time must have involved belief in an afterlife and the existence of the spirits somewhere in the cosmos, where they probably would be united with divine powers. Although we cannot decode these beliefs, the passage graves and the cult of the dead at this time represent a phase that is of religious-historical significance. A more comprehensive religious world of ideas was created based upon their belief in an afterlife. Several indicators point towards the importance of the sun in this connection (Kaul *et al.* 2002, 134), and reference can be made to the orientation of the Irish passage grave Newgrange and the way in which the sunlight falls in the middlemost of the three chambers on the shortest day of the year (O'Kelley 1982). Attempts have been made to identify the same orientation amongst the Nordic passage graves, but observations of passage openings in the Swedish passage graves suggest that they are instead orientated towards the rising of the moon at certain times of the year (Hårdh & Roslund 1991). Where the passage grave construction reached its largest scale, long-range links at an advanced organisational level existed between the centres, such as in Ireland and on the Iberian Peninsula (Eogan 1990). The construction of passage graves in Northern Europe can be regarded as a faint echo of its development in Western Europe, although it is a manifestation of the same social and ideological development.

Up until this stage, we have considered the archaic chief as a group leader, whose power and influence depended upon his ability to create surpluses, enter into alliances and manage crisis situations, either involving internal or external conflicts. He did not have a monopoly upon religion, but strived with others to demonstrate that his special position was favoured by supernatural forces. This role contrasts with a hierarchy, in which the leader is an active mediator between the supernatural world and the people. It points the way towards complex chiefdoms and kingdoms, in which the leader can have the status of a god. We are probably a long way from this stage of development at this time of the Neolithic. But the construction of passage graves may reflect the emergence of a leadership whose dominance was associated with a special competence within the religious sphere, such as making contact with the supernatural world through the spirits of the dead. This would mean a shift to a different chieftain status, where the leader knew and could communicate to the rest of the society what the divine powers required in order for the people to achieve well-being and progress. On the basis of such authority, the leader's power could grow. He could direct the workforce, and influence how the production was undertaken and how it was distributed. This could hardly have been possible without the dissemination of a common ideology (*cf.* Bradley 1990, 63). A material expression of a common mindset and common criteria for correctly achieving this is demonstrated by the distribution of the very uniform Klintebakke style within ceramic production, which, with a few exceptions, is found in the distribution area of the passage graves in South Scandinavia.

If we are correct in assuming that at the beginning of the Middle Neolithic, a hierarchy based upon both lineage and religious authority emerged, it would have created another social reality and perhaps a more fixed social structure. It also appears to coincide with the change in settlement, which from this point became more concentrated. Whilst dolmens are generally scattered across the landscape and reflect the dispersed nature of the settlement up until then, the location of the passage graves is different, such as in West Zealand, where it points towards centralisation (Schülke 2015, 193). There are, however, many examples of continuity in the construction of megalithic tombs, from simple dolmens to passage graves, as is the case at Lønt (Gebauer 2014). In East Jutland, there is a tendency for megalithic tombs to be concentrated in clusters, both near to residential sites and central sites in the form of causewayed enclosures (Madsen 1982, 214). One of the largest concentrations of megalithic tombs is located around the causewayed enclosure at Sarup on Funen (N.H. Andersen 1997, 89 ff., 2009; 2015). The dolmens are roughly contemporary with Sarup I, whilst the passage graves are of a similar date as Sarup II (N.H. Andersen 2018, 51). Near the causewayed enclosure at Büdelsdorf in Holstein, there is a concentration of megalithic tombs at Borgstedt. Comparison of the pottery that was recovered from both sites has revealed contemporaneity between activities at the causewayed enclosure and the megalithic tombs (Hage 2016, 271). There is no better example of the connection between these two kinds of monuments.

Distribution maps of dolmens, extended dolmens, grand dolmens and passage graves within the Mecklenburg area reflect a change from scattered to more concentrated settlement in the Middle Neolithic, during which the number of passage graves increases in certain areas where there was already settlement in the Early Neolithic (Schuldt 1972, 102, Maps 3-6; Wunderlich 2019). In Scania, the passage graves and dolmens are concentrated in clusters in a similar way (M. Larsson 1988a; Tilley 1996, 130, fig. 3.18; Andersson *et al.* 2016, 93 f.).

The passage graves on Bornholm are also concentrated in locally-defined areas, where dolmens were previously erected. 'Megalithic settlements' emerged, five of which can be identified on Bornholm, where more than one preserved passage grave is located near contemporary settlements, and three settlement areas include one or two dolmens (fig. 7.31). Burial and settlement concentrations are most clearly evident on the border between the parishes of Rutsker and Klemensker and in the parishes of Nylars and Ibsker, whilst settlements and burials are more scattered in the south-eastern part of the island.

The construction of passage graves required a greater degree of organisation than was required for the construction of long barrows and round dolmens, and the precondition for such work being undertaken must have been that the individual who was responsible had even more resources at his disposal. But such a project also required know-how, which is reflected in the uniform architecture of the passage graves and their complex construction (Dehn 2015). Specialists who were experienced in such construction must have been involved. During the short period of probably no more than 100-200 years, which it took to erect the passage graves, there was perhaps an equally short-lived general organization, which could provide the necessary expert knowledge and assistance for the construction work, and from which the inspiration for this work came.

Vasagård – megalithic burials and causewayed enclosures

At Vasagård, west of Læså, around 25 m from the northernmost ditch of the causewayed enclosure, is a long barrow, which contains a dolmen chamber and a passage grave (fig. 7.30:1-2). The two chambers, which both have an entrance facing to the south-east towards the causewayed enclosure, may have been surrounded by their own round barrows, as is apparently confirmed by georadar scanning (Hansen 1914, 50). The long barrow that now covers the chambers may have been erected at a later date, probably at some point in the Bronze Age. The dolmen must have been constructed at approximately the same time as the causewayed enclosure. We have previously touched upon the question of the distance between settlement, non-megalithic long barrows and dolmens, and a correlation has been identified at several locations. But no investigations have been undertaken under or around the two stone-built chambers of the long barrow at Vasagård. However, around 120 m south-south-west and 72-84 m west of the causewayed enclosure, a trial excavation in 2007 revealed settlement remains, in the form of postholes and a cultural layer containing finds dating to EN C/MN AI, whilst in and around the segmented ditches south-east of the long barrow, finds were recovered from both EN C and the beginning of MN A (see page 72 ff.).

Palisade enclosures

During the c. 400 years between the construction of the causewayed enclosures, c. 3400-3300 BC, and the end of MN AIII, c. 2900 BC, no new construction activity can be detected at Vasagård, apart from the erection of the passage grave c. 3200 BC. On the other hand, there was activity of some size, especially in MN AIII, which can be discerned from the finds in the fills of the segmented ditches. In a late part of MN AIII, however, the ditches of the causewayed enclosure were re-excavated, indicating renewed use of the structure. But the plans quickly changed, as the ditches were once again filled with the dug-up material and sealed with a stone layer. Mixed in with the stones in two of the ditches at Vasagård West were large quantities of animal bones, which, on the basis of a preliminary examination, are mainly from oxen.

Shortly after the ditches were filled up and sealed, expansion of the site began, both east and west of the river, but in this case with palisades instead of segmented ditches. This occurred at the start of MN AV, around or shortly after 2900 BC. Whilst the causewayed enclosure extended over areas to the east and west of the river, of respectively 1.7 and 1.1 ha, the palisade enclosure now covered 5.7 ha east of the river and 8.76 ha west of the river. Several palisade enclosures were constructed, presumably due to one phase falling into disrepair and having to be reconstructed, but the areas that they enclosed were approximately the same (fig. 7.32). The palisades could be constructed in closely-placed, double courses, like the northernmost ones west of the river, or in pairs of palisades courses located a considerable distance apart, like the southernmost enclosure west of the river. All the investigated palisade courses can be dated to MN AV, 2900-2800 BC. Further to the southwest, where an entrance was probably located, fragments of decorated burnt daub were found. Within the palisades both east and west of the river were circular post structures, which have been interpreted as cult houses. These were removed again after use, as all the bearing posts were pulled up after some time. In one of the cult houses, the only one that so far has been excavated west of the river, was a flat 'altar stone', and the daub on this building was decorated (Nielsen *et al.* 2015, 60 f., figs. 13-14).

These circular constructions are not the only evidence of rituals within the palisade enclosure. The uppermost layers of the interrupted ditches, above the sealed stone layers, resembled settlement layers, as they contained very fragmented pottery sherds, flint waste and burnt animal bones. But the same layers also contained around 400 complete and fragmented, small decorated stone slabs, most of which featured a sun motif, so-called 'sunstones' (fig. 7.33), whilst others were decorated with images of what may be plants and elements of the agrarian landscape (Kaul *et al.* 2016). Three stone slabs with sun motifs were also found in the postholes of the cult house that was excavated to the west of the river, including one of the largest sunstones (Nielsen *et al.* 2015, fig. 12). The worship of the sun as one of the divine forces of nature at this time is not surprising when we look back to the observatory-like cult structures that were associated with the Stichbandkeramik Culture of the fifth millennium BC, such as Quenstedt/Schalkenburg and the Goseck Circle in Saxony-Anhalt (Behrens & Schröter 1980, 93 ff.; Bertemes & Northe 2012), and when we recall the English henge monuments, some of which are also orientated towards the positions of the sun at midsummer and midwinter, such as Stonehenge. But traits linking the Nordic causewayed enclosures, palisade enclosures and circular cult houses with such structures are yet to be identified. On the other hand, there are parallels between the sun motifs on the small stone slabs and the mysterious art that Irish megalithic tombs are decorated with, such as on the kerbstones surrounding the passage grave Dowth in the Boyne Valley, onto which similar motifs in the form of 'enclosed rays' have been carved, as well as on one of the kerbstones surrounding the nearby passage grave Knowth, which is decorated with ray motif surrounded by circular motifs (Eogan 1990, fig. 21; Eogan & Aboud 1990, Pl. V). In the same area

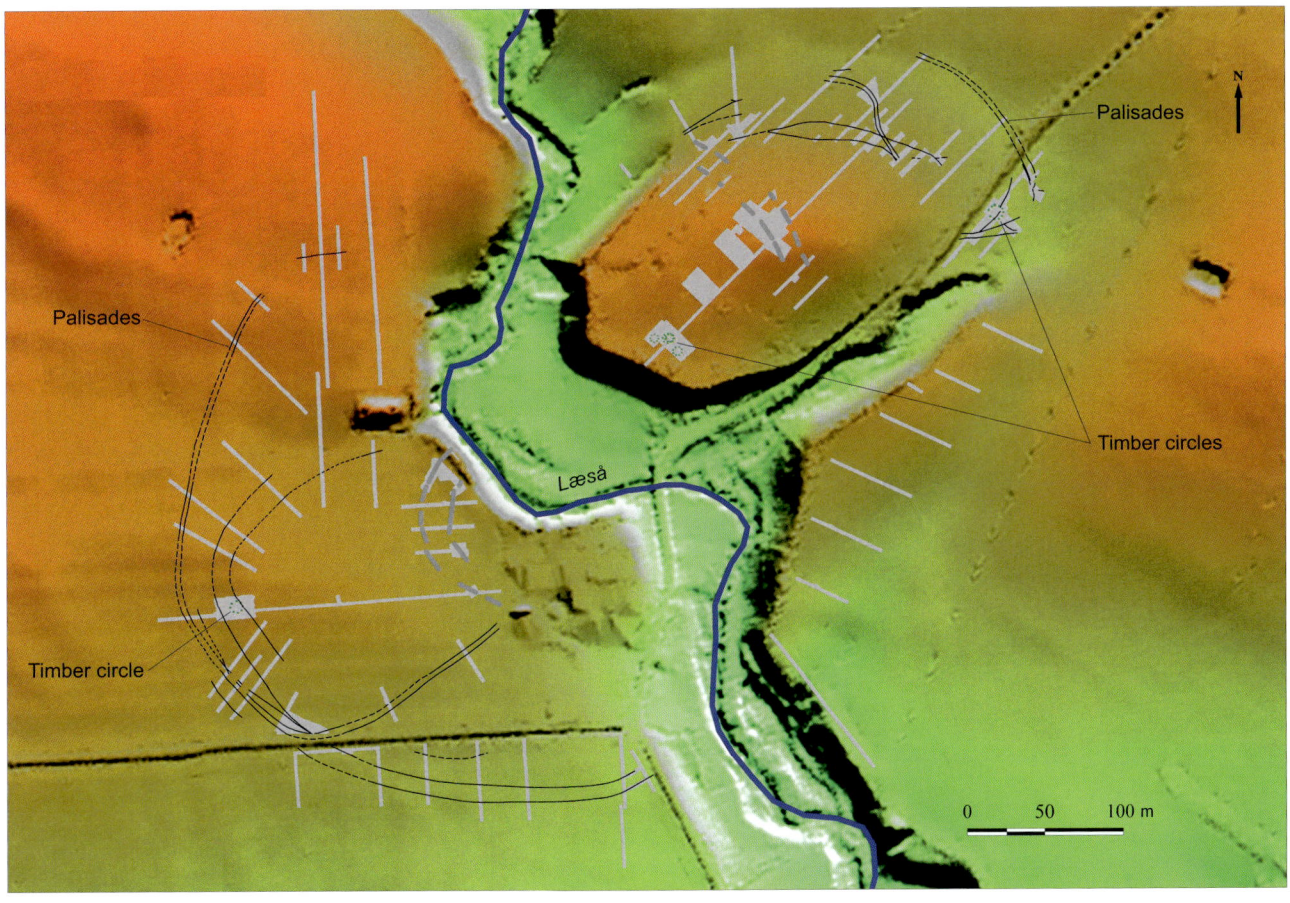

Fig. 7.32. Vasagård. Palisade enclosures from the late TRB Culture. Graphics: Michael S. Thorsen.

is the passage grave Newgrange, the 'roof box' of which allows rays of the midwinter sun to shine into the central chamber of the passage grave (O'Kelley 1982, 93 ff.).

The palisade enclosures, which were constructed at Vasagård around the earlier causewayed enclosure, belong to a group of structures that are described as the second generation of enclosed sites, and which are found in Southern Sweden and at a few sites in Denmark (Svensson 2002; Brink 2009). On Bornholm, a structure of the same type is located at Rispebjerg, only 8 km ESE of Vasagård (Kaul *et al.* 2002; Nielsen *et al.* 2014b). Rispebjerg is surrounded by numerous palisades, and a large number of circular post-built constructions have been identified. It was here that the decorated 'sunstones' were first discovered. No traces of an earlier causewayed enclosure have been identified at this site, even though its topographical location on a high plateau and near to a water course is similar to that of Vasagård East. Rispebjerg is located in the middle of an area in the south-eastern part of the island, where during MN AI settlements were located and megalithic tombs were constructed in a more scattered pattern than at the other megalithic settlement areas (fig. 7.31).

The palisade enclosures at Vasagård and Rispebjerg both belong to the late Funnel Beaker Culture, MN AV, c. 2900-2800 BC, which on Bornholm is known as the Vasagård phase. Only a few settlements dating to this period have been recorded on Bornholm. The palisade enclosures do not appear to have had a large hinterland, which suggests that they may have been permanently inhabited, as two

Fig. 7.33. 'Sunstone' of slate from Vasagård Vest. Photo John Lee, the National Museum. 1:1.

Fig. 7.34. Burnt flint chisels from circular structure at Vasagård East. Photo Michael S. Thorsen.

independent, fortified and perhaps mutually competing settlements. In this case, these would not be the only examples of settlements covering extensive areas dating to MN AV (Skaarup 1985, 365). Some of the settlements from this period are located at causewayed enclosures like Vasagård. If we turn our attentions to Central Europe, there is a general tendency for settlement during this period to be concentrated in larger and fewer settlements, which are located at dominant points in the terrain and are sometimes fortified (P.O. Nielsen 2004, 28 f.).

In MN AV, the circulation of flint axes increased after a period corresponding with MN AII-III, during which the number of flint axe hoards and individual finds of flint axes is very low, reflecting a cessation of the tradition of ritual deposition of selected objects. But from c. 2900 BC, thick-butted axes of Lindø and Valby type (group A) were produced in large quantities, and these were deposited like the thin-butted flint axes, both in hoards and individually. This type of axe dominated the burial finds in Western Denmark, along with chisels, thin-bladed axes and pointed-butted hollow-edged axes, both in passage graves and stone-packing graves (Davidsen 1978, 126 ff., P.O. Nielsen 1979; Fabricius & Becker 1996, 196 ff.). The thick-butted axe in particular once again became a symbol and sought-after object of exchange, and was sometimes made in an oversized version, although to nowhere near the same extent as the thin-butted flint axes. There are however examples of the deposition of hoards consisting of numerous flint axes. The largest of these was found at Knud in the eastern part of Southern Jutland; it contained 78 thick-butted axes and 20 other flint objects (P.O. Nielsen 1979, 38; Ebbesen 1981).

During the course of the Neolithic, another practice emerged, which probably should also be considered as sacrifice: the burning of flint implements. Burnt flint has been found at both Vasagård and Rispebjerg, but the quantity is greatest inside the palisade enclosure at Vasagård East, where fragments of burnt, thick-butted flint axes of group A and flint chisels were scattered across the surface. Burnt flint implements have also been found in the postholes of the circular buildings (fig. 7.34), which may indicate that the burning of the flint tools and/or deposition of them, wholly or as fragments, were part of the rituals that took place in these buildings.

In Sweden, in recent years, focus has been placed upon finds of 'burnt offerings' from a number of periods of the Neolithic. Burnt flint implements have been retrieved from two sites in Scania. On a hill at Svartskylle, several burnt thin-butted flint axes from late EN II were recovered, and at Kverrestad, a number of different burnt objects were found, most of which could be attributed to the Battle Axe Culture, as well as burnt human bones (L. Larsson 2002b). A third site, Stensborg, has been excavated in Östra Södermanland, Central Sweden, and dated to the Early Neolithic, c. 3600-3400 BC. Here, it is thought that there was a gathering place, where the burning of flint implements and also cereal grains occurred, as stages of sacrificial rituals (L. Larsson 2011; Larsson & Broström 2011). At a settlement at Strandby, south of Sarup on Funen, a large number of burnt fragments of flint implements have also been found, including thin-butted axes, as well as pottery from the Troldebjerg phase (N.H. Andersen 2009, 29).

The ritual deposition of flint objects that occurred on Bornholm in the Early Neolithic was a costly investment, which was expected to achieve the favour of the supernatural powers, and the same can be said of the destruction of flint tools by burning. "It could have been an act which was meant primarily to legitimate power by impressing representatives of another community" as Lars Larsson suggests (2011b, 80). But there must also have been another background: a particular pattern of action, which involved fire and transformed the object that was to be sacrificed into a different state of ritual character (L. Larsson 2011a). Burnt flint tools dating to the late Funnel Beaker Culture were used in connection with the burial cult. In Jutland, there are 17 examples of burnt axes and chisels that have been deposited near the kerbstones of megalithic tombs (Ebbesen 2011, 358). During excavation of the dolmen Trollasten in Scania, small hoard deposits were found, which contained burnt human and animal bones, burnt fragments of thick-butted, and medium- and thin-bladed flint axes, as well as other objects (Strömberg 1968, 119 ff.). The depositions at the megalithic tombs may be offerings or *pars pro toto* cremation burials, indicating a different context to the burnt flint at Vasagård and Rispebjerg, unless we interpret the temporary, circular buildings as charnel houses associated with the burning of bodies and death cult. On the burnt fragments of decorated daub recovered from the circular building at Vasagård West, besides concentric curved patterns surrounded by rays, there are also small rosettes, which are possibly small sun images, in the middle of which small pieces of burnt bone have been impressed (Nielsen *et al.* 2014, fig. 18; Nielsen *et al.* 2015, fig. 14). These bone fragments were so small that it cannot be determined whether they were animal or human. As well as its decorative effect, there must be a symbolic meaning behind this motif, and it is tempting to regard it as an image of the deceased's association with the sun. In this case, the symbolism is related to the images on the sunstones, which may also express this, or which may have had a different meaning in connection with the worship of the sun.

The finds material from the two palisade enclosures at Vasagård and Rispebjerg bring the ritual activities very much into the foreground. There are considerable quantities of finds from both sites, although only a small proportion of both assemblages have so far been analysed. New material from further excavations may very well alter the picture and enable other interpretations to be proposed. But we currently interpret these sites as central structures, whose defences were constructed under a strong central leadership, which was responsible for the rituals, including the offering of flint implements by burning. These rituals were associated with a religious faith that involved a sun cult.

The end of the Funnel Beaker Culture

As elsewhere in South Scandinavia, the Funnel Beaker Culture enters its final phase from MN BI, c. 2800 BC, at the same time as the beginning of the Single Grave Culture in Jutland. This phase is represented at the settlements at Limensgård and Ndr. Grødbygård, which both contain preserved house sites dating to the period c. 2800-2600 BC (P.O. Nielsen 1999). The pottery develops based upon the vessel forms in MN AV, as represented at Vasagård and Rispebjerg (Vasagård style), but also differs from these in terms of form and decorative motifs (Grødby style). At the end of the period, a new style emerges amongst the pottery, and influences and elements from the Globular Amphora Culture and early Corded Ware groups on the Continent to the south and south-east can be identified (Nielsen & Nielsen in prep.).

Production and distribution of thick-butted A axes was followed by an equally intense production of B axes, whose sloping and thinner butts meant that they were hafted in a different way than the A axes. The A axes dominated in MN AV, whilst the B axes appeared in MN BI (P.O. Nielsen 1979). On Bornholm, the B axes are associated with the late Funnel Beaker Culture, c. 2800-2600 BC. B axes are found in greater quantities in Scania and on Bornholm than A axes, and only in these two areas are they present in hoards. But the B axes and the associated new hafting method had a wider distribution, as in 14 examples, B axes and imitations of these are found as grave goods in early Jutlandic single graves (Iversen 2015, fig. 4.8). The largest deposit of flint axes from Bornholm, the Brogård hoard containing thick-butted axes of Group B, was recovered in the river valley just south-west of Rispebjerg, not far from the Øle Å water course (P.O. Nielsen 1979, 23, fig. 20). In the Early Neolithic, ritual deposition of complete flint axes in bogs, lakes or water courses, as well as near large stones, was common, and the latter form of deposition in particular was also practiced in the late Funnel Beaker Culture.

Summary: Six stages of social development

Although this book primarily focuses upon the Early Neolithic on Bornholm, the focus on the social development has encouraged us to look forward to the end of the Funnel Beaker Culture, in order to obtain a coherent perspective of this development. We have proposed a development that can be divided up into a number of stages, and as part of this have examined the economic, social and ideological factors that were involved in the formation of hierarchical societies. On Bornholm, six stages of development are represented, even though development can also be observed within each stage:

I. The first stage, c. 3950-3800 BC, corresponds with the first settlement on Bornholm, during which there was immigration of farmers, who brought with them the full agricultural 'package', which made it possible to establish agriculture in most places on the island within around 150 years. During the migration phase, the population may have had a leadership similar to that which also existed in the Michelsberg and Chasséen cultures during periods of population expansion. But in addition, the society was probably loosely organised, and the farmers were partially autonomous, with equal opportunity to acquire possessions.

II. In the second stage, c. 3800-3500 BC, status differences between the families emerged, each of which legitimised its position based upon lineage. Status was achieved through competitive feasting and construction of burial monuments, in the form of non-megalithic long barrows. Alliances were entered into between individuals of the same rank, both on Bornholm and during journeys elsewhere, and the contacts involved exchange of prestige objects, especially flint axes, but also copper axe blades.

III. In the third stage, c. 3500-3300 BC, the demand for competitive feasting increased alongside the transition to the construction of dolmens. The development of agriculture led to the taking into use of more land, and intensified the competition for the right to land, which led to the establishment of local leadership and the construction of causewayed enclosures. At the same time, there are signs of the first group formation, and the settlement on Bornholm now developed in different areas than before, although these can only be clearly deciphered in the next stage.

IV. In the fourth stage, c. 3300-2900 BC, settlement increased in the areas where the first dolmens had been constructed, and dolmens with entrances and passage graves were constructed. The burial cult became exclusive and was intended for prominent families, amongst which status positions emerged in the form of local leaders. A religious cosmology was established, based upon the mysterious burial cult. Ceramic production flourished, but the circulation of flint axes as status symbols declined. The number of settlements declined, although the settlements themselves increased in size.

V. In the fifth stage, in MN AV, c. 2900-2800 BC, technological and stylistic changes occur in the material culture. The high-quality and richly-decorated pottery disappears. The circulation of flint axes in the form of thick-butted A axes picks up again. The rituals now include the burning of axes and other flint implements. Palisade enclosures and circular cult houses are constructed, and a sun cult is associated with these. A strong, central leadership bases its power upon the control of both production and religion.

VI. During the last period of the Funnel Beaker Culture, MN BI, c. 2800-2600 BC, the circulation and ritual deposition of thick-butted B axes increases, to an extent and character that is reminiscent of the circulation of thin-butted flint axes in stage II. There are perhaps indications that autonomous leader types emerge during MN BI, whose status, as during the Early Neolithic, is reflected in their ability to acquire coveted prestige objects. At the same time, connections are established with the areas to the south of the Baltic, with societies influenced by the Globular Amphora Culture and Corded Ware groups, from which influences within ceramic production can be detected. During a short period, probably at the end of MN BI, there is once again an opening up to new social arrangements and external connections. This can be seen as a prelude to the changes that take place around 2600 BC, at the beginning of the Battle Axe Culture on Bornholm.

Elsewhere, group formation and territorial leadership positions developed earlier than on Bornholm, as the first causewayed enclosures in Jutland are dated to

c. 3650-3500 BC. On Bornholm, the third stage corresponds with what we understand as simple or archaic chiefdoms. The competition between aspiring chiefs from the dominant families resulted in the establishment of the first local leader positions. With the fourth stage, the power of the elite families was consolidated, and simple chiefdoms were replaced by more permanent leaders, whose duties included maintaining and dealing with the sacred universe. This is also reflected in the fifth stage, during which enclosures of a new type appear and the circulation of flint axes once again becomes important. During this and the sixth stage, some of the same tendencies are reflected as in the Early Neolithic, relating to the circulation and ritual sacrifice of flint axes, as well as the construction of gathering places, an activity that seems to have ended in MN BI.

The six stages, which are presented here based upon the material from Bornholm and its distribution patterns, can be compared with the development in other areas of the Nordic Funnel Beaker Culture. They also broadly correspond with the development within other cultural groups in Western and Central Europe. An approximately contemporary course of development occurred in Central Germany, where similar stages of social development have been identified (Müller 2001).

The emergence of Corded Ware societies in Scandinavia and Central Europe resulted, in a number of places, in a complete collapse of the social structure that had developed within the Funnel Beaker Culture. This can be regarded as a consequence of the need to produce surpluses for use in a ritual context becoming too much of a strain (Madsen 1990, 37). The changes also occurred on Bornholm, although slightly later than elsewhere and after a transitional phase, c. 2800-2600 BC (Nielsen & Nielsen 1990, 65 ff.). The centralisation of settlement that took place during the Funnel Beaker Culture in the Middle Neolithic was replaced by a completely different, scattered settlement pattern after the establishment of the Battle Axe Culture on Bornholm (F.O. Nielsen 1989). It was as if the development had to start from the beginning.

Sources of inspiration

The introduction of agriculture in Scandinavia has long been regarded as a steady development over a long period within the indigenous hunter-fisherman-gatherer communities, which were in contact with agricultural societies south of the Baltic. Contrary to this view, we instead propose a development that occurred over a short period within the area that was occupied by the early Funnel Beaker Culture, c. 4100-3800 BC, both north and south of the Baltic. This is seen against the background of the previous development on the European Continent. We believe that migration was part of this development, which could help explain why the process occurred so quickly. The notion that agriculture and cattle breeding was introduced on Bornholm without migration was inconceivable to the authors from the start. Migration models to explain the spread of agriculture around 4000 BC have also been proposed elsewhere in recent years, most energetically and with great effect by Alison Sheridan to explain the Neolithisation process in the British Isles (Sheridan 2010). Lasse Sørensen's work (2014), which uses similar arguments in relation to Scandinavia, has also been a source of inspiration.

Within Nordic archaeology, there has been a widespread reluctance to explain the social development as we have done here, proposing the formation of chiefdoms as a social category at a specific stage of the development during the Neolithic, corresponding with the time when the construction of causewayed enclosures began. But this is not the first time that this interpretation has been proposed. In 1982, Kristian Kristiansen presented a model that was based on Marxist thinking, which suggested that 'territorial chiefdoms' emerged within the Funnel Beaker Culture c. 3400 BC, at the same time as causewayed enclosures and megalithic tombs were constructed (Kristiansen 1982, 258 ff. 1984; 1991). For Kristiansen, this social system lasted until the arrival of the Battle Axe Culture c. 2800 BC, which "reflects the reversion of a chiefly territorial clan organisation into a segmentary organisation suited to predatory expansion" (with reference to Sahlins 1961). The authors recall the discussion that surrounded Kristiansen's model at the time, as well as the interpretation's relevance. It was met with both acceptance and rejection (M. Larsson 1988a, 33; 1988b, 56; Madsen 1991).

Knowing the find material better than anyone else, Jørgen Skaarup published his survey of the Neolithic on the islands south of Funen in 1985. He presented a picture of the Early Neolithic that in many ways corresponds to the one outlined in this book, taking into account the various find categories and how some of them signalled the accumulation of surplus and reflected the behaviour of individuals with leading positions such as 'petty chiefs' (Skaarup 1985, 358 (419)).

Christopher Tilley pointed out a tendency towards growing social inequality during the course of the Early Neolithic and interpreted the construction of megalithic tombs as an expression of competition, regarding this as competition between territorial groups (Tilley 1996, 115). With Pär Nordquist's book *Hierarkiseringsprocesser*, inspired by historical materialism and Paul Wason's *The Archaeology of Rank* (1994), the question of chieftain hierarchies reappeared, and the earliest chieftainship was again placed at the transition between the Early and Middle Neolithic (Nordquist 2001, 147). In recent decades, however, an evolutionist view has not been popular within archaeology. However, this has not prevented studies being undertaken of cultural change and the emergence of elite-dominated societies, but without reference to anthropology's division into developmental stages (Vandkilde 2007).

Late in the writing process, we became aware of an important article that provides an overview of the extensive and fruitful excavations undertaken in south-western Scania in recent years, which today is one of the most important areas for investigating the development of Early Neolithic society in South Scandinavia (Andersson *et al.* 2016). The three authors of the article, Magnus Andersson, Magnus Artursson and Kristian Brink, discuss several of the themes covered in this book, and arrive at many of the same possible interpretations, such as concerning the increasing hierarchisation and the formation of simple chiefdoms in the Early Neolithic societies. In another important paper, which appeared at the end of the writing process, the authors advocate for the rise of hierarchies in the Funnel Beaker Culture in South Scandinavia (Price & Gebauer 2017).

In his major work on Danish megalithic tombs, Klaus Ebbesen describes the society that constructed the megalithic tombs in Scandinavia as 'Denmark's first chieftain society' with reference to social systems in Polynesia and Melanesia (Ebbesen 2011, 545-53). As early as in his article about halberds, Ebbesen uses the term 'chieftainship' (1994, 123). He has been criticised for this (Gebauer 2012), but is himself aware of the problems associated with using social categories borrowed from theoretical anthropology (Ebbesen 2011, 545). He therefore interprets the archaeological source material on its own terms and regards the elite formation as emerging on the basis of many of the indicators that we have also used in this work. But Ebbesen differs in that he sees a primitive chieftain society as emerging "independently in the Danish area" (*idem,* 553), whereas we believe that the preconditions for development of hierarchically divided societies should be looked for further back in time and outside Scandinavia.

We have primarily been inspired by the development on the European Continent in the second half of the fifth millennium, which coincides with the beginning of the Central European Middle Neolithic or Copper Age. The process can be regarded as a shift away from the social forms of the Linear Pottery Culture farmers and the introduction of a more complex social organisation. Hierarchies emerged at different times, but also at the same time. For example, the Cerny Culture, with its extravagant, long, non-megalithic burial mounds, developed partially simultaneously with the rich, high-status burials at Varna in Bulgaria (Constantin *et al.* 1997). Other inspiration has come from the JADE project, which has outlined the connections between elite-dominated societies in Europe at a time when axes of precious stone types circulated in Western Europe, whilst copper and gold objects spread from South-East Europe (Klassen *et al.* 2012). It seems obvious to associate Northern Europe with the circulation of prestige items, as jade axes were imported and copied within the Funnel Beaker Culture, and especially when people in South Scandinavia participated in the circulation and perhaps also the production of metal items (Klassen 2004).

We do not believe that an egalitarian society was responsible for the construction of monumental tombs and causewayed enclosures, but it was a society characterised by competition for land, resources and prestige. Whether we are correct in describing this period's leaders as 'archaic chiefs' will probably be debated. But it is difficult not to see the development within the Funnel Beaker Culture from around 3300 BC until c. 2800 BC as being characterised by ever more centralisation in the hands of an elite, whose power was derived from their lineage and religious authority.

We have hardly reached the assumption of the emergence of the archaic chiefdom in the Neolithic without inspiration from analogies, in the form of both prehistoric and historically-known agricultural societies, in which the emergence of chiefdoms has occurred against a background of population growth and increased competition. Examples of these can be found in many places, but here we will just mention a few examples from the other side of the world.

The Maori people arrived in New Zealand c. AD 1200, sailing from Polynesia in canoes. They were hunters and fishermen, but also practised horticulture and cultivated root vegetables, such as taro, kumara (sweet potato) and yams. The earliest communities may have consisted of small groups bounded together by common lineage, but also later, when the society was organised into tribes, lineage played a significant role in the social status of the individual. The separate communities could be of different composition and size, but the responsibility of leadership generally rested with a chief and a council of elderly priests (Davidson 1984, 149 ff.). The Maoris constructed fortified sites, pas, sometimes with extensive defences consisting of ditches, ramparts and a palisade, which could be repeated as outer and inner elements of the fortification (Best 1975). Pas were preferably located at the centre of the settled area and were multifunctional gathering places. The population did not always live in their pa, but gathered there in numbers of up to several hundreds for common rituals or protection against external attacks. The chief usually had his residence there, which was often placed high up in the terrain. Pas could cover several hectares and some contained gardens where kumara were cultivated. Stocks of root vegetables were stored in pits at the pa. Of the c. 7,000 pas, both large and small, that have been registered in New Zealand,[3] 98% are located within the area where horticulture was practised, primarily on the North Island.

Aileen Fox has compared the Maori pas with English hillforts dating to the Iron Age, such as Maiden Castle and Hambledon Hill (Fox 1976, 53 ff.), with which there are certain structural similarities. But she could also have made comparisons with English, as well as Scandinavian, causewayed enclosures, given that there are greater similarities with these when the cultural context is examined. In both cases, the fortified structures were constructed by societies undergoing development a few centuries after their establishment in new surroundings, and in a situation in which there was competition for resources and prestige. One of the aims of the Maori pa was to protect the community's food resources. We believe that this may also have been one of the aims of the European causewayed enclosures.

Another example taken from ethnography is the construction of megalithic tombs as a stage of lavish feasts in an agricultural society. Tom Harrisson, 'The Barefoot Anthropologist', was employed by the Sarawak Museum in northern Borneo in the period 1947-1966. He describes the *irau* rituals of the Kelabit people, whose feasts were held by the young in honour of their parents, either in their old age or after death. This ritual constantly occupied people's consciousness. The culmination of the ritual was the holding of enormous feasts lasting several days, in which several hundred guests participated. During the course of the feast, a burial monument for the host family was constructed in the form of a megalithic tomb, with the young men of higher rank taking part in this. The whole arrangement could take up to two years to prepare. "It follows then, that this style of burial is not for everyone. Only the upper class can normally perform; and this they *must* do, to maintain position by Kelabit standards. Only so can they command the respect and the labour-help which preserve status and its advantages, practical and spiritual. Conversely, the higher the persons to be commemorated, the bigger the feast and the larger the effort expected of the guests in return, usually" (Harrisson 1958, 697). We consider the irau rituals a useful analogy for dolmen construction in Northern Europe, and its social and economic background.

Reference can also be made to recent ethno-archaeological studies aimed at illuminating the function of ritual feasts in the creation of social structure within various indigenous societies on the islands of South-East Asia (Jeunesse 2016; Jeunesse *et al.* 2016; Jeunesse & Denaire 2017; *cf.* Nielsen & Sørensen 2018).

Testing such analogies may also result in differing opinions about how well such analogies reflect social conditions within the Funnel Beaker Culture. Maria Wunderlich has recently studied megalith-building activities in Nagaland, north-eastern India, among the Angami and Lhota Naga, where competitive behaviour is reflected in the arrangement of feasts and the construction of megalithic monuments. Wunderlich is testing the analogy on the Funnel Beaker settlements and megalithic tombs in eastern Schleswig-Holstein and western Mecklenburg, where she does not identify any signs of individual hierarchy in house building or grave finds. She instead emphasises the representative character of the monuments, which could be interpreted as reflecting competition between different communities (Wunderlich 2017, 2019). This conclusion diverges from the one we propose here, that monument construction took place in a society characterised by differences in social rank. In the Early and Middle Neolithic, high social rank does not seem to be expressed by valuable furnishings in individual burials in contrast with what can be observed in later periods. The graves in the non-megalithic long barrows, dolmens and passage graves are sometimes well furnished with objects, but this is not always the case. We believe that it is the monumental burial itself that reveals differences in social status, between individuals as well as groups. Those who had access to enough resources could control events, such as funerary feasts and the construction of monuments. The monuments were not built for all members of society.

Notes

1. Division of EN I into a and b also occurs in other chronologies (Müller 2011b, fig. 4; Mischka *et al.* 2014, fig. 2), but here the two sub-phases have different contents.
2. We use the term 'non-megalithic long barrow' here as a general term for structures with oblong, trapezoid, rectangular, oval or, like in the Cerny Culture, keyhole-shaped ground plans, even though it cannot, in all cases, be documented that these were covered by a mound. The same applies to some of the South Scandinavian structures (N.H. Andersen 2015, 119).
3. The number of pas in New Zealand is stated by Davidson as being between 4000 and 6000 (1984, 184). By 2006, the figure had increased to c. 7000 (Nigel Prickett, pers. comm.).

The division of Bornholm into parishes.

8. Catalogue. Finds from the Early Neolithic on Bornholm

Under each of the following catalogue entries, the descriptions are ordered by place number (6 digits for respectively county, district and parish), followed by the site number, which enables access to the database *Fund og Fortidsminder* at the following web address: http://www.kulturarv.dk/fundogfortidsminder/

Abbreviations:
BMa – Bornholms Museum, Rønne, inventory nos. in the register kept between 1893 and 1971
BMR – Bornholms Museum, Rønne, file nos. from 1972
EN – Early Neolithic
LN – Late Neolithic
MN – Middle Neolithic
NM – the National Museum of Denmark, Copenhagen
NNU – *Nationalmuseets Naturvidenskabelige Undersøgelser* – The National Museum, Environmental Archaeology
SNM – *Statens Naturhistoriske Museum*

Finds list I

SETTLEMENT FINDS

During the examination of the collections at the National Museum of Denmark (NM) and Bornholms Museum (BMR), material has been recorded from 56 sites on Bornholm, which have produced finds that are characteristic of settlement dating to the Early Neolithic. The finds are from both collection and excavations. Some of the finds groups are small, for example only consisting of a few sherds of pottery, such as those from excavations of graves or settlements dating to periods other than EN, whilst other finds groups are large and were recovered during excavations of EN settlement sites. It is expected that these will be published separately and they are therefore only briefly described here.

1. Hammeren 1

060101-139a. Allinge-Sandvig parish. – NM A8557-63, A10734-42, A10788-92, A10998-11004, A11453-86, A11948-77, A22140, A38541, A43025(29?)-55. – BMa 135, 587, 593, 1338-44, 2648. (E. Vedel 1897, 1-2, 105-107. – C.J. Becker 1947, 161-164; 1951, 179. – Skaarup 1973, 132-133).

The settlement on the north-west coast of Hammeren was the first settlement on Bornholm with finds dating to the Neolithic to be thoroughly investigated. At this site, finds dating to the Ertebølle Culture and several periods of Neolithic have been collected and excavated. Systematic excavations were undertaken in 1891-93, and reports on these by J.A. Jørgensen can be found in the National Museum's archive. During the excavations in 1891-93, an up to 40 cm-thick cultural layer was recorded, which lay on top of sand and was itself also overlain by a sand layer. The Neolithic antiquities were found within the cultural layer, but it was otherwise not possible to separate them stratigraphically.

a. The decorated pottery sherds included a small collection of sherds of thin-walled, short-necked funnel beakers, some with a horizontal row of very small indentations just under the rim (fig. 3.27:2) (NM A11977, BMa H135) and others with two horizontal rows of indentations under the rim (fig. 3.27:3) (BMa H135).

b. Sherds of funnel beakers decorated with horizontal two-ply cord impressions under the rim (Becker 1947, fig. 36.1). There are also sherds of funnel beakers with a neck height of at least 7 cm, which are decorated with two-ply cord in the form of horizontal zones of 2-6 parallel cord impressions, separated by zones with vertical cord impressions (fig. 3.27:4) (BMa 2648).

c. Several sherds of pottery vessels decorated with whipped cord impressions (fig. 3.27:6). A rim sherd with short whipped cord impressions across its upper edge has hanging, concentric semicircles and horseshoe-shaped impressions made with two-ply cord (C.J. Becker 1947, fig. 36.2 and here fig. 3.27:5). Seven body sherds are decorated with vertical, parallel lines, with the spaces between filled with diagonal lines, all in whipped cord (fig. 3.27:7-8) (BMa H135, 587). There are also various belly sherds with vertical stripes (NM A10742).

d. BMa 2648. Sherd extending from the rim to the upper part of the belly of a thin-walled beaker with flared profile, with finger impressions at the front edge of the rim, under which are 6 horizontal lines of two-ply cord, below these groups of vertical lines and under these 5 horizontal lines in the same technique. The vessel should be categorised as an unusual form, for which there are no parallels amongst the Danish finds.

The settlement is located on the north-west coast of Hammerknuden, on the same sandy plateau as the ruins of Salomon's Chapel. – *Dating*: Sherds of funnel beakers of types I (and perhaps II), III and IV/V are present. Periods EN A1-2, EN B and EN C are therefore represented at the settlement. There are also a large number of sherds dating to the Middle Neolithic Funnel Beaker Culture, Pitted Ware Culture tanged arrowheads, pottery from the Boat-axe Culture and LN flint.

2. Tingbakke

060101-192. Allinge-Sandvig parish. – BMR 1752. – Privately collected during gravel quarrying.

One rim sherd of a funnel beaker decorated with horizontal lines of two-ply cord, divided by undecorated zones.

It was found in a sandy area on the side of Tingbakke, Hammeren. – *Dating*: EN B.

3. Madsebakke

060101-129. Allinge-Sandvig parish. – BMR 2889. – Excavated by Palle Ø. Sørensen in 2005 in connection with investigations of the area NW of the cliff with rock carvings.

One rim sherd of a funnel beaker decorated with horizontal lines of two-ply cord.

Found during excavation of features associated with the area of rock carvings at Madsebakke. The sherd was found at the bottom of a fill at the northern end of the cliff with rock carvings. – *Dating*: EN B.

4. Hebro, Tornbygård

060104-21. Klemensker parish. – BMR 866. – Collected during survey by F.O. Nielsen 28/10 1981.

Ceramic material: 1 rim sherd of a short-necked funnel beaker decorated with three horizontal rows of small fine indentations, 3 undecorated rim sherds, 1 base sherd, 1 belly sherd and 49 body sherds. Edge fragment of a clay disc with a number of finger/nail impressions along the edge of the upper surface. – *Flint*: 1 butt fragment of an unpolished axe, 1 blade scraper, 1 flake scraper, 1 blade knife with gloss patination along both side edges, 1 backed flake knife, 1 transverse arrowhead and 30 pieces of flint waste and cores, 10 of which are fire affected. Most of ball flint waste is of flint nodules, one fragment is of Kristianstad flint.

Found on a low sand hill covering c. 1 ha, 150 m south of Baggeå and 21 m above sea level. – *Dating*: EN A.

5. St. Knudegård

060104-55. Klemensker parish. – NM A5395b. – Collected by J.A Jørgensen in 1881. Report also by Jørgensen 29/5 1882. (E. Vedel 1897, 109 no. 4. – C.J. Becker 1947, 164).

Two rim sherds decorated with horizontal lines of two-ply cord under the rim, one also with vertical lines in the same technique (the latter illustrated in C.J. Becker 1947, fig. 39a).

Found on a sand hill, Torpebakkerne, 107 m above sea level – *Dating*: EN B.

6. Kokkedal

060104-57. Klemensker parish. – BMR 2178. – Collected by volunteer archaeologists in 1989. – Excavation in 1994 and report 6/5 1994 by F.O. Nielsen.

Ceramic material: Sherds of funnel beakers decorated with horizontal rows of indentations under the rim, and beakers with horizontal and vertical lines of two-ply cord, sherds of collared flasks and lugged jars, as well as clay disc fragments with finger impressions on the edge. Several of the funnel beakers have knobs on the shoulder. There are also a few sherds of pottery with rim beads containing finger impressions, as well as sherds decorated with whipped cord. – *Flint*: The imported flint includes fragments of polished axes, 2 two-sided and 11 four-sided, a few transverse arrowheads, scrapers and blade knives. There were only few flakes from flint nodules, but a few more fragments of Kristianstad flint. See overview of the finds from cultural layers and features in Table 3.3.

The finds are both from collection and excavation of a finds-rich cultural layer, which covered a few postholes and other features. The site is located on the west-facing slope of a sand hill, 105 m above sea level – *Dating*: Most of the finds can be dated to EN B. A few, however, date to EN A and EN C.

7. Sorgenfri

060104-186. Klemensker parish. – BMR 1394. – NM I 5952/84. – Collected by Michael Thorsen in 1982-84.

a. 1394x7-17, 28-30. *Pottery*: Joining parts of the neck and belly of a large funnel beaker, 8 rim and neck sherds decorated with 1-2 horizontal rows of small and large indentations (fig. 8.1:1-2), 15 rim and neck sherds decorated with horizontal and vertical lines in two-ply cord (fig. 8.1:3,5), 20 undecorated rim sherds, 1 neck-belly sherd of vessel with two horizontal rows of small, angular indentations under the neck-belly transition (fig. 8.1:4), 1 lugged sherd of a lugged jar and c. 200 other undecorated sherds.

b. 1394x1-6,19, 21-27. *Flint*: The imported flint consists of 35 flakes and fragments of polished axes, 5 transverse arrowheads, two of which are made from flakes of polished axes, 29 blades and blade fragments, 1 blade scraper, 2 backed flake knives, 10 pieces with retouch, 265 flakes and 35 fire-affected pieces. There are 8 pieces from ball flint nodules, a number of which are fire affected. 23 flakes are of Kristianstad flint.

Found in very undulating and sandy terrain 117 m above sea level. – *Dating*: There are a number of rim

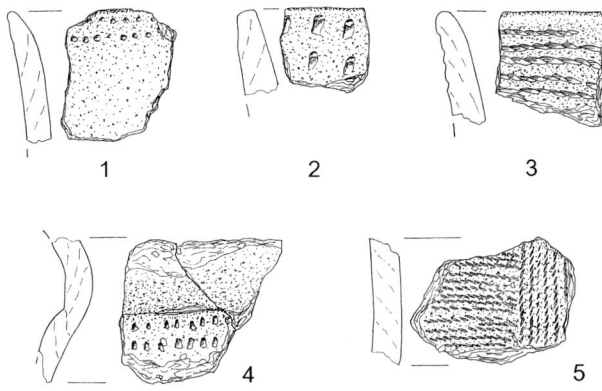

Fig. 8.1. Pottery sherds from Sorgenfri (Finds list I no. 7). Eva Koch del. 1:2.

sherds with indentations, especially the very small indentations found on type I funnel beakers, whilst the cord-decorated sherds must be from funnel beakers of type III. The finds therefore date to both EN A1 and EN B.

8. Marevadgård

060104-198. Klemensker parish. – BMR 1105. – NM I 6067/85. – Collected by volunteer archaeologists in 1987-89, after which Neolithic features and cremation burials dating to the Iron Age were recorded. – Excavation in 1994 and report 29/4 1994 by F.O. Nielsen.

A cultural layer containing finds dating to EN was excavated, under which postholes were found. In the cultural layer were ard marks containing charcoal, which was ^{14}C dated to the Late Bronze Age (K-5370-71). In a natural depression at the foot of the hill to the south, ancient soil layers were excavated, and a section was also recorded through two stratigraphically-divided cultivation horizons containing ard marks.

a. BMR1105x26, 55, 56, 63. *Pottery*: 10 rim sherds and 9 neck sherds from funnel beakers decorated with 1, 2 or 3 horizontal rows of large or small indentations, 4 undecorated rim sherds, 6 body sherds with remains of a lug, 4 sherds of the collar of a collared flask and 296 undecorated sherds. – *Flint*: The imported flint consisted of 8 flakes of polished axes, including 1 blade fragment of a four-sided axe, 1 blade knife, 1 double scraper and 34 flakes, including 8 fire-affected pieces. Of ball flint there were 3 flakes, and of Kristianstad flint 12 flakes. – Group a is made up of unstratified finds collected from the settlement area at the top of the hill.

b. BMR1105x64. *Pottery*: 2 rim sherds and 2 neck sherds of short-necked funnel beakers decorated with both 2 and 3 horizontal rows of indentations, as well as 60 undecorated sherds. – *Flint*: The imported flint consists of 2 flakes of polished axes, 1 blade knife and 1 flake. The Kristianstad flint consists of 2 cores and 2 flakes. – Finds group b is from the cultural layer at the top of the hill.

c. BMR 1105x41-43, 49-52, 54. *Pottery*: 12 rim sherds and 3 neck sherds of funnel beakers decorated with horizontal rows of indentations, 3 undecorated rim sherds, 1 neck sherd from a collared flask and 285 undecorated sherds. – *Flint*: The imported flint consists of 4 flakes from polished axes, 1 blade knife and 13 flakes. 1 flake is from a ball flint nodule and 1 core and 5 flakes are of Kristianstad flint. – Finds group c is from the postholes under the cultural layer.

d. BMR 1105x197, 201-217. *Pottery*: 4 rim sherds and 5 neck sherds of funnel beakers decorated with 1-4 horizontal rows of indentations, 1 rim sherd with horizontal lines of two-ply cord in separate zones, 3 undecorated rim sherds, 2 lugged sherds, 1 sherd with a knob under the neck-belly transition and 283 undecorated sherds. – *Flint*: The imported flint consists of 4 flakes of polished axes, 2 transverse arrowheads, 1 blade and 10 flakes. The flint from nodules consists of 9 flakes. The Kristianstad flint is made up of 4 cores and 32 flakes. – *Granite*: 1 complete and 1 fragment of the lower stone of quern stone and 2 fragments of rubbing stones. Crushing stones: 6 complete and two fragments. – *Sandstone/quartzite*: 1 grindstone fragment. – C. 1000 pieces of charcoal. – Finds group d is from an excavation of a depression containing ancient soil layers at the foot of the hill to the south.

Apart from the above-mentioned finds, further settlement material was collected in 1988-90 (BMR 1105x67-68, 89-139, 144-157, 160-194).

The settlement is located 95 m above sea level, in the south-westernmost part of Torpebakkerne, on a hill covering 120 × 120 m, which is bounded by water courses on two sides. – *Dating*: The pottery is very fragmented, and does not include any full profiles, so the rim diameter/neck height ratio cannot be measured on the funnel beakers. Characteristics that are typical of type I funnel beakers, such as rim beads with finger impressions, are apparently absent. On the other hand, many of the decorated rim sherds have indentations similar to the decoration that is found on type II funnel beakers from the Vallensgård I settlement. Amongst the large quantities of sherds, only a few are decorated with lines of two-ply cord, or are fragments from collared flasks. Most of the finds must therefore date to EN A2, and a lesser amount to EN B.

9. Skrubbegård

060104-221. Klemensker parish. – BMR 1710. – Survey and retrieval of finds from drain ditches. Report by G. Møller Larsen 20/11 1985. Finds donated to BMR by Dorte Dam.

BMR 1710x1-17. Sherds of funnel beakers, including 1 rim and 1 body sherd decorated with horizontal rows of vertical indentations, 3 rim sherds decorated with horizontal lines of two-ply cord and 1 body sherd with horizontal and vertical lines of two-ply cord. – The flint objects include 1 transverse arrowhead.

The settlement is located 105-115 m above sea level on a south-facing slope, where the soil alternates between sand and clay. – *Dating*: The cord-decorated sherds should be dated to EN B.

10. Pileskoven
060104-229. Klemensker parish. – BMR 1832. – Excavation of settlement in 1990 and report 20/4 1990 by F.O. Nielsen.

During excavation of cultural layers and depressions, features and finds were found dating to EN, MN AII, the Late Bronze Age and Early Roman Iron Age. The largest feature uncovered during the excavation was a c. east-west-orientated fill measuring 6 × 15 m, which was of irregular, rectangular shape (fig. 3.19). At the bottom of the depression, the clay subsoil was covered by a thin layer of ash and charcoal. In the middle of the depression, this layer was covered by burnt daub. The greatest concentration of this was observed as a c. 10 cm-thick layer immediately N and NE of a large stone, the layer measuring c. 3.4 × 3.0 m. Towards the E, more scattered daub extended a further 4.5 m. East of the large stone, a layer of unburnt clay was also observed, covering c. 1½ m². Several pottery concentrations were located within the daub layer and the ash layer (nos. 13, 27.1, 37.3 and 43.3). The feature is interpreted as the site of a building with a sunken floor and daubed walls. Around the large stone in the western part of the building, 5 crushing stones and hammerstones, as well as 4 fragments of quern stones, were found. Several of the stones were sooted. In the burnt layer, remains of a few charred cereal grains were also found.

The bottom layer of the depression only contained sherds of Early Neolithic pottery, whilst sherds from vessels dating to MN AII were also found in the upper layer of the depression. Several sherds of Middle Neolithic pottery were found in the small fills E and W of the large depression. The Early Neolithic finds from the daub layer and ash layer at the bottom of the depression are as follows:

Pottery: Rim sherds of a large funnel beaker with a rim diameter of c. 36 cm, decorated with vertical lines of two-ply cord divided by undecorated zones (nos. 27:1, 42:3, fig. 3.20:1); several rim and neck sherds with respectively horizontal and vertical lines of two-ply cord (no. 43:3, fig. 3.20:3); part of the neck of a large funnel beaker of type III with a rim diameter of c. 32 cm and a neck index of 39, decorated with horizontal lines of two-ply cord in groups of three, which are separated by undecorated zones (nos. 48:3, 44:2, fig. 3.20:2); neck fragment of a small funnel beaker with 9-10 horizontal lines in two-ply cord below the rim (fig. 3.20:4); many rim sherds of different funnel beakers decorated with two-ply cord impressions like the above-mentioned examples; rim sherds of a funnel beaker decorated with groups of short, vertical thin lines originating from the rim; and 1 rim sherd with 1 horizontal row of finger impressions. – *Flint*: The bottom layer of the depression contained 1 scraper and 1 crested blade knapped from a polished flint axe with a rounded side edge and domed broad surfaces, as well as a few flakes. There were a few flakes of Kristianstad flint. In the upper layers of the depression, a few flakes of flint nodules and Kristianstad flint were found, but almost no imported flint. A number of quartz flakes were, however, present.

The settlement is located 70 m above sea level south of the top of a small hill, which rises c. 6 m above the surrounding area. Towards the east, the settlement area is divided by a small depression and a spring located on another higher hill, Duebjerg. The soil in the area varies considerably. The ridge where the excavation was undertaken consists of stony moraine, whilst north and south of this are areas of light sandy soil. – *Dating*: The neck index can only be measured on a single, large vessel fragment (fig. 3.20:2), but it is very clear that a number of the neck fragments are from type III funnel beakers. Apart from a single sherd with a row of finger impressions under the rim, the bottom layers of the depression did not contain any sherds from beakers with indentations together with the cord-decorated pottery. The construction and use of the house site should be dated to EN B. There are four AMS ^{14}C dates:

1) Charcoal of apple, rowan or hawthorn (*Pomaceae*) (AAR-10261): 4960±65 BP, cal. 3800-3650 BC (1σ), 3950-3640 BC (2σ). – 2). Charcoal of hazel (*Corylus avellana*) (AAR-10262): 5038±49 BP, cal. 3950-3770 BC (1σ), 3960-3710 BC (2σ). – 3) Burnt macrofossil remains, unidentified (Ua-55724): 4513±37 BP, cal. 3350-3110 BC (1σ), 3360-3090 BC (2σ). – 4) Charcoal, unidentified (Ua-55725): 4786±31 BP, cal. 3640-3530 BC (1σ), 3650-3510 BC (2σ).

The dates of nos. 1 and 2 suggest an early date for the cord-decorated pottery from EN B, and date no. 3 probably reflects the activity at the site during MN. The fourth date is the only one that is placed within EN B (3650-3500 BC). See discussion in chapter 3, p. 66.

11. Ø. Pilegård
060104-355. Klemensker parish. – BMR 2168. – Collected during surface survey by F.O. Nielsen in 1987 and 1989.

a. BMR 2168x1. Collected in 1989: 1 rim sherd and 1 body sherd decorated with horizontal lines of two-ply cord, 1 body sherd decorated with oblong, vertical indentations and 42 other sherds. – 1 transverse arrowhead and 72 other pieces of flint.

b. BMR 2168x2. Collected in 1989: 1 rim sherd decorated with horizontal lines of two-ply cord, 1 body sherd decorated using the same technique, with the lines separated by undecorated zones, and 21 other sherds. – 23 pieces of flint.

c. BMR 2168x4. Collected in 1987: 2 sherds, including a rim sherd from a funnel beaker with a bead under the rim, in which there are oblong, triangular indentations. – 87 pieces of mainly imported flint, including flakes of polished axes.

Found on a high, sandy hilly area c. 120 m above sea level. – *Dating*: The cord-decorated pottery under a and b should be dated to EN B.

12. Gothegård

060104-356. Klemensker parish. – BMR 2169. – During survey work in 1991, F.O. Nielsen identified a charcoal-rich cultural layer containing a small amount of flint waste and a few undecorated Neolithic sherds, as well as a ploughed-damaged pit containing a small amount of charcoal and fire-cracked stones. Only 5 cm of the pit was preserved under the plough layer. This contained:

BMR 2169x1-2. A flared rim sherd from a medium-sized type II funnel beaker. The vessel is decorated with three horizontal rows of oblong, rectangular indentations that are placed close to the rim. Rim diam./neck height: c. 17/5.5 cm.

Found at the north-east-facing foot of an oblong hilly area, c. 110 m above sea level on sandy soil. – *Dating*: EN A2.

13. Torpegård

060104-381. Klemensker parish. – BMR 2170. – Collected by G. Møller Larsen and Ruth Feldbo in 1989 (privately owned).

a. 1 rim sherd of a funnel beaker with a horizontal row of curved indentations and 1 rim sherd with a row of double, oblong indentations under the rim. Neck sherd with 1 or 2 horizontal rows of finger/nail impressions under the rim. A neck-belly sherd with zones containing several rows of small indentations under the transition between the neck and belly. One sherd with a lug, probably from a lugged flask.

b. 3 rim sherds from funnel beakers with horizontal rows of indentations under the rim: 1 with three rows of small, oblong indentations, 1 with 4 rows of small rectangular indentations and 1 with 3 rows of double, small, dot-shaped indentations. The latter has a neck-shoulder profile that is characteristic of type I funnel beakers.

Found in a gravel quarry and excavation of a tree-throw on sandy soil, 107 m above sea level. – *Dating*: EN A, and part of the material can be dated to EN A1.

14. Smedegade, Klemensker

060104-393. Klemensker parish. – BMR 3358. – Excavated by Finn Ole Nielsen and Michael Thorsen in 2005 (F.O.S. Nielsen 2006a, 44-46). Summary plan fig. 3.30.

a. BMR 3358x7-62. Finds from cultural layer. *Ceramic material*: Sherds of funnel beakers, lugged jars, lugged flasks and collared flasks, as well as clay disc fragments. A few of the many sherds could be joined together into measurable neck and shoulder areas of funnel beakers (fig. 3.32:1). The cultural layer contained 599 undecorated and 899 decorated rim sherds, 98 sherds with lugs and 119 kg of undecorated body sherds, as well as 35 clay disc fragments. The recording of 689 rim sherds from 118.75 m², constituting the most finds-rich quarter of the area, produced the following percentages for rim decoration:

Undecorated rims	22.8 %
Horizontal bead with finger impressions	0.6 %
Horizontal rows of finger impressions	4.6 %
Horizontal rows of indentations	65.9 %
Two-ply cord impressions	6.1 %

Flint: The cultural layer contained 2744 pieces of flint, which can be divided up into 8 fragments of polished, thin-butted axes, 243 flakes and blades with polished facets, 7 fire-affected halberd fragments (fig. 3.40:3), 22 transverse arrowheads, 36 scrapers, 1 flake borer, 1 core, 54 blades and blade fragments, and 2380 flakes. Two large fragments, part of the blade and butt of the same thin-butted, polished flint axe were found in the cultural layer in the eastern part of the excavation area, only 25 cm apart (fig. 3.38). Amongst the implements and flakes, imported flint dominates compared to that from flint nodules and Kristianstad flint. – *Other stone*: 12 quern stones and quern stone fragments, including 2 rubbing stones, 17 grindstones and grindstone fragments, 22 crushing stones and 20 hammerstones. – *Burnt daub*: The cultural layer contained c. 8 kg of burnt daub, most of which was concentrated in a c. 7 × 5 m area in the south-west of the excavation area. The cultural layer also contained burnt bone, charcoal, charred hazelnut shells and charred cereal grains.

b. BMR 3358x71. Finds from hole for probable roof-bearing post A10, c. 0.5 m in diameter and 0.2 m deep *Ceramic material*: 3 rim sherds of funnel beakers decorated with 3 horizontal rows of closely-placed, oblong impressions under the rim (fig. 3.33:1), 1 rim sherd of funnel beaker with at least 2 horizontal rows of D-shaped impressions under the rim, 1 rim sherd with 3 horizontal rows of diagonal, oblong impressions, 1 sherd of the neck and upper part of the belly of an undecorated type II funnel beaker (fig. 3.33:2), joining parts of the neck of a lugged jar and several undecorated sherds. Most of a clay disc with finger impressions along the edge, which is up to 2 cm thick and 19.5 cm in diameter (fig. 3.33:3). The following were also found: 1 g of hazelnut shells and 78 charred cereal grains, including 12 grains of naked six-row barley (*Hordeum vulgare var. nudum*), 7 grains of ordinary wheat (*Triticum aestivum*), 11 grains of emmer (*Triticum dicoccum*) and 15 grains of unidentified wheat (*Triticum sp.*), identified by Peter Steen Henriksen (NNU j.no. A9488). One wheat grain is AMS ^{14}C dated to (Ua-55181) 4951±32 BP, cal. 3770-3670 BC (1σ), 3790-3650 BC (2σ).

c. BMR 3358x72. Finds from hole for probable roof-bearing post A11. Upon excavation, the hole proved to be only 0.1 m deep. *Pottery*: Sherds from the neck and upper part of the belly of type II funnel beaker, with 3 horizontal rows of indentations under the rim (fig. 3.32:2), and 26 undecorated body sherds. *Flint*: 1 flake of polished axe, 1 flake with cortex and use retouch on the edges, 9 flakes, mostly of imported flint, 1 of which is fire affected, and 1 flake of Kristianstad flint. The following were also found: 33 g of hazelnut shells and 1 g of charred cereal grain, including 1 grain of einkorn (*Triticum monococcum*) and 1 grain of unidentified wheat (*Triticum sp.*), identified by Peter Steen Henriksen (NNU j.no. A9488). One wheat grain has been AMS ^{14}C dated to (Ua-55182) 4963±32 BP, cal. 3780-3700 BC (1σ), 3800-3650 BC (2σ).

d. BMR 3358x78. Finds from fill A17, including mixed content near uprooted tree. *Pottery:* Remains of the neck and side of undecorated funnel beaker of type II with gradual transition between neck and belly (fig. 3.32:3). In addition: 1 rim sherd with a thin, horizontal bead under the rim in which there are finger impressions, 1 rim sherd with indentations on the rim, 1 rim sherd with 3 horizontal rows of closely-placed, oblong indentations, 7 undecorated rim sherds, 2 body sherds from the same or 2 different, presumably Middle Neolithic, vessels with whipped cord impressions, as well as 126 undecorated body sherds. *Flint:* 1 small, transverse-retouched blade and 2 flakes.

e. BMR 3358x102. Finds from hole for probable roof-bearing post A42, which when excavated turned out to be only 0.17 m deep. *Pottery*: Neck sherds from funnel beaker decorated with horizontal and vertical two-ply cord impressions and indentations into the rim (fig. 3.32:4), 2 sherds with the same decoration and 34 undecorated body sherds. *Flint*: 1 flake.

f. BMR 3358x124. Finds from posthole A66, which was 0.34 m in diameter and 0.38 m deep. *Ceramic material*: 1 rim sherd of a funnel beaker with a flared, thickened rim, under which are 3 horizontal rows of short, vertical indentations (fig. 3.40:1), as well as 3 neck sherds with horizontal rows of oblong indentations, 21 small body sherds and 3 clay discs. *Flint:* 1 fire-affected fragment of a 5.2 cm-wide and 1.8 cm-thick halberd polished on both sides (fig. 3.40:2). The fragment was found in the middle of the posthole at a depth of 0.1 cm. 1 flake scraper from a flint nodule, 2 flakes of imported flint and 1 flake of Kristianstad flint. The posthole also contained many fragments of burnt daub.

g. BMR 3358x143. Finds from pit A88, which was 55 cm in diameter and 27 cm deep, with vertical sides and a flat bottom. *Pottery*: 1 rim sherd of a funnel beaker with 3 horizontal rows of small, oval indentations under the rim, 1 rim sherd with 2 horizontal rows of small, round indentations and 1 undecorated rim sherd. In addition, a neck sherd with indentations, a handle fragment and 1 sherd of a vessel with a round bottom, as well as 33 undecorated body sherds. A soil sample contained 14 g of burnt cereal grains, 81 % of which were of naked six-row barley (*Hordeum vulgare var. nudum*) and 9 % emmer (*Triticum dicoccum*). There were also a few grains of glumed six-row barley (*Hordeum vulgare var. vulgare*) and ordinary wheat (*Triticum aestivum*), identified by Peter Steen Henriksen (NNU j.no. A9488). One grain of naked barley is AMS ^{14}C dated to (Ua-55183) 4917±32 BP, cal. 3710-3650 BC (1σ), 3770-3640 BC (2σ).

h. BMR 3358x154, 155, 156. Finds from features A99 and A100, which when excavated proved to be the same fill, probably an animal burrow, whose contents are presumably mixed: *Pottery*: Sherds from the neck and upper belly of a type II funnel beaker with 3 horizontal rows of indentations under the rim (fig. 3.39:1), 2 rim sherds with at least 2 horizontal rows of oblong indentations under the rim, 1 rim sherd with at least 3 horizontal two-ply cord impressions, 2 undecorated rim sherds, 1 neck/belly sherd and 45 undecorated body sherds of thin- and thick-walled vessels. – *Flint:* 5 fragments of polished flint axes, including the middle part of a thin-butted axe that is 2.5 cm thick (fig. 3.39:2), 3 transverse arrowheads (fig. 3.39:3-5), 6 flake scrapers (fig. 3.39:6-8), 1 atypical backed flake knife, 47 flakes of mostly imported flint, including 8 fire-cracked pieces, 3 flakes of Kristianstad flint and 5 flakes from flint nodules. Finds no. 156 consists of a number of charred plant remains: 18 g of hazelnut shells and 27 charred cereal grains, including 11 grains of naked six-row barley (*Hordeum vulgare var. nudun*), 3 grains of ordinary wheat (*Triticum aestivum*), 3 grains of emmer (*Triticum dicoccum*) and 1 grain of unidentified wheat (*Triticum sp.*), identified by Peter Steen Henriksen (NNU j.no. A9488). A grain of emmer has been AMS ^{14}C dated to (Ua-55184) 4904±32 BP, cal. 3700-3650 BC (1σ), 3770-3630 BC (2σ).

i. BMR 3358x190. Finds from pit A70, which measured 0.95 × 0.5 m on the surface and was 0.17 m deep. *Pottery*: At the top was an undecorated funnel beaker/lugged beaker placed with its bottom facing upwards. The vessel, which is 18 cm high and has a rim diameter of 22.4 cm, has half of the rim missing, but is otherwise complete (fig. 3.35-36). There are four short, vertical beads formed by finger pinching under the transition between the neck and belly; these resemble lugs, but the vessel is otherwise undecorated. The pit also contained (x128): 4 small sherds, 2 of which are neck sherds of funnel beakers with impressions under the rim. – *Flint:* 1 blade fragment of a polished flint axe and a flake scraper of ball flint.

j. BMR 3358x191. *Pottery*: Small funnel beaker of type II decorated with 2 rows of vertical indentations or stab-and-drag grooving under the rim. Part of the vessel rim is missing, but it is otherwise complete. 10 cm high, with rim diameter of 8.6 cm (fig. 3.37). Found lying on its side in the cultural layer.

During excavation in advance of the levelling of a garden area, a cultural layer, postholes and various fills associated with an Early Neolithic settlement were found. A total area of 500 m² was investigated. Finds groups b-i described above are from 8 of the 19 excavated and recorded features found under the cultural layer, see fig. 3.30. Several of the postholes must have been associated with house structures, and the excavator estimates that at least 6 houses were located within the investigated area, and that a number of these burnt down. The settlement is located high up on a sandy plateau 112 m above sea level. *Dating*: There are a few sherds of type I funnel beakers, but the majority of the measurable pottery fragments are from funnel beakers of type II. There are also a number of sherds of vessels decorated with two-ply cord and rows of long indentations under the rim, which are characteristic of type III funnel beakers. Most of the material should therefore be dated to EN A2, a smaller proportion to respectively EN A1 and EN B.

15. Baggård

060104-276. Klemensker parish. – BMR 3469. – Excavation by F.O. Nielsen and P.O. Nielsen in 2011 associated with raw material extraction.

BMR 3469. *Pottery*: 11 rim sherds of funnel beakers with one or two rows of indentations under the rim, 9 rim and neck sherds with a row of nail or finger impressions under the rim, on one sherd the impressions are in a low, added bead, 3 undecorated rim sherds, one from a short-necked funnel beaker of type I, 1 rim sherd of a flask with a slightly inturned rim, 1 rim sherd of a bowl with a rounded rim and 315 undecorated body sherds, 1 with a preserved food residue. – *Flint*: 1 blade with use-wear (gloss patination), 6.5 cm long, 1 blade, 4.8 cm long, 58 flakes, most of which are fire affected, including 3 blade fragments and 6 flakes with polished facets. 1 hammerstone or crushing stone, 5 × 5 × 3.5 cm, of Kristianstad flint or related material. – *Other stone*: 1 crushing stone of beach-rolled granite with two opposite-facing crushing surfaces, 7.5 × 6 × 4 cm, 1 small fire-affected fragment of a possible quern stone or rubbing stone. – *Other material*: C. 30 small pieces of burnt clay. A small collection of burnt bone. 2 pieces of charcoal.

Found in a fill, which was 1.8 m long, 0.65 m wide and up to 0.5 m deep, that had the character of a tree-throw, on sandy soil and flat terrain c. 17 m above sea level. – *Dating*: EN A1.

16. Møllehøj

060105-53. Olsker parish. – BMR 3310. – Collected by Klaus and Kasper Thorsen in 1988.

Pottery: Body sherds decorated with horizontal lines of two-ply cord, and sherds with both horizontal and vertical lines in the same technique. – *Flint*: 1 fire-affected scraper, 1 transverse arrowhead and a number of flakes.

Found on a sandy hill 119 m above sea level. – *Dating*: EN B. – A pointed-butted axe of fine-grained rock was found in the same field, see Finds list IV no. 44.5.

17. Pilegård

060105-86 and -188 Olsker parish. – BMR 1078 and 1401. – Found during the excavation of a cemetery dating to the Roman and Early Germanic Iron Age (report by Lars Kempfner-Jørgensen 25/3 1984). During surface stripping, an up to 10 cm-thick soil layer was identified, which contained Early Neolithic pottery and flint waste. The cultural layer extended down the hill to the south-west. A number of features could be dated to EN, including a few postholes and a pit:

BMR 1078x11. Finds from posthole/pit, feature 5, 2nd layer from above: A rim sherd decorated with horizontal lines of two-ply cord and a body sherd with remains of indentations.

BMR 1078x12. Find from posthole/pit, feature 5, 3rd layer from above: A neck sherd of a funnel beaker decorated with horizontal lines of two-ply cord, cut by vertical lines of the same technique.

BMR 1078x15. Collected during surface shovelling, almost exclusively from the south-western part of the excavation area: *Pottery*: 1 belly sherd decorated with vertical lines of two-ply cord separated by undecorated zones, 1 rim sherd decorated with horizontal lines of two-ply cord, 1 rim sherd and 6 neck sherds decorated with horizontal lines of two-ply cord, 1 undecorated rim sherd, 1 sherd of a flat base and 62 undecorated body sherds.

The following finds are from surface collection undertaken by Klaus Thorsen and Michael Thorsen in 1983-84 in connection with a survey near the Iron Age cemetery. The finds were later submitted to BMR:

BMR 1401x1. *Pottery*: A neck sherd decorated with two rows of small, round indentations under the rim and 11 neck sherds decorated with horizontal lines of two-ply cord.

BMR 1401x2. *Flint*: The Senonian and Danian flint consists of 26 flakes and fragments of polished axes, 1 borer, 1 scraper, 1 retouched piece, 1 blade, 8 axe body flakes and 168 pieces of flint waste. – Of ball flint: 1 blade-like flake and 37 other flakes. – Kristianstad flint: 22 flakes. – Unidentified flint: 36 fire-affected pieces.

Collected 1985-86: *Ceramic material*: 3 rim sherds of probably the same, medium-sized funnel beaker decorated with horizontal lines of two-ply cord. 1 rim sherd and two body sherds decorated with horizontal lines of two-ply cord divided by undecorated zones. 1 body sherd decorated with concentric curves of whipped cord. 1 fragment of a clay disc with oblong impressions on the edge. – *Flint*, imported: Three transverse arrowheads, an 8.2 cm-long blade and a small core borer.

Collected in 1988: *Pottery*: A rim sherd with a horizontal bead on the rim in which there are square indentations. 3 rim sherds with indentations, one with an expanded rim, under which is a horizontal row of oblong, diagonal indentations. 12 rim sherds and 4 neck sherds decorated with horizontal lines of two-ply cord. 3 rim sherds and 2 neck sherds decorated with vertical lines of two-ply cord. 2 rim sherds and 1 body sherd decorated with horizontal and vertical lines of two-ply cord. One belly sherd decorated with vertical lines of two-ply cord in between which are undecorated zones. 2 body sherds decorated with vertical lines of whipped cord. 1 lugged sherd. – *Flint*, imported: 2 transverse arrowheads.

Found at the top of a sandy, slightly sloping, south-east-facing hill c. 100 m above sea level. – *Dating*: The numerous sherds of vessels decorated with different patterns in two-ply cord place most of the finds group in EN B. The finds under f and g include sherds of vessels decorated with whipped cord, one of which with suspended semicircles, indicating that there is also material from EN C.

18. Klippehøj

060105-191. Olsker parish. – BMR 1405. – Excavation by F.O. Nielsen *et al.* of cemetery dating to the Iron Age. The finds are from the settlement pit excavated in zone G in 2010.

BMR 1405. *Ceramic material*: 1 undecorated sherd of the neck and rim of a small, short-necked type I funnel beaker. 1 sherd of funnel beaker with 2 rows of small indentations under the rim. 1 rim sherd with a row of small, irregular indentations close to the rim, almost in the rim itself. 1 undecorated neck sherd and 1 neck/belly sherd from funnel beakers. 1 lugged sherd. 116 undecorated body sherds, including 2 with burnt food residues. 5 small pieces of burnt clay. – *Flint*, imported: 1 flake. Ball flint: 1 flake. 3 other flint flakes, one which is fire affected. – *Burnt bone*: 3 small pieces.

Found on the west-facing slope of a hilly area, c. 88 m above sea level in a boulder clay area. Dating: EN A1.

19. Karlshøj

060105-199. Olsker parish. – BMR 1704. – Collected up until 1989 by G. Møller Larsen and Dorte Dam in a settlement area containing house sites dating to the Roman Iron Age:

BMR 1704x7. 4 rim sherds from funnel beakers, 1 decorated with a horizontal row of diagonal indentations, 2 with 2 rows of indentations and 1 with 3 rows of small round indentations. The latter is from a type II funnel beaker (rim diameter/neck height: 13/3.3 cm).

BMR 1704x8. Two body sherds decorated with horizontal lines of two-ply cord.

BMR 1704x21. An undecorated rim sherd of a short-necked funnel beaker, 1 rim sherd of funnel beaker with 2 horizontal rows of indentations and 1 small body sherd with parallel lines of two-ply cord.

Found on a sandy ridge 90 m above sea level – *Dating*: EN A2 and EN B.

20. Engvang

060106-144. Rutsker parish. – BMR 2476x1.

Sherds of funnel beakers found at a burial place containing burnt patches dating to the Late Roman Iron Age (C.J. Becker 1947, 166).

Rim sherds of medium-sized, short-necked funnel beaker with very flared neck and two low, horizontal beads under the rim, in which there are vertical nail impressions. 1 rim sherd of a funnel beaker with a neck height of almost 10 cm, the uppermost half of which is decorated with horizontal two-ply cord impressions. Rim sherd of a pottery vessel decorated with horizontal and vertical lines of two-ply cord.

Found on the southern slope of a sandy plateau 105-110 m above sea level. – *Dating:* Finds group a should be dated to EN A1, whilst the two cord-decorated sherds under b should be placed in EN B.

21. Møllebjerg/V. Rosendalegård NØ

060106-161. Rutsker parish. – BMR 1627. – Collected by René Rose in 1990-91 in an area where a settlement dating to the Viking period and Early Middle Ages was excavated in 1995-96 by Henrik Høier, who also wrote the report.

BMR 1627x312-313. *Pottery*: A rim sherd with 1 horizontal row of indentations, 1 rim sherd with indentations at the edge of the rim, 1 rim sherd with zones of horizontal lines in two-ply cord, separated by undecorated zones, and 8 undecorated rim sherds.

BMR 1627x314-316. *Pottery*: One neck sherd with fine, horizontal lines of two-ply cord, 2 neck sherds with horizontal rows of indentations, 1 belly sherd with vertical lines of whipped cord, 7 belly sherds with vertical belly stripes, 1 base sherd and 78 undecorated sherds.

BMR 1627x317-323. *Flint*, imported: 33 flint flakes of polished axes, 14 blades and blade fragments, 6 scrapers and c. 275 flakes. Kristianstad flint: 72 flakes, including 4 burnt. Ball flint: 24 flakes, including 4 burnt, and 9 additional burnt flint flakes.

The site is located on a sandy hilly area c. 99 m above sea level. – *Dating:* EN C.

22. Vester Rosendalegård

060106-173. Rutsker parish. – BMR 2071. – Excavation of settlement pit 2-6/4 1992 and report 10/4 1992 by F.O. Nielsen.

BMR 2071x4-6. The upper layers of the pit. *Ceramic material*: 417 fragments of pottery and clay discs, including neck and belly sherds decorated with indentations, whipped cord and vertical belly stripes, a few with zoned decoration. There are also fragments of a clay disc that is decorated on both sides. – *Flint*: 50 pieces of imported flint and 16 fragments of Kristianstad flint, including a scraper. – *Other stone*: 5 crushing stones/hammerstones, 3 grindstone fragments, 1 quern stone fragment and 1 fragment of a four-sided axe.

BMR 2071x7-9. The middle layers of the pit, 'the waste layer'. *Ceramic material*: 788 fragments of pottery and clay discs, including sherds of funnel or lugged beakers, decorated with indentations and different patterns in whipped cord, as well as vertical belly stripes, both consisting of vertical grooves and vertical lines of whipped cord, which can be divided by narrow, vertical stripes with crosslines. A few sherds of vessels with zoned decoration. – *Flint*: 225 pieces of imported flint, including 9 polished axe fragments, 7 scrapers and 3 blades/blade knives. The Kristianstad flint consists of 17 cores and flakes, and of ball flint there were 6 flakes. – *Other stone*: 8 crushing stones/hammerstones, 3 grindstone fragments, 1 quern stone fragment, 1 fragment of a four-sided axe and 1 neck fragment of a battle axe of Fredsgårde type. 16 small fragments of amber were also found.

BMR 2071x10-13. The lowest layers of the pit. *Ceramic material*: 158 sherds/fragments of pottery vessels and clay discs, most of which are undecorated, a few decorated sherds with indentations, whipped cord, or vertical belly stripes. One clay disc fragment has finger impressions on its upper surface and another fragment is decorated on both sides. – *Flint*: 6 pieces of imported flint, 3 pieces of Kristianstad flint and 1 fragment of a ball flint nodule. – *Other stone*: 10 crushing stones/hammerstones, 2 grindstone fragments and 3 quern stone fragments.

The pit, which was interpreted as a clay extraction pit, measured 5 × 6 m on the surface and was 1 m deep. The site is located high up in a hilly area c. 99 m above sea level, at the transition between sand and clay. – *Dating*: Three sherds of funnel beakers decorated with two-ply cord, from the middlemost and bottom layers, may date to EN B, whilst most of the finds are from EN C/MN AIa.

23. Skovgård

060106-184. Rutsker parish. – BMR 2457. – Collected by Mogens Jensen and excavated by Finn Ole Nielsen in 2014.

a. BMR 2457x7. Finds from cultural layer (A1): *Pottery*: 1 neck-belly sherd of funnel beaker with gradual transition between neck and belly, 1 rim sherd of a funnel beaker of type III with 2 horizontal rows of oblong indentations under the rim, 2 neck sherds of funnel beakers decorated with horizontal lines of two-ply cord, 1 lug fragment of a lugged jar and 65 undecorated sherds. – *Flint*: 1 scraper and 9 flakes. – *Quartz*: 2 pieces.

b. BMR 2457x8-14. Finds from cooking pit and collected in the area south and west of gravel pit: *Pottery*: 1 decorated rim sherd, 17 body and base sherds, including 7 decorated, and 1 lugged sherd. – *Burnt daub*: 2 pieces. – *Flint*: 1 flake of polished axe, 1 blade knife, 1 core, 26 flakes and 4 pieces of burnt flint. 1 piece of Kristianstad flint. – *Quartz*: 5 pieces.

c. BMR 2457x15-55. Finds from excavation of cultural layers, postholes and tree-throws: *Ceramic material*: 43 decorated rim sherds, 5 of which have added beads under the rim in which there are finger impressions (fig. 3.10:5), whilst the rest are decorated with 1 or 2 rows of indentations, although 1 rim sherd has 5 horizontal rows of indentations (fig. 3.10:2-4). 49 undecorated rim sherds and 21 neck-belly sherds with both gradual and sharp transition between the neck and belly (fig. 3.10:1). 3 decorated sherds, and 1377 undecorated body and base sherds. 11 lugged sherds, most of which are from lugged jars. 4 clay disc fragments with finger impressions along the edge (fig. 3.10:6). – *Burnt daub*: c. 2.5 kg. – *Flint*: Imported: 1 fragment of a pointed-butted flint axe of type 2 with very domed broad surfaces (fig. 3.10:7) and 17 polished flakes, 4 scrapers, 2 blades, 1 blade knife and 60 flakes. – Flint nodules: 2 scrapers, 1 oblong arrowhead and 15 flakes. – Kristianstad flint: 12 pieces. – Unidentified and burnt flint: 29 pieces. – *Granite*: 2 quern stone fragments and 2 crushing stones. – *Quartz*: 2 fragments. – *Burnt bone*: c. 65 g. – *Charred cereal grains*: 51 fragments, 12 of which were identified by Peter Steen Henriksen as club wheat (note dated 5 March 2015). Two of these grains have been AMS ^{14}C dated: 1) (Ua-55726) 5084±32 BP, cal. 3960-3800 BC (1σ), 3970-3790 BC (2σ). – 2) (Ua-55727) 5016±30 BP, cal. 3940-3710 BC (1σ), 3950-3700 BC (2σ).

Found and excavated at the edge of a sand and gravel quarry on a hill 101 m above sea level. The excavated finds (c) include sherds from funnel beakers with early types of rim decoration: applied beads under the rim with finger impressions and 1-2 rows of indentations, including rows of very small indentations. Together with the fragment of the pointed-butted flint axe, this indicates an early date. The finds from the cultural layer (a), however, show that later pottery is also represented, some of which is decorated with two-ply cord. – *Dating*: EN A1 and EN B.

24. Borgen

060107-98. Rø parish. – BMR 1393. – NM I 5954/84. – Collected by G. Møller Larsen on several occasions from 1959 onwards. The finds were later donated to Bornholms Museum, where in 1988 they were registered in a number of groups:

BMR 1393x1-11, marked 'Borgen 1959'. *Pottery*: Remains of neck and shoulder of an undecorated, short-necked funnel beaker (fig. 8.2:2), 1 rim sherd

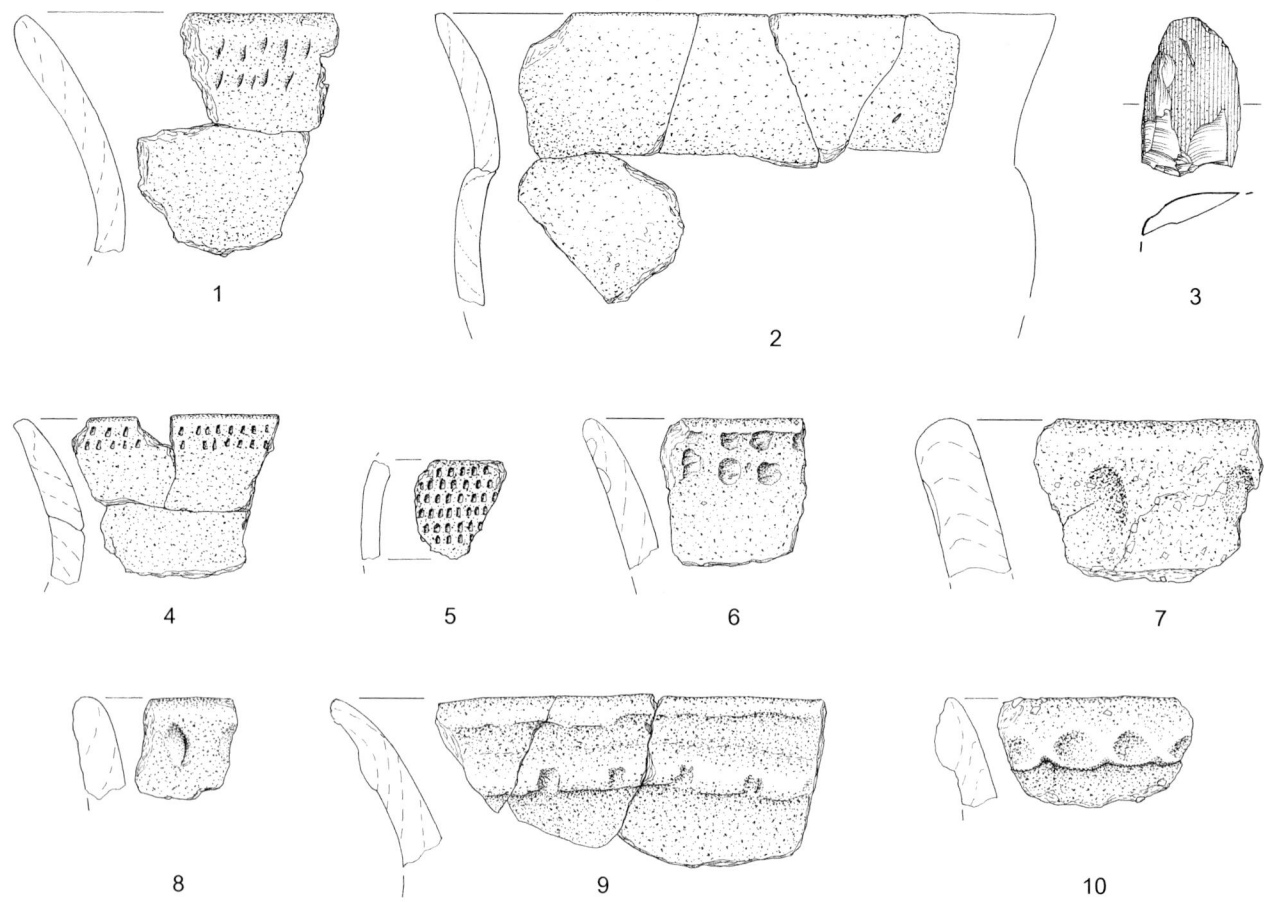

Fig. 8.2. Pottery sherds and fragment of polished flint axe (3) from Borgen (Finds list I no. 24). Eva Koch del. 1:2.

with horizontal bead under the rim in which there are indentations (fig. 8.2:9), 1 rim sherd with two rows of vertical nail impressions (fig. 8.2:1), 1 rim sherd of a thick-walled vessel with a horizontal row of finger impressions (fig. 8.2:7), 1 rim sherd with two horizontal rows of small, square indentations, 1 rim sherd with indentations made with a ribbed implement at the front edge of the rim, under which is a horizontal row of similar impressions, 5 undecorated rim sherds, 26 undecorated neck-belly sherds and 210 undecorated body sherds. There are also two rim sherds in a more compact fabric with impressions under the rim, which most likely date to MN, the rim of a sieve, probably dating to the Late Bronze Age, and a base sherd, which is also not of a Neolithic date. – *Senonian and Danian flint*: 27 flakes and fragments of polished axes, including a piece of the edge of a pointed-butted axe (fig. 8.2:3) and a fragment of a four-sided axe with a flat broad surface; 4 scrapers, one from a flake of a polished axe, 2 are blade scrapers, and the other has a double cutting edge; 1 backed flake knive, 1 core and 51 flakes, 15 of which are fire affected. – *Ball flint*: 2 scrapers, 1 blade and 53 flakes, 30 of which are fire affected.

BMR 1393x12-18, marked 'Borgen H'. *Ceramic material*: 1 rim sherd with 1-2 horizontal rows of very small indentations, 5 undecorated rim sherds, one body sherd with the lug of a lugged jar and two fragments of other lugs, 10 neck-belly sherds, the base of a vessel with a concave base and c. 200 undecorated body sherds. There is also a clay disc fragment with small impressions on the edge.

BMR 1393x19-26, marked 'Borgen H. 1981'. *Pottery*: A rim sherd of a large vessel with a horizontal bead under the rim in which there are finger impressions (fig. 8.2:10), and a belly sherd with horizontal rows of small, fine impressions (fig. 8.2:5). There are also sherds of vessels from periods other than EN: A few rim and body sherds of very coarse, thick-walled vessels, sherds of the shoulder of a vessel decorated with comb impressions from MN AIII and 20 very coarse body sherds. – *Flint*: A fragment of a polished flint axe with a flat broad surface.

BMR 1393x27-36, marked 'Borgen V. 1981'. *Pottery*: 1 sherd of a funnel beaker with a gradual transition between the neck and belly, sherds of the neck of a lugged flask or jar, two rim sherds with a horizontal bead with finger impressions, 8 rim sherds with different types of indentations, 22 undecorated rim sherds of funnel beakers, 35 neck/belly sherds and base sherds, and more than 200 undecorated body sherds. – From later periods than EN: Two rim sherds in a more compact fabric, probably dating to MN, and sherds of a sieve, probably of a Late Bronze Age date. – *Stone*: A grindstone of sandstone.

The finds are from cultural layers, which are not described in detail, located at the edge of a gravel quarry at Borgen, in undulating terrain, 95 m above sea level, within Rø Plantage. – *Dating*: The Early Neolithic pottery vessels which dominate the finds group, include remains of funnel beakers with rim and shoulder profiles corresponding with type I (fig. 8.2:2), that together with the added beads with finger impressions, indicate a date within EN A1. But there are also rim sherds from funnel beakers with a higher, flared neck corresponding with type II (fig. 8.2:4), which together with horizontal rows of nail and finger impressions without beads under the rim, suggest a EN A2 date. The dating of the Early Neolithic finds from this site solely to EN A is supported by the fact that amongst the quite large quantities of ceramic material there is not a single sherd from a cord-decorated vessel. A small proportion of both the pottery and flint material also dates to MN AIII, and a few sherds to the Late Bronze Age.

25. Salene
060107-126. Rø parish. – BMR 1840. – Collected by Michael S. Thorsen in 1983.

BMR 1840x2. A neck sherd of funnel beaker decorated with parallel, horizontal lines of two-ply cord.

Found on the coastal cliff at Salene, 15-20 m above sea level, just NW of the mouth of Bobbe Å, in a mixed freshwater deposit near the coast. – *Dating*: EN B. Sherds of Ertebølle pottery were found in a cooking pit.

26. Båstedbakken
060107-128. Rø parish. – BMR 1512. – Collected by Michael S. Thorsen up until 1985 and taken to the museum in 1996.

Two neck sherds of funnel beakers decorated with horizontal lines of two-ply cord. – Flakes of four-sided polished flint axes.

Part of a large collection of finds from different periods found in a sandy hilly area, 97 m above sea level and close to the site of Grønvang (no. 29). – *Dating*: EN B.

27. Åløkken
060107-138. Rø parish. – BMR 2166. – Finds from a pit excavated in 1989 by F.O. Nielsen.

BMR 2166x1. Finds from the pit: 4 rim sherds of short-necked type I funnel beakers (one sherd with a rim diameter/neck height: 21/3 cm, neck index: 14.3, fig. 3.3:1), 3 of which are undecorated and 1 has two horizontal rows of quite small indentations near the rim (fig. 3.3:2); 166 undecorated body sherds; 1 fragment of a clay disc with finger impressions on the edge (fig. 3.3:3); and 1 broken, tongue-shaped object of fired clay, which may be the shaft of a clay spoon (fig. 3.3:4). – *Flint*: 1 flake of a polished axe and 5 flakes. – The pit also contained burnt bone and charcoal. 5 pieces of charcoal from the pit have been identified by Claus Malmros, NM, as alder (*Alnus sp.*), ash (*Fraxinus excelsior*), oak (*Quercus sp.*) and lime (*Tilia sp.*) (NNU A 8501). A piece of an ash branch has been AMS ^{14}C dated (AAR-9466): 5011±46 BP, cal. 3930-3710 BC (1σ), 3950-3700 BC (2σ).

BMR 2166x2. Unstratified finds. *Pottery*: An undecorated rim sherd of a short-necked funnel beaker and 66 undecorated body sherds. – *Flint*: A wide blade scraper of Senonian flint and several other pieces.

The site is located on the south-eastern slope of a sandy hill, 98 m above sea level. – *Dating*: The funnel beaker sherds from the pit (a) come from type I vessels and should be dated to EN A1.

28. Tyskegård
060107-63. Rø parish. – BMR 1506, 2281. – Finds collected by private collector Gert Møller Larsen and transferred to the museum in 1995.

A rim sherd of a medium-sized funnel beaker decorated with horizontal lines of two-ply cord, separated by undecorated zones. A few other small sherds are decorated with indentations and two-ply cord. – The collected material also consists of 113 undecorated sherds of varying character and date, 3 fragments of burnt clay, 2 blades, 1 scraper, 1 flake from a polished flint axe, 12 pieces of imported flint, 14 pieces of ball flint, 3 pieces of Kristianstad flint and 1 piece of matt flint.

Found in a hilly area, 100 m above sea level and c. 300 m north-west of Tyskegård, where sandy soils alternate with clay soils. – *Dating*: EN B.

29. Grønvang
060107-105. Rø parish. – BMR 1714. – Finds from a field survey by private collector Klaus Thorsen, who later handed in the finds to the museum.

BMR 1714x1. 1 rim sherd decorated under the rim with a row of vertical, oblong indentations.

BMR 1714x2. A body sherd decorated with horizontal lines of fine, two-ply cord.

Found 95 m above sea level on a sandy hill, which slopes down towards the north-west, close to the site of Båstedbakken (no. 26). 1.3 kg of undecorated pottery sherds were also found, dating to the Neolithic and Viking period, as well as a few pieces of flint, both imported flint and ball flint, as well as a few fragments of burnt daub. – *Dating*: The cord-decorated sherd dates to EN B.

30. Bakkegård
060203-195. Pedersker parish. – BMR 1926. – Finds from inspection of drainage ditches in the spring of 1986 by Dorte Dam and others, submitted to the museum in 1998.

A small rim sherd decorated with horizontal lines of two-ply cord.

Found along with other pottery and flint at a site where finds from several different periods were recovered. It is located on a west-facing elevated area of sandy soils, c. 30 m above sea level. – *Dating*: EN B.

31. Frydenlund/Dyrkobbel

060203-163. Pedersker parish. – BMR 2165. – Collected by F.O. Nielsen in 1987.

A rim sherd with an applied bead under the rim, in which there are finger impressions. – 1 transverse arrowhead. – Flint waste.

Collected on a small ridge just NE of Dyrkobbel, c. 39 m above sea level. – *Dating*: EN A1.

32. Solhøj

060205-40 and -221. Åker parish. – BMR 1549.

1. Surface collection from the area of the Solhøj property. Finds in private collector Solveig Andersen's collection.

a. Solhøj NØ, sb. 40. 1 rim sherd decorated with 2 horizontal rows of D-shaped indentations. 1 rim sherd decorated with horizontal lines of two-ply cord.

b. Solhøj N, sb. 221. A rim sherd decorated with 2 horizontal rows of D-shaped indentations. 1 rim sherd and 1 neck sherd decorated with horizontal lines of two-ply cord. 2 clay disc fragments with impressions on the edge.

2. Finds from the National Museum's trial excavation in 1987 at sb. 221. – NM A53228/SOx9.

1 rim sherd decorated with horizontal lines of two-ply cord.

Nos 1 and 2 were found close to one another on the upper part of the sandy plateau 'På Løkker', 36 m above sea level. – *Dating*: A number of periods within EN may be represented by the material that was collected, but the cord-decorated sherds from funnel beakers should be dated to EN B.

33. Vallensgård I-III

Vallensgård I. 060205-197. Åker parish. – NM A53160. – See detailed discussion in this volume.
Vallensgård II. 060205-438. Åker parish. – BMR 1619. – Surface collection in 1981.

1 rim sherd decorated with two horizontal rows of semicircular indentations. 1 rim sherd decorated with whipped cord impressions. 1 body sherd from vessel dated to MN AI-III. 1 fragment of a thin-butted flint axe and 1 butt fragment of an Early Neolithic battle axe (fig. 6.2:1).

Vallensgård III. 060205-235. Åker parish. – BMR 1700. – Surface collection in 1986.

1 rim sherd decorated with 2 horizontal rows of oval indentations, as shown in fig. 2.8.4a, and 1 rim sherd decorated with three horizontal rows of small, rectangular indentations, as shown in fig. 2.8.5b, both probably from type II funnel beakers. A blade fragment of a thin-butted flint axe.

Vallensgård I-III are situated on sandy soil 80-84 m above sea level, see fig. 2.15. – *Dating*: More than one period of the EN is represented, including EN A2, B and C, as well as the first part of MN A.

34. Limensgård/Rævekulebakke

060205-198. Åker parish. – NM 5166/83, inv. no. A53446. – BMR 1002, 1081. – Excavation in 1984-89 by the authors for the National Museum in collaboration with Bornholms Museum. House sites dating to the Early, Middle and Late Neolithic were excavated, as well as settlement remains and burials from later periods (F.O. Nielsen & P.O. Nielsen 1985, 1986 a and b; P.O. Nielsen 1999; Nielsen & Nielsen 2014c; 2019).

a. Finds from Rævekulebakke pit AD, excavated in 1987: Early Neolithic material was found secondarily deposited in the uppermost layer of a shallow pit, which was c. 75 cm in diameter and 15 cm deep. *Pottery*: Undecorated sherds of the neck of a short-necked lugged flask; 2 rim sherds of funnel beakers, one decorated with a horizontal row of narrow, oblong, vertical indentations, the other with 2 rows of similar indentations; 2 rim sherds and 1 body sherd decorated with horizontal lines of two-ply cord. – *Flint*: 1 transverse arrowhead, and 1 scraper from a flake of a polished axe. – Report by Lars Jørgensen 3/12 1987, p. 16.

b. Finds from cultural layer FK, excavated in 1987 and 1989. *Pottery*: 81 rim and neck sherds of funnel beakers, 11 of which are decorated with 1 or more horizontal lines of indentations under the rim, and 40 are decorated with horizontal lines of two-ply cord, three sherds also with vertical lines. To this can be added 844 body and base sherds, and 2 small clay disc fragments. – *Flint*: 221 pieces, consisting of 162 fragments of imported Senonian flint, 52 pieces of ball flint and 7 fragments of Kristianstad flint. The imported flint consists of 22 pieces with traces of polishing, including fragments of four-sided axes, which are either pointed butted or early thin butted, as well as 3 blades, 1 of which is retouched, 2 scrapers and 3 possible borers made from flakes.

c. Finds from house site FJ, excavated in 1989. The house site, which was covered by cultural layer FK, consisted of a row of five roof-bearing posts (fig. 3.7). From posthole FJ1: 1 rim sherd of a thick-walled vessel with impressions under the rim and 6 undecorated sherds. – From posthole FJ3: Sherds from the lower body of a lugged vessel with a broken-off lug. – From posthole FJ4-5: 6 undecorated sherds and one flint flake. – Charred cereal grains were collected from posthole FJ3-5, and identified by David Robinson, NM, as naked barley (*Hordeum vulgare* var. *nudum*), wheat (*Triticum* sp.) and bread wheat (*Triticum aestivum*). One of the cereal grains from posthole FJ3 is AMS ^{14}C dated (OxA-2895): 5000 ± 70 BP, calibrated 3940-3700 BC (1σ), 3950-3650 BC (2σ).

Finds from various cultural layers and postholes: At least 25 sherds of funnel beakers decorated with horizontal lines of two-ply cord; 1 neck sherd of funnel beaker decorated with horizontal and vertical lines of two-ply cord; 1 sherd of a funnel beaker with indentations under the rim; 1 sherd of a collared flask; 9 clay disc fragments with finger impressions on the edge.

The Early Neolithic finds were recovered from most of the excavated area, but were mainly concentrated in the northern part, near the plough-damaged burial mound, Rævekulebakke, and in cultural layer FK, in the far north-east, near house sites FJ and FH. The settlement is located 39 m above sea level on a hill, where the soil consists of fine, clayey sand. – *Dating*: Cultural layer FK contained a few sherds of short-necked type I funnel beakers and a number of sherds of funnel beakers decorated with two-ply cord, which based upon the rim and neck profiles here and elsewhere at the settlement must be of type III. The settlement began during EN A1, in which house site FJ should be placed. The finds from pit AD and most of the other finds date to EN B.

35. Vasagård East

060205-203. Åker parish. – NM A53159. – BMR 816. – Excavations in 1988, 1993 and 2012-18 of a causewayed enclosure from EN C – MN AIII and a palisade enclosure from MN AV by F.O. Nielsen, P.O. Nielsen and Michael S. Thorsen (P.O. Nielsen 1999, 153; Kaul *et al.* 2002; P.O. Nielsen *et al.* 2014a; P.O. Nielsen *et al.* 2015).

VAS 128. An undecorated neck/belly sherd of a type IV funnel beaker (fig. 3.24).
Found in the lowest layer of ditch AJ in the outer row of ditches of a causewayed enclosure.

VAS 2978. Remains of the neck and upper part of the belly of an Early Neolithic funnel beaker of type III, decorated under the rim with 6-7 horizontal two-ply cord impressions. Found in trial trench XVI, north of the causewayed enclosure, in 2015.

The site is located on a hill 44-45 m above sea level, where the soil consists of boulder clay mixed with gravel. – *Dating*: EN B and C.

36. Ndr. Grødbygård

060205-205. Åker parish. – BMR 948 and 1399. – Report of 16/12 1987 by Lars Jørgensen on the excavation of an Iron Age cemetery and Neolithic settlement in 1984-85 (Kempfner-Jørgensen & Watt 1985). – Combined research and rescue excavation in 1984-93, in an area of settlement and burial places dating to the Neolithic, Bronze Age and Iron Age (Nielsen & Nielsen 1991; 2014b; 2019). In 1988, c. 225 m² of a cultural layer containing Early Neolithic finds was excavated (BMR 948x1250-1856).

Only the pottery finds have so far been examined. 1200 decorated sherds from Early Neolithic vessels can be divided up as follows: 10 rim sherds have a horizontal row of finger impressions under the rim, and 1 of these also has an applied bead. 258 rim sherds have one or more horizontal rows of indentations under the rim, of which 169 sherds have short and 89 oblong indentations. 769 rim sherds of funnel beakers have two-ply cord impressions in horizontal lines, but also in vertical lines, as well as alternating horizontal and vertical lines. 68 sherds are decorated with whipped cord and 82 are from vessels with vertical belly stripes. 12 sherds are from collared flasks. The cultural layer also contained the following:

a. BMR 948x281. One side of a funnel beaker decorated with 4 horizontal lines of two-ply cord under the rim, with a rounded shoulder and flat base without a pronounced base (fig. 3.28). Rim diameter/neck height: c. 22/7 cm (neck height 31.8 % of rim diameter).

b. BMR 948x1289. A complete, 9.5 cm-high funnel beaker decorated with a horizontal row of diagonal indentations under the rim and with vertical channelling on the belly (fig. 3.29:1).

c. BMR 948x1261. A 13.5 cm-long butt fragment of a polished, thin-butted flint axe of type IIIA (fig. 3.29:2).

d. BMR 948x1295. A 9.3 cm-long neck fragment of a thin-butted axe of fine-grained rock, pecked and polished, but with one irregular broad surface (fig. 3.29:3).

The settlement is located on a sandy plateau south of the watercourse Grødby Å, 36 m above sea level. – *Dating*: A small number of vessels with finger impressions under the rim should be dated to EN A1, and most of the sherds with horizontal rows of short impressions to EN A1-A2. The most commonly-occurring decoration, however, is two-ply cord impressions, which must indicate that most of the settlement material dates to EN B. Vessels decorated with whipped cord and vertical belly stripes are datable to EN C. One funnel beaker (a) has a vessel form that places it in type II, although its decoration is typical of type III vessels. It must therefore be regarded as an intermediate form and dated to EN A2/EN B. The complete funnel beaker (b) is of type IV and should be dated to EN C.

37. Kællingeby Vest

060205-444. Åker parish. – BMR 3623. – Collected and excavated by private collector Finn Bakke Hansen in 2010 in a field that was ploughed after being set aside for a long period.

BMR 3623. *Pottery*: 30 rim sherds from funnel beakers with indentations under the rim. 1 rim sherd with indentations in the rim. 5 undecorated rim sherds, 1 from a funnel beaker of type I. 9 rim sherds of funnel beakers with up to 10 horizontal lines of two-ply cord under the rim. – *Flint*, imported: 39 fragments and flakes of polished axes, a number of which are four-sided in cross section. 1 fragment of a four-sided, polished flint chisel. 2 blades and 1 blade fragment. 4 flake scrapers, 2 of which are made from fragments of polished flint axes. 7 transverse arrowheads, 2 of which are made from fragments of polished axes. To these can be added several hundred flakes of imported flint (238 g), ball flint (813 g) and Kristianstad flint (169 g).

Most of the finds were recovered from a c. 40 cm-thick cultural layer on clayey sand soils, in an area of flat terrain c. 44 m above sea level. – *Dating*: A number of Neolithic periods may be represented by the numerous finds from the field surface and the cultural layer. Rim sherds from type 1 funnel beakers and rim sherds with horizontal impressions of two-ply cord indicate that much of the material should be dated to respectively EN A1 and EN B.

38. Sandemandsgård

060301-47. Knudsker parish. – BMR 2116. – Finds retrieved during rescue excavation associated with construction work, undertaken 12-19/10 1992 by Martin Appelt, who also wrote the report of 6/11 1992.

a. BMR 2116x4-15, x17-32. *Pottery*: 48 undecorated rim sherds, 2 sherds of which are from the neck of a lugged jar; 1 rim sherd with applied bead with finger impressions and 1 rim sherd with a row of nail impressions; 7 rim sherds of funnel beakers decorated with a horizontal row of round or angular indentations; 10 rim sherds with 2 rows, 1 rim sherd with 3 rows and 1 rim sherd with 4 rows of indentations; 17 sherds with lugs; 1 neck/belly sherd with a knob at the top of the belly; 1 fragment of a clay disc with finger impressions in the edge; and 912 other undecorated sherds. – *Flint*: 15 flakes and fragments of polished flint axes, of which 2 fragments include preserved parts of domed broad surfaces and equally domed narrow surfaces, probably of pointed-butted axes of type 2; 5 blades and 92 other pieces of imported flint; 19 fragments of ball flint; 2 cores and 28 pieces of Kristianstad flint. – *Quartzite*: 1 core of coarse-grained, red-brown quartzite, which measures 14 × 13.5 × 11.2 cm (fig. 3.9), and 38 flakes. – *Other stone*: 2 hammerstones. – Fragments of daub.

b. BMR 2116x16. *Pottery*: 29 undecorated rim sherds; 2 rim sherds with 1 row of finger/nail impressions; 2 rim sherds of funnel beakers with 1 horizontal row of indentations and 2 rim sherds with 2 rows of indentations; and 5 sherds with lugs. – *Flint and other stone*: 2 fragments of polished flint axes and 48 other pieces of imported flint; 6 fragments of ball flint; 1 core and 16 flakes of Kristianstad flint; and 2 flakes of quartzite. – Fragments of daub.

c. BMR 2116x33. *Pottery*: 38 undecorated rim sherds, including rim sherds of a large funnel beaker (fig. 3.8:5) (rim diameter/neck height: c. 34/6 cm) and a small funnel beaker (fig. 3.8:1) (rim diameter/neck height: c. 13.8/3.7 cm); 2 rim sherds of funnel beakers decorated with 1 horizontal row of indentations, 4 rim sherds with 2 rows, 3 rim sherds with 3 rows and 1 rim sherd with 4 rows of indentations (fig. 3.8:2-4); 1 fragment of the neck of a lugged jar (fig. 3.8:6) and sherds with lugs. – *Flint*: 1 flake of a polished flint axe, 1 blade and 34 other pieces of imported flint, 1 piece of ball flint, 7 fragments of Kristianstad flint, 6 pieces of burnt flint. – *Other stone*: 1 fragment of a grindstone. – Fragments of daub.

The above finds numbers represent most of a large quantity of finds, which are from pits, postholes, a burnt layer and from surface cleaning in the southern part of the excavation area (x4-15, x17-32). Features and finds in this area may be from one or more house sites, without it being possible to establish the shape and extent of these. Other finds are from a pit (x16) and a cultural layer (x33), which was partially excavated. There were also later elements at the site, consisting of settlement remains dating to the Late Bronze Age and Early Iron Age, as well as fills containing mixed material. One pit, for example, contained sherds of short-necked funnel beakers, a fragment of a collared flask and a sherd from a Bronze Age vessel (x6). – *Dating*: Parts of a funnel beaker with a gradual transition between the neck and belly should possibly be attributed to EN A0 (fig. 3.8:1). In addition, only a few vessel parts can be measured, whilst several neck profiles correspond with type I funnel beakers, which together with the degree and method of decoration place most of the finds in EN A1.

39. Stubbeløkken

060301-130. Knudsker parish. – BMR 3707. – Excavation by Anders Pihl in January 2015.

BMR 3707x33. Finds from pit A98: *Pottery*: Rim sherds of a funnel beaker with 2 horizontal rows of angular indentations under the rim and a gradual transition between the neck and belly. 3 rim sherds of different funnel beakers with 2 horizontal rows of indentations under the rim. 1 rim sherd of a funnel beaker with 4 horizontal rows of small, round indentations under the rim and notches in the rim itself (fig. 3.14:1-4). 3 undecorated rim sherds and 11 neck/belly sherds. The side of a lugged beaker with lugs close to the transition between the neck and belly (fig. 3.14:5). 232 undecorated body and base sherds. Several of the pottery vessels are coarsely tempered with crushed feldspar. – *Burnt clay*: 2 small pieces. – *Flint*: 2 flakes of imported flint, one of which is polished. 1 large, fire-affected piece of a core or an axe, and 1 fire-affected piece of unidentified flint. 1 unworked piece of ball flint. – *Quartzite*: 1 flake. – *Bone*: 1 tooth fragment.

Pit A98 was excavated on gravelly soil c. 50 m above sea level in connection with a quarry extension. The pit was 87 cm in diameter and 35 cm deep, with a flat, stone-lined bottom. The fill was dark at the top and lighter at the bottom; charcoal samples were taken from both layers for dating, see below. Within an area of c. 2300 m² around the pit, tree-throws and depressions were identified containing undecorated sherds of Early Neolithic character and a small amount of flint, including a flake from the body of an axe, in the form of an 8 cm-long blade. – *Dating*: The funnel beaker neck fragments are not large enough to enable the neck index to be measured. Based upon the decoration, which consists of indentations but does not include two-ply cord impressions, a date within EN A1-2 is indicated. There are three AMS ¹⁴C dates of material from the pit (charcoal identified by Claudia Baittinger, NM):

1) From the bottom layer (3707x74-1), nutshell (*Corylus avellana*) (AAR-25002): 4941±28 BP, cal. 3761-3662 BC (1σ), 3775-3655 BC (2σ).

2) From the upper layer (3707x33-5), charcoal (*Quercus* sp.) (AAR-25003): 4734±29 BP, cal. 3631-3384 BC (1σ), 3635-3378 BC (2σ).

3) From the upper layer (3707x33-5), charcoal (*Quercus* sp.) (AAR-25004): 4779±31 BP, cal. 3637-3528 BC (1σ), 3643-3390 BC (2σ).

The dating of the bottom layer of the pit is placed in EN A2, whilst the two dates for the upper layer lie within EN B – EN C, although these periods are otherwise not represented by the pottery. This may indicate that there was some contamination of the upper layers of the pit with charcoal from later activity at the site.

40. Højegård

060302-114. Nyker parish. – BMR 1681. – Excavated by Michael S. Thorsen in April 2010.

BMR 1681x10. Finds from the ploughsoil near pit A16. *Pottery:* 9 rim sherds of large funnel beakers with an applied bead with finger impressions under the rim; 3 rim sherds of a medium-sized funnel beaker with finger impressions in the rim, under which is an applied, horizontal bead with finger impressions; 4 rim sherds of large funnel beaker with a horizontal bead under the rim in which there are oblong/triangular indentations; 4 rim sherds of medium-sized funnel beakers with a row of oblong/irregular indentations under the rim, one with closely-placed notches in the rim itself; 4 rim sherds of a small funnel beaker with two horizontal rows of indentations under the rim; 1 rim sherd of a small funnel beaker with a horizontal row of small, triangular indentations under the rim; 6 undecorated rim sherds, one from a lugged jar; 3 sherds from the upper part of the belly of a funnel beaker with a horizontal row of large, deep, double, triangular indentations at the transition between neck and belly; 3 neck/belly sherds, two of which constitute most of the side of a small funnel beaker; 1 lug of a lugged flask; and 230 body sherds, two of which have indentations and the rest are undecorated, including sherds up to 1.3 cm thick. In addition, 1 fragment of a clay disc. – *Flint*: 3 flakes of polished flint axes, one with use retouch on a straight edge, 1 scraper of Senonian flint with remains of cortex on its upper surface, 3 fragments of fire-affected flint, 1 core and 1 flake of Kristianstad flint. – *Quartzite*: 1 beach-rolled fragment used as a hammerstone.

BMR 1681x11. Finds from pit A16. *Pottery*: 2 rim sherds of a large funnel beaker with a horizontal bead with finger impressions under the rim; 2 rim sherds of small funnel beakers, one with notches in the edge, the other with a horizontal row of closely-placed, round indentations under the rim; 5 rim sherds of funnel beakers with 2 rows of round/D-shaped indentations, one with notches in the rim itself; 2 undecorated rim sherds; 1 neck/belly sherd of a large funnel beaker with a horizontal row of double, vertical indentations at the transition between the neck and belly; and 130 undecorated body sherds. – *Flint*: 1 fire-affected fragment of a large scraper of imported flint and 1 flake of Senonian flint with cortex. – *Other stone*: 1 fragment of a polished, two-sided axe of fine-grained diabase (fig. 3.6). – *Burnt bone*: 2 small pieces.

The above finds were recovered during the excavation of a small pit and the ploughsoil around it. The site is located on sandy soil 16 m above sea level. – *Dating*: All vessel profiles and types of rim decoration can be attributed to type 1 funnel beakers, which dates the material to EN A1.

41. Lillegård

060302-127. Nyker parish. – BMR 2164. – Excavation by F.O. Nielsen in January 1990. The following objects were found during excavation of a pit, which measured 2.55 × 0.9 m, and was c. 0.2 m deep:

a. BMR 2164x1. *Pottery*: Sherds of the neck and upper part of the belly of an undecorated lugged beaker (rim diameter 14 cm, neck height 3.7 cm); 10 undecorated rim sherds; 8 rim sherds of funnel beakers with 1 or 2 horizontal rows of finger impressions; 29 rim and body sherds decorated with 2-4 rows of square indentations, also 1 rim sherd with curved, 1 with D-shaped and 3 with small round indentations; 1 rim sherd with fine, horizontal lines of two-ply cord; 1 small belly sherd with vertical stripes, in between which are zip patterns; 5 neck/belly sherds with knobs just under the transition between the neck and belly; and c. 526 other sherds. – *Flint*: 1 flake of a polished axe, 7 pieces of imported flint, 1 piece of ball flint, 4 pieces of matt flint, 1 piece of Kristianstad flint and 1 fragment of fire-affected flint. – Under the same number: Charcoal from the bottom layer of the pit. This included three pieces identified by Claus Malmros, NM, as pome (*Pomaceae*) and oak (*Quercus sp.*) (NNU A 8500). A branch fragment of pome is AMS ¹⁴C dated (AAR-9465): 4910±55 BP, cal. 3760-3640 BC (1σ), 3810-3630 BC (2σ).

b. BMR 2164x2. *Pottery*: Joining sherds of a medium-sized funnel beaker with 4 horizontal rows of short, oblong indentations under the rim (fig. 3.13:1) (rim diameter 19 cm, neck height 5.6 cm); 5 rim and neck sherds with horizontal rows of square indentations; and c. 233 other sherds. – *Flint*: 1 flake of a polished axe, 1 blade and 1 flake of imported flint, 1 piece of ball flint and 1 fragment of fire-affected flint.

c. BMR 2164x3. *Pottery*: Joining sherds of a large funnel beaker (rim diameter c. 34.4 cm, neck height 6.5 cm) decorated with 2 horizontal rows of finger impressions under the rim (fig. 3.13:3).

d. BMR 2164x3B. *Pottery*: 1 rim sherd with a horizontal line, 1 rim sherd with indentations, 1 neck/belly sherd of a lugged beaker and 44 other sherds. – *Flint*: 1 flake of a polished axe, 2 flakes of imported flint, 12 pieces of ball flint, 1 scraper of matt flint, 1 piece of Kristianstad flint and two fragments of fire-affected flint.

e. BMR 2164x3C. *Pottery*: Joining sherds of the neck and belly of an undecorated lugged beaker (fig. 3.13:2) (rim diameter 14 cm, neck height 4.9 cm), 1 undecorated rim sherd and 13 other sherds. 1 fragment of a clay disc with finger impressions on the edge. – *Flint*: 1 piece of ball flint.

A humic cultural layer in the uppermost part of the pit (x1) contained numerous sherds of Early Neolithic funnel beaker pottery, but only a small amount of flint. In the bottom layer of the pit (x2) were the remains of two funnel beakers (x2 and x3), which may have been deposited complete or as large sherds. The large funnel beaker with finger impressions under the rim (x3) was found close to a posthole (x3B), and in the fill of another posthole (x3C) were large fragments from a third vessel, an undecorated lugged beaker. During collection of finds from the surface of adjacent areas, sherds dating to both EN and MN were found. The site is located on a sandy plateau 44 m above sea level, north of the watercourse Blykobbe Å. – *Dating*: EN A2: Funnel beakers of both types I and II are represented, but most sherds are from type II vessels. – EN B: A single cord-decorated sherd. – EN C and MN A: A few sherds.

42. St. Myregård II
060303-117. Nylars parish. – NM A53217. – BMR 1400. – Excavation in August-September 1987 of an early Middle Neolithic settlement (P.O. Nielsen 1989, 15-16).

a. MX II 140/85: Sherds of the rim, neck, belly and base of a medium-sized, undecorated funnel beaker, rim diameter/neck height: 17.7/5 cm. The profile is convex-concave and the rim flared (fig. 3.1:2).

b. MX II 140/85: Neck/belly sherds from a large, thick-walled funnel beaker with convex-concave profile and flared neck (fig. 3.1:1).

Found together with a number of other sherds from the two vessels during excavation of trial holes aimed at defining the extent of the Middle Neolithic settlement. The sherds were found in a cultural layer under the ploughsoil in trial hole 140/85. The same cultural layer covers an area of c. 80 × 55 m and otherwise mainly contained settlement material dating to MN AIb. The above-mentioned finds must be associated with activities that took place long before the Middle Neolithic settlement was established. The site is located on a flat plain 20 m above sea level, on soils consisting of coarse meltwater sand. – *Dating*: Based upon their characteristic, flared profile, both funnel beakers can be classified as type 0, which places the finds in EN A0.

43. Møllebo
060303-255. Nylars parish. – BMR 779. – Excavated by private collector Carl Lau. Submitted to the museum in 1980.

BMR 779x1. *Pottery*: 1 undecorated neck sherd of a medium-sized, thin-walled funnel beaker with flared neck, type II (rim diameter/neck height: c. 24/5.5 cm); 1 undecorated rim sherd of a similar vessel and 2 other undecorated rim sherds; 1 rim sherd with indentations on top of the rim; 3 rim sherds with a low outer rim bead, in which there are wide finger impressions; 4 rim sherds of a vessel with a low outer rim bead, in which there are irregular and D-shaped indentations, apparently made with a nail; 2 rim and neck sherds with 1 horizontal row of deep, D-shaped indentations; 1 rim sherd of a small funnel beaker with fine incisions on top of the rim and 2 horizontal rows of small, oval indentations under the rim; 2 rim and neck sherds with 2 horizontal rows of indentations; 2 body sherds with various indentations; 4 neck/belly sherds; 88 undecorated sherds; and 2 sherds of a collared flask. 1 fragment of a clay disc. – *Flint*: 4 pieces of imported flint, including 2 that have been retouched, apparently for use as gunflint, 2 pieces of fire-affected flint, 3 pieces of ball flint, 1 large scraper and 14 other pieces of matt flint.

Found near an *in situ* stone on the innermost part of the sandy plateau between Stampen and Arnager, c. 645 m from the coast and 16 m above sea level. – *Dating*: The first-mentioned funnel beaker sherd, and probably a number of the others, can be dated to EN A2.

44. Hjuleregård
060303-670. Nylars parish. – BMR 3509. – Excavated in 2007 and 2009 by Michael S. Thorsen.

BMR 3509x16. Feature A9 was a pit that contained the following: *Pottery*: Part of the neck of a large, undecorated funnel beaker of type I, with a neck height of 6.9 cm and rim diameter of 38 cm (fig. 3.2:1). Several rim sherds of undecorated funnel beakers, including one with a neck height of c. 5 cm and a rim diameter of 24 cm. 1 rim sherd of a medium-sized funnel beaker with horizontal, applied bead with finger impressions, c. 1 cm under the rim (fig. 3.2:2). 1 rim sherd of a medium-sized funnel beaker with a horizontal row of small, triangular indentations close to the rim (fig. 3.2:3). 1 rim sherd of a large funnel beaker with flaring rim and a horizontal row of finger impressions under the rim. 17 rim sherds of at least 3 funnel beakers with slightly thickened, flaring rims and more or less clear finger impressions just under the rim. 2 body sherds with a knob. 1 undecorated rim sherd and 244 undecorated body and base sherds. – *Flint*: 1 irregular blade, 4.9 cm long, knapped from a polished flint axe. 2 small flakes of imported flint, one polished. – There are also 35 pieces of fired clay, 22 g of burnt bones and charcoal.

The burnt bones have been examined by Pernille Bangsgaard, SNM, who counted 58 very burnt or calcinated bone fragments, 3 of which could be identified as part of a cranium and 2 as fragments of pig metatarsal (*Sus* sp., domestic pig or wild boar). The rest of the bone fragments could not be identified by species, but, on the basis of size and morphology, are apparently from the same overall animal category: medium-sized mammals (based upon an e-mail of 18 April 2017).

A charcoal sample contains branches of hazel, the stone fruit family, oak, lime and mistletoe, as identified by Claus Malmros, NM. AMS ^{14}C dates:

1) Charcoal of hazel (*Corylus avellana*) (AAR-15011): 5064±25 BP, cal. 3943-3801 BC (1σ), 3951-3796 BC (2σ).

2) Charcoal of mistletoe (*Viscum album*) (AAR-15012): 5058±25 BP, cal. 3941-3799 BC (1σ), 3950-3792 BC (2σ).

BMR 3509x00. Feature B was a pit that contained the following: *Pottery:* 11 undecorated rim sherds, 5 neck/belly sherds and c. 120 undecorated body sherds, probably from the same funnel beaker of an early type.

BMR 3509x22. Feature C1 was a pit with a diameter of 1.25 m, which contained the following: *Pottery:* 4975 g sherds consisting of 8 sherds of the neck of a medium-sized, undecorated funnel beaker like that shown in fig. 3.2:1, 2 rim sherds of funnel beakers with horizontal beads with finger impressions under the rim, 1 rim sherd with 2 horizontal rows of irregular, short indentations, 6 undecorated rim sherds, 1 neck/belly sherd and 281 undecorated body sherds. – *Flint*: 1 fire-affected flake. The finds also included 8 g of charcoal, 1 piece of burnt bone and 1 fragment of burnt clay.

Found in connection with the extension of the property. Within a c. 120 × 75 m area, a number of fills were recorded, 17 of which were excavated. The soil consists of clay, and the site is located 68 m above sea level. – *Dating*: EN A1.

45. Strandvejen, Rønne

060304-39. Rønne parish. – BMR 2028. – Registration of privately-owned finds recovered before 1980.

Sherds of the neck of a large funnel beaker decorated with 3 × 3 horizontal lines of two-ply cord separated by undecorated zones.

Found during digging 'just above the gravel' in a garden c. 15 m above sea level, along with an undecorated neck/belly sherd, diverse flint flakes and a polished stone axe fragment. – *Dating*: EN B.

46. Bornholms Lufthavn

060304-123. Rønne parish. – BMR 3819. – Excavation by Anders Pihl in 2015.

BMR 3819x3 from pit A7. *Pottery*: 2 rim sherds, probably from the same large type II funnel beaker, decorated under the rim with 2 horizontal rows of finger impressions, 1 body sherd with possible decoration, 3 neck-belly sherds and 41 undecorated body and base sherds. – *Flint*: 12 pieces of ball flint, 4 of which are fire affected.

BMR 3819x4, unstratified finds A11. *Pottery*: 2 body sherds from a small, thin-walled vessel.

BMR 3819x5 from pit A6. *Pottery*: 3 decorated rim sherds with curved indentations under the rim, 1 body sherd decorated with parallel lines of two-ply cord, 1 neck-belly sherd with pronounced transition between the neck and belly, probably from a type III funnel beaker, 1 body sherd with a vertical handle, which is probably from a lugged jar, and 12 undecorated body sherds. – *Flint*: Imported: 1 polished flake. Ball flint: 7 flakes, 1 of which is fire affected. Unidentified flint: 1 flake.

Found during excavation associated with the extension of the airport car park, on flat terrain and sandy soil, 15 m above sea level – *Dating*: The pottery from A7 can be dated to EN A2 and the pottery from A6 to EN B.

47. Gamleborg

060305-155. Vestermarie parish. – NM A45071-83. – During the excavation of the castle Gamleborg, in Almindingen forest, Neolithic finds were recovered at several locations. The excavator, Ole Klindt-Jensen, mentions five such sites in a note dated 27/6 1958, in which no. 5, which was located around the middle of the plateau occupied by the castle, is described as associated with most finds. The following objects were found here:

NM A45082. Rim sherds and neck-body sherds from a funnel beaker decorated under the rim with two horizontal rows of vertical nail impressions (fig. 8.3).

The sherds were found in sandy soil on rocky

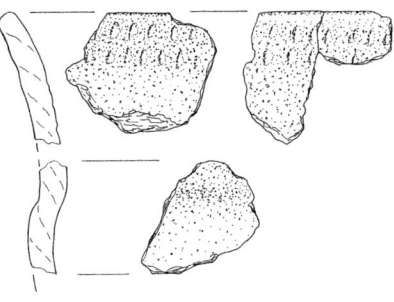

Fig. 8.3. Sherds of funnel beaker from Gamleborg (Finds list I no. 47). Eva Koch del. 1:2.

ground, at a depth of c. 25 cm, together with various other sherds, as well as a tanged flint arrowhead of Middle Neolithic type, 2 scrapers, 1 blade and 2 flakes of polished flint tools, c. 50 fragments of waste flint and 4 fire-affected flint fragments. – *Dating*: The finds from the site include objects from several phases of the Neolithic, but the funnel beaker sherds should be dated to EN A.

48. Grisby

060403-130. Ibsker parish. – NM A34594. – Becker 1947, 164 and fig. 39.2.

Rim sherd of a large funnel beaker decorated with zones of vertical, parallel lines of whipped cord.

Found at a coastal settlement where finds from the Ertebølle Culture and other periods were also recovered. – *Dating*: EN C.

49. Dalshøj

060403-135. Ibsker parish. – BMR1639. – In connection with the laying of a water pipeline, Finn Ole Nielsen inspected the excavated pipeline trench on 8/12 2001, and observed a pit that was 1.8 m long and 0.25 m deep measured from the bottom of the ploughsoil. The fill of the pit was light grey and contained charcoal. The finds consisted of the following:

Pottery: 1 neck/belly sherd of a short-necked funnel beaker with a neck index of 24; 1 rim sherd of medium-sized funnel beaker decorated with 1 horizontal row of finger impressions c. 1 cm under the rim; 1 rim sherd of a medium-sized funnel beaker with finger impressions near the rim; 3 rim sherds of funnel beakers with 1 horizontal row of indentations under the rim; 1 rim sherd of funnel beaker with 2 horizontal rows of indentations under the rim; 1 sherd of the upper part of the belly of a vessel decorated with 2 horizontal rows of small indentations at the top of the belly; 3 sherds from an undecorated, open bowl; 1 body sherd with a round knob; and 227 undecorated body and base sherds of thick- and thin-walled vessels. 2 sherds of clay discs with finger impressions on the edge. – *Flint*: 1 scraper, 3 cm long, of an oblong, large flake. – *Quartzite*: 2 flakes, but of different material. – *Slate*: 1 flat piece, 4.6 × 4.9 cm, originally triangular, but with one corner missing. Along the preserved edges on one side are c. 0.5 cm-long incisions. – *Burnt daub*: 13 pieces. – *Bone*: 1 fragment of a tubular bone.

The pit was located c. 60 m above sea level on boulder clay. – The first-mentioned neck fragment can be measured and is from a type II funnel beaker. The other rim sherds are decorated with indentations that are found on funnel beakers of this type. The use of a horizontal row of finger impressions in the vessel wall under the rim, without an applied bead, is most often found on type II funnel beakers. The decoration consisting of two horizontal rows of indentations on the upper part of the belly is only known from a few other finds of pottery from EN A (see this list no. 7 (fig. 8.1:4) and no. 40). The finds also include sherds from an open bowl, a form that is otherwise only rarely represented at settlements on Bornholm dating to EN. – *Dating*: EN A2.

50. Holkemyr/Frennemark

060404-12. Svaneke parish. – Found during geological investigations in 1894 by K. Rørdam for D.G.U. (Rørdam 1895. *Cf*. Vedel 1897, 2-3, 107-09).

C. 20 pottery sherds, including rim sherds of a type II funnel beaker decorated with two horizontal rows of oblong, slightly diagonal indentations. There are also a few pieces of flint waste.

The finds are from the middlemost of three cultural layers in the beach ridge, which is located 110 m from the coast, and the highest point of which lies 7 m above sea level. – *Dating*: EN A2.

51. Svaneke Boldbane/Frennemark

060404-15. Svaneke parish. – BMa 2421.

1 rim sherd from a funnel beaker decorated with zones of horizontal lines of two-ply cord, which are separated by undecorated zones. 5 undecorated sherds.

Found during an excavation in 1930 on soils consisting of marine-deposited sands and gravels. – *Dating*: EN B.

52. Nørre Sandegård

060405-154. Østerlars parish. – NM A43239. – Found during excavations by C.J. Becker in 1948-52. At the same site, finds have been recovered dating to the Maglemosian Culture, Middle Neolithic Funnel Beaker Culture, Battle Axe Culture and Late Neolithic, and there are also Bronze Age and Iron Age burial places (Becker 1990, 40-45).

a. A complete funnel beaker with a flared profile decorated with horizontal two-ply cord impressions (fig. 3.18), and also many fragments of vessels of the same type, with the same type of cord impressions in both horizontal and vertical zones. 2 rim sherds are decorated with horizontal rows of indentations under the rim (Becker 1990 Pl. 14-17).

b. Remains of a funnel beaker of type V with diagonal indentations near the rim and vertical belly stripes (Becker 1990 Pl. 18:362). There are also rim sherds from two large funnel beakers decorated with whipped cord impressions (Becker 1990 Pl. 16:92, 147, 366 and 17:309).

Found in settlement layers, which were disturbed by later burials, but also overlain and protected by these. The settlement was located a short distance from the coast on sandy soil, c. 10 m above sea level. – *Dating*: Finds group a was attributed by C.J. Becker to 'the Siretorp group', but this material should be dated to EN B. Finds group b contains a complete funnel beaker, which C.J. Becker dated to the Virum group. The funnel beaker, together with the two vessels decorated with whipped cord impressions, should be dated to EN C/ MN AI.

53. Gudhjem Syd

060405-182. Østerlars parish. – BMR 1392. – Collected in April 1984 by private collector G. Møller Larsen in an area of development. The finds were subsequently handed in to BMR in several portions:

a. BMR 1392x1-10, 'unstratified finds'. *Pottery*: Remains of the neck and shoulder of a large funnel beaker decorated with 1 row of finger impressions under the rim (fig. 8.4:1). Remains of the neck and shoulder of a medium-sized funnel beaker decorated with 2 rows of vertical nail impressions under the rim, with 1 or 2 round knobs on the upper part of the shoulder. Joining parts of a base with a slightly concave underside probably belong to the same vessel (fig. 8.5). 2 rim sherds

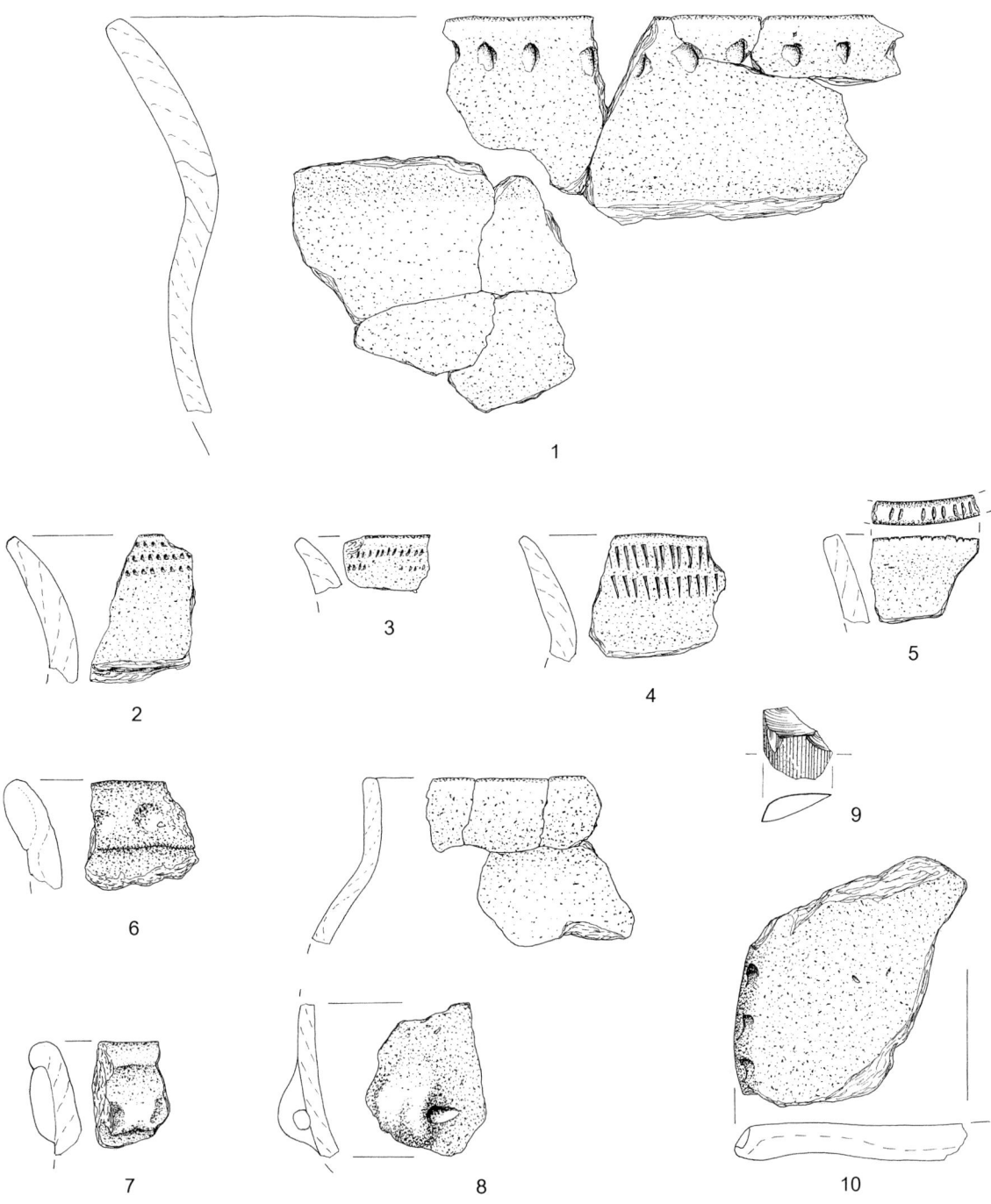

Fig. 8.4. Sherds of funnel beakers (1-7), sherds of lugged jar (8), fragment of polished flint axe (9) and fragment of clay disc (10) from Gudhjem Syd (Finds list I no. 53). Eva Koch del. 1:2.

225

of large funnel beakers with a wide, horizontal bead under the rim with finger impressions (fig. 8.4:6-7), 1 rim sherd of a funnel beaker with 3 horizontal rows of small indentations (fig. 8.4:2), 1 rim sherd with 2 rows of oblong indentations (fig. 8.4:4) and 2 rim sherds with short indentations under the rim (fig. 8.4:3), 1 rim sherd with transverse notches in the upturned rim (fig. 8.4:5), 4 undecorated rim sherds and 31 undecorated body sherds. Remains of a small lugged jar include parts of the neck and a body sherd with a lug, which has a vertical groove on its outer surface (fig. 8.4:8).

b. BMR 1392x14-16, from 'waste layer'. *Pottery*: 5 rim sherds of a large funnel beaker with 1 row of finger impressions below the rim (like fig. 8.4:1 and probably from the same vessel). 3 rim sherds of a medium-sized funnel beaker with 2 rows of vertical nail impressions under the rim (like fig. 8.5 and probably from the same vessel). 1 large base sherd and 78 undecorated body sherds. 1 clay disc fragment with finger impressions on the edge (fig. 8.4:10).

c. BMR 1392x17-41, from different features and layers: *Pottery*: 2 decorated and 6 undecorated rim sherds, and 332 undecorated body sherds, not all of Neolithic date. – *Flint*: A transverse arrowhead and 37 flakes, one of which is knapped from a polished axe, probably pointed butted (fig. 8.4:9). – *Other stone*: 4 crushing stones and a small hammerstone. – In addition, there were 20 pieces of burnt daub.

Found on flat, sandy terrain 20 m above sea level and c. 375 m from the coast, partly under a layer of drifting sand. The material is from cultural layers, pits and postholes that are not described in detail. The postholes are not definitely Neolithic, as finds from the Bronze and Iron Age were also found at the site. – *Dating*: Finds groups a and b include remains of funnel beakers with neck and shoulder profiles corresponding with type I. Together with the sherds of large vessels with a horizontal bead with finger impressions under the rim and the lugged jar with a short neck, this points towards a date within EN A1. The ratio between neck height and rim diameter, however, places the medium-sized funnel beaker (fig. 8.5) at the transition between types I and II. Dating of the Early Neolithic material from the group solely to EN A is supported by the fact that there is not a single sherd with cord decoration amongst the large quantities of pottery.

54. Nørre Sandegård Vest

060405-183. Østerlars parish. – BMR 1409. – Found in 1987 during excavations of a cemetery dating to the Late Germanic Iron Age (Jørgensen & Nørgård Jørgensen 1997, with discussion of the Neolithic finds and their distribution, see page 15 and fig. 8). A limited c. 10 × 10 m area around graves nos. 7 and 26 included an earlier cultural layer containing Early Neolithic pottery (report by Lars Jørgensen 21/5 1988).

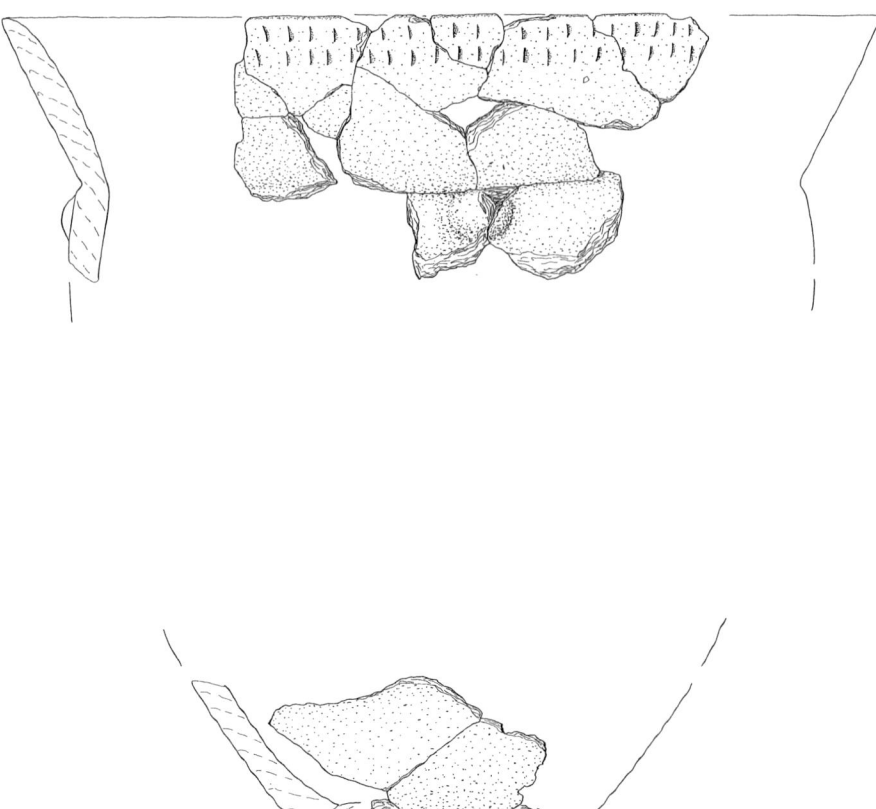

Fig. 8.5. Remains of funnel beaker from Gudhjem Syd (Finds list I no. 53). Eva Koch del. 1:3.

BMR 1409x753. Finds from a tree-throw under graves 25 and 26: *Pottery*: 5 rim sherds, a number of which are from the same vessel, with oblong indentations under the rim. 1 rim sherd with notches on the edge, under which are small V-shaped indentations. 6 undecorated rim sherds, 2 neck-belly sherds, 2 flat bases and 83 undecorated body sherds. – *Flint*: 2 flakes of ball flint. – *Other material*: A small amount of burnt bone, as well as charred hazelnut shells and charcoal.

BMR 1409x755. Finds from posthole, feature 67: *Pottery*: 5 sherds, 1 of which is a rim sherd of a short-necked funnel beaker with a horizontal row of oblong indentations under the rim.

BMR 1409x862. Finds from the fill of grave 7: *Pottery*: 1 undecorated rim sherd of a medium-sized type I/II funnel beaker (rim diameter/neck height: 26/5.3 cm). 2 rim sherds of small beakers with 1 row of small indentations just under the rim. 3 rim sherds with 1 horizontal row of vertical indentations. 1 rim sherd with 2 horizontal rows of diagonal, oblong indentations. 2 rim sherds with a horizontal bead with finger impressions under the rim. 4 neck/belly sherds with a flat shoulder profile, which characterises type I funnel beakers. 115 undecorated sherds.

Found within a limited area of moraine sand, 20 m above sea level and c. 200 m from the coast. – *Dating*: EN A. Some traits, like the applied bead under the rim with finger impressions and the flat shoulder profile, point towards EN A1, whilst the undecorated rim sherd recorded under no. x862 can be placed at the boundary between funnel beakers of types I and II.

55. Snekkebjerg

060405-229. Østerlars parish. – BMR 3139. – Excavated in 2001-05 by Ulla Lund Hansen and Christina R. Seehusen.

BMR 3139x25. *Pottery*: 1 body sherd with parallel lines of two-ply cord.

BMR 3139x26. *Pottery*: Undecorated body sherds. – *Flint*: 1 flake of a polished flint axe. 1 small flake axe, one side of which is formed by the striking platform, the other by continuous retouch. The edge is sloping and has pieces missing as a result of its use. 23 flint flakes, including at least 1 piece of ball flint and 1 piece of Kristianstad flint.

Found in cultural layers and a few features, in a sandy elevated area during the excavation of a Late Iron Age cemetery. Flint flakes and pottery sherds from a Neolithic settlement were found all over the hill. – *Dating*: EN B.

56. Jættebro

060406-133. Østermarie parish. – BMR 916. – Excavated in 2004, 2005 and 2007 by Michael Vennersdorf and Michael S. Thorsen.

a. BMR 916x167, 323 and 325 from feature A209. *Pottery*: Parts of the neck of a large funnel beaker with an estimated rim diameter of 52 cm. Under the rim is an applied bead with finger impressions, which are pinched together so that the impressions are almost triangular in shape (fig. 3.5:3). Parts of the neck of a funnel beaker with a rim diameter of 20 cm and neck height of 3.5 cm, with a horizontal row of finger impressions under the rim (fig. 3.5:2). Parts of the neck of a small, undecorated funnel beaker with a rim diameter of 12 cm and neck height of 3 cm (fig. 3.5:1). 2 rim sherds with a horizontal row of small, square indentations. Several rim sherds of the above-mentioned vessels or from funnel beakers with the same decoration. 1 fragment of a clay disc with finger impressions on the edge. The ceramic material, which in total weighs 5103 g, also includes many, uncounted, undecorated body and base sherds. 5 sherds from Iron Age vessels represent contamination. – *Flint*: A fire-affected fragment of a two-sided, polished, pointed-butted flint axe (type 1). A small blade and 6 flakes from polished flint axes, 1 transverse arrowhead, 4 flakes of imported flint, 3 other flakes (fire affected, unidentified) and 4 flakes of Kristianstad flint. – *Amber*: Small fragments. – The fill was of irregular appearance on the surface, measuring at most 3.5 × 2.15 m, and was 0.4 m deep. The bottom was a regular round shape, and the fill was dark grey in colour, and mixed with charcoal and burnt bone. The bottom layer, which was darkest in colour, contained the largest pieces of charcoal and the neck of the small funnel beaker no. 325 (fig. 3.5:1). Amongst the material from the charcoal layer at the bottom of the pit (no. 167), 43 pieces have been identified as oak (*Quercus sp.*) and 14 as belonging to the rose family (*Rosaceae*) by Claudia Baittinger and Jonas Ogdal Jensen, NM (NNU j.nr. A8637). 1 piece of charcoal of *Rosaceae*, consisting of an annual ring, was AMS ^{14}C dated, which gave the result (Ua-55180): 5020±33 BP, cal. 3940-3710 BC (1σ), 3950-3700 BC (2σ). Wiggles in the calibration curve give an uncertain distribution, which under 1σ is divided into two 'peaks', one in the interval 3940-3870 BC (35.4 %) and the other in the interval 3810-3760 BC (28.4 %).

b. BMR 916x169 from feature A211: *Pottery*: 1 small rim sherd decorated with 3 horizontal rows of small, oblong indentations and 1 small fragment of a rim sherd with one or more horizontal rows of indentations. – The fill was of oval appearance on the surface, measuring 1.55 × 0.9 m, and was only 0.2 m deep. It consisted of grey-black, sandy soil.

Finds from the Early Neolithic settlement were recovered during the excavation of burials dating to the Roman Iron Age. Apart from the above-mentioned features containing finds from EN, a fill, feature A344, was excavated, which contained a few decorated sherds of vessels dating to MN A1, as well as flint flakes, burnt bone and charcoal. The settlement is located c. 50 m above sea level on moraine soil, a short distance from a stream bed. – *Dating*: On the basis of the rim profiles and decoration of the funnel beakers, which correspond with type I, the material from feature A209 can be dated to EN A1.

Finds list II

INDIVIDUAL FINDS OF POTTERY VESSELS

1. 'Bornholm'

06.00.00. – NM 2878. – Madsen 1868 Pl. 44.10; Becker 1947, 44, find no. 96.

Short-necked, lugged flask with flat bottom and two opposite-facing lugs on the upper part of the belly. Height: 19 cm (fig. 8.6).

Sent to the museum in 1833 without further information, other than that it was found on Bornholm. As noted by C.J. Becker (1947, 44), remains of peat inside the vessel indicate that it came from a bog. – *Dating*: EN A.

2. Kofoedsgård 1

060104. Klemensker parish. – NM A40026. – *Antiqvariske Annaler* 4. Bind, 1827, 386; Madsen 1868, Pl. 44.9; Becker 1947, 44 no. 98; Glob 1952 nr. 66.

Short-necked, lugged jar with flat base. Just under the middle of the belly are 4 lugs. Height: 21.3 cm (fig. 8.7).

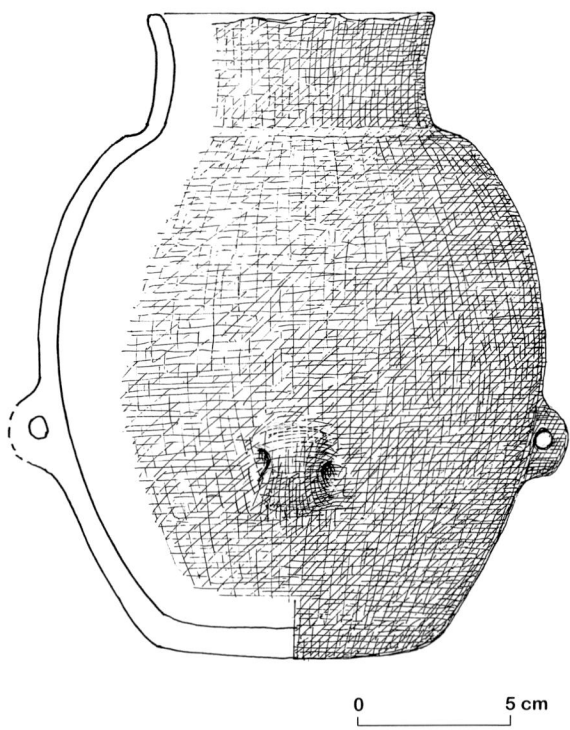

Fig. 8.7. Lugged jar from Kofoedsgård (Finds list II no. 2). H. Ørsnes del. 2:5.

Acquired in 1827. Found in a bog at a depth of 12 feet (c. 3.75 m). According to a report by Prince Christian Frederik (later Christian VIII) to Den Kgl. Commission til Oldsagers Opbevaring, dated 31 December 1824, the lugged jar was found together with a number of smaller vessels, a human head of small dimensions, pieces of several human crania and fossilised bones, including of dog, goat and pig. Estimated elevation: 100-103 m above sea level.– *Dating*: EN A.

3. Kofoedsgård 2

060104. Klemensker parish. – BMa 614. – Müller 1918, no. 43; Glob 1952 no. 7.

An almost complete funnel beaker with a slightly expanded rim, under which are 4 horizontal lines formed by two-ply cord impressions (fig. 8.8). Under this are groups of 5 vertical lines in the same technique. Height: 11 cm. Rim diameter/neck height: 9.8/4.2 cm. The neck height is 42.8 % of the rim diameter, corresponding with funnel beakers of type III.

Found c. 1850 on a gravel hill east of Kofoedsgård. Estimated elevation: 100-103 m above sea level. – *Dating*: EN B.

4. Simlegårds Bakker (Simblegaardsbakken)

060104-29A. Klemensker parish. – BMa 724. – Ebbesen 1974.

An almost complete, short-necked funnel beaker decorated with 2 horizontal rows of oblong impressions

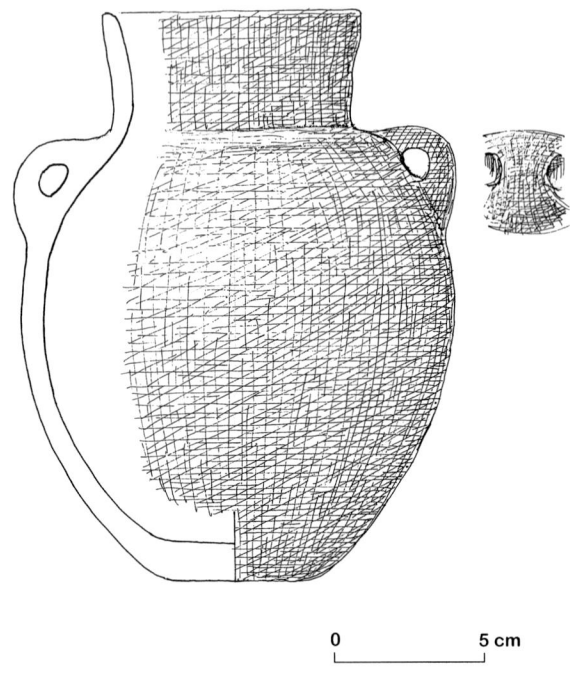

Fig. 8.6. Lugged flask from 'Bornholm' (Finds list II no. 1). H. Ørsnes del. 2:5.

Fig. 8.8. Funnel beaker from Kofoedsgård (Finds list II no. 3). After S. Müller 1918, fig. 43. 1:2.

under the rim. Height: 8.5 cm, rim diameter/neck height: 7.5/2 cm. The neck height is 26.6 % of the rim diameter, corresponding with funnel beakers of type II.

The vessel was sent to Bornholms Museum without further information, other than it was found on the hill 'Simblegaardsbakken'. In 1881, J.A. Jørgensen found flint objects on Simlegårds Bakker, although again the location is not precisely identified. A small collection of finds at Bornholms Museum is listed under no. 580: A small conical blade core; a fragment of a polished flint axe; a small blade; and a rim sherd from a funnel beaker decorated near the rim with 3 horizontal rows of small round indentations. Probable elevation: 110-127 m above sea level. – *Dating*: EN A2 (the pottery vessel BMa 724).

5. Vallensgård

060205. Åker parish. – NM A19305. – Müller 1913, 316 fig. 82; Müller 1918, no. 45.

An almost complete funnel beaker with a slightly expanded rim, under which are 8 horizontal lines formed by two-ply cord impressions (fig. 2.14). Somewhat unusually, there are cord impressions in the same technique on the underside of the flat base, in the form of 6 short, parallel lines. Vessel height: 12 cm, rim diameter/neck height: 12/5 cm. The neck height is 41.6 % of the rim diameter, corresponding with type III funnel beakers.

The information does not identify where the vessel was found except at Vallensgård. The surface of the vessel has an uneven, black colour, suggesting that it was originally located in a bog. It is therefore possible that the finds location was in the bog Vallensgård Mose. The land at Vallensgård lies between 75 and 89 m above sea level. – *Dating*: EN B.

6. The Baltic Sea north-east of Bornholm

BMR 3419. Lugged jar, 25 cm high. Found by fisherman Louis Kofoed, Melsted, in May 1929, whilst he was fishing in 56-fathom deep waters (fig. 5.13A).

7. The Baltic Sea south-east of Bornholm

NM j.nr. 5399/84. – S. Nielsen 1975. – Lugged jar, 40 cm high. Recovered during trawling by skipper Peter Larsen, Snogebæk, in the summer of 1968, c. 20 nautical miles south-east of Bornholm (fig. 5.13B).

8. The Baltic Sea west-north-west of Bornholm

NM A51090. Lugged jar, 20.8 cm high, caught during trawling at Nygrund, 6-7 nautical miles west-north-west of Hammer Havn, by John Seerup, Sandvig, around 1st June 1984 (fig. 5.13C).

Finds list III

FINDS FROM BURIALS

1. Bjørnebakkerne I

060104-181. Klemensker parish. – BMR 645, 2167. –Excavation by F.O. Nielsen in May 1979. Report also by F.O. Nielsen 14/6 1979.

Sherds from the neck and transition between the neck and belly of a medium-sized type III funnel beaker (rim diameter/neck height: 17/6.3 cm), decorated with two horizontal rows of indentations under the rim, above small, short indentations, and below these oblong indentations (fig. 7.21). Body sherds of a slightly larger funnel beaker probably of the same type. 1 transverse arrowhead.

Found in an elongated, slightly rounded and almost pointed-bottomed pit, which was orientated SE-NW (fig. 7.20). At the south-eastern end were two large stones and under these was a concentration of charcoal. Below and along the sides of the pit were a number of small stones. A possible posthole was observed. The feature was interpreted as a possible grave. It may alternatively have been a facade ditch or post pit of a non-megalithic long barrow (see below no. 2 Runegård East). – Finds including sherds from a collared flask were collected on 8/11 1981. The finds location was on a gravel ridge 105 m above sea level – *Dating*: The funnel beaker sherds can be dated to EN B.

2. Runegård East

060205-202. Åker parish. – BMR 677. – Excavation in 1982 and report by Margrethe Watt. The aim of the excavation was to investigate settlements containing house sites dating to the Early Iron Age and Viking period (Watt 1982). The excavation involved both large-scale surface excavations and trial trenches. A large quan-

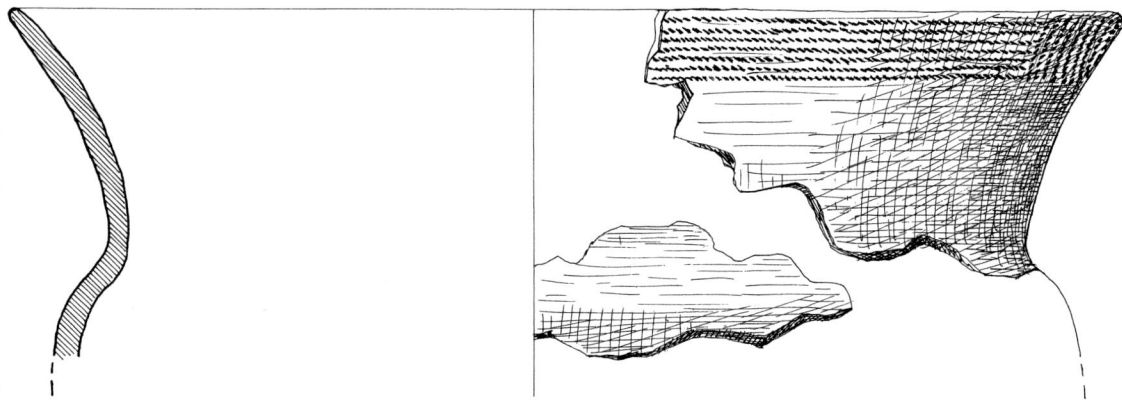

Fig. 8.9. Neck of large funnel beaker from Simenehøje (Finds list III no. 3). H. Ørsnes del. 1:4.

tity of Neolithic finds was recovered within the area (Kempfner-Jørgensen & Watt 1985, 94 ff.). In one of the trial trenches, Neolithic feature 1305 was uncovered and contained the following:

An almost complete funnel beaker, found as sherds and restored (fig. 7.23). It has an expanded rim, under which are 4 groups of 3 horizontal lines formed by two-ply cord impressions, interrupted by groups of vertical lines in the same technique. Vessel height: 11.4 cm, rim diameter/neck height: 11.1/5.7 cm. The neck height is 51.3% of the rim diameter, corresponding with type III funnel beakers.

The Neolithic feature 1305 is described in the report as follows (fig. 7.22): *A possibly disturbed EN C burial. On the surface, it had the appearance of a collection of stones that mostly consisted of head-sized, rounded fieldstones. Around these was a faint, oblong fill measuring c. 2.6 m. The fill was N-S orientated. Within this fill, there was a posthole at the north end, which was circular with a diameter of 55 cm (i.e. later than 'the burial'). A corresponding small post (?) containing a brown-violet, charcoal-rich fill was also observed at the southern end. A small funnel beaker with cord decoration was found between the uppermost layer of stones. A N-S section was placed along the grave and its western half was removed. At the bottom, the oblong fill was very diffuse, as it almost exclusively consisted of dug-up subsoil. At level 115 (i.e. 42 cm below the surface of the subsoil) the fill had clearly divided into two, with the southern part most obvious and apparently forming a circular hole, which had a layer of light brown, charcoal-mixed sand at the bottom. Both this fill and the more diffuse one to the north contained a number of head-sized fieldstones of the same type as those that covered the surface. Apart from the pottery vessel, no other finds were recovered. The feature should possibly be interpreted as a Neolithic grave (stone packed), which was destroyed by tree-throws in the past. The feature is certainly very disturbed.* – Alternatively, this feature can be interpreted as a short, stone-filled facade ditch of an E-W-orientated non-megalithic long barrow, which contained two substantial posts, whose removal caused disturbance, which the excavator interpreted as being naturally caused (see discussion p. 181 f.). – *Dating*: The feature is dated by the small, cord-decorated type III funnel beaker to EN B (fig. 7.23).

3. Simenehøje/Nyker Plantage

060302-112. Nyker parish. – BMa 1395. – Inspection in 1959 by C.J. Becker, who acquired the find for BMR in the same year.

Sherds from the neck of a very large type II funnel beaker (rim diameter over 40 cm, neck height 12.5 cm), decorated under the rim with 7 horizontal lines of two-ply cord, interrupted by zones of vertical lines (fig. 8.9).

Found on sandy soil at the foot of a small natural hill 110 m above sea level, north-west of the highest point at Simenehøje. The sherds of pottery were found at a shovel's depth and on top of stones, which may have formed a pavement. – No flint was recovered at this location. – *Dating*: The funnel beaker's neck index of 22.5, assuming that the rim diameter was measured correctly, places it in type II. Its size, however, makes this type classification questionable, so it may either date to EN A2 or EN B.

Finds list IV

AXES OF FLINT AND OTHER STONE MATERIALS

Pointed-butted flint axes, individual finds

Type 1

1. Smørmosegård, Vestermarie, 060305-93. NM A105. Partly polished, two-sided pointed-butted flint axe, 14.4 cm long (fig. 4.1). Donated to the National Museum in 1866 by the farmer's two sons.
2. 'Bølshavn', Østermarie. BMa 1761. Unpolished, two-sided pointed-butted flint axe, 21.1 cm long. Purchased from a seller. Apparently found at Bølshavn.

3. Karlshøj/Kleven, Klemensker matr. 32b. BMa 1971. Unpolished, two-sided pointed-butted flint axe, 17.3 cm long.
4. Myseregård, Rutsker matr. 26a. Privately owned. Polished, two-sided pointed-butted flint axe, 14 cm long, blade damaged in modern period. Found just to the south-east of a hilly area with EN pottery, close to an old watercourse/spring running towards Fuglesangen.
5. Stamperegård, Østermarie matr. 75a. Privately owned. Polished, two-sided, pointed-butted flint axe, 15.2 cm long. Found in the meadow south of the county road.

Type 2
6. Bornholm, without any other information about the finds circumstances. Acquired in 1893 from a private collection. NM A11829. Polished, pointed-butted flint axe, 15.8 cm long, with brownish patination (P.O. Nielsen 1977, fig. 2b).
7. Runegård, Åker matr. 34. NM A19973 (previously BMR 1205). Very finely polished, pointed-butted flint axe with brownish patination, 22.1 cm long.
8. Lille Krashavegård, Klemensker, 060104-160. NM A42740 (marked Vedel 1871). Polished and resharpened, pointed-butted flint axe of four-sided form, but with very domed broad surfaces, 12 cm long (fig. 8.10). Found in a field at Freehold farm no. 21 at a depth of 1 foot (c. 30 cm).
9. Engegård, Nylars matr. 4a. BMa 34. Polished, pointed-butted flint axe with irregular cross section, 13.2 cm long.
10. Ø. Pilegård, Klemensker matr. 34a. BMa 202. Polished and resharpened, pointed-butted flint axe with an almost trapezoid cross section. Cf. settlement Ø. Pilegård (Finds list I no. 11).
11. Torpebakkerne, Rosendalegård's land in Rutsker, matr. 31a. BMa 746. Polished, pointed-butted flint axe with asymmetrical cross section, 21.3 cm long and with damaged blade.
12. Kirkebogård, Klemensker matr. 78a. BMR 924. Polished and resharpened, pointed-butted flint axe with asymmetrical cross section, 11.7 cm long.
13. Kofoedgård Lynglod, Klemensker, matr. 175df. BMa 1119. Polished, pointed-butted flint axe with irregular, rounded cross section, 18.3 cm long.
14. Risen, Østerlars matr. 33a. BMa 1324. Polished and sharpened, pointed-butted flint axe with very domed broad surfaces, 15.2 cm long.
15. Piberegård Lynglod, Klemensker matr. 175hb. BMa 1746. Polished, pointed-butted flint axe with very domed broad surfaces, 15.4 cm long.
16. Lynggård, Olsker matr. 34b-f or c. BMa 1917. Polished and resharpened, four-sided pointed-butted flint axe, 11.5 cm long. "Found 12 feet (c. 3.8 m) deep in a marl pit".

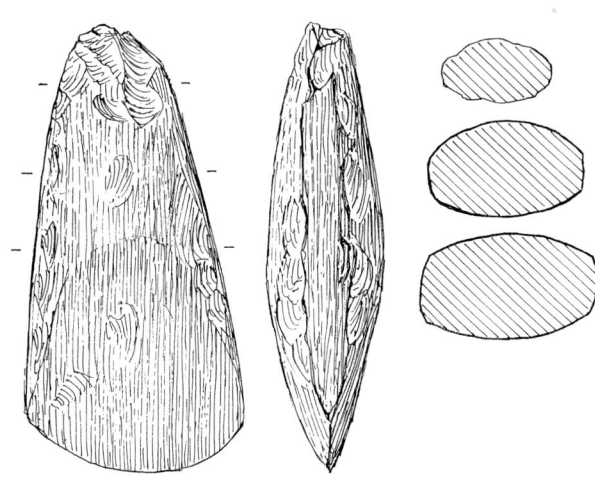

Fig. 8.10. Pointed-butted flint axe of type 2 from Lille Krashavegård (Finds list IV no. 8). 1:2.

17. Lindeskoven, Rø matr. 41. BMa 1977. Polished, pointed-butted flint axe with rounded oval cross section, 13.3 cm long.
18. Birkely, south of Vallingebjerg, Åker matr. 196t. BMa 2136. Polished and resharpened, pointed-butted flint axe with irregular cross section, 12.3 cm long and with damaged blade.
19. Smålyngen, Pedersker matr. 80. BMa 2333. Polished, pointed-butted flint axe with asymmetrical cross section, 13.1 cm long, with slightly damaged blade.
20. Fredshvile, Klemensker, matr. 126. Privately owned. Unpolished, pointed-butted flint axe, knapped as two sided, but due to its short, wide form is probably an unpolished preform for a type 2 axe (fig. 4.3). Length 15.7 cm. Found during harrowing a few years after the retrieval of four-sided axe no. 27 in approximately the same place.
21. Fredshvile, Klemensker, matr. 126. Privately owned. Polished, pointed-butted flint axe, 14.2 cm long. Found around 1952 in a depression in the rocks near a blasted-off stone, in approximately the same place as axe no. 13.
22. Skåningehøj, Klemensker, 060104-214. Privately owned (BMR 878). Polished, pointed-butted flint axe, 16.7 cm long. Found on a small sandy raised area near Skåningehøj, on the land of Vester Pilegård.
23. Søvang, Klemensker matr. 78c. Privately owned (BMR 904). Polished, pointed-butted flint axe with oval cross section, c. 13 cm long. Found in 1980, during excavation south of the house at Bedegadevej 18.
24. Sjælemosen, Olsker matr. 14a. Privately owned. Polished, pointed-butted flint axe, 14 cm long (fig. 4.2). Found in 1983 in shallow water by Klaus Thorsen.

25. Ndr. Dyndebygård, Povlsker matr. 38-39. Privately owned. Polished and resharpened, pointed-butted flint axe with irregular cross section, 11.5 cm long.
26. Rispebjerg (Rispebjerg Huse), Povlsker matr. 49f. Privately owned. Polished, pointed-butted flint axe with rounded cross section, 11.3 cm long.
27. Munkerup, Østermarie matr. 189a. Privately owned. Polished, pointed-butted flint axe with irregular cross section, 12.2 cm long.
28. Myregård, Østermarie matr. 63a. Privately owned. Polished, pointed-butted flint axe with irregular cross section, 18.3 cm long.

Type 3

29. Vellensby, Nylars. NM MLXV, acquired in 1823. Polished, four-sided, pointed-butted flint axe, 30.3 cm long (fig. 4.6). Found under a large stone.
30. Melgård, Rutsker, 060106-143. NM 8854, acquired in 1845. Polished and resharpened, four-sided, pointed-butted flint axe, 9.7 cm long. Found in "the ground of a destroyed burial mound", which contained stone coffin burials dating to the Bronze Age.
31. Klinten (Klinteskov), Vestermarie, 060305-81. NM A125. Polished, four-sided pointed-butted flint axe, 16.5 cm long. Found in the fill of a burial mound containing Iron Age graves.
32. Bornholm, without further information about the finds circumstances. NM A11828. Acquired in 1893 from a private collection. Polished, four-sided flint axe, 17.8 cm long, with grey, slightly brown patination.
33. Lindholmsgård, Rø matr. 35. BMa 395. Polished, four-sided, pointed-butted flint axe, 12 cm long.
34. Dalslunde, Østermarie matr. 52a. BMa 621. Polished and resharpened, four-sided, pointed-butted flint axe, 12.9 cm long.
35. Brommegård, Rø matr. 37a. BMa 1373. Polished and resharpened, four-sided, pointed-butted flint axe, 15.1 cm long.
36. Fredshvile (?), Klemensker, matr. 126. Privately owned. Polished, four-sided, pointed-butted flint axe, 18.4 cm long (fig. 4.5). Found by the father of the person who found nos. 12 and 27, although the finds location is uncertain.
37. Risholm, Klemensker, 060104-236. Privately owned (BMR 2029). Polished, four-sided, pointed-butted flint axe, 18.1 cm long. A grindstone was found in the same field.
38. Brunsbjerg, Petersborgvej, Olsker. Privately owned. Polished and sharpened, four-sided, pointed-butted flint axe, 12.1 cm long.
39. Møllehøj, Olsker matr. 5b. Privately owned. Polished, four-sided, pointed-butted flint axe, with a repaired but unpolished blade, 16 cm long. Settlement finds at the same location (Finds list I no. 16).
40. Lynggård, Rø matr. 7a. Privately owned. Polished and sharpened, four-sided, pointed-butted flint axe, 11.5 cm long.
41. Ndr. Dyndebygård, Povlsker matr. 38-39. Privately owned. Polished, four-sided flint axe, 15.5 cm long. Found around 1965 in a meadow between Bro and Rispebjerg, west of Ndr. Dyndebygård.

Pointed-butted axes of materials other than flint, individual finds

42. Smålyngen, Pedersker. NM A620. Four-sided, pointed-butted axe of fine-grained rock, 18.7 cm long. Found during ploughing of previously uncultivated plot of land.
43. Snogebæk, Poulsker, 060204-54. NM A44893. Four-sided, pointed-butted axe of fine-grained rock, 15 cm long.
44. Lillehave, Åker matr. 38b. NM A53361. Four-sided, pointed-butted axe of quartzite, 18.7 cm long. The blade is bifacially sharpened and not repolished (fig. 4.7). Found in a cultivated field.
44.1. Strangegård, Klemensker. BMa 885. Butt end of four-sided, pointed-butted axe of fine-grained rock.
44.2. Pilegård, Nyker. BMa 1209. Four-sided, pointed-butted axe of fine-grained rock, 19.9 cm long, with very domed broad surfaces.
44.3. Skovfryd, Nyker, matr. Nr. 79q. BMR 1656. Four-sided, pointed-butted axe of fine-grained stone, 13.7 cm long, with wide narrow surfaces and domed broad surfaces. Found south of Hallemarken and north-east of Dyndegård.
44.4. Klemenskro, Klemensker. BMa 1933. Four-sided, pointed-butted axe of fine-grained stone, 14.2 cm long.
44.5. Risbyvang, Klemensker. Privately owned. Irregular, four-sided, pointed-butted axe of sandstone with iron content, 13.5 cm long, resharpened.
44.6 Skovvang, Olsker. Privately owned. Cylindrical, partially four-sided, pointed-butted axe of fine-grained rock, resharpened, with very domed broad surfaces, 17 cm long. Found at the settlement of Møllehøj (Finds list I no. 16).
44.7. Runegård, Åker. Privately owned. Butt end of pointed-butted axe of fine-grained rock, four-sided but with a very round cross section.

Hoard finds containing pointed-butted axes

45. Ravnekær, Almindingen, Vestermarie, 060305-415. Privately owned (NM j.nr. 6647/87. BMR 1566).
(1) Two-sided, pointed-butted flint axe of light grey Senonian flint, partially polished on the broad surfaces and superficially polished on the narrow surfaces, 11.5 cm long. The blade is slightly curved like an adze blade (fig. 4.4:1).
(2) Two-sided, pointed-butted flint axe of grey Senonian flint with only a small amount of polishing

on one broad surface, in the highest areas, 12.8 cm long. The blade is knapped so that it curves like an adze blade (fig. 4.4:2).

(3) Two-sided, pointed-butted flint axe of grey Senonian flint, 12.5 cm long. The blade is straight, but with secondary working on both sides (fig. 4.4:3).

(4) Flake axe or small, thin-bladed axe of grey Danian flint, 8.1 cm long, formed from a large, pointed-butted axe (fig. 4.4:4).

(5) Small, four-sided, pointed-butted axe of light grey-green, fine-grained rock, 9.2 cm long (fig. 4.4:5).

(6) Flake axe of light grey Senonian flint, formed from a polished, pointed-butted flint axe, 10.3 cm long. The blade is very blunt and probably broken in its present form (fig. 4.4:6).

The axes were found in 1947 during the digging of a hole for a fence post in Statsskoven, along with 6 or 7 other similar axes, in a rock cleft.

Flint axes with a butt width measuring 4 cm, individual finds

46. Pilegård, Bodilsker. BMa 176. Polished, four-sided flint axe, 20.6 cm long.
47. Melsted. BMa 331. Polished and sharpened, four-sided flint axe, with one of the blade corners missing, 14 cm long. Found near Melsted.
48. Pedersker. BMa 419. Polished, four-sided axe, 18.7 cm long.

Thin-butted flint axes, individual finds

Type I

49. Østermarie, 060406-73A. NM A825. Unpolished, thin-butted flint axe, 21.3 cm long. Both edges are rounded on one broad surface.
50. Gammeltoftegård, Østermarie, 060406-166. NM A15008 (previously BMa 642). Polished, thin-butted flint axe with asymmetrically knapped butt, 35.8 cm long. Found in 1896 at a depth of 1 foot (c. 30 cm) under the surface next to a large stone. A similar axe was found in the same place a few years before.
51. Lille Krashavegård, Klemensker matr. 29c. BMa 1207. Polished and resharpened, thin-butted flint axe, 13 cm long. Found in a depression.
52. St. Dammegård, Klemensker matr. 32a. BMa 1210. Polished and resharpened, thin-butted flint axe, 15.1 cm long. Found in the soil just east of the farm.
53. Vestergård, Vestermarie matr. 82a. BMa 2349. Polished, thin-butted flint axe, whose butt end has been reshaped, 15.6 cm long.
54. Brogård, Nyker matr. 9a. BMa 2440. Polished, thin-butted flint axe, one blade corner missing, 15.4 cm long.
55. Vallensgård Mose, Åker. BMa 2632. Polished, thin-butted flint axe with damaged blade, 22.3 cm long. Found in the bog in the 1920s.
56. Ladegård, Klemensker matr. 58a. Privately owned. Partially polished, thin-butted flint axe, 16 cm long.
57. Fredenslyst, Klemensker matr. 28t. Privately owned. Polished and resharpened, thin-butted flint axe, 14.1 cm long. Found in the spring of 1986 during stone collection.
58. Sommeregård, Povlsker matr. 35a. Privately owned. Polished and resharpened, thin-butted flint axe with very domed broad surfaces, 15.2 cm.
59. St. Myregård, Pedersker. Privately owned. Polished and resharpened, thin-butted flint axe, 16.2 cm long. Found NE of St. Myregård.
60. Nordre Ellebygård, Østermarie matr. 70. Privately owned. Polished and resharpened, thin-butted flint axe, 13.1 cm long. Found west of the farm, close to the westernmost marl pit.
61. Brøddegård, Rø. Privately owned. Polished and resharpened, thin-butted flint axe, 13.3 cm.

Type I-II

62. St. Myregård, Nylars matr. 13-14a. Privately owned. Polished and resharpened, thin-butted flint axe, 21.3 cm long.

Type II

63. Nylars. NM 27473 (Fr.VII 4833). Polished, thin-butted flint axe, 35.5 cm long. Found in a bog in Nylars parish.
64. Freehold farm no. 5 (Lille Myregård), Knudsker, 060301-67. NM 27475 (Fr.VII 4832). Polished, thin-butted flint axe, 35.5 cm long.
65. Lille Myregård, Pedersker. NM A3322. Unpolished, thin-butted flint axe, 31.1 cm long. Found during agricultural work.
66. Bjørnebakken, Klemensker. BMa 85. Polished and resharpened, thin-butted flint axe, 20.5 cm long.
67. Glappe, Østermarie. BMa 397. Polished and resharpened, thin-butted flint axe, 19.3 cm long.
68. Mønstergård, Østermarie. BMa 681. Polished, thin-butted flint axe, 32 cm long.
69. Bodelyngen, Åker s. BMa 1089. Unpolished, thin-butted flint axe knapped from two diametrically opposite edges, 28.3 cm long.
70. Arbejdslyst, Åker. BMa 1421. Polished, thin-butted flint axe, 32 cm long. Found in one of the outlying fields of the parish, probably matr. 196eu.
71. Dambo, Klemensker matr. 32c. BMa 1554. Unpolished, thin-butted flint axe knapped from only two striking platforms on the same broad surface, 29.5 cm long.
72. Frennegård, Ibsker. BMR 1560x6. Polished and resharpened, thin-butted flint axe with broken blade, 30.3 cm long. Found around 1900 on the farm's land.

73. Vasegårdsmosen, Pedersker matr. 42a. BMa 1902. Polished and resharpened, thin-butted flint axe, 34.2 cm long. Found during the draining of the bog.
74. Østermarie 060406-173. BMa 2636. Polished, thin-butted flint axe, 31.2 cm long. Found during ploughing of a meadow.
75. Rutsker Højlyng. Privately owned. Fragment (part of blade) of a polished and slightly resharpened, thin-butted flint axe with almost completely parallel narrow sides, 16 cm long. The damage to the blade may have occurred in modern times. Found in 1985, in a depression WSW of Landlyst.
76. Vallensgård, Åker matr. 1æ, 1u. Privately owned. Polished, thin-butted flint axe, 26.6 cm long. Found during ploughing in 1953-55, in the middle of the boundary between the two land register units (matrikler).
77. The Sports Hall, Åkirkeby. Privately owned. Butt fragment of polished, thin-butted flint axe, 16 cm long. Found in 1993, south of the Sports Hall in a spraying track.
78. Stålegård, Åker matr. 69. Privately owned. Polished, thin-butted flint axe, 32.2 cm long. Found in July 1981 during ploughing at the edge of a low hill, near a large stone at the edge of a duck pond.
79. Mønstergård, Østermarie matr. 211 (the farm itself). Privately owned. Polished, thin-butted flint axe with damaged and repaired edge, 17.5 cm long.
80. St. Knudegård, Klemensker, 060104-232. Privately owned (NM 7088/90). Polished, thin-butted flint axe, 36 cm long (fig. 5.5). Found around 1960 during the draining of a small bog NW of the farm.

Type II-IIIA

81. Lappegård, Ibsker matr. 64a. BMa 282. Polished and resharpened, thin-butted flint axe with parts of the edge broken off, 22.4 cm long. Found on the surface of a field.
82. Rødbjerg, Klemensker. BMa 1866. Polished and resharpened, thin-butted flint axe, 34.5 cm long. Found during excavation of a ditch.
83. Gammel Dam, Rutsker matr. 95. BMa 2604. A polished and resharpened, thin-butted flint axe with a damaged and repaired blade area which has not been repolished, 16.2 cm long.
84. Lille Præstegårdsmosen, Klemensker matr. 4a. Privately owned (BMR 896). Polished and resharpened, thin-butted flint axe, 17.4 cm long.
85. Højegård, Knudsker. Privately owned (BMR 2287). Polished thin-butted flint axe, 28.1 cm long. One blade corner has broken off.
86. Vestergård, Østermarie matr. 98a. Privately owned. Fragment (part of the butt) of polished, thin-butted flint axe, 20.3 cm long.

Type IIIA

87. Freehold farm no. 15 (Kaggård), Rutsker s. NM A62. Polished thin-butted flint axe, 36.8 cm long. Found around 1852 in a hollow in the field.
88. Steensgård, Vestermarie matr. 48a. NM A365. Polished, thin-butted flint axe, 26.5 cm long (fig. 5.7). Found during the digging of a ditch in a previously uncultivated area. The axe was located in a stone layer.
89. Nyker, 060302-74. NM A576. Polished and resharpened, thin-butted flint axe, 19.8 cm long. Found in an outlying field plot of Hallemarken in Nyker, around 1 foot (30 cm) below the surface and placed diagonally under a large stone. A short distance away was another similar axe.
90. Freehold farm no. 3 (Maegård), Olsker. NM A731. Polished, thin-butted flint axe, 31.8 cm long. Found close to a large stone and c. 1/2 foot (c. 15 cm) under the surface.
91. Lyngen, Povlsker Plantage. NM A5897. Polished, thin-butted flint axe with damaged blade, 36 cm long.
92. Nylars. NM A15007. Polished, thin-butted flint axe, 34 cm long. Found during ploughing of a field in Nylars close to a boghole. A large preform for an axe was found near the axe.
93. Skrubbegård, Klemensker s. NM A20302. Polished, thin-butted flint axe, 40.5 cm long.
94. Vellensgård, Nyker, 060302-106. NM A42736 (marked Vedel 1871). Polished, thin-butted flint axe, resharpened and with later damage to the blade, 15.5 cm long. Found during the excavation of a ditch at a depth of c. 2 feet (c. 60 cm) in the soil.
95. Freehold farm no. 32 (Fåregård), Olsker, 060105-166. NM A42743 (marked Vedel 1871). Unpolished, thin-butted flint axe, slight damage to blade and butt, 18 cm long. Found at the bottom of a pond.
96. Bakkegård, Klemensker matr. 30a. BMa 94. Partially polished thin-butted flint axe with reknapped but not repolished blade, 18.4 cm. Found during cultivation of plot east of the farm.
97. Bjørnegård, Klemensker, matr. 87a. BMa 105. Polished and resharpened, thin-butted flint axe, with one blade corner missing, 22.5 cm long.
98. Rosendalegård, Rutsker. BMa 224. A 15 cm-long butt fragment of a partially polished, thin-butted flint axe. Found on the farm's land.
99. Stenbaltregård, Pedersker. BMa 266. Polished, thin-butted flint axe with reknapped blade without repolishing, 24 cm long.
100. Stenbaltregård (?), Pedersker. BMa 267. Polished, thin-butted flint axe, 19.6 cm long.
101. Lyngen, Ibsker s. BMa 275. Partially polished, thin-butted flint axe with damaged blade, 24.5 cm long. Found during digging work.

102. Østermarie. BMR 276. Polished and sharpened thin-butted flint axe with reknapped blade without repolishing, 19.5 cm long. Found during digging work.
103. S. Bedegadegård, Klemensker matr. 26a. BMR 396. Polished, thin-butted flint axe with reknapped blade without repolishing, 20.6 cm long.
104. Dalslunde, Østermarie. BMR 620. Polished and resharpened, thin-butted flint axe with slightly damaged blade, 32.3 cm long.
105. Langemyr, Åker. BMR 735. Polished, thin-butted flint axe, 25.8 cm long. Found in a bog.
106. Døvredal, Bodilsker. BMR 1047. Polished and much resharpened, thin-butted flint axe, 15.4 cm long.
107. Nørregård, Vestermarie matr. 55a. BMa 1051a. Polished, thin-butted flint axe with damaged blade, 20 cm long.
108. Sdr. Dyndebygård, Povlsker matr. 36a. BMa 1142. Polished, thin-butted flint axe, 25.5 cm long.
109. Sdr. Dyndebygård, Povlsker matr. 36a. BMa 1213. Polished, thin-butted flint axe with reknapped edge without repolishing, 25 cm long.
110. Bæla, Rutsker. BMa 1347. Polished and resharpened, thin-butted flint axe, 18.3 cm long. Found at the edge of a pond during its cleaning.
111. Frennegård, Ibsker. BMR 1560x7. Heavily resharpened, thin-butted flint axe, 11.8 cm long. Found around 1900 on the farm's land.
112. Risbygård, Klemensker, matr. 62-64a. BMa 1591. Unpolished, thin-butted flint axe, 22.7 cm long. Found in the farm's fields.
113. Vejrmøllegård, Åker. BMa 1638. Polished and resharpened, thin-butted flint axe, 27.7 cm long. Ploughed up near a house NW of Vejrmøllegård.
114. Julegård, Klemensker. BMa 1715. Polished and resharpened, thin-butted flint axe, 18 cm long. Found on the farm's land.
115. Glappe Mølle, Østermarie. BMa 1720. Irregularly shaped, partially polished, thin-butted flint axe, 25.6 cm long. Found in a pile of broken stones.
116. Degnegård, Rø matr. 23c. BMa 1725. A polished and resharpened, thin-butted flint axe, with broken butt, 19.2 cm long. Found on the farm's land.
117. Siegård, Østermarie matr. 35a. BMa 1802. The butt of a thin-butted flint axe with repaired and resharpened blade, 13.4 cm long. Found in the western part of the farm's fields.
118. 'Hellig Kvinde', Østermarie. BMa 1853. Polished and resharpened, thin-butted flint axe, 23 cm long. Found near 'Hellig Kvinde' between Listed and Bølshavn during the digging up of stones for breaking them up.
119. Ravnebækhuset, Rutsker matr. 46d. BMa 1880. Polished and resharpened, thin-butted flint axe, 18.1 cm long. Found in 1918 in a ploughed field near Lusekullen west of Ravnebæk, a stream which runs between the plots of land in question.
120. Lynggård, Pedersker matr. 64. BMa 2013. Polished, thin-butted flint axe with reknapped blade without repolishing, 22.5 cm long. Collected north of the farm.
121. Freehold farm no. 9 (Bredsensgård), Olsker. BMa 2080. Polished, thin-butted flint axe, 23.8 cm long. Found on the farm's land.
122. Kodal, Ibsker matr. 149. BMa 2219. Polished, thin-butted flint axe, 26 cm long. Found in 1915.
123. Smålyngen, Pedersker. BMa 2332. Polished, thin-butted flint axe with reknapped blade without repolishing, 26.5 cm long.
124. Ø. Rosendalegård, Rutsker matr. 31a. Privately owned. Polished and resharpened, thin-butted flint axe.
124a. Muredam Øst, Klemensker. BMR 3906x1. Unpolished and unpatinated, thin-butted flint axe, 28.8 cm long. One of the blade corners has been damaged in modern times, but the axe is otherwise complete.
125. St. Dammegård, Klemensker matr. 32a. Privately owned. Polished, thin-butted flint axe, 32.2 cm long. Found in 1989 under an old stable wing at the farm.
126. Kannikegård, Klemensker matr. 88a. Privately owned (BMR 895). Polished, thin-butted flint axe, 25 cm long. Found west of the farm in a depression.
127. Kirkebogård, Klemensker, matr. 78a. Privately owned. Fragment (butt) of polished, thin-butted flint axe, 14 cm long.
128. Marevadgård, Klemensker, 060104-41. Privately owned (BMR 895). Polished and resharpened, thin-butted flint axe, 16.9 cm long. Found during ploughing near the waterworks.
129. Ladegård, Klemensker matr. 58a. Privately owned. Partially polished, thin-butted flint axe, 26.8 cm long.
130. Ladegård, Klemensker matr. 58a. Privately owned. Fragment (blade fragment) of polished, thin-butted flint axe, 13.3 cm long.
131. Lille Krashavegård, Klemensker matr. 29a. Privately owned. Unpolished, thin-butted flint axe, 25.3 cm long. Found in a depression in a large meadow area WNW of the farm.
132. Bækkegård, Klemensker matr. 25a + 61g. Privately owned. Polished and resharpened, thin-butted flint axe, 23.6 cm long, with slightly damaged blade.
133. Petersborg, Klemensker matr. 15m. Privately owned. Polished, thin-butted flint axe, 28.3 cm long. Found south of Petersborg.
134. Gothegård, Klemensker matr. 13a. Privately owned. Butt fragment of polished, thin-butted flint axe, 19.6 cm long. Found NE of the farm, at the east end of the bog.
135. Rosenhøj, Klemensker. Privately owned. Unpol-

ished, thin-butted flint axe, 25.5 cm long. Found in 1936 during the excavation of a ditch near the new county road between Klemensker and Rø.
136. Ø. Rosendalegård, Rutsker matr. 31a. Privately owned. Polished and resharpened, thin-butted flint axe, 18.9 cm long. Probably found south-west of the farm.
137. Bøgely, Rø matr. 108ag, approximately. Privately owned. Polished and highly resharpened, thin-butted flint axe, 14.5 cm long.
138. Almindingsvej, Åker. The viaduct north of Åkirkeby. Privately owned. Polished, thin-butted flint axe, 26 cm long.
139. Store Nydam, Almindingen. Privately owned. Polished and resharpened, thin-butted flint axe, 15.4 cm long.
140. Nyker matr. 3bn. Privately owned. Polished, thin-butted flint axe, 28.8 cm long, with golden brown patination.
141. Nyker matr. 7f. Privately owned. Polished and resharpened, thin-butted flint axe, 19.1 cm long.
142. Engegård, Nylars, 060303-202. Privately owned (BMR 2077). Polished, thin-butted flint axe, 44 cm long.
143. Kirkebogård, Østermarie matr. 88. Privately owned. Polished and resharpened, thin-butted flint axe, 20 cm long. Based upon the patination, the axe must have been located in a wetland.
144. Vestergård, Østermarie matr. 98a. Privately owned. Fragment (blade) of polished, thin-butted flint axe, 14 cm long.

Type IIIA-B
145. Freehold farm no. 31 (Sdr. Stensebygård), Bodilsker. NM A939. Unpolished, thin-butted flint axe, 33.1 cm long.
146. Freehold farm no. 56 (Kronegård), Tingsted, Vestermarie, 060305-131. NM A42741 (marked Vedel 1871). Polished and resharpened, thin-butted flint axe with later damage to the blade, 16.9 cm long.
147. Brogård, Olsker. Privately owned. Polished, thin-butted flint axe, 18.9 cm long. Found c. 100 m east of the farm, close to an old clay pit.
148. Kjølleregård, Bodilsker matr. 42a. Privately owned. Unpolished, thin-butted flint axe, 30 cm long. Found during ploughing south of the farm.
149. Vellensbygård, Nylars matr. 16-17a. Privately owned. Thin-butted flint axe with partially completed polishing, 30.3 cm long. Found in 1930 during ploughing on a hill south of the farm, where a gravel pit is now located.

Type IIIB
150. St. Myregård, Pedersker. BMa 548. Unpolished, thin-butted flint axe with damaged blade, 31 cm long. Found in a bog at St. Myregård.

151. Allinge. BMa 582. Thin-butted flint axe, mostly unpolished but with partial polishing of one broad surface, 32 cm long. Found during the digging of a well at a depth of 4 feet (c. 126 cm) below ground.
151a. Risegård's land, Østermarie. BMa 1912. Heavy, thin-butted flint axe, partially polished on the broad surfaces and with repaired but not repolished blade, 27.2 cm long. Found in the same place as no. 169, next to a rock face with rock carvings, at a depth of c. 2 feet (c. 63 cm). Next to the axe was charcoal and black ash.
152. Frennegård, Ibsker. BMR 1560x5. Unpolished, thin-butted flint axe, 23.9 cm long. Found around 1900 on the farm's land.
153. Fredensbo, Ibsker, 060403-186. BMR 1938. Partially polished, thin-butted flint axe, 27.6 cm long. Found during the draining of the field.
154. Sjælemosen, Olsker matr. 14a. BMa 2032. An unpolished, thin-butted flint axe, 30 cm long. Found in the bog.
155. Brogård, Olsker. Privately owned. An unpolished, thin-butted flint axe, 31.3 cm long. Found c. 100 m east of the farm.
156. Ny Skovgård, Olsker matr. 8. Privately owned. Polished, thin-butted flint axe, 29 cm long. Found during ploughing west of the farm's garden.

Type IIIB-VI
157. Nylars. NM A2989. A partially polished, thin-butted flint axe, 36.5 cm long. Found during the excavation of a ditch.
158. Klemensker Plantage, Klemensker matr. 175. BMa 2178a-b. Two polished and sharpened, thin-butted flint axes, respectively 17.5 and 13.5 cm long. It is not known whether they were found together.
159. Vallensgård Mose, Åker s. BMa 2631. Unpolished, thin-butted flint axe with modern damage on the neck and blade, 21.7 cm long. Found in the bog in the 1920s.
160. Rågelundsgård, Østerlars matr. 58a. Privately owned. Fragment (part of blade) of polished and resharpened, thin-butted flint axe, 15.6 cm long. Found near the county road between Østerlars and Gudhjem.

Type VI
161. Brøddegård, Rø matr. 6 (or Olsker matr. 40). NM 6695. Unpolished, thin-butted flint axe, 29 cm long.
162. Vestermarie? BMa 137. A polished, thin-butted flint axe with reknapped blade without repolishing, 22.9 cm long.
163. Smedegård, Nyker matr. 13a. BMR 429. Unpolished, thin-butted flint axe, 17.8 cm long.
164. Degnegård, Rø matr. 23c. BMa 1726. Polished and resharpened, thin-butted flint axe, 19.8 cm long. Found on the farm's land.

165. Grubbegård, Pedersker matr. 41. Privately owned. Polished thin-butted flint axe with reknapped but unpolished blade, 20.4 cm long. Found in c. 1972 during sowing in what was originally a wetland.
166. Elledal, Almindingensvej 25, Østermarie matr. 98b. Privately owned. Butt fragment of polished, thin-butted flint axe, 12.1 cm long. The axe was collected at the watercourse Gyldenså.

Types VI-VII
167. Bondegård, Rø matr. 19a. BMa 1495. Partially polished, thin-butted flint axe, 16.3 cm long. Found around 1897 on the farm's land.
168. Sydvang, Stensebyvej 13, Bodilsker matr. 5a. Partially polished, thin-butted flint axe, 15.7 cm long. Found around 1940 in a drainage ditch south of the farm's garden. Privately owned.

Type VII
169. Risegård's land, Østermarie. BMa 1013. Partially polished, thin-butted flint axe with a slightly outward curved blade, 17.2 cm long. Found just under the ground surface next to a rock face with rock carvings.
170. Brødreengen, Vallensgård, Åker. Privately owned. Heavy, thin-butted flint axe with polished broad surfaces and unpolished narrow surfaces, 24.2 cm long, with cortex on the butt. One of the blade corners has broken off. Found during ploughing in the bog, probably after 1966.

Hoard finds containing thin-butted flint axes
171. Freehold farm no. 9 (Blæsbjerggård), Nyker. NM A943-44. One unpolished and one partially polished thin-butted flint axe of type VI/VII, respectively 20.1 and 22 cm long. Found together at a depth of 3 feet (c. 90 cm) next to a large stone (Nielsen 1977, 128 no. 130).
172. Almindingen, Østermarie. NM A8272-73. Two polished, thin-butted flint axes, both of type IIIA and both 36.6 cm long. One of the axes, however, has very narrow and parallel narrow sides, and can therefore perhaps be attributed to type IV (Nielsen 1977, 125-26 no. 89). Found together at a depth of 2 feet (c. 60 cm) east of Almindingen, in a forestry area owned by the state.
173. Bredsensgård, Olsker. NM A10806-07. Two unpolished, thin-butted flint axes, one of which is 33.4 cm long and of type IIIA, the other, which is 34.5 cm long, cannot be identified more closely than as type IIIA/B. The axes were found at the edge of a small boghole at the foot of a hill, probably close to each other at a shallow depth (Nielsen 1977, 125 no. 67).
174. Stavehøl, Østerlars matr. 17b. NM A25658-63. Hoard consisting of six very small, thin-butted flint axes of type I, five of which are polished and one unpolished.
(1) Unpolished, thin-butted axe, 16.8 cm long. The final knapping has only been undertaken from two side edges on the same side of the axe (fig. 5.2:1).
(2) Thin-butted axe with polished broad surfaces and partially polished narrow surfaces, 15.7 cm long. With asymmetrically resharpened blade produced by reknapping one of the broad surfaces closest to the blade, without repolishing (fig. 5.2:2).
(3) Thin-butted axe polished on all four sides, 16.9 cm long, with asymmetrically resharpened blade produced by reknapping of one broad surface closest to the blade without repolishing (fig. 5.2:3).
(4) Thin-butted axe polished on all four sides, 16.2 cm long. One blade corner has broken off (fig. 5.2:4).
(5) Thin-butted axe polished on all four sides, 14.2 cm long, resharpened and repolished on both sides, with finely polished blade area. One blade corner has broken off (fig. 5.2:5).
(6) Thin-butted axe polished on all four sides, 12.9 cm long, resharpened and repolished on both sides, with finely polished blade area. But there was subsequent symmetrical resharpening of the blade, which has not been repolished (fig. 5.2:6).
Found on a plot belonging to Freehold farm no. 12 in 1909 or before. According to the farm owner's account, at a depth of up to 40 cm below the ground surface, a rectangle made up of small stones was found, which was covered by two thin slabs. Inside the coffin were the six flint axes with their blades turned outward, like in a six-pointed star shape. The location is described as 'near a slope opposite a rather steep stream bank'. The axes were transferred from Bornholms Museum to the National Museum in 1909 (Nielsen 1977, 122 no. 24).
175. Brødreengen, Vallensgård, Åker, 060205-175. BMa 378-79. See chapter 2, find no. 1.
176. Bakkely, Lille Bakkegård, Olsker. BMa 2104:1-7. Hoard with thin-butted axes of type I, II and I/IIIA.
(1) Polished, thin-butted flint axe of type I, 29.6 cm long (fig. 5.3:1).
(2) Polished and resharpened thin-butted flint axe of type II with broken-off blade, 24 cm long (fig. 5.3:2).
(3) Four-sided, thin-butted flint axe of type I with polishing started near the blade, 25.2 cm long (fig. 5.3:3).
(4) Unpolished, thin-butted flint axe of type I/III, 25 cm long (fig. 5.3:4).
(5) Four-sided, unpolished, thin-butted axe with slightly outward curved blade, 15.5 cm long (fig. 5.3:5).
(6) Polished and resharpened, thin-butted flint

axe of type I, with broken-off butt, 13 cm long (fig. 5.3:6).

(7) Two-sided, unpolished flint axe, 24.7 cm long, probable a preform for a thin-butted flint axe of type I (fig. 5.3:7).

The axes were found in a crevice on the land of Freehold farm no. 17. They were found together in the crevice, which sloped steeply down. Both above and below the axes, the crevice was filled with fist-sized stones, which also formed a layer that covered the axes. Acquired in 1928 (Nielsen 1977, 122 no. 22).

177. Vallensgård, Åker. BMa 2227a-b. See chapter 2, find no. 4.
178. Brødreengen, Vallensgård, Åker, 060205-199. Privately owned (NM 525/68). See chapter 2, find no. 2.
179. Brødreengen, Vallensgård, Åker, 060205-199. Privately owned. See chapter 2, find no. 3.

Hoards containing thin-bladed flint axes

180. Hallegård, Nyker. NM A788-89. Hoard with two thin-bladed axes.

(1) Thin-bladed flint axe of type b1, polished on all four sides and 13.8 cm long (fig. 5.4:1).

(2) Thin-bladed flint axe of type b1, polished on the broad surfaces and partially on the narrow surfaces, 12.3 cm long and slightly resharpened (fig. 5.4:2). Found in 1869 during the excavation of a ditch in a field. The axes had been placed upright beside one another in a small stone coffin, in a 1 foot (c. 30 cm) square, covered by a quite large, flat stone and filled with ash and charcoal (S. Müller 1886, 218 no. 14; Vedel 1886, 250; Rech 1979, 70 and 110 no. 203, here incorrectly named "Hanegaard").

Thin-butted axes of material other than flint

181. Arnager, Nylars. NM A38795. Thin-butted axe of fine-grained rock, 12 cm long. The blade is very damaged.
182. Bukkegård, Poulsker. BMa 268. Thin-butted axe of fine-grained rock, 22.3 cm long, with domed broad surfaces. Well preserved, but with evidence of use indicated by small pieces that have broken off the blade. Found on the north side of Rispebjerg.
183. Vasegård, Ibsker. BMa 1153. Thin-butted axe of fine-grained rock, 13 cm long. The butt is somewhat irregular and pointed. One broad surface is more domed than the other.
184. Klippedam, Østerlars. BMa 1501. Thin-butted axe of fine-grained rock, 22.7 cm long. It has been broken into two pieces. The broad surfaces are domed.
185. St. Klintegård, Vestermarie. Privately owned. Pecked preform for a heavy, thin-butted axe of fine-grained rock, 28 cm long. The butt is pointed. Large pieces have broken off the blade.
186. Dyrstenshøj, Klemensker. BMa 1763. Thin-butted axe of fine-grained rock, 15.2 cm long. One broad surface is more domed than the other. The blade is damaged on one side, which is thought to have been rectified by knapping and polishing.
187. St. Myregård, Pedersker, matr. 16a. Privately owned. Thin-butted axe of fine-grained rock, 14 cm long. With wide narrow surfaces and slightly domed broad surfaces. The butt is pointed. The blade slopes, which must be the result of damage that has been rectified by knapping and polishing.
188. Rabækkegård, Ibsker. Privately owned. A 9.8 cm-long blade of what, on the basis of the parallel narrow sides, must have been a thin-butted axe of fine-grained rock. The broad surfaces are very domed.
189. Rævekulebakke, Limensgård, Åker, 060205-198. Privately owned. An 8 cm-long blade area of what, based upon the parallel narrow sides, must have been a thin-butted axe of fine-grained rock. Irregular, with slightly domed broad surfaces. The blade is damaged. Found during collection at the settlement area (Finds list I no. 34).

Finds list V

STONE BATTLE AXES

The Early Neolithic battle axes from Central Europe and South Scandinavia have been examined and divided into types by M. Zápotocký (1992) and, in relation to Denmark, K. Ebbesen (1998). Reference is made to the typological divisions of both authors. Two shaft-hole axes from Bornholm which appear in Zápotocký's catalogue (Finds list I nos. 580 and 623) are not included here, as the authors do not consider them to be Early Neolithic battle axes. Illustrations of the axes can be seen in fig. 8.11, where they are numbered in the same way as in the list below.

Zápotocký's Group FI-II

1. Hjorthøj, Østerlars (matr. 44ng). Privately owned (now missing). A 12.9 cm-long preform for a battle axe with incompletely bored-through shaft hole.

Zápotocký's Group FIII, Ebbesen type I

2. Kokkedal, Klemensker. BMa 1158. A 15.5 cm-long battle axe with a started shaft hole. Slightly damaged on the blade and both broad surfaces near the shaft hole.
3. Gudhjem. NM 3798. A well-preserved, 17.7 cm-long battle axe (Zápotocký 1992, Finds list I no. 593 and Table 21.9).
4. Klemensker. BMa 2051. Half of a battle axe, which has broken at the shaft hole. The object measures 9.1 cm from the break to the broken-off blade.

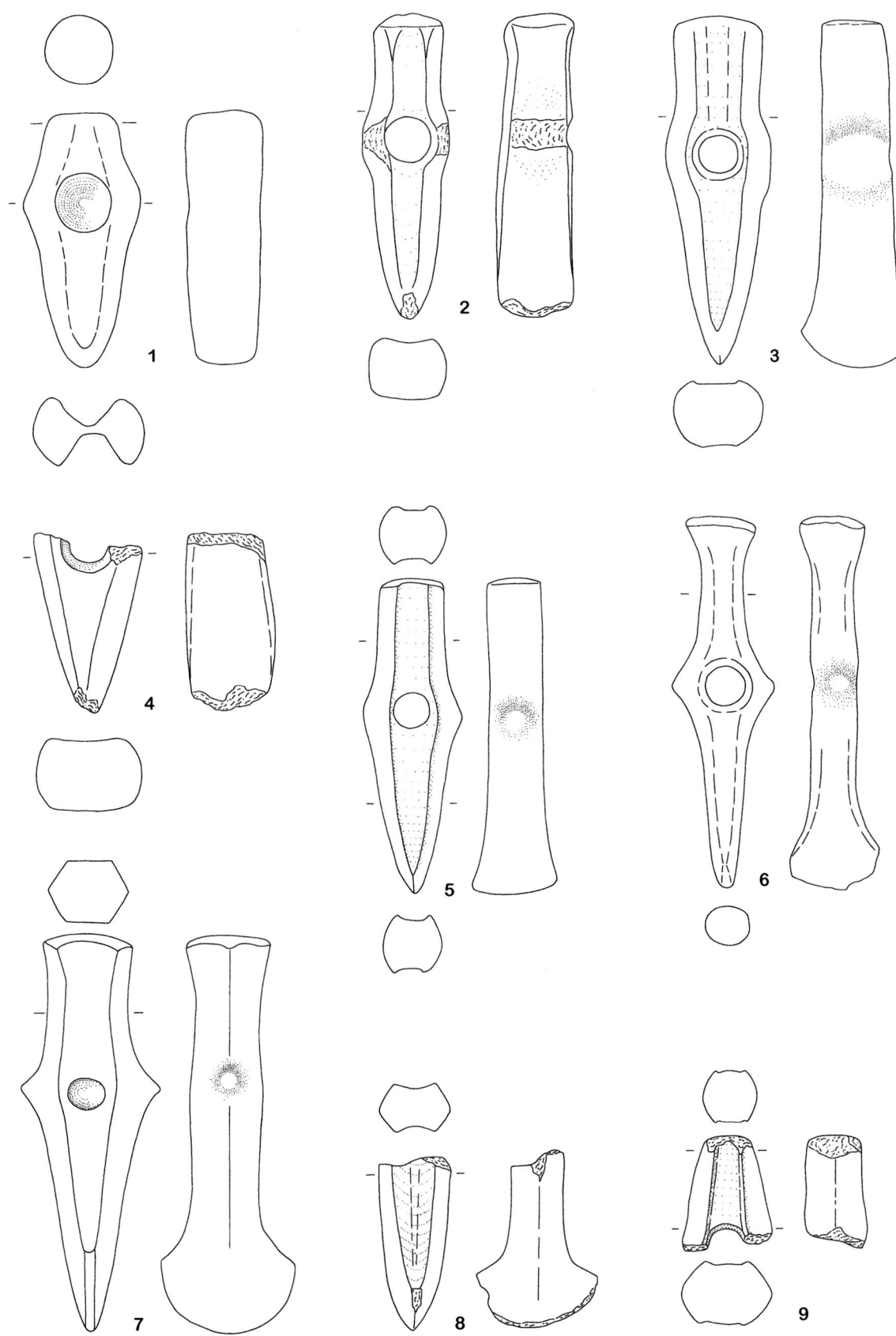

Fig. 8.11. Early Neolithic battle axes (Finds list V nos. 1-15). 1:3.

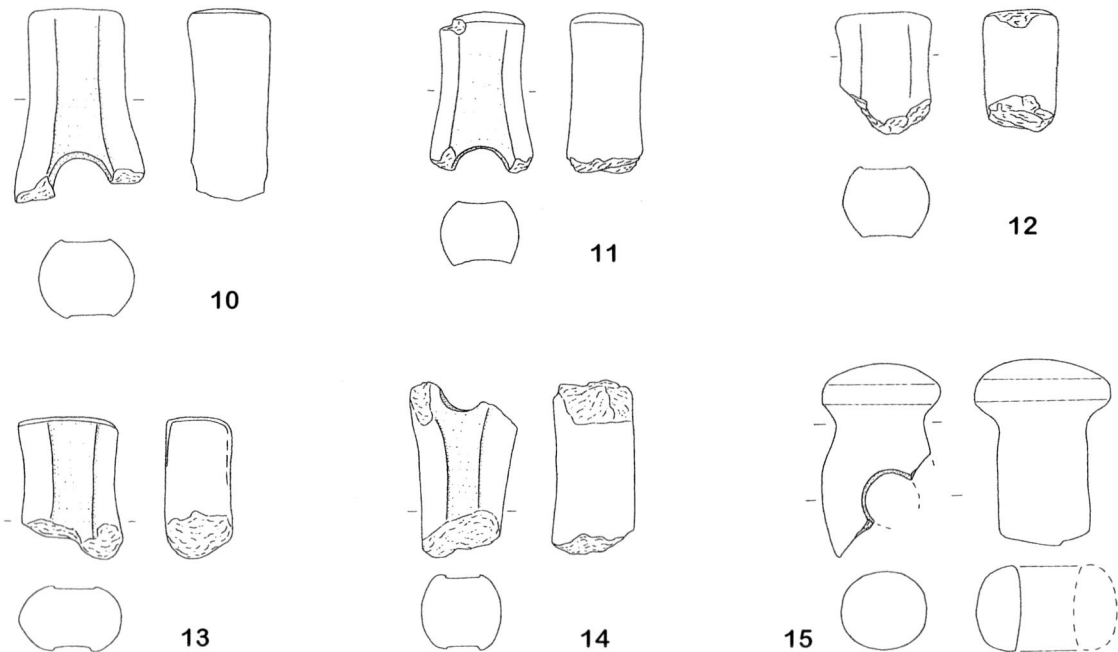

Západotocký's Group FIV, Ebbesen type II

5. Vestermarie. NM A11037. A well-preserved, 16 cm-long battle axe (fig. 6.1:1) (Zápotocký 1992, Finds list I no. 643 and Table 30.1. Ebbesen 1998, 106).
6. Ellevang, Sdr. Ellebygård, Vestermarie. BMR 2086. An 18.9 cm-long battle axe, the surface of which is partially broken off. One of the blade corners has broken off (fig. 6.1:3). Found in a spring together with rib bones (not preserved).
7. Smedegård, Åker. Privately owned. A well-preserved, 20.2 cm-long battle axe with started shaft hole (fig. 6.1:2). Found near a spring, c. 500 m SW of Smedegård.
8. Rødbjerg, Tornbygård, Klemensker. Privately owned. A 9 cm-long fragment of part of the blade of a battle axe with broken-off pieces along the blade.

Západotocký's Group FIII-IV, Ebbesen's types I-II

9. Smålyngen, Pedersker. BMa 341. A 6 cm-long fragment of the blade or butt of a battle axe, which has broken off at the shaft hole.
10. Lindet, Østermarie. BMa 1910. An 8 cm-long butt fragment of a battle axe, which is broken off at the shaft hole.
11. Vallensgård II. Privately owned. A 6.6 cm-long butt fragment of a battle axe, which is broken off at the shaft hole (fig. 6.2:1). Collected from the field surface.
12. Vallensgård. BMR 1618. A 5 cm-long butt fragment of a battle axe, which is broken off at the shaft hole. Collected from the field surface.
13. Pedersker? BMR 518x3. A 5.9 cm-long butt fragment of a battle axe, which is broken off at the shaft hole.
14. Ellesgård, Østermarie. BMa 410. A 7.2 cm-long fragment of the blade or butt of a battle axe, which is broken off at the shaft hole.

Západotocký's Group KVIII

15. Myregård, Pedersker. Privately owned. A 7.8 cm-long fragment of the butt of a battle axe with a butt-knob, broken at the shaft hole (fig. 6.2:2).

Finds list VI

FLINT HALBERDS

1. Biskopsenge, Ibsker, 060403-143. NM A2842 (fig. 8.12:1). Acquired in 1877. A 30.7 cm-long, symmetrical halberd with brown patination. Complete, with the exception of the outermost point, which probably broke off in prehistoric times. Notches on one edge are without patination and must be damage of a more recent date. Produced by fine, regular pressure flaking, and with polishing on both sides near the base and at the point. Found near a large stone in one of the fields at Grynegård.
2. Bakkegård, Klemensker. BMa 197 (fig. 8.12:2). A 17 cm-long halberd with dark brown patination. It is coarsely knapped and curved when viewed from the edge. Broken at the base, where the break is patinated, so the damage probably occurred in prehistoric times. Found north of Bakkegård.
3. Ø. Pilegård, Klemensker. BMa 200 (fig. 8.12:3). The point of a halberd, 13.9 cm long. Regular in shape. A piece of the base has broken off, and the break has the same light grey patination as the rest of

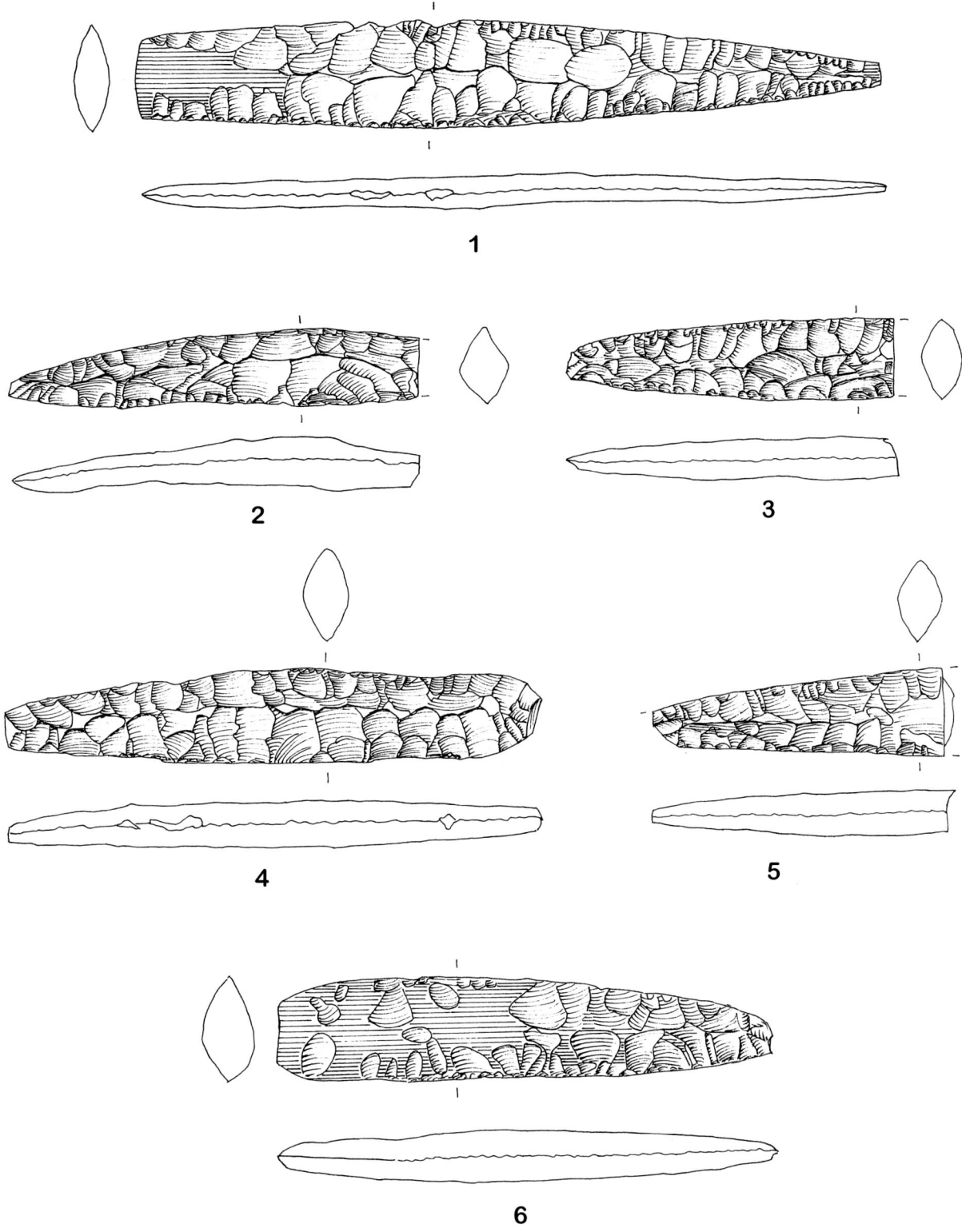

Fig. 8.12. Halberds of flint (Finds list VI nos. 1-6). 2:5.

the surface of the halberd. The break therefore probably occurred in prehistoric times. The point is slightly damaged. Rust marks on both sides have been caused by agricultural implements. Found on the hill east of the farm.

4. Dammegård, Pedersker. BMa 1952 (fig. 8.12:4). Halberd, which is complete apart from its broken point, 22.3 cm long. The halberd was originally regular in shape, but has many notches at the edges, probably resulting from its intensive use.

The whole surface, including the break near the point, is patinated in the same light brown colour, so the damage must have occurred in prehistory. The halberd is not polished, but the raised areas are very worn. Found c. 1890 in one of the farm's fields.

5. Thoruppegård, Klemensker. BMa 2360 (fig. 8.12:5). The point of a halberd, 12.7 cm long. Regular in shape, with light grey patination and small rust patches caused by agricultural implements. The halberd is broken around the middle, and the surface of the break has the same patination as the rest of the surface. This damage therefore probably occurred in prehistoric times. The point is broken, and here the surface of the break is not patinated, which may indicate that this damage occurred in more recent times. Found in one of the farm's fields.
6. Klippely, Klemensker. Privately owned. Complete halberd, 20.6 cm long (fig. 6.5 and 8.12:6). Not completely regular in shape, with large broken-off pieces. Partially polished, mainly on one side. The surface is not heavily patinated, its colour varying between light and dark grey. Damage, in the form of pieces that have broken off from the point and base, probably occurred in prehistoric times.
7. Lille Dammegård, Klemensker. BMR 3488x1. An 11 cm-long, roughly knapped halberd fragment or perhaps more likely a preform for a halberd, with a break at both ends. Not especially patinated.

Finds list VII

COPPER AXES
1. Vester Bedegadegård, Klemensker, 060104-237. NM A52087. Pointed-butted axe of copper, 17.8 cm long, with pointed oval cross section. The surface is corroded (fig. 4.8:2-3). Found in 1992, in a hollow on the surface of a field (Vandkilde 1996, 474 no. 873; Klassen 2000, no. 34, with metal analysis; Klassen 2010).
2. Slusegård, Pedersker, 060203-136. NM B3459. Flat axe blade of copper, 12.3 cm long (fig. 7.26:2). Found by J.A. Jørgensen in a flat, sandy field north of Slusegård and sent to the National Museum in 1884 (Aner & Kersten 1977, no. 1476; Vandkilde 1996, no. 53; Klassen 2000, no. 10 with metal analysis).
3. Nexø, with no precise finds location. BMa 2189. Axe blade of copper, 10.6 cm long. Corroded and with uneven surface (fig. 7.26:1). Given to the museum in 1935 (Aner & Kersten 1977, no. 1464 I; Vandkilde 1996, no. 52; Klassen 2000, no. 59). No metal analysis.

Bibliography

Ahlström, T. 2009. *Underjordiska dödsriken*. Coast to coast books no. 18. Göteborgs Universitet, Institutionen för arkeologi, Göteborg.

Andersen, N.H. 1997. *The Sarup Enclosures. The Funnel Beaker Culture of the Sarup site including two causewayed camps compared to the contemporary settlements in the area and other European enclosures*. Jysk Arkæologisk Selskabs skrifter XXXIII:1. Højbjerg.

Andersen, N.H. 1999. *Saruppladsen. Sarup vol. 2*. Jysk Arkæologisk Selskabs Skrifter XXXIII:2, Moesgård Museum, Højbjerg.

Andersen, N.H. 2000. Kult og ritualer i den ældre bondestenalder. *Kuml* 2000, 13-57.

Andersen, N.H. 2009. Sarupområdet på Sydvestfyn i slutningen af 4. årtusinde f. Kr. In Schülke, A. (ed.) *Plads og rum i tragtbægerkulturen. Bidrag fra Arbejdsmødet på Nationalmuseet, 22. september 2005*. Nordiske Fortidsminder Ser. C, bind 6, Det Kongelige Nordiske Oldskriftselskab, København, 25-44.

Andersen, N.H. 2013. Die Grabenanlagen von Sarup (Dänemark). In Meller, H. (ed.) *3300 BC. Mysteriöse Steinzeittote und ihre Welt*. Landesmuseum für Vorgeschichte, Halle, 222-29.

Andersen, N.H. 2015. Frydenlund – Early Neolithic settlement and "barkaer" structures in the Sarup area. In Brink, K., Hydén, S., Jennbert, K., Larsson, L. & Olausson, D. (eds) *Neolithic Diversities. Perspectives from a conference in Lund, Sweden*. Acta Archaeologica Lundensia Series in 8°, No. 65, 117-27.

Andersen, N.H. 2018. Sarup revisited. Archaeological reality and realities of archaeology. *Acta Archaeologica* 89, 31-62.

Andersen, N.H. 2019. House sites under burial monuments in the Sarup area of South-West Funen. In Sparrevohn, L., Kastholm, O.T. & Nielsen, P.O. (eds) *Houses for the Living. Two-aisled Houses from the Neolithic and Early Bronze Age in Denmark*. Nordiske Fortidsminder Vol. 31:1. The Royal Society of Northern Antiquaries, Copenhagen, 133-44.

Andersen, N.H. & Madsen, T. 1978. Skåle og bægre med storvinkelbånd fra yngre stenalder. Overgangen mellem tidlig- og mellemneolitikum. *Kuml* 1977, 131-60.

Andersen, S.H. 1991. Norsminde. A "Køkkenmødding" with Late Mesolithic and Early Neolithic Occupation. *Journal of Danish Archaeology* 8, 1989, 13-40.

Andersen, S.H. 1993. Bjørnsholm. A Stratified Køkkenmødding on the Central Limfjord, North Jutland. *Journal of Danish Archaeology* 10, 1991, 59-96.

Andersen, S.H. 1994. Norsminde, ein Muschelhaufen mit später Ertebølle- und früher Trichterbecherkultur. In Hoika, J. (ed.) *Beiträge zur frühneolithischen Trichterbecherkultur im westlichen Ostseegebiet. 1. Internationale Trichterbechersymposium in Schleswig vom 4. bis 7. März 1985*. Untersuchungen und Materialien zur Steinzeit in Schleswig-Holstein 1, 11-49. Neumünster.

Andersen, S.H. 2000. 'Køkkenmøddinger' (Shell Middens) in Denmark: a Survey. *Proceedings of the Prehistoric Society* 66, 361-84.

Andersen, S.H. 2007. Shell middens ("Køkkenmøddinger") in Danish Prehistory as a reflection of the marine environment. In Milner, N., Craig, O.E. & Bailey, G.N. (eds) *Shell Middens in Atlantic Europe*. Oxbow Books, Oxford, 31-45.

Andersen, S.H. 2008. The Mesolithic – Neolithic transition in Western Denmark seen from a kitchen midden perspective. A survey. In Fokkens, H., Coles, B.J., Van Gijn, A.L., Kleijne, J.P., Ponjee, H.H. & Slappendel, C.G. (eds) *Between Foraging and Farming*. Analecta Prehistorica Leidensia 40, 67-74.

Andersen, S.H. 2009. *Ronæs Skov. Marinarkæologiske undersøgelser af en kystboplads fra Ertebølletid*. Jysk Arkæologisk Selskabs Skrifter 64, Nationalmuseet / Moesgård Museum, Højbjerg.

Andersen, S.H. 2011. Kitchen middens and the early pottery of Denmark. In Hartz, S., Lüth, F. & Terberger, T. (eds) *Frühe Keramik im Ostseeraum – Datierung und Sozialer Kontext. Internationaler Workshop in Schleswig vom 20. bis 21. Oktober 2006*. Bericht der Römisch-Germanischen Kommission 89, 2008 (2011), 191-215.

Andersen, S.H. 2013. *Tybrind Vig. Submerged Mesolithic settlements in Denmark*. Moesgård Museum / The National Museum of Denmark / Jutland Archaeological Society Publications Vol. 77, Højbjerg.

Andersen, S.H. & Johansen, E. 1992. An Early Neolithic Grave at Bjørnsholm, North Jutland. *Journal of Danish Archaeology* 9, 1990, 38-58.

Andersen, S.T. 1991. Natural and Cultural Landscapes Since the Ice Age. Shown by Pollen Analyses from Small Hollows in a Forested Area in Denmark. *Journal of Danish Archaeology* 8, 1989, 188-99.

Andersen, S.T. 1992. Early- and middle-Neolithic agriculture in Denmark: Pollen spectra from soils in burial mounds of the Funnel Beaker Culture. *Journal of European Archaeology* 1, 153-80.

Andersen, S.T. 1993. Early agriculture. In Hvass, S. & Storgaard, B. (eds) *Digging into the Past. 25 Years of Archaeology in Denmark*. The Royal Society of Northern Antiquaries / Jutland Archaeological Society, Højbjerg, 88-91.

Andersson, M., Artursson, M. & Brink, K. 2016. Early Neolithic Landscape and Society in South-West Scania – New Results and Perspectives. *Journal of Neolithic Archaeology*, 19 July 2016. www.j-n-a.org, 23-114.

Aner, E. & Kersten, K. 1977. *Bornholms, Maribo, Odense und Svendborg Amter. Die Funde der älteren Bronzezeit des nordischen Kreises in Dänemark, Schleswig-Holstein und Niedersachsen Band III*. København/Neumünster, Wachholtz Verlag.

Apel, J. 2001. *Daggers Knowledge & Power. The Social Aspects of Flint-Dagger Technology in Scandinavia 2350-1500 cal BC*. Coast to coast-book 3, Uppsala.

Apel, J.-E., Bäckström, Y., Hallgren, F., Knutsson, K., Lekberg, P., Olsson, E., Steineke, M. & Sundström, L. 1995. Fågelbacken och trattbägarsamhället. Samhällsorganisation och rituella samlingsplatser vid övergången till bofast tillvaro i östra Mellansverige. *TOR* 27:1, 47-132.

Arbogast, R.-M. 1998. Contribution de l'archéozoologie du site Michelsberg de Mairy (Ardennes) à l'étude de l'origine de la variabilité des faunes du Néolithique récent du Nord de la France. In Biel, J., Schlichtherle, H., Strobel, M. & Zeeb, A. (eds) *Die Michelsberger Kultur und ihre Randgebiete – Probleme der Entstehung, Chronologie und des Siedlungswesens. Kolloquium Hemmenhofen, 21.-23.2.1997 (Jens Lüning zum 60. Geburtstag)*. Materialhefte zur Archäologie in Baden-Württemberg 43, Stuttgart, 135-42.

Bägerfeldt, L. 1992. *En studie av neolitikum på Gotland. Problem och konsekvenser utifrån undersökningen av en dös och neolitiska lösfynd*. ARKEO-Förlaget, Gamleby.

Bagge, A. & Kaelas, L. 1950. *Die Funde aus Dolmen und Ganggräbern in Schonen, Schweden. Bd. I, Das Härad Villand*. Kungl. Vitterhets Historie och Antikvitets Akademien, Stockholm.

Bagge, A. & Kjellmark, K. 1939. *Stenåldersboplatserna vid Siretorp i Blekinge*. Kungl. Vitterhets Historie och Antikvitets Akademien, Stockholm.

Bakker, J.A. 1976. On the possibility of reconstructing roads from the TRB period. *Berichten ROB* 26, 63-91.

Bakker, J.A. 1992. *The Dutch Hunebedden. Megalithic Tombs of the Funnel Beaker Culture*. International Monographs in Prehistory, Archaeological Series 2. Ann Arbor, Michigan.

Bakker, J.A., Vogel, J.C. & Wislański, T. 1969. TRB and other C_{14} Dates from Poland (ca 4350-1350 BC and 800-900). *Helinium* 9, Part A 3-27, Part B 209-238.

Balcer, B. 1983. *Wytwórczość narzędzi krzemiennych w neolicie ziem Polski*. Polska Akademia Nauk, Wrocław.

Ballin, T.B. 2013. Felsite axeheads reduction. The flow from quarry pit to discard/deposition. In Mahler, D.L. (ed.) *The Border of Farming. Shetland and Scandinavia. Papers from the symposium in Copenhagen September 19th to the 21st 2012*. Northern Worlds, The National Museum of Denmark, Copenhagen, 73-91.

Barclay, G.J., Brophy, K. & MacGregor, G. 2002. A Neolithic building af Claish Farm near Callander, Stirling Council, Scotland, U.K. *Antiquity* 76, 23-24.

Bastian, W. 1961. Das jungsteinzeitliche Flachgräberfeld von Ostorf, Kreis Schwerin. *Jahrbuch für Bodendenkmalpflege in Mecklenburg* 1961, 7-130.

Bayliss, A., Healy, F., Whittle, A. & Cooney, G. 2011. Neolithic narratives: British and Irish enclosures in their timescapes. In Whittle, A., Healy, F. & Bayliss, A. (eds) *Gathering Time. Dating the Early Neolithic Enclosures of Southern Britain and Ireland*, Vol. 2, Oxbow Books, Oxford & Oakville, 682-847.

Beck, M.R. 2013. Højensvej Høj 7 – en tidligneolitisk langhøj med flere faser. *Aarbøger for nordisk Oldkyndighed og Historie* 2011-2012, 33-117.

Becker, C.J. 1947. Mosefundne Lerkar fra yngre Stenalder. *Aarbøger for nordisk Oldkyndighed og Historie* 1947, 1-318.

Becker, C.J. 1951. Den grubekeramiske kultur i Danmark. *Aarbøger for nordisk Oldkyndighed og Historie* 1950, 153-274.

Becker, C.J. 1952. Maglemosekultur paa Bornholm. *Aarbøger for nordisk Oldkyndighed og Historie* 1951 (1952), 96-177.

Becker, C.J. 1955. Stenalderbebyggelsen ved Store Valby i Vestsjælland. Problemer omkring tragtbægerkulturens ældste og yngste fase. *Aarbøger for nordisk Oldkyndighed og Historie* 1954, 127-97 (for English version see Becker 2002).

Becker, C.J. 1956. A Neolithic Antler Weapon from Rye Aa, North Jutland. *Acta Archaeologica* 27, 148-53.

Becker, C.J. 1975. Hovedlinier i Bornholms oldtidshistorie. *Bornholmske Samlinger* 1975, 1-41.

Becker, C.J. 1990. *Nørre Sandegård. Arkæologiske undersøgelser på Bornholm 1948-1952*. Det Kgl. Danske Videnskabernes Selskab, Historisk-filosofiske Skrifter 13. København.

Becker, C.J. 1993a. Flintminer og flintdistribution ved Limfjorden. *Kort- og råstofstudier omkring Limfjorden*. Limfjordsprojektet, Rapport nr. 6, Århus, 111-134.

Becker, C.J. 1993b. Cult houses of the Funnel Beaker Culture. In Hvass, S. & Storgaard, B. (eds) *Digging into the Past. 25 Years of Archaeology in Denmark*. The Royal Society of Northern Antiquaries / Jutland Archaeological Society, Aarhus, 110-11.

Becker, C.J. 2002. The Early Neolithic Settlement at Store Valby, West Zealand. In Fischer, A. & Kristiansen, K. (eds) *The Neolithisation of Denmark. 150 years of debate*, 145-64. J.R. Collis Publications, Sheffield.

Behrens, H. 1973. *Die Jungsteinzeit im Mittelelbe-Saale-Gebiet.* Veröffentlichungen des Landesmuseums für Vorgeschichte in Halle, Bd. 27. Berlin.

Behrens, H. & Schröter, E. 1980. *Siedlungen und Gräber der Trichterbecherkultur und Schnurkeramik bei Halle (Saale).* Veröffentlichungen des Landesmuseum für Vorgeschichte in Halle 34. Berlin.

Bellwood, P. 2005. *First Farmers. The Origins of Agricultural Societies.* Blackwell Publishing, Malden (USA), Oxford (UK), Carlton (AUS).

Bellwood, P. & Oxenham, M. 2008. The Expansions of Farming Societies and the Role of the Neolithic Demographic Transition. In Bocquet-Appel, J.-P. & Bar-Yosef, O. (eds) *The Neolithic Demographic Transition and its Consequences.* Springer-Verlag, N.Y., 13-34.

Bennike, P. 1985. *Palaeopathology of Danish Skeletons. A Comparative Study of Demography, Disease and Injury.* Akademisk Forlag, København.

Bennike, P. 1999. The Early Neolithic Danish bog finds: a strange group of people! In Coles, B., Coles, J. & Jørgensen, M.S. (eds) *Bog Bodies, Sacred Sites and Wetland Archaeology. Proceedings of a conference held by WARP and the National Museum of Denmark, in conjunction with Silkeborg Museum, Jutland, September 1996.* WARP Occasional Paper 12, Exeter, 27-32.

Bennike, P. 2003. Ancient Trepanations and Differential Diagnoses: A Re-evaluation of Skeletal Remains from Denmark. In Arnott, R., Finger, S. & Smith, C.U.M. (eds) *Trepanation. History – Discovery – Theory.* Swets & Zeitlinger, Lisse, The Netherlands, 95-115.

Bennike, P. & Alexandersen, V. 2007. Population Plasticity in Southern Scandinavia. From Oysters and Fish to Gruel and Meat. In Cohen, M.N. & Crane-Kramer, G.M.M. (eds) *Ancient Health. Skeletal Indicators of Agricultural and Economic Intensification.* American Journal of Physical Anthropology vol. 138:4, 130-48.

Bennike, P. & Ebbesen, K. 1987. The Bog Find from Sigersdal. Human Sacrifice in the Early Neolithic; with a contribution by Lise Bender Jørgensen. *Journal of Danish Archaeology* 5, 1986, 85-115.

Bennike, P., Ebbesen, K. & Jørgensen, L.B. 1986. Early neolithic skeletons from Bolkilde bog, Denmark. *Antiquity* LX, 199-209.

Beran, J. 1998. Die Michelsberger Fundgruppen in Mitteldeutschland. In Biel, J., Schlichterle, H., Strobel, M. & Zeeb, A. (eds) *Die Michelsberger Kultur und ihre Randgebiete. Probleme der Entstehung, Chronologie und des Siedlungswesens. Kolloquium Hemmenhofen 21.-23.2.1997.* Materialhefte zur Archäologie 43, Stuttgart, 73-83.

Beran, J. 2000. Der mitteldeutsche Raum als Grenzland vorgeschichtlicher Kulturkreise in Jung- und Endneolithikum. In Beier, H.-J. & Einicke, R. (eds) *Varia Neolithica I.* Beiträge zur Ur- und Frühgeschichte Mitteleuropas 22, Weissbach, 121-32.

Beran, J. & Wetzel, G. 2014. Die neolithische Siedlung der Michelsberger Kultur Wustermark 21, Lkr. Havelland. *Veröffentlichungen zur brandenburgischen Landesarchäologie* 46, 2012 (2014), 37-141.

Berggren, Å., Högberg, A., Olausson, D. & Rudebeck, E. 2016. Early Neolithic flint mining at Södra Sallerup, Scania, Sweden. *Archaeologia Polona* 54, 167-80.

Berglund *et al.* 1991a. Berglund, B.E., Malmer, N. & Persson, T. 1991. Landscape-ecological aspects of long-term changes in the Ystad area. In Berglund, B.E. (ed.) *The Cultural Landscape during 6000 years in southern Sweden – the Ystad Project.* Ecological Bulletins 41, 405-24, Copenhagen.

Berglund *et al.* 1991b. Berglund, B.E., Larsson, L., Lewan, N., Olsson, G.A. & Skansjö, S. 1991. Ecolocical and social factors behind the landscape changes. In Berglund, B.E. (ed.) *The Cultural Landscape during 6000 years in southern Sweden – the Ystad Project.* Ecological Bulletins 41, 425-45, Copenhagen.

Berglund, B.E. & Welinder, S. 1972. Stratigrafin vid Siretorp. *Fornvännen* 1972, 73-93.

Bertemes, F. 1991. Untersuchungen zur Funktion der Erdwerke der Michelsberger Kultur in Rahmen der kupferzeitlichen Zivilisation. In Lichardus, J. (ed.) *Die Kupferzeit als historische Epoche. Symposium Saarbrücken und Otzenhausen 6.-13.11.1988.* Saarbrücker Beiträge zur Altertumskunde 55, Rudolf Habelt, Bonn, 441-64.

Bertemes, F. & Northe, A. 2012. Goseck – Die "erste" Kreisgrabenanlage in Sachsen-Anhalt. In Bertemes, F. & Meller, H. (eds) *Neolithische Kreisgrabenanlagen in Europa/Neolithic Circular Enclosures in Europe. Internationale Arbeitstagung 7.-9. Mai 2004 in Goseck (Sachsen-Anhalt).* Tagungen des Landesmuseums für Vorgeschichte Halle Bd. 8, 11-39.

Best, E. 1975. *The Pa Maori. An account of the fortified villages of the Maori in pre-European and modern times; illustrating methods of defence by means of ramparts, fosses, scarps and stockades.* A.R. Shearer, Wellington (reprint of first edition 1927).

Boelicke, U. 1977. Das neolithische Erdwerk Urmitz. *Acta Praehistorica et Archaeologica* 7/8, 1976/77, 73-121.

Bogaard, A. 2004. *Neolithic Farming in Central Europe. An Archaeobotanical Study of Crop Husbandry Practices.* Routledge, London.

Bogucki, P. 1993. Animal traction and household economies in Neolithic Europe. *Antiquity* 67, no. 256, 492-503.

Boujot, C. & Cassen, S. 1993. A Pattern of evolution for the Neolithic funerary structures of the west of France. *Antiquity* 67, 477-91.

Brace, S., Diekmann, Y., Booth, T.J., van Dorp, L., Faltyskova, Z., Rohland, N., Swapan Mallick, S., Olalde, I., Ferry, M., Michel, M., Oppenheimer, J., Broomandkhoshbacht, N., Stewardson, K., Martiniano, R., Walsh, S., Kayser, M., Charlton, S., Hellenthal, G., Armit, I., Schulting, R., Craig, O.E., Sheridan, A., Pearson, M.P., Stringer, C., Reich, D., Thomas, M.G. & Barnes, I. 2019. Ancient genomes indicate population replacement in Early Neolithic Britain. *Nature Ecology & Evolution*, vol. 3, May 2019, 765-771, www.nature.com/natecolevol.

Bradley, R. 1990. The *Passage of Arms. An archaeological*

analysis of prehistoric hoards and votive deposits. Cambridge Univ. Press, Cambridge.

Bradley, R. 2005. *Ritual and Domestic Life in Prehistoric Europe.* Routledge, London & N.Y.

Brandt, G., Haak, W., Adler, C.J., Roth, C., Szécsényi-Nagy, A., Karimnia, S., Möller-Rieker, S., Meller, H., Ganslmeier, R., Friederich, S., Dresely, V., Nicklisch, N., Pickrell, J.K., Sirocko, F., Reich, D., Cooper, A., Alt, K.W. & The Genographic Consortium 2013. Ancient DNA Reveals Key Stages in the Formation of Central European Mitochondrial Genetic Diversity. *Science* vol. 342, 257-61.

Brinch Petersen, E. 1974. Gravene ved Dragsholm. Fra jægere til bønder for 6000 år siden. *Nationalmuseets Arbejdsmark* 1974, 112-20.

Brinch Petersen, E. 2008. Warriors of the Neolithic TRB-Culture. In Sulgostowska, Z. & Tomaszewski, A.J. (eds) *Man – Millennia – Environment. Studies in honour of Romuald Schild.* Institute of Archaeology and Ethnology, Polish Academy of Sciences, Warszawa, 33-38.

Brinch Petersen, E. 2015. Diversity of Mesolithic Vedbæk. *Acta Archaeologica* 86:1 (Acta Archaeologica Supplementa XVI), 19-202.

Brink, K. 2009. *I palissadernas tid. Om stolphål och skärvor och sociala relationer under yngre mellanneolitikum.* Malmöfynd nr. 21, Malmö Museer.

Brown, A. 2007. Dating the onset of cereal cultivation in Britain and Ireland: the evidence from charred cereal grains. *Antiquity* 81, no. 314, 1042-52.

Brøndsted, J. 1937. *Danmarks Oldtid I, Stenalderen.* København.

Brück, J. 1999. Ritual and rationality: some problems of interpretation in European archaeology. *European Journal of Archaeology* vol. 2, no. 3, 313-44.

Casati, C., Sørensen, L. & Vennersdorf, M. 2004. Current research of the Early Mesolithic on Bornholm. In Terberger, T. & Eriksen, B.V. (eds) *Hunters in a changing world.* Rahden/Westfahlen, 113-32.

Casati, C. & Sørensen, L. 2006. Bornholm i ældre stenalder. Status over kulturel udvikling og kontakter. *Kuml* 2006, 9-58.

Cassen, S., Boujot, C. & Vaquero, J. (eds) 2000. *Éléments d'architecture. Exploration d'un tertre funéraire à Lannec er Gadouer (Erdeven, Morbihan). Constructions et reconstructions dans le Néolithique morbihannais. Propositions pour une lecture symbolique.* Chauvigny.

Cassen, S. 2012. L'objet possédé, sa représentation: mise en contexte general avec steles et gravures. In Pétrequin, P., Cassen, S., Errera, M., Klassen, L., Sheridan, A. & Pétrequin, A.-M. (eds) *Jade. Grande haches alpines du Néolithique européen. V^e et IVe millénaires av. J.-C.* Tome 2. Besançon, 1310-1353.

Cassen, S., Boujot, C., Bella, S.D., Guiavarc'h, M., Le Pennec, C., Martinez, M.P.P., Querré, G., Santrot, M.-H. & Vigier, E. 2012. Dépôt bretons, tumulus carnacéens et circulation à longue distance. In Pétrequin, P., Cassen, S., Errera, M., Klassen, L., Sheridan, A. & Pétrequin, A.-M. (eds) *Jade. Grande haches alpines du Néolithique européen. V^e et IVe millénaires av. J.-C.* Tome 1. Besançon, 918-95.

Cederschiöld, L. 1949. En yxa av kristianstadsflinta från Jylland. *Fornvännen* 44, 53.

Chambon, P. & Thomas, A. 2010. The first monumental cemeteries of western Europe: the "Passy type" necropolis in the Paris basin around 4500 BC. www.jungsteinSITE.de, October 19th 2010.

Childe, V.G. 1957. *The Dawn of European Civilization.* London, Routledge & Kegan Paul.

Chmielewski, W. 1952. *Zagadnienie grobowców kujawskich w świetle ostatnich badań.* Biblioteka Muzeum Archeologicznego w Łodzi 2, Łódź.

Christensen, C. 1990. Stone Age Dug-out Boats in Denmark: Occurrence, Age, Form and Reconstruction. In Robinson, D.E. (ed.) *Experimentation and Reconstruction in Environmental Archaeology. Symposia of the Association for Environmental Archaeology No. 9. Roskilde, Denmark, 1988,* 119-141. Oxbow Books, Oxford.

Christensen, C. 1995. The Littorina Transgressions in Denmark. In Fischer, A. (ed.) *Man and Sea in the Mesolithic. Coastal settlement above and below present sea level.* Oxbow Books, Oxford, 15-22.

Colas, C., Manolakakis, L., Thevenet, C., Baillieu, M., Bonnardin, S., Dubouloz, J., Farruggia, J.-P., Maigrot, Y., Naze, Y. & Robert, B. 2007. Le monument funéraire Michelsberg ancient de Beaurieux "La Plaine" (Aisne, France). *Cahiers d'archéologie romande* 108, 329-34.

Constantin, C., Mordant, D. & Simonin, D. 1997. La culture de Cerny et le chalcolithique de la terminologie européenne. In Constantin, C., Mordant, D. & Simonin, D. (eds) *La Culture de Cerny. Nouvelle économie, nouvelle société au Néolithique. Actes du Colloque International de Nemours 9-10-11 mai 1994.* Mémoires du Musée Préhistoire d'Ile-de-France n° 6. Nemours, 701-10.

Cooney, G., Bayliss, A., Healy, F., Whittle, A., Danaher, E., Cagney, L. Mallory, J., Smyth, J., Kador, T. & O'Sullivan, M. 2011. Ireland. In Whittle, A., Healy, F. & Bayliss, A. (eds) *Gathering Time. Dating the Early Neolithic Enclosures of Southern Britain and Ireland,* Vol. 2, Oxbow Books, Oxford & Oakville, 562-669.

Copley, M.S., Berstan, R., Dudd, S.N., Doherty, G., Mukherjee, A.J., Straker, V., Payne, S. & Evershed, R.P. 2003. Direct chemical evidence for widespread dairying in prehistoric Britain. *Proceedings of the National Academy of Science* 100 no. 4, 1524-29.

Copley, M.S. & Evershed, R.P. 2007. Organic residue analysis. In Benson, D. & Whittle, A. (eds) *Building Memories: The Neolithic Cotswold Long Barrow at Ascott-under-Wychwood, Oxfordshire.* Oxbow Books, Oxford, 283-88.

Craig, O. E., Steele, V.J., Fischer, A., Hartz, S., Andersen, S.H., Donohoe, P., Glykou, A., Saul, H., Jones, D.M., Koch, E. & Heron, C.P. 2011. Ancient lipids reveal continuity in culinary practices across the transition to agriculture in Northern Europe. *Proceedings of the National Academy of Science, USA* 108, 17910-15.

Czekaj-Zastawny, A. 2015. Imported Danubian pottery in the Late Mesolithic context in Dąbki. In Kabaciński, J., Hartz, S., Raemaekers, D.C.M. & Terberger, T. (eds) *The Dąbki Site in Pomerania and the Neolithisation of the North European Lowlands (c. 5000-3000 calBC)*. Rahden/Westfalen, 219-32.

Czekaj-Zastawny, A., Kabaciński, J. & Terberger, T. 2013a. Geneza kultury pucharów lejkowatych w kontekście przemian kulturowych w Europie północnej w V tys. BC (Origin of Funnel Beaker Culture in the light of cultural transformations in Northern Europe in the 5th millennium BC). *Przegląd archeologiczny* 61, 189-213.

Czekaj-Zastawny, A., Kabaciński, J. & Terberger, T. 2013b. The Origin of the Funnel Beaker Culture from a southern Baltic coast perspective. In Kadrow, S. & Włodarczak, P. (eds) *Environment and subsistence – fourty years after Janusz Kruk's "Settlement studies…"* Studien zur Archäologie in Ostmitteleuropa / Studia nad Pradziejami Europy Środkowej 11. Institute of Archaeology, Rzeszów University. Dr. Rudolf Habelt, Bonn, 409-28.

Czekaj-Zastawny, A. & Kabaciński, J. 2015. The early Funnel Beaker culture at Dąbki. In Kabaciński, J., Hartz, S., Raemaekers, D.C.M. & Terberger, T. (eds) *The Dąbki Site in Pomerania and the Neolithisation of the North European Lowlands (c. 5000-3000 calBC)*. Rahden/Westfalen, 203-17.

Czerniak, L. 2012. After the LBK. Communities of the 5th millennium BC in North-Central Europe. In Gleser, R. & Becker, V. (eds) *Mitteleuropa im 5. Jahrtausend vor Christus. Beiträge zur Internationalen Konferenz in Münster 2010*. Westfälische Wilhelms-Universität Münster. Lit Verlag Dr. W. Hopf, Berlin, 151-74.

Czerniak, L. 2018. The emergence of TRB communities in Pomerania. *Prace i Materiały Muzeum Archeologicznego i Etnograficznego w Łodzi*, Seria Archeologiczna 47, 2016-2017, 103-30.

Czerniak, L. & Pyzel, J. 2011. Linear Pottery farmers and the introduction of pottery in the southern Baltic. In Hartz S., Lüth F. & Terberger, T. (eds) Early Pottery in the Baltic. Dating, Origin and Social Context. International Workshop at Schleswig from 20th to 21st October 2006. *Bericht der Römisch-Germanischen Kommission* 89, 2008 (2011), 347-360.

Czerniak, L. & Rzepecki, S. 2015. Research on the origin of the TRB culture in east Pomerania. Pottery from Bielawki, site 5, Pelplin commune. *Gdańskie studia archeologiczne* 5, 40-57.

Damm, C.B. 1991. Burying the Past: An Example of Social Transformations in the Danish Neolithic. In Garwood, P., Jennings, D., Skeates, R. & Toms, J. (eds) *Sacred and Profane. Proceedings of a Conference on Archaeology, Ritual and Religion, Oxford 1989*. Oxford University Committee for Archaeology, Monograph No. 32, Oxford, 43-49.

Danaher, E. 2009. *Monumental Beginnings: the archaeology of the N4 Sligo inner relief road*. National Roads Authority, Scheme Monographs 1, Dublin.

Daniel, G.E. 1958. *The Megalith Builders of Western Europe*. London, Hutchinson.

Darvill, T. 1996. Neolithic buildings in England, Wales and the Isle of Man. In Darvill, T. & Thomas, J. (eds) *Neolithic Houses in Northwest Europe and Beyond*. Oxbow Monographs 57, 77-111. Oxford.

Davidsen, K. 1978. *The Final TRB Culture in Denmark. A Settlement Study*. Arkæologiske Studier vol. V, Akademisk Forlag, København.

Davidson, J. 1984. *The prehistory of New Zealand*. Longman Paul, Auckland.

Dehn, T. 2015. The megalithic construction process and the building of passage graves in Denmark. In Laporte, L. & Scarre, C. (eds) *The Megalithic Architectures of Europe*. Oxbow Books, Oxford/Philadelphia, 59-68.

Delor, J.-P., Genreau, F., Heurtaux, A., Jacob, J.-P., Leredde, H., Nouvel, P. & Pellet, C. 1997. L'implantation des nécropoles monumentales, au sud du Bassin Parisien. In Constantin, C., Mordant, D. & Simonin, D. (eds) *La Culture de Cerny. Nouvelle économie, nouvelle société au Néolithique. Actes du Colloque International de Nemours 9-10-11 mai 1994*. Mémoires du Musée Préhistoire d'Ile-de-France nº 6. Nemours, 381-95.

Dibbern, H. 2016. *Das trichterbecherzeitliche Westholstein: Eine Studie zur neolithischen Entwicklung von Landschaft und Gesellschaft*. Frühe Monumentalität und soziale Differenzierung 8. Verlag Dr. Rudolf Habelt, Bonn.

Domańska, L. 1995. *Geneza krzemieniarstwa kultury pucharów lejkowatych na Kujawach*. Katedra Archeologii Uniwersytetu Łódzkiego, Łódź.

Domańska, L. & Kośko, A. 1983. Łącko, woj. Bydgoszcz, stanowisko 6 – obozowisko z fazy I ("AB") kultury pucharów lejkowatych na Kujawach. *Acta Universitatis Lodziensis. Folia Archaeologica* 4, 3-55.

Duhamel, P. 1997. La Nécropole monumentale Cerny de Passy (Yonne): Description d'ensemble et problemes d'interpretation. In Constantin, C., Mordant, D. & Simonin, D. (eds) *La Culture de Cerny. Nouvelle économie, nouvelle société au Néolithique. Actes du Colloque International de Nemours 9-10-11 mai 1994*. Mémoires du Musée Préhistoire d'Ile-de-France nº 6. Nemours, 397-448.

Ebbesen, K. 1974. Bornholms første bønder. *Bornholmske Samlinger* 1974, 55-58.

Ebbesen, K. 1979. *Stordyssen i Vedsted. Studier over tragtbægerkulturen i Sønderjylland*. Arkæologiske Studier Vol. VI. Akademisk Forlag, København.

Ebbesen, K. 1981. Det store offerfund fra Knud. *Nordslesvigske Museer* 1981, 29-43.

Ebbesen, K. 1982. Yngre stenalders depotfund som bebyggelseshistorisk kildemateriale. In Thrane, H. (ed.) *Om yngre stenalders bebyggelseshistorie. Beretning fra et symposium, Odense 30. april – 1. maj 1981*. Skrifter fra Historisk Institut, Odense Universitet, nr. 30, 60-79.

Ebbesen, K. 1984. Tragtbægerkulturens grønstensøkser. *Kuml* 1984, 113-53.

Ebbesen, K. 1985. Bornholms dysser og jættestuer. *Bornholmske Samlinger* II. Rk. Bd. 18, 175-211.

Ebbesen, K. 1990. The Long Dolmen at Grøfte, South-West Zealand. *Journal of Danish Archaeology* 7, 1988, 53-69.

Ebbesen, K. 1994. Tragtbægerkulturens dolkstave. *Aarbøger for nordisk Oldkyndighed og Historie* 1992, 103-36.

Ebbesen, K. 1998. Frühneolithische Streitäxte. *Acta Archaeologica* 69, 77-112.

Ebbesen, K. 2002. Neolitiske ravperler i Västergötland. *in Situ. Västsvensk Arkeologisk Tidskrift* 2002, 85-126.

Ebbesen, K. 2007. *Danske dysser – Danish Dolmens*. Forlaget Attika, København.

Ebbesen, K. 2009. *Danske Jættestuer*. Forfatterforlaget Attika, København.

Ebbesen, K. 2011. *Danmarks Megalitgrave* Bind 1,1-2. Forfatterforlaget Attika, København.

Ebbesen, K. & Mahler, D. 1980. Virum. Et tidligneolitisk bopladsfund. *Aarbøger for nordisk Oldkyndighed og Historie* 1979, 11-61.

Eliade, M. 1958. *Patterns in Comparative Religion*. Sheed & Ward, London.

Eliade, M. 1959. *The Sacred & The Profane. The Nature of Religion. The Significance of Religious Myth, Symbolism, and Ritual within Life and Culture*. Harcourt, Brace & World, N.Y.

Eogan, G. 1990. Irish Megalithic Tombs and Iberia: Comparisons and Contrasts. In *Probleme der Megalithgräberforschung. Vorträge zum 100. Geburtstag von Vera Leisner*. Madrider Forschungen Bd. 16. Walter de Gruyter, Berlin/N.Y., 113-37.

Eogan, G. & Aboud, J. 1990. Diffuse Picking in Megalithic Art. In *La Bretagne et l'Europe préhistoriques. Mémoire en hommage à Pierre-Roland Giot*. Revue archéologique de l'Ouest, Supplément nº 2, 121-40.

Eriksen, P. & Andersen, N.H. 2014. *Stendysser. Arkitektur og funktion*. Ringkøbing Skjern Museum / Moesgaard Museum / Jysk Arkæologisk Selskabs Skrifter 85. Aarhus.

Eriksen, P. & Gebauer, A.B. 2016. Nyt om kulthuset og de store stengrave ved Tustrup. *Museum Østjylland Årbog* 2016, 98-107.

Fabricius, K. & Becker, C.J. 1996. *Stendyngegrave og Kulthuse. Studier over Tragtbægerkulturen i Nord- og Vestjylland*. Arkæologiske Studier vol. XI, Akademisk Forlag, København.

Fairweather, A.D. & Ralston, I.B.M. 1993. The Neolithic timber hall at Balbridie, Grampian Region, Scotland: the building, the date, the plant macrofossils. *Antiquity* 67, 313-23.

Fernandes, D.M., Strapagiel, D., Borówka, P., Marciniak, B., Żądzińska, E., Sirak, K., Siska, V., Grygiel, R., Carlsson, J., Manica, A., Lorkiewicz, W. & Pinhasi, R. 2018. A genomic Neolithic time transect of hunter-farmer admixture in central Poland. *Nature, Scientific Reports* 8:14879, 1-11. DOI:10.1038/s41598-018-33067-w

Fischer, A. 1982. Trade in Danubian Shaft-Hole Axes and the Introduction of Neolithic Economy in Denmark. *Journal of Danish Archaeology* 1, 7-12.

Fischer, A. 1983. Handel med skolæstøkser og landbrugets indførelse i Danmark. *Aarbøger for nordisk Oldkyndighed og Historie* 1981, 5-16.

Fischer, A. 2002. Food for Feasting? An evaluation of explanations of the neolithisation of Denmark and southern Sweden. In Fischer, A. & Kristiansen, K. (eds) *The Neolithisation of Denmark. 150 years of debate*, 343-93. J.R. Collis Publications, Sheffield.

Fischer, A. & Kristiansen, K. (eds) 2002. *The Neolithisation of Denmark. 150 years of debate*. J.R. Collis Publications, Sheffield.

Fischer, A., Olsen, J., Richards, M., Heinemeier, J., Sveinbjörnsdóttir, Á.E. & Bennike, P. 2007. Coast-inland mobility and diet in the Danish Mesolithic and Neolithic: evidence from stable isotope values of humans and dogs. *Journal of Archaeological Science* 34, 2125-50.

Fischer, C. 1976. Tidlig-neolitiske anlæg ved Rustrup. *Kuml* 1975, 29-72.

Fleming, A. 1973. Tombs for the Living. *Man* 8, no.2, 177-93.

Forssander, J.-E. 1938. Den spetsnackiga flintyxan. *Winther-Festskrift*, 15-39. København.

Fox, A. 1976. *Prehistoric Maori Fortifications in the North Island of New Zealand*. Longman Paul, Auckland.

Friederich, S. & Hoffmann, V. 2013. Die Rinderbestattung von Profen – mit Rad und Wagen. In Meller, H. (ed.) *3300 BC. Mysteriöse Steinzeittote und ihre Welt*. Landesamt für Denkmalpflege und Archäologie / Landesmuseum für Vorgeschichte, Halle, 83-84.

Friedman, J. & Rowlands, M. 1977. Notes towards an epigenetic model of evolution of 'civilization'. In Friedman, J. & Rowlands, M. (eds) *The Evolution of Social Systems*. Duckworth, London, 201-76.

Gabałówna, L. 1970. Wyniki analizy C-14 węgli drzewnych z cmentarzyska kultury pucharów lejkowatych na stanowisku 1 w Sarnowie – z grobowca 8 i niektóre problem z nimi związane. *Prace i Materiały Muzeum Archeologicznego i Etnograficznego w Łodzi*, Seria Archeologiczna nr. 17, 77-91.

Gebauer, A.B. 2012. Danske stenalderhøvdinge? En anmeldelse af K. Ebbesens "Danmarks Megalitgrave". *Kuml* 2012, 205-215.

Gebauer, A.B. 2014. Meanings of monumentalism at Lønt, Denmark. In Furholt, M., Hinz, M., Mischka, D., Noble, G. & Olausson, D. (eds) *Landscapes, Histories and Societies in the Northern European Neolithic*. Frühe Monumentalität und soziale Differenzierung, Band 4, Bonn, 101-12.

Geschwinde, M. & Raetzel-Fabian, D. 2009. *EWBSL. Eine Fallstudie zu den jungneolithischen Erdwerken am Nordrand der Mittelgebirge*. Beiträge zur Archäologie in Niedersachsen 14, Rahden/Westfalen.

Gidlöf, K., Dehman, K.H. & Johannson, T. 2006. *Citytunnelprojektet. Almhov – delområde 1*. Malmö Kulturmiljø, Rapport nr. 39, Malmö.

Glob, P.V. 1952. *Danske Oldsager* II. *Yngre Stenalder*. København.

Glob, P.V. 1967. *Danske Oldtidsminder*. Gyldendal, København.

Glykou, A. 2016. *Neustadt LA 156. Ein submariner Fundplatz des späten Mesolithikums und frühesten Neolithikums in Schleswig-Holstein. Untersuchungen zur Subsistensstrategie der letzten Jäger, Sammler und Fischer an der norddeutschen Ostseeküste*. Untersuchungen und Materialien zur Steinzeit in Schleswig-Holstein und im Ostseeraum aus dem Archäologischen Landesmuseum und dem Zentrum für Baltische und Skandinavische Archäologie in der Stiftung Schleswig-Holsteinische Landesmuseen Schloss Gottorf, Band 7. Wachholtz Verlag, Kiel/Hamburg.

Glørstad, H. 2009. The Northern Province? The Neolithisation of Southern Norway. In Glørstad, H. & Prescott, C. (eds) *Neolithisation as if history mattered. Processes of Neolithisation in North-Western Europe*, 135-68. Bricoleur Press, Lindome.

Glørstad, H. & Prescott, C. (eds) 2009. *Neolithisation as if history mattered. Processes of Neolithisation in North-Western Europe*. Bricoleur Press, Lindome.

Gräslund, B. 1994. Prehistoric Soul Beliefs in Northern Europe. *Proceedings of the Prehistoric Society* 60, 15-26.

Gron, K.J., Montgomery, J. & Rowley-Conwy, P. 2015. Cattle Management for Dairying in Scandinavia's Earliest Neolithic. *PLoS ONE* 10(7): e0131267. doi:10.1371/journal.pone.0131267.

Gron, K.J., Montgomery, J., Nielsen, P.O., Nowell, G.M., Peterkin, J.L., Sørensen, L. & Rowley-Conwy, P. 2016. Strontium isotope evidence of early Funnel Beaker Culture movement of cattle. *Journal of Archaeological Science: Reports* 6, 248-251.

Gron, K.J., Gröcke, D.R., Larsson, M., Sørensen, L., Larsson, L., Rowley-Conwy, P. & Church, M.J. 2017. Nitrogen isotope evidence for manuring of early Neolithic Funnel Beaker Culture cereals from Stensborg, Sweden. *Journal of Archaeological Science: Reports* 14, August 2017, 575-79.

Gron, K.J. & Rowley-Conwy, P. 2017. Herbivore diets and the anthropogenic environment of early farming in southern Scandinavia. *The Holocene* 27 (I), 98-109.

Gron, K.J. & Sørensen, L. 2018. Cultural and economic negotiation: a new perspective on the Neolithic Transition of Southern Scandinavia. *Antiquity* 92, 364, 958-74.

Gronenborn, D. 2007. Beyond the models: 'Neolithisation' in Central Europe. In Whittle, A. & Cummings, V. (eds) *Going over. The Mesolithic-Neolithic Transition in North-West Europe*. Proceedings of the British Academy 144, 73-98. Oxford Univ. Press, Oxford / N.Y.

Gronenborn, D. 2016. Some thoughts on political differentiation in Early to Young Neolithic societies in western central Europe. In Meller, H., Hahn, H.P., Jung, R. & Risch, R. (eds) *Arm und Reich – Zur Ressourcenverteilung in prähistorischen Gesellschaften / Rich and Poor – Competing for resources in prehistoric societies*. 8. Mitteldeutscher Archäologentag vom 22. bis 24. Oktober 2015 in Halle (Saale). Tagungen des Landesmuseums für Vorgeschichte Halle, Band 14/I, 61-75.

Grönwall, K.A. 1903. Flintens naturlige Forekomst paa Bornholm og de bornholmske Stenaldersredskaber. *Aarbøger for nordisk Oldkyndighed og Historie* 1903, 316-19.

Grönwall, K.A. & Milthers, V. 1916. *Kortbladet Bornholm*. DGU I. Rk. Nr. 13. København.

Gruber, G., Carlsson, T. & Gill, A. 2016. Crops, Cattle and Human DNA. The Motala Site and the Mesolithic-Neolithic Transition in Östergötland, Southern Sweden. *Current Swedish Archaeology* vol. 24, 81-106.

Grygiel, R. 1984. The household cluster as a fundamental social unit of the Brześć Kujawski Group of the Lengyel Culture in the Polish Lowlands. *Prace i Materiały Muzeum Archeologicznego i etnograficznego w Łodzi, Seria Archeologiczna* 31, 43-334.

Grygiel, R. 2008. *Środkowy neolit, grupa Brzesko-Kujawska kultury Lendzielskiej (Middle Neolithic, the Brześć Kujawski Group of the Lengyel Culture). Neolit i początki epoki brązu w rejonie Brześcia Kujawskiego i Osłonek*. Lódź.

Grygiel, R. 2018. The Funnel Beaker culture in the Brześć Kujawski and Osłonki Region (Kuyavia). *Prace i Materiały Muzeum Archeologicznego i etnograficznego w Łodzi, Seria Archeologiczna* 47, 2016-2017, 177-201.

Gurstad-Nilsson, H. 2001. En neolitisering – två förlopp. Tankar kring jordbrukskulturens etablering i Kalmarsundsområdet. In Magnusson, G. (ed.) *Möre, historien om ett småland*. Kalmar läns museum, Kalmar, 129-64.

Hage, F. 2016. *Büdelsdorf / Borgstedt. Eine trichterbecherzeitliche Kleinregion*. Frühe Monumentalität und soziale Differenzierung 11. Institut für Ur- und Frühgeschichte der CAU Kiel /Verlag Dr. Rudolf Habelt, Bonn.

Hallgren, F. 2008. *Identitet i praktik. Lokala, regionala och överregionala sociala sammanhang inom nordlig trattbägarkultur*. Coast to coast-book 17, Uppsala.

Hamard, D. 1989. Le village michelsberg des Hautes Chanvières à Mairy (Ardennes), II. L'outillage en silex. *Gallia préhistoire* 31, 119-26.

Hampel, A. 1989. *Die Hausentwicklung im Mittelneolithikum Zentraleuropas*. Universitätsforschungen zur Prähistorischen Archäologie 1. Bonn.

Hansen, P.V. & Madsen, B. 1983. Flint Axe Manufacture in the Neolithic. An Experimental Investigation of a Flint Axe Manufacture Site at Hastrup Vænget, East Zealand. *Journal of Danish Archaeology* 2, 43-59.

Hansen, S.I. 2014. Bornholms jættestuer. In Nielsen, P.O., Nielsen, F.O.S. & Adamsen, C. (eds) *Solstensøen. På sporet af Bornholms bondestenalder*. Bornholms Museum, Nationalmuseet & Wormianum, Rønne, 47-80.

Harrisson, T. 1958. A Living Megalithic in Upland Borneo. *The Sarawak Museum Journal* VIII, 694-702.

Hartz, S. 2011. From pointed bottom to round and flat bottom – tracking early pottery from Schleswig-

Holstein. In Hartz, S., Lüth, F. & Terberger, T. (eds) Frühe Keramik im Ostseeraum – Datierung und Sozialer Kontext. Internationaler Workshop in Schleswig vom 20. bis 21. Oktober 2006. *Bericht der Römisch-Germanischen Kommission,* 89, 2008, 241-76.

Hartz, S., Lübke, H. & Heinrich, D. 2000. Frühe Bauern an der Küste. Neue ¹⁴C-Daten und aktuelle Aspekte zum Neolithisierungsprozeß im norddeutschen Ostseeküstengebiet. *Praehistorische Zeitschrift* 75, 129-52.

Hartz, S., Heinrich, D. & Lübke, H. 2002. Coastal farmers – the neolithisation of northernmost Germany. In Fischer, A. & Kristiansen, K. (eds) *The Neolithisation of Denmark. 150 years of debate,* 321-40. J.R. Collis Publications, Sheffield.

Hartz, S. & Lübke, H. 2005. Zur chronostratigraphischen Gliederung der Ertebølle- und frühesten Trichterbecherkultur in der südlichen Mecklenburger Bucht. *Bodendenkmalpflege in Mecklenburg-Vorpommern* 52, 119-44.

Hartz, S. & Lübke, H. 2006. New Evidence for a Chronostratigraphic Division of the Ertebølle Culture on the southern Mecklenburg Bay. In Kind, C.J. (ed.) *After the Ice Age. Settlements, Subsistence and Social Development in the Mesolithic of Central Europe.* Materialhefte zur Archäologie in Baden-Württemberg 78. Theiss, Stuttgart, 61-77.

Hartz, S., Lübke, H. & Terberger, T. 2007. From fish and seal to sheep and cattle: new research into the process of neolithisation in northern Germany. In Whittle, A. & Cummings, V. (eds.) *Going Over – The Mesolithic-Neolithic Transition in Northwest Europe.* Proceedings of the British Academy 144, 567-94. Oxford Univ. Press, Oxford.

Hatting, T. 1978. Lidsø. Zoological remains from a Neolithic settlement. In Davidsen, K., *The Final TRB Culture in Denmark. A Settlement Study.* Akademisk Forlag, København, 193-207.

Hayden, B. 1990. Nimrods, Piscators, Pluckers and Planters: The Emergence of Food Production. *Journal of Anthropological Archaeology* 9, 31-69.

Hayden, B. 2014. *The Power of Feasts, from Prehistory to the Present.* Cambridge Univ. Press, Cambridge.

Hayden, B. & Villeneuve, S. 2010. Who Benefits from Complexity? A View from Futuna. In Price, T.D. & Feinman, G.M. (eds) *Pathways to Power. New Perspectives on the Emergence of Social Inequality.* Fundamental Issues in Archaeology. Springer, N.Y./Dordrecht/Heidelberg/London, 95-145.

Hedges, R.E.M., Housley, R.A., Bronk, C.R. & van Klinken, G.J. 1991. Radiocarbon dates from the Oxford AMS system: Archaeometry Datelist 13. *Archaeometry* 33:2, 279-296.

Heinemeier, J., Heier Nielsen, S. & Rud, N. 1993. Danske AMS ¹⁴C dateringer, Århus 1992. *Arkæologiske Udgravninger i Danmark* 1992, 291-95.

Heinemeier, J. & Rud, N. 2000. AMS ¹⁴C dateringer, Århus 1999. *Arkæologiske Udgravninger i Danmark* 1999, 296-313.

Helbæk, H. 1955. Store Valby – Kornavl i Danmarks første neolitiske Fase. *Aarbøger for nordisk Oldkyndighed og Historie* 1954, 198-204.

Helms, M.W. 1988. *Ulysses' Sail. An Ethnographic Odyssey of Power, Knowledge, and Geographical Distance.* Princeton Univ. Press, Princeton, N.J.

Herbaut, F. 2000. Les Haches Carnacéennes. In Cassen, S., Boujot, C. & Vaquero, J. (eds) *Éléments d'architecture. Exploration d'un tertre funéraire à Lannec er Gadouer (Erdeven, Morbihan). Constructions et reconstructions dans le Néolithique morbihannais. Propositions pour une lecture symbolique.* Chauvigny, 387-96.

Hernek, R. 1989. Den spetsnackiga yxan av flinta. *Fornvännen* 83, 1988, 216-23.

Hirsch, K., Klooss, S. & Klooss, R. 2008. Der endmesolithisch-neolithische Küstensiedlungsplatz bei Baabe im Südosten der Insel Rügen. *Bodendenkmalpflege in Mecklenburg-Vorpommern, Jahrbuch* 55, 2007, 11-51.

Holten, L. 2009. Åbninger til en anden virkelighed. Megalitanlæg som mediatorer mellem her og hisset. In Schülke, A. (ed.) *Plads og rum i tragtbægerkulturen. Bidrag fra Arbejdsmødet på Nationalmuseet, 22. september 2005.* Nordiske Fortidsminder Ser. C, bind 6, Det Kongelige Nordiske Oldskriftselskab, København, 159-77.

Högberg, A. & Olausson, D. 2007. *Scandinavian Flint – an Archaeological Perspective.* Aarhus University Press, Aarhus.

Højlund, F. 1979. Stenøkser i Ny Guineas Højland. Betydningen af prestigesymboler for reproduktion af et stammesamfund. *Hikuin* 5, 31-48.

Hulthén, B. & Welinder, S. 1981. *A Stone Age Economy.* Stockholm.

Hårdh, B. & Roslund, C. 1991. Passage Graves and the Passage of the Moon. In Jennbert, K., Larsson, L., Petré, R. & Wyszomirska-Werbart, B. (eds) *Regions and Reflections in Honour of Märta Strömberg.* Acta Archaeologica Lundensia Ser. in 8°, N° 20, 35-43. Lund.

Isern, N., Zilhão, J., Fort, J. & Ammerman, A.J. 2017. Modeling the role of voyaging in the coastal spread of the Early Neolithic in the West Mediterranean. *Proceedings of the National Academy of Sciences of the United States of America.* https://doi.org/10.1073/PNAS 1613413114

Iversen, J. 1941. Landnam i Danmarks Stenalder. En pollenanalytisk Undersøgelse over det første Landbrugs Indvirkning paa Vegetationsudviklingen. *Danmarks Geologiske Undersøgelse,* II, Nr. 66, 1-68. København.

Iversen, J. 1949. The Influence of Prehistoric Man on Vegetation. *Danmarks Geologiske Undersøgelse,* IV, Bd. 3, Nr. 6, 1-25. København.

Iversen, J. 1954. The Late-Glacial Flora of Denmark and its Relation to Climate and Soil. *Studies in Vegetational History in honour of Knud Jessen 29ᵗʰ November 1954.* Danmarks Geologiske Undersøgelse, II, Nr. 80, 87-119.

Iversen, R. 2015. *The Transformation of Neolithic Societies. An Eastern Danish Perspective on the 3ʳᵈ Millennium BC.* Jutland Archaeological Society Publications 88, Højbjerg.

Jacobsson, B. 1986. The Skogsdala Dolmen. A Long Dolmen beneath a Bronze Age Burial Mound at Skogsdala, South Scania, Sweden. *Meddelanden från Lunds universitets historiska museum* 1985-86 (*Papers of the Archaeological Institute University of Lund* 1985-86). New Series Vol. 6, 84-114.

Jankowska, D. 1980. *Kultura pucharów lejkowatych na Pomorzu środkowym. Grupa Łupawska*. Uniwersytet im. Adama Mickiewicza w Poznaniu, Seria Archeologia nr. 17, Poznań.

Jankowska, D. 1990. *Społeczności strefy południowo-zachodniobałtyckiej w dobie neolityzacji*. Uniwersytet im. Adama Mickiewicza w Poznaniu, Seria Archeologia nr. 33, Poznań.

Jansen, J. 1820. *Beskrivelse over de på Bornholm, efter den Kongelige Commission til Oldsagers Opbevaring foranstaltede Udgravninger af Høye mm.* Det Kongelige Bibliotek Ny kgl. Saml. 726 e, 4to.

Jażdżewski, K. 1932. Zusammenfassender Überblick über die Trichterbecherkultur. *Praehistorische Zeitschrift* 23, 77-110.

Jażdżewski, K. 1936. *Kultura pucharów lejkowatych w Polsce zachodniej i środkowej*. Poznań.

Jażdżewski, K. 1984. *Urgeschichte Mitteleuropas*. Wrocław/Warszawa/Kraków/Gdańsk/Łódź.

Jennbert, K. 1984. *Den produktiva gåvan. Tradition och innovation i Sydskandinavien för omkring 5300 år sedan*. Acta Archaeologica Lundensia Series in 4º, Nº 16. Lund.

Jensen, H.J. 1994. *Flint Tools and Plant Working. Hidden Traces of Stone Age Technology. A use wear study of some Danish Mesolithic and TRB implements*. Aarhus Univ. Press, Aarhus.

Jessen, K. 1929. Bemærkninger om Skovens Historie paa Bornholm. *Botanisk Tidsskrift* 40, 474-76.

Jeunesse, C. 2010a. Die Michelsberger Kultur. Eine Kultur ohne Friedhöfe. In Lichter, C. (ed.) *Jungsteinzeit im Umbruch. Die "Michelsberger Kultur" und Mitteleuropa vor 6000 Jahren*. Badisches Landesmuseum, Karlsruhe, 90-95.

Jeunesse, C. 2010b. Das Erdwerk von Mairy und seine grossen Gebäude. In Lichter, C. (ed.) *Jungsteinzeit im Umbruch. Die "Michelsberger Kultur" und Mitteleuropa vor 6.000 Jahren*. Badisches Landesmuseum Karlsruhe, 62.

Jeunesse, C. 2016. A propos des conditions de formation des assemblages osseux archéologiques dans les sociétés pré-littéraires disparues européennes (Néolithique et Protohistoire). Une analyse ethnoarchéologique dans deux sociétés vivantes de l'Asie du Sud-Est. *Journal of Neolithic Archaeology* 18, 2016, 23-64 [doi 10.12766/ jna.2016.2].

Jeunesse, C., Le Roux, P. & Boulestin, B. (eds) 2016. *Mégalithismes vivants et passes: approches croisées* (Living and Past Megalithisms: interwoven approaches). Oxford (Archaeopress Archaeology).

Jeunesse, C. & Denaire, A. 2017. Origine des animaux sur pied, circuit de la viande. La formation des assembles osseux dans le context d'une fête traditionnelle à Sumba (Indonésie). Une enquête etnoarchéologique. *Bulletin de la Société prehistorique française* 114:1, 115-136.

Johannsen, N.N. 2006. Draught cattle and the South Scandinavian economies of the 4th millennium BC. *Environmental Archaeology* vol. 11, no. 1, 35-48.

Johannsen, N.N. & Kieldsen, M. 2014. En stendyngegrav ved Kvorning. Fund, kontekst og betydning. *Kuml* 2014, 9-28.

Johannsen, N. & Laursen, S. 2010. Routes and Wheeled Transport in Late 4th-Early 3rd Millennium Funerary Customs of the Jutland Peninsula: Regional Evidence and European Context. *Praehistorische Zeitschrift* 85, 15-58.

Johansen, K.F. 1917. Jordgrave fra Dyssetid. *Aarbøger for nordisk Oldkyndighed og Historie* 1917, 131-47.

Johansen, K.L. 2006. Settlement and Land Use at the Mesolithic-Neolithic Transition in Southern Scandinavia. *Journal of Danish Archaeology* 14, 201-23.

Johansson, A.D. 1999. Ertebøllekulturen i Sydsjælland. *Aarbøger for nordisk Odkyndighed og Historie* 1997, 7-88.

Johansson, P. 2003. *The Lure of Origins. An Inquiry into Human-Environmental Relations, Focussed on the "Neolithization" of Sweden*. Lunds University, Lund.

Jordan, P. & Zvelebil, M. 2009. Ex Oriente Lux: The Prehistory of Hunter-Gatherer Ceramic Dispersals. In Jordan, P. & Zvelebil, M. (eds) *Ceramics Before Farming. The Dispersal of Pottery Among Prehistoric Eurasian Hunter-Gatherers*. Publications of the Institute of Archaeology, University College London, Walnut Creek, California, 33-89.

Jørgensen, L. & Nørgård Jørgensen, A. 1997. *Nørre Sandegård Vest. A Cemetery from the 6th-8th Centuries on Bornholm*. Nordiske Fortidsminder Ser. B, Vol. 14. Det Kgl. Nordiske Oldskriftselskab, København.

Kabaciński, J. & Terberger, T. 2011. Pots and pikes at Dąbki 9, Koszalin district (Poland) – the early pottery on the Pomeranian coast. In Hartz, S., Lüth, F. & Terberger, T. (eds) Frühe Keramik im Ostseeraum – Datierung und Sozialer Kontext. Internationaler Workshop in Schleswig vom 20. bis 21. Oktober 2006. *Bericht der Römisch-Germanischen Kommission*, 89, 2008, 361-92.

Kaelas, L. 1953. Den äldre megalitkeramiken under mellan-neolitikum i Sverige. *Antikvariska Studier* V, Kungl. Vitterhets Historie och Antikvitets Akademiens Handlingar 83, 7-77. Stockholm.

Kanstrup, M., Thomsen, I.K., Mikkelsen, P.H. & Christensen, B.T. 2012. Impact on charring on cereal grain characteristics: linking prehistoric manuring practice to $\delta^{15}N$ signatures in archaeological material. *Journal of Archaeological Science* vol. 39, 2533-40.

Kanstrup, M., Holst, M.K., Jensen, P.M., Thomsen, I.K. & Christensen, B.T. 2014. Searching for long-term trends in prehistoric manuring practice. $\delta^{15}N$ analyses of charred cereal grains from the 4th to the 1st millennium BC. *Journal of Archaeological Science* vol. 51, 115-25.

Karsten, P. 1994. *Att kasta yxan i sjön. En studie över rituel tradition och förändring utifrån skånska neolitiska offerfynd*. Acta Archaeologica Lundensia Series in 8º, No. 23. Stockholm.

Kaul, F. 1988. Neolitiske gravanlæg på Onsved Mark, Horns Herred, Sjælland. *Aarbøger for nordisk Oldkyndighed og Historie* 1987, 27-83.

Kaul, F., Nielsen, F.O. & Nielsen, P.O. 2002. Vasagård og Rispebjerg. To indhegnede bopladser fra yngre stenalder på Bornholm. *Nationalmuseets Arbejdsmark* 2002, 119-138.

Kaute, P., Schindler, G. & Lübke, H. 2005. Der end-mesolithisch/frühneolithische Fundplatz Stralsund-Mischwasserspeicher – Zeugnisse früher Bootsbautechnologie an der Ostseeküste Mecklenburg-Vorpommerns. *Bodendenkmalpflege in Mecklenburg-Vorpommern, Jahrbuch* 52, 2004, 221-41.

Kempfner-Jørgensen, L. & Watt, M. 1985. Settlement Sites with Middle Neolithic Houses at Grødby, Bornholm. *Journal of Danish Archaeology* vol. 4, 87-100.

Kihlstedt, B., Larsson, M. & Nordqvist, B. 1997. Neolitiseringen i Syd-, Väst- och Mellansverige – social och idelogisk förändring. In Larsson, M. & Olsson, E. (eds) *Regionalt och interregionalt. Stenåldersundersökningar i Syd- och Mellansverige*. Riksantikvarieämbetet, Arkeologiska undersökningar, Skrifter nr. 23, 85-133.

Kind, C.-J. 2010. Diversity at the Transition—A View from the Mesolithic. In Gronenborn, D. & Petrasch, J. (eds) *Die Neolithisierung Mitteleuropas: Internationale Tagung / The Spread of the Neolithic to Central Europe*, 449-460. Mainz, Verlag des Römisch-Germanischen Zentralmuseums.

Kinnes, I. 1982. Les Fouaillages and megalithic origins. *Antiquity* 56, 24-30.

Kirby, M. 2011. Lockerbie Academy: Neolithic and Early Historic timber halls, a Bronze Age cemetery, an undated enclosure and a post-medieval corn-drying kiln in south-west Scotland. *Scottish Archaeological Internet Report* 46. www.sair.org.uk

Kjærum, P. 1967. The chronology of the passage graves in Jutland. *Palaeohistoria* vol. XII, 1966, 323-33.

Kjærum, P. 1971. Skavangedyssen. In Nørlykke, C. (ed.) *Brudstykker, Holger Friis tilegnet på firsårsdagen 15. oktober 1971*. Historisk Samfund for Vendsyssel, Hjørring, 63-71.

Klassen, L. 1999. Prestigeøkser af sjældne alpine bjergarter. En glemt og overset fundgruppe fra ældre stenalders slutning i Danmark. *Kuml* 1999, 11-51.

Klassen, L. 2000. *Frühes Kupfer im Norden. Untersuchungen zu Chronologie, Herkunft und Bedeutung der Kupferfunde der Nordgruppe der Trichterbecherkultur*. Jutland Archaeological Society Publications 36, Moesgård Museum, Aarhus.

Klassen, L. 2002. The Ertebølle Culture and Neolithic continental Europe: traces of contacts and interaction. In Fischer, A. & Kristiansen, K. (eds) *The Neolithisation of Denmark. 150 years of debate*, 305-17. J.R. Collis Publications, Sheffield.

Klassen, L. 2004. *Jade und Kupfer. Untersuchungen zum Neolithisierungsprozess im westlichen Ostseeraum unter besonderer Berücksichtigung der Kulturentwicklung Europas 5500-3500 BC*. Jutland Archaeological Society Publications 47, Moesgård Museum, Aarhus.

Klassen, L. 2010. Kobberøksen fra Vester Bedegadegård på Bornholm. In Andersen, M. & Nielsen, P.O. (eds) *Danefæ. Skatte fra den danske muld*. Nationalmuseet & Gyldendal, København, 39-43.

Klassen, L. 2014. *Along the Road. Aspects of Causewayed Enclosures in South Scandinavia and Beyond*. East Jutland Museum / Moesgaard Museum, Aarhus Univ. Press.

Klassen, L., Cassen, S. & Pétrequin, P. 2012. Alpine axes and early metallurgy. In Pétrequin, P., Cassen, S., Errera, M., Klassen, L., Sheridan, A. & Pétrequin, A.-M. (eds) *Jade. Grande haches alpines du Néolithique européen. V^e et IVe millénaires av. J.-C*. Tome 2. Besançon, 1280-1309.

Klassen, L. & Nielsen, P.O. 2010. En skolæstøkse fra Åmosen. Import af varer af eksotiske stenarter i sen jægerstenalder og tidlig bondestenalder, 5400-3800 f. Kr. In Andersen, M. & Nielsen, P.O. (eds) *Danefæ. Skatte fra den danske muld*. Nationalmuseet & Gyldendal, København, s. 34-38.

Knarrström, B. 1997. Neolitisk flintteknologi i et skånsk randområde. *Carpe Scaniam. Axplock ur Skånes förflutna*. Riksantikvarieämbetet, Arkeologiska Undersökningar, Skrifter nr. 22, 7-25.

Knight, V. 1998. Moundville as a diagrammic ceremonial center. In Knight, V.J. & Steponaitis, V.P. (eds) *Archaeology of the Moundville chiefdom*. Smithsonian Institution Press, Washington D.C., 1-25.

Knoche, B. 2013. Riten, Routen, Rinder – Das jungsteinzeitlische Erdwerk von Soest im Wegenetz eines extensiven Viehwirtschaftsystems. In Melzer, W. (ed.) *Neue Forschungen zum Neolithikum in Soest und am Hellweg*. Soester Beiträge zur Archäologie 13, 119-74.

Knutsson, H. 1995. *Slutvandrat? Aspekter på övergången från rörlig til bofast tillvaro*. Aun 20. Societas Archaeologica Upsaliensis. Uppsala.

Koch, E. 1998. *Neolithic Bog Pots from Zealand, Møn, Lolland and Falster*. Nordiske Fortidsminder Ser. B, Vol. 16, København.

Koch, E. 1999. Neolithic offerings from the wetlands of eastern Denmark. In Coles, B., Coles, J. & Jørgensen, M.S. (eds) *Bog Bodies, Sacred Sites and Wetland Archaeology. Proceedings of a conference held by WARP and the National Museum of Denmark, in conjunction with Silkeborg Museum, Jutland, September 1996*. WARP Occasional Paper 12, Exeter, 125-31.

Kofod, K.M. 1917. To bornholmske Storgaardes Historie. *Bornholmske Samlinger* Bd. 11, 107-66.

Kossian, R. 2005. *Nichtmegalithische Grabanlagen der Trichterbecherkultur in Deutschland und den Niederlanden*. Veröffentlichungen des Landesamtes für Denkmalpflege und Archäologie Sachsen-Anhalt

– Landesmuseum für Vorgeschichte 58, I-II, Halle (Saale).

Kreuz, A., Märkle, T., Marinova, E., Rösch, M., Schäfer, E., Schamuhn, S. & Zerl, T. 2014. The Late Neolithic Michelsberg Culture – just ramparts and ditches? A supraregional comparison of agricultural and environmental data. *Praehistorische Zeitschrift* 89 (1), 72-115.

Kristensen, I.K. 1991. Storgård IV. An Early Neolithic Long Barrow near Fjeldsø, North Jutland. *Journal of Danish Archaeology* 8, 1989, 72-87.

Kristiansen, A.M. 2000a. Langhøjen ved Rokær – variation over et tema. In Hvass, S. & Det Arkæologiske Nævn (eds) *Vor skjulte kulturarv. Arkæologien under overfladen. Til Hendes Majestæt Dronning Margrethe II 16. april 2000.* Det Kgl. Nordiske Oldskriftselskab & Jysk Arkæologisk Selskab, 44-45.

Kristiansen, A.M. 2000b. Nye skikke. *Skalk* no. 4, 5-10.

Kristiansen, K. 1982. The Formation of Tribal Systems in Later European Prehistory: Northern Europe, 4000-500 B.C. In Renfrew, C., Rowlands, M.J. & Segraves, B.A. (eds) *Theory and Explanation in Archaeology.* Academic Press, N.Y., 241-80.

Kristiansen, K. 1984. Ideology and material culture: an archaeological perspective. In Spriggs, M. (ed.) *Marxist Perspectives in Archaeology.* Cambridge Univ. Press, Cambridge, 72-100.

Kristiansen, K. 1991. Chiefdoms, states, and systems of social evolution. In Earle, T. (ed.) *Chiefdoms, Power, Economy, and Ideology.* Cambridge Univ. Press, Cambridge, 16-42.

Kristiansen, K. 1998. *Europe before history.* Cambridge Univ. Press, Cambridge.

Kristiansen, K. 2010. Decentralized Complexity: The Case of Bronze Age Northern Europe. In Price, T.D. & Feinman, G.M. (eds) *Pathways to Power. New Perspectives on the Emergence of Social Inequality.* Fundamental Issues in Archaeology. Springer, N.Y./Dordrecht/Heidelberg/London, 169-92.

Kristiansen, K. & Larsson, T.B. 2005. *The Rise of Bronze Age Society. Travels, Transmissions and Transformations.* Cambridge Univ. Press, Cambridge.

Kruk, J. & Milisauskas, S. 1999. *Rozkwit i upadek społeczeństw rolniczych neolitu* (the Rise and Fall of Neolithic Societies). Instytut Archeologii i Etnologii Polskiej Akademii Nauk, Kraków.

Kukawka, S. 2015. Początki kultury pucharów lejkowatych na niżu Polskim. *Folia Praehistorica Posnaniensia* XX, 277-300.

Lang, R. 1985. *Gotlands tunnackiga flintyxor.* Uppsats i påbygnadskurs i arkeologi särskilt nordeuropeisk vid Stockholms Universitet.

Larsson, L. 1992a. Neolithic Settlement in the Skateholm Area, Southern Scania. *Meddelanden från Lunds universitets historiska museum* 1991-1992 (*Papers of the Archaeological Institute University of Lund* 1991-1992), New Series Vol. 9, 5-44.

Larsson, L. 1992b. Façade for the Dead. A Preliminary Report on the Excavation of a Long Barrow in Southern Scania. *Meddelanden från Lunds universitets historiska museum* 1991-1992 (*Papers of the Archaeological Institute University of Lund* 1991-1992). New series Vol. 9, 45-56.

Larsson, L. 2002a. Undersökningen av Jättegraven. In Larsson, L. (ed.) *Monumentala gravformer i det äldsta bondesamhället.* University of Lund, Department of Archaeology and Ancient History, Report Series No. 83, Lund, 7-33.

Larsson, L. 2002b. Feuer und Beile. Bewusste Zerstörung von Flintgeräten im Neolithikum. *Archäologisches Korrespondenzblatt* 32, 345-56.

Larsson, L. 2007. Mistrust traditions, consider innovations? The Mesolithic-Neolithic transition in southern Scandinavia. In Whittle, A. & Cummings, V. (eds) *Going over. The Mesolithic-Neolithic Transition in North-West Europe.* Proceedings of the British Academy 144, 595-616. Oxford Univ. Press, Oxford / N.Y.

Larsson, L. 2011a. The ritual use of axes. In Davis, V. & Edmonds, M. (eds) *Stone Axe Studies III.* Oxbow Books, Oxford, 203-14.

Larsson, L. 2011b. Water and fire as transformation elements in ritual deposits of the Scandinavian Neolithic. *Documenta Praehistorica* XXXVIII, 69-82.

Larsson, L. 2014. Neolithic transformations: relationships between society and landscape. In Furholt, M., Hinz, M., Mischka, D., Noble, G. & Olausson, D. (eds) *Landscapes, Histories and Societies in the Northern European Neolithic.* Frühe Monumentalität und soziale Differenzierung, Band 4, Bonn, 197-206.

Larsson, L. & Broström, S.-G. 2011. Meeting for Transformation. A Locality for Ritual Activities During the Early Neolithic Funnel Beaker Culture in Central Sweden. *Current Swedish Archaeology* 19, 183-201.

Larsson, M. 1984. *Tidigneolitikum i Sydvästskåne. Kronologi och bosättningsmönster.* Acta Archaeologica Lundensia, Series in 4° N° 17. Lund.

Larsson, M. 1985. *The Early Neolithic Funnel Beaker Culture in South-west Scania, Sweden. Economic and Social Change 3000-2500 B.C.* BAR International Series 264, Oxford.

Larsson, M. 1988a. Megaliths and Society. The Development of Social Territories in the South Scanian Funnel Beaker Culture. *Meddelanden från Lunds universitets historiska museum* 1987-1988 (*Papers of the Archaeological Institute University of Lund* 1987-1988), New Series Vol. 7, 19-39.

Larsson, M. 1988b. Exchange and Society in the Early Neolithic in Scania, Sweden. In Hårdh, B., Larsson, L., Olausson, D. & Petré, R. (eds) *Trade and Exchange. Studies in Honour of Berta Stjernquist.* Acta Archaeologica Lundensia Series in 8°, N° 16, 49-58.

Larsson, M. 1992. The Early and Middle Neolithic Funnel Beaker Culture in the Ystad area (Southern Scania). Economic and social changes, 3100-2300 BC. In Larsson, L., Callmer, J. & Stjernquist, B. (eds) *The Archaeology of the Cultural Landscape. Field work and research in a South Swedish rural region.* Acta Archaeologica Lundensia Series in 4°, N° 19, 17-90. Lund.

Larsson, M. 1997a. See Kihlstedt, B. *et al.* 1997.

Larsson, M. 1997b. Från det vilda till det tama. Aspekter på neolitiseringen i Sydsverige. In Åkerlund, A., Bergh, S., Nordbladh, J. & Taffinder, J. (eds) *Till Gunborg. Arkeologiska samtal.* Stockholm Archaeological Reports Nr 33, 349-59.

Larsson, M. 2013. Brave New World, the Paths Towards a Neolithic Society in Southern Scandinavia. In Larsson, M. & Debert, J. (eds) *NW Europe in Transition. The Early Neolithic in Britain and South Sweden.* BAR International Series 2475. Archaeopress, Oxford, 37-42.

Larsson, M. 2015. Agency, creolization and the transformation of tradition in the constitution of the earliest Neolithic in southern Scandinavia. In Brink, K., Hydén, S., Jennbert, K., Larsson, L. & Olausson, D. (eds) *Neolithic Diversities. Perspectives from a conference in Lund, Sweden.* Acta Archaeologica Lundensia Series in 8º, No. 65, 75-79.

Larsson, M., Lemdahl, G. & Lidén, K. 2012. *Mot en ny värld, Yngre stenålder i Sverige 4000-1700 f. Kr.* Studentlitteratur, Lund.

Larsson, M. & Rzepecki, S. 2003. Pottery, Houses and Graves. The Early Funnel Beaker Culture in Southern Sweden and Central Poland. *Lund Archaeological Review* 8-9, 2002-2003, 1-22.

Last, J. 2013. The End of the Longhouse. In Hofmann, D. & Smyth, J. (eds) *Tracking the Neolithic House in Europe. Sedentism, Architecture, and Practice,* 261-82. Springer, N.Y./Dordrecht/Heidelberg/London.

Laurelut, C. 1989. Le village michelsberg des Hautes Chanvières à Mairy (Ardennes), III. Étude de la céramique. *Gallia Préhistoire* 31, 129-37.

Laurelut, C. in press. Mairy – settlement, monumentality and sociocultural complexity in the Meuse valley during the first half of the 4th millennium BC. To appear in the proceedings of the EAA Conference in Helsinki 2012.

Lewis, J.P., Ryves, D.B., Rasmussen, P., Olsen, J., Knudsen, K.-L., Andersen, S.H., Weckström, K., Clarke, A.L., Andrén, E. & Juggins, S. 2016. The shellfish enigma across the Mesolithic-Neolithic transition in southern Scandinavia. *Quaternary Science Reviews* 151, 315-20.

Liep, J. 1991. Great man, big man, chief: a triangulation of the Massim. In Godelier, M. & Strathern, M. (eds) *Big men and great men. Personification of power in Melanesia.* Cambridge Univ. Press, Cambridge, 28-47.

Lind, T. 1936. Fra Bornholms Museum. *Bornholmske Samlinger* Bd. 24, 240-53.

Lindqvist, C. 1997. Ansarve hage-dösen. Tvärvetenskapliga aspekter på context och den neolitiska förändringen på Gotland. In Åkerlund, A., Bergh, S., Nordbladh, J. & Taffinder, J. (eds) *Till Gunborg. Arkeologiska samtal.* Stockholm Archaeological Reports Nr 33, 361-78.

Lindqvist, C. & Possnert, G. 1997. The subsistence economy and diet at Jakobs/Ajvide and Stora Förvar, Ekstra Parish and other Prehistoric dwelling and burial sites on Gotland in long-term perspective. In Burenhult, G. (ed.) *Remote Sensing,* Vol. I. Theses and Papers in North European Archaeology 13:a, Stockholm, 29-90.

Linton, R. 1936. *The Study of Man.* D. Appleton-Century Company, N.Y.

Lipson, M. *et al.* (57 authors) 2017. Parallel palaeogenomic transects reveal complex genetic history of early European farmers. *Nature* 551, 368-372.

Liversage, D. 1981. Neolithic Monuments at Lindebjerg, Northwest Zealand. *Acta Archaeologica* 51, 1980, 85-152.

Liversage, D. 1992. *Barkær. Long Barrows and Settlements.* Arkæologiske Studier IX, København.

Lübke, H. 1998. Die dicken Flintspitzen aus Schleswig-Holstein. Ein Beitrag zur Typologie und Chronologie eines Grossgerätetyps der Trichterbecherkultur. *Offa* 54/55, 1997/98, 49-95.

Lübke, H. 2005. Ergänzende Anmerkungen zur Datierung der Einbäume des endmesolithisch/frühneolithischen Fundplatzes Stralsund-Mischwasserspeicher. *Bodendenkmalpflege in Mecklenburg-Vorpommern, Jahrbuch* 52, 2004, 257-61.

Lübke, H., Lüth, F. & Terberger, T. 2009. Fischers or farmers? The archaeology of the Ostorf cemetery and related Neolithic finds in the light of new data. *Bericht der Römisch-Germanischen Kommission* 88, 2007, 307-38.

Madsen, A.P. 1868. *Afbildninger af Danske Oldsager og Mindesmærker. Stenalderen.* København.

Madsen, B. 1984. Flint Axe Manufacture in the Neolithic: Experiments with Grinding and Polishing of Thin-Butted Flint Axes. *Journal of Danish Archaeology* 3, 47-62.

Madsen, T. 1975. Tidlig-neolitiske anlæg ved Tolstrup. *Kuml* 1973-74 (1975), 121-154.

Madsen, T. 1978. Toftum ved Horsens. Et "befæstet" anlæg tilhørende tragtbægerkulturen. *Kuml* 1977, 161-84.

Madsen, T. 1982. Settlement Systems of Early Agricultural Societies in East Jutland, Denmark: A Regional Study of Change. *Journal of Anthropological Archaeology* 1, 197-236.

Madsen, T. 1990. Changing patterns of land use in the TRB Culture of South Scandinavia. In Jankowska, D. (ed.) *Die Trichterbecherkultur. Neue Forschungen und Hypothesen. Material des Internationalen Symposiums Dymaczewo, 20-24 September 1988,* Teil I, Poznań, 27-41.

Madsen, T. 1991. The social structure of Early Neolithic society in South Scandinavia. In Lichardus, J. (ed.) *Die Kupferzeit als historische Epoche. Symposium Saarbrücken und Otzenhausen 6.-13.11.1988.* Saarbrücker Beiträge zur Altertumskunde 55, Rudolf Habelt, Bonn, 489-96.

Madsen, T. 1994. Die Gruppenbildung im frühesten Neolithikum Dänemarks und ihre Bedeutung. In Hoika, J. (ed.) *Beiträge zur frühneolithischen Trichterbecherkultur im westlichen Ostseegebiet. 1. Internatio-*

nale Trichterbechersymposium in Schleswig vom 4. bis 7. März 1985. Untersuchungen und Materialien zur Steinzeit in Schleswig-Holstein 1, 227-37. Neumünster.

Madsen, T. 2019. Pots for the ancestors. The structure and meaning of pottery depositions at passage graves. In Müller, J., Hinz, H. & Wunderlich, M. (eds) *Megaliths – Societies – Landscapes. Early monumentality and Social Differentiation in Neolithic Europe* Vol. 3. Frühe Monumentalität und soziale Differenzierung 18. Institut für Ur- und Frühgeschichte der CAU Kiel / Verlag Dr. Rudolf Habelt, Bonn, 893-920.

Madsen, T. & Jensen, H.J. 1982. Settlement and land use in Early Neolithic Denmark. *Analecta Praehistorica Leidensia* 15, 63-86.

Madsen, T. & Petersen, J.E. 1984. Tidligneolitiske anlæg ved Mosegården. Regionale og kronologiske forskelle i tidligneolitikum. *Kuml* 1982-83 (1984), 61-120.

Malmer, M.P. 1962. *Jungneolithische Studien*. Acta Archaeologica Lundensia, Series in 8º, Nº 2. Lund.

Malmer, M.P. 2002. *The Neolithic of South Sweden, TRB, GRK, and STR*. The Royal Swedish Academy of Letters, History and Antiquities, Stockholm.

Malinowski, B. 1922. *Argonauts of the Western Pacific*. Studies in economics and political science no. 65, London.

Marolle, C. 1989. Le village michelsberg des Hautes Chanvières à Mairy (Ardennes), I. Étude préliminaire des principales structures. *Gallia préhistoire* 31, 93-117.

Marolle, C. 1998. Le site de Michelsberg des "Hautes Chanvières" avec bâtiments et enceinte à Mairy, Ardennes – France. In Biel, J., Schlichtherle, H., Strobel, M. & Zeeb, A. (eds) *Die Michelsberger Kultur und ihre Randgebiete. Probleme der Entstehung, Chronologie und das Siedlungswesens. Kolloquium Hemmenhofen, 1997 (Jens Lüning zum 60. Geburtstag)*. Materialhefte zur Archäologie in Baden-Württemberg 43, 21-28.

Mathiassen, T. 1948. *Danske Oldsager I, Ældre Stenalder*. Gyldendal / Nordisk Forlag, København.

Mathieson, I. et al. (38 authors) 2015. Genome-wide patterns of selection in 230 ancient Eurasians. *Nature* 528, 499-503.

Mauss, M. 1990. *The Gift. The form and reason for exchange in archaic societies*. Routledge, London.

Meurers-Balke, J. 1983. *Siggeneben-Süd. Ein Fundplatz der frühen Trichterbecherkultur an der holsteinischen Ostseeküste*. Offa-Bücher 50, Neumünster.

Meyer, M. & Raetsel-Fabian, D. 2006. *Neolithische Erdwerke im Überblick*. www.jungsteinSITE.de

Midgley, M.S. 1985. *The Origin and Function of the Earthen Long Barrows of Northern Europe*. BAR International Series 259. Oxford.

Midgley, M. 1992. *TRB Culture. The First Farmers of the North European Plain*. Edinburgh Univ. Press, Edinburgh.

Midgley, M.S. 1997. The Earthen Long Barrow Phenomenon of Northern Europe and its Relation to the Passy-Type Monuments of France. In Constatin, C., Mordant, D. & Simonin, D. (eds) *La Culture de Cerny. Nouvelle économie, nouvelle société au Néolithique. Actes du Colloque International de Nemours 9-10-11 mai 1994*. A.P.R.A.I.F, Nemours, 679-85.

Midgley, M.S. 2000. The Earthen Long Barrow Phenomenon in Europe: Creation of Monumental Cemeteries. *Památky archeologické – Supplementum* 13 (*In Memoriam Jan Rulf*). Prague, 255-65.

Midgley, M.S. 2011. Early farming and the creation of community: the case of northern Europe. In Hadjikoumis, A., Robinson, E. & Viner, S. (eds) *The Dynamics of Neolithisation in Europe. Studies in honour of Andrew Sherratt*. Oxbow Books, Oxford, 264-89.

Mikkelsen, V.M. 1954. Studies in the sub-atlantic history of Bornholm's vegetation. In *Studies in Vegetational History in honour of Knud Jessen*. Danmarks Geologiske Undersøgelse II. Række. Nr. 80, 210-29.

Mikkelsen, V.M. 1966. Bornholms natur, beboere og naturfredning gennem tiderne. *Bornholmske Samlinger* II:2, 9-47.

Mikkelsen, V.M. 1991. *Borrelyngen on Bornholm, Denmark. A heath on rocky ground. Exploitation and vegetation from antiquity to the present day*. The Royal Danish Academy of Sciences and Letters, Biologiske Skrifter 38. Copenhagen.

Milisauskas, S. & Kruk, J. 1982. Die Wagendarstellung auf einem Trichterbecher aus Bronocice in Polen. *Archäologisches Korrespondenzblatt* 12, 141-44.

Milthers, V. 1930. *Bornholms Geologi*. Danmarks Geologiske Undersøgelse. V. Række, Nr. 1.

Mischka, D., Furholt, M., Hinz, M., Noble, G. & Olausson, D. 2014. Foreword: Landscapes, Histories and Societies in the northern European Neolithic. In Furholt, M., Hinz, M., Mischka, D., Noble, G. & Olausson, D. (eds) *Landscapes, Histories and Societies in the Northern European Neolithic*. Frühe Monumentalität und soziale Differenzierung, Band 4, Bonn, 11-16.

Mischka, D., Roth, G. & Struckmeyer, K. 2015a. Michelsberg and Oxie in contact next to the Baltic Sea. In Kabaciński, J., Hartz, S., Raemaekers, D.C.M. & Terberger, T. (eds) *The Dąbki Site in Pomerania and the Neolithisation of the North European Lowlands (c. 5000-3000 calBC)*. Archäologie und Geschichte im Ostseeraum 8, Rahden/Westfahlen, 465-78.

Mischka, D., Roth, G. & Struckmeyer, K. 2015b. Michelsberg and Oxie in contact next to the Baltic Sea. In Brink, K., Hydén, S., Jennbert, K., Larsson, L. & Olausson, D. (eds) *Neolithic Diversities. Perspectives from a conference in Lund, Sweden*. Acta Archaeologica Lundensia Series in 8º, No. 65, 241-50.

Montelius, O. 1899. *Der Orient und Europa* I, Stockholm.

Mordant, D. 1997. Le complexe des Réaudins à Balloy: Enceinte et nécropole monumentale. In Constantin, C., Mordant, D. & Simonin, D. (eds) *La Culture de Cerny. Nouvelle économie, nouvelle société au Néolithique. Actes du Colloque International de Nemours 9-10-11 mai 1994*. Mémoires du Musée Préhistoire d'Ile-de-France nº 6. Nemours, 449-79.

Müller, J. 2001. *Soziochronologische Studien zum Jung- und Spätneolithikum in Mittelelbe-Saale-Gebiet (4100-2700 v.Chr.). Eine sozialhistorische Interpretation prähistorischer Quellen.* Vorgeschichtliche Forschungen 21, Rahden/Westf.

Müller, J. 2004. Zur Innovationsbereitschaft mitteleuropäischer Gesellschaften im 4. Vorchristlichen Jahrtausend. In Fansa, M. & Burmeister, S. (eds) *Rad und Wagen. Der Ursprung einer Innovation. Wagen im Vorderen Orient und Europa.* Philipp von Zabern, Mainz a.R., 255-64.

Müller, J. 2011a. Early pottery in the North – a southern perspective. In Hartz, S., Lüth, F. & Terberger, T. (eds) Frühe Keramik im Ostseeraum – Datierung und Sozialer Kontext. Internationaler Workshop in Schleswig vom 20. bis 21. Oktober 2006. *Bericht der Römisch-Germanischen Kommission,* 89, 2008, 287-99.

Müller, J. 2011b. *Megaliths and Funnel Beakers: Societies in Change 4000-2700 BC.* Drieendertigste Kroon-Vordracht, gehouden voor de Stichting Nederlands Museum voor Anthropologie en Praehistorie te Amsterdam op 8 april 2011. Amsterdam.

Müller, S. 1886. Votivfund fra Sten- og Bronzealder. *Aarbøger for nordisk Oldkyndighed og Historie* 1886, 216-51.

Müller, S. 1888. *Ordning af Danmarks Oldsager. Stenalderen.* Kjøbenhavn.

Müller, S. 1913. Sønderjyllands Stenalder. *Aarbøger for nordisk Oldkyndighed og Historie* 1913, 169-322.

Müller, S. 1918. *Oldtidens Kunst i Danmark. Stenalderens Kunst.* Kjøbenhavn.

Münther, V. 1945. Sprækkedale og Diabasintrusioner på Bornholm. *Meddelelser fra Danmarks geologiske Forening* 10.5, 641-45.

Nickel, C. 1998. Michelsberger Skelettreste – Gräber ... oder was sonst? In Biel, J., Schlichtherle, H., Strobel, M. & Zeeb, A. (eds) *Die Michelsberger Kultur und ihre Randgebiete – Probleme der Entstehung, Chronologie und des Siedlungswesens. Kolloquium Hemmenhofen, 21.-23.2.1997 (Jens Lüning zum 60. Geburtstag).* Materialhefte zur Archäologie in Baden-Württemberg 43, Stuttgart, 151-58.

Nielsen, A.V. 1967. Landskabets Tilblivelse. In *Danmarks Natur* Bind 1, Politikens Forlag, København, 251-344.

Nielsen, F.O. 1988. Bornholms bebyggelse i yngre stenalder – et forskningsprojekt. *Fra Bornholms Museum* 1987-1988, 63-72.

Nielsen, F.O. 1989. Nye fund fra stridsøksetiden på Bornholm. In Larsson, L. (ed.) *Stridsyxekultur i Sydskandinavien. Rapport från det andra nordiska symposiet om Stridsyxetid i Sydskandinavien 31.X – 2.XI 1988.* University of Lund Institute of Archaeology, Report Series No. 36, 89-101.

Nielsen, F.O.S. 1996a. *Forhistoriske interesser.* Bornholms Amt, Teknisk Forvaltning, Rønne.

Nielsen, F.O.S. 1996b. Før Aakirkeby blev købstad. Arkæologiske efterretninger om fund fra oldtid og tidlig middelalder. *Bornholmske Samlinger* III Rk. 10. Bd., 197-216.

Nielsen, F.O. 1997. The Neolithic Settlement on Bornholm. In Król, D. (ed.) *The Built Environment of Coast Areas during the Stone Age. The Baltic Sea-Coast Landscapes Seminar, Session No. 1,* 119-127. Gdansk.

Nielsen, F.O.S. 2001. Nyt om Maglemosekultur på Bornholm. In Lass Jensen, O., Sørensen, S.A. & Møller Hansen, K. (eds) *Danmarks Jægerstenalder – status og perspektiver,* 85-99. Hørsholm Egns Museum.

Nielsen, F.O.S. 2006a. Bornholms Museums antikvariske arbejde 2004-2005. *Bornholms Museum – Bornholms Kunstmuseum* 2004-2005, 39-72.

Nielsen, F.O. 2006b. *Fortidsminder på Bornholm.* Bornholms Regionskommune, Natur & Miljø, Allinge.

Nielsen, F.O. & Nielsen, P.O. 1986a. En boplads med hustomter fra mellem- og senneolitikum ved Limensgård, Bornholm. In Adamsen, C. & Ebbesen, K. (eds) *Stridsøksetid i Sydskandinavien.* Arkæologiske Skrifter 1, 175-193. København.

Nielsen, F.O. & Nielsen, P.O. 1986b. Stenalderhuse ved Limensgård på Bornholm. *Nationalmuseets Arbejdsmark* 1986, 36-48.

Nielsen, F.O. & Nielsen, P.O. 1990. The Funnel Beaker Culture on Bornholm. In Jankowska, D. (ed.) *Die Trichterbecherkultur – Neue Forschungen und Hypothesen. Material des Internationalen Symposiums Dymaczewo, 20 – 24 September 1988.* Teil I, 54-72. Poznań.

Nielsen, F.O. & Nielsen, P.O. 1991. The Middle Neolithic Settlement at Grødbygård, Bornholm. A local society in times of change. In Jennbert, K., Larsson, L., Petré, R. & Wyszomirska-Werbart, B. (eds) *Regions and Reflections in Honour of Märta Strömberg.* Acta Archaeologica Lundensia Ser. in 8, No 20, 51-65. Lund.

Nielsen, F.O. & Nielsen, P.O. 2019. Two-aisled houses from the Early, Middle and Late Neolithic on Bornholm. In Sparrevohn, L.R., Kastholm, O.T. & Nielsen, P.O. (eds) *Houses for the Living. Two-aisled Houses from the Neolithic and Early Bronze Age in Denmark.* Nordiske Fortidsminder Vol. 31:1. The Royal Society of Northern Antiquaries, Copenhagen, 95-113.

Nielsen, F.O. & Nielsen, P.O. in prep. *Limensgård. Houses from the Early, Middle and Late Neolithic on Bornholm.*

Nielsen, J.N. 2000. *Sejlflod – ein eisenzeitlisches Dorf in Nordjütland,* I-II. Nordiske Fortidsminder Serie B, Vol. 20:1-2. København.

Nielsen, P.O. 1977. Die Flintbeile der frühen Trichterbecherkultur in Dänemark. *Acta Archaeologica* vol. 48, 61-138.

Nielsen, P.O. 1979. De tyknakkede flintøksers kronologi. *Aarbøger for nordisk Oldkyndighed og Historie* 1977, 5-71.

Nielsen, P.O. 1984. Flint Axes and Megaliths – the Time and Context of the Early Dolmens in Denmark. In Burenhult, G. (ed.) *The Archaeology of Carrowmore. Environmental Archeology and the Megalithic Tradition at Carrowmore, Co. Sligo, Ireland.* Theses and Papers in North-European Archaeology 14, Stockholm, 376-87.

Nielsen, P.O. 1985a. De første bønder. Nye fund fra den tidligste tragtbægerkultur ved Sigersted. *Aarbøger for Nordisk Oldkyndighed og Historie* 1984, 96-126.

Nielsen, P.O. 1985b. Review of Jutta Meurers-Balke: Siggeneben-Süd. Ein Fundplatz der frühen Trichterbecherkultur an der holsteinischen Ostseeküste. Offa-Bücher 50, Neumünster. *Journal of Danish Archaeology* 4, 202-03.

Nielsen, P.O. 1989. Neolitiske bopladser. Udgravningsmetodiske eksempler fra nye undersøgelser. *Arkæologiske udgravninger i Danmark* 1988, 11-32. København.

Nielsen, P.O. 1994. Sigersted und Havnelev. Zwei Siedlungen der frühen Trichterbecherkultur auf Seeland. In Hoika, J. (ed.) *Beiträge zur frühneolithischen Trichterbecherkultur im westlichen Ostseegebiet. 1. Internationale Trichterbechersymposium in Schleswig vom 4. bis 7. März 1985*. Untersuchungen und Materialien zur Steinzeit in Schleswig-Holstein 1, 289-324. Neumünster.

Nielsen, P.O. 1997. Keeping Battle-Axe People away from the Door: Neolithic House-Sites at Limensgård and Grødbygård, Bornholm. In Król, D. (ed.) *The Built Environment of Coast Areas during the Stone Age. The Baltic Sea-Coast Landscapes Seminar, Session No. 1*, 196-208. Gdansk.

Nielsen, P.O. 1998. De ældste langhuse. Fra toskibede til treskibede huse i Norden. *Bebyggelsehistorisk tidskrift* Nr. 33, 1997, s. 9-30. Borås 1998.

Nielsen, P.O. 1999. Limensgård and Grødbygård. Settlements with house remains from the Early, Middle and Late Neolithic on Bornholm. In Fabech, C. & Ringtved, J. (eds) *Settlement and Landscape. Proceedings of a conference in Århus, Denmark, May 4-7 1998*, 149-165. Jutland Archaeological Society / Aarhus University Press.

Nielsen, P.O. 2004. Causewayed camps, palisade enclosures and central settlements of the Middle Neolithic in Denmark. *Journal of Nordic Archaeological Science* 14, 19-33.

Nielsen, P.O. 2009. Den tidligneolitiske bosættelse på Bornholm. In Schülke, A. (ed.) *Plads og rum i tragtbægerkulturen. Bidrag fra Arbejdsmødet på Nationalmuseet, 22. september 2005*. Nordiske Fortidsminder Ser. C, bind 6, 9-24. Det Kongelige Nordiske Oldskriftselskab, København.

Nielsen, P.O. 2019. The development of the two-aisled longhouse during the Neolithic and Early Bronze Age. In Sparrevohn, L., Kastholm, O.T. & Nielsen, P.O. (eds) *Houses for the Living. Two-aisled longhouses from the Neolithic and Early Bronze Age in Denmark*. Nordiske Fortidsminder Vol. 31:1, 95-113. The Royal Society of Northern Antiquaries, Copenhagen / University Press of Southern Denmark.

Nielsen, P.O., Andresen, J. & Thorsen, M.S. 2015. Vasagård på Bornholm – palisader, solsten og et 4.900 år gammelt, dekoreret kulthus. *Nationalmuseets Arbejdsmark* 2015, 50-63.

Nielsen, P.O. & Nielsen, F.O.S. 2014a. De første bønder på Bornholm. In Nielsen, P.O., Nielsen, F.O.S. & Adamsen, C. (eds) *Solstensøen. På sporet af Bornholms bondestenalder*. Bornholms Museum, Nationalmuseet & Wormianum, Rønne, 15-46.

Nielsen, P.O. & Nielsen, F.O.S. 2014b. Grødby. Toskibede huse og runde anlæg. In Nielsen, P.O., Nielsen, F.O.S. & Adamsen, C. (eds) *Solstensøen. På sporet af Bornholms bondestenalder*. Bornholms Museum, Nationalmuseet & Wormianum, Rønne, 119-50.

Nielsen, P.O. & Nielsen, F.O.S. 2014c. Limensgård. Storbyggeri i flere faser. In Nielsen, P.O., Nielsen, F.O.S. & Adamsen, C. (eds) *Solstensøen. På sporet af Bornholms bondestenalder*. Bornholms Museum, Nationalmuseet & Wormianum, Rønne, 159-86.

Nielsen, P.O. & Paulsen, H. 2014. At bygge og bo i et stenalderhus. In Nielsen, P.O., Nielsen, F.O.S. & Adamsen, C. (eds) *Solstensøen. På sporet af Bornholms bondestenalder*. Bornholms Museum, Nationalmuseet & Wormianum, Rønne, 151-58.

Nielsen, P.O., Nielsen, F.O.S. & Thorsen, M.S. 2014a. Vasagård. Stenalderbøndernes samlingsplads ved Læsåen. In Nielsen, P.O., Nielsen, F.O.S. & Adamsen, C. (eds) *Solstensøen. På sporet af Bornholms bondestenalder*. Bornholms Museum, Nationalmuseet & Wormianum, Rønne, 81-103.

Nielsen, P.O., Nielsen, F.O.S. & Thorsen, M.S. 2014b. Rispebjerg. En centralplads fra sen tragtbægerkultur. In Nielsen, P.O., Nielsen, F.O.S. & Adamsen, C. (eds) *Solstensøen. På sporet af Bornholms bondestenalder*. Bornholms Museum, Nationalmuseet & Wormianum, Rønne, 107-18.

Nielsen, P.O. & Sørensen, L. 2018. The Formation of Social Rank in the Early Neolithic of Northern Europe. *Acta Archaeologica* vol. 89, 15-29.

Nielsen, S. 1975. Et nyt fund af en øskenkrukke fra havet ved Bornholm. *Bornholmske Samlinger*, 2. Rk., Bd. 8, 79-84.

Niesiołowska, E. 1994. Einige Probleme der frühen Trichterbecherkultur in Polen. Die Sarnowo-Stufe und die Pikutkowo-Phase. In Hoika, J. (ed.) *Beiträge zur frühneolithischen Trichterbecherkultur im westlichen Ostseegebiet. 1. Internationale Trichterbechersymposium in Schleswig vom 4. bis 7. März 1985*. Untersuchungen und Materialien zur Steinzeit in Schleswig-Holstein 1, 32546. Neumünster.

Noe-Nygaard, N., Price, T.D. & Hede, S.U. 2005. Diet of aurochs and early cattle in southern Scandinavia: evidence from ^{15}N and ^{13}C stable isotopes. *Journal of Archaeological Science* 32, 855-71.

Nordqvist, B. 1997. See Kihlstedt, B. et al. 1997.

Nordquist, P. 2001. *Hierarkiseringsprocesser. Om konstruktionen av social ojämlikhet i Skåne, 5500-1100 f. Kr.* Studia Archaeologica Universitatis Umensis 13. Arkeologiska institutionen, Umeå universitet.

Nyegaard, G. 1985. Faunalevn fra yngre stenalder på øerne syd for Fyn. In Skaarup, J., *Yngre stenalder på øerne syd for Fyn*. Langelands Museum, Rudkøbing, 426-66.

O'Kelley, M.J. 1982. *Newgrange. Archaeology, art and legend*. Thames and Hudson, London.

Olausson, D.S. 1983a. Lithic Technological Analysis

of the Thin-butted Flint Axe. *Acta Archaeologica* 53, 1982, 1-87.

Olausson, D.S. 1983b. *Flint and groundstone axes in the Scanian Neolithic. An evaluation of raw materials based on experiment.* Scripta Minora, Regiae Societatis Humaniorum Litterarum Lundensis, 1982-1983:2. Lund.

Olausson, D. 1997. Craft specialization as an agent of social power in the South Scandinavian Neolithic. In Schild, R. & Sulgostowska, Z. (eds) *Man and Flint. Proceedings of the VIIth International Flint Symposium Warszawa – Ostrowiec Świętokrzyski, September 1995.* Institute of Archaeology and Ethnology, Polish Academy of Sciences, Warszawa, 269-77.

Olausson, D. 2000. Talking Axes, Social Daggers. In Olausson, D. & Vandkilde, H. (eds) *Form Function & Context. Material culture studies in Scandinavian archaeology.* Acta Archaeologica Lundensia Series in 8°, No. 31, Lund, 121-33.

Österholm, I. 1989. *Bosätningsmönstret på Gotland under stenåldern. En analys av fysisk miljö, ekonomi och social struktur.* Theses and Papers in Archaeology 3, Stockholm.

Österholm, S. 1997. Forntidens båtar – ett försök med eksperimentell arkeologi. In Burenhult, G. (ed.) *Ajvide och den moderna arkeologin.* Natur och Kultur, Falköping, 161-71.

Oswald, A., Dyer, C. & Barber, M. 2001. *The Creation of Monuments. Neolithic Causewayed Enclosures in the British Isles.* English Heritage, Swindon.

Papiernik, P. 2012. Sprawozdanie z badań wykopaliskowych na stanowisku 20 w Redczu Krukowym, pow. Włocławski, woj. Kujawsko-Pomorskie. *Prace i Materiały Muzeum Archeologicznego i Etnograficznego w Łodzi,* Seria Archeologiczna nr. 45, 2010-2012, 195-238.

Papiernik, P. & Płaza, D.K. 2018. *Od epoki kamienia do współczesności. Badania archeologiczne w Redczu Krukowym na Kujawac.* Wydawnictwo Fundacji Badań Archeologicznych Imiena Profesora Konrada Jażdżewskiego 26. Łódź.

Patton, M.A. 1991. Axes, Men and Women: Symbolic Dimensions of Neolithic Exchange in Armorica (northwest France). In Garwood, P., Jennings, D., Skeates, R. & Toms, J. (eds) *Sacred and Profane. Proceedings of a Conference on Archaeology, Ritual and Religion, Oxford 1989.* Oxford University Committee for Archaeology, Monograph No. 32, Oxford, 65-79.

Patton, M. 1993. *Statements in Stone. Monuments and Society in Neolithic Brittany.* Routledge, London and N.Y.

Pedersen, L. 1997. They put fences in the sea. In Pedersen, L., Fischer, A. & Aaby, B. (eds) *The Danish Storebælt since the Ice Age – man, sea and forest.* Copenhagen, A/S Storebælt Fixed Link, 124-43.

Persson, P. 1998. *Neolitikums början. Undersökningar kring jordbrukets introduktion i Nordeuropa.* Göteborg, Institutionen för arkeologi.

Petersen, E.B. see Brinch Petersen, E.

Petersen, K.S. 1993. Environmental changes recorded in the Holocene molluscan faunas from Djursland, Denmark. *Scripta Geologica, Special Issue* 2, 359-69. Leyden.

Petersen, P.V. 2001. Grisby – en fangstboplads fra Ertebølletid på Bornholm. In O. Lass Jensen, S. A. Sørensen & K. Møller Hansen (eds) *Danmarks jægerstenalder – status og perspektiver.* Hørsholm Egns Museum, 161-174.

Petersson, H. 1999. Where did all the farmers come from? *Journal of Danish Archaeology* 13, 1996-97, 179-90.

Petersson, H. 2009. The processual legacy and new directions in Scandinavian Neolithic research. In Glørstad, H. & Prescott, C. (eds) *Neolithisation as if history mattered. Processes of Neolithisation in North-Western Europe,* 169-91. Bricoleur Press, Lindome.

Petré, R. & Strömberg, M. 1958. Prehistoric and Mediaeval settlements sites at Råga Hörstad, Asmundtorp. *Meddelanden från Lunds Universitets Historiska Museum,* 52-90.

Pétrequin, P., Gauthier, E. & Pétrequin, A.-M. 2010. Les haches en silex de type Glis-Weisweil en France, en Suisse et en Allemagne du Sud-Ouest. Des imitations de haches alpines à la transition V^e-IVe millénaires av. J.-C. In Matuschik, I., Strahm, C., Eberschweiler, B., Fingerlin, G., Hafner, A., Kinsky, M., Mainberger, M. & Schöbel, G. (eds) *Vernetzungen. Aspekte siedlungsarchäologischer Forschung. Festschrift für Helmut Schlichtherle zum 60. Geburtstag.* Freiburg im Breisgau, 237-52.

Pétrequin, P. et al. 2012a. Pétrequin, P., Cassen, S., Errera, M., Klassen, L., Sheridan, A. & Pétrequin, A.-M. (eds) 2012. *JADE. Grande haches alpines du Néolithique européen. V^e et IVe millénaires av. J.-C.* Tome 1-2. Besançon.

Pétrequin, P. et al. 2012b. Pétrequin, P., Cassen, S., Klassen, L. & Valcarce, R.F. 2012. La circulation des haches carnacéennes en Europe occidentale. In Pétrequin, P., Cassen, S., Errera, M., Klassen, L., Sheridan, A. & Pétrequin, A.-M. (eds) *Jade. Grande haches alpines du Néolithique européen. V^e et IVe millénaires av. J.-C.* Tome 2. Besançon, 1015-1045.

Pickard, C. & Bonsall, C. 2007. Late Mesolithic coastal fishing practices. The evidence from Tybrind Vig, Denmark. In Hård, B., Jennbert, K. & Olausson, D. (eds) *On the road. Studies in honour of Lars Larsson.* Acta Archaeologica Lundensia in 4°, No. 26. Almqvist & Wiksell, Stockholm, 176-83.

Pitts, M. 1996. The Stone Axe in Neolithic Britain. *Proceedings of the Prehistoric Society* 62, 311-71.

Pollex, A. 1998. Ein neolithisches Rinderskelett von Penkun, Lkr. Uecker-Randow. Bemerkungen zur Interpretation sogenannter Rinderbestattungen. *Bodendenkmalpflege in Mecklenburg-Vorpommern, Jahrbuch* 1997, Bd. 45, 103-128.

Pospieszny, Ł. 2010. Living with the Ancestors: Neolithic Burial Mounds of the Polish Lowlands. In Kiel Graduate School "Human Development in Landscapes" (ed.) *Landscapes and Human Development: The Contribution of European Archaeology. Proceedings of* the International Workshop "Socio-Environmental Dynamics over the last 12,000 Years: The Creation of Landscapes (1st-4th April 2009)". Universitätsforschungen zur prähistorischen Archäologie 191. Rudolf Habelt, Bonn, 143-57.

Preuß, J. 1966. *Die Baalberger Gruppe in Mitteldeutschland*. Veröffentlichungen des Landesmuseum für Vorgeschichte in Halle 21, Berlin.

Price, T.D. 1996. The first farmers of southern Scandinavia. In Harris, D.R. (ed.) *The origins and spread of agriculture and pastoralism in Eurasia*. London, 346-62.

Price, T.D. 2000. The introduction of farming in Northern Europe. In Price, T.D. (ed.) *Europe's First Farmers*. Cambridge University Press, Cambridge, 260-300.

Price, T.D. 2015. *Ancient Scandinavia. An Archaeological History from the First Humans to the Vikings*. Oxford Univ. Press, Oxford.

Price, T.D., Ambrose, S.H., Bennike, P., Heinemeier, J., Noe-Nygaard, N., Petersen, E.B., Petersen, P.V. & Richards, M.P. 2007. New Information on the Stone Age Graves at Dragsholm, Denmark. *Acta Archaeologica* 78:2, 193-219.

Price, T.D. & Bar-Yosef, O. 2010. Traces of Inequality at the Origins of Agriculture in the Ancient Near East. In Price, T.D. & Feinman, G.M. (eds) *Pathways to Power. New Perspectives on the Emergence of Social Inequality*. Fundamental Issues in Archaeology. Springer, N.Y./Dordrecht/Heidelberg/London, 147-68.

Price, T.D. & Gebauer, A.B. (eds) 2005. *Smakkerup Huse. A Late Mesolithic Coastal Site in Northwest Zealand, Denmark*. Aarhus University Press, Århus.

Price, T.D. & Gebauer, A.B. 2017. The Emergence of Social Inequality in the Context of Early Neolithic Northern Europe. In Hansen, S. & Müller, J. (eds) *Rebellion and Inequality in Archaeology*. Human Development in Landscapes 11. Universitätsforschungen zur prähistorischen Archäologie 308, Habelt, Bonn, 135-52.

Price, T.D. & Noe-Nygaard, N. 2009. Early Domestic Cattle in Southern Scandinavia and the Spread of the Neolithic in Europe. In Finlay, N., McCartan, S., Milner, N. & Wickham-Jones, C. (eds) *From Bann Flakes to Bushmills. Papers in honour of professor Peter Woodman*. Oxford Books, Oxford, 198-210.

Randsborg, K. 1974. Social Stratification in Early Bronze Age Denmark: a Study in the Regulation of Cultural Systems. *Praehistorische Zeitschrift* 49, 38-61.

Randsborg, K. 1975. Social Dimensions of Early Neolithic Denmark. *Proceedings of the Prehistoric Society* 41, 105-18.

Randsborg, K. 1979. Resource distribution and the function of copper in Early Neolithic Denmark. In Ryan, M. (ed.) *Proceedings of the Fifth Atlantic Colloquium*, Dublin, 303-18.

Rasmussen, K.L. 1993. Radiocarbon Datings from the Bjørnsholm Site, North Jutland. *Journal of Danish Archaeology* 10, 93-96.

Rasmussen, P. 2005. Mid- to late-Holocene land-use change and lake development at Dallund Sø, Denmark: vegetation and land-use history inferred from pollen data. *The Holocene* 15.8, 1116-29.

Rasmussen, P., Hansen, H.J. & Nielsen, L.B. 1998. Kulturlandskabets udvikling i et langtidsperspektiv. To sjællandske områder gennem de sidste 6000 år. *Nationalmuseets Arbejdsmark* 1998, 101-14.

Ravn, M. 2011. The Early Neolithic Volling site of Kildevang – its chronology and intra-spacial organisation. In Hartz, S., Lüth, F. & Terberger, T. (eds) Frühe Keramik im Ostseeraum – Datierung und Sozialer Kontext. Internationaler Workshop in Schleswig vom 20. bis 21. Oktober 2006. *Bericht der Römisch-Germanischen Kommission* 89, 2008 (2011), 135-63.

Ravn, M. 2012. Kildevang – en tidligneolitisk Volling boplads i Østjylland. In Kaul, F. & Sørensen, L. (eds) *Agrarsamfundenes ekspansion i nord. Symposium på Tanums Hällristningsmuseum, Underslös, Bohuslän, d. 25.-29. maj 2011*. Nordlige Verdener, Nationalmuseet, København, 31-43.

Rech, M. 1979. *Studien zu Depotfunden der Trichterbecher- und Einzelgrabkultur des Nordens*. Offa-Bücher Band 39. Karl Wachholtz Verlag, Neumünster.

Reimer, P.J., Bard, E., Bayliss, A., Beck, J.W., Blackwell, P.G., Bronk Ramsey, C., Buck, C.E., Cheng, H., Edwards, R.L., Friedrich, M., Grootes, P.M., Guilderson, T.P., Haflidason, H., Hajdas, I., Hatté, C., Heaton, T.J., Hogg, A.G., Hughen, K.A., Kaiser, K.F., Kromer, B., Manning, S.W., Niu, M., Reimer, R.W., Richards, D.A., Scott, E.M., Southon, J.R., Turney, C.S.M., van der Plicht, J. 2013. IntCal13 and MARINE13 radiocarbon age calibration curves 0-50000 years cal BP. *Radiocarbon* 55(4), 1869-87.

Renfrew, C. 1973. *Before Civilization. The Radiocarbon Revolution and Prehistoric Europe*. Jonathan Cape, London.

Renfrew, C. 1977. Alternative models for exchange and spatial distribution. In Earle, T.K. & Ericson, J.E. (eds) *Exchanges systems in prehistory*. London, Academic, 71-90.

Renfrew, C. 1987. *Archaeology and Language. The Puzzle of Indo-European Origins*. Jonathan Cape, London.

Richards, M.P. & Koch, E. 2001. Neolitisk kost. Analyser af kvælstof-isotopen ^{15}N i menneskeskeletter fra yngre stenalder. *Aarbøger for nordisk Oldkyndighed og Historie* 1999, 7-17.

Robson, H.K., Steele, V.J., Meadows, J., Koch, E., Nielsen, P.O., Fischer, A., Hartz, S., Saul, H., Heron, C. & Craig, O. (in prep.). Organic residue analysis of Neolithic 'bog pots' demonstrates mixed processing of foodstuffs.

Rostholm, H. 1982. *Oldtiden på Herning-egnen*. Herning Museum, Herning.

Rowley-Conwy, P. 1984. The laziness of the short-distance hunter: the origins of agriculture in western Denmark. *Journal of Anthropological Archaeology* 3, 300-24 (reprinted in Fischer & Kristiansen 2002, 273-87).

Rowley-Conwy, P. 2003. No fixed abode? Nomadism in the northwest European neolithic. In Burenhult, G. & Westergaard, S. (eds) *Stones and bones: Formal disposal of the dead in Atlantic Europe during the Mesolithic-Neolithic interface 6000-3000 BC*. British Archaeological Reports, International Series 1201, 115-43. Oxford.

Rowley-Conwy, P. 2004. How the West Was Lost. A Reconsideration of Agricultural Origins in Britain, Ireland, and Southern Scandinavia. *Current Anthropology* 45, Supplement (Special Issue: Agricultural origins and dispersal into Europe), 83-113.

Rowley-Conwy, P. 2011. Westward Ho! The spread of agriculture from Central Europe to the Atlantic. *Current Anthropology* 52, 431-51.

Rowley-Conwy, P. 2014. Foragers and Farmers in Mesolithic/Neolithic Europe, 5500-3900 cal. BC: Beyond the anthropological comfort zone. In Foulds, F.W.F., Drinkall, H.C., Perri, A.R., Clinnick, D.T.G. & Walker, J.W.P. (eds) *Wild Things. Recent Advances in Palaeolithic and Mesolithic Research*. Oxbow Books, Oxford & Philadelphia.

Rudebeck, E. 1986. *Ängdala. Flintgruvor från yngre stenåldern, S. Sallerup. Utgrävningar 1977-81*. Rapport nr. 1, Malmö Museer, Malmö.

Rudebeck, E. 2000. *Tilling Nature, Harvesting Culture. Exploring Images of the Human Being in the Transition to Agriculture*. Acta Archaeologica Lundensia Series in 8°, No. 32. Stockholm.

Rudebeck, E. 2002a. En tidigneolitisk långhög i Kristineberg. In Larsson, L. (ed.) *Monumentala gravformer i det äldsta bondesamhället*. University of Lund, Department of Archaeology and Ancient History, Report Series No. 83, Lund, 77-109.

Rudebeck, E. 2002b. Likt och olikt i de sydskandinaviska långhögarna. In Larsson, L. (ed.) *Monumentala gravformer i det äldsta bondesamhället*. University of Lund, Department of Archaeology and Ancient History, Report Series No. 83, Lund, 119-46.

Rudebeck, E. 2010. I trästodernas skugga – monumentala möten i neolitiseringens tid. In Nilsson, B. & Rudebeck, E. (eds) *Arkeologiska och förhistoriska världer*. Malmö Museer, 83-251.

Rudebeck, E. & Macheridis, S. 2015. The proper way of dwelling at the Early Neolithic gathering site of Almhov in Scania, Sweden. In Brink, K., Hydén, S., Jennbert, K., Larsson, L. & Olausson, D. (eds) *Neolithic Diversities. Perspectives from a conference in Lund, Sweden*. Acta Archaeologica Lundensia Series in 8°, No. 65, 173-87.

Rydbeck, O. 1918. Slutna mark- og mossfynd från stenåldern i Lunds Universitets Historiska Museum. *Från Lunds Universitets Historiska Museum*, 1-66.

Rzepecki, S. 2004. *Społeczności środkowoneolititycznej kultury pucharów lejkowatych na Kujawach*. Uniwersytet im. Adama Mickiewicza w Poznaniu, Materiały do syntezy pradziejów Kujaw nr. 12, Poznań.

Rzepecki, S. 2011. *The Roots of Megalithism in the TRB Culture*. Łódź.

Rørdam, K. 1895. Beretning om en geologisk Undersøgelse paa "Frænnemark" ved Svaneke paa Bornholm. *Danmarks Geologiske Undersøgelse* Nr. 7, *Mindre Meddelelser* I, 3-14.

Sahlins, M.D. 1961. The segmentary lineage: an organization of predatory expansion. *American Anthropologist* 63, 322-45.

Sahlins, M.D. 1963. Poor man, rich man, big man, chief: Political types in Melanesia and Polynesia. *Comparative Studies in Society and History* vol. V:3, 285-303.

Sahlins, M.D. 1974. *Stone Age Economics*. Tavistock Publications, London.

Salomonsson, B. 1963. An Early Neolithic Settlement Site from S.W. Scania. *Meddelanden från Lunds Universitets Historiska Museum* 1962-63, 65-122.

Salomonsson, B. 1970. Die Värby-Funde. Ein Beitrag zur Kenntnis der ältesten Trichterbecherkultur in Schonen. *Acta Archaeologica* Vol. XLI, 1970, 55-95.

Scarre, C. 2007. Changing places: monuments and the Neolithic transition in western France. In Whittle, A. & Cummings, V. (eds) *Going over. The Mesolithic-Neolithic Transition in North-West Europe*. Proceedings of the British Academy 144, 243-61. Oxford Univ. Press, Oxford / N.Y.

Scarre, C. 2010. Westeuropa im 5. u. 4. Jahrtausend v. Chr. Ein Überblick. In Lichter, C. (ed.) *Jungsteinzeit im Umbruch. Die "Michelsberger Kultur" und Mitteleuropa vor 6000 Jahren*. Badisches Landesmuseum, Karlsruhe, 141-48.

Schenck, T. 2014. Hunter-gatherers with funnel-beakers: Experimental implications for the adoption of pottery in Early Neolithic Southern Norway. In Furholt, M., Hinz, M., Mischka, D., Noble, G. & Olausson, D. (eds) *Landscapes, Histories and Societies in the Northern European Neolithic*. Frühe Monumentalität und soziale Differenzierung, Band 4, Bonn, 275-88.

Schier, W. 2009. Extensiever Brandfeldbau und die Ausbreitung der neolithischen Wirtschaftweise in Mitteleuropa und Südskandinavien am ende des 5. Jahrtausend v.Chr. *Praehistorische Zeitschrift* 84 (1), 15-43.

Schoeninger, M.J., DeNiro, M.J. & Tauber, H. 1983. Stable nitrogen isotope ratios of bone collagen reflect marine and terrestrial components of prehistoric human diet, *Science* 220, 1381-83.

Schuldt, E. 1972. *Die mecklenburgischen Megalithgräber. Untersuchungen zu ihrer Architektur und Funktion*. Beiträge zur Ur- und Frühgeschichte der Bezirke Rostock, Schwerin und Neubrandenburg 6, Berlin.

Schülke, A. 2009. The social use of space during the Early Neolithic in Northwest Zealand. In Glørstad, H. & Prescott, C. (eds) *Neolithisation as if history mattered. Processes of Neolithisation in North-Western Europe*, 217-56. Bricoleur Press, Lindome.

Schülke, A. 2014. Three concepts of burying the dead – different types of megalithic monuments and their ritual and social significance. In Furholt, M., Hinz, M., Mischka, D., Noble, G. & Olausson, D. (eds) *Landscapes, Histories and Societies in the Northern Eu-*

ropean Neolithic. Frühe Monumentalität und soziale Differenzierung, Band 4, Bonn, 113-23.
Schülke, A. 2015. The diversity of settings. Ritual and social aspects of tradition and innovation in megalithic landscapes. In Brink, K., Hydén, S., Jennbert, K., Larsson, L. & Olausson, D. (eds) *Neolithic Diversities. Perspectives from a conference in Lund, Sweden*. Acta Archaeologica Lundensia Series in 8°, No. 65, 188-99.
Schulting, R.J. 1998. Sighting the sea: stable isotope evidence for the transition to farming in northwestern Europe. *Dokumenta Praehistorica* XXV, 203-18.
Schunke, T. & Viol, P. 2014. Die "Schiepziger Gruppe" – eine Fundlücke wird gefüllt. In Meller, H. & Friederich, S. (eds) *Salzmünde-Schiepzig – ein Ort, zwei Kulturen. Ausgrabungen an der Westumfahrung Halle (A143)*, Teil I. Archäologie in Sachsen-Anhalt, Sonderband 21/1, Halle (Saale), 113-21.
Schwabedissen, H. 1979. Die "Rosenhof-Gruppe". Ein neuer Fundkomplex des Frühneolithikums in Schleswig-Holstein. *Archäologisches Korrespondenzblatt* 9, 167-72.
Schwabedissen, H. 1981. Zwei frühneolithische Gefässe von Klenzau, Kreis Ostholstein, und deren Beziehung zur "Rosenhof-Gruppe." *Offa* 38, 41-51.
Service, E.R. 1971. *Primitive Social Organisation. An Evolutionary Perspective*. Studies in Anthropology. Random House, N.Y. (second edition).
Sheridan, A. 2010. The Neolithisation of Britain and Ireland: the Big Picture. In Finlayson, B. & Warren, G. (eds) *Landscapes in Transition*. Oxbow, Oxford, 89-105.
Sheridan, A. 2013. Early Neolithic Habitation Structures in Britain and Ireland: A Matter of Circumstance and Context. In Hofmann, D. & Smyth, J. (eds) *Tracking the Neolithic House in Europe. Sedentism, Architecture, and Practice*, 283-300. Springer, N.Y./Dordrecht/Heidelberg/London.
Sherratt, A. 1981. Plough and Pastoralism: aspects of the secondary products revolution. In Hodder, I., Isaac, G. & Hammond, N. (eds) *Pattern of the Past: Studies in honour of David Clarke*. Cambridge Univ. Press, Cambridge, 261-306.
Sherratt, A. 1990. The genesis of megaliths: monumentality, ethnicity and social complexity in Neolithic north-west Europe. *World Archaeology* 22:2, 147-67.
Sjögren, K.-G. 2003. *"Mångfalldige uhrminnes grafvar…" Megalitgravar och samhälle i Västsverige*. Gotarc series B. Gothenburg archaeological theses No. 27. Göteborg.
Sjögren, K.-G. 2012. Neolitisering i Västsverige – en översikt över källäget. In Kaul, F. & Sørensen, L. (eds) *Agrarsamfundenes ekspansion i nord. Symposium på Tanums Hällristningsmuseum, Underslös, Bohuslän, d. 25.-29. maj 2011*. Nationalmuseet, København, 73-86.
Sjögren, K.-G. 2014. Mortuary Practices, Bodies and Persons in Northern Europe. *Oxford Handbooks Online*, Oxford University Press, 1-13.

Sjögren, K.-G. 2015. News from Frälsegården. Aspects of Neolithic burial practices. In Brink, K., Hydén, S., Jennbert, K., Larsson, L. & Olausson, D. (eds) *Neolithic Diversities. Perspectives from a conference in Lund, Sweden*. Acta Archaeologica Lundensia Series in 8°, No. 65, 200-10.
Sjögren, K.-G. 2017. Modeling Middle Neolithic Funnel Beaker Diet on Falbygden, Sweden. *Journal of Archaeological Science Reports* 12, 295-306.
Sjögren, K.-G. & Price, T.D. 2013. Vegetarians or meat eaters? Enamel $\delta^{13}C$ and Neolithic diet at the Frälsegården passage tomb, central Sweden. In Bergerbrant, S. & Sabatini, S. (eds) *Counterpoint: Essays in Archaeology and Heritage Studies in Honour of Professor Kristian Kristiansen*. BAR International Series 2508. Archaeopress, Oxford, 43-52.
Sjöström, A. & Pihl, H. 2002. Örnakulladösen. In Larsson, L. (ed.) *Monumentala gravformer i det äldsta bondesamhället*. University of Lund, Department of Archaeology and Ancient History, Report Series No. 83, Lund, 47-76.
Skaarup, J. 1973. *Hesselø – Sølager. Jagdstationen der südskandinavischen Trichterbecherkultur*. Arkæologiske Studier vol. 1, København.
Skaarup, J. 1975. *Stengade. Ein langeländischer Wohnplatz mit Hausresten aus der frühneolithischen Zeit*. Meddelelser fra Langelands Museum, Rudkøbing.
Skaarup, J. 1985. *Yngre stenalder på øerne syd for Fyn*. Meddelelser fra Langelands Museum, Rudkøbing.
Skousen, H. 2008. *Arkæologi i lange baner: undersøgelser forud for anlæggelsen af motorvejen nord om Århus 1998-2007*. Moesgård Museum, Højbjerg.
Smyth, J. 2014. *Settlement in the Irish Neolithic: new discoveries at the edge of Europe*. Prehistoric Society Research Paper 6, Oxbow Books, Oxford.
Smyth, J. R. & Evershed, R.P. 2015a. Milking the megafauna: using organic residue analysis to understand early farming practice. *Environmental Archaeolgy*, DOI: 10.1179/1749631414Y.0000000045 [online journal]
Smyth, J. & Evershed, R. 2015b. The molecules of meals: new insight into Neolithic foodways. *Proceedings of the Royal Irish Academy* 115C, 27-46.
Sokal, R., Oden, N. & Wilson, C. 1991. Genetic evidence for the spread of agriculture in Europe by demic diffusion. *Nature* 351, 143-145. DOI:10.1038/351143a0
Sparrevohn, L.R. 2009. Omkring en å. Tragtbægerkulturens særlige steder. In Schülke, A. (ed.) *Plads og rum i tragtbægerkulturen. Bidrag fra Arbejdsmødet på Nationalmuseet, 22. september 2005*. Nordiske Fortidsminder Ser. C, bind 6, Det Kongelige Nordiske Oldskriftselskab, København, 45-65.
Spielmann, K.A. 2008. Crafting the sacred: Ritual places and paraphernalia in small-scale societies. In Wells, E.C. & McAnany, P.A. (eds) *Dimensions of Ritual Economy*. Research in economic anthropology vol. 27, 37-72.
Stafford, M. 1999. *From Forager to Farmer in Flint. A Lithic Analysis of the Prehistoric Transition to Agri-*

culture in Southern Scandinavia. Aarhus University Press, Århus.

Stenberger, M. 1943. *Das Grabfeld von Västerbjers auf Gotland*. Kungl. Vitterhets Historie och Antikvitets Akademien, Stockholm.

Steppan, K. 1998. Archäozoologische Untersuchung der Säugetiere aus den Gräben der Michelsberger 'Erdwerke' in Bruchsal, Landkreis Karlsruhe. Die Bedeutung der Haus- und Wildsäugetiere im Rahmen der jungneolithischen Ernährungswirtschaft in Südwestdeutschland. In Biel, J., Schlichtherle, H., Strobel, M. & Zeeb, A. (eds) *Die Michelsberger Kultur und ihre Randgebiete – Probleme der Entstehung, Chronologie und des Siedlungswesens. Kolloquium Hemmenhofen, 21.-23.2.1997 (Jens Lüning zum 60. Geburtstag)*. Materialhefte zur Archäologie in Baden-Württemberg 43, Stuttgart, 143-50.

Stjerna, K. 1911. Före hällkisttiden. *Antikvarisk Tidskrift för Sverige* 19, 2,1-164.

Stjernquist, B. 1965. An Early Neolithic settlement site at Simris in S.E. Scania. *Meddelanden från Lunds Universitets Historiska Museum* 1964-65, 32-70.

Strathern, M. 1970. Stone Axes and Flake Tools: Evaluations from Two New Guinea Highland Societies. *Proceedings of the Prehistoric Society* 35, 1969, 311-29.

Strömberg, M. 1968. *Der Dolmen Trollasten in St. Köpinge, Schonen*. Acta Archaeologica Lundensia, Series in 8°, N° 7, Lund.

Strömberg, M. 1971. *Die Megalithgräber von Hagestad. Zur Problematik von Grabbauten und Grabriten*. Acta Archaeologica Lundensia, Series in 8°, N° 9, Lund.

Sundström, L. 2003. *Det hotade kollektivet. Neolitiseringsprocessen ur ett östmellansvensk perspektiv*. Coast to coast-books no. 6, Uppsala.

Sørensen, L. 2012. Fremmede økser som sædekorn for neolitisering. In Kaul, F. & Sørensen, L. (eds) *Agrarsamfundenes ekspansion i nord. Symposium på Tanums Hällristningsmuseum, Underslös, Bohuslän, d. 25.-29. maj 2011*. Nationalmuseet, København, 8-30.

Sørensen, L. 2014. *From Hunter to Farmer in Northern Europe. Migration and adaptation during the Neolithic and Bronze Age*. Acta Archaeologica Supplementa Vol. XV. Oxford.

Sørensen, L. 2015. Endnu et indspark i neolitiseringsdebatten. Aktuel status inden for spredningen af agrarsamfundene. *Arkæologisk Forum* nr. 33, 32-36.

Sørensen, L. in press. New theoretical discourses in the discussion of the neolithisation process in South Scandinavia during the late 5th and early 4th millennium BC – an identification of learning processes, communities of practice and migrations. *Documenta Prehistoria*, forthcoming.

Sørensen, L. & Karg, S. 2014. The expansion of agrarian societies towards the North – new evidence for agriculture during the Mesolithic/Neolithic transition in Southern Scandinavia. *Journal of Archaeological Science* 51, 98-114.

Sørensen, S.A. 2019. Tabt, kasseret eller ofret? – En foreløbig præsentation af et kystbundet deponeringsområde i Syltholmfjorden på Lolland. *Gefjon* nr. 4, 152-75.

Tabaczyński, S. 1972. Gesellschaftsordnung und Güteraustausch im Neolitikum Mitteleuropas. Neolithische Studien I, Berlin.

Taffinder, J. 1998. *The Allure of the Exotic. The social use of non-local raw materials during the Stone Age in Sweden*. Aun 25. Uppsala.

Tauber, H. 1981. ^{13}C evidence for dietary habits of prehistoric man in Denmark. *Nature* 292, 332-22.

Tauber, H. 1986. Analysis of stable isotopes in prehistoric populations. In Herrmann, B. (ed.) *Innovative Trends in der prähistorischen Anthropologie. Beiträge zu einem internationalen Symposium vom 26. Februar bis 1. März 1986 in Berlin (West)*. Mitteilungen der Berliner Gesellschaft für Anthropologie, Ethnologie und Urgeschichte, Band 7, 31-38.

Terberger, T., Hartz, S. & Kabaciński, J. 2009. Late hunter-gatherer and early farmer contacts in the southern Baltic – a discussion. In Glørstad, H. & Prescott, C. (eds) *Neolithisation as if history mattered. Processes of Neolithisation in North-Western Europe*. Bricoleur Press, Lindome, 257-97.

Terberger, T. & Kabaciński, J. 2010. The Neolithisation of Pomerania – a critical review. In Gronenborn, D. & Petrasch, J. (eds) *Die Neolithisierung Mitteleuropas / The Spread of the Neolithic to Central Europe. International Symposium, Mainz 24 June-26 June 2005*. Römisch-Germanisches Zentralmuseum Mainz, Tagungen Band 4. Verlag RGZM, 375-405.

Thorpe, I.J. 1996. *The Origins of Agriculture in Europe*. Routledge, London & N.Y.

Thorpe, N. 2009. Becoming Neolithic in Southern Britain. In Glørstad, H. & Prescott, C. (eds) *Neolithisation as if history mattered. Processes of neolithisation in North-Western Europe*. Bricoleur Press, Lindome, 23-63.

Tilley, C. 1996. *An ethnography of the Neolithic. Early prehistoric societies in southern Scandinavia*. New studies in archaeology, Cambridge Univ. Press., Cambridge.

Troels-Smith, J. 1953. Ertebøllekultur – Bondekultur. Resultater af de sidste 10 Års Undersøgelser i Aamosen, Vestsjælland. *Aarbøger for nordisk Oldkyndighed og Historie* 1953, 5-62.

Usinger, H. 1978. Bölling-Interstadial und Laacher Bimstuff in einem neuen Spätglazial-Profil aus dem Vallensgård Mose/Bornholm. Mit pollengrössenstatistischer Trennung der Birken. *Danmarks Geologiske Undersøgelse, Årbog 1977* (1978), 5-29.

Vandkilde, H. 1996. *From Stone to Bronze. The Metalwork of the Late Neolithic and Earliest Bronze Age in Denmark*. Jutland Archaeological Society Publications XXXII, Aarhus.

Vandkilde, H. 2007. *Culture and change in central European prehistory, 6th to 1st millennium BC*. Aarhus Univ. Press, Aarhus.

Vedel, E. 1886. *Bornholms Oldtidsminder og Oldsager*. København.

Vedel, E. 1897. *Efterskrift til Bornholms Oldtidsminder og Oldsager*. København.

Vigne, J.-D. 2008. Zooarchaeological Aspects of the Neolithic Diet Transition in the Near East and Europe, and Their Putative Relationships with the Neolithic Demographic Transition. In Bocquet-Appel, J.-P. & Bar-Yosef, O. (eds) *The Neolithic Demographic Transition and its Consequences*. Springer-Verlag, N.Y., 179-205.

Vogt, J. 2009. Der Fundplatz Brunn 17 im Landkreis Mecklenburg-Strelitz. Ergebnisse einer Grabung unter besonderer Berücksichtigung der trichterbecherzeitlichen Funde und Befunde. In Terberger, T. (ed.) *Neue Forschungen zum Neolithikum im Ostseeraum*. Archäologie und Geschichte im Ostseeraum 5, Rahden/Westfalen, 135-236.

Wahl, J. 2010. Wenige Knochen, viele Fragen. Auf der Suche nach den Menschen der Michelsberger Kultur. In Lichter, C. (ed.) *Jungsteinzeit im Umbruch. Die "Michelsberger Kultur" und Mitteleuropa vor 6000 Jahren*. Badisches Landesmuseum, Karlsruhe, 96-101.

Wason, P. 1994. *The Archaeology of Rank*. New studies in Archaeology. Cambridge Univ. Press.

Watt, M. 1982. Huse og grave fra vikingetid ved Runegård i Grødby. *Fra Bornholms Museum 1982*, 25-34.

Welinder, S. 1985. *Tunnackiga stenyxor och samhälle i Mellansverige 5000 B.P.* Varia 11. Universitetets Oldsaksamling, Oslo.

Welinder, S. 1997. The Stone Age Landscape of Coastal Southeast Sweden at the Neolithic Transition. In Król, D. (ed.) *The Built Environment of Coast Areas during the Stone Age. The Baltic Sea-Coast Landscapes Seminar, Session No. 1*, Gdansk, 87-97.

Wenger, E. 1998. *Communities of practice. Learning, meaning and identity*. Cambridge Univ. Press, Cambridge.

Wentink, K. 2006. *Ceci n'est pas une hache. Neolithic Depositions in the Northern Netherlands*. Leiden. M. Phil. thesis (http://edna.itor.org/nl/projecten/a00308/)

Wentink, K., van Gijn, A. & Fontijn, D. 2011. Changing contexts, changing meanings: Flint axes in Middle and Late Neolithic communities in the northern Netherlands. In Davis, V. & Edmonds, M. (eds) *Stone Axe Studies* III. Oxbow Books, Oxford, 399-408.

Wiklak, H. 1983. Wyniki badań wykopaliskowych w osadzie i na cmentarzysku kultury pucharów lejkowatych na stanowisku 1A w Sarnowie, województwo Włocławskie. *Prace i Materiały Muzeum Archeologicznego i Etnograficznego w Łodzi, Seria Archeologiczna* nr. 30, 167-91.

Winther, J. 1943. *Blandebjerg*. Langelands Museum, Rudkøbing.

Wiślański, T. 1986. The role of Pomerania in the Neolithic. In Malinowski, T. (ed.) *Problems of the Stone Age in Pomerania*. Archeologia Interregionalis, Warszawa, 47-67.

Wiślański, T. & Czarnecki, M. 1970. Osada kultury pucharów lejkowatych w Kosinie, pow. Pyrzyce (stanowisko 6). *Materiały zachodniopomorskie* 16, 73-105.

Wunderlich, M. 2017. Megalithic monuments and equality. In Hansen, S. & Müller, J. (eds) *Rebellion and Inequality in Archaeology*. Human Development in Landscapes 11. Universitätsforschungen zur prähistorischen Archäologie Band 308. Verlag Dr. Rudolf Habelt, Bonn, 154-71.

Wunderlich, M. 2019. Social implications of megalithic constructions – A case study from Nagaland and Northern Germany. In Müller, J., Hinz, H. & Wunderlich, M. (eds) *Megaliths – Societies – Landscapes. Early monumentality and Social Differentiation in Neolithic Europe* Vol. 3. Frühe Monumentalität und sociale Differenzierung 18. Institut für Ur- und Frühgeschichte der CAU Kiel / Verlag Dr. Rudolf Habelt, Bonn, 1133-51.

Wyszomirska, B. 1988. *Ekonomisk stabilitet vid kusten. Nymölla III. En tidigneolitisk bosätning med fångstekonomi i nordöstra Skåne*. Acta Archaeologica Lundensia, Series in 8° Nr 17. Lund.

Zápotocký, M. 1992. *Streitäxte des mitteleuropäischen Äneolithikums*. VCH, Acta Humaniora, Weinheim.

Zich, B. 1993. Die Ausgrabung chronisch gefärdeter Hügelgräber der Stein- und Bronzezeit in Flintbek, Kreis Rendsburg-Eckernförde. Ein Vorbericht. *Offa* 49/50, 1992/93, 15-31.

Zimmermann, H. 1998. Pfosten, Ständer und Schwelle und der Übergang vom Pfosten- zum Ständerbau – Eine Studie zu Innovation und Beharrung im Hausbau. *Probleme der Küstenforschung im südlichen Nordseegebiet* Band 25, 9-241.

Zvelebil, M. 1996. The agricultural frontier and the transition to farming in the circum-Baltic region. In Harris, D.R. (ed.) *The Origins and Spread of Agriculture and Pastoralism in Eurasia*, 323-45. University College London Press.

Zvelebil, M. 1998. Agricultural Frontiers, Neolithic Origins, and the Transition to Farming in the Baltic Basin. In Zvelebil, M., Dennell, R. & Domańska, L. (eds) *Harvesting the Sea, Farming the Forest. The Emergence of Neolithic Societies in the Baltic Region*, 9-27. Sheffield Archaeological Monographs 10, Sheffield Academic Press.

Zvelebil, M. & Rowley-Conwy, P. 1984. Transition to Farming in Northern Europe: A Hunter-Gatherer Perspective. *Norwegian Archaeological Review* 17:2, 104-28.

Åberg, N. 1913. *Kalmar läns stenålder*. Meddelanden från Kalmar läns fornminnesförening VI.

Authors' addresses

Poul Otto Nielsen,
The National Museum,
Ancient Cultures of Denmark and the Mediterranean,
Frederiksholms Kanal 12,
DK-1220 Copenhagen K
poul.otto.nielsen@natmus.dk

Finn Ole Sonne Nielsen,
Bornholms Museum,
Sct. Mortensgade 29,
DK-3700 Rønne
fon@bornholmsmuseer.dk

Nordiske Fortidsminder
Serie B – in quarto

Bind 1. Ebbe Lomborg: Die Flintdolche Dänemarks. Studien über Chronologie und Kulturbeziehungen des südskandinavischen Spätneolithikums (1973).
Bind 2. Thorkild Ramskou: Lindholm Høje. Gravpladsen (1976).
Bind 3. Olaf Olsen & Holger Schmidt: Fyrkat. En jysk vikingeborg. Bind I: Borgen og bebyggelsen / Fyrkat, A Viking Fortress in Jutland. Vol I: The Fortress and the Buildings. With a contribution by Hans Helbaek: The Fyrkat Grain. A geographical and chronological study of rye (1977).
Bind 4. Else Roesdahl: Fyrkat. En jysk vikingeborg. Bind II: Oldsagerne og gravpladsen / Fyrkat, A Viking Fortress in Jutland. Vol. II: The Finds and the Cemetary (1977).
Bind 5. Klaus Ebbesen: Tragtbægerkultur i Nordjylland / Trichterbecherkultur in Nordjütland (1978).
Bind 6. Birgitte Bille Henriksen: Lundby-holmen. Pladser af Maglemose-type i Sydsjælland / the Lundby Islet. Sites of Maglemose-Type in South Zealand. With a contribution by Knud Rosenlund (bone material) (1980).
Bind 7. Knud Andersen, Svend Jørgensen & Jane Richter: Maglemose hytterne ved Ulkestrup Lyng (1982).
Bind 8. Berit Jansen Sellevold, Ulla Lund Hansen & Jørgen Balslev Jørgensen: Iron Age Man in Denmark (1984).
Bind 9. Lise Bender Jørgensen: Forhistoriske textiler i Skandinavien / Prehistoric Scandinavian Textiles (1986).
Bind 10. Ulla Lund Hansen: Römischer Import im Norden. Waren-austausch zwischen dem Römischen Reich und dem freien Germanien (1987).
Bind 11. Mogens Ørsnes: Ejsbøl I. Waffenopferfunde des 4.-5. Jahrh. nach Chr. (1988).
Bind 12. Danmarks Middelalderlige Skattefund ca. 1050 – ca. 1550 / Denmark's medieval treasure-hoards c. 1050 – c. 1550 (1992).
Bind 13. Ulla Lund Hansen et alii: Himlingøje – Seeland – Europa. Ein Gräberfeld der jüngeren römischen Kaiserzeit auf Seeland, seine Bedeutung und internationalen Beziehungen. With contributions by Verner Alexandersen, Bernhardt Beckmann, Haldis Johanne Bollingberg, Kristian Dalsgaard, Mogens Schou Jørgensen, Anne Kromann, Ulla Mannering, Per Nørnberg, Berit Jansen Sellevold, Ole Stilborg, Marie Stoklund & Ingrid Sørensen (1995).
Bind 14. Lars Jørgensen & Anne Nørgård Jørgensen: Nørre Sandegård Vest. A Cemetary from the 6th-8th Centuries on Bornholm. With contributions by Ulla Mannering (textiles) and Claus Malmros (wood analyses) (1997).
Bind 15. Jørgen Jensen: Fra Bronze- til Jernalder / From Bronze Age to Iron Age. A chronological study (1997).
Bind 16. Eva Koch: Neolithic Bog Pots from Zealand, Møn, Lolland and Falster (1998).
Bind 17. Anne Nørgård Jørgensen: Waffen und Gräber Typologische und chronologische Studien zu Skandinavischen Waffengräbern 520/30 bis 900 n.Chr. (1999).
Bind 18. Svend Nielsen. The Domestic Mode of Production – and Beyond. An archeological inquiry into urban trends in Denmark, Iceland and Predynastic Egypt (1999).
Bind 19. Per Ethelberg et alii: Skovgårde. Ein Bestattungsplatz mit reichen Frauengräbern des 3. Jhs. n.Chr. auf Seeland. With contributions by Ulla Lund Hansen, Ide Demant, Pia Bennike, Verner Alexandersen, Tove Hatting, Annette Adomat & Gerd Nebrich (2000).
Bind 20, 1-2. Jens N. Nielsen: Sejlflod. Ein eisenzeitliches Dorf in Nordjütland. Bd. 1-2: Katalog der Grabfunde (2000).
Bind 21. Fritze Lindahl: Symboler i guld og sølv. Nationalmuseets fingerringe 1000-1700-årene / Symbols of Gold and Silver. Rings in the Danish National Museum (2003).
Bind 22. Flemming Kaul: Bronzealderens religion. Studier af den nordiske bronzealders ikonografi / The Religion of the Bronze Age. Studies of the iconography of the Nordic Bronze Age (2004).
Bind 23. Birgit Als Hansen & Morten Aaman Sørensen: Ornamenterede middelalderlige gulvfliser i Danmark / Ornamented medieval floor-tiles in Denmark (2005).
Bind 24. Eva Hübner: Jungneolitische Gräber auf der Jütischen Halbinsel. Typologische und chronologische Studien zur Einzelgrabkultur (2005).
Bind 25. Morten Axboe: Brakteatstudier (2007).

Bind 26. Hans Mikkelsen og Michael Andersen (red.): Hedensted Kirke. Undersøgelser og restaureringer (2016).

Bind 27. Søren A. Sørensen: The Kongemose Culture (2017).

Bind 28. Marzena J. Przybyła: Pressblechverzierte spätkaiserzeitliche Trachtbestandteile in Südskandinavien (2018).

Bind 29. Torben Sarauw: Bejsebakken – En nordjysk bebyggelse fra yngre jernalder og vikingetid (2019).

Bind 30. Bjarne Henning Nielsen, Tine Nord Raahauge & Peter Steen Henriksen/Jan Harild: Smedegård – a village mound from the Early Iron Age near Nors in Thy, north-west Denmark (2019).

Bind 31:1-2. Lotte Reedtz Sparrevohn, Ole Thirup Kastholm & Poul Otto Nielsen (eds.): Houses for the Living. Two-aisled houses from the Neolithic and Early Bronze Age in Denmark. Vol. 1 – Text, Vol. 2 – Catalogue (2019).